the best" will do!

Colleen
Christmas, '92

Italy

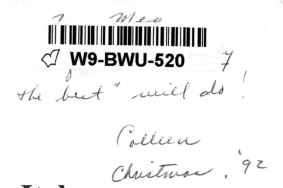

at its best

BY ROBERT S. KANE

The World at Its Best Travel Series
BRITAIN AT ITS BEST
FRANCE AT ITS BEST
GERMANY AT ITS BEST
HAWAII AT ITS BEST
HOLLAND AT ITS BEST
HONG KONG AT ITS BEST
ITALY AT ITS BEST
LONDON AT ITS BEST
NEW YORK AT ITS BEST
PARIS AT ITS BEST
SPAIN AT ITS BEST
SWITZERLAND AT ITS BEST
WASHINGTON, D.C. AT ITS BEST

A to Z World Travel Guides
GRAND TOUR A TO Z: THE CAPITALS OF EUROPE
EASTERN EUROPE A TO Z
SOUTH PACIFIC A TO Z
CANADA A TO Z
ASIA A TO Z
SOUTH AMERICA A TO Z
AFRICA A TO Z

Robert S. Kane

THIRD EDITION

Italy at its best

PASSPORT BOOKS
a division of *NTC Publishing Group*
Lincolnwood, Illinois USA

More praise for Robert S. Kane . . .

"The strength of Kane's books lies in their personal flavor and zestful writing style. He doesn't shy away from expressing opinion, is strong on culture, art, and history, along with dining and shopping."

—Jack Schnedler, *Chicago Sun-Times*

"Kane's books take the reader beyond the expected. His works are carefully researched, succinctly presented and opinionated."

—Jane Abrams, *New York Daily News*

"Kane is a man of perception and taste, with a knowledge of art, architecture and history. He doesn't spare the occasional sharp evaluation if something is less than highest quality."

—Lois Fegan, *Jersey Journal*

"Anyone going should take one of Bob Kane's books."

—Paul Jackson, *New York Post*

"Kane's candor, conciseness and credibility have made his books among the top selling in the travel field—a must for travelers."

—Joel Sleed, *Newhouse News Service*

"Kane does not mince words. His choices, ranked according to price, service, location and ambiance, are selective; he provides opinions."

—Ralph Gardner, *San Antonio Express-News*

"Kane wanders the globe, testing pillows, mattresses and, in some cases, abominable food in order to be a faithful guide, writing his own observations, and leaving nothing to ghost writers or a band of behind-the-scenes reporters; Kane's unafraid to recommend some places and condemn others."

—Maria Lisella, *The Travel Agent*

Published by Passport Books, a division of NTC Publishing Group.
4255 West Touhy Avenue, Lincolnwood (Chicago), Illinois 60646-1975. U.S.A.

Manufactured in the United States of America.
Library of Congress Catalog Card Number: 92-60397

2 3 4 5 6 7 8 9 ML 9 8 7 6 5 4 3 2 1

For Enza Cirrincione

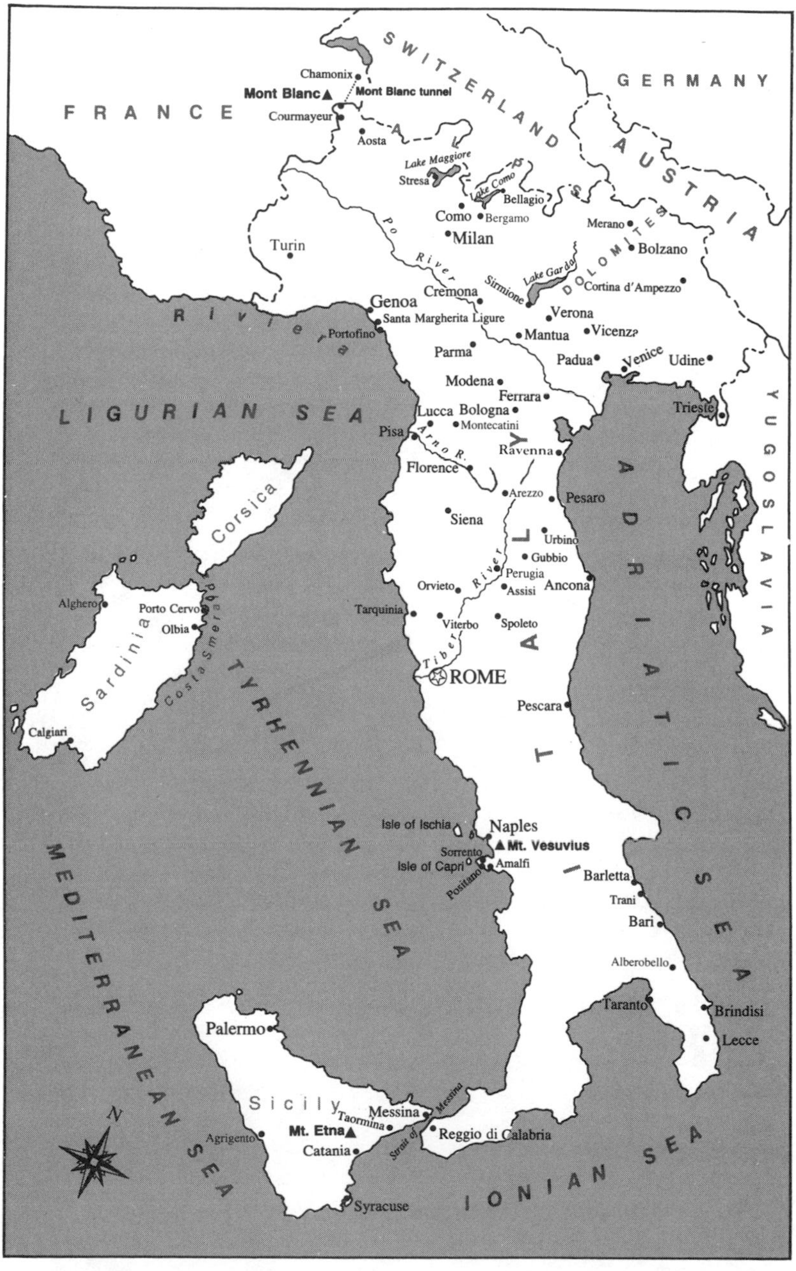

FRANCE
SWITZERLAND
GERMANY
AUSTRIA
YUGOSLAVIA
ITALY
Chamonix
Mont Blanc
Mont Blanc tunnel
Courmayeur
Aosta
Lake Maggiore
Stresa
Lake Como
Bellagio
Como
Bergamo
Milan
Merano
DOLOMITES
Bolzano
Turin
Po River
Lake Garda
Sirmione
Cortina d'Ampezzo
Cremona
Genoa
Santa Margherita Ligure
Portofino
Riviera
Verona
Mantua
Vicenza
Parma
Padua
Venice
Udine
Modena
Ferrara
Trieste
LIGURIAN SEA
Lucca
Bologna
Montecatini
Pisa
Arno R.
Ravenna
Florence
Corsica
Arezzo
Pesaro
Siena
Urbino
Gubbio
Perugia
Assisi
Ancona
Orvieto
Alghero
Porto Cervo
Olbia
Sardinia
Costa Smeralda
Tarquinia
Viterbo
Spoleto
Tiber River
ROME
ADRIATIC SEA
Pescara
Calgiari
TYRHENNIAN SEA
Isle of Ischia
Naples
Mt. Vesuvius
Sorrento
Isle of Capri
Amalfi
Positano
Barletta
Trani
Bari
MEDITERRANEAN SEA
Alberobello
Taranto
Brindisi
Palermo
Lecce
Sicily
Messina
Taormina
Strait of Messina
Agrigento
Mt. Etna
Reggio di Calabria
Catania
IONIAN SEA
Syracuse
N

Contents

Foreword

Italy: The Big Picture

I am as guilty as my countrymen—or at least have been, up to now—with the same essentially myopic view of the Italian travel scene's potential that began with Grand Tourists out of England in the eighteenth century and set a rigid pattern. When you went to Italy, you kept to the established circuit: Rome, of course; Naples and its bay; centrally situated Florence; northerly Venice; and—more recently—Milan.

Splendid, as far as they go. Indeed, I confess to sufficient fascination for these Big Leaguers to have made of them some years back the subject of *Italy A to Z*, my first book about Italy. And I've never tired of returning to them, in the course of a quarter-century of Italian exploration.

On recent visits, though, I began to take in less celebrated places, Trieste to Taormina, and to understand that the beaten Italian path was but an Italian sampler. Later, traveling extensively in the course of researching this book, the pieces of the pattern fell into place, and I came to appreciate the extraordinary wealth—art and architecture, culture and cuisine—that had evolved in the clutch of long-contentious city-states that settled enough of their differences only in the middle of the last century to become, politically at least, a united Italy.

That, at least, is how Italians you meet along the way are fond of putting it. They insist that the contemporary republic is more constitutional than actual, with more differences than similarities among its component parts. There is something to their argument. Parma, quietly elegant, is hardly a carbon copy of exuberant Palermo. A resident of southeasterly Bari will no doubt require a period of adjustment in Bolzano, where German is a co-official language. The mosaic-embellished churches of Ravenna are a long way indeed from the Rome of the Renaissance and the Baroque. French-accented Turin would seem to have little in common with the Ionian seaport of Taranto. Can residents of a small island like, say, southerly Capri identify with those of a small city like, say, northerly Cremona?

Travel Italy extensively enough and you perceive that its outwardly disparate sectors interrelate to an extent that many Italians—so much closer to the situation than objective observers like ourselves, from abroad—will not concede. It was, to be sure, the clan Gonzaga that made Mantua a city to be feared, while the Este family was responsible for Ferrara's opulence, and Dukes of Montefeltro developed Urbino. Pisa battled Lucca, Sardinia's kings ruled in absentia from Turin. Medieval popes governed much of the territory north of Rome. Spaniards, for a while, reigned over Naples; Hapsburgs, Trieste. Earlier kings in southerly Apulia and Sicily were of Germanic and Gallic origin.

Then you consider common antecedents. The clever early Etruscans created many communities. Gifted Greeks settled much of the south. The later Romans populated the entire peninsula. War was near-constant, with warriors often nonpeninsular. But it became clear, as time passed, that geography was a uniting factor in Italy's favor. It was small enough for Christianity to have become entrenched, and for the Romans' Latin to evolve as the modern Italian language.

The creativity of the Italian Middle Ages was national—albeit with variations—rather than regional. The Renaissance, born in the Florence of the Medici, came to flower throughout Italy, the while it influenced the rest of Europe.

Later centuries—Mannerist, Baroque, Rococo, and beyond, have hardly been less dynamic or inventive. What becomes apparent to the traveler who goes beyond the Big City basics of today's Italy, to contemporarily less reputed provincial points, is the extent of a cultural wealth unsurpassed in any other country. To the Doges' Palace of Venice, add ducal palaces of Mantua, Modena, and Gubbio, to cite but three. To Rome's St. Peter's and Venice's St. Mark's, add treasure-filled cathedrals of Lecce, Orvieto, and Siena, to name another trio. To museums that are household words—Florence's Uffizi, Milan's Brera, Naples' Capodimonte—add those of Bologna, Genoa, and Padua, of many, many in the provinces. And opera houses: Catania's and Verona's surpass in beauty those of Florence and Rome; and they are but a pair.

Creature comforts? I suspect you will be as comfortable at the Costa Smeralda's Cala di Volpe Hotel as in cosmopolitan Milan's Duca di Milano, and that you will dine as deliciously at Courmayeur's La Maison de Filippo, in the Alps, as at Ranieri, smack in the center of Rome. Which leaves the Italians themselves. Surely you will find hosts in lesser cities—say, Syracuse or Spoleto—with not a whit less of the undefinable charm that, as much as anything else, draws us to Italy, whatever the particulars of our itinerary.

ROBERT S. KANE

1

Italy

A Mini A to Z

ADDRESSES: *Italian Government Travel Offices* are located in the United States at 630 Fifth Avenue, New York, NY 10111; 500 North Michigan Avenue, Chicago, IL 60611; and 360 Post Street, San Francisco, CA 94108, as well as at 3 Place Ville Marie, Montreal, Quebec, Canada. These offices—among whose functions is to provide the prospective traveler in Italy with gratis information and literature—are part of a worldwide network, whose headquarters—*Ente Nazionale Italiano per il Turismo*—known simply as ENIT (*ay-neet*)—are at Via Marghera 2, Rome. Worth knowing about, too, is the *Italian Cultural Institute* (Istituto Italiano di Cultura), a government agency sponsoring film showings, concerts, art exhibitions, and cultural exchanges; its U.S. offices are at 686 Park Avenue, New York, NY 10022 and 1 Charlton Court, San Francisco, CA 94123. Business travelers may find the *Italian Trade Commission,* another government agency, helpful; it is at 499 Park Avenue, New York, NY 10022. Within Italy, the traveler finds two types of tourist offices. If it is operated by a province—Italian counterpart of a U.S. county—it is called an *Ente Provinciale di Turismo;* if it is under the aegis of a city or town, it has a longer name, usually *Azienda Autonoma di Soggiorno e Turismo.* Addresses of these offices appear in chapters following.

AIRLINES: Several airlines link the U.S. and Italy with transatlantic service to Milan (in the north) and southerly Rome, so that you may commence an Italian journey in Milan, work your way south and return to the U.S. from Rome. Or vice-versa. Within Italy, domestic air routes embrace a remarkably extensive network, Trieste to Naples, Venice to Brindisi.

BREAKFAST is a distinctly minor meal in Italy (you must not expect the croissants and brioches of France or the delicious assorted breads of Germany), usually a caffè completo—which means simply an undistinguished pair of rolls and coffee, served with milk, butter, and jam (in some—not all—hotels included in the room rate). The most common addition to this standard repast is a boiled egg. But bigger hotels will serve fried or scrambled eggs, toast, fruit, and fruit juices (Italy's oranges—especially the blood-red ones—when fresh-squeezed, result in delicious juice), all, of course, at additional cost. There are exceptions to this pattern in certain hotels—the estimable Jolly chain especially—with buffet breakfasts served in dining and/or breakfast rooms. In hotels of every category, though, you may have breakfast brought to your room, ordering it the night before through the concierge, or—in bigger hotels—by means of the American-invented menus that you place on the outer doorknob before retiring.

BUSES: Aside from those of package tours that you will have booked before you left home, and the usual day and half-day bus sightseeing in bigger cities, long-distance buses operate intercity on a scheduled basis; they can be an excellent—and inexpensive—alternative to trains, planes, or rented cars, and are, in my experience, clean, comfortable (with reclining seats), and efficiently operated. Additionally, Europabus and other companies operate buses with guides aboard between certain key cities (Venice-Padua-Florence, for example) with concentrated sightseeing at points en route.

CLIMATE: Expect, roughly, the kind of four-season, temperate-zone weather of the United States, but with milder winters and longer, hotter summers, especially in Rome and Naples, along with excessive summer and early-fall humidity in those cities. Generally, spring and autumn are the kindest Italian seasons, late summer the most uncomfortable, with August—when everything is crowded, what with so many Italians and other Europeans vacationing—the month to avoid if at all possible. Fahrenheit averages:

	Winter (February)	Spring (May)	Summer (July)	Fall (October)
Rome	52	70	82	65
Florence	47	67	81	63
Milan	40	66	75	56
Naples	54	70	83	66
Venice	48	67	77	60

CLOTHES: This is Europe's best-dressed country, bar none. No other Europeans—not the French, not the British—have quite the sense of style of the Italians, especially urban Italians, with Rome and Milan leading. And I'm speaking of men (Italian males are the world's vainest—but with taste) as well as women. Be as informal as you like during the day—especially in summer and early fall—but dressier—in better places at least—after dark. In the case of papal audiences at the Vatican: jackets and ties for the gents, covered heads and arms for the ladies.

CREDIT CARDS are generally accepted in many—but by no means all—restaurants, chain department stores, and many—but by no means all—shops. But they are not yet as widely accepted as in the United States; I still come across restaurateurs and shopkeepers, even in big cities, unfamiliar with them. Most popular are *American Express, Diners Club, Visa,* and *MasterCard.*

CURRENCY: *The lira* (plural: *lire*). Inquire about rates for it from bank and currency-exchange firms in the U.S. or Canada before departure; you may want to buy some in advance. In Italy, best rates are obtained at change-offices identified by the word *Cambio* and banks (you absolutely *must* have your passport with you), but hotel cashiers also change money. Take the bulk of your funds in traveler's checks—they're the safest—with plenty in twenty-dollar denominations—they're the most convenient. Denominations of the lira include 1000-, 5000-, 10,000-, 50,000-, and 100,000-lire notes, with the occasional low-denomination coin turning up. *Tip:* Because prices are in the thousands and tens of thousands of lire, you'll find it *very* convenient to have a pocket- or purse-size calculator with you to convert to or from dollars.

CUSTOMS: Entering Italy. Generally, Italian customs officers assume what you're taking in is your own business; you're allowed personal effects, of course: two cartons of cigarettes, two bottles of wine in addition to a bottle of liquor, as many as two still cameras and a movie camera, a reasonable amount of film for your own use, and gifts and doodads you may have picked up in other countries during the course of your travels, whose final resting place will be your own home base.

Returning to the United States. Each individual may bring back $400 worth of purchases duty free. That is allowable once every 30 days, provided you've been out of the country at least 48 hours. If you've spent more than $400 you'll be charged a flat 10 percent duty on the next $1000 worth of purchases. Remember, too, that antiques, duly certified to be at least 100 years old, are admitted duty free and do not count as part of your $400 quota; neither do paintings, sculptures, and other works of art, of any date, if certified as original; it's advisable that certification from the seller or other authority on their authenticity accompany them. Also exempt from duty, but as a part of the $400 quota: one quart of liquor. And—this is important—there is no restriction on how much one may bring in beyond the $400 limit, so long as the duty is paid.

DEPARTMENT STORES, SHOPS, AND SUPERMARKETS: The first—department stores—tend to be mediocre south of Florence, but they improve phenomenally in northern cities; major chains such as *Coin, La Rinascente,* and *Upim* are geared to local customers, which means that they can be better value than boutiques priced for foreigners. I make mention of their locations in many of the chapters following. I make shopping suggestions in some detail, and by category, in chapters on the Big Five cities—Rome, Florence, Milan, Naples, Venice—and I capsulize the shopping scene in chapters dealing with a number of other cities. The supermarket—*supermercato,* in Italian—is happily ubiquitous, and a source not only of snack items, but of wines, for hotel-room aperitifs.

DRIVING: Take your own car, rent one in advance of arrival or on the scene, or buy a new Italian car. U.S. licenses are valid if you're driving your own car, but for rentals you need an International Driving License; however, these are obtainable after arrival in Italy upon presenting your home license to a frontier or provincial outlet of the *Automobile Club d'Italia* (ACI), the motorist's best friend in Italy, with a *Phone Assistance Center* at Via Magenta, 5, Rome, whose number for English-speaking questioners is (06) 4212. If, while driving, your car breaks down, dial 116 from the nearest phone, and ACI's closest office will be dispatched to help. There are some 3000 miles of splendidly engineered *autostrade,* or superhighways (on which tolls are paid), with gas stations popping up periodically, as well as decent modern motels and links of the Autogrill chain, for sustenance. Ask your home auto club, travel agent, and/or car-rental firms like Avis and Hertz for driving details in advance of departure.

ELECTRICAL CURRENT: Confusing. There are two types of voltage, 115 AC and 220 AC. You don't know what voltage your hotel has until you arrive, so the transformer you may have brought along for your shaver, hair dryer, or whatever may or may not work. Additionally, you'll want to carry an adapter plug to be attached to the *flat* prongs of your American-purchased appliances so that it will fit into *round* Italian holes. American department stores sell kits containing a transformer and a variety of adapter shapes. Alternatively, you may buy an Italian-made appliance for use during your journey upon arrival in Italy.

GEOGRAPHY: A country the size of Arizona may not seem very big, but the Italian boot you became familiar with in elementary school geography class is some 760 miles long, and for most of its length between 100 and 150 miles wide, with France, Switzerland, Austria, and Yugoslavia its neighbors to the northwest, north, and east; the Tyrrhenian Sea (Mare Tirreneo) flanking its western shore, the Ionian Sea (Mare Ionio) directly south of the boot, and the Adriatic Sea (Mare Adriatico) lapping its eastern shore. Coastline all told exceeds 5300 miles, and Italian territory includes the Mediterranean's two largest islands, Sardinia and Sicily, along with many small ones. This is a land of mighty peaks (the Italians call Mont Blanc, on the frontier with France, Monte Bianco), volcanic peaks (Etna, for example, in Sicily, and Naples's Vesuvius), a chain of mountains—the Apennines—that extend through the center, and terrain that ranges from gloriously mountain-backed northern lakes like Como and Maggiore through to the palm-planted squares in cities of the near-subtropical south.

There are some 59 million Italians living in a democratic, multiparty republic (Parliament comprises the 630-member Chamber of Deputies and the 315-member Senate), divided into precisely 20 *Regioni*, which I wager you have *not* learned in school. Roughly equivalent to American states (and subdivided into provinces—counterparts of our counties) they are (with Regional capitals in parentheses): Valle d'Aosta (Aosta), Piedmont (Turin), Liguria (Genoa), Lombardy (Milan), Veneto (Venice), Trentino-Alto Adige (Trento), Friuli-Venezia Giulia (Trieste), Emilia-Romagna (Bologna), Tuscany (Florence), Umbria (Perugia), Marche (Ancona), Lazio (Rome), Abruzzo (L'Aquila), Molise (Campobasso), Campania (Naples), Apulia (Bari), Basilicata (Potenza), Calabria (Catanzaro), Sicily (Palermo), and Sardinia (Cagliari). (So that you will not think I am using the word "region" generically when I refer to a Region of Italy, in the pages following, I employ the Italian *Regione* (plural: *Regioni*).

HOLIDAYS are a pleasure for working Italians, but can present problems for traveling foreigners with shops, most restaurants, and museums closed. Besides Christmas, New Year's, and Easter, take note of Labor Day (May 1, with parades in the cities), Liberation Day (April 25), Assumption Day (August 15), and Saint Stephen's Day (the day after Christmas).

HOTELS: About the hotels in this book: I have either lived in, dined in, drunk in, and/or thoroughly inspected the hotels carefully selected for evaluation in these pages; they are divided into three price groups: *Luxury, First Class,* and *Moderate.* Italians rank with the very top-rung European hoteliers—French, German, and Swiss. Invariably, at least in my not inconsiderable experience, they take as much pride in running modest pensiones or second-class hotels as luxury houses. When an Italian hotel—of any category—is well operated, everything works well, reception to room service. And overwhelmingly, cleanliness is next to godliness.

Hotels operated by crack American chains like *Hilton International, Sheraton, Inter-Continental* and its *Forum* division, and *Best Western* (whose Italian affiliates are locally owned) will not be unfamiliar to transatlantic visitors. But there are other chains, Italian and international—with hotels Italy-wide—for which orientation is warranted. *Ciga Hotels,* without any question the preeminent Italian hotel company, concentrates on luxury-category hostelries such as Venice's legendary Gritti Palace and Rome's landmark Excelsior. *Bettoja Hotels* is an exclusively Roman chain, by which I mean that its fourth-generation Bettoja family president, Angelo, skillfully operates precisely a handful of hotels, two of which are the flagship Mediterraneo and the more modest Nord, all in the convenient Stazione Termini quarter of the capital. *Jolly Hotels'* well-operated houses extend from Turin in the north to Bari in the south; they are in the First Class category.

Leading Hotels of the World (head office: 747 Third Avenue, New York, NY 10017), international rather than Italian, and an association of privately owned luxury hotels rather than a chain, has 20-plus Italian affiliates; a few examples are Lake Como's Villa d'Este, a trio of Costa Smeralda resorts, and such city hotels as Florence's Savoy and Verona's Due Torri. *Relais et Châteaux* (U.S. office: 2400 Lazy Hollow, Houston, Texas 77063)—still another international association, and French-founded—specializes in pricey smaller spots often—but not always—in the countryside; about 20 are in Italy. London-based *Orient Express Hotels* (U.S. office: 1155 Avenue of the Americas, New York, NY 10036) has a small but choice Italian representation, with Venice's Cipriani Hotel its kingpin. That leaves an outstanding American firm—*E* (for Elizabeth Adams) *& M* (for Martha Morano) *Associates,* 211 East 43rd Street, New York, NY 10017—which has pioneered in representing Italian hotels (Rome's Bettoja chain, Venice's Monaco e Grand Canal Hotel among them) that bespeak charm and personality.

LANGUAGE: Italians, realizing that—unlike English, French, German, and Spanish—their language is the sole official tongue of but one country (their own), make an effort at learning foreign languages.

Those with whom you come in contact—in hotels, caffès, restaurants, shops, air terminals—will be fluent in English. Where the Italian you encounter does not speak your language, he or she will welcome whatever Italian you have at your command. That, together with gestures, makes communication not only possible, but frequently enjoyable. There is a good deal of French, some German, too. And it is worth emphasizing that even Italians who have not studied Spanish can understand that language—closest of the Romance tongues to their own—with little difficulty. *Tip:* Before you go, pick up a copy of *Just Enough Italian,* one of Passport Books' excellent *Just Enough* phrasebook series; or study the language, in advance of your departure, with Passport's *Just Listen 'n Learn Italian*—a three-cassette-and-textbook kit.

OPEN HOURS: Except for hotels, restaurants, certain museums (in Rome and the north), and transport terminals, Italy closes down for lunch. *Restaurants* generally serve lunch between 12:30 and 2:30 P.M. (Italians rarely eat before 1 P.M.), usually opening for dinner at 7 P.M., through 10 to 11 P.M.; Italians rarely dine before 8 P.M. You *shop* between about 8:30 A.M. and about 12:30 P.M., resuming about 3:30 P.M. through to about 7:30 P.M., Monday through Saturday. I say "about" because there are variations of a half-hour either way; especially in the north where midday breaks can be shorter, and in the case of department stores, which—bless them—often have shorter lunch hours than shops, or stay open the day long. *Banks* generally are open from 8:30 A.M. to 1:30 P.M., Monday through Friday, but may also keep afternoon hours; your hotel will know. *Post offices* are open from 8 A.M. to 2 P.M., and bear in mind that if your hotel concierge has no stamps, increasingly the case, tobacco shops (*tabacchi*) stock them. *Churches* tend to keep the same hours as shops, more or less. That leaves *museums.* If "Nazionale" is in the title, the museum is operated by the Italian government and will, with rare exceptions, close at 2 P.M., Tuesday through Saturday, which means you had better be there by 1:30, when ticket sales usually cease. National museums close on Mondays and holidays, but may also be open on Sundays from 9 A.M. to 1 P.M., which means you had better be at the ticket window by 12:30. The other key museum term is "Civico." When part of a title, it signifies that operation is municipal. Generally speaking, from Florence southward, a Museo Civico's hours will be just as limited as those of a Museo Nazionale; that is to say, closed in the afternoon, with very few exceptions, the most significant being city-operated museums in Rome which in recent seasons have been open nonstop the day long Tuesdays through Saturdays, closing at 1 P.M. Sundays and Mondays. Municipal museums *north* of Florence generally have afternoon as well as morning open-hours, and the traveler with limited time is in their debt. What a boon it would be for tourism in Italy if Italian government museums would follow the municipal museums' footsteps! Florence's Galleria degli Uffizi has pioneered in this respect, for which it rates an enthusiastic bravo.

OPERA AND FESTIVALS: Of the European countries, only Germany comes close to Italy, with respect to opera. Every Italian city of any substance, as you will read in the chapters following, invariably has a ravishingly beautiful opera house—and performances of quality on its stage, with Milano's La Scala, Naples's San Carlo, and Rome's Teatro dell' Opera the Big Three, a dozen mid-category, and many others as well. The catch is that the season is limited—November or December through May, sometimes into June. This is alleviated in some cities with alfresco summer seasons, and by the institution of the music festival, of which the top two are Florence's Maggio Musicale (in May) and Spoleto's Festival dei Due Mondi (mid-June/mid-July), but there are easily a score more, Aosta through Viterbo. Note, too, that opera is supplemented by ballet and symphonic concerts. Italian Government Travel Offices have advance schedules for major houses, and certain American travel agents may be able to order tickets in advance. None in hand upon arrival, ask your hotel concierge for help, or stand out in front of the theater an hour or so before curtain—as I have done upon occasion, with success—watching for ticket holders wanting to sell.

PASSPORTS: Necessary for admittance to Italy, and to be presented to U.S. Immigration upon your return. Apply at Department of State Passport Offices in a dozen-plus cities (look under U.S. Government in the phone book) or—in smaller towns—at the office of the clerk of a federal court, and at certain post offices. Allow four weeks, especially for a first passport (valid for ten years), for which you'll need a pair of two-inch-square photos and birth certificate or other proof of citizenship. There's a $55 fee (subject to change) for first passports; renewals are cheaper. If you're in a hurry when you apply, say so; Uncle Sam will usually try to expedite if you can show documentation indicating imminent departure. Upon receipt of your passport, sign your name where indicated, fill in the address of next of kin, and keep this valuable document with you—*not packed in a suitcase*—as you travel. In case of loss, contact local police, nearest U.S. embassy or consulate (in Italy, these are located in Rome, Florence, Genoa, Milan, Naples, Palermo, and Trieste), or the Passport Office, Department of State, Washington, D.C. 10524.

PASTA: "A pasta a day keeps the doctor away." That's my tried and tested motto in the course of Italian travels. And I have a confession to make: Some days—naturally, in the course of duty, on behalf of readers—I have been known to have pasta both at lunch *and* dinner. And I am not unlike many, many Italians in this respect; ask them what they most miss when leaving Italy and the answer, invariably, is a daily pasta-fix. Fattening? Well in my case—consumed largely in lieu of desserts other than fresh fruits, in tandem with the considerable walking involved in on-scene exploration—it definitely is not.

Shapes of pasta (below) are limitless,with different shapes responding to different types of sauces. Still other pasta points: There are dry (pasta asciutta) and fresh pastas, green pasta (pasta verde), and also pasta colored with tomatoes and other vegetables. Many species of noodles are made with eggs, although the bulk of pastas are composed of flour and water. Key term, with respect to the degree of doneness in the preparation of all pasta, is *al dente*—to the teeth, firm and chewy, rather than overcooked and porridgey.

When to order pasta? Italians tend to include it among first courses, or *primi,* as they are called. But restaurant staffs in Italy are wonderfully permissive. Have it to start, or, if you prefer, as a *secondo,* or entrée. Whenever you like.

My friend and colleague, Jean Anderson, with coauthor Elaine Hanna—in *The New Doubleday Cookbook* (Doubleday)—categorize the various species of pasta with such clarity—I have not come across any such breakdown, even in books devoted exclusively to Italian cookery I have consulted—that I want to share their summary with you. With some paraphrasing and pruning by me, they see the pasta scene this way: *spaghettis* include capellini, spaghettini, vermicelli, fusilli, spirali, and spaghetti proper; *flat and ribbon shapes* embrace linguine, taglierini, fettuccine, and lasagne; the *noodle* group comprises tagliatelle, trenette, and others of varying widths; such *stuffed pasta* as ravioli, cappelletti, panzerotti, agnolotti, and tortellini; tubular *macaronis* like bucatini, penne, rigatoni, ziti, cannelloni, and manicotti; *fancy-shaped* farfalline (little bows), farfalle (bigger bows), conchiglie (seashell macaroni), and ear-shaped orecchiette; and such *soup pastas* as stelle (stars), stelline (little stars), quadruccini (little squares), conchigliette (little seashells), and pastina (tiny bits of dough). You're bound to come across these—and still other types of pasta, as well as such pasta substitutes as risotto (stir-fried rice) and crespelle (crêpes served stuffed)—in the course of an Italy-wide trip. (See Restaurants, below.)

PORTIERE is the Italian for concierge; they are, by and large, among Europe's most knowledgeable; ask them for help with anything from train and plane reservations to opera bookings. They're bound to have a free supply of maps of the town and, in the case of the bigger cities, a gratis What's-on-This-Week (or This Month) booklet, which tourist offices generally do not stock.

RATES for selected hotels (where I've stayed, or which I've inspected) and restaurants (where I've eaten) are categorized as *Luxury, First Class,* and *Moderate;* these terms translate pretty much into what they would mean in the U.S., adjusted, of course, to the purchasing power of the dollar with respect to the Italian lira at the time of your visit.

RESTAURANTS: Of the European cuisines it is the Italian—or at least a modified version thereof—with which we are most familiar in the United States. Or at least *think* we are. By that I mean to say we can be ridden with stereotypes. Pasta (above) is, to be sure, a delightful dimension of an Italian trip; it is invariably comforting and delicious, and I must admit to succumbing to a daily fix as I travel through Italy. But it is only a phase—just a phase—of the brilliant Italian cuisine, which ranks with French and Chinese among the Global Big Three. Italians, by and large, open their meal with a first course, or primo, of pasta, soup, or hors d'oeuvres (which they term antipasto), going to a main course, or secondo, that may be fish or seafood, meat (veal and lamb are popular, but broiled beefsteaks and grilled sausages are invariably superb, too), or poultry (with turkey supplementing chicken and duck). Contorni—vegetables—are an Italian specialty. No chefs in Europe, save the French and the Greeks, toss a green salad with more finesse. Desserts? I wager there's not a restaurant in Italy ever without a big bowl of macedonia di frutta—fresh fruit cup. Cheese—the grainy Parmesan, especially—is a popular dessert substitute. And there is always a selection of cakes and pastries, not as celebrated, perhaps, as those of France, Britain, Germany, or Austria, but hardly to be despised. Which leaves staples like coffee (strong espresso, frothy cappuccino), crusty bread, wines (below) that are world class, as are Italian-invented, globally emulated pizza, and gelato—the planet's most irresistible (and in my view, best) ice cream.

Let me emphasize that Italians are primarily à la carte-orderers in restaurants. (Table d'hôte, or "tourist," menus are available, but popular mainly in resorts that are filled with foreign visitors on budgets.) Just because Italians open with pasta, soup, or antipasto and continue with an entrée doesn't mean that *you* must. Order what you like; if you opt for a meal comprising, say, pasta and a salad; or soup followed by pasta; or simply an omelet, so be it. A word on *terminology.* Most eating places are ristoranti, but there are trattorie, too. A trattoria is simply a restaurant less elaborate in menu and décor than a ristorante. Caffès serve sandwiches, hot snacks, coffee, tea, hot chocolate, soft drinks, ice cream, wine, and spirits. And places called bars are hardly different from caffès, with quite as much variety; indeed, many city dwellers take their breakfast—rolls and coffee—in them, as indeed you can.

ROME (ANCIENT) TO REPUBLIC (CONTEMPORARY): Which is to say, history: Chapter 2 (Rome) deals the most extensively with what has gone before, the better to appreciate what remains today; chapters on others of the Big Five cities—Florence, Milan, Naples, and Venice—also deal with background in some detail; elsewhere I capsulize, but sufficiently, I hope, to provide you with perspective for intelligent on-scene exploration.

S.I.P. is the Italian telephone company's acronym. You see it displayed in phone-filled shops—often, please note, in railway stations. These are the least expensive places to make overseas or long-distance phone calls; operators assist, and there are no service charges. Phone home from your hotel room *collect;* having the call charged to your hotel account can be outrageously expensive. *Calling from a pay phone* requires that you buy a token, or gettone, at a caffè, tobacconist, or newsstand; dial first, wait for your party to answer, and *only then* drop the gettone in the slot.

TIPPING: Rome and the south constitute a region where tips play a much more important part in the traveler's life than is the case in the north. You must not feel offended if your southerly tips never seem to be adequate; conveying that impression to tippers is simply a part of the southern lifestyle. Stand firm by what you think is fair, proper, and reasonable, albeit not excessive—for porters in air terminals, train stations, and at hotels; hotel doormen who actually hail you a cab (not just opening the door of one parked but inches away), room-service waiters (minimal amounts if fat service charges are automatically tacked onto the check), and concierges, but only if they've performed special services for you. Only if you like, add 5 percent for waiters when a service charge has been added to the check; 15 percent if it has not; 15 percent to taxi drivers *only* if they have *not* charged supplementi, in which case no tip is necessary; small change for coffee or a snack while standing at a bar, and to gas station attendants who clean your windshield. That said, it should not be necessary to add—but I am doing so because some Americans allow themselves to be intimidated abroad—that tips are for cordial, efficient service. At no time are they obligatory in Italy—or anywhere.

TOURS, TOUR OPERATORS, TRAVEL AGENTS: Agents, first: Select one who is affiliated with the American Society of Travel Agents (ASTA), and ideally, who knows Italy firsthand. For a first trip, some travelers are happy with a package; operators making a particular specialty of Italy—whose packages may be booked through retail travel agents—include American Express, Catholic Travel Office/Hodgson Travel Service, Central Holiday Tours, CIT Tours, Donna Franca Tours, Globus-Gateway, Italia-Adagio, Maiellano Tours, and Vavolizza Travel. In studying brochures, note the *location* of hotels—ideally, you want to be *central;* places *actually visited* (not passed by, on the bus); and *free time* at your disposal, especially in cities. An introductory package behind you, consider return visits on your own—to where *you* want to go, at *your* speed.

TRAINS: They do, to be sure, go just about everywhere. First class is of course costlier than second, but is in my view the *only* way to travel on Italian rails. Best trains run between major cities—Rome/Naples, Rome/Florence, Florence/Milan, for example, some of which are first-class-cum-extra-supplement Pendolino or Trans European Express (TEE) trains, the cream of the crop. After Pendolino and TEE, the best are so-called Rapidos (some of which are all-first-class, with advance booking required). They may or may not be all that *rapido,* but are at least swifter than slower Express and Diretto trains; these last to be resorted to *only* when absolutely and utterly necessary. As for amenities like dining cars, snack bars, or even simple refreshment carts on wheels, please note that these are distinctly sometime things, found only on certain trains; inquire when booking, and emulate the Italians—*always* travel with snack food. Seat reservations are possible for certain trains departing from big cities—hotel concierges know which ones—and *whenever you can reserve, do so* or risk standing even in first class. Italian State Railways—whose symbol is *FS,* for *Ferrovie Italiane dello Stato*—sells two types of reduced-fare tickets from U.S. offices of CIT Tours (at 666 Fifth Avenue, New York, NY 10019; and 6033 West Century Boulevard, Los Angeles, CA 90045) that are *not* available in Italy; one, called BTLC, is valid for unlimited travel for periods of 8 to 30 days, and is a very good deal; the other, termed Kilometric, is so zanily and needlessly complex, involving so much paperwork at each station and aboard as well (plus payments of supplements for Rapidos), that I cannot recommend it. Note that railroad personnel invariably speak only Italian, and that sleeping cars are available on certain long-distance trains. Something else again is the privately operated *Venice Simplon-Orient-Express*—a super-luxury service utilizing elegantly refurbished stock from the legendary old Orient Express—that runs between London, Paris, Zürich, and Venice, stopping in Italy at Florence on the way to Venice, and upon return from Venice at Milan.

WINES, by Max Drechsler: Italy is the greatest wine-producing country in the world; every province of every *Regione* of Italy makes wine. As far back as 800 B.C. the Etruscans had become vintners, and winemaking has continued uninterrupted. Grapes grow everywhere, and rare is the farmer who doesn't produce wine, if only for his own consumption.

In 1965, laws were enacted comparable to those of France that regulate consistency of winemaking. Wines meeting established standards are entitled to use the designation Denominazione di Origine Controllato (DOC); they must be made in a precisely defined area, from specified grapes, aged and bottled according to set rules. The same name can apply to a red or a white, dry or sweet, still or sparkling. So specify when ordering, to be sure. While the DOC system is a dependable guide, remember that there are many good wines throughout the country that are not so designated. Wines that follow are table wines, all dry, mainly to accompany meals, though many whites among them make excellent aperitifs.

Apulia—heel of the Italian boot—produces more wine than any other *Regione;* they tend to be more aggressive than refined. Try Castel del Monte and Castel Mitrano (red), and Locorotondo, Leverano, and Donna Marzia (white). *Campania* wisely uses volcanic soil from Mt. Vesuvius—well suited for grapes; best wines still come from areas developed by ancient Romans, including the islands of Capri and Ischia. Try Taurasi and Episcopio (red); Lacryma Christi and Ischia (white). *Emilia Romagna* produces wines in quantity, including Lambrusco, well known to Americans, albeit thin, often sweetish, and to be avoided. Try Sangiovese di Romagna and Gutturnio dei Colli Piacentini (red); Albana di Romagna and Trebbiano di Romagna (white).

Friuli–Venezia Giulia, in the northeast around Trieste, produces excellent wines, thanks to a climate created by proximity of the Dolomites to the Adriatic. Try Cabernet and Merlot (red); Pinot Bianco and Pinot Grigio (white). *Latium,* centered on Rome, produces wines best drunk young; they can be agreeable if not distinguished, and include Cecubo, Falerno, and Torre Ercolana (red); Frascati, Colli Albani, and Castelli Romani (white). *Liguria,* embracing Genoa and the Riviera, has limited vineyard area but grows more than a hundred types of grapes. Try Rossese di Dolceacqua and Pornassio Ormeasco (red); Vermentino and Pigato (white). *Lombardy's* wines rank with the best, and several are excellent, reds especially. Try Sassella, Grumello, Inferno, and Frecciarossa (red); Frecciarossa, Lugana, and Clastidio (white). *Marche's* sole wine of repute is Verdicchio, famous as much for its amphora-shaped bottle as for its flavor.

Piedmont wines are quite in a class by themselves, Italy's finest, and mostly red. Try Barolo, Barbaresco, Gattinara, Barbera, and Dolcetto D'Alba (red); Cortese and Gavi (white). *Sardinia* wines can be heavy but satisfactory. Try Cannonau and Carignano del Sulcis (red); Torbato and Vermentino di Gallura (white). *Sicily's* wines, esteemed by the ancient Romans, include Corvo and Etna (red); Corvo and Etna (white).

Trentino–Alto Adige, on the Austrian border, produces Austrian-influenced wines, some of them notable. Try Cabernet and Santa Maddalena (red); Traminer Aromatico and Pinot Bianco (white). *Tuscany's* Chianti is Italy's most famous wine, for long bottled in straw-covered flasks, whose contents were grapy and insignificant. Now, it appears more often in claret-shaped bottles and can rank with the best reds in France or Spain, especially when marked Chianti Classico, Chianti Classico Riserva, or—a step lower—Chianti Putto. Try Brunello di Montalcino—a truly great wine—and Vino Nobile di Montepulciano (red); Vernaccia di San Gimignano, Galestro, and Elba (white).

Umbria's weather is dependable; most of its wines are good from year to year. Try Castello di Montoro and Torgiano (a.k.a. Rubesco) (red); Orvieto and Torgiano (white). *Valle d'Aosta* grows grapes terrace-style, on mountain slopes. Try Donnaz and Torrette (red); Blanc de Morgex and Vin du Conseil (white). *Veneto* leads Italy's *Regioni* in the number of DOC wines; they tend to be light and refreshing. Try Bardolino, Valpolicella, and Cabernet (red); Soave, Bianco di Custoza, and Tocai Bianco (white). Italy also produces sparkling wines, most famous of which is Asti Spumanti, a sweet, champagne-like beverage; the dry Brut Spumanti (the Cinzano firm's Principe di Piemonte brut is excellent—and truly dry); and three celebrated aperitif wines—Vermouth (dry white and sweet red), sherrylike Marsala, and Campari. This last is often combined in a tall glass with ice and soda, and is the basis of two classic cocktails—Americano (with sweet Vermouth and club soda) and Negroni (with sweet Vermouth, club soda, and a dollop of gin).

2

Rome/Roma

Eternal Lures of the Eternal City

BACKGROUND BRIEFING

For the generation I have known it, Rome has been the most changeless of the capitals. Return when you will, and the skyline as seen from the Pincio, in the Borghese Gardens, is quite as you have always remembered it, with the dome of St. Peter's dominating, as it has for centuries, and as surely it will for many centuries more. The municipal authorities—whose oft-seen symbol, "SPQR" (Senatus Populusque Romanus), dates back to a Senate that met twenty-five hundred years ago—have not had the success they would like in restricting the automobile from the core of the city. (Although cars are forbidden between 6 A.M. and 10:30 A.M., traffic continues to be horrendous.) But they have kept the skyscraper out in the newer peripheral sections. Central Rome remains, rather miraculously, the Rome of the Caesars, of the great Renaissance-era quattrocento, of the beautiful Baroque centuries, even of the later nationalists' Risorgimento that resulted in the city becoming capital of a modern, united Italy.

It is not necessary in Rome, as in other cities, to make special excursions to an "old town." You are already there. Your hotel is within walking distance of where your Roman hosts' ancestors lived more than half a millennium before Christ was born. The rather gruesome Romulus and Remus legend having to do with the founding of Rome is no more than that: legend. You may remember that these twins were brought up at first by a female wolf on whose breasts they fed, later by a shepherd, and that Romulus, after doing in his sibling twin, set about founding the town that took its name from his, populating it with local passersby whom he mated with ladies of the neighboring Sabine tribe, these last having nothing to say in the matter.

THE ETRUSCANS' ROME

There is more sense in the historians' reports that it was the ancient Etruscans who gave the settlement its name—the very same Roma it is called today—in the seventh century B.C. The Roman Republic was formed in 509 B.C. and by 272 B.C. Rome had the whole Italian peninsula under its control, as you discern from prefatory paragraphs in succeeding chapters of this book. Then came the conquest of Carthage, whose ruins still are to be seen on the Tunisian coast, across the Mediterranean. All of the Hellenistic states fell to Rome. Asia Minor, Egypt, Greece, Spain, and Gaul followed, so that by the time Julius Caesar (102–44 B.C.) took over as dictator, Rome controlled the entire Mediterranean world. Caesar intelligently reformed what had become a strife-ridden state, with a program that ranged from the granting of citizenship rights to the Spaniards and Gauls to intensified public building on the home front. But his good works ended with his assassination, and within decades the republic had become the empire.

Its first emperor, Octavian Augustus, was extraordinarily competent; he set a course of peace and prosperity that lasted for two centuries. Rome, despite the stigma of the institution of slavery, had long since accepted the culture of the Greeks whom it had conquered, and had continued to extend its frontiers. This was the period of such emperors as the high-living but nonetheless efficient Nero, whose reign ended with his suicide; of Hadrian, the sophisticated administrator and reorganizer; and of Marcus Aurelius, at once a fine ruler and a philosopher-teacher.

THE SPLENDOR OF IMPERIAL ROME

Imperial Rome—visualized today from its remarkable core-of-town remains—was a luxurious and architecturally splendid city of a million population whose life revolved around the market center that was the Forum and the entertainment center that was the Colosseum, and whose upper classes knew central heating, efficient sanitation, and running water.

Both republic and empire were studded with immortals—Lucretius (poetry), Caesar (history), Cicero (author of the first Latin prose, with his *Orations*), Virgil (poetry as exemplified by the *Aeneid*), Horace (poetry and satire), Livy (history), and Pliny the Younger (prose).

It ended in 476—the fateful year when a barbarian upstart named Odoacer was able to dethrone Romulus Augustinius. Politically, Rome was overlarge and overwieldy. Spiritually, there was the conflict of the new Christianity with the old Roman religion. Morally, there was the spectacle of a slavery-dependent society, sloppy-rich at the top, and with the masses at once morale-poor and economically impoverished.

Which is hardly to write classical Rome off as a decadent bust. We are still, a couple of millenniums later, greatly in its debt. We learned from the enormous empire Rome administered for centuries how sophisticated governments are organized and run. We inherited legal codes that were the first to espouse the principle that better a guilty man go free than an innocent man be adjudged guilty.

The Latin language, from which all of the Romance languages sprang—not to mention other languages with Romance connections, like our own—is a major Roman legacy. And so, for that matter, was the rich culture—embodying art, architecture, philosophy, and literature—that the Romans adopted from the Greeks and passed along to posterity.

The Rome of the Great Popes

Rome, as an empire, moved east to the Byzantium that the Emperor Constantine renamed Constantinople, after himself. But within the city the power that was increasingly to be reckoned with was that of the leaders—or pontiffs—of the rapidly growing Christian Church, who gave Rome an eminence in the area of religion that it had lost in matters political. Still, the early medieval centuries saw tremendous decline. Gregory I, the sixth-century pope who was one of the greatest Romans of them all, started the city back on the road to greatness. The later establishment of the Holy Roman Empire, with German emperors assuming their crowns in Rome, gave the city a renewed prestige, if not the political power it once knew. But the Middle Ages were not Rome's proudest. There were incessant squabbles between factions vying for the papacy that resulted in periodic turmoil and a variety of types of government.

Coincident with the arrival of the fifteenth century, moral standards in the papal court sank to a level that made easy the appeal of the Reformation. Withal, this period—the fifteenth century, or quattrocento—was the Golden Age of the arts in Italy, of popes like Sixtus IV, Innocent VIII, Leo X, Clement VIII, whose patronage of the arts, possibly not always with spiritual motivations, resulted in the employment of such geniuses as Michelangelo and Raphael in the papal courts. They created much of the Rome that we know today, and their successors, in the Baroque period of the seventeenth and early eighteenth centuries—Bernini, for example—added to the city's still-evident splendor.

Savoy Kings, Mussolini, Today's Republic

By the time Napoleon invaded Rome at the end of the eighteenth century, its papal rulers had made of it one of the great cities of the world. Intervening decades saw popes in and popes out. At one point

Mazzini—one of the three great leaders of the nineteenth-century Risorgimento movement for Italian unity, along with Garibaldi and Cavour—headed a short-lived Italian republic. But in 1870, Rome became capital of a united Italian kingdom under the House of Savoy. King Victor Emmanuel II that year moved into Quirinale Palace, displacing Pope Pius IX, who retreated to the Vatican to complete the longest pontificate in history.

From that year until 1929, the Vatican and the Italian government were angry with each other, the popes not recognizing during all that period the loss of their imperial sovereignty. (With the 1929 Lateran Treaty, they agreed to sovereignty only over Vatican City.)

Fascism marched into Rome—and Italy—in 1922 with Benito Mussolini, who promptly took over the government (leaving the little king, Victor Emmanuel III, a puppet and creating for himself the title of Il Duce). Mussolini became at once an imperialist (snatching Ethiopia in the face of the League of Nations' condemnation), racist (emulating the anti-Semitism of fellow dictator Hitler), Axis partner (with his admired Hitler), and supplier of troops to Francisco Franco's insurgent Spanish Civil War troops.

Italy joined Germany in World War II, to suffer losses so severe that Mussolini's own people overthrew him, executed him in 1945 at Lake Como, and ended the war on the Allied side. At war's end King Victor Emmanuel fled the country for Egypt (where he died a few years later), leaving the throne to his son Umberto. Umberto's reign was not long—from May 19 to June 13, 1946. A referendum voted the monarchy out of existence.

Republican Italy, in the north at least, has made remarkable economic progress. The long-impoverished south remains behind the rest of the country in many economic and social areas. The seventies saw the beginning of a southern development fund, and reforms in education and housing. But the same decade saw ultimately successful agitation in the city that is the seat of the worldwide Roman Catholic Church, for divorce, birth control, and legal abortion. Years of negotiation culminated in a 1984 concordat with the Vatican—replacing that of 1929—that ended Catholicism's status as Italy's state religion. This new concordat guarantees religious freedom for Italians, makes religious education in schools optional, and divests Rome of its status as a "holy city," which had allowed church-imposed bans of films, books, and plays.

This is a city that has known Octavian Augustus and Julius Caesar, Virgil and Horace, Napoleon and Mazzini, the Victor Emmanuels and Mussolini, Gregory I and John XXIII, Michelangelo and Bernini. It can take work stoppages and challenges to spiritual dogma, and the comings and goings of late-twentieth century premiers: Rome remains the Eternal City.

ON SCENE

Lay of the Land: The wise visitor to Rome walks until his feet kill him and he can go no farther. He then relaxes over an espresso in a caffè and resumes. There is always the door of a newly discovered church to open, with who-knows-what great art or architecture within. Or a newly noticed shop to case. Or a restaurant that looks inviting. Rome is at once the Romans themselves—attractive, animated, amusing—and the Rome they and their ancestors have created. Take a look at whatever map you have and find the north-south thoroughfare called *Via del Corso.* It is Rome's principal street, and its extremities are easy-to-remember landmarks. At the north is *Piazza del Popolo,* with central obelisk, trio of churches, and location just beneath the Pincio Hill of the Borghese Gardens. The southern extremity of Via del Corso is *Piazza Venezia.* You cannot miss it because it is dominated by the massive nineteenth-century wedding cake that is the Vittorio Emanuele Monument. Palazzo Venezia, onetime office of the dictator Mussolini and now a museum, is opposite the monument, and what is left of ancient Rome is just behind it: the Forums, Capitoline Hill, and, more distant, the Colosseum.

Retrace your steps on Via del Corso about two thirds of the way back to Piazza del Popolo, until you come to *Via Condotti,* on your right. It is at once the heart of the smartest shopping area in town and leads to *Piazza di Spagna*—the Spanish Steps area—which is where you're likely to bump into Cousin June or your college classmate or the couple you sat with on the bus your first day in town. There are flower vendors in the plaza, and the splendid steps leading up to the Church of Santa Trinità dei Monti are congested the summer long with souvenir-selling youngsters from various points of the planet.

From Piazza di Spagna, you may proceed to Piazza del Popolo by *Via del Babuino,* the main antiques-shop street of Rome, or along *Via Margutta,* another fashionable thoroughfare running parallel with Babuino. Now you're wondering how to get to Via Vittorio Veneto, of which you've heard. Ascend the Spanish Steps to *Via Sistina,* taking Sistina (another interesting shopping area) to *Via Francesco Crispi,* turning left on that street until you reach *Via Ludovisi* with the Eden Hotel on its corner. Walk down Via Ludovisi a couple of blocks, and you've reached *Via Veneto.* Continue to its summit, and you bump smack into Villa Borghese—the Borghese Gardens. Walk downhill on Via Veneto and you pass a number of hotels as well as the ex-royal palazzo that serves as the American Embassy; follow Via Veneto's curve and you are at *Piazza Barberini* with its landmark Triton fountain by Bernini.

From Piazza Barberini, you may take shop-lined *Via del Tritone* westward to Via del Corso—where you began. Or you may walk south on *Via Quattro Fontane* to the massive Basilica of Santa Maria Maggiore, thence a few blocks to its right and *Stazione Termini,* the strikingly contemporary main railway station. St. Peter's and the Vatican are across the Tiber. You may take either of two bridges, one leading directly to the circular fortress-landmark that is Castel Sant' Angelo. The other is closer to *Via della Conciliazione,* which leads to *Piazza San Pietro* and the basilica, with the Vatican Museums to the right of St. Peter's as you approach. On this same side of the river, but considerably below St. Peter's and the Vatican, is the mellow *Trastevere* quarter, which you will want to amble about, perhaps in connection with a lunch or dinner.

THE ESSENTIAL ROME

One man's Rome is not necessarily another's. Still, based on visits and revisits over the years, these dozen destinations are counseled to the short-time visitor, the newcomer not tarrying for long, as the essence—or at least an essence—of the city.

Città Vaticano–San Pietro and Cappella Sistina: Who knows, if the pope were to commission a headquarters today for the Catholic faith, what might be constructed? Italy is not without distinguished contemporary architects, artists, and artisans. Still, the likelihood is that the result might be an inverted shoebox, with a travertine face. There is no disputing the good luck of the Church to have built when it did, reaping the genius of the Renaissance.

No great global monument is more easily distinguished, more a part of its environment. Interminable spats with the Vatican over the centuries notwithstanding, Roman city fathers have left St. Peter's dome to dominate the skyline. One sees it from almost everywhere in town. And as you walk to it from the Tiber, you realize that you cannot separate it from the piazza fronting it and bearing its name. One's spiritual faith, or even a total lack of it, is not all that important, when it comes to the world's smallest country. St. Peter's Basilica, laying aside its function as No. 1 Catholic place of worship (only the pope may officiate at mass from the high altar), is Rome at its most reassuring, its most stable, yes—even more so than the core-of-town remnants of the ancient empire—its most eternal.

It took well over a century to build. By the time it was consecrated by Pope Urban VIII in 1626, collaborators had included Michelangelo (the still-ascendable dome and the marble *Pietà*—the Virgin with Christ descended from the Cross—which crossed the Atlantic to the 1964–65 New York World's Fair and made news again in 1972 when it was damaged by a Hungarian fanatic), Bernini (the brilliant altar canopy or baldachin, and the piazza, without), and Raphael (the façade). From stem to stern, length exceeds 600 feet. The dome is almost 400 feet high.

There's a lot to take in—richly decorated chapels (daily masses are said in Cappella del Coro), papal tombs, monumental sculpture, and, more impressive than any of the component parts, splendid scale.

There is a Treasury, with relics and ornaments, and, in the Grotto, entered from the left of the basilica, a maze of papal tombs spanning the history of the church, from St. Peter to John Paul I. Both basilica and piazza—the colonnaded oval that is a mid-seventeenth-century Bernini creation—are impressive enough empty, or nearly so. Still, both deserve attendance in the course of a papal-led mass, ceremony, or audience (100,000 in the square is not an unusually high figure).

Cappella Sistina, the Sistine Chapel, a part of the Vatican Museums complex (of which more later), goes back to the early sixteenth century. It is the site of meetings of the College of Cardinals, when a new pope is elected. If your visit is a summer one, prepare for a mob scene in the Sistine. Indeed, every part of it except the ceiling—which Michelangelo began painting in 1508, and which was the subject of a controversial 1980s restoration—will be occupied. Have a good look around. The end wall is Michelangelo's interpretation of the Last Judgment, while the ceiling embraces his Creation and Prophets. The right and left walls are by other artists—Botticelli most especially, but also Luca Signorelli, Pinturicchio, and Ghirlandaio. But the Sistine is, more than anything else, Michelangelo, a masterwork that even upon repeated revisits remains one of the great interiors of a city where great interiors are commonplace. The crowds are understandable.

Ancient Rome—Colosseo and Pantheon: There is no question but that strolls through the Forums are rewarding. Still, there are two absolute requisites of the old empire. Both are well enough preserved, these many centuries later, for the nonarchaeologist visitor to immediately perceive this city as it was some two millenniums past. The Colosseum is sufficiently intact to be appreciated for what it was: seat of the action, with gladiators vs. lions and other fun and games, dating back to the first century, and with a seating capacity of some fifty thousand—not bad if you consider that ancient Rome had a population of about a million.

It is difficult to believe that work was begun on the Pantheon almost three decades before Christ was born. It is the only 100 percent shipshape ancient Roman building. Its domed, colonnaded exterior is in such good condition that it could be neo-classic. But it's the real thing. The unusual proportions of the dome are not fully appreciated until one steps inside. The Pantheon is now a church, and contains the tombs of the painter Raphael and of monarchs of the House of Savoy.

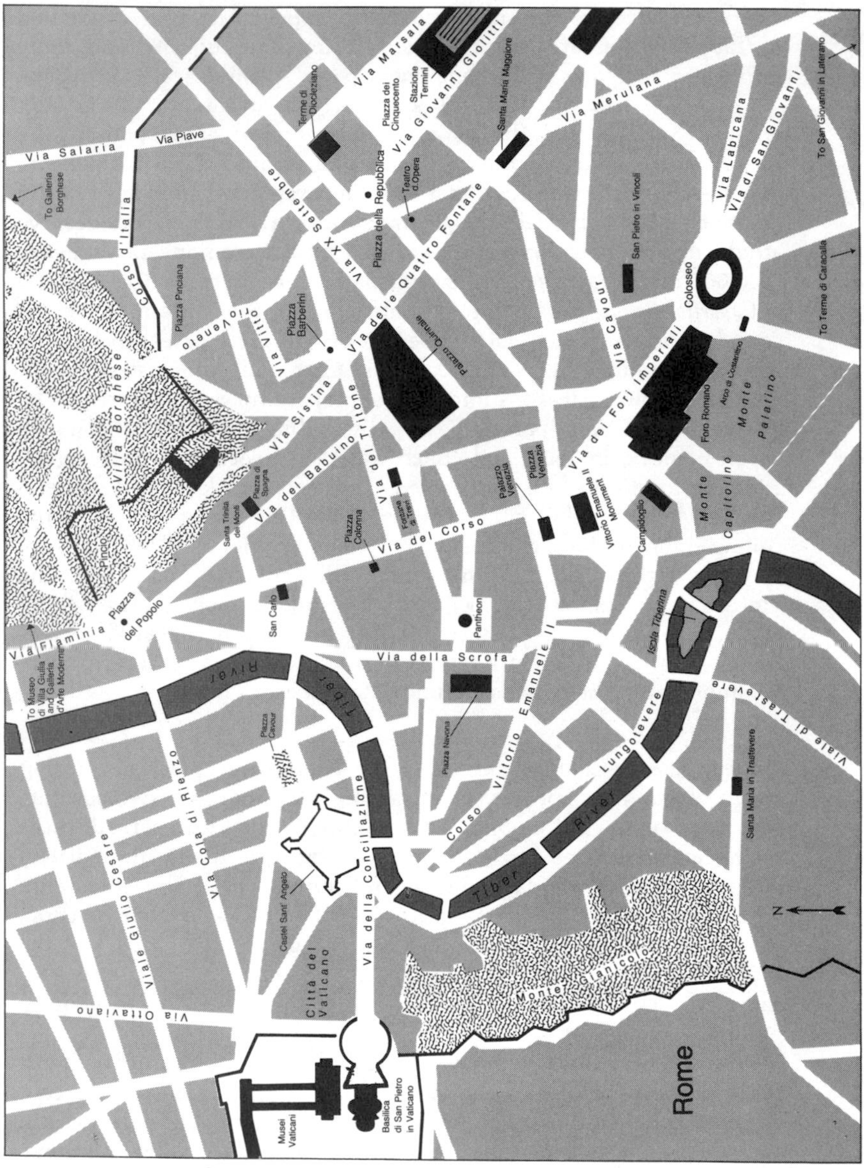
Rome
Via Salaria
Via Piave
Via Marsala
Stazione Termini
Via Giovanni Giolitti
Piazza dei Cinquecento
Terme di Diocleziano
Santa Maria Maggiore
Via Merulana
Via Labicana
Via di San Giovanni
To San Giovanni in Laterano
To Galleria Borghese
Corso d'Italia
Via XX Settembre
Piazza della Repubblica
Teatro d.Opera
Via delle Quattro Fontane
San Pietro in Vincoli
Colosseo
To Terme di Caracalla
Piazza Pinciana
Via Veneto
Via Vittorio
Piazza Barberini
Palazzo Quirinale
Via Cavour
Via dei Fori Imperiali
Arco di Costantino
Foro Romano
Monte Palatino
Villa Borghese
Via Sistina
Via del Tritone
Via del Babuino
Piazza di Spagna
Santa Trinità dei Monti
Fontana di Trevi
Piazza Colonna
Via del Corso
Palazzo Venezia
Piazza Venezia
Vittorio Emanuele II Monument
Campidoglio
Monte Capitolino
Pincio
Piazza del Popolo
Via Flaminia
San Carlo
Pantheon
Isola Tiberina
Via della Scrofa
Corso Vittorio Emanuele II
To Museo di Villa Giulia and Galleria d'Arte Moderna
River Tiber
Piazza Navona
Lungotevere
Viale di Trastevere
Santa Maria in Trastevere
Piazza Cavour
Via Cola di Rienzo
Viale Giulio Cesare
Castel Sant' Angelo
Via della Conciliazione
Città del Vaticano
Via Ottaviano
Monte Gianicolo
Musei Vaticani
Basilica di San Pietro in Vaticano
N

Two of the five major basilicas—Santa Maria Maggiore and San Paolo Fuori le Mura: "Basilica" is the title given to certain churches by the pope as a special honor. (It is not to be confused with "cathedral," a church—which may or may not be a basilica—that is the seat of a bishop.) Rome has a higher proportion of basilicas than any other city. Of these, five, in addition to St. Peter's, are considered top-rank, for a variety of reasons—historical and ecclesiastical. The interiors of the lot are formidably severe, immense, and virtually chairless. (Do not plan on resting weary feet.) San Giovanni in Laterano, or St. John Lateran; San Pietro in Vincoli, or St. Peter in Chains; and San Lorenzo Fuori le Mura (St. Lawrence's Outside the Walls) are later described. The other two follow St. Peter's, up here in this honor group of requisite Roman attractions. One, *Santa Maria Maggiore* (St. Mary Major), is called to the reader's attention at this point for several reasons. First is that it is the major *(maggiore)* church in Rome named for St. Mary, of many, many, many. (There are more St. Mary's churches in Rome than those by any other name.) The second is that it is so heart-of-town, fronting Piazza Santa Maria Maggiore, as central a Rome landmark as, say, the nearby railway station, which is close only geographically; in age, some fifteen centuries separate the two. Santa Maria Maggiore goes back to A.D. 431, although it has been several times remodeled. It's a mix of styles, with a Baroque façade, a Renaissance campanile (the tallest in town), and a multiperiod interior with a magnificent coffered ceiling, fine mosaics, a number of chapels, and, as in the case of all major basilicas, tremendous scale.

San Paolo Fuori le Mura (St. Paul's Outside the Walls), on Via Ostiense, is special for two reasons: First is size. This is the largest church in town after St. Peter's. Second is beauty. This is the loveliest of the major basilicas, with a Romanesque cloister that frames a garden of quiet charm, and a mosaic frieze of popes, St. Peter to John XXIII. Though originally ancient, most of the church one sees today is mid-nineteenth century, a meticulous restoration that took two and a half decades to complete, following an 1823 fire.

A pair of requisite museums: Museo Nazionale Romano–Baths of Diocletian and Galleria Nazionale d'Arte Antica–Palazzo Barberini: Thanks to the global repute of the Vatican Museums—which persist, even in the late twentieth century, in covering the genitals of nude sculptures with fig leaves, but which are otherwise estimable—museums of Rome proper are among the most undervisited of any capital in Europe. They are also among the Continent's very best, and, I might add, often devoid of fig leaves. I am fond enough of them to have singled out a score-plus of favorites that are dealt with in later pages. At this point, though, I single out two representatives as requisites. They have been selected not only because of their exhibits—one deals with ancient Rome, the other with the Italian Renaissance—but because of absolutely smashing settings.

Museo Nazionale Romano–Baths of Diocletian (Piazza della Repubblica) comprises the baths themselves—a complex of high-ceilinged, splendidly proportioned halls and patios, built seventeen centuries ago (when it accommodated some three thousand bathers)—and a collection of classical art (earmarked, alas, for eventual transfer to new quarters on Piazza Cinquecento) that ranks with that of the National Archaeological Museum in Naples: mosaics, frescoes, sarcophagi, and sculpture—both busts and full figures, ranging from a *Satyr Looking at His Tail* to an *Amazon Leaping on a Fallen Gaul.* Take note, too, of the odd group, *Gaul Killing Himself after Having Killed His Wife,* of the head of a gorgeous goddess who may or may not have been Aphrodite, of a geometric mosaic simply called *Whirling Disc,* of a seated pugilist. It is worth noting (nobody in the museum is going to tell you) that also created out of the ancient baths—or at least from one of the baths' immense halls—is the Church of Santa Maria degli Angeli (later described). Its architect was Michelangelo himself. Museum and church have completely separate entrances and there are no signs directing the visitor from one to the other.

Galleria Nazionale d'Arte Antica–Palazzo Barberini is one of two component parts of the national ancient-art museum. (The other, in Palazzo Corsini, is recommended on a later page.) Barberini is heart-of-town (13 Via Quattro Fontane). It is sumptuous Baroque (Carlo Maderno and, later, Bernini were its designers and the great builder-pope, Urban VIII was its original occupant). The paintings are sumptuous too—mostly Renaissance and mostly Italian (with seventeenth- and eighteenth-century Italian works among others, in Palazzo Corsini). Barberini's treasures are abundant—Tintoretto's *Jesus and the Adulterous Woman;* Lotto's *Portrait of a Young Man;* Raphael's seductive lady, *La Fornarina;* Piero di Cosimo's exquisite *La Maddalena;* Titian's *Venus and Adonis;* a Holbein of *Henry VIII.* But paintings on the walls are not all. The ceiling of the immense ballroom, called *Il Trionfo della Gloria,* and painted by Pietro da Cortona, is a glorious triumph indeed, and surely the No. 2 ceiling in town, after that by Michelangelo in the Sistine Chapel.

A Renaissance palace—Palazzo Farnese: Aside from those palazzi now doing duty principally as art museums, there are others to be regarded principally for their architecture and decoration. Palazzo Farnese (Piazza Farnese) was begun in 1514 by Antonio Sangallo the Younger—using building materials from the Colosseum, of all places. But it was completed by Michelangelo. The entire structure is a work of genius—architectural proportions, arched entrance vestibule, super-high ceilings, frescoed and tapestried reception rooms. The White Room was where Sweden's Queen Christina lived after her abdication in the mid-seventeenth century, when she left Sweden for Rome and became a Catholic. For long the French Embassy, and open to the public every Sunday morning, the palazzo has, in recent seasons, closed its doors to visitors. In the hope that a future ambassador will again open its doors, I bring it to your attention at this point, and suggest that if you would like to have a look in the interim, you request permission from the Ambassador's secretary, by telephone, upon arrival in Rome. *Bonne chance!*

A square and a fountain—Piazza Navona and Fontana di Trevi: No Italian city, indeed no European city, is more beautifully endowed with these beloved appurtenances of urban life. Piazza Navona is the most romantic in town. Bernini's glorious Fontana dei Fiumi dominates, but there are seventeenth-century palaces and churches (including Sant' Agnese, later described), restaurants, and caffès. Until a little over a century ago the square was flooded on summer Sundays, becoming Rome's—if not Europe's—No. 1 swimming pool. Fontana di Trevi is the richest such in the world, ever since the world learned from a film, *Three Coins in the Fountain,* back in the 1950s, of the old legend decreeing that if you threw a coin into Trevi (presumably with your back to it) you were bound to return to Rome. On one visit, I happened by at about ten in the morning. The water had been turned off and the fountain's pool drained, while sanitation men (bank tellers, they should be called) gathered up the previous day's haul. There appeared to be enough to keep a visitor in Rome for an entire season. Coins or no, the mid-eighteenth-century fountain is Rome's most dramatic, with its exuberant, Baroque, chariot-drawn Neptune surrounded by playing gusts of water.

A suburban excursion— Villa d'Este at Tivoli: Despite the spectacular crenelated towers of its fifteenth-century fortress and a few mellow churches, the town of Tivoli would not be worth the boring twenty-mile drive eastward from Rome. It is Villa d'Este that makes it an exceptional excursion destination. What happened was that an ambitious sixteenth-century cardinal named Ippolito d'Este (whose mother was Lucrezia Borgia) thought he had enough money and power to land himself the papacy. While still a young man, he served at the court of François I, in France. Back home, he found himself governor of Tivoli, whose official residence was—at least for this man whose home had been the French royal court—a relatively plain ex-monastery. What he did, then, was build Villa d'Este, with the collaboration of a brilliant team—architect Piero Ligorio and a slew of designers, artists, artisans, and—not to be overlooked—landscapists. It was these last—the garden planners—who are responsible for Villa d'Este's lasting fame. The house is a fine

Renaissance country villa, but in and of itself, it would never draw the crowds that come. They want to see the fountain-filled formal gardens. If you except Petrovorets, Peter the Great's horticultural fantasy at his country palace outside St. Petersburg, there is nothing else—anywhere—that can touch them. And you do not need a great deal of time—half a day all told will do it. There is a great central Fountain of Dragons, or Girandole, a walkway (verdant and sparkling, bordered by no less than a hundred fountains), grottoes and fishponds, grand stairways and sprinkled sculpture.

BEYOND THE BASICS: SELECTED MUSEUMS

Earlier on in this chapter I include two Roman museums—National Gallery-Palazzo Barberini and Roman National-Baths of Diocletian—among requisites for even the most abbreviated of Roman visits. In that same honor group the Sistine Chapel—actually a part of the Vatican Museums complex—is also included. Now come a score more, as recommended for their settings—palaces, villas, town houses, even a castle—as for their contents.

Castel Sant'Angelo (Lungotevere Castello) is a Roman surprise package, at least to the many visitors who believe that the ancient circular mausoleum-cum-fortress-cum-papal-palace on the right bank of the Tiber near the Vatican is today no more than a historical landmark, to be admired for its derring-do façade. Well, step inside. Up you go on the ramps that connect the various levels, in which are housed exhibits ranging from armor, guns, and swords to Renaissance paintings and frescoes, with a series of sumptuous papal apartments the real treats, most especially the so-called Cupid and Psyche Room with its Del Vaga frieze, and a carved and gilded ceiling of unusual beauty.

Galleria Borghese (Viale del Museo Borghese) houses a remarkable group of paintings and sculpture collected by Cardinal Borghese in the seventeenth century—not long after most of these works were created. The beautiful gallery was designed for the purpose for which it is still being used. The cardinal knew how to pick paintings—Raphael's *Deposition from the Cross,* Titian's *Sacred and Profane Love,* Caravaggio's *Madonna dei Palafrenieri,* Botticelli's *Three Angels Singing,* Bernini's *Self-Portrait,* a Carpaccio *Courtesan,* a Bellini *Madonna, St. John the Baptist* as interpreted both by Veronese and Bronzino. But these are just a handful of what is a major Italian collection.

Galleria Farnesina (Via della Lungara) occupies an exemplary early-sixteenth-century mansion whose interior decorators included Raphael and Il Sodoma (both of whom painted striking frescoes), not to mention other ravishing works. To be combined with Palazzo Corsini, just opposite and below described.

Galleria Nazionale d'Arte Moderna (Viale delle Belle Arti) is hardly in a league with New York's MOMA, Paris's Pompidou, Amsterdam's Stedelijk, or even Milan's or Stockholm's lesser-known modern-art museums. On hand are representative works of such foreigners as Braque, Cézanne, Courbet, de la Fresnaye, Degas, Mondrian, Van Gogh, and Utrillo. There are several galleries devoted to their Italian contemporaries—mostly unknown to visitors from abroad, but not without interest.

Goethe Museum (Via del Corso 18) is worth a brief inspection, even to non-Goethe fans, if only because it provides one an opportunity to see the interior of a central Rome town house of considerable vintage. Goethe was in residence from 1786 to 1788, and the place is crammed with objects relating to his stay and its influence on his work.

Keats-Shelley Memorial House (Piazza di Spagna 26) is perhaps of more interest to English-speaking visitors than the Goethe house, above. Still, aside from its architecture (it went up in 1725) and limited furnishings, it is mainly for Keats, Shelley, and Byron buffs, with memorabilia of all three English poets, each having lived in Rome. (Only Keats was in residence in this house; it was where he died in 1821, while on an extended visit with painter Joseph Severn.)

Museo Barracco (Corso Vittorio Emanuele 168) embraces a curious variety of periods. It occupies a sixteenth-century palace that, if hardly exuding warmth and charm, is nonetheless soberly grand. It is named for a late-nineteenth century baron who gathered together its exhibits, which are mostly sculpture of Egyptian, Roman, and Etruscan times, paling in contrast to the Barracco's high point: its coffered ceilings. City of Rome is the landlord.

The Museo Capitolino (on Piazza del Campidoglio—a Michelangelo-designed square in the heart of ancient Rome) is adjacent to Palazzo del Senatore—Rome's Town Hall, which is not open to visitors. Still, its exterior double staircase is a sight in and of itself, and so is the statue in the center of the square of Emperor Marcus Aurelius; it goes back some eighteen centuries, during which time few equestrian sculptures have surpassed it. Operated by the City of Rome, the Capitolino is noted for its ancient sculpture, with *Statue of the Dying Gaul* the most memorable single work, along with a lovely Venus and a sculpture from Etruscan times (some twenty-five centuries ago) of the notorious she-wolf who mothered Rome's legendary founders, Romulus and Remus. Gems of the Pinacoteca, or picture gallery, include a Michelangelo self-portrait, a Bellini *Youth,* Titian's *Baptism of Christ,* and—again relating to Rome's founding—Rubens's *Finding of Romulus and Remus,* in the midst of taking nourishment from their wolf-mother's breast. There are works, as well, by Veronese, Tintoretto, Giovanni Bellini, Caravaggio, Annibale Carracci, and Guercino among the Italians; and by such foreigners as France's Poussin and Spain's Velázquez. When you've absorbed the museum, and if the day is fine, sit for a spell on one of the stone benches of the piazza, and gaze at the panorama of Rome, spread out below.

Museo Nazionale d'Arte Orientale (Via Merulana 248) occupies the second floor of a somber palace, not far from Santa Maria Maggiore. Many Western cities—Toronto, Paris, Stockholm, to name a few—have far more substantial Asian art collections. Still, if you are in the neighborhood, climb the staircase and have a look. (The guards, who often have few customers, cannot help but be perked up by your visit.) There is good early Persian pottery, Indian and Nepalese sculpture, Thai Buddha heads, and, occupying most of the space, considerable Chinese work—paintings, ceramics, statues, textiles.

Museo Nazionale delle Arti e Tradizioni Popolari (Piazzale Giuseppe Marconi 10) is a considerable distance from central Rome, in the EUR section, named for the international exposition Mussolini intended to mount in 1940. Although there is later construction in the area, built for the 1960 Olympics and including Nervi's Palazzo dello Sport, the neighborhood is essentially Mussolini Modern, which, no matter what else one thinks of this lasting manifestation of Italian fascism, is substantial. The museum is devoted to Italian folk art, by *Regione*—furniture, clothes, ceramics, rugs, needlework, woodenware, painting and prints, religious articles, toys, and dolls. And there is a fabulous full-scale Venetian gondola.

Palazzo Braschi (Piazza San Pantaleo 10) is the museum of the history of Rome, chockablock with paintings and pottery and sculpture, and other objects—from mosaics to a papal throne—illuminating the background of the city. Still, setting supersedes exhibits. Palazzo Braschi is a late-eighteenth-century structure that was built to house a papal nephew. The main stairway is neo-Renaissance, but the various rooms put one in mind of eighteenth-century England's Robert Adam. Every salon has frescoed ceilings and walls, massive eighteenth-century paintings, and fine eighteenth-century furniture. Lovely.

Palazzo Corsini (Via della Lungara 10) continues underappreciated. Located on the right bank of the Tiber near Trastevere, it went up in the early eighteenth century for Pope Clement XII's family, replacing an earlier palace that had been the home of Sweden's self-exiled Queen Christina in the seventeenth century. (A plaque outdoors states that "La Regina Christina di Svezia mori in questa stanza il 19 aprile 1689" and is accompanied by the same text in a Swedish translation, explaining that the queen died within.) At any rate, the opulent Corsini is repository of the mostly seventeenth-century paintings of the Galleria Nazionale d'Arte Antica, the remainder of which is housed in earlier-recommended Palazzo Barberini. To see? I counted five Caravaggios, including his matchless *St. John the Baptist,* other Italians like Reni and Carracci, Giordano, and Strozzi; and more foreign art than one often sees in Italian museums—Van Dyck, Rubens, de Hooch, Murillo, Brueghel. Not to mention the palace itself, its painted ceilings a major Roman treat. (And earlier-recommended Galleria Farnesina is just across the street.)

Galleria Doria Pamphili (a.k.a. Palazzo Doria Pamphili): I don't think there's any question but that this is Rome's most eccentrically operated museum. And finding it is not easy. It's on a square called Piazza del Collegio Romano, which is just west of Via del Corso (at its Piazza Venezia end). Take Via Lata from the Corso, and in a moment you're on the square housing the Doria Pamphili. Its building is designated only by a bronze plaque that says *Galleria* and *I-A.* Before making the trip, double-check the odd hours, which, traditionally, have been Tuesday, Friday, Saturday, and Sunday only, from 10 A.M. to 1 P.M. But wait; the foregoing are hours for that portion of the gallery—in a Baroque-era mansion that had been home to Pope Innocent X and others of the Pamphili clan—displaying a brilliant but oddly uncelebrated collection of paintings, which include a Velázquez of the house's papal occupant, Titian's *Herodias,* and works as well by Tintoretto, Correggio, Raphael, Giordano, Reni, Giovanni Bellini, Del Sarto, and Bassano—among the Italians; and Teniers, Rubens, Quentin Massys, Brueghel, Van Dyck, Dürer, and Lorrain among the foreigners. A hall of mirrors, smaller than that of Versailles but hardly less splendid, with a sumptuously frescoed ceiling, edges these galleries, so that all visitors are able to take it in. But there's more: the palace's private apartments. You must arrive by no later than 10:30 A.M., and upon arrival buy a ticket for a tour of these apartments, in addition to the ticket of general admission. Between 10:30 and 11, one of the palazzo's handful of guards (usually exclusively

Italian-speaking) wanders through, asking tour ticket holders to join him or her. You are led through a series of chambers—mostly decorated (like the hall of mirrors) and furnished in eighteenth-century, a hundred or so years after the house was built. The smoking room, first on the expedition, has a coffered ceiling, tapestries on walls, and leather-covered chairs. A portrait of Columbus by Jan Gossart dominates the second room, named for the mariner Andrea Doria. Crystal chandeliers hang from the ceiling of the ballroom, with silk-brocade walls, original parquet floor, and a frescoed ceiling. From Sala di Bal, you pass through a series of smaller rooms—one in yellow with needlepoint-tapestry panels surfacing walls; one in red, highlighted by Brueghel paintings of each of the four seasons; another in green, with painted chairs typical of Rococo Venice, and paintings attributed to Longhi. Tour's end finds you in the family chapel, with a ceiling frescoed mostly in tones of gray, seventeenth-century marble altar, stations of the cross of majolica pottery and gilt-framed; and instead of pews, eighteenth-century armchairs upholstered in red damask. It's quite a show. As well it should be. There are two admission fees—one for the art collection, another to see the gallery's state rooms.

Galleria Spada (Piazza Capo di Ferro 3) is difficult to find and does anything but encourage visitors. With so much great art elsewhere in Rome, the Spada is not an essential destination. There is no excuse for an art museum not labeling its paintings. You must consult duplicated lists of artworks, few of which are available in each room. Within are a quartet of galleries, containing paintings—Del Sarto, Bassano, Tintoretto are among the artists—frescoes, and furniture. Room No. 3 is the most elaborate; every inch of it is busily decorated.

Palazzo Venezia (Piazza Venezia) is possibly the most bypassed museum in central Rome. It is pointed out as a fine specimen of fifteenth-century architecture and as a former home not only of Renaissance popes and later Venetian ambassadors, but of this century's dictator Benito Mussolini—who harangued the Romans from a balcony. Within, though—once one finds the entrance, which is not easy—is a museum of the decorative arts: furniture, tapestries, ceramics, metalwork, even armor, mostly all Italian Renaissance. Recent seasons have seen the Venezia serving a second function: its long disused reception halls—high-ceilinged, still with original decorations—are now put to use for short-term exhibitions. If such a show is underway when you're in Rome, take it in. And, upon exiting, pop into the Palazzo's separately entered *Cappella dell' Adorazione,* a Baroque jewel of a chapel, so tiny it seats only twelve.

Musei Vaticani (Viale Vaticano): The Vatican Museums complex (gained by the sole entrance on Viale Vaticano) can overwhelm if one lets it. To some visitors, a look at the paintings in its Pinacoteca represents the Rome museum scene in toto. To others, too many of its component parts are undertaken at a single time, with resulting museum fatigue of the worst kind. Ideal tack is to divide the Vatican Museums into several inspections. The *Sistine Chapel*, a part of the group, is earlier recommended as a Roman requisite. It and the Pinacoteca evince the most visitor interest. The latter dates to the eighteenth century, when Pope Pius VI began systematically to collect and group together paintings from various parts of the Vatican. Much later, in the early 1930s, Pope Plus XI built a modern building for the collection, which now numbers some 500 paintings, representing Italian art through the centuries. There are exquisite Giottos and Fra Angelicos, Bellini and Da Vinci, Titian and Raphael, Caravaggio and Bordone, and as a bonus a surprising group of French Impressionists. The *Raphael Rooms* (Stanze di Raffaello) are not so well known as the Sistine Chapel but are quite as special. They house a series of frescoes on various themes—mostly biblical and classical. The adjacent *Raphael Loggias* are a gallery full of religious-theme paintings based on designs by the master but executed by his students. *Museo Pio-Clementino* is a treasure trove of classical sculpture, with that of *Laocoön and His Sons*—being gruesomely strangled by snakes—perhaps the outstanding piece. *Chiaramonti's* highlights are busts of the Roman emperors, in a sumptuously decorated gallery. The extraordinarily beautiful *Library* is elaborately frescoed, full of fascinating manuscripts and globes. The *Borgia Apartments* are a suite of rooms that for long constituted the papal residence; chief decorator was the artist Pinturicchio (who painted a series of frescoes in the late fifteenth century). The *Papal*—or *Nicholas V—Chapel* had no less a master than Fra Angelico as its decorator. There are a *Tapestry Gallery*, an *Egyptian Gallery*, and an *Etruscan Gallery*, all top-drawer.

Villa Giulia (Piazza di Villa Giulia 9) is of dual interest. The handsome house had been the sixteenth-century summer retreat of Pope Julius III. In and of itself, it is a delight of no mean aesthetic value. Exhibits are of quite another era—mostly superb pottery of the extraordinarily gifted Etruscans (who preceded the ancient Romans) indoors, with a gem of a meticulously reconstructed Etruscan temple in the capacious garden.

BEYOND THE BASICS: SELECTED CHURCHES

It is to its everlasting credit that the Catholic Church, in its headquarters city, has never considered art and architecture incompatible with dogma. Quite the contrary. Even the earlier medieval churches, of which some remain, set aesthetic standards. Then, with the Renaissance, and upon the return of the seat of the papacy to Rome from

France's Avignon, the city began to blossom as an artistic as well as spiritual center, under art-minded pontiffs like Sixtus IV, Julius II, and Leo X in the fifteenth and sixteenth centuries. There was no stopping, though, with that era. Roman church construction continued under popes like Urban VIII in the seventeenth century and Benedict XIV in the eighteenth. Rome today, as a consequence, is a veritable maze of churches, from the biggest and grandest, St. Peter's, through to charming, albeit uncelebrated, Baroque parishes in every corner of the older precincts. (Of contemporary churches in the suburbs the less said—aesthetically, at least—the better.) So as to give the newcomer an idea of the magnitude of the church plant, if that it may be called, I have suggested as Roman requisites earlier on in this chapter, not only St. Peter's, but two of the five so-called major basilicas. Each of this quintet could easily serve as sole principal place of worship in any leading city. But in Rome this group is but frosting on the cake. Scores more churches are artistically, architecturally, and historically worthwhile. From this overwhelming total, I single out some forty of a group of many more that I have visited.

That said, let me add this word: Simple exteriors can conceal opulent interiors. Pop into whatever churches you pass by. Relatively few of those in the central city will disappoint; more often than not they are exemplary on architectural lines, with art treasures as well. You may enter when masses are being said, but *quietly* and *unobtrusively.* At other periods, don't hesitate to query priests or sacristans for details, in whatever languages are at your disposal. (Many clergy speak English, French, or German.)

Churches close for long midday breaks, but when a church is open, one can generally count on a priest being on duty, if not in the church proper, then in the sacristy *(sacrestia),* where—in more cases than with today's museums—postcards and even guidebooks of the subject structure are on sale. (Look for postcards in automatic wall dispensers, too.) Location of sacristies? They are usually behind closed doors to either side of the main part of the church, or to the rear; don't be afraid to snoop about. Only rarely are there signs directing one to them.

For that matter—and of more import—only occasionally are there easily discernible, clearly legible signs on the exteriors of churches so that you know their names. Too often, posters advising of special activities in other churches are what strike one's eye. To ascertain the name of a church, step into its vestibule, the tiny passage that no Italian church is without, through which one proceeds to the interior. Most vestibules have bulletin boards on which the church's name and time of masses are indicated. In Italian, of course. Which is why I give the Italian names of churches, there being little gained in translating, say, Santa Maria del Popolo into St. Mary of the People.

Sant' Agnese in Agone (Piazza Navona): If you are not up on St. Agnes's tribulations, it's worth noting that she is said to have been forced to disrobe on Piazza Navona just before her execution. She was saved from humiliation only by Providential aid, with her long hair unfurling and curtaining her naked body from stares of the assembled curious. This Baroque church commemorating her agony is handsomer without; two side towers frame a central dome, the lot beautifully blending into the beautiful square. Inside, look up at frescoes lining the cupola.

Sant' Agostino in Campo Marzio (Via di Sant' Agostino) is originally fifteenth-century and was rebuilt in the eighteenth, with a façade embracing both Renaissance and Baroque motifs. The interior dazzles, with a dozen side chapels, beautifully decorated cupola and high altar, and paintings by Caravaggio *(Madonna dei Pellegrini)* and Raphael *(Isaiah)*—among them.

Sant' Andrea al Quirinale (Via del Quirinale), bearing the name and in the shadow of the presidential (and ex-papal) palace, does not disappoint. It's a little gem of Baroque, the work of no less a master than Bernini.

Santa Brigida (Piazza Farnese) is for viewing in conjunction with a visit to earlier-recommended Palazzo Farnese. It has a blue ceiling dotted with gold stars, and there is an exquisite gilded sunburst over the altar. Dazzling.

San Carlo al Corso (Via del Corso) gives one a clue to its importance with the towering dome (the work of Pietro da Cortona) behind its Baroque façade. Within, one is overwhelmed by tremendous size—high and long and wide—and ceaseless decoration, the chief delights of which are sculpted angels at every turn.

San Carlo alle Quattro Fontane (a neighbor of Sant' Andrea al Quirinale, above) is at the intersection named for its quartet of Baroque fountains, one on each corner. It's a case of big things coming in small packages—Baroque, with an unusual oval-shaped dome, and a winsome galleried cloister.

Santa Cecilia in Trastevere (Piazza di Santa Cecilia) embraces a variety of styles, and they all come together nicely, from early mosaics to Baroque sculpture, most certainly including frescoes by Pinturicchio, a Romanesque campanile, and a joyfully tranquil courtyard.

San Clemente (Piazza di San Clemente), a near neighbor of the Colosseum, is named after the fourth pope, who died toward the end of the first century, only decades after the first pope, St. Peter. The two-level Basilica of San Clemente is somewhat newer. It embraces a twelfth-century street-level church and a fresco-decorated fourth-century subterranean church: a treasure trove of sculpture, mosaics, and frescoes. Irish Dominicans have operated San Clemente for almost three centuries; nowhere in Rome does one hear lovelier English spoken, although there are still more Irish priests at San Silvestro in Capità (below).

SS. Cosma e Damiano (Via in Miranda, adjacent to Foro Romano) is a basilica at once boasting great age and great art. It goes back to the fourth century, with later additions. The standout work is a sixth century mosaic, over the apse, of Christ, Saints Peter and Paul, and two martyrs. But there are half a dozen side chapels with paintings and a Renaissance frescoed ceiling. The adjacent monastery is the mother house of that branch of the Franciscans known as the Third Order Regular of St. Francis—and has been since 1512.

Il Gesù di Roma (Piazza del Gesù) is world headquarters church of the Society of Jesus. It is a masterful late-sixteenth–early-seventeenth-century work that has served as prototype for Jesuit churches around the world. The immense Baroque interior is one of the most lavish in Rome, with quantities of gold and jewels in the décor, a lapis lazuli-embellished tomb with the remains of St. Ignatius Loyola (the Jesuits' founder), splendid frescoes, and superbly decorated side chapels.

San Giovanni in Laterano (Piazza di San Giovanni in Laterano)—or St. John Lateran—is one of the five major basilicas along with Santa Maria Maggiore, San Pietro in Vincoli, San Paolo Fuori le Mura, and San Lorenzo Fuori le Mura. St. John Lateran dates to the first Christian emperor, Constantine. (Although its façade is eighteenth century, and a lot within is from other epochs.) The surrounding complex includes the palace wherein was signed the 1929 Lateran Treaty between the Vatican State and the Italian Government. The church itself—immense, formal, and formidable—is designated the Cathedral of Rome. Gilded wood ceiling and mosaic-decorated apse highlight the interior, but what one wants most to see is the thirteenth-century cloister, among the handsomest in town. (What one may—or may not—want to see is the nearby *Scala Santa,* a staircase in a Renaissance building that is supposed to contain the actual steps—twenty-eight of them—used by Jesus when he went before Pontius Pilate for sentencing. For this reason, there are faithful who climb this Holy Staircase on their knees; note the relic-filled chapel at the top, closed to the public but visible through windows, and gained, also, by a second, unsanctified stairway.)

San Girolamo della Carità (Via di Monserrato) adjoins church-dotted Piazza di Santa Caterina della Rota, near Piazza Farnese and its earlier-recommended palace. Its interior, with marble employed as you may not have seen it elsewhere, is among the more sumptuous in Rome.

San Giuseppe dei Falegnami (Forum Romano) can easily, not unlike SS. Luca e Martina (below), be passed by, given the competing splendor of the Forum ruins. Still, it was in the dungeonlike, still visitable *priogone* below this church that Saints Peter and Paul were imprisoned (you want to have a look).

Above, the little Renaissance church has a gilded coffered ceiling, balconied walls, and an angel-framed Baroque organ.

Sant' Ildefonso (Via Sistina) is too often passed by. Walking this street you're generally en route to or from the Spanish Steps, which lead down from it. But a pause in this church can be rewarding. It's a small Renaissance jewel and interestingly multilingual. By that I mean masses are said in Spanish as well as Italian, while confessions are heard, additionally, in English and Portuguese.

San Lorenzo Fuori le Mura (Piazzale San Lorenzo) occupies a place of honor among Rome churches; it is one of the handful of major or Patriarchal Basilicas, so called because their patriarchs, or leaders, have always been popes. Least well known of the quintet, San Lorenzo, not far east of the main railway station, was created by uniting two distinct, albeit adjacent, Romanesque churches, with its single modern addition the tomb of Italy's respected post–World War II premier, Alcide de Gasperi. Behind a colonnaded façade is the tomb not only of St. Lawrence, but those of Saints Stephen and Justin. The bishop's throne is mellow thirteenth century. But loveliest of all is an equally aged cloister, double-storied and serene. The *Catacombs of Cyraica*—or at least what remains of these third-century subterranean burial chambers—are adjacent, visitable through a trio of entrances, with original paintings the principal embellishments.

SS. Luca e Martina (Forum Romano) is so tiny that you might pass it by while ambling through the Forum. Don't. This elegant Baroque confection was the work of painter Pietro da Cortona. A very high dome frames a very small, crucifix-shaped interior, quite severe save for sublime da Cortona paintings backing the side altars.

San Luigi dei Francesi (Piazza di San Luigi dei Francesi) labels itself also as St. Louis des Français; it is the French national church in Rome. (You may hear mass *en français tous les dimanches à* 10:30.) The Renaissance façade is striking. So, for that matter, is the interior, whose special treasures are a trio of massive Caravaggio paintings in the last chapel on the left and a series of Domenichino frescoes—the subject is St. Cecilia—in the second chapel on the right. *Vive la France!*

San Marco (Piazza San Marco alongside Palazzo Venezia), originally fourth century, was rebuilt in the ninth and remodeled in the fifteenth and seventeenth centuries. A Romanesque belfry stands alongside it, but it is medieval mosaics within—of Christ and the Apostles, along the walls of the apse—that draw—and awe—one, the eye being led to them through a series of graceful arches framing the single nave.

Santa Maria degli Angeli (Piazza della Repubblica) is a part of the earlier-recommended Museo Nazionale Romano–Baths of Diocletian—the part of these ancient Roman baths that Pope Pius IV commissioned Michelangelo to turn into a church. And a remarkable church it is, with an immense, high-ceilinged, colonnaded Renaissance interior that remains very grand—if hardly warm or inviting. (Even though both museum and church are carved out of the old baths, each has a separate entrance, and there are no signs to help one get from one to the other. If you've inspected the museum first, the church entrance is to the museum's left.)

Santa Maria dell' Anima (Via della Pace 20) is to my knowledge the only Catholic church in town that keeps its doors locked during open hours. This may or may not have to do with the fact that it's the Deutsche Nationalkirche in Rome. (Masses are said in German.) At any rate, after one finds the bell, the German-speaking Italian sacristan opens up. (The price of his postcards is *per Stuück*, or by the card.) There is a little gem of a courtyard, filled with lovingly tended plants. And, within, the smallish interior yields treasures, including Raphael frescoes, a papal tomb (Hadrian VI), and a rather super high altar.

Santa Maria d' Aracoeli sul Campidoglio is notable for its location (on the Capitoline Hill just next door to the earlier-recommended Michelangelo-designed Musei Capitolini), its façade (somberly striking, virtually unadorned buff-colored brick), the main approach to it up a dramatic flight of 124 steps that were built in 1348, its essentially Renaissance interior (with a memorable ceiling of that era), and works of art by Donatello and Bernini, among others. All told, this basilica goes back fifteen centuries. Franciscans have run it since the thirteenth century, and so that I don't frighten you away by my mention of those steep 124 steps, let me note that there is another entrance on Piazza del Campidoglio.

Santa Maria in Cosmedin (Piazza della Bocca della Verità) is on a square named for its best-known appurtenance, the decorative cover of a drain hole in its entryway. Bocca della Verità translates as Mouth of Truth. The sculpted cover is of a man's face, with a big opening for the mouth. Legend has long decreed that anyone holding his hand in the mouth while swearing to tell the truth, but not so doing, would find himself minus a hand; the mystically endowed jaws of the mouth would chop it off.

Santa Maria di Loreto and Ssma. Nome di Maria (Piazza Venezia at Via dei Fori Imperiali) are so tiny, in contrast to the fussy bulk of the Vittorio Emanuele Monument, that they are easily passed by. Neither individually nor taken together could they be called important. Still, this pair of domed octagonal churches—Baroque twins, you might call them—are charmers as much within—frescoes and mosaics decorate them—as for their façades. Usually one or the other is open.

Santa Maria Nova (Via Sacra), in the heart of ancient Rome, goes back to the tenth century, but except for its medieval campanile is now mostly Baroque, with a multicolored coffered ceiling its outstanding feature, and a fifth-century painted *Madonna and Child* its most charming surprise.

Santa Maria degli Angeli (Piazza Esedra) is a stunner of a Baroque beauty—immense and architecturally superior, with trompe-l'oeil altars, Corinthian capitals atop columns of the nave, and dazzling frescoes surfacing side walls by such artists as Lotto, sculpture by Houdon, and the high altar—with a papal tomb—by Michelangelo.

Santa Maria della Vittoria (Via XX Settembre, not far from Quirinale Palace) is a high Baroque masterwork—especially within—by Moderno, with a gilded sunburst on its high altar, Bernini's sculpture of St. Theresa in ecstasy, and half a dozen art-filled side chapels. Special.

Santa Maria del Popolo (Piazza del Popolo) is one of the trio of churches on this great oblong of a square (later described). Of the three it is the oldest and finest, thanks to great art within. This is an essentially

Renaissance structure, with Baroque additions. To be especially noted are frescoes by Pinturicchio in two chapels and the main-church ceiling; the Raphael-designed Chigi Chapel; a *Nativity* by Piombo, and two Caravaggios in still another chapel. While you're in the piazza, pop in, also, to the Baroque near-twins—*Santa Maria dei Miracoli* and *Santa Maria in Montesanto.*

Santa Maria in Traspontina (Via della Conciliazione) is a Baroque beauty on the street leading to St. Peter's—in case you were wondering if the great basilica has any competition in its immediate neighborhood. The answer is yes. This is but one of a number, with a finely coffered ceiling, imposing dome, and crown-topped altar.

Santa Maria in Trastevere (Piazza Santa Maria in Trastevere) is a landmark whose Romanesque façade is known to countless diners in restaurants across the square it fronts. Go in. Lures are a coffered ceiling, Byzantine altar, and a nave delineated by chunky neo-Ionic columns.

Santa Maria dell' Umiltà (Via dell' Umiltà 30) is the beautifully embellished Baroque chapel of a Dominican convent that was turned over to the American Catholic bishops in the mid-nineteenth century by Pope Pius IX. Until 1953, it was the North American College in Rome; in that year, a much larger college building was opened on Janiculum Hill, in the Vatican, to house the college's undergraduate students. The smaller graduate group now uses the Via dell' Umiltà building as headquarters. It also contains the Bishops' Office for United States Visitors to the Vatican, operated by the U.S. Conference of Catholic Bishops. For Catholics, this is where parish priests write in advance for tickets to Wednesday-morning papal audiences. Others may write to this office in advance, or call there in person, to arrange for tickets (they are free).

Santa Maria in Vallicella (Piazza della Chiesa Nuova) is a place of special charm. Pietro da Cortona decorated the ceiling, cupola, and apse frescoes with grace and style. Rubens painted three pictures; even the marble floor is noteworthy.

Santa Maria in Via (Via Santa Maria in Via, near Piazza Colonna) is ravishing Baroque, with a splendidly frescoed ceiling framing its nave, spectacular high altar, and no less than eight side chapels, with those immediately to the right and left of the high altar especially beautiful.

Santa Maria in Via Lata (Via del Corso at Via Lata) is another Roman church (see SS. Luca e Martina above) graced by the hand of Baroque painter Pietro da Cortona, who redesigned what had been a much older structure. Small but adroitly proportioned, the interior is rich with detail, a coffered ceiling and frescoed walls the standouts. A refreshing pause from the Corso shops.

Santa Maria della Vittoria (Via XX Settembre) is surpassed in the exuberance of its décor by no other Roman Baroque church. It is mostly the work—as regards interior design—of Carlo Maderno, with a major exception of frescoes by Domenichino and a breathtaking sculpture—*St. Theresa in Ecstasy*—by Bernini. There is a ceiling fresco framed by sculpted angels, and a gleaming gilded sunburst dominates the high altar.

San Pietro in Montorio (Piazza San Pietro in Montorio) is atop Janiculum Hill, with super views of the Vatican and Rome. The church is Renaissance with a quartet of paintings by Sebastiano del Piombo, a chapel by Bernini, and, in its little courtyard, a circular, classic-style temple by Bramante.

San Pietro in Vincoli (Via degli Anibaldi) is the major basilica of St. Peter in Chains, so named because it is the repository of chains of St. Peter's Jerusalem and Roman imprisonments; they are contained in a glass-walled bronze casket in front of the main altar. The pewless, multi-period sanctuary is severely handsome and dominated by Michelangelo's oversized, powerful statue of a stern, long-bearded Moses—principal reason for a visit.

Santa Pudenziana (Via Urbana) is a bit of Early Christian Rome. In other words, a rarity. Parts of it date to the fourth and fifth centuries, including, from the latter, a still-graphic mosaic. The campanile is Romanesque, but most of the church was restored in the sixteenth century and is still essentially as it was then. Special.

Quattro Coronati (Via del Querceti) is an away-from-the-center combination church-convent that sees few contemporary visitors. One enters as callers have since medieval times. You knock at the entrance of a convent of cloistered nuns. A revolving metal box—surely as old as the church itself—is silently turned outward to meet your gaze. You open it and, bending to look within, find an equally venerable key, with the veiled face of a silent nun in the darkened background. The key opens the church, which in turn leads to a serene garden-cloister that (along with one of the chapels—San Silvestro) is one of the most memorable of Roman destinations. On leaving, one returns the key the same way.

San Silvestro in Capite (Piazza San Silvestro in Capite) is a Baroque enchantment. One enters through an unexpected front yard. The church, under a ravishing ceiling fresco, is walled in *faux-marbre,* and fringed by half a dozen side chapels; first on the left has paintings by Francesco Trevisani, which the Irish Pallottine priests—a detachment of them along with Italian students runs the place—regard as the principal treasures. Mass is said in English, with an Irish lilt to it.

Santa Susanna (Via XX Settembre): What one most remembers about Santa Susanna—apart from the not unimportant fact that it is operated by American Paulist fathers, whose mother church is the big, gray, neo-Gothic St. Paul the Apostle on New York City's Ninth Avenue—is a pair of absolutely enormous frescoes on both of its principal inner walls by Baldassar Croce, responsible for a number of other luminous works as well. But chief credit for this Renaissance masterwork of a church goes to Carlo Maderno, in charge of its stem-to-stern restoration in the late sixteenth century. Masses are said in Yank-accented English, and there's a worth-knowing-about bulletin board used by resident Americans to buy, sell, swap, rent, or whatever.

San Teodoro (Via di San Teodoro) is in ancient Rome, beneath Palatine Hill, and is itself appropriately ancient. Strikingly circular in design, it dates to the seventh century, if only partially. An important mosaic excepted, it is mostly Renaissance restoration.

SSma. Trinità (Via Condotti): A church on mercantile Via Condotti? Why not? Even more mercantile Via del Corso has several. Condotti's Holy Trinity is a minuscule but gorgeous Baroque work, its dome framing an oval space ringed by tiny chapels. Confessions are heard in English.

Santa Trinità dei Monti (Via Trinità dei Monti), atop the Spanish Steps, and with twin campaniles, has been a Rome landmark since it went up some four centuries ago. By and large, it is best appreciated from without, which is just as well, as it appears rarely to be open, except for fashionable weddings, when uninvited visitors are rudely banned entry. Such, at least, has been my experience.

A ROMAN MISCELLANY

Arco di Costantino went up seventeen centuries ago to commemorate a military victory of the forces of Emperor Constantine. It remains almost completely intact, beautifully carved and inscribed, with its bas-reliefs variations on a theme of valor in battle. Location is opposite the Colosseum.

Castelli Romani—Roman Castles—is the collective name of a group of picturesque little towns in the Alban Hills, or Colli Albani, southeast of town. They make for a nice day-long excursion in the warm-weather months, when the pope is invariably in residence at his summer palace in *Castel Gandolfo.* Traditionally he holds audiences on Wednesday mornings, along the lines of those held the rest of the year in the Vatican. If I had but two choices to make on a Castelli Romani outing, the first would be to Castel Gandolfo, for a walk round the pretty little square, a look at the Baroque papal palace (by the same Carlo Maderno who designed St. Peter's) from without its walls, and a view of the immense water-filled crater way below. There are agreeable little caffès for refreshment, most especially the local wine—white, crisp, and fruity. And the domed church on the square—designed by Bernini and with plaques commemorating papal visits—is special. I would return to Rome, then, by means of the road through other regional towns, stopping at *Frascati,* which gives its name to the most celebrated of local white wines. There is a bustling central sector—you might want to walk about, investigate shops and caffès, and pop into the cathedral. And there are a number of elaborate Renaissance mansions, most especially *Villa Aldobrandini,* in an open-to-visitors terraced park.

Catacombs of San Callisto: Catacombs, nothing more than the fancy name for underground cemeteries, are not everyone's idea of fun. Still, they are not without historic, theological, or, for that matter, architectural interest. There are four major groupings in and about Rome. Most important are those of San Callisto, out on the ancient Appian Way. They go back to the second century and are named for a pope who suffered martyrdom in the Trastevere quarter of the city. A band of priests are the contemporary custodians of San Callisto, guiding small groups from a ground-level reception area (with a chapel) into the depths. What you see is an elaborate maze of chambers, decorated with frescoes and containing tombs of about a dozen early popes. There is, as well, a niche marking the site where St. Cecilia was originally buried, along with a copy of the statue by Carlo Maderno that stands alongside her burial place at the Basilica of St. Cecilia in Trastevere.

Contemporary architecture: The Parioli sector, north of the Borghese Gardens and home to the *Foreign Affairs Ministry*, is Mussolini Modern, that is, overscaled and built to last (if not necessarily to please aesthetically). In this same northern area is *Foro Italico*, post–World War II name for the prewar Foro Mussolini, with a range of buildings including the immense *Olympic Stadium* and the much smaller, and adjacent, sculpture-encircled *Stadio dei Marmi*. Still more remnants of the Mussolini era are to be found south of town, in the *EUR area*, the initials standing for Esposizione Universale di Roma, Il Duce's planned 1940 Fascism Fair, which, because of the war, never came off. Still, the buildings in the exaggerated style of the period remain, most especially the *Palazzo della Civilità del Lavoro*, with its façade a maze of arched windows set in white marble. The architecture of the period has a heavy-handed look that, if not felicitous, at least says a lot more for its designers than much of the plasticlike construction of later decades, which is represented in this area by *Palazzo dello Sport*, built for the 1960 Olympics.

Fontane (Fountains): Along with Viterbo (chapter 40) Rome is the most fountain-filled of cities. *Fontana di Trevi* is earlier recommended in The Essential Rome. *Fontana dei Fiumi* is the Bernini masterwork—actually a trio of fountains with a central obelisk—that dominates Piazza Navona. One of its two neighboring fountains, *Fontana del Moro*, whose central figure of a Moor, dolphin in hand, is also by Bernini. So, for that matter, are *Fontana del Tritone*—surely the most dramatic of the smaller Roman fountains—on Piazza Barberini, and less celebrated *Fontana delle Api* (Bees' Fountain) at the Via Veneto intersection. *Fontana delle Tartarughe*, a sixteenth-century treasure by the sculptor Landini, on Piazza Mattei, is named after the bronze turtles drinking from its waters. *Fontana delle Naiadi* is the circular attention-getter in Piazza della Repubblica. *Le Quattro Fontane* are located at the intersection of Via del Quirinale and the street called Quattro Fontane. The four fountains are Baroque conceits, one each on the side of the buildings flanking the crossing, and—imitation being the sincerest form of flattery—have been copied in Palermo (chapter 24).

The Forums (Roman and Imperial) and Palatine Hill: I have earlier recommended the Colosseum and Pantheon as the best of ancient Rome because they are the most intact of its souvenirs, the easiest to come to grips with. The recently restored (1988) arch of Constantine, dating to 315 A.D. and a Colosseum neighbor, is noteworthy too. The Forums, Roman (the original) and Imperial (its successor), are ruins of the ancient city, in part restored. Many visitors content themselves with vistas of the contiguous area they occupy, from a distance. A better way to take in this beautiful area is to walk down Via dei Fori Imperiali, linking the Colosseum and Piazza Venezia with the Roman Forum on one side and the Imperial Forums on the other. Each forum area keeps specific open hours, museum-style. Foro Romano (Roman Forum) requisites include the 100-foot high *Trajan Column, Marcus Aurelius Column, Arch of Septimius Severus* (all restored in 1988) as well as remains of two once-lovely temples—*Antonio e Faustina* and *Castore e Polluce.* Fori Imperiali (Imperial Forums) musts are *Basilica di Massenzio,* especially its trio of magnificent arches, and the hundred-foot column, *Colonna Traiano,* which dominates the Foro Traiano area. History-studded Palatine Hill, from which there is a splendid panorama of the forum, is not without substantial monuments. See the frescoes in *Casa di Livia,* what is left of a once vast stadium, and, just above it, *Domus Flavia,* the remarkable Imperial Palace.

Isola Tiberina is a much ignored island of some little beauty smack in the waters of the Tiber, near Piazza Venezia and the forums. Approach by bridge from either riverbank. Have a look at the *Church of San Bartolomeo,* on the site in one form or another for a millennium.

Ostia (less than twenty miles from town) means two things to Romans. First, and the oldest by a couple of millenniums, is *Ostia Antica*—the excavations (begun near the turn of the century) of a remarkable ancient port city. The other is *Ostia Lido,* Rome's No. 1 seaside resort. Ostia Antica operates with specified hours. My suggestion is to start out in its museum, with documentation as well as objects—including evocative frescoes—that explain the ancient city's significance. Then amble about, taking in mosaic-decorated baths, once-imposing forum, mosaic trademarks of various ancient merchants in Piazzale delle Corporazioni, and theater, used for contemporary performances in summer. Ostia Lido, jammed by Romans in the warm-weather months (they reach it in half an hour by train from Stazione Termini) embraces beaches and facilities for changing.

Palazzi (Palaces) are frequently put to public use in Rome, and a number so employed are called to your attention elsewhere in this chapter. Others, not necessarily open to the public but worth an inside peek if you can manage it, and certainly an exterior appraisal, include *Palazzo* *della Cancelleria* (Piazza della Cancelleria), a Renaissance masterwork built under papal auspices and still Vatican property, of especial style and elegance, both as regards its colonnaded façade and its inner courtyard; *Palazzo Chigi* (Piazza Colonna), severely handsome, beautifully proportioned, late-Renaissance in era, currently housing Italian cabinet offices; *Palazzo Madama* (Piazza Madama), Roman outpost of the powerful Florentine Medici, who rarely stinted on building budgets, seventeenth century outside, eighteenth within, and now the Senate, or Upper House, of the Italian Parliament; *Palazzo Montecitorio* (Piazza di Montecitorio), seat of the Lower House of Parliament, immense, formidable, and dating back to Bernini (mid seventeenth century); and *Palazzo Margherita* (Via Veneto), an elaborate neo-Renaissance beauty out of the late nineteenth century that once housed a queen but is now the embassy of a republic, to wit, the United States of America. Most significant of the lot is *Palazzo del Quirinale,* the history of Rome for the last four centuries all in a single building that went up in 1574 as a papal summer palace, remaining the pontiff's home until about a century ago when Rome became the capital of the unified Kingdom of Italy. Savoyard monarchs then replaced popes until after World War II, when the current republic succeeded the monarchy and the palace became seat of the presidents of Italy, with interiors—completed over a period of several centuries—magnificent, most particularly the high-ceilinged, fresco-walled Sala Regia. We must be optimists and hope that an Italian president will follow the practice of American presidents—in the case of Washington, D.C.'s, White House—and institute regular visitors' hours for the Quirinale. Ask your hotel concierge, in any case, how to go about requesting permission for a special tour. At any rate, try popping into the Quirinale's across-the-square neighbor, eighteenth century *Palazzo della Consulta.* It had been a papal ministry—the Foreign Ministry and the Ministry of African Affairs—during the period when Italy controlled Ethiopia and Libya, and is now a law court.

Parchi (Parks): There are a number on the fringes of town—*Monte Mario,* in the north (its landmark for travelers is the Cavalieri Hilton Hotel), is a good example—but for most visitors, *Villa Borghese* (Borghese Gardens) best exemplifies verdant Rome. It is a vast green named for the seventeenth-century cardinal whose estate it was. Within it are three earlier-recommended museums as well as *Giardino Zoologico* (Rome's zoo and a delightful destination for half a sunny day). Its Pincio sector is entered from Piazza del Popolo, and from Porta Pinciana, atop Via Vittorio Veneto.

Piazze (Squares) not otherwise brought to your attention are many. Let me concentrate on a handful. *Piazza Barberini* is so near Via Vittorio

Veneto that many visitors get to know it—and its earlier-recommended Bernini-designed Fontana del Tritone. *Piazza Colonna* straddles busy Via del Corso—Rome's main street—and is distinguished by the Marcus Aurelius column in its center, earlier-described Palazzo Chigi, and colonnaded Palazzo Wedekind. *Piazza della Repubblica,* still also called by its former name of Piazza dell' Esedra, is graced by the earlier-mentioned Fountain of the Naiads. *Piazza del Popolo* is one of the city's great Baroque squares, at the terminus of Via del Corso, and with three first-rank churches, earlier recommended. *Piazza del Quirinale* is dominated by the presidential palace, not to mention neighboring palaces as well as churches, a number of which are earlier described. There is a central obelisk and, thanks to the elevation, splendid vistas. *Piazza di Spagna* is, along with Via Veneto, the most visitor-trod territory in town. The 137 magnificent steps of *Scalinata della Trinità dei Monti* lead from the square to Via Sistina. The steps are eighteenth century and the fountain in the square is more than a century older. *Piazza Venezia* is also of requisite visitor interest. First, because of the landmark, a turn-of-century mock-classic horror, that is a monument to King Victor Emmanuel II and is known locally as Vittoriano; second, because of earlier recommended Palazzo Venezia; third, because the square is a terminus of important Via del Corso; and fourth, because it is the entry point to ancient Rome (above). *Piazza di Santa Maria in Trastevere is* the heart of the across-the-Tiber Trastevere quarter, with a disproportionate quantity of restaurants and venerable monuments. *Piazza del Campidoglio* was designed by Michelangelo and houses a trio of palaces, one of which is now a museum, earlier recommended.

Stazione Termini (Piazza Cinquecento): It is a pity that the Italians have not taken post-World War II architecture more seriously; ugly modern apartment buildings similar to those the world over excepted, there has been little important public construction—nothing to match the output of Mussolini Modern in the 1930s. Stazione Termini, the main station, is modern Roman design at its most striking—long, sleek, and of a piece, an immense marble rectangle whose exterior is an easily identifiable landmark and whose interior is at once coolly severe and utterly functional.

Vatican City (Città del Vaticano) is essentially, for the visitor at least, tours of St. Peter's Basilica and the Vatican Museums, earlier recommended. At this point it might be worth noting that this compact enclosure of just under 109 acres (even tiny Monaco is four times as large), with a population of about a thousand, is a sovereign state, under terms of agreements with Italy, most especially the Lateran Agreement signed in 1929, incorporated into the Constitution of the postwar

Italian Republic in 1947, whose 1984 replacement I summarize on an earlier page. The concordats define Vatican City to include St. Peter's, the Vatican Palace (the papal residence to the right of St. Peter's as you approach it), the museum complex, the gardens, and adjacent structures, as well as a group of thirteen buildings outside the Vatican, including the Basilicas of St. John Lateran, St. Paul's Outside the Walls, and Santa Maria Maggiore (see Selected Churches, above), and the summer papal palace at Castel Gandolfo (see Castelli Romani, above).

Vatican City exchanges diplomats with some seventy countries. President Franklin Roosevelt sent the first U.S. presidential personal representative, and President Reagan the first U.S. ambassador. (Visitors in search of embassies in Rome must always specify whether they want the embassy accredited to the Italian Republic or to the Vatican; many countries have both, and the latter are located in Rome proper just as are the former.)

Tiny resident populace notwithstanding, there are Vatican laws, postage stamps (you may mail cards and letters home from the Vatican, and they may well arrive sooner than if posted from Italy), coins, a newspaper (foreign press and diplomats watch papal trends in *Osservatore Romano)*, trains, and—most apparent of all to visitors—soldiers. These last are the Swiss Guards (they come mostly from the French-speaking part of Switzerland), who still wear—at least for dress—uniforms designed half a millennium ago by no less distinguished a couturier than Michelangelo; hats are iron helmets with scarlet pompons, tunics and trousers are in wide vertical strips of blue and orange, with leggings to match. Hands are white-gloved; one invariably holds a long wrought-iron halberd, with a battle-ax at its extreme end.

Actual work of administration of the state, in matters temporal, is entrusted to the secretary of state; he serves under the pope on behalf of the Pontifical Commission, whose members are cardinals. Spiritual affairs are the business of the Roman Curia, a group of boards headed by cardinals, each with its own specialty, and all under the direction of the pope, who is elected to office by the College of Cardinals (they hold their elections in the Sistine Chapel) and remains in office for life. The pope (*Il Papa,* in Italian) has but a single temporal title: Sovereign of the State of Vatican City. But his spiritual titles are considerable: Bishop of Rome, Vicar of Jesus Christ, Successor of St. Peter, Prince of the Apostles, Supreme Pontiff of the Universal Church, Patriarch of the West, Primate of Italy, Archbishop and Metropolitan of the Roman Province. Pope No. 1 was St. Peter (he arrived in Rome A.D. 42), and John Paul II was elected in 1978; in between were nearly 300 popes and antipopes. There are two principal Vatican languages—Italian, the language of the state, and, more important because it is the language of papal encyclicals and other major documents, Latin, the official language of the Holy See. The populace, which includes some actual citizens of the Vatican state holding Vatican passports, is mostly Italian in origin but includes imported clergy from many countries, as well as the Swiss Guard.

Villa Adriana (Tivoli) is frequently but not always combined on excursions out of the capital with Villa d'Este in the same town of Tivoli, and honored, in this chapter, as a requisite of The Essential Rome (above). Hadrian's Villa dates to the second century, occupies a sprawling estate, and embraces a remarkable-enough assortment of ruins, as well as the museum recommended for orientation in advance of touring about. Withal, unless one is a scholar, the magic that should emanate from any imperial palace is absent.

AFTER DARK

Opera: Like other major Italian cities, Rome disappoints late-spring through early-autumn opera buffs who would like to hear their favorites sung in its opera house. Principal seasons for this performing art are traditionally November through May. Locale is *Teatro dell' Opera* (Piazza Benjamino Gigli)—multitiered, elaborate, elegant. The company has its own ballet troupe and its opera repertory is heavy on Italians—Verdi, Puccini, Donizetti.

Concerts: The first-rate *Accademia Filarmonica Romana* generally plays at *Teatro Olimpico* (Piazza Gentile da Fabriano)—late fall through early spring. In the summer, try to take in a concert at *Basilica di Massenzio in* Fori Imperiali, a magnificently proportioned fourth-century souvenir of Emperor Constantine. Still other concerts take place at *Auditorio Pio* (Via della Conciliazione). Atmospheric churches often double as concert halls, too.

Movies: Rome is headquarters to a globally celebrated film industry and has no dearth of cinemas; some fifty are first-run houses, but at almost all the sound tracks of imported films are dubbed into Italian. A notable exception, where imported English-language movies are shown with the original sound tracks (and with printed Italian titles), is *Cinema Pasquino* (Vicolo del Picole 19).

Legitimate theater: The capital is the national center of the thriving Italian theater. Plays are, of course, presented in Italian, but language is never a barrier for true theater lovers who are curious about details of production, like sets, costumes, music when present, direction, acting.

Principal theaters are the *Sistina* (Via Sistina 124), *Eliseo* (Via Nazionale 183), *Quirino* (Via Marco Minghatti 1), and *Valle* (Via del Teatro Valle 23).

Papal audiences: Traditionally, the pope holds a mass audience Wednesday mornings in the strikingly contemporary Audience Hall adjacent to St. Peter's Basilica (to the left as you approach on Via della Conciliazione). In summer, these move to the papal palace at suburban Castel Gandolfo, covered on an earlier page. Admission is by gratis ticket only. Audiences are arranged and operated by the Prefettura della Casa Pontifica, at the Vatican. American Catholics may arrange in advance for admission through parish priests. Americans, Catholic and otherwise, may also apply for tickets upon arrival in Rome, through the Bishops' Office for United States Visitors to the Vatican, in the earlier-described Casa dell' Umiltà, Via dell' Umiltà 30, in central Rome. (If you know what Wednesday you would like to attend, write in advance; the postal zone is 00187, Roma.) To say that these audiences are the greatest show in Rome is not to be disrespectful. One's religious faith or lack of same notwithstanding, attendance at a papal audience provides one with a grasp of the extraordinary universality, the multinational, multilingual, multiracial composition of the Catholic Church. The pope, in scarlet cape and white biretta, traditionally welcomes—and later briefly addresses—his visitors in Italian, French, English, German, Spanish, and Portuguese after his entrance and a tour around the hall, during which he bestows his blessings. Invariably, there is a sprinkling of vividly costumed cardinals—representing every major racial group—in attendance. Adding more color is a complement of helmeted Swiss Guards. I repeat: It's quite a show. But if you can't make it, keep in mind that traditionally the pope, when in residence, greets Sunday visitors, recites the Angelus, and bestows the Apostolic Blessing from the balcony of his palace, overlooking Piazza San Pietro (to the right of St. Peter's as you approach); the scheduled time is noon, so be in place a few minutes before, to watch aides hang a brown velvet banner with the papal shield on the pontiff's balcony. (The Sunday blessing is transferred to Castel Gandolfo in July and August, along with Wednesday audiences.)

SETTLING IN

Aldrovandi Hotel (Via Aldrovandi 15) rates A for atmosphere, for starters. A 90-year-old palazzo for long a private school, it shelters 143 rooms and suites—highlighted with eighteenth-century furniture and accessories. The grill-restaurant is reliable and the bar can be lively. Member, Leading Hotels of the World. *First Class.*

Alexandria Hotel (Via Vittorio Veneto 18) is well situated, with a nifty lobby and comfortable rooms, breakfast and bar; no restaurant. Good value. *Moderate.*

Ambasciatori Palace Hotel (Via Vittorio Veneto 70) has a smart location just opposite the American Embassy. The lobby (note the 1920s murals) is among the more beautiful in town; the restaurant moves to a canopied terrace in summer, and accommodations—150 good-size rooms and 14 suites—are elegant. *Luxury.*

Anglo Americano Hotel (Via Quattro Fontane 12) is an elderly 120-room house with an inspired central location—some rooms overlook Palazzo Barberini—that has been completely—and handsomely modernized. All rooms have bath, and the lobby is welcoming. Breakfast only. *First Class.*

Atlantico Hotel (Via Cavour 23) has a cheery lounge and the advantage of a lobby passage connecting it to next-door Hotel Mediterraneo (they are both part of the well-run Bettoja chain), whose restaurant and bar it shares. All 77 rooms are perky-modern-functional, and with bath. Situation is near Stazione Termini. Very pleasant. *First Class.*

Atlas Hotel (Via Rasella 3) has a heart-of-everything location and behind its traditional façade are nearly half a hundred rooms with bath, pretty lobby-lounge-bar, and a super roof garden for sun-cum-views. Breakfast only. *First Class.*

Bernini Bristol Hotel (Piazza Barberini): Walking through Piazza Barberini, you can be so caught up with the beauty of Bernini's Triton Fountain, in its center, that you can pass right by the hotel that overlooks the square. Well, don't. The Bernini Bristol is an old-school hotel (it dates to 1874 in its original quarters) that is just the right size for a luxury house—125 traditional-style rooms and 14 smashing suites—and with just the right location: Via Veneto leads from it in one direction, Via Sistina (and thence Via Condotti) in another, Via Barberini and the art treasures of Palazzo Barberini in still another. The recently refurbished restaurant is authentically Roman, its heavily international clientele notwithstanding (and it moves to the roof in summer—a special treat). The lobby bar is handsome and the staff kindly. *Luxury.*

Bologna Hotel (Via Santa Chiara 4) occupies a fine eighteenth-century house, very central, that has been converted into a good-looking hotel, with an antique-filled lounge, bar, compact but comfortable rooms. Breakfast only. *Moderate.*

Boston Hotel (Via Lombardia 47), in the Veneto area, has attractive bedrooms, 121 in all, handsome lobby, restaurant, bar. And agreeable service. *First Class.*

Cavalieri Hilton International Hotel (Via Cadiolo 101), in the smart Monte Mario residential section, is a considerable distance from central Rome, but with gratis hotel-operated bus service to and from Piazza di Spagna. It has emerged handsomer than ever from a relatively recent $12 million stem-to-stern refurbishing. Its 400 modern rooms, many with sumptuous views, have been restyled in pastels with warm-toned furnishings and new marble baths. There's a variety of places to dine, drink, dance, hold meetings, and shop, and a honey of a pool in the beautiful garden that is a distinct bonus in summer. Among the better-looking of this quality chain's properties around the world—and I know most Hilton Internationals, from Barbados to Manila. *First Class.*

Cecil Hotel (Via Francesco Crispi 55) is at once central (you're but steps from Via Sistina) and contemporary. This is a small modern house with baths in 28 of the 32 rooms, and breakfast, albeit no restaurant. Good value. *Moderate.*

Columbus Hotel (Via della Conciliazione 33) is a fifteenth-century cardinal's palazzo-turned-hotel, and within the shadow of St. Peter's. Public rooms are museum-caliber—one, for example, with a ceiling painted by Pinturicchio, others with magnificent wall frescoes. Still, the category is not luxury; 80 of the 100 relatively plain bedrooms have baths, however, and there are both restaurant and bar. Popular with visiting clerics, but all are welcome. *First Class.*

Condotti Hotel (Via Mario de' Fiori 37) is small in room count (total is 21) but big on looks (this is a part of Amadeo Ottaviani's small but smart chain, with the ambience of a deft traditional-contemporary meld) and service. Not to mention location: heart of the smartest of shopping quarters. Breakfast only. *Moderate.*

Daria Pensione (Via Sicilia 24) is just off Via Vittorio Veneto, with fussily but amusingly decorated public rooms (pictures occupy every available inch of wall space), kind management, spotless look, and 27 rooms, all with bath. Breakfast only. *Moderate.*

De la Ville Hotel (Via Sistina 69) attracts first with location: on a central street that's a hop and a skip from the summit of the Spanish Steps. Setting is a palazzo out of the last century that Forum Hotels, a division of the global, New York-based Inter-Continental chain, has refurbished with a sure sense of style. Public spaces retain traditional ambience and include an inviting cocktail lounge—you sink into pale-blue-upholstered club chairs—edging the lobby, and, up a flight, a handsome restaurant and adjacent bar overlooking the hotel's pretty patio. My most recent inspection reveals that the nearly 200 rooms and suites have emerged from redecoration as one of the handsomest in town, their color schemes pastel, their textiles small-patterned, their baths updated, and, in a number of instances, their terraces affording super views. Friendly staff, too. *First Class.*

Dinesen Hotel (Via Porta Pinciana 18, near Via Veneto) has 84 rooms, half of which have their own baths. There's a loyal British repeat clientele who appreciate its good location and value. Breakfast only. *Moderate.*

D'Inghilterra Hotel (Via Bocca di Leone 14) went up as a palazzo in the early sixteenth century, and was not always as smart as is the case today. It is just off Via Condotti and a step from the Spanish Steps. It's an early Roman home of mine and has been spiffily refurbished in recent years. Lounges are rather giddily Italian–Victorian, and there's a congenial bar. Fiercely loyal international repeat clientele. Breakfast only. *First Class.*

D'Italia Hotel (Via Quattro Fontane 155) is just opposite Palazzo Barberini in central Rome, with 50 rooms, half with private facilities. Breakfast only. *Moderate.*

Eden Hotel (Via Ludovisi 49) is among the smaller of the grander hotels; on scene since 1889, its ambience is intimate and relaxing. There are two restaurants, including a rooftop one affording fine vistas; cozy bar, too, as well as 115 rooms and suites. Those I have inspected—including the Borghese Suite, smartly Art Deco in tones of palest lavender—are attractive. Location, midway between Via Veneto and Piazza di Spagna, is positively inspired. *Luxury.*

Eliseo Hotel (Via Porta Pinciana 30): Ascend to the terminus of Via Veneto, turn left and you've arrived at the well-situated Eliseo—with its front rooms facing the park called Villa Borghese. This is an elderly house that has been transformed into an appealing hotel. Public spaces include a honey of a picture-windowed rooftop restaurant and a terraced bar. Those of the half hundred rooms and suites I've inspected are delightfully eighteenth century in style, and with good baths. Very nice indeed. Best Western. *First Class.*

Excelsior Hotel (Via Vittorio Veneto 125): A case might well be made for the premise that development of Via Veneto as the core of trendy Rome can be credited to the prescient chaps—gamblers, you might well call them—who erected the Excelsior—a 322-room, 44-suite palace of a hotel—in a part of the city that was, in 1906, open country. Rome was emerging as capital of the united Italy—and drawing international visitors, even before World War I. It thrived during the Twenties (a Holy Year in 1925 helped matters) and again after World War II, when Via Veneto—dominated by the Excelsior—became synonymous with *la dolce vita*—a phrase popularized by Federico Fellini in a film by that name. Today's Excelsior is a consequence of the Ciga Hotels chain's extensive floor-by-floor renovation that has carefully retained the turn-of-century look of the hotel, while the amenities for which Ciga is known—beginning with excellently equipped bathrooms—have been updated. The lobby floor—with its ever-bustling entrance hall, a ballroom-size lounge off of which lead a trio of actual ballrooms (the capital's most celebrated), both popular bar and small but excellent and recently restyled restaurant, with Caffè Doney (see Daily Bread, below) adjacent—is an intrinsic dimension of contemporary Rome. Accommodations range from absolutely fabulous suites (you could, if the occasion arose, review troops from the twin balconies of Suite 104/5!) beyond to generous-size (and charming) twins and doubles overlooking the Veneto, to smaller inside singles. The Excelsior, operated by a mostly long-on-scene staff of pros, is special. *Luxury.*

Flora Hotel (Via Vittorio Veneto 191) is near the top of the Veneto hill, and is an absolute charmer of an old-timer, dignified and correct but at the same time friendly and warm. Rooms and suites—200 in all—tend to understatement rather than excess in décor, and many offer dazzling views. There's a cocktail lounge but no restaurant; breakfast only. *First Class.*

Forum Hotel (Via Tor de' Conti 25) is not large—there are 80 rooms and suites—but it is attractive, not only because of its tasteful décor but because of its ace-in-the-hole location just opposite Foro Romano, which makes its Forum-view rooms and restaurant (dealt with on a later page) special. A treat is the roof garden bar-lounge. *First Class.*

Grand Hotel (Via Vittorio Emanuele Orlando 3) is an elderly beauty with more style in one room than many hotels have in a dozen. Its situation—overlooking the landmark fountain of Piazza Esedra—could not be more central. Nor could its credentials be more impeccable, for it was the legendary César Ritz who built the hotel, which opened in 1894 as the first in Italy with electric lights. Before long, kings of Italy, based in not-far-distant Quirinale Palace, began housing royal guests at the Grand. And so it evolved as a Roman meeting place of consequence. Ciga Hotels, its proprietors over a period of decades, have maintained it meticulously. Its high-ceilinged central lounge is, certainly to this observer, quite the handsomest public space of any in a Roman hotel. The bar leading from it, now smartly Luigi XVI in style, the recently redecorated restaurant (evaluated on a later page) and Le Pavillon (Rome's snazziest snack bar) are lookers, as well. Those of the score of suites I have inspected—especially including a big one in blue and ivory facing Piazza Esedra and a smaller one in yellow-covered Empire furniture—are lovely, as are those of the 175 bedrooms I have either inhabited or inspected. (Most are doubles; the Grand has but ten singles.) A Ciga hotel that's a member of Leading Hotels of the World. *Luxury.*

Hassler Hotel (Piazza Trinità dei Monti 6) has an advantage of location: atop the Spanish Steps. There are just over a hundred rooms and suites (those with front views, looking out over the city, are the choicest, most especially some 20 with terraces, but all of the accommodations I've inspected are attractive and with excellent baths), a rooftop restaurant evaluated on a subsequent page, and a bar that moves to the garden in summer, becoming, for me at least, the Hassler at its most charming. Member, Leading Hotels of the World. *Luxury.*

Imperiale Hotel (Via Vittorio Veneto 24) is a well-situated, good-looking house that is not so big (there are only 84 rooms, many of which are oversized) that it can't provide pleasant service. Restaurant, bar. *First Class.*

Internazionale Hotel (Via Sistina 79) was where I put up on a long-ago Roman trip during a time when it was clean but very simple. Recent seasons have seen it handsomely refurbished; 33 of its 36 rooms have baths; bar and breakfast room. Location is perfect—just down Via Sistina from the Spanish Steps. *Moderate.*

Jolly Hotel Vittorio Veneto (Corso Italia 1) is modern-look handsome. There are 200 rooms, all with super baths, commodious lobby, cocktail lounge that seems even bigger, inviting restaurant (the Jollys serve delicious Italian fare), façade that is among the better of Rome's modern exteriors, and a convenient location just off Via Veneto. Polished Jolly know-how is reflected in management and service, not to mention a typically Jolly breakfast buffet—which will set you up for a busy morning. *First Class.*

Jolly Leonardo da Vinci Hotel (Via dei Gracchi 324) is attractive—big lobby and adjacent lounges, restaurant and bar, inviting rooms and suites. And bouquets of fresh flowers in the public rooms. The location is interesting: just a few minutes' walk across Ponte Regina Margherita from central Piazza del Popolo, on the Vatican side of the Tiber, in a residential quarter. *First Class.*

Londra e Cargill Hotel (Piazza Sallustio 18, and to many Romans simply the "Londra") deserves better acquaintance. It first came to my attention when I was billeted there as a press delegate to the ASTA World Travel Congress, held in Rome in 1985. I've been a fan ever since. Location is a pretty little square a few short blocks east of Via Veneto, to the rear of the vast walled garden of the American Embassy. Façade is traditional but the Londra's interiors—lobby-lounge, congenial bar, convenient restaurant—are contemporary, as are those of the 105 rooms I have either inhabited or inspected, the lot of them with up-to-the-minute baths. And the staff smiles. *First Class.*

Lord Byron Hotel (Via de Notaris 5) is, to be sure, a ten- or fifteen-minute drive from the center, in an attractive residential quarter. Ideally, you've the use of a car (although there is gratis shuttle service to and from Via Veneto), and a yen for tranquil quarters in what is, when all is said and done, one of Europe's most frenetic capitals. Flagship of the small albeit smart chain of Ottaviani Hotels, the Lord Byron deftly teams fine eighteenth-century antiques and paintings with contemporary furnishings, textiles, and, upon occasion, wallpapers, the lot employed with a deft sense of style and color. A consequence is a set of interiors that are among the best-looking you'll encounter in Rome, lobby-lounges and bar, upwards to the 40 rooms and ten suites, downward to an extraordinary restaurant that is reviewed on a subsequent page. Proprietor Amadeo Ottaviani, along with his head honcho, Roland Brecht, operate the Byron with what can only be called tender loving care. The staff, reception through restaurant, is as skilled as it is smiling. This is a special place. Member, Leading Hotels of the World. *Luxury.*

Madrid Hotel (Via Mario de' Fiori 93) is a winner, with but 24 rooms and 8 suites, all with bath, and well located (Via Condotti is around the corner). Breakfast is included in the room rate, but there's no restaurant. *Moderate.*

Majestic Hotel (Via Vittorio Veneto 50)—relatively recently, and thoroughly, renovated—is traditional-style, with a quiet ambience. The eighteenth-century-style lobby, with a frescoed ceiling, is pleasant, the restaurant moves to a terrace in summer, and there's a bar-lounge. Nice rooms, too; 100 all told. *Luxury.*

Marini Strand Hotel (Via del Tritone 17)—a near-neighbor of Fontana di Trevi—is, to understate, at the center of the Roman action. This is an attractive old-school house with high-ceilinged lobby, convenient restaurant, convivial little bar, and 118 rooms; those I have inspected are traditionally decorated and well-equipped. Nice. *First Class.*

Massimo d' Azeglio Hotel (Via Cavour 18) is No. 2 in the Bettoja chain, just after the Mediterraneo (below). Thoroughly refurbished, it is also the oldest, dating back to 1875, with a restaurant—later described—that is exceptional, convivial bar, spacious lobby and lounges, 210 well-equipped rooms, and friendly service—thanks in large part to personal, always-on-the-scene direction of president Angelo Bettoja, third-generation head of the chain, who knows America and Americans well, in part because Signora Bettoja is American-born. (Connects with the San Giorgio, another Bettoja house, next door.) *First Class.*

Mediterraneo Hotel (Via Cavour 15)—biggest and most impressive of the Bettoja quintet (see Massimo d'Azeglio Hotel, above) is flagship of the fleet, with 367 rooms and suites (some of those higher up have terraces affording sublime views of the city), lobby that's a stellar specimen of Italian Art Deco and still with its original mosaics, comfortable cocktail lounge, 21 Restaurant (evaluated on a later page), and the relatively recently created terraced caffè on the roof. I have always found Mediterraneo service warm and gracious, and visit after visit my verdict is constant: the best concierges in Rome. Then there is the matter of location: Stazione Termini, the main train station, and the air terminal to its side, are but steps away. And it is worth my mentioning that the Mediterraneo is the headquarters of Lo Scaldavivande—nine-day cooking course packages, directed and taught by Jo (Mrs. Angelo) Bettoja, U.S.-born and the author of a celebrated book of Italian cookery; the package is usually offered five times each spring and summer. *First Class.*

Michelangelo Hotel (Via Stazione San Pietro 14) is a modern 200-room house whose distinctive feature is location: it's in the very shadow of St. Peter's—which was designed by the genius for whom the hotel is named. Rooms are light and bright; public rooms including restaurant and bar—capacious. *First Class.*

Mondial Hotel (Via Torino 127) is midway between Piazza della Repubblica and the Opera. The look is ultra-mod—lobby, restaurant, bar-lounge, and 77 compact, but well-equipped, bedrooms. A bonus: an entire side of the hotel's color brochure constitutes one of the best maps of Rome I have come across. *First Class.*

Nardizzi Americana Pensione (Via Firenze 38)—a hop and a skip from the train station and Piazza Repubblica—is a find for the low-budget traveler, on scene some six decades, with neat-as-a-pin rooms (not all with bath), comfy lounge, agreeable breakfast room, and tabs that include the first meal of the day. Friendly. *Moderate.*

Nazionale Hotel (Piazza Montecitorio) fronts the splendid broad square named for the palace housing the lower chamber of the Italian Parliament. It is small enough—there are 78 rooms—to be intimate, and there's an air of elegance, too, in the traditional-style lobby, the blue-, brown-, and white-hued lounge. Restaurant and bedrooms are in the same color scheme. *First Class.*

Nord Hotel (Via Giovanni Amendola 3) is a functional, up-to-date, 200-room house, the least elaborate of the Bettoja Rome quintet. Which is not to say that it's not nice. Just that it's not fancy, and is without restaurant or bar, as are so many in its category. Location is the Stazione Termini area. Breakfast only. *Moderate.*

Pace Elvezia Hotel (Via IV Novembre 104): Any hotel whose name translates as Swiss Peace has to have something going for it. Pace Elvezia's is a location near Piazza Venezia, cozy public spaces, and 64 rooms, most of which have baths. Breakfast only. *Moderate.*

Parco di Principe Hotel (Via G. Frescobaldi 5) is quite the most imaginatively designed of the modern Roman hotels. Dominant color is green and the setting is a capacious green garden—with a broad terrace and outdoor pool—on the Via Mercadante side of the Borghese Gardens, which is a fairish walk to the Via Veneto. One whole window-wall of the restaurant overlooks the garden. There are just over 200 rooms and suites. *First Class.*

Pensione Suisse (Via Gregoriana 56) is indeed Swiss-operated, as its name suggests, well situated near the Spanish Steps, with baths or showers in nearly half of its 28 neat rooms. Breakfast only. Good value. *Moderate.*

Plaza Hotel (Via del Corso 126) was built in 1860 with what must then have been the most knock-'em-dead public rooms in Rome, and it has maintained them well ever since. The main lounge, with its crystal chandeliers and neo-Renaissance ceiling, must surely have first served as a very grand ballroom. Entrance hall and adjacent smaller lounges are equally dazzling, and there's a bar, but no restaurant. Bedrooms—there are 240 with bath—are less elaborate but okay; many have brass beds. Breakfast only. *First Class.*

Quattro Fontane Hotel (Via Quattro Fontane 149) is nicely situated between Palazzo Barberini and Palazzo Quirinale. There are 50 rooms with bath; doubles are small, but value is good. Pretty lounge, with a coffered ceiling. Breakfast only. *Moderate.*

Quirinale Hotel (Via Nazionale 7) is a hop and skip from the Opera, with which it is connected by both tradition and a tunnel—heavily trafficked after performances by patrons en route to the Quirinale for refreshment. The hotel, dating back to 1865, is graced with a quiet inner garden where lunch is served in summer. There are 189 rooms and suites, restaurant, bar. *First Class.*

Raphael Hotel (Largo Febo 2, near Piazza Navona) is a fine old building, converted with imagination into a 100-room hotel. The look is provincial-traditional, blended with contemporary. Antiques are scattered about in lounge, restaurant, bar, and roof garden where guests may have drinks and breakfast in summer. Directly next door is the venerable Church of Santa Maria della Pace; rooms on the church side overlook its cloister. *First Class.*

Regina Hotel Baglioni (Via Vittorio Veneto 72) is diagonally opposite the American Embassy. Updated bedrooms—they total 134—are among the more desirable in town, and there's a striking, high-ceilinged lobby. Restaurant, bar. *First Class.*

San Giorgio Hotel (Via G. Amendola 61) is a gem of a period piece, the period being the 1930s. There are a handsome high-ceilinged lobby, lounge, bar, breakfast room, and nearly 200 attractively furnished rooms. A passage leads into earlier-recommended Hotel Massimo d'Azeglio, with its exceptional restaurant (later described). Both of these houses are part of the Bettoja chain. *First Class.*

Savoia Hotel (Via Ludovisi 15, and known also as the Savoy) fronts on Via Veneto and is among the smarter of the clutch of hotels opposite the landmark American Embassy. A lovely lobby is illuminated by a network of Murano crystal chandeliers, the bar-lounge draws Romans as well as hotel guests, there are both a restaurant and a coffee shop, and those of the 110 bedrooms and 5 suites that I've inspected are attractively traditional in style and well-equipped. A pleasure. *First Class.*

Scalinata di Spagna Hotel (Piazza Trinità dei Monti 17) is just opposite posh Hotel Hassler, and with luck you'll have nabbed a room with views over the Spanish Steps quite as panoramic as the Hassler's best. But there's a catch to this attractive, albeit eccentrically operated, hotel. Only half of the 14 rooms have complete private baths; the remainder have shower and sink but no toilet. You want a room with a full bath? You've got to be lucky; they're first-come-first-served, with rates the same as those without. *Moderate.*

Senato Hotel (Piazza del Pantheon 73): No hotel in Rome is situated opposite a more historic monument; the Pantheon, after all, dates to Roman times. The Senato, despite an impressive façade, is unpretentious but neat, with a bar leading from the lobby-lounge and baths attached to a number of its functional rooms. Breakfast only. *Moderate.*

Sheraton Roma Hotel (Viale del Pattinaggio): Credit Sheraton with pulling off a neat trick: creation of a country resort-cum-convention-center in the city. Or, at least, near the modern EUR quarter of the city—five miles south of the center, in the direction of Fiumicino Airport. The Sheraton complex embraces 680 intelligently equipped rooms, 20 suites, and a pair of restaurants (one, Tre Fontane, is esteemed for Italian cuisine, the other is adept at Stateside-style hamburgers). There are, as well, an outdoor pool and caffè, tennis and squash, jogging track, health club–sauna, convention facilities for 1800, parking for 800 cars, Alitalia ticketing counter. Aside from business guests, the Sheraton is ideal for motorists visiting Rome as part of a larger Italian itinerary. Shuttle buses to and from town. *Luxury.*

Sistina Hotel (Via Sistina 136), located on convenient Via Sistina, near the Spanish Steps, is small (27 rooms) but stylish, thanks to thorough renovation as a result of its becoming part of the smart Ottaviani chain. There's a bar (but no restaurant) and breakfast is served on a pretty terrace in good weather. *Moderate.*

Sitea Hotel (Via Gregoriana 56) is near both Piazza di Spagna and Via Sistina. There are 29 rooms, 10 of which have baths. Nice lounge, capacious terrace. Breakfast only. *Moderate.*

Texas Pensione (Via Firenze 47): That's what I said, pardner: Texas. Thirteen of 17 rooms have baths. Antiques are scattered throughout, especially in the bar-lounge, with a wood-burning fireplace that makes it popular at cocktail time in the cool months. Breakfast only. *Moderate.*

Trinità dei Monti Pensione (Via Sistina 91) has a score of rooms, almost all with bath, and an agreeable bar-lounge. This is a simple place; lures are central location and low price. *Moderate.*

Tritone Hotel (Via dei Tritone 210)—a hop and a skip from Piazza Colonna and the central shopping quarter—is smallish (there are 42 clean-lined rooms with bath) but convenient, and sound value. Breakfast only. *Moderate.*

Veneto Hotel (Via Piemonte 63) has named itself after a major street—Via Veneto—the better to impress you with its location on the next street away, parallel with it. This is a modern house with restaurant, bar-lounge, and 45 well-equipped rooms. *Moderate.*

Visconti Palace Hotel (Via Cesi 37) is well located—near Piazza Cavour and Castel Sant' Angelo—and comfortable, with 250 okay rooms. Breakfast only. *First Class.*

DAILY BREAD

As with other matters, one eats in Rome as do the Romans. Rome has its own specialties: gnocchi alla romana—semolina-based dumplings; spaghetti alla carbonara (with bacon and eggs) and all' amatriciana (with bacon); cannelloni—wide canal-shaped pasta with an appropriate sauce and melted-cheese topping; the deep-fried seafood melange called fritto misto; the veal, cheese, and ham entrée known as saltimbocca; richly sauced fettuccine alla romana; stracciatella—a delicious egg-drop soup; chicken either alla diavola or alla cacciatore; roast suckling pig; novel ways of preparing lamb (abbacchio al forno is the delicious local lamb roast); and vegetables like artichoke and broccoli. Sunday sustenance note: Many if, indeed, not most—restaurants outside of those in hotels shutter Sundays; plan in advance.

SELECTED RESTAURANTS

44 (Via Flavia 44; Phone 465-0222) makes a specialty of pizza (the plain cheese species is excellent), but pasta is reliable, too. Opt for veal piccata as an entrée, to be accompanied by the house red. Friendly and central. *Moderate.*

Alemagna (Via del Corso at Piazza Colonna) is a big bakery-confectionery-caterer kind of establishment, run by the people who make the sweet panettone bread widely exported to the United States at Christmas. The species of gelati (ice cream) and sherbet are limitless. There are candies, tiny frosted cakes, sandwiches, minipizzas, and counters of antipasti. Pasta dishes take up another cafeteria-style counter. And, best of all, there is the drink called frullati di frutti: strawberries, peaches, bananas, pears, apples, apricots, lemons, oranges, and grapefruits are combined in a blender with milk, sugar, and maraschino liqueur. Think of me when you order one. *Moderate.*

Alfredo alla Scrofa (Via della Scrofa 104; Phone 654-0163) is one of the "original" Alfredos that made fettuccine alla romana—pasta in a rich cream-and-butter sauce, tossed at table—into a world-renowned dish. It's called fettuccine al triplo burgo here, and it's delicious. So is just about everything else, especially the chicken-breast preparation called petto di pollo al cardinale, and roast lamb—abbacchio arrosto. There's a good fritto misto—mixed fried seafood—too. Photos of luminary customers line the walls, but ordinary mortals are treated rather haughtily, albeit with dispatch. The outdoor terrace is recommended in warm weather. *First Class.*

Al Moro (Vicolo delle Bollette 13; Phone 678-3995) appeals from the moment one enters. Walls are white and garnished with strings of garlic bulbs and onions. The place hums with modish Romans who know where to go for Roman specialties served with panache. Ignore spaghetti al Moro (the surprise is bacon and eggs) at your peril; grilled veal chops are super, too; so is veal with tomato sauce and prosciutto. And nowhere in Rome is the Parmesan cheese more deliciously crumbly or served with better bread. *First Class.*

Andrea (via Sardegna 28; Phone 482-1891) makes ordering easy; the menu is à la carte and not overextended. There are antipasti and soups, but my counsel is to open with pasta—spaghetti with basil-accented tomato sauce, linguine al pesto, or one of the risotti. Roast chicken, osso bucco with rice and mushrooms, and veal scaloppini are among entrées.

And you needn't order a sweet; a waiter will appear with a generous-size platter of chocolates, candied fruit (including grapefruit and orange peel, dried apricots, and figs), and a plate of *biscotti*—dessert biscuits—as well. Super. *First Class.*

Aurora 10 (Via Aurora 10; Phone 474-2779) has a cordial staff and a talented chef, with such good things to eat as tortellini in broth, risotto, saltimbocca, and mixed seafood platter. Consider one of the excellent dessert wines as an accompaniment to your sweet. Off Via Veneto. *First Class.*

Babington's Tea Room (Piazza di Spagna 23) is an across-the-square neighbor of the house in which Keats lived, and it may well be almost as old. Despite, or perhaps because of, the Anglo name, clientele is mostly Roman, who come to sample good cakes and pastries, tea, and cappuccino. Go at 5 or 6 P.M. and you would think they were giving the stuff away. But with the exception of a fancy tea spot in Paris called Angelina, it appears to me to set a world record when it comes to steep tabs for places of its type. *First Class.*

Bernini Bristol Hotel Ristorante (Piazza Barberini; Phone 463-051) is among the better—and the best located—of the hotel dining rooms. The serving staff is top-rank, but you go primarily for the cuisine. Order à la carte, if you like, but consider also the good-value Suggerimenti dello Chef—the daily table d'hote lunches and dinners, which might open with gnocchi, risotto, or shrimp cocktail, offer main courses of canard à l'orange, the classic duck dish known in Italy as anitra all'aranci, or vitello tonnato (cold veal in tuna sauce), with a choice of tempting desserts from a wheeled-to-table trolley. *First Class/Luxury.*

Dal Bolognese (Piazza del Popolo 1; Phone 361-1426): Lure here is the rich, cream-based cuisine of Bologna. Sit under the big canopy outside and watch crowds in the Baroque piazza, or dine within, observing contemporary art on wood-paneled walls. Service is as kind and expert as the fare—and has been, these many years. Try specialties: misto di pasta—a combination plate with tortellini, tortelli, and lasagne verde; giambonetti cremolati—veal in a typically Bolognese cream sauce; and polpettone di vitello—balls of minced veal subtly sauced. Granita, a type of sherbet (try the raspberry or the lemon) makes a lovely, light dessert. There's a good red house wine. In my view, visit after visit, one of Italy's best restaurants. *First Class.*

La Buca di Ripetta (Via di Ripetta 36; Phone 321-9391) does not, alas, accept credit cards; you must have sufficient cash to shell out for such dishes as the day's soup or risotto, penne arrabbiata, a variety of veal and beef entrées, satisfactory salads, and reasonably priced carafe wines. Whatever I have had was very good. *First Class.*

Caffè Berardo (Piazza Colonna) is heart-of-town. The ice creams are special. So are the whole glacéed oranges. Good pizza, too. Romans love the plum cake—English-style and English-spelled. *Moderate.*

Caffè di Colombia (Piazza Navona): A pair of Piazza Navona restaurants are later counseled. But for a coffee or an ice-cream break, this is a traditional-style place in a glorious setting. *Moderate.*

Caffè Doney (in the Excelsior Hotel—but with its own entrance from the street, at Via Vittorio Veneto 125; Phone 4708): If you're going to experience a Via Veneto caffè—they are pricier than most counterparts elsewhere in town—there's no question but that it should be Doney, meticulously operated by the Ciga Hotels chain like the hotel in whose premises it is situated, and the reigning *regina* of the cluster of watering holes crowding Veneto pavements. Of course, you may settle for an espresso at a table on the street or—more interestingly, in the company of Roman regulars at the bar, inside—but Doney is justifiably celebrated for made-on-premises pastries (they are not all that costly, and you want to have a look at options, in the glass case inside, before selecting) and for its own ice creams and sherbets, relatively reasonably priced. If you're either famished or flushed—better yet, both—consider a sandwich (ham-and-cheese is the best buy), a burger, or an omelet. Italian-made apéritifs—Campari or vermouth, for example—are the cheapest alcoholic drinks. *First Class.*

Caffè Giolitti (Via degli Uffici del Vicario 40) is, more than anything else, a gelateria. By that I mean that after you've eaten its ice cream (especially the chocolate) not even the brownie-fudge back home at Baskin-Robbins is going to mean much to you. Sherbets—particularly the lemon—are matchless, too. There are ravishing pastries, as well as sandwiches and drinks. *Moderate.*

Caffè Greco (Via Condotti 80), which had passed its sixteenth birthday the year our Declaration of Independence was signed, remains, decade in and decade out, the most convenient locale in town for the study and observation of beautiful Romans. Coffee, snacks, drinks, what-have-you. Wonderful looking, too, especially the Art Nouveau style (called "Liberty" in Italy) restaurant to the rear of the standup bar. *Moderate/First Class.*

Caffè Pellachia (Via Boncompagni 49) is typical of any number of quite ordinary—but quite nice—caffès near, but not on, tourist-trod Via Vittorio Veneto, that are much less expensive than the Veneto's. *Moderate.*

Campana (Vicolo della Campana 18; Phone 656-7820) calls its quarters the oldest of any restaurant in town; the building housing this typically Roman, solid, and unpretentious place goes back to the sixteenth century. Everything is delicious, especially such dishes as fettuccine con funghi (mushrooms), grilled fish, roast lamb, veal in a number of ways. *First Class.*

Cannavota (Piazza San Giovanni in Laterano 20; Phone 775-007) typifies bourgeois Roman dining: too fussily decorated perhaps, with a staff that takes itself seriously and rarely smiles. One goes for the food and good value. The cold table is a honey; try one of the contorni (a choice of spinach, peppers, chicory, or mushrooms) or open with a pasta specialty like rigatoni alla Rigore or bucatini alla Cannavota, which is thick spaghetti in a seafood sauce. Scaloppe alla verbena, lemon-flavored veal, is delicious. Basilica of St. John Lateran is across the square. *First Class.*

La Capricciosa (Largo dei Lombardi 8) is a convenient spot, just off Via del Corso, especially appealing in summer, thanks to its outdoor terrace. It makes a specialty of pizza, but the menu runs a wide gamut. *First Class.*

Carpes (Via Veneto 116; Phone 482-7107) is a sensible heart-of-town choice, with excellent sauces atop pastas, first-rate gnocchi, and such entrées as grilled scampi and filet of veal. Friendly. *First Class.*

Cesarina (Via Piemonte 109; Phone 488-007) is a big, busy, noisy, immediately likable place. A house specialty is a tripartite pasta plate—tortellini, lasagne, and ravioli verde. Misto Cesarina—deep-fried fritto misto of vegetables and hot stuffed tomatoes—is inspired. So is sautéed veal piccata. Cesarina is bigger on deserts than much of its competition; Semifreddo Cesarina embraces soft vanilla ice cream, zuppa inglese (trifle), and chocolate sauce. *First Class.*

Checchino dal 1887 (Via Monte Testaccio 30; Phone 574-6318): Unless you're being driven, or have your own car, you'll need a pricey taxi to reach this away-from-the-core restaurant. The specialty is Roman dishes—based on tripe, oxtail, and sweetbreads—and there are such regulars as mixed antipasto, the egg-drop soup called stracciatella, familiarly sauced pastas, and veal. Withal, nothing is outstandingly delicious enough, in my experience, to warrant the excursion to and from the center of Rome, and some dishes disappoint (grilled pork chop, for example). I can't counsel this one. *First Class.*

La Corte dei Leoni (Via San Basilio 70, at Piazza Barberini; Phone 481-9005) is conveniently situated and makes a specialty of pizzas in considerable variety and roasts prepared in a wood-burning oven. *First Class.*

Crisciotti al Boschetto (Via del Boschetto 30; Phone 474-4770), though not far from the core of the city, and inexpensive, is a case of getting what you pay for: neither attractive nor delicious nor especially welcoming, at least in my experience. I can't counsel this one. *Moderate.*

La Cupella (Via Sardegna 39; Phone 538-7686) is strategically situated in a street just off Via Veneto. Its kicker is a fabulous antipasto buffet. Pasta is delicious (I counsel the tomato-sauced gnocchi). And so are roasts. *First Class.*

D' Angelo (Via della Croce 29; Phone 678-3924) is at once restaurant, pasticceria, gelateria. There is a proper menu in the dining area (ravioli is creditable) but service there is slow and erratic; you're better off in the course of a day's shopping in this area, centered on Via Condotti, ordering a snack from the bar, following with a scrumptious pastry (the selection is enormous) or ice cream. *Moderate.*

Da Giovanni (Via Salendra 1; Phone 485-950) is congenial and with fare that pleases. Fettuccine e scaloppine alla Giovanni is the veal and pasta house specialty, but the assorted antipasto platter and the day's soups are good, too; so are such pastas as tuna-sauced spaghetti and fettuccine alla bolognese. This is a good spot for sausages (delicious grilled, as throughout Italy). Macedonia di frutta—fruit cup—is the indicated dessert. *Moderate.*

Da Mario (55 Via della Vite; Phone 678-3818) makes sense for lunch when you've been shopping the Piazza di Spagna quarter. Start with choices from an all-you-can-eat buffet. Pasta is first-rate; ditto hearty beef and veal entrées. *First Class.*

Da Vicenzo (Via Castel Fidardo 4; Phone 484-596) specializes in fish, but entrées like osso bucco and veal scaloppine are counseled, as well. Central. *First Class.*

Il Delfino (Corso Vittorio Emanuele 67) is a massive cafeteria that accepts credit cards and that fills the bill for a modest lunch on the run. Note that there's a well-priced three-course menu that might run to lasagne or a chicken entrée, with fresh fruit for dessert. Central. *Moderate.*

L'Eau Vive (Via Monterone 85; Phone 654-1095) is to the Vatican what Washington's La Maison Blanche is (or at least, was) to the White House—a buzzy, gossipy place of nourishment for bigwigs. Cuisine is tastily French-inspired and served by waitresses who are members of a missionary order and wear French Colonial costumes. Despite its popularity with Vatican brass, location—a splendid Renaissance palazzo which had housed a long-ago pope—is in central Rome, near the Pantheon. *First Class.*

Elettra (Via Principe Amedeo 74; Phone 474-5397) typifies the old-school, ever-reliable, central Rome *ristorante:* nothing fancy but operated by pros, with alert service and delicious fare. Antipasto misto is a super opener, or opt to begin with a pasta specialty—spaghetti carbonara or tagliatelle alla ghiottona, with its sauce based on mushrooms. Your entrée might well be the house's veal masterwork, costoletta Elettra, or grilled breast of chicken. Fairly priced wines. *First Class.*

Esedra (Via Principe Amedeo 27; Phone 488-2853): You've come from the Opera and you're famished. Esedra is a near neighbor. Soup, spaghetti al pomodoro, and well-roasted chicken might be the ingredients of a satisfactory meal. *First Class.*

Taverna Flavia (Via Flavia 9; Phone 481-7787) draws as smart a crowd as one is likely to encounter in Rome, unpretentious décor notwithstanding. The lure is absolutely super food—such as vegetable soup (zuppa di verdura) and saltimbocca romana. And note the Italian bread transformed via the grill into hot toast. *First Class.*

Fontanella (Largo Fontanella di Borghese; Phone 678-3849) is a delicious touch of Tuscany in the capital. One's fellow diners are invariably affluent Romans, talky and enthusiastic—as well they might be. There's a great mosaic mural of Florence dominating the décor within, and an outdoor terrace for summer meals. Good things to eat include salame toscano—a plate with several types; pappardella alla toscana—noodles under a pair of sauces; tacchino modo nostro—turkey "our style"; anitra—or duck—cooked with olives; and the classic Tuscan standby, broiled steak. *First Class.*

Forum Hotel Roof (Via Tor de' Conti 25; Phone 679-2446) has nothing less than Foro Imperiali as the subject matter of the panorama offered lunchers and/or diners, enclosed in winter, al fresco in warm weather. There are good-value piatti del giorno—daily blue plates. Of the pastas, try cannolicchi alla Forum; of the meats, scaloppine alla Forum. And of the sweets, pera alla bell' Elena, ice cream-cum-chocolate sauce over poached pears. *First Class.*

Frattina (Via Frattina 14; Phone 473-862) is a bar-caffè that caters to weary shoppers in a heavily mercantile area near Piazza di Spagna. Cool off on a hot day with a plate of ice cream at an outdoor table. *Moderate.*

Galeassi (Piazza Santa Maria in Trastevere; Phone 580-3775) is smack in the heart of Trastevere, on its finest square, facing its finest church. In summer you eat under a canopy on the piazza, and you eat well. Consider such tasty pasta dishes as penne all' arrabbiata or agnolotti, house-style fish specialties like spigola dorata, or fried calamari—the squid so beloved of Romans. *First Class.*

George's (Via Marche 7; Phone 484-575) began life after World War II under auspices of a transplanted Englishman; thus its Anglo name. Contemporarily, it emerges as authentically Roman, with superbly sauced pastas (try the rigatoni), succulent lamb and veal, and an ambience that is, to me, quite the most relaxing in the Veneto quarter. Summer garden. *First Class.*

Gemma e Maurizio (Via Marghera 39 near Stazione Termini; Phone 491-230): My friend Fiorenza Cruciani, who worked at E.N.I.T. headquarters across the street, introduced me to this unpretentious but delightful trattoria—which she and her colleagues patronized at lunch. Soups and pastas are super, no less so the veal scaloppine. Have the house wine. And rest assured, Gemma and Maurizio will take good care of you. *Moderate.*

Giggi Fazi (Via Lucullo 22) is a good place to see Roman families—Mamma, Pappa, Granny, and the kids—enjoying a meal. The entire hierarchy—maître d', captains, waiters—makes a point of chatting with guests. Don't be surprised at the odd-appearing menu; you're looking at Roman dialect. Pollo spezzato co'll peperoni (chicken with peppers) and fiji de lapecona a la spiedo (lamb chops with chicory) are both good. *First Class.*

Giovagno (Piazza d'Aracoeli 7; Phone 476-843) is strategically sited opposite the Vittorio Emanuele monument, is smallish and unassuming, and takes no credit cards. But Romans in the neighborhood pack it for lunch, with good reason. Open with a pasta like bucatini, opt for piccata of veal as an entrée. And do not omit dessert; Giovagno's are special. *First Class.*

Girarrosto (Via Campania 29; Phone 482-1899)—its walls busily hung, and topped by shelves of wine—prides itself on its Tuscan origins. It features Florentine beefsteaks, Parma ham, Tuscan-sauced pastas, and what might well be Italy's best baby lamb chops. Everything I've tasted is delicious, but you must expect the place to be crowded (mostly by foreigners) and very noisy, to the point where a meal can be more tasty than relaxing. *First Class.*

Il Golosone (Via Flavia 66, other locations): Ice-cream cones and cups—fig and melon are among unusual flavors. *Moderate.*

Grand Hotel Ristorante (Via Vittorio Emanuele Orlando 3; Phone 4709) is a special space (it emerged from an elegant redecoration in the late eighties) that edges what is arguably the handsomest hotel lobby-lounge in town. Consider a festive meal built around an à la carte with such tempters as smoked sturgeon among starters, an unusually delicious cream of broccoli au gratin among soups, risotto combined with ham and fennel, along with entrées including truffled chicken breast and a hearty roast veal. Fine wines, impeccable service. To summarize, in my view Rome's No. 1 splurge restaurant. Bravo! *Luxury.*

Hassler Hotel Roof (Trinità dei Monti 6; Phone 679-2551) makes no pretense of being typically Roman. It has for long catered to affluent Americans intent on a festive meal combined with a panorama of the city from the summit of a hotel situated atop the Spanish Steps. The staff is English-speaking, and there are menu cards in English. Even though you may order non-Italian dishes—shrimp cocktail, Russian caviar, consomme with sherry, roast chicken, grilled lamb chops, poached sea bass with Hollandaise sauce—there are plenty of authentic national specialties, the range risotto al radicchio, polenta pasticciata, and tonnarelli conca d'oro through such entrées as saltimbocca and seafood fritto misto. *Luxury.*

Hostaria dell' Orso (Via Monte Brianzo 93; Phone 656-4250): One goes to the Hostaria neither for food, which is pedestrian, nor for service, which can be patronizing. (Affluent steak-and-baked-potato Americans have a way of demoralizing restaurant staffs.) Tabs are high, but one looks upon a dinner as an expensive evening, with something to eat and drink, at a magnificent antique of a house. The Hostaria goes back more than half a millennium and embraces three sumptuously furnished levels—bar-lounge as you go in; restaurant up a flight; and *boîte* topside. Inspect the furnishings, objects, and paintings of all three. *Luxury.*

Marte (Piazza in Campo Marzio; Phone 722-8306) is a sensible heart-of-old-Rome choice for an alfresco lunch or dinner in warm weather or a cozy meal at other times of the year. The soups are good—try the minestrone. And so are any number of pasta choices. *First Class.*

Massimo d'Azeglio Hotel Ristorante (Via Cavour 18; Phone 4816-101): This century-old hotel and restaurant (a part of the Bettoja chain) is a Roman institution, the atmospheric restaurant especially. Business people in the area like to stop in for lunch. Pasta is inordinately tasty; try the spaghetti all' amatriciana, here flavored with ham and truffles. Grilled fresh trout is another house specialty. The piatti del giorno are invariably good bets: osso bucco con risotto and scaloppine al vino bianco, for example. Grills are always available, and of the desserts, banana flambé is exceptional. Agile service. *First Class.*

Mastrostefano (Piazza Navona 94; Phone 654-1669) starts out with an inspired location on one of the great Baroque squares of Europe, continues with décor—the comparison is to a docked Art Deco ship of the 1930s—concludes with delicious food and skilled service. Cannelloni and fagotto (spinach-filled ravioli) are delicious pasta choices. And the osso bucco is an indicated entrée. Order the house Frascati to accompany your meal. In warm weather, sit on the terrace. *First Class.*

Il Matriciano (Via dei Gracchi 55; Phone 321-3040) sees to it that you lunch or dine satisfactorily. Menu à la carte and relatively limited, so that it is easy to order a meal of, say, minestrone, ravioli teamed with ricotta and spinach, roasted porcini mushrooms, and veal chops—or, from the seafood menu—shrimps, swordfish, sole, or perhaps, the excellent fritto misto. *First Class/Luxury.*

Da Necci (Piazza dell' Oratorio 50; Phone 562-3376) is a typically old-fashioned, typically Roman place; a brick fireplace dominates its arched, stuccoed interior. In summer, dinner on the piazza is indicated. Food is unexceptional but veal with peppers is a good bet. *First Class.*

Nuova Stella (Via Manin 50; Phone 474-5520) is family-operated and friendly enough, but the food—salads, pasta, chicken—is only so-so, at least in my experience. Big draw is price—carafe wine, for example, just has to be among the least expensive such in Rome. *Moderate.*

Osteria Margutta (Via Margutta 82; Phone 679-8190): The winsome Art Nouveau front attracts, as you walk along, hungry at the termination of a Via Margutta or Piazza di Spagna shopping tour. And so you pop in. Penne al tonno—quill-shaped pasta with a tuna sauce—is a propitious opener, the fish of the day, simply grilled, to follow, a refreshing Frascati accompanying. Desserts are wheeled over on a cart. Nice waiters. *First Class.*

Panzironi (Piazza Navona 74; Phone 396-976): Although I have long been partial to Piazza Navona's Mastrostefano, there are times—on sunny days—when it can be packed. Panzironi, its near-neighbor, is a worthy alternative for a meal, ideally at an outside table, in one of Europe's most inspired squares. Consider pasta e fagioli—macaroni and bean soup—as an opener, roast lamb as an entrée, the house Frascati, and perhaps an ice-cream dessert. *First Class.*

Passetto (Via Zanardelli 14; Phone 654-3696) is a dignified old-timer. You enter on Via Zanardelli, but if it's summer, aim for a table at the rear on the covered terrace overlooking Piazza Sant' Apollinare—much more amusing than the stuffy dining room. Spaghetti all' amatriciana, made here with bacon, tomato, and white wine, is a specialty. So is the tacchina novellia con ciporine—a turkey dish. Abbacchio d'Abruzzi is tasty baby lamb. *Luxury.*

Pesa (Via Garibaldi 18; Phone 58-09-236) is in the quarter of town that might be called Trenchermen's Trastevere. This is an atmosphere house of yore. Open with prosciutto and melon, follow with the pasta platter—a trio of the day's choices. Continue with still another platter—of seafood, including jumbo shrimp. Dessert is served in the same fashion—a vast tray of watermelon, figs, apricots, and peaches will be brought to the table. Fun. *First Class.*

Peppone (Via Emilia 58; Phone 493-976) is, like Piccolo Mondo (below), worth knowing about if you're headquartering in or around nearby Via

Veneto. It's smallish but inviting—the look is rough-plastered walls with wrought-iron accents—and the staff is old-school and kindly. Stracciatella—the Italian counterpart of China's egg-drop soup—makes for a bracing first course; so, indeed, does spaghetti salsa pomodoro e basilico. With veal entries reliable. And the house wine is well-priced. *First Class.*

Piccolo Mondo (Via Aurora 39, near Via Veneto; Phone 485-680) is an old personal favorite, for long popular with neighborhood regulars as well as guests from hotels in the neighborhood. The draw is an attractive environment—a clutch of contiguous brick-walled and barrel-vaulted chambers, with outdoor tables on the street in fine weather—and a congenial green-vested staff that serves up well-cooked fare from an extensive à la carte. A memorable meal might consist of tortellini in brodo—the classic Italian consommé with filled pasta—to open, a fabulous abbacchio, or roast of lamb, cacciatore style, with house wine to accompany, and fruit for dessert. *First Class.*

Porto di Ripetta (Via di Ripetta 250; Phone 3612-376) is intimate in scale, appealing of décor, and with seafood its specialty; marinare dal mare is a favored entrée. And the cellar is extensive. *First Class.*

Ranieri (Via Mario de' Fiori 26; Phone 579-1592) is a step from Via Condotti. It's an old-timer—smallish, intimate, and with a history that goes back to the middle of the last century. The restaurant is named for a one-time chef of Queen Victoria, who took over only after his subsequent employer, Empress Carlotta of Mexico, lost her husband to a firing squad—and her own reason. Cannelloni all' casalinga—the house's own—is four-star; so is the veal dish called costoletta di vitello all' imperiale, and the chicken, Massimiliano style. Torta deliziosa, a cake enveloped with chocolate cream and bitter chocolate shavings, is indeed deliziosa. In my view—confirmed each time I return—this is one of Italy's best restaurants. *Luxury.*

Relais le Jardin (Lord Byron Hotel, Via de Notaris 5; Phone 360-9541) occupies extraordinarily handsome subterranean quarters. Massive Renaissance paintings in splendidly gilded frames complement an otherwise contemporary space, with cotton-slipcovered club chairs flanking flower-centered tables. The sure hand of proprietor Amadeo Ottaviani (the Lord Byron is the flagship hotel of his small chain) has been at work in the look of the Relais, in the selection of a crackerjack staff (there's no better service in Rome, at least that I know), and in the creation of a menu that is part nouvelle, or *nuova* (grouped on the side of the menu headed La Creativa) and part classic Italian (called La Tradizione); a meal composed of dishes from both parts is a sound idea. Open with smoked salmon unusually garnished or blinis teamed with caviar under a subtle lemon sauce, continue with spaghetti whose *nuova* sauce is based on mushrooms and provolone cheese, or ravioli stuffed with a red caviar and duck, in preparation for such entries as scampi baked on a bed of lettuce and spinach, or roast lamb—*presalé* as you remember it from Normandy—served with an artichoke-and-fresh-mint purée accompanied by deftly prepared zucchini. The Relais's dessert spectacular embraces chocolate and apple cakes, vanilla ice cream, and crème caramel, and you skip it at your peril. Exceptional wines. In my experience, this is one of Italy's best restaurants—well worth the quarter-hour's drive from the center. *Luxury.*

Romolo (Via Porta Settimana 8; Phone 588-284) is an ancient Trastevere house, which, legend decrees, is where the painter Raphael lived with his mistress, La Fornarina, and where he drank wine with fellow-artist Sebastiano del Piombo. These many centuries later, Romolo thrives partly because of the legend, partly on consistently good cuisine (if not service, which can be disagreeable). Withal, this is as good a place as any to sample trippa alla romana, the local tripe specialty, not to mention more prosaic dishes like grilled pork chops. And there is no gainsaying the success of the antipasto; it's delicious. *First Class.*

Sabatini (Piazza di Santa Maria in Trastevere 18; Phone 582-026) is a Trastevere landmark, facing the Church of Santa Maria in Trastevere, on its broad piazza. The look is of natural brick walls supporting venerable beamed ceilings. What one wants to order here is fish, simply grilled, preceded by the superb seafood antipasto or clam-sauced spaghetti alle vongole. (There are actually two Sabatinis; the second is entered at adjacent Vicolo Santa Maria in Trastevere, and has its own phone: 581-8307.) *First Class.*

Sans Souci (Via Sicilia 20; Phone 493-504) could be a set from an Astaire and Rogers movie. It is not, of course, that old. But I suspect it dates at least to the early seventies and that its popular proprietor, Bruno Borghesi, has been adamant about its remaining quite as it was from the time of the opening. Sans Souci is not subtle. Walls are mirrored and fitted with enormous crystal sconces, whose illumination is complemented by candles inserted in silver deer centering each of the tables, the lot of them set with the orange-bordered porcelain that is Richard-Ginori's most celebrated pattern. Waiters—there appear to be a veritable regiment of them—are uniformed in brown tails to match the brown leather of the chairs in which their customers are seated. And massed floral arrangements are dotted about. You may open with a drink in the little bar up front, taking your time to peruse an elaborate bill of fare that, I want to emphasize, is essentially Italian—international clientele and the restaurant's French name notwithstanding. Carpaccio and prosciutto con melone are ideal appetizers. Order your risotto with any of half a dozen accents: mushrooms, asparagus, Parmesan cheese among them. And pastas: Tagliolini—a variation on the noodle theme—are deliciously sauced, and one of a number. Grilled giant shrimp are memorable; ditto medaglioni di vitello. With beef—including châteaubriand prepared for two—as reliable as veal. Your waiter will wheel up a *carrozza* of cakes. But I urge that you consider prepared-at-table crespelle, or crèpes, or that you order one of Sans Souci's soufflés; chocolate, with a vanilla sauce, is sublime. And study the wine list with care; it's top of the line. *Luxury.*

El Toulà (Via della Lupa 29; Phone 687-3498) is a good looker with a sense of style and fare mostly emanating from the Veneto region of the north. Which means that this is a good source of risotto, to mention but one tasty possibility. Very smart. *Luxury.*

21 (Mediterraneo Hotel, Via Cavour 15; Phone 464-051) is the restaurant of the flagship hotel (above) of Rome's Bettoja chain, which knows a thing or two about the kind of food Romans—and their visitors—enjoy. Setting is striking Art Deco—one wall is covered with an original mosaic—staff smiles, and the à la carte menu (always with daily specials appended) tempts. Antipasto from the *carrello* is the prototypical Roman opener. But insalata caprese—of mozzarella, tomato, and basil—is light and lovely. Rome's own stracciatella—clear soup topped with eggdrops and cheese—is inspired at 21. So are such pastas as bucatini ai tre formaggi (with a three-cheese sauce), tuna-sauced penne, tonnarelli with a salmon sauce, and Milanese-style risotto. Entrées are treats, tacchino Valdostano (turkey Aosta style) and rostini annegati ai Soave (veal chops with a wine sauce) especially. *First Class.*

Da Vicenzo (Via Castel Fidardo 4) is an attractive—and delicious—source of seafood; the day's catch is invariably a good bet. *First Class.*

SHOPPER'S ROME

Rome is the most stylish of the European capitals, where one seeks smartness, quality, and design. And finds them. Shopping is concentrated in Via del Corso, the popular-price Main Street connecting

Piazza del Popolo with Piazza Venezia; Via Nazionale, another middle-level street joining Piazza della Repubblica with Piazza Venezia; smart Via Condotti, at the foot of the landmark Spanish Steps (Piazza di Spagna), leading to Via del Corso; also-fashionable streets parallel with Condotti (like Via Frattina) and leading from it (like Via Belsana, Via Bocca di Leone and Via Mario de' Fiori); and adjacent, also-posh thoroughfares like Via Sistina, Via del Tritone, Via del Babuino, and Via Margutta.

ANTIQUES: Unless you know old things, it is not a bad idea to make the rounds with someone who does, for there are many ingeniously executed copies of Italian antique furniture, not to mention paintings; Italians are extraordinarily skilled in those areas. Have whatever you buy authenticated by means of a written notation from the seller. (You will want this for U.S. customs, in any event, to qualify your purchase of anything more than a century old for duty exemption.) No matter how fancy the shop, it is always wise to ask if the price quoted is indeed the final price. It also pays to ask questions about age, origin, workmanship, and the like. Good dealers are glad to answer, and you learn a lot in the process.

Antarte (Via del Babuino 55) deals in sixteenth- and seventeenth-century Italian furniture, sculpture, and paintings. *Angelo Vivanti* (Via del Babuino 138) mixes English objects with Italian, with smaller bibelots dotted about and the range several centuries. *Carlo Lampronti* (Via del Babuino 42) is heavy on eighteenth-century paintings and furniture, even older ceramics. *Botteguccia* (Via Margutta 34) offers drawings and prints of the nineteenth century, furniture that's older, small stuff. *Cuena* (Via Margutta 53) occupies the very grand ground floor of a massive palazzo, with diverse stock—capitals of ancient columns, venerable sculpted heads, gilded furniture, much of it Italian, of the eighteenth and nineteenth centuries. *Flea Market* (actually called *Porta Portese,* for the still-standing arches of an ancient gate, its principal entrance) is a Sundays-only proposition, with the location left bank of the Tiber, near the Trastevere quarter. It is smaller than Paris's Marché aux Puces, but at least as much fun, with entire families searching out buys; really old objects are rare. From a jumble of notes, I have alphabetized merchandise I encountered on a half-day's visit: antiques (precious few), army surplus, auto parts, books (used), brass and copper, china, coins, dolls, gadgets (kitchen and other), handkerchiefs (Chinese), jeans (spelled *jinz* on one stall), jewelry (used, if not necessarily old), knitwear, leather, olives, paintings (mostly contemporary and mostly dreadful), peanuts (in shells), radios, scarves, shoes (including sandals and sneakers), suede jackets, sunglasses, telephones, totes, typewriters (aged), watches (old pocket), and yarn. *Granmercato Antiquario Babuino* (Via del Babuino 150) is a massive space sheltering stalls of a couple score dealers vending an extraordinary range of wares, ivory and jewelry, old prints and old silver, paintings and furniture. Every piece is ticketed with price and century of origin. *Martinoja* (Via del Babuino 107) zeroes in on the eighteenth century, with lovely paintings and furniture.

AUCTIONS: *Sotheby's* (Piazza di Spagna 90) exhibits three days in advance of sale.

BARBER/HAIRDRESSER: There are, of course, countless choices. A favorite of mine is *I Barberini* (Piazza Barberini 53); at once central, and with fairly reasonable tabs. Book an appointment by phoning 488-0869.

BOOKS: *Rizzoli* (Largo Chigi, off Piazza Colonna) is the very same that Americans know from its several U.S. branches. The Rome store is enormous, with big selections of art books, which the Italians print beautifully.

CHINA AND GLASS: *Richard-Ginori* (Via Condotti 71) is Italy's leading designer-manufacturer of porcelain, going back to the eighteenth century, and with stores throughout the country and abroad. The beautiful merchandise (dinner services are the specialty but there is a lot more) here compensates for the unsmiling sales staff. *Fornari* (Via Frattina 44) is another excellent porcelain source.

CHILDREN'S CLOTHES: *Pre-Natal* (Via della Croce 17) makes its point with witty, moderately tabbed duds for kids. *Tablo* (Piazza di Spapa) is *the* place for the high-style child; everything is beautiful, beautifully made, and costly.

MEN'S AND WOMEN'S CLOTHING: *Battistoni* (two Via Condotti locations between Vias Bocca di Leone and Belsana) vends conservative clothing—men's and women's—of high quality, and at a price. *Beltrami* (Via Condotti 19) is striking looking, with strikingly designed men's and women's clothes and accessories; expensive. *Da Vinci* (Via del Corso 89) carries finely woven men's wool sweaters, at fair prices. *Emilio Pucci* (Via Campania 59) retains a loyal female American following: expensive clothes and accessories, a long-on-scene clothing shop. *Étienne Aigner* (Piazza di Spagna) specializes in understated smart clothes and accessories, both men's and women's, with leather gifts as well; costly. *Eddy Monetti* (Via Condotti 63) has shops in major Italian cities, with customers who can afford, say, $100-plus for a necktie. *Brioni* (Via

Barberini 79) is at once a source of custom-tailored men's clothing (usually completed in three days), but with ready-to-wear as well, and haberdashery. *Fila* (Via Capole Case 24 at Piazza di Spagna) makes a specialty of stylish sportswear—golf jackets, baseball caps, tees and sweats, small luggage. *R. Piatelli* (Via Condotti 20)—on scene, it avers, since 1880—has developed superb taste since that time in men's and women's clothing; have a look, by all means. *Bac and Harry* (Via XX Settembre, Via del Gambero 29, other locations): Trendy menswear. *Duglas* (Via XX Settembre 42) terms itself—and accurately—a source of *eleganza maschile. Polidori* (Via Condotti 61) is a source of million-lire men's suits. Equate *Stuart* (Via Vittoria 8) with smart men's clothing. *Franceschini's* (Via del Corso 98) men's sportswear is good-looking and expensive, with shoes as well (including Cole-Haans imported from the U.S.). *Roxy* (on both Via Frattina and Via Veneto, and other major cities) has the best-value silk neckties of any that I know in Italy; those of *Gioffer* (Via Frattina) are also inexpensive, but not, in my view, up to Roxy's. *Gianni Versace* (Via Borgognona and Via Bocca di Leone) is the epitome of contemporary alta moda, male as well as female. Top designers' shops on Via Borgognona include *Gianfranco Ferre, Givenchy, Laura Biagiotti,* and *Fendi. Luisa Spagnoli* (Via Frattina and Via Veneto) is an Italy-wide women's wear chain; smartly styled, middle-category. *Max* (Via Bocca di Leone 7) has smashing neckties, makes up shirts to order. *Mila Schön* (Via Condotti 64), for long a top couturier, sells both men's (relatively recently—and with dashing neckties) and women's clothes. So does *Salvatore Ferragamo* at separate Via Condotti shops. *Mimosa* (Via del Corso 135) typifies the popular-priced women's clothing shop, of which Via del Corso has many. *Nazareno Gabrielli* (Via Condotti 41) is among the newer of the Condotti stores, with two floors of glitzy men's and women's sportswear; expensive. *Raineri Gattinoni* (Via Sistina 42): women's sportswear, modish and costly. *Sporting Club* (Via Frattina 92) lures ladies with silks and sportswear; not inexpensive. *Testa* (Via Frattina 105) is a long-on-scene vendor of well-designed, well-constructed men's wear, with smart suede jackets. *Tommassina Sistinalla* (Via Sistina 104): lovely, lacy lingerie. *Ungaro* (Via Bocca di Leone 24) is the name of a talented couturier; this is his Rome shop. Ditto his neighbor, *Valentino* (Via Bocca di Leone 18)—for women's things, with a men's shop on Via Condotti. *Barone* (Via del Corso 323) has good-value, moderate-price men's clothing and accessories. A final clutch of rankers for clothing, on Via Condotti: *Piatelli* (men's and women's tailored duds), *Campanile,* with both men's and women's clothing; *Trussardi,* Rome link of a clothing chain—men's and women's both; and *Max Mara,* known for its ladies' wear.

DEPARTMENT STORES: *La Rinascente* has two outlets—the smaller on centrally situated Piazza Colonna, fronting Via del Corso, with women's clothing and accessories on main, second, and third floors; men's wear on 1 (a flight up), and children's clothing and accessories on 4. Much bigger—occupying seven selling floors—is *La Rinascente* on Piazza Fiume, away from the center. *Coin* (Piazza le Appio; Via Le Libia 61; other locations) offers good-value house-brand clothing for all the family; name brands and housewares, too, with a speedy alteration service for your purchases. Though much smaller, *Standa,* a link of another chain on Via del Corso, is worth exploring for its moderately priced women's and men's clothing, accessories, and shoes. And the *Upim* branch on Via Nazionale has buys in housewares as well as clothing.

FOODSTUFFS: *Alemagna* (Piazza Colonna) is a national chain whose units embrace caffès and retail shops that are sources of packaged cookies and candies. *Perugina* (Via Condotti 12) is a celebrated Perugia candymaker; tempting chocolates imaginatively packaged. *Street markets* are a joy of Rome. *Mercato Rionale* occupies the vast square called Campo dei Fiori—fruits and vegetables, as well as fresh-caught fish, among much more, make this an ideal place to study the ingredients of the Italian table. *Piazza San Cismato* is a people-packed, food-filled Trastevere market—lots of fun. Still another open market is on *Via della Pace,* near Piazza Navona.

GLOVES: No one makes them as masterfully as the Italians; the butter-soft calfskin ones are ideal gifts: light in weight, invariably good value. *Merola* (Via del Corso 143) has, in my view, the best glove buys in town, with respect to both quality and price. *The Glove Shop* (Via Vittorio Veneto 106) is a long-on-scene source. *Sermoneta* (Piazza di Spagna) has big glove selections on its main floor, good-quality small leather goods—wallets and the like—upstairs.

HANDICRAFTS: *Bella Coppa* (Via dei Coronati 8) was founded by an enterprising American couple, Mr. and Mrs. Kellogg Smith, ex-*Cleveland Press,* to fill a gap in this area, with attractive pottery, textiles, woodwork from all regions of the republic.

JEWELRY AND SILVER: *Allessandrelli* (Via Vittoria 33) protects its gold jewelry by having customers pass through two locked rooms to enter and depart. Understandable; their wares are costly. *Mario Buccellati* (Via Condotti 30) is a Florentine firm with typically heavy Florentine-style silver; other pieces as well; in New York, too. *Bulgari* (Via Condotti 10) is celebrated for its high-style jewelry, fashioned of gold, silver, and precious stones; with foreign branches, New York among them. *Cartier*

(Via Condotti 17) is a link of the classy, Paris-based multinational chain—diamonds and other gems and gold fashioned into jewelry and watches. *Van Cleef and Arpels*—like Cartier and also on Via Condotti—has far-reaching branches, with jewelry and watches the stock in trade. *Luana Francisci* (Via di Ripetta 258) vends its own strikingly contemporary-design brooches, bracelets, rings, and earrings, based on gold and diamonds, but with colored stones employed as well. *Bozart* (Via Bocca di Leone 4) sells its own-design costume jewelry, pricey but interesting.

LEATHER AND LUGGAGE: *Antonio Antinori* (Via Francesco Crispi 45) is a breath of Florence, with the northern city's gold-decorated leatherware—desk sets, especially; luggage, too. *Caresa* (Via del Tritone 117) has big stocks, as well as suede jackets and coats. *Val Corso* (Via del Corso 151) attracts with moderate tabs for a range of leather goods. *Pelletteria Excelsior* (Via Veneto 12) is a sound source of leather and luggage—billfolds through trunks. *Ginocchi* (Via Sistina 35): Good looking bags, wallets, and other objects, the lot smartly styled, if not inexpensive. *Emma Testa* (Via Sistina 58) terms her wares altamoda—and high-style they are. *Gucci* (Via Condotti 8 for clothing and shoes and Via Condotti 77 for leather goods, scarves, and ties) is at the top of every American and Japanese visitor's list of Rome requisites, right up there with St. Peter's. If you can't spot fellow-Yanks in Rome by their clothes or speech, you can tell them by their Gucci shopping bags. Prices are lower than in U.S. branches (and occasionally there are closeout sales of discontinued models, ties and shoes especially). But they are not cheap. If you don't find what you want at the Rome Gucci, there are branches in Milan, Naples, Perugia, Venice, Bari, and Porto Cervo, with the original stores in Florence.

LINENS, EMBROIDERY, AND FABRICS: *Emilia Bellini* (Via Condotti 77) is a long-established firm with linens embroidered and otherwise, of surpassing beauty. *Frette* (Piazza Colonna) is for very smart, very pricey bed linens; in New York, too. *Pratesi* (Piazza di Spagna) is the prototype of high-style bed linen and towels, the designs contemporary, the prices steep; also in New York. *Luisa Rubelli* (Via del Babuino 86) sells exquisitely made reproductions of antique brocades and damasks, by the meter. *Lisio* (Via Sistina 25) specializes in silks and taffetas by the meter; tassels, too.

PRINTS AND ETCHINGS: *Olga Bruno* (Via del Governo Vecchio 38) has for long sold fine old and rare books, engravings, and maps: a treasure trove in an area dotted with explorable shops in this same fascinating category. *Plino Marecchia* (Piazza Navona) is a maze of aged etchings; you'll want to browse and browse. Have a look too, at *Osvaldo Coccaza* (Via Vittoria 76).

RELIGIOUS ARTICLES: *Via della Conciliazione*—a street, not a shop—leads from the Tiber to St. Peter's and is Religious Goods Row, with one shop after another full of this kind of merchandise, with little discernible difference, one from the other, at least to an inexpert eye. *Lelli Garey* (Piazza Farnese 104) is an Italian woman with a British husband whose shop is popular with English-speaking visitors from both sides of the Atlantic.

SHOES are sold at virtually every turn, in this as in all Italian cities. A few of the more interesting shops: *Fratelli Rossetti,* a pricey national chain, with New York, London, and Paris branches, and very good-looking shoes, men's and women's both, and *Tanino Crisci,* another expensive chain, are both on Via Borgognona. *Mada* (Via della Croce 39) is tiny but has elegant women's shoes at untiny tabs. *Marco* and *Tradote* are typical of a number of Corso shoe shops, with both men's and women's models at moderate prices. *Raphael Salato* (Piazza di Spagna): beautifully designed, well crafted, expensive; both men's and women's. *Campanile* is another Via Condotti source of fine shoes as well as luggage. *Morosilu* (Via Francesco Crispi) has good-value, moderate-category shoes; ditto *Pollini* (Via Frattina 22). *Dal Co'* (Via Vittoria 65): Tasteful women's footwear. *Campanile* (Via Condotti 58) is stylish albeit costly; shoes cost upwards of $200 per pair.

TEXTILES: *Meconi* (Via Cola di Rienzi 309) is worth knowing about if you'll be having suits, sport jackets, or shirts custom-made; wool, cotton, and other materials for women's clothing as well—all by the meter. Near the Vatican.

INCIDENTAL INTELLIGENCE

Airports/air terminal: Leonardo da Vinci International Airport at Fiumicino *(fyou-me-cheeno),* 22 miles from town, is connected by train with *Stazione Ostienze,* itself linked by Line B of the metro, or subway, with *Stazione Termini* (Piazza del Cinquecento), the main railroad station, which is so outstanding architecturally that it is accorded space on an earlier page. *Getting about:* Ideally, you position yourself in a central hotel so that you may walk virtually everywhere; that is always my plan. Taxis are metered and plentiful except, of course, at rush hours; hotel doormen can be expert at snagging them, or phone 3875, remembering that there are *supplementi* (extras) for baggage, being summoned by phone, riding after 10 P.M. and on holidays, airport rides to cover the driver's journey back to town, and heaven knows what all else. When in Rome (or for that matter, anywhere in Italy), emulate the locals, who let *supplementi* take the place of tips. Grandly named *Metropolitana* is the relatively modest two-line metro, or subway system; Line A connects the Vatican with such points as Stazione Termini, Via Veneto, Piazza di Spagna, and Piazza del Popolo; while Line B links Stazione Termini with earlier-described Ostia, stopping intermediately at stations near the Colosseum and the EUR quarter, among others. Of the *bus routes* (board at the back, buy your ticket either from a machine or a human seller, invalidating it in the machine at the central door, as you exit), No. 33 is touristically popular (it includes Basilica of Santa Maria Maggiore among stops); so are No. 4 (which takes in Basilica San Giovanni in Laterano); No. 32 (Forum Romano is among its stops); No. 75 (Trastevere quarter); No. 118 (Baths of Caracalla, Colosseum, Catacombs of St. Calixtus); and—worth knowing about—No. 60, covering the core of central Rome. *What's on:* Ask your hotel concierge for current issues of *Un Ospite di Roma: A Guest in Rome* and *Carnet di Roma,* for up-to-the-minute open hours of museums and monuments, opera and concert schedules, other intelligence. *The press:* Don't let language difficulties keep you from perusal of such dailies as *Il Giornale d'Italia, Il Messaggero,* the Vatican's influential *Osservatore Romano,* and Rome editions of such distinguished papers as Milan's *Corriere della Sera* and Turin's *La Stampa. Non-Catholic places of worship* include American Episcopal Church (Via Nazionale), Church of England (Via del Babuino—an extraordinarily beautiful specimen of British Gothic Revival transplanted to Italy), Methodist (Via Firenze), Baptist (Via del Teatro Valle), Society of Friends (Via Napoli), Russian Orthodox (Via Palestro), and Jewish (Great Synagogue, Lungotevere Cenci). *English-speaking Catholic priests* operate earlier-described Church of Santa Susanna (Via XX Settembre), Church of San Clemente (Piazza di San Clemente), and Church of San Silvestro in Capite (Piazza San Silvestro in Capite), among others. *Further information:* Ente Nazionale Italiano per Il Turismo (ENIT) has a counter in its headquarters' lobby (Via Marghera 2) for information on travel throughout Italy. For information on Rome: Ente Provinciale per il Turismo di Roma, Via Parigi 5, as well as at Aeroporto Leonardo da Vinci and Stazione Termini.

3

Assisi

Home of the First Franciscan

BACKGROUND BRIEFING

Think about it: What Catholic saint—even including Apostles like Peter, Andrew, James, and John, contemporaries of Jesus—has captured the imagination of the world—non-Christian as well as Christian—in quite the manner of the Assisi-born son of a rich medieval cloth merchant?

And ask yourself a second question: What other European city is as indelibly associated in the public mind with a saint as is Assisi? Think Assisi and you think St. Francis. And vice-versa. Indeed, were it not for the saint, still-small Assisi—its scenic situation on the spur of a hill in the central Apennines of Umbria notwithstanding—would be less celebrated and less visited than any number of still obscure towns nearby.

Its pre-Franciscan history is not unlike those of its neighbors. Prehistoric Umbrians were succeeded by Etruscans who, as long ago as the third century B.C., lost a decisive battle to invading Romans, one of whose buildings—a still splendidly colonnaded temple—now sees service as a church in the heart of contemporary Assisi.

Come the Middle Ages, and the Romans' Asisium had become the Italians' Assisi, from time to time battling not-far-distant city-states like Perugia (chapter 26)—which at one point held Francis prisoner—and Spoleto (chapter 30), the while achieving the wealth that, as status-seeking medieval Italians, they spent on construction of churches, forts, and palaces.

Later centuries of domination by the Papal States prior to the mid-nineteenth-century formation of the pan-Italian monarchy were part of a peninsular pattern. But the relatively brief life of Francis—he was born in 1182 and died in 1226, at the age of 44—was not. The boy's French-born mother had had him baptized Giovanni (John) during the absence of his father, Pietro di Bernardone, on one of the business journeys he made often to France. But Pietro was such a Francophile—having married a Frenchwoman and become wealthy in large part because of his dealings with the French—that he renamed their son Francesco—by no means common at that time—inadvertently creating a vogue for a name that remains popular to this day, female as well as male, in all the Western languages.

No Catholic saint's life is more familiar. As a youth Francis was well educated, well dressed, and experienced in the ways of battle. At twenty-two he had served a year as war prisoner of the Perugians, and returned home ill, from a battle in distant Apulia. Shortly thereafter, he parted with his family, became an ascetic, and the small band of followers that he gathered around him constituted the nucleus of a religious order whose mostly brown-robed friars (not to mention nuns of the Franciscan-affiliated Poor Clares, established by St. Clare, an Assisi contemporary of Francis) have these many centuries operated from churches and monasteries around the world.

Within two years of his death, Francis was beatified. Half a century after, the basilica containing his tomb was consecrated, and the Franciscans began calling in great artists to decorate it. The still-small town—Assisi's population embraces about 6000 living within its medieval walls, 25,000 beyond—is dotted with places associated with the saint, whose globally familiar Sermon to the Birds exemplifies an eternal message of universal love and universal peace.

It is not for nothing that the Vatican has long since decreed the Basilica of San Francesco both a Patriarchal Basilica—on a par with Rome's top five (San Pietro, San Giovanni Laterano, Santa Maria Maggiore, San Paolo Fuori le Mura, San Lorenzo), as well as a Papal Chapel, where the liturgy is celebrated by direct authority of the pope. Nor that, still later, Francis was designated the patron saint of Italy.

ON SCENE

Lay of the Land: First, prepare yourself for tour buses. They dot the Assisi terrain and their passengers crowd it. (When they are present, in full force, it is not always easy to find space in a restaurant at lunchtime.) But don't despair; this relatively compact town—unlike most shrines that I know—is as much a lure for its art and architecture as for its religious significance. And to its credit, powers that be have not allowed it to become tacky. There is nothing, for example, like the long row of souvenir stalls visually polluting the Duomo complex in Pisa (chapter 27) or similarly ugly stands that have, in recent seasons, sprung up around Venice's Piazza San Marco (chapter 37). Eight Middle Ages gates punctuate still-intact city walls, enclosing a rectangular-shaped area dominated by a fairy-tale fortress, *Rocca Maggiore* by name, almost directly overhead as one looks north from the beautiful central square—part of it Roman—*Piazza del Comune.* Main Street, appropriately called *Via San Francesco,* cuts west from the square to the *Basilica San Francesco* complex. And *Via San Gabriele* (later becoming *Viale Alessi*) connects Piazza del Comune with the walled town's eastern edge. Virtually any Assisi street makes for an atmospheric stroll—*Via San Rufino* leads northeast to *Piazza San Rufino* and the *Duomo. Corso Mazzini* leads to *Piazza Santa Chiara* and the *Basilica of Santa Chiara.* Narrow lanes—Gothic arches overhead and over doorways of their houses—include *Vicolo Superiore di Sant' Andrea, Vicolo degli Sposti,* and *Vicolo del Pozzo della Mensa;* wider streets like *Via Montecavallo* and *Via Perlici* are quite as lovely. And there are several points with important Franciscan associations not far out of town.

Basilica of San Francesco (Piazza San Francesco) is not for up-one-aisle-to-the-altar, return-via-the-other-aisle kind of inspection. It comprises two churches, upper and lower. And each is the equivalent of a major art museum by any kind of international standard. There are more beautiful Italian Gothic façades than the basilica's (that of Assisi's Duomo, below, is one such). But the art within is brilliant. Start in Chiesa Inferiore, or *Lower Church.* After noting a framed robe, hair shirts, and sandals that Francis had worn, and his tomb (a 1932 replacement of the original), take in *Cappella San Martino,* with ten scenes of St. Martin's life frescoed in the fourteenth century by Simone Martini; there's a double portrait of St. Francis and St. Clare at the entrance. Observe the nave art, most especially Maestro di San Francesco's *St. Francis Preaching to the Birds,* scenes in the life of St. Mary Magdalen in the chapel named for her, painted by Giotto in 1310; works in the right transept, including Giottos of the *Nativity and Crucifixion;* a bearded St. Francis by Simone Martini; and a *Madonna and Child with Angels and St. Francis* (the saint's face therein is much reproduced) by Cimabue; and in the left transept, frescoes by Pietro Lorenzetti, including a celebrated *Stigmata of St. Francis.*

Chiesa Superiore, or *Upper Church,* is more of a piece. By that I mean, aside from exuberantly decorated vaults and a superbly carved Renaissance choir, its principal treasures are a series of 28 frescoes all by Giotto delineating incidents in St. Francis's life that line the nave. They are in chronological sequence, starting with No. 1 at the high altar end of the right aisle as you enter, ending with No. 28, just opposite. Giotto was such a consummate storyteller and such a talented painter, with an eye as much for color as for architectural and other detail, not to mention facial expression, that each of this group invites attention; you will find yourself buying postcard reproductions of favorites, afterward, in the big basilica shop. The lineup begins with Francis honored by an Assisi citizen spreading his cloak before him, continues with Francis giving away his own cloak, and goes on to other events of note, such as renouncing an inheritance by giving his clothes to his father, Pope Innocent III approving of the Franciscan order, the sermon to the birds, the stigmatization, and the canonization.

Duomo (a.k.a. Church of San Rufino, Piazza San Rufino) boasts quite the handsomest façade in town, elegant Romanesque, with no less than a trio of rose windows separated from as many portals—note the sculpted lunettes over each and lions flanking the center portal—by a beautifully arched loggia. The interior is late Renaissance, although there are older objects, the baptismal font—where St. Francis and St. Clare were both baptized—among them. And there is a treasure-filled museum.

Basilica of Santa Chiara (Piazza Santa Chiara), thirteenth-century Gothic, with the biggest buttresses you are ever likely to encounter, is considerably smaller than San Francesco, but appears to draw quite as many visitors—so expect crowds. You'll no doubt have to queue to visit St. Clare's subterranean tomb; and to enter the side chapel wherein is situated the twelfth-century painted crucifix reputed, so legend decrees, to have spoken to St. Francis when it hung in the Church of San Damiano (below). A multilingual nun behind a grille greets each visitor to the chapel and gives him or her a little card with a prayer of St. Francis, printed in major languages, which says, in part: ". . . Give me right faith, firm hope, perfect charity, and profound humility, with wisdom and perception . . ."

Templo di Minerva/Church of Santa Maria Sopra Minerva (Piazza del Comune) could not have been any more beautiful when it was erected by the Romans nineteen centuries back; its six Corinthian columns support a still-superb portico, and shield the entrance to the Baroque-era church inside.

Pinacoteca Civica (Palazzo dei Priori, Piazza del Comune): Assisi's art museum is located in a fourteenth-century palace. Draws are frescoes and paintings, of which Ottaviano Nelli's riveting *Madonna and Child with Saints,* and Matteo da Gualdo's moving *Crucifixion* stand out; venerable sculpted fragments too.

Forum e Museo Romano (Via Portica) complements Templo di Minerva (above) as still another aspect of Roman Assisi. It occupies, rather imaginatively, the crypt of what had been the Church of San Nicolà, exhibiting busts and tablets, torsos and tombs, and there's a passage to what remains of the city's Roman Forum.

Basilica of Santa Maria degli Angeli (two and half miles southwest of town) is massive, domed, elaborate Baroque. Within it has been placed, ingeniously, tiny Cappella della Porziuncola, the Romanesque chapel alongside which Francis lived with early followers for several years, and where St. Clare took her first nun's vows. Also in the basilica is Cappella del Transito, where Francis died; it contains a Della Robbia statue of the saint; still more Della Robbias are in the crypt. The basilica's museum has portraits of Francis both by Cimabue and Maestro di San Francesco, and there are, as well, a frescoed cloister, plus a pair of art-filled refectories. It's quite a show.

Church of San Damiano and Eremo delle Carceri are important for associations with St. Francis, and in the case of the former, St. Clare, as well. San Damiano (just below Porta Nuova, the city's southeast gate) is where the painted crucifix now in the Basilica of Santa Chiara, above, is said to have, legend decrees, spoken to Francis in the name of God, impelling him to serve the church. Later, St. Clare and nuns of her then newly founded order lived in San Damiano; their choir and refectory still are to be seen, and there is a flower-filled cloister. The Carceri Hermitage (two miles from town) is the site of a grotto to which Francis made retreats and of a cloister centered with a long-dry well that tradition says became filled with water as a result of Francis's prayers; setting is an emerald slope of Monte Subasio, overlooking Assisi.

SETTLING IN

Subasio Hotel (Via Frate Elia 2) is perfectly situated between the Basilica of San Francesco and the core of town, with gracious lobby-lounges, a restaurant that moves from a high-arched cellar to a broad terrace-cum-view in warm weather, convenient snack bar that serves prix-fixe steak-and-fries lunches, and not quite 70 rooms and suites, with those in front affording memorable panoramas. Kind and professional staff. Lovely. *First Class.*

Fontebella Hotel (Via Fontebella 25) is venerable from without—the building is originally Baroque—with 47 pleasant rooms with bath, attractive public spaces that include an atmospheric restaurant and congenial cocktail lounge, and friendly service. *First Class.*

Umbra Hotel (Via degli Archi 6): I like the Umbra's location, on a street just off central Piazza del Comune, and I like the stylishly traditional décor of its lobby, bar-lounge, bedrooms (they total 25), and restaurant worthy of comment in a later paragraph. *First Class.*

Giotto Hotel (Via Fontebella 41) is a hotel to be reckoned with, given fine views from its valley-view rooms, congenial bar-lounge, capacious restaurant (at its best in summer when it occupies a broad terrace), and service from smiling pros. On my last inspection, not all 72 rooms had baths. *Moderate/First Class.*

Dei Priori Hotel (Corso Mazzini 15) is heart-of-the-Assisi action, in a thoroughly—and tastefully—refurbished house of considerable pedigree. Décor is nineteenth-century, in the lobby, lounge, and restaurant, and there are 28 neat rooms with bath. Friendly. *Moderate.*

San Pietro Hotel (Piazza San Pietro 5) lies in the shadow of a landmark church whose name it takes. Lobby is neatly contemporary, the 46 rooms are bath-equipped, and the restaurant is of sufficient interest to warrant later comment. *Moderate.*

San Francesco Hotel (Via San Francesco 48) has spotlessness in its favor, along with a view of the Basilica for which it is named, from front rooms. But the lobby is tiny, lounge and restaurant, well, vivid; service perfunctory, those of the 44 rooms I've inspected small, and with emphasis on groups. Only if you must. *Moderate.*

DAILY BREAD

Buca di San Francesco (Via Brizi 1; Phone 812-204) could not be more typically Old Assisi. It occupies a core-of-town medieval mansion with a terrace appended that is put to good use in summer. Risotto quattro formaggi—with a sauce embracing four cheeses—is a fine starter; grilled sausages, with a tomato salad, are a good entrée selection. Accompany with the house wine. *First Class.*

Taverna dell' Arco da Bino (Via San Gregorio 8; Phone 812-283) makes its home in the high-ceilinged, stone-walled ground floor of a house dating to the twelfth century. For dinner, order a specialty—girarrosto—from the spit; chicken and lamb are good bets. Open with the house's cannelloni or the egg-drop soup called stracciatella. At lunch, omelets-cum-French fries are popular. *First Class.*

La Fortezza (Vicolo della Fortezza; Phone 812-418) is the well-operated enterprise of a husband-wife team; the latter is chef, the former out front. Grilled specialties are tasty. *Moderate.*

Il Frantoio (Via Illuminati, adjacent to Fontebella Hotel; Phone 812-977): Ideally, you choose Il Frantoio on a starry evening, so that you may dine on the terrace, for views of the valley below. The pasta called paglia e fieno—straw and hay—is indicated as a first course, with roast veal or chicken cacciatore among the entrées. Well-priced wines. *Moderate.*

Subasio Hotel Ristorante (Via Frate Elia 2; Phone 812-206) is attractive (part venerably brick-walled, part in a picture-windowed pavilion) and moves to a garden in warm weather. Fare is exceptional—antipasto with a mix of hams and salamis; spaghetti alla carbonara (with a ham-and-egg sauce). And if you've ordered red wine, conclude with a cheese platter including parmigiano, fontina, and bel paese. *First Class.*

Umbra Hotel Ristorante (Via degli Archi 6; Phone 812-240) is so central, handsome, and with such good food that you want to know about it. Order bruschetta—toasted garlic bread, lightly anointed with olive oil—to accompany your antipasto or soup. Risotto, Umbrian-style, is good, too. *First Class.*

Da Otello (Piazzetta Chiesa Nuova; Phone 812-415) makes a specialty of pizza, with a variety of toppings. Central. *Moderate.*

Caffè Minerva (Piazza del Comune) draws the thirsty and foot-weary. Have a coffee, a drink, and perhaps a little sandwich. *Moderate.*

Caffè Trovellesi (Piazza del Comune) is fun in summer when its tables occupy space in the square. *Moderate.*

INCIDENTAL INTELLIGENCE

If your approach is by train, don't be alarmed if you don't observe Assisi upon alighting. The railway station, on the Foligno–Terontola line, is three miles from town, with which it's connected by bus. *Further information:* Azienda Autonoma Comprensoriale di Cura Soggiorno e Turismo, Piazza del Comune 12, Assisi.

4

Bari

and Apulia's Coastal Cathedrals

BACKGROUND BRIEFING

With one notable exception—Venice—and a pair of relatively minor ones—Trieste and Ravenna—Americans rarely cross the relatively narrow Italian peninsula to cities of the Adriatic coast. Which is hardly to say that the rest of the world has been of the same disposition over the centuries.

On the contrary. Take Bari, leading port of the southeast, capital of the *Regione* we call Apulia in English (Puglia in Italian), and a good-looking metropolis adept in roughly equal portions at commerce, culture, and cuisine.

Not surprising, if you take into consideration the role of colonizers and invaders over long centuries. Warlike Illyrians came south from their Balkan homeland in prehistoric times. Later, Greeks crossed the Atlantic (Bari's Museo Archeologico is packed solid with their handiwork). They were followed by hardly less creative Romans. Ensuing centuries saw Goths, Lombards, Normans, and Byzantines on scene. Bari's strategic situation, an opening to the Middle East, lured Crusaders to it; many sailed from its harbor along with that of the southerly Apulian port of Brindisi (chapter 16). The Middle Ages saw the city controlled by the gifted Hohenstaufen dynasty out of Germany's Swabia. (Frederick II's thirteenth-century castle remains a still-in-use landmark.)

The charm of today's Bari is that it wears its checkered past as a badge of honor, as proud of the grid pattern of its commercial quarter (left over from the Napoleonic period) as of the Romanesque basilica where repose bones of its patron saint, Nicholas, brought from the Middle East some nine hundred years ago.

ON SCENE

Lay of the Land: Tree-lined boulevards edged by gracious public buildings; an authentically venerable *Città Vecchia,* or Old Town; smart shopping streets, pedestrian and otherwise; waterfront promenades: Bari has them all. Streets to concentrate on are a pair of boulevards perpendicular to each other: *Corso Vittorio Emanuele,* going east–west, linking *Piazza Garibaldi* with *Porto Vecchio,* or Old Port, and with such eye-filling buildings out of the last century as opposite-each-other *Palazzo del Governo* (provincial) and *Palazzo di Città* (municipal) as well as classic-style *Teatro Piccinni,* and *Corso Cavour,* as much for fine shops as for palazzi housing the *Banco d'Italia and Chamber of Commerce,* with its standout *Teatro Petruzzelli,* an all-Europe ranker, rich with gilt embellishment and splendid sculpture. *Via Sparano* is the principal pedestrians-only shopping street; *Via Argiro* is shop-lined too, and leads to *Piazza Roma* and the railway station. And do drive along the waterfront's *Lungomare Nazario Sauro.*

Basilica di San Nicola (Piazza di San Nicola): It is a toss-up which is the more significant—San Nicola or the Duomo. They are both beautiful specimens of what has come to be called Apulian Romanesque, but San Nicola is older by almost a century (1089)—and gets credit it well deserves for being the prototype for churches built in this part of Italy during this prolific church-building period. It was the arrival in Bari of the remains of St. Nicholas in 1087—a shipload of pious sailors were the bearers—that impelled construction of this church. The saint is buried in the crypt; observe capitals of the columns—no two alike—supporting the vaults, and the Byzantine icon of the saint—in gold and black—at his tomb. The church proper is one of the more exquisitely somber in Christendom, with the only décor the architecture, if you except a gilded-wood ceiling—a felicitous Baroque addition—embedded with paintings. Sculpture stands out in Apulian Romanesque, no more so than in San Nicola. Study the ciborium, or arched canopy, a masterwork in stone on the high altar; exquisitely embellished bishop's throne; lavishly carved frames of doors and windows; and still more sculpture—along with silver, scrolls, and paintings—in the basilica's museum.

Church of San Gregorio (Largo Urbano, next door to San Nicola) is smaller than its immediate neighbor, but not to be skipped. Another Romanesque beauty, it typifies the kind of lovely church dotted about the old quarter of the city, with the capitals on the columns of its nave exceptional.

Duomo (Piazza Odegitria): This Romanesque building bore up beautifully from the twelfth century through to the terms in office of a run of eighteenth-century archbishops who decided the time was ripe for "modernization," which meant—at that period—transformation to the Baroque. Only at the turn of the present century, and only because some stucco of the transept disintegrated (to reveal the original cupola) did authorities determine to restore the building to its original splendor: a rose window over the portal, the arcades of the south wall, nave and high altar, frescoed crypt. We are in their debt.

Castello Normanno-Svevo (Piazza Federico 2 di Svavia): I recommend, on a later page of this chapter, an excursion to Castel del Monte, architecturally one of the superior castles of medieval Europe. But that is hardly to counsel nonattendance at this heart-of-Bari reminder of the swashbuckling era of Frederick II who, some seven hundred years ago, refashioned an even older fortification. This is a massive trapezoid, double-towered, thick-walled, its moat now a finely manicured garden, the chambers flanking its quiet inner court part government offices, part a museum of venerable paintings from throughout Apulia that have been recipients of on-site restoration.

Museo Archeologico (Piazza Umberto 1) occupies the interminably rambling upper floor of Palazzo Ateneo, a University of Bari building (with a library exhibiting precious manuscripts, below). There are perfectly beautiful objects to be viewed in this museum, but they are so infelicitously presented—displays are jam-packed and without enough dividers to break them up—that the going can be heavy. What I do in such museums is arbitrarily select the occasional piece that catches my eye and concentrate on it, continuing then to similarly selected exhibits in other sections. There are masses of miraculously undamaged Bari-area Greek ceramics—kraters, vases, plates—with exquisite terracotta-and-black designs. And the sculpture is formidable, too.

Pinacoteca Provinciale (Palazzo della Provincia, Lungomare Nazario Sauro) shares space with government offices, on the second floor of a nondescript building. But there is nothing nondescript about an overwhelming proportion of the paintings. You'll find a good deal of work by Apulian artists whose names are unfamiliar. But remain alert, as you move about, for Bartolommeo Vivarini's *Annunciation;* Paris Bordone's *Sacra Conversazione,* an immense *Madonna* by Veronese, with tiny angels hovering about, against a background of blue clouds; a Tintoretto of *Saint Roch;* an unusual Giovanni Bellini of *St. Peter,* Bible in hand, daggers in both his head and heart; and still another *St. Peter* by Giordano.

Castello del Monte (23 miles southwest of Bari) ranks, in its way, with the great ones of Wales—like Conwy and Caernarvon—in the pecking order of European medieval castles. It remains, seven and a half centuries following its construction by the still-respected Swabian King Frederick II, an architectural marvel, with the octagon its inspired motif throughout. Basic shape is octagonal, and at each corner the wall is punctuated by an octagonal tower. The interior—though unfurnished—is masterful, with eight main-floor chambers, each in the outline of a trapezoid, and a similarly designed second story.

A quintet of coastal cathedrals: There are, actually, more than five of these utterly lovely Romanesque masterworks easily within a 50-mile drive northwest of Bari. Ideally, one devotes a solid day to a selection of them, in some cases visiting nearby museums and still other churches, pausing for lunch and coffee breaks in the process. But I want to emphasize that distances are so minimal that it's possible to visit my cathedral quintet in a morning or an afternoon. Indeed, I don't know of any comparably compact area of Europe where a traveler can observe as many outstanding works of venerable architecture—each in a separate town—as in the area of Bari. An itinerary? Start with the most distant point, the pretty port town of *Barletta,* proceeding to its Piazza del Duomo to see the thirteenth-century cathedral, with an abnormally tall and slim nave, six-level campanile that towers over the town, and an interior whose principal embellishment is an elegant ciborium on the high altar. Nearby, the Church of Santo Sepolcro, parts of it eleventh century, is somber and impressive; no less so, though, than Barletta's celebrated Colossus, a fabulous freestanding statue in bronze, fifteen feet high, of a long-ago Roman emperor. If by any chance it's open, have a look at the opulent interior of Teatro Comunale Curci; no small Italian town has an opera house to surpass it. Don't miss the massive, Swabian-built castle at the edge of town near the water. And note the pair of next-door museums on Via Cavour—Civico (paintings) and Archeologico.

Continue to *Trani,* whose nine-hundred-year-old Duomo literally skirts the sea, at the edge of a peninsula, core of town. There's a high arch at the base of the needlelike campanile, attached to the cathedral, a honey of a rose window, beneath which is a bronze door almost as old as the church. Also seaside, but a hop and skip distant, is a thirteenth-century castle, relatively small for Apulia, but impressive. If you've time, take in the Church of Ognissanti, a Romanesque beauty.

Ruvo di Puglia is an engaging inland town, based on contiguous squares, Piazza Carollotti and Piazza Regina Margherita. Its underappreciated collection of ancient Greek pottery—all of it from the neighborhood—is nearby in Museo Jatta (Piazza Bovio). End at the Duomo, on the square taking its name, and with the most dazzling façade of any of our quintet. A pair of ferocious animals guard the intricately carved main portal, beneath a rose window. Rows of columns, each with a lovely capital, flank the nave.

Bitonto, closer to the sea than Ruvo, albeit inland, is home to the most exquisitely detailed of our cathedral group, a treasure of Romanesque dating to the twelfth century. You want to take a walk around the façade before entering, noting the bas-relief over the main portal, unusual contour of the multilevel campanile, splendidly carved loggia. Within, marble pulpit, galleried nave, and marble-columned crypt are all significant.

That leaves No. 5, *Palo del Colle,* a friendly little town, whose onetime cathedral has reverted to the status of parish church (it is now called Chiesa Matrice). Still, a rose by any other name. This is a smashing Romanesque structure, with an especially elegant campanile and a gracefully arched nave.

Alberobello and its trulli: Regional tourism authorities make much of this area of Apulia, the reason being its dwellings. They are called trulli, and it is their quaint, cutesy-pie design—circular, of whitewashed stone blocks (joined without mortar), and topped with dark stone conical roofs—that attracts visitors. The singular of trulli is trullo, and if I may, let me say that if you've seen one trullo, you've seen them all. A small town called Alberobello is the most substantial of the trulli communities, with its *Church of Sant' Antonio* perhaps the most elaborate of its structures. But unless you are in the neighborhood—Alberobello is about 30 miles southeast of Bari—don't bother.

SETTLING IN

Jolly Hotel (Via Giulio Petroni 15): You like this one from the moment of arrival in the attractive, oversized lobby, on an agreeable street a hundred yards from the railway station, and an easy walk to Piazza Roma and the core of Bari. There are 164 carefully equipped rooms with excellent baths, a restaurant so good that I provide additional comment on a later page, friendly bar-lounge, and—important this—reception/concierge staff than which I have found none more congenial or skilled anywhere in Italy. *First Class.*

Palace Hotel (Via Lombardi 13) is a modern house, whose smartly designed interior—based on geometric motifs embracing brown, blue, and beige throughout—appeal, as do a central Bari situation, just over 200 pleasant rooms, attractive restaurant, and busy bar at the far end of the lobby. *Luxury.*

Grand Hotel et d'Oriente (Corso Cavour 32) blends an intricately detailed, traditional façade with a sprightly mod-look interior embracing high-ceilinged lobby, red-hued cocktail lounge, earth-toned bedrooms. Location is central. Breakfast only. *First Class.*

Ambasciatori Hotel (Via Omodeo 51) is a high-rise surrounded by greenery of a park edging the University of Bari campus, a ten-minute drive from the center. The look is very contemporary indeed, with nicely furnished rooms, rooftop restaurant-cum-view, cocktail bar. *First Class.*

Executive Business Hotel (Corso Vittorio Emanuele 201) is small—there are only 21 rooms—but stylish modern in look, making excellent use of materials such as plastic and tile. Beds in all of the rooms fold into the wall, so that those chambers—each equipped with an executive desk—are ideal for business meetings. Showers but not tubs in the baths. Bar and breakfast. Central. *First Class.*

Sheraton Nicolaus Hotel (Via Rosalba 27) is, alas, south of the center, albeit full-facility, with 175 nice rooms, restaurants, bar, and indoor pool. *Luxury.*

Hotel Boston (Via Piccinni 155) is a clean-lined house, with 72 bath-equipped rooms, cocktail lounge, and breakfast service. Central. *Moderate.*

Victor Hotel (Via Nicolai 71) welcomes with an inviting modern lobby, has 75 rooms with bath, bar-lounge, breakfast. Quite central. *Moderate.*

DAILY BREAD

La Pignata (Via Melo 9; Phone 23-2481) represents Italian Modern at its most sophisticated, with accents of orange and red smartly accenting white walls. You are impressed upon entry with staff smiles and a groaning antipasto buffet, which tastes as good as it looks. Sample it, and for the remainder of your meal—plan on a multicourse lunch or dinner—put yourself in the hands of the maître d', sampling Apulian specialties, as, for example, orecchiette a cime di rape (the ear-shaped Apulian pasta with a turnip-green sauce); tortiera alla Barese, a soup based on mussels, tomatoes, and pecorino cheese; cozze fritte alla Pugliese—fried mussels; zucchine alla Poverella—a casserole dish; and braccioletti alla Barese, a veal masterwork. Apulian wines are featured. In my view, one of Italy's best restaurants. *Luxury.*

Sorso Preferito (Via de Nicolò 46; Phone 23-57-47): Red linen on the tables, black wrought-iron chandeliers, superagile waiters, an agreeable buzz in a busy space vibrant with contented *Baresi,* come to enjoy themselves. As well they might. The antipasto platter embraces mini-pizzas, a warm spinach-and-pepper combination, sizzling fritters of varying types. A favored entrée is grilled sausages served with a salad. But there are Apulian-style roasts and fish, as well. Bread is typically Apulian—coarse and cut into great chunks. And the house red is lovely. In my view, one of Italy's best restaurants. *First Class.*

La Provolina (Lungomare Starita 19) is one of a number of restaurants overlooking the harbor with fish and seafood specialties. Take your choice of anything from the water, noting that the catch of the day, simply grilled, is invariably good, with a local white wine. *First Class.*

Jolly Hotel Ristorante (Via Giulio Petroni 15; Phone 36-43-66): Openers here set the standard. While you're perusing the spiffily designed menu, the waiter comes with piping hot bruschette—garlic bread lightly anointed with olive oil and peppers. You continue with a nicely textured galantine, or, perhaps, a pasta like tortellini panna e prosciutto—with ham-flecked cream sauce. The Jolly's Châteaubriand with sauce Béarnaise is esteemed, desserts are extravagant, and the wine list one of the most complete in town. *First Class.*

Vecchia Bari (Via Dante Alighieri 47; Phone 521-6496), with its expertise at promotion—you're greeted by a pile of multilingual color brochures when you enter—has achieved a degree of recognition with foreign visitors. It is smallish, with red-and-white checked cloths covering tightly spaced tables. Service, at least in my case, was patronizing, and barely civil, with those dishes I sampled undistinguished. I can't recommend this one. *First Class.*

Motta (Corso Vittorio Emanuele 121) is a well-located outpost of a national caffè chain, indicated for a coffee, snack, or lunch break. *Moderate.*

Caffè Guerrieri (Corso Cavour 131) is a strategic shopper's retreat; coffee, pastries, cold drinks on hot days. *Moderate.*

Il Fagiano (Viale Toledo 9, in the village of Selva di Fasano; Phone 799-157) is called to your attention as a worthwhile lunch point, should you be touring in the neighborhood of Alberobello (above). This is quite a grand country house, with dining rooms scattered about the ground floor, whose focal point is an attractive bar-lounge, pleasant for aperitifs the while seated on overstuffed chairs and sofa. The menu is relatively limited for a restaurant of this category, but the chef is skilled. You open with an on-the-house order of what the French call *amuse-gueules*—tiny hot canapes. Orecchiette in a basil-flavored sauce is creditable. And veal dishes—nodini di vitello (a steak) and piccata di vitello al limone (a medaillon, simply sautéed)—are good bets. The cellar abounds in Apulia vintages, and if you've ordered a red, end with local cheeses served from a cart. *First Class.*

SOUND OF MUSIC

Teatro Petruzzelli (above) is eminently visitable for performances of opera, ballet, symphonic, and other concerts. Check, as well, for what's playing at also-beautiful *Teatro Piccinni.*

SHOPPER'S BARI

Pedestrians-only Via Sparano and boulevardlike Corso Cavour are interesting strolling territory. And so are neighboring streets; *Upim* department store is on busy Via Piccinni and its major competitor, *Standa,* is on palm-centered Corso Vittorio Emanuele. Other shops of interest include *La Borsetta* (women's clothing) on Corso Vittorio Emanuele; *Fantastico* (women's) and *Trione* (men's) on Via Argiro; *Fendi* (mostly women's) and *Trussardi* (men's) on Via Principe Amadeo; *Cam* (men's) on Via Piccinni; and a branch of Florence-origin *Gucci* (leather, men's and women's clothes, accessories) on Via Sparano.

INCIDENTAL INTELLIGENCE

Bari is a major east-coast transport terminus, with domestic air service. Aeroporto Bari–Palese is five miles from town. Car-carrying passenger ships link Bari with points both in Yugoslavia (including Dubrovnik) and in Greece (including Corfu). *Further information:* Azienda Autonoma di Soggiorno e Turismo: Via Melo 253, Bari; Via Gabbiani 4, Barletta; Piazza della Repubblica, Trani.

5

Bologna

Underappreciated Art, Famed Food

BACKGROUND BRIEFING

When you consider the succession of upheavals Bologna has survived in the course of a couple of millenniums plus, from beginnings as the pre-Christian Etruscan community called Felsina, through to severe World War II bombings, its contemporary unruffled lifestyle—correct, cultured, and, with respect to its extravagant cuisine, delicious—is indeed remarkable.

No more so than its look: this wealthy, progressive northern metropolis is capital of the *Regione* of Emilia Romagna and seat of a nine-hundred-year-old university that's a century senior to Oxford, assiduously retains the contours of a medieval town, its uncelebrated trademark a pair of towers (Pisa, after all, has only one such) that lean in opposite directions.

The Bolognese—some 420,000 all told—regard the tilts of their *Torri Pendenti* as though they were perfectly normal occurrences. No question about it: this city takes things in stride. And there are and have been many things: they range from weather (this is Italy's wettest town, which counts some 20 miles, all told, of arcades, or *portici,* sensibly underpinning its buildings) to an interminable succession of wars.

The name derives from the Romans; they called their thriving colony *Bononia.* Post-Roman hegemony was nothing if not diverse. Byzantines succeeded Romans in the sixth century, to be followed by domination of the Papal States—overthrown by the Bolognese, who established a militarily and intellectually respected *comune* in the twelfth century, by which time enough wealth had accumulated for towers of churches and battlements of palaces to create a skyline not all that different from what one sees this very day.

Powerful families and factions—of the kind that emerged in city-states Italy-wide—came to the fore in the Renaissance, when there were tugs of war among adherents of such clans as the Bentivoglio, whose most remembered scion, Giovanni, controlled the city from 1462 through to 1506, a 44-year period during which building flourished and intellectuals peopled the Bentivoglio court. Unpopular papal rule resumed in the early sixteenth century, continuing until the late eighteenth—despite a number of unsuccessful revolts during a period that saw the last coronation by a pope—in Bologna—of a Holy Roman Emperor, in this case, the great Charles V.

Today's Bologna, preoccupied with industry, education, government, and science (there's a nuclear research enterprise) does not accord the promotion of tourism high priority. Nonetheless, a visit can be effortless (virtually every Italian train of consequence seems to pass through centrally situated Bologna), comfortable (there are good hotels), tasty (there is no dearth of creditable restaurants), enjoyable (the low-key Bolognese can be very friendly), and—to understate—eye-opening.

ON SCENE

Lay of the Land: Thank the flat terrain for making Bologna an easy walking city. Thank earlier Bolognese for having built so beautifully, and for embellishing what they built with extraordinary art. And thank today's Bolognese for preserving it all. An irregular ring of contiguous thoroughfares, each a *viale* (boulevard), albeit variously named, encloses the historic core, whose nerve center, appropriately labeled *Piazza Maggiore,* or Major Square, is flanked by a clutch of brilliant palaces—one is the art-rich city hall—as well as a church that is among the planet's largest. Adjacent *Piazza Nettuno* is named for its Renaissance fountain, topped by a giant likeness of the Roman god of the sea, *Piazza Porta Ravegnana.* A short walk northeast is the site of the *Torri Pendenti,* the two leaning towers you'll want to observe: twelfth-century *Torre degli Asinelli,* almost 300 feet high and with a stairway to its summit; and half-as-tall, eleventh-century *Torre Garisenda,* with a tilt greater (three yards plus, toward the northeast) than its neighbor (about a yard and a half westward). Major streets lead from Piazza Maggiore. *Via Indipendenza*—hotel-, restaurant-, and shop-lined, and concluding at *Piazza XX Settembre* and the main railway station, *Stazione Centrale*—extends north; *Via Rizzoli,* one of the principal shopping streets, goes east; *Via Ugo Bassi,* also important for shops, leads west; *Strada Maggiore,* to the southeast, is flanked by fine old palaces and indicated for atmospheric strolls. *Via Zamboni* is a northeasterly street on which one passes *Teatro Comunale,* the opulent opera house; Renaissance-era *Palazzo Poggi,* principal University of Bologna building; and *Pinacoteca Nazionale,* at the intersection of *Via delle Belle Arti*. Note, too, that *Via Farini*, not far south of the leaning towers, is a Bolognese Bond Street—brimming with pricey boutiques.

Palazzo Comunale (a.k.a. Palazzo Accursio, Piazza Maggiore) is the ideal interior with which to become acquainted with the grandeur of medieval Bologna. The broad brick-crenelated façade—a mammoth clock in its tower—is sufficiently imposing to prepare you for the scale of the interior. This is a dual-purpose building. It is Bologna's city hall *and* a repository—on its second floor, gained by a splendid ceremonial staircase—of a mix of art and artifacts, in a series of decorated dazzlingly high-ceilinged salons. There are paintings by artists whose names you know—like Tintoretto and Signorelli—and by others, Bolognese not familiar to you, including interpretations of the *Crucifixion and Annunciation*, as well as gargantuan frescoes and superb furniture from both Baroque and Renaissance periods.

Basilica of San Petronio (Piazza Maggiore) is what the Italians term *stupendo*, meaning both enormous (it's one of the largest extant) and splendid. This is easily the city's No. 1 church, as much for its size—nearly 400 feet long, more than 180 feet wide, close to 150 feet high—as for its design (it took almost three centuries, beginning in the late fourteenth, to complete, and even so, the façade is only partially finished) and its art. Jacopo della Quercia's sculpted lunette above the main portal is stunning, and after walking past giant red-brick pillars supporting a handsomely vaulted nave, pause to admire the brilliant gilded crucifix on the high altar, memorably frescoed chapels (especially those by Giovanni da Modena in Cappella dei Magi), and scenes by Lorenzo Costa in two others, as well as a sculpted *Saint Petronius* by Sansovino, in still another. No wonder this was the church selected for the papal coronation of Holy Roman Emperor Charles V, four and a half centuries ago.

Pinacoteca Nazionale di Bologna (Via delle Belle Arti 56), with its arcaded Renaissance façade, surprises the visitor with a modern, clean-lined interior, ideal foil for a collection of art—medieval through Baroque—that is one of Italy's most important, with emphasis on painters of the Bologna school. There are other artists as well—a ravishing Raphael of *St. Cecilia*; a Giotto of the *Virgin and Child Enthroned*; works by Parmigianino and Lorenzo Monaco. But mostly the painters are Bolognese, celebrated ones like Guido Reni, Domenichino, and the Carracci cousins—Lodovico, Agostino, and the best known, Annibale; but others, perhaps new to us, like Giovanni da Bologna, Jacopino da Bologna, and Vitale da Bologna, with all of whose work it is a pleasure to become acquainted. The work of the related Carracci and of their colleagues was the subject of an enormous special exhibition—*The Age of Correggio and the Carracci*—in the late 1980s, at New York's Metropolitan Museum of Art, with paintings on loan from Bologna's Pinacoteca Nazionale and other Italian museums.

Museo Civico Medievale (Via Monzoni 4) is, to start, an atmospheric palazzo; its galleries with beamed ceilings and its public areas with frescoed walls surround a colonnaded courtyard. The exhibits stun—stone crosses and venerable books, carved ivory and bronze jewelry, stained glass and stone-carved tombs, heads of medieval popes in bronzes. There are two treasury-filled floors, with the ruins of a Roman-era stone wall in the basement. As you depart, ask to be directed to the museum's *Palazzo Fava,* whose walls are highlighted with frescoes by the sixteenth-century Carracci brothers, Annibale and Lodovico.

Basilica of San Domenico (Via Garibaldi): Churches in Italy operated by Franciscans and Dominicans are rarely small, and invariably art-filled. Here in Bologna, the Dominicans have a special reason for the grandeur of their Gothic-façade, Baroque-interior house of worship: the Spanish-born saint—his name was Domingo de Guzmán and his early missionary work was in thirteenth-century France—is buried within. St. Dominic's tomb is an elaborately sculpted Renaissance sarcophagus in an equally elaborate chapel. Far more moving, to me at least, is an unostentatious portrait of the saint—in the black-and-white habit of his order, red missal in hand, his head framed by a gold halo—by an unknown medieval master that is almost Impressionistic in its simplicity. There are, as well, works by Michelangelo (three sculptures) and by Filippino Lippi and Guido Reni, who is buried in San Domenico.

Complesso Santo Stefano (Piazza Santo Stefano) is a unique-to-Bologna complex of utterly beautiful Romanesque churches and chapels. *San Vitale e Agricola,* with its virtually unadorned brick interior, is perhaps the finest.

Church of San Francesco (Piazza Malpighi) is, to be sure, not as art-filled as San Domenico (above) but its scale is so marvelous—pair of campanili; massive flying buttresses supporting a massive apse; vast, triple-nave interior; charming cloister—that you may want to pay your respects.

Church of San Giovanni in Monte (Via Farini) looks smallish and unprepossessing from without, but you want to have a look, if only for the rich cache of art: Vitale da Bologna's *Madonna and Child,* Lorenzo Costa's *Madonna Enthroned with Saints,* Ercole dei Roberti's *Pietà,* and Jacopino da Bologna's painted crucifix.

Metropolitana di San Pietro (Via Indipendenza) is Bologna's cathedral, an essentially Baroque structure notable principally for the generous proportions of its high and wide single-nave interior, for the fine detailing of its plasterwork, and for a reputed *Annunciation* by Lodovico Carracci.

Palazzo Archiginnasio (Via dell' Archiginnasio 8) is a smasher of a Baroque palace created as a multifunction University of Bologna facility and embracing a two-level cortile whose coats of arms are those of long-ago professors and students; a library whose high walls are also embellished with a marvelous mix of insignia; an eminently visitable chapel and—most visually exciting of the inner spaces—an anatomy theater, splendidly paneled, its larger niches filled with full-length sculptures, and its smaller ones with busts. Special.

Museo Civico Archeologico (Via dell' Archiginnasio 2) occupies a porticoed onetime hospital, its halls crammed—and I mean crammed in the old-fashioned museum sense—with exhibits of Etruscan art (sculptures, ceramics, metalwork), Roman (marble torsos, busts), and other cultures, golden tiaras through bronze helmets. Everything—the Egyptian objects of course excepted—is local.

Palazzo della Mercanzia (Piazza della Mercanzia) may well be the first Chamber of Commerce you visit that is situated in a fourteenth-century Gothic palace. Although it is not officially open to visitors in the manner of a museum, the chap at the desk will show you through, the while you admire coffered ceilings, walls of exquisitely worked leather (some of them frescoed), and an impressive stairwell.

SETTLING IN

Baglioni Hotel (Via Indipendenza 8)—heart of town—is a beloved old-timer known throughout the Italian peninsula, which closed for several years in the mid-eighties for an extensive restoration and refurbishing—the cost was $7 million—that was concluded in time for a 1987 reopening. Originally built as a town palazzo by a cardinal in 1738, today's Baglioni retains frescoes by Carracci as part of an interior highlighted by crystal-chandeliered public spaces. The restaurant (below) is handsome, the bar-lounge once again a principal Bologna gathering place. And there are 130 beautifully detailed rooms and suites, with fine baths. Member, Leading Hotels of the World. *Luxury.*

Royal Hotel Carlton's (Via Montebello 8) generously proportioned lobby is high-ceilinged and set off by a sweeping circular staircase, with both the deeply upholstered brown-leather furniture and the reception staff welcoming. The 250 tastefully furnished, carefully equipped suites and rooms feature big baths, and like public spaces, are in tones of gold and brown. There's a super cocktail lounge—you sink right into the tan leather chairs—and popular restaurant, as well. Location is a quiet street near Via Indipendenza. *Luxury.*

Jolly Hotel (Piazza XX Settembre) is a contemporary 172-room link—traditionally furnished—of the ever-reliable nationwide chain, conveniently close to the main railway station as well as to Via Indipendenza. Big lobby, cocktail lounge, restaurant. *First Class.*

Milano Excelsior Hotel (Via Pietramellara 51) is a hop and a skip from the main railway station. The look is contemporary, and there are 84 rooms and suites, small restaurant, and bar-lounge. *First Class.*

Internazionale Hotel (Via Indipendenza 60): I wish this attractive house had a restaurant, although given its central situation it is close to many. Behind the handsome porticoed façade is a looker of a modern lobby and adjacent cocktail lounge; 140 attractive rooms. Breakfast only. *First Class.*

Corona d'Oro Hotel (Via Guglielmo Oberdan 12) is an atmospheric palazzo of respectably advanced age that has been deftly transformed into a honey of a hotel. The lobby-lounge is of-the-moment, albeit with original stucco work. There are 35 neat rooms; bar and breakfast but no restaurant. Central. *Moderate.*

Roma Hotel (Via D'Azeglio 9) is well located near Piazza Maggiore, and likable. There's a pleasant lobby-bar-lounge, along with 83 neat rooms; a restaurant as well. *Moderate.*

Regina Hotel (Via Indipendenza 51) is an arcaded structure of yore without, pertly modern inside, with 61 rooms and a bar-caffè that moves out front in summer. Breakfast only. *Moderate.*

Palace Hotel (Via Montegrappa 9) is close to Via Ugo Bassi's shops and the main square. There are 113 functional rooms, bar-lounge, but no restaurant. *Moderate.*

DAILY BREAD

Tre Frecce (Strada Maggiore 19; Phone 231-200) takes pride of place in this selected group of evaluated Bolognese restaurants for three reasons. First is its situation on one of the most beautiful of the city's streets (see above), lined with palazzi of advanced age (of which the restaurant building—of Middle Ages origin—is one). Second—and this brings up a point worth being informed of not only in Bologna but throughout Emilia Romagna—is the matter of bread. The unfortunate preferred type, in restaurants at least, is a hard, flaky sort of sweetish cracker, twisted as a pretzel might be, but in different designs. Happily, some—not all—restaurants have ordinary Italian bread, but *you must ask for it:* the magic term is *pane comunale,* or city bread. And Tre Frecce is one of these. And third, it is the ideal venue for an on-scene introduction to the city's specialties including its celebrated pasta, the stuffed (with meat, cheese, herbs) tortellini, which are a variation on the theme of ravioli—and are not only addictive (sometimes in *brodo,* or broth, or variously sauced) but may appear in other guises, as tortelli (pumpkin-filled), capellini, tortelloni, and agnellotti. Lasagne, delicious at Tre Frecce, is also of local origin. The bologna sausage we associate with the city's name is locally termed *mortadella* and is invariably a part of the mixed antipasto. For entrées, consider *bollito misto* (a meld of boiled meats), chicken and rabbit casseroles, superbly prepared veal and pork specialties, most definitely including grilled sausages, a Tre Frecce standout, along with the minifritters that come as an on-the-house appetizer. Lovely service. *First Class.*

Diana (Via Indipendenza 24; Phone 231-302): If the staff—maitre d', captains, fast-moving waiters, the lot of them—would only learn to smile and attempt a pleasantry or two with customers, this restaurant would be an unalloyed pleasure. As it is, you put up with the near-surliness because the invariably packed Diana is attractive to look upon—long and light and airy—because it is central, and because the food is excellent. Everything is freshly prepared—asparagi alla Bismarck (asparagus topped with a sunnyside egg), super soups (including the verdura, or vegetable), the traditional pastas (I include risotto alla parmigiana in that category), and classic entrées (try the grilled veal steak). You'll notice how the clientele—as many Bolognese as visitors—gobble up the exceptional desserts. Excellent wine list. *First Class.*

Carracci (Baglioni Hotel, Via Indipendenza 8; Phone 225-445) makes a specialty of regional dishes, starting with antipasto misto all' Emiliana—an apt opener. Lasagne al forno is among the pastas, and if you haven't had turkey in Italy, Carracci is the place to try petto di tacchinella alla Petroniana. The grilled veal chop is commendable, too. *First Class.*

Cesari (Via dei Carbonesi 8; Phone 237-710) is what the French would term a *restaurant du quartier,* unpretentious and frequented by a clientele of locals known to the staff. Located on an interesting and aged street not far from Piazza Maggiore, it is friendly and fun, bottles of wine lining its paneled walls, tables close together (customers get to talk to each other that way), welcoming management, and super vittles, including a wagon laden with antipasto wheeled to table, superlative tortellini alla panna (in cream sauce), a range of scalloped veal preparations, truffle-accented, if you like. If you've ordered a red wine, save some to accompany a chunk of Parmesan cheese, to conclude. *First Class.*

Al Montegrappa da Nello (Via Montegrappa 2; Phone 36-331) is on a tiny extension of Via Indipendenza, with a narrow entrance that belies its considerable size—gracefully arched rooms on the main floor and basement, as well. This is a congenial spot, with swift service and excellent fare. A meal might run to lasagne verde, costolette alla Bolognese (a delicious veal chop), with perhaps zuppa inglese for dessert. Well-priced wines. *Moderate/First Class.*

Duttour Balanzon (Via Fossalta 3; Phone 232-998) is indicated for a satisfying lunch while you're exploring the historic core. It's cavernous, crystal-chandeliered and multichambered, with a counter for tavola calda, or short-order dishes, and table service, as well. Open with a mix of local salamis, continuing with tortellini alla Bolognese, its sauce a cream-tomato-cheese combination; or try strete, mini-mini stuffed pasta. *Moderate.*

La Torre (Corte Galluri 5; Phone 222-448) is good to know about, not only for its reliable soups, pastas, and entrée specials-of-the-day, but because it is well priced and central. *Moderate.*

Luciano (Via Nazario Sauro 19; Phone 231-249) has achieved a degree of celebrity, the reasons for which can elude at least one sampler of its fare. My experiences with its antipasto and a duck specialty—to name two dishes—were disappointing, and there is no *pane comunale* to be had, even upon request. Pluses are smart modern décor, agreeable service, creditable wines. *First Class.*

Caffè della Galleria (Galleria Cavour, just off Via Farini) is indicated for coffee or a cold drink at one of its outdoor tables, at least when the sun shines. *Moderate.*

Caffè Tiffany (Via Rizzoli 67) beckons with outdoor tables from which you watch the passing parade, the while partaking of refreshment. *Moderate.*

Caffè Jolly (Piazza della Porta Ravegnena): I don't know of an easier way to seep in the phenomena of Bologna's leaning towers than an alfresco table here. Ice cream is the prepackaged kind; the species memorably named "Blob" is very nice indeed. *Moderate.*

SOUND OF MUSIC

Teatro Comunale (Largo Respighi 1) is among the esteemed eighteenth-century opera houses, in a country with not a few such, with a vast single-aisled orchestra and four levels of galleries, the lot under a frescoed ceiling centered by a giant chandelier. Go for opera, ballet, a concert—whatever you can get a ticket for.

Teatro Duse (Via Cartoleria 42) presents dance companies as well as plays. How about attempting Shaw's *Saint Joan* as *Santa Giovanna,* in Italian, of course?

SHOPPER'S BOLOGNA

Department stores are excellent, including *Coin* (Via Marconi) and *Upim,* on Via Rizzoli, whose many other shops include *Richard-Ginori* (porcelain) and *Boni* (men's clothing). Via Mazzini is important for such shops as *Giorgio Armani* (high-style men's and women's clothing) and *Old England* for the English-inspired clothes beloved of Italians. And *Gucci,* a branch of the Florence-based leather-clothing-and-accessories house, is in Galleria Cavour. But in my view the most interesting shopping street is Via Farini, with such boutiques as *L'Uovo* (porcelain and pottery dinnerware), *Principe* (custom-made men's shirts), *Dario* (kids' clothes), *Lauriti* (furs), and *Valier* (high-style women's clothing).

INCIDENTAL INTELLIGENCE

Bologna's Borgo Panigale Airport is four miles north of town; domestic and international flights. *Further information:* Ente Provinciale per il Turismo, Via Leopardi 1, Bologna.

6

Bolzano

Italy mit Schlag und Strudel

BACKGROUND BRIEFING

Guten tag or *Buon giorno:* you take your pick of daily greetings in the bilingual city of Bolzano, equidistant from the Austrian city of Innsbruck, due north just beyond the Brenner Pass, and Italy's Verona (chapter 38), due south. Setting is a verdant valley beneath snowy mountains, just west of the high Dolomites and Cortina d'Ampezzo (chapter 8), a spectacular 65-mile drive east along the Grande Strada delle Dolomiti.

Not that Bolzano's linguistic fluency has come about without problems. Far from it. When you are located at a point where two distinctive tongues are spoken, a situation can develop whereby Giovanni may want to express himself in Italian while Johann prefers German. How do you compromise? It's not always easy. So Bolzano—capital of one of two provinces of the Trentino-Alto Adige *Regione*—has learned the hard way, over long centuries. It goes back half a millennium after the start of the Christian era when Teutonic invaders came from the north, upsetting the tranquility of a long-Roman area, of course bringing with them their own language.

From that time until as recently as the years immediately following the Second World War, the issue of language has been paramount. Bolzano was part of the Bishopric of Trento, culturally Italian through the fifteenth century, after which it was for long ruled by the Germanic Hapsburgs. The nineteenth century saw the area variously Austrian, Bavarian, Italian, and once more Austrian. Then, just after World War I, it again turned Italian, intensely so by reason of the forced Italianization policy of dictator Benito Mussolini, under which German-speakers were forced to use the Italian language even to the point of Italianizing their names; and Italian-speaking citizens were shipped up from the south to tip the population balance in the ethnic Italians' favor.

The post–World War II constitution of the then-new Italian Republic assured the *Regione* special semiautonomous status, and placed both languages on an equal legal status, granting each group education in its mother tongue (you go either to a school with Italian or German as the language of instruction, studying the other tongue as a second language); and guaranteeing legality to place-names in both languages. (Thus, Bozen is the official German-language name for Bolzano, and Süd-Tyrol [South Tyrol in English] is the German equivalent of the Italian Alto Adige.) As the visitor in Bolzano learns, bilingualism extends even to restaurant menus, where names of pasta sauces are duly translated, so that no diner's linguistic—or nationalistic—sensibilities may be offended.

There are, to be sure, older people, who remain stubbornly monolingual in Bolzano, which is more Italian- than German-speaking (in the countryside, the situation is reversed). But younger people whom you encounter in hotels, restaurants, and bigger shops will be bilingual, often switching from one language to the other even in casual conversations with friends that you'll overhear in public places. Make no mistake about it. This is not your everyday Italian destination. Call it Bolzano or Bozen, as you will. *Una rosa,* oops, *eine Rose,* by any name: it's distinctive. And, having provided a bit of background on skills with respect to its pair of national languages, I am obliged to add that there's considerable fluency in still a third: English.

ON SCENE

Lay of the Land: Although, as I mention earlier, place-names are in both languages, I shall simplify matters by using only the Italian in this chapter, as elsewhere in this book. The core of town occupies an area enclosed on the west by the Talvera River, and on the south by the Isarco River. It is centered by Piazza Walther, whose landmark is the tall Duomo spire. The railroad station is but steps to the south, on *Viale Stazione.* The principal shopping street—Via Portici—is immediately north, lined by Baroque houses, mostly converted—and with style—into mercantile establishments. Walk west on Via Portici and you find yourself in *Piazza delle Erbe,* centered by a Rococo fountain topped by a crowned Neptune and leading to busy *Via Museo,* an extension of Portici (with one of two Bolzano links of the Coin department store chain) and continuing to *Ponte Talvera,* spanning the river for which it's named, with *Passeggiata Lungo Talvera*—a lovely riverside promenade—perpendicular to it. Take the bridge across the river following *Corso Libertà,* just opposite, and you're soon in Piazza Gries, named for the quarter in which it is situated, with a pair of art-filled churches, below recommended, nearby.

Church of San Francesco (Via Francescani), despite World War II, for me at least, is the most beautiful in town. Originally fourteenth-century Gothic, its standouts are frescoes of early Franciscans. Move then to the cloister of the adjacent monastery, arcades superbly arched, continuing into Cappella della Vergine, for the complex's masterworks: nine panels of an altar carved in wood, then painted and gilded, by a man named Hans Hocker, in 1500. The central—and largest—panel is a *Nativity*, the others, though smaller, are hardly less sublime.

Duomo (Piazza Walther): The lacy Gothic campanile of the Duomo is quite its handsomest feature, but I am partial, also, to the broad, steeply pitched roof, and the diamond design of its black and white tiles, as well as the Romanesque portal. Although there are frescoes of the Giotto school, and considerable other art inside, the early-sixteenth-century pulpit and a later Baroque high altar are especially memorable.

Church of San Domenico (Piazza Domenicani) emerges, despite post-World War II restoration, with consistent Gothic charm—beautifully brick-edged vaults, fragments of original frescoes in its cloister, fourteenth-century frescoes by the school of Giotto in Cappella San Giovanni, and an interesting painting of St. Dominic, founder of the order, by no less a master than Guercino.

Palazzo Mercantile (Via Argentieri) shelters the Chamber of Commerce, a stunner of a Baroque palace, wherein you want to beeline for the Aula Grande, or Great Hall, resplendent with respect to scale and décor, opulently chandeliered, its walls lined with paintings of long-ago princes. Special.

Museo Civico (Via Cassa di Risparmio, at Via Museo) is a treat; four not-so-small floors of a Baroque palazzo with everything—ancient bronze lamps through silver-trimmed Baroque rifles—local. Exhibits here can be evocative—a painted Romanesque crucifix; a medieval polychrome *Madonna*, long-legged Child on her knee; sad-eyed *Saint Peter* holding a giant gold key; proper portraits of proper city fathers extending over the centuries; gaily decorated porcelain stoves; skillfully crafted furniture.

Abbazia dei Benedettini di Muri (Piazza Gries, across the Talvera, in Gries) is a clutch of buildings making up a Benedictine Abbey. What you want to see are the beautiful altars (seven all told) and the vaulted frescoes—the lot created in the eighteenth century by Martin Knoller—in the Church of Sant' Agostino.

Parocchiale di Gries (Via Knoller, Gries) is the Romanesque-Gothic parish church just across Piazza Gries from the abbey (above), and eminently visitable if only because of the splendid 1475 altar—carved wood, gilded and painted—by Alto Adige's most celebrated artist, Michael Pacher, with its central panel a joyous *Coronation of the Virgin.*

Collalbo is an Alpine village high above Bolzano, on an extraordinary plateau called Renon, at an elevation of some 3600 feet. The coward's way is to make the trip by car. Much more fun—and so convenient—is to journey via cable car. Simply proceed to *Finivia del Renon,* the cable car station on Via Renon, just down the street from the railway station. Cars depart frequently, and in less than half an hour you reach the station at *Sopra Bolzano,* where you transfer to a Toonerville Trolley-type train, for a slow but scenic quarter-hour's ride to the resort village of Collalbo, from which views of the city and the surrounding mountains and valleys are positively ethereal. Plan the trip so as to arrive for lunch at one of the hotel restaurants recommended below. Or, if you like, remain overnight, awakening in time to see the sun rise.

Castel Roncolo (Via Sant Antonio, at the northern edge of Bolzano) is a medieval landmark of a castle precipitously perched atop a cliff a good five-minute walk up from the road—but with a caffè at journey's end—that has been on scene since 1237. Alas, there is no furniture, but frescoes of the early fifteenth century, relating daily life of that era, are decided compensation.

Merano, fifteen miles northwest of Bolzano (and like Bolzano with a corresponding German name: Meran), is a resort town that makes for an easy day-long or overnight excursion. Again not unlike much larger Bolzano, it occupies a scenic valley, with the campanile of its *Duomo* (Piazza del Duomo) a central landmark. The Duomo's gabled façade is not unlike those of Renaissance Holland; and the same Baroque painter, Martin Knoller, whose altars are recommended (above) at the Benedictine Abbey in the Gries section of Bolzano, is here represented. From the cathedral, stroll past shops on lively Via dei Portici, continuing along attractive Corso della Libertà (running parallel with it). You'll be hungry enough for a hearty lunch (making sure you try a local wine), at moderately priced, country-style *Meraner Weinkost* (Corso della Libertà 35; Phone 30-578). In the afternoon, consider a hike along the unique-to-Merano *passeggiate,* or promenades, flanking the in-town *Passirio River,* one of which ascends *Monte Benedetto,* high above the city. If you've wheels, drive out (two miles) to *Castel Tirolo,* for 800 years straddling its own summit, and with an interesting interior. Overnight? *Aurora Hotel* (Passeggiata Lungo Passirio 38) is core-of-Merano, full facility and *Moderate.*

Trento, capital of the Trentino region some 30 miles south of Bolzano, makes for an absorbing day's outing. Utilizing central *Piazza del Duomo* as a focal point, inspect that square's fine *Duomo,* as old as nine centuries and with a chapel in which the sixteenth-century papal-led Council of Trent—opposing increasingly popular Protestantism—took place. *Via Roma,* the main shopping street, leads to *Castello del Buon Consiglio,* which went up five centuries back as the bishop's palace, and now houses the *Trentino National Museum* in its elaborate interior, with period paintings and furnishings the lures. Should you decide to overnight, the restaurant-equipped *Accademia Hotel* (Vicolo Colico, *First Class*) is a good choice; its dining room is busy with loquacious locals at midday.

SETTLING IN

Parkhotel Laurin (Via Laurino 4) is quite the epitome of the unabashedly old-fashioned luxury house—turn-of-century, with high-ceilinged public lobby, ballroom-size bar-lounge, commendable Belle Époque Restaurant, lovely bedrooms (no two alike, and those I have inspected are tastefully traditional), with a swimming pool in the garden, and a heart-of-the-city situation. *Luxury.*

Alpi Hotel (Via Alto Adige) is strikingly contemporary, smartly capacious lobby through attractive rooms. There's a wood-beamed, marble-columned restaurant and a congenial bar. Central. *First Class.*

Grifone/Grief Hotel (Piazza Walther) could not be more heart-of-the-Bolzano-action, on its principal square, occupying a pair of contiguous structures, both mellow with age, albeit smartly updated (alas, a minority of rooms are without baths), restaurant that moves to a summer garden, bar popular with locals, strategically placed sidewalk caffè on the square; swimming pool in the garden. *First Class.*

Luna/Mondschein Hotel (Via Piave 15) is attractive and central (not far from the shops of Via dei Portici), with 84 rooms (most bath-equipped), restaurant that takes up summer residence in the garden, and bar-lounge. *Moderate.*

Città/Stadt Hotel (Piazza Walther) is rambling, elderly, and with a lobby that could do with some brightening up, at least on my most recent inspection, but with the advantage of baths in all rooms, bar-lounge, restaurant, and central Piazza Walther location. *Moderate.*

Bemelmans-Post Hotel (Collalbo, on the Ritten plateau above Bolzano) leads the Collalbo pack, agreeably Tyrolean. There are 50 neat rooms; specify if you want a terrace and a bath—not all were so equipped on my last inspection; garden, swimming pool, tennis, as well as a reliable restaurant and cozy bar. *Moderate.*

DAILY BREAD

Kaiserkron (Piazza della Mostra 1; Phone 970-0770) presents cuisine that melds German/Austrian, Italian, and French-origin *Nouvelle.* Open, for example, with smoked breast of duck, a delicate artichoke pâté, or a trout salad (substituting pasta if you like). Entrées are delicious: stuffed filet of salmon, various cuts of veal and beef, as are vegetables and salads; mousse au chocolat typifies the sweets. Wines are the best of the region. If it's summer, ask for a table on the Piazza della Mostra terrace. In my view, one of Italy's best restaurants. *First Class.*

Tabasco (Via Crispi 9; Phone 26-562): Part of the charm of bilingual Bolzano is ordering Italian-style cuisine from the German-language side of restaurant menus. Tabasco—smartly vaulted in a contemporarily decorated space that's part of a venerable core-of-town structure—is as good a spot as any to ask for Terlaner weinsuppe/zuppa al vino bianco/white wine soup; pennette feinschmeckerart/pennette al buongustaio/pennette gourmet style; or, among the entrées, piccata mit zitrone/piccata al limone/veal medaillon with lemon sauce. I might add that—in any language—everything that I've sampled is very good. *First Class.*

Da Abramo (Piazza Gries 16; Phone 301-41) is indicated for lunch in the course of, say, a half-day's exploration across the river, in Gries, with fare authentically Italian, including a vegetarian antipasto, fresh salmon among entrées, and, to conclude, the smashing strawberry soufflé. *First Class.*

Grifone/Grief Hotel Caffè (Piazza Walther): Take an outdoor table, and for the price of an espresso you've views of the Bolzano passing parade and the Duomo spire. *Moderate.*

Caffè Monika (Via della Mostra 17) offers a panorama of the Bolzano shopping scene from its alfresco tables on an animated pedestrians-only street. *Moderate.*

Röter Adler (Via Goethe 34) typifies the Austrian-style inns where locals like to spend evenings, over a leisurely beer or two. Near Piazza Walther. Atmospheric and *Moderate.*

Dolomiten Hotel Ristorante (Collalbo, on the Renon plateau) makes for a hearty lunch stop in the course of a day's outing in Collalbo. Nowhere in the region is it more difficult to believe that you're in Italy rather than Austria. Of course, the owning-family members who serve you speak Italian, but they'll ask for your order in German, and if you're wise you'll have a typically Teutonic lunch of, say, *Wienerschnitzel und frites, mit* the local *weisswein. Moderate.*

Caffè Lintner (Collalbo): No time for a proper lunch in the course of your Collalbo outing? Settle, then, for something to drink and pastry on the terrace of Lintner. The mountain views are smashing. *Moderate.*

SOUND OF MUSIC

There's considerable concert and other musical activity at Bolzano's *Teatro Concordia* (Piazza Cristo Re) and *Conservatorio* (Piazza Domenicani) and the Tourist Office (address below) publishes monthly programs of events.

INCIDENTAL INTELLIGENCE

Further information: Azienda di Soggiorno e Turismo, Piazza Walther 8, Bolzano; Stazione Sopra Bolzano, Collalbo; Corso della Libertà 45, Merano.

7

Como and Maggiore

Pleasures of Two Great Lakes

BACKGROUND BRIEFING

It is odd, our hesitant attitude toward European lakes. Blessed with so many, as we are on our continent—not a few Americans, myself included, learned to swim in lakes, rather than pools or oceans—we rarely go out of our way to inspect inland bodies of water with transatlantic addresses. Oh, yes, there are a few acceptable exceptions: romantic Windermere and its sister-lakes in the north of England are upon occasion worked into itineraries taking Yanks north to Scotland; we simply dare not offend the Irish by disdaining a jog in a horse-drawn carriage around the indisputably scenic lakes of Killarney; and we pay a modicum of attention to history-laden Constance, considered visitable if only because its multinational waters lap the shores of Germany, Switzerland, and Austria.

Italian lakes? For Americans, they seem more inaccessible than is actually the case. The two dealt with in this chapter are easily reached from Milan (chapter 19), to which we may fly nonstop from America, and they're just down the road from Swiss points like Lugano and Locarno. Why go? Combine attributes of the lakes of Ireland, Britain, and Middle Europe—romance, beauty, history—tacking on the phenomenon of almost Mediterranean-type gardens (the climate is mild the year round), adding monuments of man—opulent villas, art-filled churches, and for that matter, in the case of Como, a proper city of considerable substance, without forgetting expertise at hotel-keeping that comes of a century of experience—and you have the reasons. You want to remember that others will have preceded you. No less an emperor than Julius Caesar sent a colony of settlers north to these shores half a century before Christ was born. (Both Plinys were Como-born and Virgil is presumed to have been a visitor.)

The post-Roman centuries saw towns rise up, trade develop, wars fought (Milan was a chronic enemy, among a number). Napoleon himself came, during the French period. Not long after, Caroline of Brunswick, uncrowned and dispossessed consort of self-indulgent King George IV of Britain, turned Lake Como's Villa d'Este into a royal residence, the while taking an Italian lover; and some decades later the same Villa d'Este served for two years as an imperial palace—the home-away-from-St. Petersburg of a Russian czarina, who came for the play of sunshine on the emerald slopes edging garden-bordered waters. There were so many others, battling Byzantines and Lombards, dynastic families like the Viscontis and Sforzas, painters and sculptors and artists to decorate palaces and churches of families like Lake Maggiore's Borromeo, which produced both a cardinal and a Renaissance saint.

Even before Belle Époque tourism began in earnest a century back, when still-great hotels like Villa d'Este and Maggiore's Îles des Borromées, as pioneers, opened their doors, there were visitors like Shelley and Goethe, Browning and Stendhal. If today's guests are mostly European, especially to Maggiore (and also to more easterly Lake Garda, whose principal town, Sirmione, is dealt with in chapter 38), there is a fairly substantial American presence on Como, closest of the big lakes to Milan, and the one I lead off with, below.

ON SCENE

LAGO DI COMO (a.k.a. Lago di Lario)

Lay of the Land: It's big: 30 miles long, two and a half miles at its widest, Y-shaped, with an astonishing beauty that results when staggering peaks—snowy atop, lushly verdant and flower-filled lower down—descend to a shoreline fringed by a profusion of man-made settlements. No. 1—*Como town*—is detailed below; the others are all accessible by road, of course, but also by frequently departing lake steamers that stop at the lot, going and coming. Of these, the most important are *Cernobbio,* so close to Como town that it is almost an extension of it (for that reason very convenient) and site of historic Villa d'Este, landmark-turned-hotel you want to visit for a drink or meal even if you're staying elsewhere; *Bellagio,* straddling a gorgeous peninsula at the point forming the center of the lake's Y-formation, hotel-, restaurant-,shop-, and caffè-dotted, with charming alleylike streets—salitas—climbing its hills; *Tremezzo,* directly across the water from Bellagio and linked to it by ferry; smaller, neighboring *Menaggio;* and—near the northern terminus of the lake—*Gravedona,* with the industrial town of *Lecco* at the lower tip of the Y-prong, on the east, corresponding to Como town on the west.

Como town's historic core—extending inward from the lake and grid-shaped—is eminently explorable, and, for that matter, shoppable. Distracting as more bucolic diversions of the lake may be, allot a day to become acquainted with this attractive, affluent, animated city, Roman-founded and a major silk-manufacturing center since the Renaissance.

If you're staying at one of the city hotels I recommend below, you'll be near broad *Piazza Cavour,* which is also where your boat will dock if you're coming in from a lakeside hotel. Simply cross the square to *Via Plinio* and within seconds you're on still another smashing square, *Piazza del Duomo,* where side by side are three of northern Italy's brilliant façades; first is the authentic-looking twentieth-century replacement of an originally Romanesque clock tower; next is beautifully arcaded, Gothic-origin *Broleto,* for long the town hall; and last is the *Duomo,* whose Gothic façade is among the better looking in the north. The Duomo's interior is a mix of epochs, much of it Renaissance and Baroque; note the splendid tapestries, some of them Flemish, unusual in an Italian cathedral; take your time with works of art, not missing Bernardino Luini's *St. Jerome,* on a chapel altar, noting, too, the frescoes and the eighteenth-century dome over the transept, by Filippo Juvara, whose work appears throughout the north.

Have a look at the *Basilica of San Fedele* (Via Vittorio Emanuele), utterly severe Romanesque—and beautiful, albeit no less so than also-Romanesque *Basilica of Sant' Abbondio,* worth the detour to Strada Regina if only for its cloister and high-altar frescoes. *Villa dell' Olmo* is easily the most elegant structure in town—a late-eighteenth-century palace, set off by appropriately formal gardens just in from the lake, which was opened by Napoleon in 1797 and now serves very well indeed as a setting for concerts and conferences. *Museo Civico Archeologico-Artistico* (Piazza Medaglie d'Oro Comasche, at the foot of Via Vittorio Emanuele) is an eighteenth-century mansion brimming with ancient Como objects, Roman through Romanesque, and later paintings.

Consider Como's *shops;* they're the ones citizens patronize, so that prices are not inflated, as they can be in heavily tourist-populated resort areas out on the lake. There are big department stores, including Upim (with an on-premises supermercato) beyond the center, on Via Giulio Cesare. Via Vittorio Emanuele and Via Bernardo Luini are full of interesting stores. At day's end, make tracks for Piazza Funiculare for the seven-minute funicular ride to the summit of *Monte Brunate*—and a memorable overall view of the city you've explored and the lake and mountains beyond.

Lakeside beauty spots you'll enjoy visiting by boat include *Villa Carlotta* (in Tremezzo) where a tour embraces both formal Italian and informal English-style gardens—azalea-filled—as well as the eighteenth-century house with Canova sculptures, paintings, tapestries, and neoclassic furniture; *Villa Melzi* (Bellagio)—for sumptuous, sculpture-filled, pool-punctuated gardens, Japanese as well as Occidental, and the interior of an impressive house, whose treasures include paintings by Rubens and Van Dyck; *Villa Serbelloni* (high above Bellagio and not to be confused with a celebrated, similarly named hotel [below] down in the village)—history-rich, now occupied by New York's Rockefeller Foundation, with a fabulous terraced garden its ace-in-the-hole; *Villa Monastero* (in Varenna)—a medieval convent, which a scandal forced Lake Maggiore-born Cardinal (later Saint) Charles Borromeo to close in the sixteenth century, and which survives as a center for scholarly congresses, its gardens and its architecture a brilliant meld; *Palazzo Gallio* (in Gravedona)—a treasure of a late Renaissance pleasure palace, a visit to which can be combined with three Gravedona churches of consequence: *Santa Maria del Tiglio,* unadulterated twelfth-century Romanesque with superb frescoes; *SS. Gusmeo e Matteo,* thirteenth-century and named for the saints whose bodies are found within it, with a masterfully frescoed ceiling; and *Santa Maria delle Grazie,* the "baby" (fifteenth century) of the trio, elaborately decorated and with a frescoed cloister.

LAGO MAGGIORE

Lay of the Land: Not far northwest of Lake Como, Maggiore—despite its name, which translates as *major*—is second in size of the Italian lakes, larger than Como to be sure, but smaller than Garda—with a length of 41 miles, a maximum width of two and a half miles, and its northern tip in Switzerland (with pretty Locarno on the shore—see *Switzerland at Its Best*). Irregularly oblong in shape—it could be a *very* wide river—its classic vacation town is hotel-filled Stresa, on its western shore. Stresa's pluses are the celebrated Îles des Borromées Hotel, which pioneered tourism on the lake a century back, and a trio of remarkable islands, a putt-putt boat ride from the shore, owned by the Borromeo family dynasty over a span of centuries. Major Maggiore (no pun intended) West Shore towns, besides Stresa, include near-to-Stresa *Pallanza* and southerly *Arona;* on the east shore it is worth noting *Laveno* (with a translake ferry service to little *Intra,* not far from Stresa), and northerly *Luino.* Again, as on Como, you may drive or take other surface transport, but the amusing way to get about is by lake steamer.

Stresa is a placid little town, made to order for relaxation. It borders the lake, with a single waterfront boulevard—variously called *Strada Statale del Sempione, Corso Umberto,* and *Corso Italia,* separating its inner precincts from the shore. A major waterfront square is *Piazza Marconi*—from where boats depart, on the one hand, and by means of which one goes inland on *Via Principe Tomaso* to *Piazza Cadorna,* and adjacent thoroughfares of the core. *Parco di Villa Pallavicino,* at the southern edge of town, is a color-drenched mix of flora (by that I mean flowerbeds as well as masses of century-old trees) and fauna (by that I mean a zoo, in which most animals are cageless, roaming free), with both restaurant and bar-caffè. The railway station is mid-town on *Via Principe di Piemonte,* and another station—one you want to head for in the course of your stay—is *Stazione Funivia Stresa-Mottarone* (Piazzale Lido) for a cable car journey to the summit of 4600-foot *Monte Mottarone*—and vistas of town, island, and lake.

Isola Bella is surely the lake's most spectacular cultural treat: a relatively compact plot of land surmounted, at one end, by an ebullient Baroque palace built—and still owned and inhabited—by the lake's preeminent clan, with a ten-level formal garden—like no other in Italy—at its other extremity. The garden—terraced, sculpted, and formally planted—is not necessarily every nature-lover's cup of tea.

And the palace, when one enters to encounter a veritable sea of plastic-covered furniture—there is a fair-sized admission fee—can initially disappoint. But one must forgive, at least partially, the owning Borromeos, in this era of mass tourism; Isola Bella visitors who would never dream of journeying to the outskirts of, say, Turin (chapter 35) to inspect isolated Palazzo Stupinigi, jam the precincts of Isola Bella as they would the Magic Kingdom at Disneyland. Once accustomed to tacky plastic protectors, though, there are pockets of beauty to be encountered. The high-ceilinged music room—a Bassano among its many paintings—was the site of the 1935 Stresa Conference at which Mussolini hosted France's Pierre Laval and Britain's Ramsey MacDonald, an oddly matched Big Three who agreed to unite against Hitler—but of course did not—with the clouds of World War II already gathering. (Their abortive resolutions decorate a wall.) The Directoire-style Sala di Napoleone is where Bonaparte, Josephine, and an entourage of 60 stayed two nights in 1797. There is an entire room full of Giordano paintings; still another, of Flemish tapestries; and half a dozen shell-embellished grottoes.

Isola dei Pescatori ("Fishermen's Island") lives up to its name with a plethora of scruffy but quite good seafood restaurants (it's fun to go for lunch) and block after block of souvenir stalls, from whose *padrones* every male visitor—and many females—above the age of three buys a yachtsman's cap; I must admit they look spiffy.

Isola Madre, least visited of the Borromeo islands, is essentially a five-terrace garden, with species running a gamut that extends from, say, grapefruit to wisteria. You land at one pier, follow the route of the brochure you're given with your admission ticket, and exit at still another, having passed by a quite-charming satellite Borromeo mansion, which you may enter, and with the option of taking refreshment at a caffè near the departure point.

Villa Taranto (Pallanza) has unusual Scottish origins, in the person of the late Neil McEachern, who was so fond both of Italy and of flowers that he bought a finger of land jutting into the lake, at Pallanza, in 1931, and set about turning it into a world-class botanical garden that is a joy to stroll—replete with terraces, waterfalls, lotus pools, and ornamental fountains. It is good exercise: there are some four miles of avenues, including those aptly named Azalea, Maple, Rhododendron, and Camellia. While you're in Pallanza, have a look, also, at *Museo Civico*—as much for its setting in eighteenth-century Palazzo Dugani, as for its Roman remnants and paintings; and at the Renaissance-era *Church of Madonna di Campagna,* lavishly frescoed throughout and with a carved wood choir. *San Carlone* is the local name given to a stupendous sculpted likeness—surely this is Italy's answer to New York Harbor's Statue of Liberty—of locally born San Carlo Borromeo (1538–1584), a member of the Borromeo family of Isola Bella fame (above), which was erected at the end of the seventeenth century, about two miles outside of Arona. Cast of bronze and copper, it's 77 feet tall and surmounts a stone base that visitors climb preparatory to ascending the statue's inner stairway, all the way up to St. Charles's neck.

Church of San Pietro in Campagna is as good a reason as any to visit attractive Luino; its principal treasure is Bernardino Luini's *Adoration of the Magi.* The Città Vecchia—or old quarter—is atmospheric; no less so is the lakefront promenade, its kicker a gilded sculpture of the Virgin.

SETTLING IN

LAGO DI COMO

Metropole Suisse Hotel (Piazza Cavour, Como town) is my in-town favorite; old (but nicely updated) and gracious, directly on the lake (ask for a room with a view), with a bar-lounge within, terrace-caffè without, and a ranking restaurant (Imbarcadero, below) adjacent. *First Class.*

Plinius Hotel (Via Garibaldi 33, Como town) is as convenient to the railway station as to Piazza Cavour, a pert, contemporary house, with an attractive lobby bar-lounge, baths in most of the 30 rooms, and friendly management. *Moderate.*

Villa d'Este Hotel (Cernobbio), whose historic significance—as a royal residence, first for Queen Caroline of Britain, later for Czarina Maria Fedorovna of Russia—I write about earlier on, retains its palatial Renaissance façade—it went up in the sixteenth century—as well as gloriously vaulted ceilings and knock-'em-dead grand stairway of its main hall, now the lobby. It has been a hotel for more than a century, and in recent years an expert management team has refined and refurbished it to the point where, in my view, it ranks with the Aga Khan's hotel-cluster on the Sardinian Costa Smeralda (chapter 9) as among Italy's finest resorts, fitting easily into a world-class league. Villa d'Este's 160 rooms and suites—no two alike—are antique-accented, with as much expertise in the area, for example, of bathroom fixtures as in the selection of drapery textiles and accessories like paintings, lamps, mirrors, and ever-present fresh flowers. One restaurant is a vast canopied, picture-windowed pavilion (whose buffet breakfasts, incidentally, are the most sumptuous in Italy, and in which men need jackets and ties at dinner). Another is an à la carte grill about which I write later; you may lunch casually around the pool and have drinks in a choice of spots, alfresco and indoors. There's boating and tennis (8 courts), waterskiing and squash, jogging trails and a gym, golf at seven nearby 18-hole courses, dancing in both nightclub (on the terrace, in summer) and disco. And a skilled, smiling staff. Member, Leading Hotels of the World. *Luxury.*

Regina Olga Hotel (Cernobbio) has location going for it both ways—its front door is just off Cernobbio's main square and views from rear rooms are over the lake. The look can be somewhat vivid in the public spaces, but there are 80 well-equipped rooms, pair of restaurants, bar-lounge, pool. *First Class.*

Villa Serbelloni Hotel (Bellagio)—not to be confused with just plain Villa Serbelloni whose gardens are open to visitors (above)—is an enchanting Belle Époque period-piece, lakefront, with high ceilings in its lobby, lounges, and restaurant (about which more later) frescoed in the style of the Renaissance, and furnished in the opulent manner of the turn of the present century. There are 95 rooms and suites, each distinctive, each charming; a mod-look bar-lounge, a honey of an outdoor pool overlooking the lake (with a beach adjacent), and sprightly service. Lovely. *Luxury.*

Ambassador Hotel (Bellagio) is directly lakefront albeit heart-of-town, with its lakeview room-cum-terraces the preferred ones; not all have baths. There's a good-value restaurant, bar-lounge, and long-on-scene management. *Moderate.*

Du Lac Hotel (Bellagio) is proud, as well it might be, of its rooftop sun terrace. Most of the 50 rooms are bath-equipped and many lakeview. Relax at the bar, and don't hesitate to try the restaurant, alfresco in warm weather. *Moderate.*

Excelsior Splendid Hotel (Bellagio) was refurbished and restored—handsomely and relatively recently. Its restaurant is convenient, and rooms—all with bath or shower—are inviting; swimming pool. *Moderate.*

Fioroni Hotel (Bellagio) is more modern than many in town, and with a cozy bar-lounge, competent restaurant, and agreeable enough rooms whose only drawback, when I last visited, was saggy mattresses. It is worth noting that this is one of the only hotels in the area, outside of Como town, that traditionally remains open all year. *Moderate.*

Bazzoni Hotel (Tremezzo) is architecturally contemporary, with good-size terraces in all of its traditional-style lakeview rooms; panoramas come with meals at the restaurant (about which more later), and there's a sun deck and bar-lounge. *Moderate.*

Grand Hotel (Tremezzo) retains its smashing turn-of-century, lakeview façade, but its interiors are quite obviously not today what they were in earlier eras. Still, this is an agreeable enough place, full-facility. *First Class.*

Victoria Hotel (Menaggio) is a beautiful old-timer that has—and relatively recently—been splendidly refurbished stem to stern, with original chandeliers and fine stuccowork of its lobby/lounge and Restaurant Le Tout Paris wisely retained, its 53 bedrooms—some terraced, many with views—stylishly contemporary, its pool in the garden a delight. Super. *First Class.*

Bellavista Hotel (Menaggio) is a neat-as-a-pin house, center of town, with a lakeview terrace, choicest of the 46 rooms are out back, and vistas of the hardly disagreeable town are viewed from the front. Bar-lounge, popular restaurant. *Moderate.*

LAGO MAGGIORE

Îles des Borromées Hotel (Stresa) opened in 1863, shortly after steamers began calling at Stresa. A bold pioneer in the field, it was conceived by a pair of brothers named Omarini who had worked in grand hotels abroad and were convinced that tourists would want to see not only the lake but the Borromean islands just opposite Stresa. The hotel's domed and intricately detailed façade—one of the finest such in Italy—happily remains, and its beautifully refurbished—and maintained—interiors are appropriately Belle Époque-accented. Location is Corso Umberto, a five-minute walk to the core of town. The 120 rooms and suites are a delight; especially the lakeview ones. Bar-lounge is congenial, outdoor pool a pleasure, the restaurant worthy of additional comment in a later paragraph. As a special bonus, there's the hotel's Centro Benessere—an extraordinarily well-equipped health and beauty spa, its range physiotherapy and sauna through hydromassage and weight reduction. *Luxury.*

Regina Palace Hotel (Stresa) is—after the Îles des Borromées—the most evocative in town, of the Stresa of yore, a proud and handsome house, with traditional-style public spaces, 175 updated rooms, restaurant, bar, pool, and Corso Umberto location. *First Class.*

Bristol Hotel (Stresa) is the farthest from the center of the Corso Umberto hostelries, a capacious modern house, balconies attached to all 250 rooms, vast chandeliered lobby, restaurant, bubbly cocktail lounge, huge pool. *First Class.*

La Palma Hotel (Stresa), another of the Corso Umberto leaders, gets good marks for its 120 good-sized terraced rooms, generous public spaces, honey of a glass-walled restaurant, and lakefront swimming pool. Very nice indeed. *First Class.*

Italie & Suisse Hotel (Stresa) has an in-town situation, on convenient Piazza Imbarcadero. Try for a corner room and don't hesitate to lunch or dine in the restaurant. *Moderate.*

DAILY BREAD

LAGO DI COMO

Imbarcadero (Piazza Cavour, adjacent to Metropole Suisse Hotel, Como town; Phone 277-341): In an impressive setting—Roman-style columns support a coffered ceiling, and the lighting is subdued—savvy waiters serve up an interesting mix of cuisines—gnocchi and well-sauced pastas as well as snails, Burgundy-style, for starters; Italian-style turkey, Gallic-style duckling, roast lamb, veal specialties among the entrées; with crêpes Albert the indicated sweet. Fine wines. *Luxury.*

Da Pietro (Piazza Duomo, Como town; Phone 263-395) is mod-look and inviting within, but more fun in warm weather when tables are laid in the square facing the Duomo; there are four table d'hôte menus, with as many prices, and an à la carte, from which you want to select the house's reputed risotto alla parmigiana. *First Class.*

Da Celestino (Viale Lungo Lario Trento 7, Como town; Phone 263-470) is conveniently close to Piazza Cavour, and with Tuscan specialties, including—in case you're homesick for beef—Florentine-style steaks. *First Class.*

Caffè Bolla (Via Bellatini, Como town) is heart-of-shopping-district, with tables, smartly covered in tan linen, spilling into the street. Have a pastry with your espresso. *Moderate.*

Caffè Monti (Piazza Cavour, Como town) is as much for refreshment as for the splendid vista of the people-packed square, with the lake as a backdrop. *Moderate.*

Villa d'Este Hotel Grill (Cernobbio; Phone 511-471) conveys what might be termed smartly low-key comfort, is located in a detached building a scenic stroll across the garden from the hotel proper, allows men to dress casually (jackets and ties are required in the main restaurant), maintains a nicely dense decibel count (everybody has a good time), and serves up superb Italian fare. Spaghetti alla siciliana, tagliolini ai frutti di mare (seafood-sauced noodles), and ravioli di verdura al burro e salvia (with vegetables, butter, and sage) are among the pastas; piccatina allo sport (the grill's own version of a veal specialty), pollo alla cacciatore (you've not had better hunter-style chicken), and filetto di manzo al dragoncello (filet of beef, in this case, tarragon-accented) typify the entrées. Fresh lake fish are good, too; desserts are the work of a master pâtissier, and no area restaurant has a finer cellar. In my view, one of Italy's best restaurants. *Luxury.*

Terzo Crotto (Cernobbio; Phone 512-304) is a case of the tail wagging the dog, in this case the restaurant of a tiny hotel being more reputed than the hostelry proper. And with good reason. The antipasto or, perhaps, a risotto, are good ideas for openers; try an entrée based on fresh-caught lake fish. *First Class.*

Trattoria del Vapore (Cernobbio; Phone 510-308) is just the ticket for a casual lunch or dinner, built upon a pasta opener, with the meat entrées—veal especially—as sensible a choice as the fish. *Moderate.*

Villa Serbelloni Hotel Ristorante (Bellagio; Phone 950-216) is evocatively Old School with respect to décor, and delicious with respect to food. Prix-fixe menus are pricier (and with an extra course) at dinner than at lunch. You might open with the house's cannelloni or trenette al pesto, continue with grilled salmon steak or fritto misto—the seafood mix—concluding with a choice of desserts. Fine wines. *Luxury.*

Terrazzo sul Lago (adjacent to Metropole Hotel, Bellagio; Phone 950-664) occupies an enormous, centrally located terrace and features well-priced prix-fixe lunches and dinners, to be consumed as you watch the passing Bellagio parade. *Moderate.*

Caffè San Remo (Bellagio): A mass of pink-linen-covered tables on a waterfront terrace. Scrumptious views. *Moderate.*

Bazzoni Hotel Ristorante (Tremezzo; Phone 40-403): Up you go to the second floor, sitting behind picture windows if it's cool, or out on the open terrace; either way, the elevation affords vistas. And accompanying fare—there's a wide choice of pastas and local fish, simply but deliciously prepared—is very good indeed. *First Class.*

Locanda dell' Isola Comacina (Isola Comacina; Phone 55-083) makes for something of a mealtime adventure. You board this island restaurant's own boat for the five-minute ride to the Locanda on Comacina Island, and a meal-with-a-view, which never varies, either at lunch or dinner: assorted antipasti including prosciutto and bresaola (dried beef), grilled trout or other fresh lake fish, roast chicken with a green salad, cheese platter, ice cream, fresh fruit, coffee, with the house white—a Soave—accompanying. Fun. *First Class.*

Le Tout Paris (Victoria Hotel, Menaggio; Phone 32-003) is the attractive restaurant of an attractive hotel (see above), worth knowing about in the course of a day's journey on the lake. Three-course fixed-price menus are good value—and tasty—but there's à la carte, as well. *First Class.*

Caffè El Timon (Tremezzo) throws in lakeside vistas (it's on the shore) with the cost of your espresso, or, if you're hungry, delicious minipizzas. Friendly. *Moderate.*

Lago Maggiore

Emiliano (Corso Italia 50, Stresa; Phone 31-396) is welcoming, smiling, and operated by what appears to be an all-female staff, at least out front.

Seafood starters are excellent—smoked salmon or a fish mousse to start, pastas like salmon-sauced tagliolini. Carefully prepared meat and seafood entrées. Everything that I have sampled is delicious. *First Class.*

Îles des Borromées Hotel Ristorante (Stresa; Phone 30-431) charms, both with its Belle Époque look and its specialties. The raw-beef treat, carpaccio, is delicious; likewise maccheroni al gorgonzola; along with entrées like fegato alla veneziana—the famed calves-liver masterwork. And wait until the *carrello di dolci* is wheeled up; I defy you to refuse a dessert. Excellent wines. *First Class/Luxury.*

Verbano (Isola Pescatori; Phone 30-396): You can't leave Stresa without having tried a fish lunch on Fishermen's Island. Verbano typifies the lot—simple but friendly and tasty, with outdoor tables in fine weather. The starters are not a strong point but entrées—fritto misto of lake fish or the sautéed trout—are first rate. Have the house white—a Frascati come north from Rome. *Moderate.*

Caffè La Verbarella (Stresa) is well located on Corso Umberto, so that you watch the crowds, taking in the pretty nearby gardens, and the lake as well. Good ice cream. *Moderate.*

SOUND OF MUSIC

Teatro Sociale (Piazza del Popolo, Como town) is an early-nineteenth-century neoclassic stunner—half a dozen Corinthian columns supporting its portico—with a well-rounded concert-opera-ballet season.

INCIDENTAL INTELLIGENCE

First thing to pick up from your hotel concierge, upon arrival, is a timetable of *Navigazione Lago di Como,* for lake steamers; you'll make good use of it. Yes, you may motor easily—from Como to Stresa; route is via Laveno, where you board a car-carrying ferry that crosses Lake Maggiore to Intra, whence you complete your journey by means of a short drive to Stresa. *Further information:* Azienda Promozione Turistica, Piazza Cavour 17, Como; Via Principe Tomaso, Stresa.

8

Cortina d' Ampezzo

Beauty in the Dolomites

BACKGROUND BRIEFING

It will take your breath away. En route. Upon departure. And more to the point of this chapter, for as long as you stay. Cortina may not be the easiest of Italian towns to reach. But you want to make the effort—and even if you're not a skier or winter-sports buff. Alpine resorts in Austria, France, Germany, Norway, and yes, Italy—have stiff competition here, with respect to creature comforts, as well as scenic vistas.

The world at large first made the acquaintance of Cortina—locals drop the "d' Ampezzo" as do visitors, almost immediately upon arrival—when it hosted the 1956 Winter Olympics. But long before that time, this heart-of-the-Dolomites village—resident population hovers at about 8000—was a settlement of some substance, from the early nineteenth century, as principal town of the still sparsely populated Ampezzano area. Tourism began later, with the turn of the present century.

Today, Cortina lures skiers November through April, and just plain nature lovers (cable cars operate all year and walks into the mountains are a pleasure) for the remaining months, when such pastimes as horseback riding, camping, even tennis and swimming are popular. But even the laziest nonathletic types are kept happy, what with the extraordinary range of hotels (standards are high in all categories), places to dine, dance, drink, and shop.

ON SCENE

Lay of the Land: Picture a vast and verdant valley, at an altitude of just over 4000 feet, encircled by jagged Dolomite peaks, centered by a single, slender church steeple. That's Cortina. Its main pedestrians-only thoroughfare, shop-lined *Corso Italia,* cuts through its core, north to south, becoming *Via Roma* as it extends southwesterly into the valley.

Via Stazione and *Via XXIX Maggio* extend east from Corso Italia, connecting it with *Largo delle Poste,* another north-south street. Then there are the mountains: the Tofane cluster, a trio, each of which exceeds 9000 feet; Pomagnon, over 7200 feet; celebrated Cristallo, extending more than 9500 feet; and Tre Cime di Lavaredo, at approximately 9000 feet. Ascending (and descending) is no problem. There were, at my last count, 7 cable cars, 19 ski lifts, 14 chair lifts, and a gondola in the neighborhood, along with facilities for ice skating and bobsledding.

Church of SS. Filippo e Giacomo (Corso Italia) is the landmark parrocchiale, or parish church, with Romanesque origins but a Baroque look, thanks to early-eighteenth-century (and, in the case of the campanile, nineteenth-century) rebuilding. Go on in to see the painting of the *Madonna and Saints* on the high altar, and elaborately frescoed side chapels.

Museo delle Regole & Galleria d'Arte Mario Rimoldi share attractive quarters at Via del Parco 1; the former is a relatively small but professionally superior presentation of Cortina's prehistoric centuries; the latter is used for changing exhibitions of the work of painters and sculpture of this very moment.

Stadio Olimpico del Ghiaccio sounds more impressive in Italian than English (Ice Stadium) and is strikingly good contemporary Italian architecture: a four-level structure that went up for the 1956 Winter Olympics, enclosing a giant ice rink on three sides. It is the easiest of the Olympics installations to visit; the others are a ski jump and a bobsled track.

By road to Bolzano (chapter 6) can be an eye-filling Italian adventure, via the 65-mile-long *Grande Strada delle Dolomiti,* cutting through an east-west cross section of the Dolomites. The route by and large follows the highway identified as SS 48 delle Dolomiti, passing through, as one proceeds, a marvelous mix of idyllic lakes like Alleghe, broad valleys like Agordino, pretty villages like Arabba, scenic mountain passes like Pordoi, soaring peaks like the Torri del Vaiolet, ending as you get closer to Bolzano, on Route 241, near Lago di Carezza. Canazei, a pretty resort, is an apt spot to pause for a hearty lunch-cum-panorama at the moderately priced Tyrol Hotel.

SETTLING IN

Cristallo Hotel (Via Menardi 42) straddles a wooded hill just above the village, in a rambling pavilion with wood-beamed public spaces that include a locally reputed restaurant, lively cocktail lounge, late-hours disco, snack bar, solarium for sunning, pair of tennis courts, outdoor swimming pool, and some 80 rooms and suites, with a décor that might be called Spiffy Rustic. *Luxury.*

Miramonti Majestic Hotel (Pezziè 103) emulates a comfortable—very comfortable—hunting lodge, with oversized lounges furnished with oversized chairs, a wickery, picture-windowed winter garden, crystal-chandeliered restaurant, bar-lounge, winter swimming pool/health club, 134 delightfully furnished rooms, and shuttle-bus service to the core of town from its elevated situation. *Luxury.*

De la Poste Hotel (Piazza Roma 14) is the only first-class house in the core of the village, and it's a winner—not too large (83 handsome rooms and suites), a range of cozy lounges, a bar that is No. 1 in Cortina, and a restaurant worthy of additional comment in a later paragraph. *First Class.*

Savoia Hotel (Via Roma 62) occupies a pair of buildings, with Via Roma dividing them. There are 142 charming rooms, no two quite alike, many with smashing mountain views. Lounges are a treat, the bar kicky, the restaurant very good indeed. *First Class.*

Splendid Venezia Hotel (Corso Italia 209), a modern house on the upper reaches of Corso Italia, is larger than it looks; there is an intimate quality belying a total of 93 well-equipped rooms, some with terraces, the better to enjoy the scenery. Public spaces, including congenial bar and restaurant, are antique-accented. *First Class.*

Majoni Hotel (Via Roma 55) is, despite a typically Alpine-style façade, so tastefully contemporary within that it appears to be higher category than is the case. Bedrooms, nearly 50 all told, are as comfortable as they are attractive; public spaces are capacious, with a white-accented bar-lounge and a restaurant in tones of brown and beige. An easy walk along Via Roma to the center. Special. *Moderate.*

Europa Hotel (Corso Italia 207): If the Europa's 52 rooms—or at least those I have seen—were larger, I would move it to near the top of this select group of evaluated hotels. As it is, with its top-of-Corso Italia location, good-looking, traditional-décor lounges, bar and commendable restaurant, and professional service, it is easily recommendable. *Moderate.*

Cortina Hotel (Corso Italia 94) is central as can be—the parish church is just opposite—with smartly contemporary lounges and bar, zingy rustic-décor restaurant and bedrooms. *First Class.*

Ancora Hotel (Corso Italia 62) is quite as central as the Cortina (above), if less trendy. There are 82 rooms (those to aim for have views of the parish church and the mountains backing it), bar-lounge, solarium, and restaurant-cum-outdoor terrace. *First Class.*

Concordia Park Hotel (Corso Italia 28) has 60 okay rooms, a restaurant—and park views. *Moderate.*

DAILY BREAD

Campanile (Piazza Venezia 2; Phone 61-777) takes its name from the bell tower of the parish church next door; you're right in the heart of town. It embraces a clutch of contiguous rooms, the lot of them wood-paneled. The menu is nothing if not eclectic, with such specialties as würstel con crauti—a kind of Cortina choucroute garni; gulasch all' Ungherese; and the very Italian—and delicious—salsiccie (grilled sausage) con polenta. Zuppa di verdura, the vegetable soup, is bracing; so is spaghetti pomodoro; and so are the veal entrées. Regional wines. *First Class.*

El Toulà (Via Ronco 123; Phone 3339) is a bit away from the center, but it's so attractive and offers such smashing mountain views as well as smashing cuisine—especially well-sauced pastas, delicious roasts, super sweets, a wide choice of regional and other Italian wines—that you're bound to have a good time. Caveat: unless matters change, or unless Cortina is devoid of visitors, you must book in advance. *Luxury.*

Trattoria da Francesco (Via XXIX Maggio 5; Phone 3821) is conveniently central, friendly, and with hearty fare, antipasto assortito through veal and lamb entrées. *Moderate.*

De la Poste Hotel Ristorante (Piazza Roma 14; Phone 4271): You've been enjoying a drink in this hotel's see-and-be-seen bar, and you're hungry.

Well, move right along to the brass-chandeliered, tapestry-hung, candle-lit restaurant and tuck into the table d'hôte, which might open with pasta e fagioli or individual pizzas, continue with grilled sole or English-style roast beef, with cheese or fruit to conclude. *First Class.*

Beppe Sello Hotel Ristorante (Via Ronco 68; Phone 3236) is the good-value dining room of a small hotel, reliable for lunches and dinners based on beef or seafood entrées. *First Class.*

Vienna (Via Roma 66; Phone 2720) is an unlikely name for a pizzeria, but the proof of the pudding, or rather of the pizza, is what counts. *Moderate.*

Caffè Embassy (Corso Italia 54) is long-esteemed for its pastries, which, when combined with coffee, are the perfect midday pick-me up. If you can't find a seat, move along to neighboring *Caffè Lovat,* a Corso Italia neighbor.

SHOPPER'S CORTINA

Cortina's Corso Italia offers above-average shopping, with the locally owned *Cooperative* department store (Cortina citizens may join and receive discounted prices) one of the finest such in any of the smaller Italian cities; there are six levels, with the mezzanine supermercato (wines as well as groceries) and the ground-floor handicrafts and housewares departments among the more interesting. Other Corso Italia shops worth knowing about include *K-2* for ski equipment and duds (good value in Italy), *Antonio* (Tyrol-style linens and accessories), *Guerresco* (a series of three shoe shops at various points along the street), and *Ritz* (with a pair of shops, one for women, one for men and boys, both with super sportswear).

INCIDENTAL INTELLIGENCE

You may fly to Milan and take a bus from there; or come north via bus from Venice; there is bus service, as well, between Cortina and Bolzano. *Further information:* Azienda Autonoma di Soggiorno e Turismo, Piazza Roma, Cortina d' Ampezzo.

9

Costa Smeralda

and Samplings of Sardinia

BACKGROUND BRIEFING

It is no wonder that Sardinians are not without xenophobic attitudes toward newcomers to their Mediterranean island. What people would not be, given a record of invaders over the centuries that reads like a survey course in world history?

Phoenicians came as early as the eighth century B.C., and were successively followed by Carthaginians, Romans, Vandals, Byzantines, Arabs, northern Italian city-states like Genoa and Pisa (Pisan Romanesque churches still dot Sardinia), Spaniards (the Catalan language from the Spanish region centered on Barcelona still is spoken in northwest Sardinia), Austrians, and—in the early eighteenth century—the royal house of Savoy, which promptly dubbed its realm the Kingdom of Sardinia, albeit mostly ruling, absentee-style, from Turin (chapter 35) until, of course, that same dynasty became the royal house—ultimately Rome-based—of a united Italy.

The post-World War II constitution of the republic allows the *Regione* of Sardinia to continue speaking its distinctive language, but instruction in Italian, the national language, is compulsory in schools. Sardinians are allowed more autonomy than is the case with *Regioni* of the *Continente*—which is what Sardinians call the mainland. But Sardinia—perhaps because of a lingering, centuries-long-induced dose of xenophobia—has never become tourist territory of global significance, in the manner, say, of Sicily, to which this book devotes three chapters. With a single major exception: the splendid, wide, white-sand beaches fringing rock-bound coves of the island's dramatically irregular northeast shore, and known—thanks to their prime developer, the fabulously rich Aga Khan—as the Costa Smeralda.

Emerald Coast, indeed. Aptly named for the greenish hue of its Tyrrhenian Sea waters, the area wraps around a promontory extending from the airport-equipped town of Olbia and includes Porto Cervo village, created by the Aga Khan's firm, Società Alberghiera Costa Smeralda (with one of the smartest clutches of shops in Italy), along with a quintet of resort hotels that, with Lake Como's Villa d'Este, constitute the best such in Italy; a Robert Trent Jones–designed golf course that's one of the most beautiful in the world and equal to the Jones courses in Hawaii; an internationally reputed yacht club, one of the finest marinas in the Mediterranean; even a cantiere, or shipyard; and, hardly insignificant, a well-operated international airline that flies in (and flies home) many of the Costa Smeralda's foreign guests.

There are of course other Sardinia resorts; 1200-bed Forte Village and 2300-bed Tanka Village, both in the south, typify enormous tourist-village developments geared to the northern European mass—and I mean mass—market.

But it was the Costa Smeralda that pioneered as a Sardinian destination of international consequence in the 1960s. And it is the Costa Smeralda that remains precisely that.

ON SCENE

Lay of the Land: The transatlantic visitor flies over to Sardinia primarily to unwind in the course of Italian travels, at the Costa Smeralda in the northeast, with the option of forays to insular Sardinian spots, such as—proceeding in a counterclockwise direction around the 160-mile-long, 70-mile-wide island—Sassari, Alghero, Cagliari, and Nuoro. Package tours are the exception to the rule; if you want to explore Sardinia, you do it, ideally, via rented car (carefully ascertaining in advance of departure the frequency of gas stations—there can be few—on your route), with public buses and some trains as alternatives.

Porto Cervo village is the nerve center of the Costa Smeralda. Life revolves around its circular Piazzetta, edged by trendy boutiques (most of them links of mainland chains) along with Sarma Supermercato, stocked with Sardinian and other Italian wines, as well as groceries. In addition, Porto Cervo is dotted with restaurants and caffès, plus a tennis club, hotel, marina, and yacht club.

Sassari, the No. 2 city, a few miles inland from the coast in northwest Sardinia, bases itself on Corso Vittorio Emanuele, the main thoroughfare, and has Spanish antecedents, as is evident in the *Duomo* (Piazza del Duomo)—or at least its Iberian-influenced Baroque façade—if not in the mix-of-periods interior. *Museo Nazionale Giovanni Sanna* (Via Roma) displays paintings by such masters as Guercino, Bassano, and Piero di Cosimo, as well as Sardinian artists; an interesting exhibit of the island's traditional crafts, and—oldest of its works—bits and pieces of ancient Sardinia, the Roman period included. *Gallo d'Oro,* located on Piazza d'Italia, the quite grand central square, is a convenient lunch stop *(Moderate)*, as is *Il Senato* (Via Mundula 2, *First Class*)—a near neighbor of the Duomo (above) and *Grazia Deledda Hotel* (Viale Dante 47, *First Class*), a modern 125-room house-cum-swimming-pool-and-restaurant *(First Class)*, is indicated for overnight.

Alghero, 15 miles southwest of Sassari, and with one of the three Sardinian airports (the other two are at Olbia and Cagliari), often strikes visitors as the most charming of the towns, in large part thanks to an atmospheric Città Vecchia flanking its harbor, stubborn retention since the Middle Ages of the Catalan language, with still more Catalan influence in remaining Spanish Gothic portions of the *Duomo* (Piazza Duomo). The Gothic-origin *Church of San Francesco* (Piazza San Francesco), has a powerfully vaulted apse. Grotto buffs head out of town (14 miles west) to Capo Caccia's *Grotta di Nettuno. Riu* (Piazza Civica; Phone 977-240, *Moderate*) is a good bet for lunch. *La Lepanto* (Via Carlo Alberto 135, Phone 079-979-116; *Luxury*) is one of Italy's leading lobster restaurants. Seaview *Carlos V Hotel* (Lungomare Valencia 24, *First Class*), an agreeable 110-room house, is ideal for overnight; it just has to be the only place in Italy where "Charles" (it is named for Holy Roman Emperor Charles V, whose domains included Sardinia) is spelled the Spanish way (with a final "s"). Olé!

Cagliari, capital and major city, saw heavy World War II bombing. One remaining old quarter, Castello, is atmospheric. The core is enclosed by water-bordering Via Roma (with a branch of the La Rinascente department store chain); broad shop-lined Via Dante runs perpendicular to it. *Museo Nazionale Archeologico* (Piazza Indipendenza) is the most important on the island, with bronze work from the Sardinian Nuraghic era, going back some ten centuries before Christ; objects, as well, from the Carthaginian, or Punic, period; gold and silver jewelry; and Sardinian paintings. The *Duomo* (Via Duomo) retains an original Romanesque campanile, but the façade is mostly a restoration; inside is multiepoch, with a pair of medieval pulpits and a treasury. The *Church of San Domenico* (Via San Domenico) is largely rebuilt; you go for the Gothic cloister. *Antica Hostaria* (Via Cavour 60; Phone 665-870; *First Class*) is a good spot to sample local specialties at lunch. If you must remain overnight, *Regina Margherita Hotel* (Viale Regina Margherita 44, *First Class*) and *Moderno Hotel* (Via Roma 159, *Moderate*) are fairly central, albeit without restaurants.

Nuoro: Sardinians are big on traditional costumes and handicrafts. If these interest you, pop into this town, 50 miles south of Porto Cervo, heading for *Museo delle Vita e delle Tradizioni Popolari Sarde* (Via Mereu 56). *Grazia Deledda Hotel* (Via Lamarmora 175; Phone 31-257, *Moderate*) is indicated for lunch (and overnight, as well, although you're not far from the Costa Smeralda). About a dozen miles out of town, at *Serra Orrio*, is a cluster of prehistoric nuraghi, conical stone houses of the ancient Sardinians—as good a place as any to see some of these, perhaps en route back to the Costa Smeralda.

SETTLING IN

Cala di Volpe Hotel (Costa Smeralda) lies between the sea and the links of the Robert Trent Jones-designed Pevero Gold Club. It is a fanciful variation on the theme of a medieval Sardinian village, a jumble of towers, turrets, loggias, and arches that shelter what is perhaps the most creative of hotel interiors on the coast—floors surfaced with hand-decorated tiles, punctuated by the actual trunks of juniper trees, mosaics in the lobby, Sardinian textiles throughout, and—most memorable touch—trompe l'oeil murals and decorations—each original—on walls, closet doors, and chests. There are 125 antique-accented rooms and suites (the Presidential has its own pool and solarium, as well as three bedrooms/baths, and two living rooms!), a fabulously large salt-water pool on a sweeping lawn, tennis courts, both piano bar and wee-hours disco, and an exceptional restaurant for dinner (as at all Costa Smeralda hotels, men do not wear jackets). Lunch is barbecue based, opening with a 50-dish antipasto buffet, and served around the pool. Lots of repeaters. May through September. Affiliated with Ciga Hotels and a member of Leading Hotels of the World. *Luxury.*

Romazzino Hotel (Costa Smeralda) is an idyllic sight from a distance, the stark white of its walls a foil for verdant countryside surrounding it on three sides, with acres of gardens, and the beach on the fourth. Indeed, this is the only hotel of the group that has its own beach for swimming, with an adjacent pool, as well. Within, there are 90 terraced rooms, their wrought-iron beds covered with handwoven red, yellow, and green spreads, with high point of décor throughout the hand-painted tiles, from a lobby map of the island to door plaques indicating room numbers. The red-chaired, multiarched restaurant is handsome, and you lunch around the pool, opting for pizza, if you like. Mid-May through mid-October. Affiliated with Ciga Hotels and a member of Leading Hotels of the World. *Luxury.*

Pitrizza Hotel (Costa Smeralda)—smallest, priciest of the group (Cala di Volpe is second most expensive, with Romazzino, Cervo Hotel, and

Cervo Tennis Club following, in that order)—is for getters-away-from-it-all, never more than 50 all told, at any given time. It embraces half a dozen villas, their capacious terraces sheltered by grapevines, with four to six rooms in each (some are duplexes) and the look one of country antiques, accessories, carpets, and textiles based on tones of beige. The detached clubhouse contains a lounge-cum-piano-bar and a terraced restaurant for candle-lit dinners (lunch is served under a pergola in the garden). Beyond, there's a swimming pool carved out of pink granite, with the hotel's own secluded beach just below. An enchanter. Open May through September. Affiliated with Ciga Hotels and a member of Relais et Châteaux. *Luxury.*

Cervo Hotel (Costa Smeralda): City dwellers—strike that out—village dwellers—this one's for you, overlooking the animated Piazzetta in Porto Cervo and designed to be a part of the village, into which it blends. I like the rooms; there are 90, all told, each with hand-carved wooden bedsteads, terra-cotta floors, and terraces. There's a super restaurant, with its terrace giving on to the harbor, while the bar-lounge's open area edges the Piazzetta. The pool, around which lunch is served, is generous-sized and there's boat service to an away-from-the-village beach. March through October. Affiliated with Ciga Hotels and a member of Leading Hotels of the World. *First Class.*

Cervo Tennis Club Hotel (Costa Smeralda) sports 16 elegant rooms, among the most contemporary in look of any of the Costa Smeralda hotels; a topnotch restaurant; cozy bar; connected indoor/outdoor swimming pools; sauna-gym; and—to get to the raison d'être—seven tennis courts, floodlit for evening play. And, yes, John McEnroe, Vitas Gerulaitis, and Ilie Nastase are among players who have used the master court. Worth noting: The Tennis Club, near the Piazzetta in Porto Cervo, is traditionally open all year. Affiliated with Ciga Hotels. *First Class.*

Sporting Hotel (Porto Rotondo), near Olbia and not far from the Porto Cervo hotels, is small (there are but 27 terraced, wicker-accented rooms facing the sea) has a rambling wood-beamed lounge, reliable restaurant called El Toula, and a convivial piano bar; and is strategically sited on a finger of land edged on one side by a white-sand beach and on the other by a yacht harbor, with a good, worth-noting seafood spot, *Paguro,* nearby. There's a swimming pool as well. Casual and congenial. Affiliated with Ciga Hotels. *First Class.*

DAILY BREAD

(*Dress Code:* The entire Costa Smeralda is sensibly casual-dressy for dinner; that means a smart shirt and slacks—but neither jacket nor tie for gents; modish, albeit informal, duds for the women.)

Cervo Grill (Piazzetta, Porto Cervo; Phone 92-003) makes a specialty of hearty lamb chops and beefsteaks and of flambéed dishes. Start with assorted salamis and conclude with a house-baked dessert, the while watching Piazzetta promenaders. *First Class.*

Il Pomodoro (Porto Cervo, adjacent to Cervo Hotel) translates as The Tomato; the specialty is pizza, with ten kinds always available, the popular tomato-and-mozzarella Margherita included. Super pastas, as well, with a limited number of meat and seafood entries. *First Class.*

Il Ristorante del Golf (Porto Cervo Golf Club; Phone 96-210) is open to nonmembers and for that matter nonplayers. But you must specify the candle-lit terrace—overlooking the links and the sea—when you book for dinner; it's popular. Lobster, roasts, steaks, and other international dishes in the evening; a fabulous buffet at the pool for lunch. *Luxury.*

Il Pescatore (Porto Vecchio of Porto Cervo; Phone 92-296): The name indicates the specialty: fish, caught today and simply grilled, and super seafood, as well, preceded, if you like, by seafood-sauced pasta. Lovely setting, especially appreciated with an outdoor table on a fine day. *First Class.*

Petronilla (Su Conca, near Porto Cervo; Phone 92-207) features local crayfish. Ideally, precede the crustaceans with crab-sauced spaghetti alla granseola, a house specialty. *First Class.*

Caffè Espresso (Passeggiata, in the Piazzetta complex, Porto Cervo) is perhaps the most versatile of the see-and-be-seen spots, open from breakfast into evening, for coffee and pastry, sandwiches and drinks. *Moderate.*

Il Portico (Piazzetta, Porto Cervo) is what the Italians call an American bar, which means it's primarily for alcoholic drinks. (The wood-paneled *Pub,* adjacent, is just as popular, and like Il Portico, open late.) *First Class.*

Cala di Volpe Hotel Ristorante (Costa Smeralda; Phone 96-083): There are à la carte specialties—grilled scampi, especially—that appeal, in this animated dinner spot, but the prix-fixe dinner includes a bountiful antipasto buffet, a pasta course, and veal, beef, and poultry entrées, as well. Super. *Luxury.*

Patrizza Hotel Ristorante (Costa Smeralda; Phone 92-000) is the most intimate and romantic of the hotel dining rooms; go for the prix-fixe dinner, hoping that zuppa di pesce (fish soup) is on the menu, ordering a dessert soufflé à la carte. *Luxury.*

INCIDENTAL INTELLIGENCE

Alisarda, founded by the Aga Khan–headed Costa Smeralda enterprises, connects Olbia with half a dozen Italian cities, including Rome and Milan, and also, in summer, half a dozen French, German, and Swiss points, serving meals on domestic flights. Additionally, Alisarda links Cagliari and Alghero with the Italian mainland and Palermo, Sicily. And passenger ships operated by Italian State Railways ply between Naples, Genoa, and other mainland points and Olbia, Cagliari, and other Sardinian ports. *Further information:* Ente Provinciale per Il Turismo, Piazza Matteotti 9, Cagliari; Viale Caprera 36, Sassari; and Piazza Italia, Nuoro; Azienda Autonoma di Soggiorno e Turismo, Piazza Porta Terra 9, Alghero; and Via Catello Piro 1, Olbia.

10

Courmayeur

Alps and Castles in Valle d'Aosta

BACKGROUND BRIEFING

Courmayeur? It sounds French. Well, this Alpine resort *par excellence* is indeed *almost* French, stretching across a valley at the foot of 15,781-foot Mont Blanc—oops, Monte Bianco, in Italian—with the fabulous seven-mile tunnel under Europe's second-highest peak just next door, connecting it with the sister resort of Chamonix, in La Belle France.

Analyze the meaning of the name and you get an idea of Courmayeur's respectably advanced age. It's not your run-of-the-mill ski town; its history goes back to Roman settlers forming a tribunal—*Curia Mayor*—within its boundaries. The Middle Ages saw the area that now constitutes Italy's smallest *Regione*—Rhode Island-sized Valle d'Aosta—become a checkerboard of invariably contentious miniduchies, their inhabitants speaking French (which is why the name Courmayeur stuck) as well as Italian, which, indeed, their mostly bilingual descendants do, to this very day. Earliest tourists were travelers come to drink no-longer-consumed mineral waters in the seventeenth century. As early as the eighteenth, climbers and explorers anxious to conquer Monte Bianco were on hand. And in the nineteenth, intrepid Britons pioneered as winter sports enthusiasts.

Completion of the extraordinary tunnel under Monte Bianco in 1965 not only opened a shorter motor route between major centers like Paris and Rome, but saw Courmayeur increase in international accessibility—and popularity. The town today remains delightfully small, with about 3000 residents (although its contiguous satellite villages, Entrèves and La Palud, are positively bucolic in contrast), but at the same time well equipped with hotels and restaurants, trendy shops, amusing caffès, a mix of discos, congenial multilingual hosts, and an extraordinary wealth of facilities, including the world's largest cable car (capacity 135 skiers and their skis), one of four; two bucket lifts; six chair lifts; a dozen-plus ski lifts; and a ski school with a faculty of 90.

Italy's prime winter resort—along with Cortina d'Ampezzo (chapter 8)—Courmayeur is so strategically situated—not only Alpine, but on the frontier with France and within easy driving distance of Valle d'Aosta's surprise-packed capital, as well as the plethora of castles erected by its medieval nobles—that it beckons the curious nonskiing traveler as well, and not only in winter; this is a town for all seasons.

ON SCENE

Lay of the Land: By and large, Courmayeur is conveniently walkable. *Via Roma,* the animated main street, is lined with caffès and oft-classy shops: Toni Cobbi (sports clothes, ski and climbing equipment), Trussardi (men's and women's clothes, accessories), Bassi (porcelain, pottery), Firma (making a specialty of sweaters), Angelini (local woodcarving, other crafts), Guichardaz (antiques); and for the makings of a picnic, La Spiga (bakery), Il Salumaio (the *Regione*'s superb salamis), and Goio (for a bottle of regional wine). Via Roma leads into *Piazza Abate Henry,* the central square easily distinguishable thanks to the campanile of the parish church. There are three principal cable-car stations: *Funivia Val Veenya* is in the pretty neighboring village of Entrèves; *Funivia Monte Bianco* (about which more later) is in La Palud, adjacent to Entrèves; but *Funivia Courmayeur* is right in town, on *Strada della Volpe.* Courmayeur is served by the railway station at *Pré St.-Didier,* a couple of miles south, while the entrance to the *Monte Bianco/Mont Blanc Tunnel* is a couple of miles north.

Church of SS. Pantaleone e Valentino (Piazza Abate Henry) is charming Baroque, but its claim to fame is its towering, weathered gray stone campanile, a Romanesque memento whose bells have been rung at regular intervals since 1392.

Museo Alpino (Piazza Abate Henry), just opposite the church (above) deals with the exploits of explorers and climbers; it's not a ski exhibit. Rather, you'll find stuffed Alpine animals, rare mountain rocks, equipment and photographs, souvenirs of celebrated climbs, and a scale model of the Courmayeur area.

By tunnel and/or cable car to France: The 11-mile tunnel (opened in 1965) connecting Courmayeur with Chamonix (subject of a chapter in

France at Its Best) involves half an hour to forty-five minutes' drive either way to and from your Courmayeur hotel, of course you must have your passport with you, for Italian and French customs, going and returning. It's agreeable to spend, say, a morning or afternoon strolling central Chamonix, in and about Place Saussure, relaxing in one of its myriad open-air café (*La Croix Blanche* and *La Taverne de Chamonix* are two such) perhaps buying a bag of pastries at the pâtisserie of *Madame Ancey*, on the square; tucking into a Gallic lunch at *First Class Restaurant La Tartiffle* (Rue Moulins; Phone 53-20-22), then returning again by means of the tunnel.

Much more exciting would be to go one way—through the breath-takingly beautiful Mont Blanc Massif—by cable car. You board Mont Blanc Cableways at La Palud (whose elevation is 4459 feet) just outside of Courmayeur and take a car—passing mountain fauna like chamois and ibex en route—to Punta Helbronner, through which the Franco-Italian frontier passes, and with a café and an observation terrace from which—the altitude is 11,358 feet—you have an overview of nearby snowy peaks (Mont Blanc of course, but others as high as 13,000 feet) and mammoth glaciers, as well. You change to a French car at that point, continuing to Aiguille du Midi station (11,434 feet), with still another observation terrace and café, before you start your descent for the final stretch—to Chamonix, at 3413 feet, somewhat lower than Courmayeur's 4016-foot altitude. Time consumed en route, with stops: approximately two hours, unless, of course, you're a skier, in which case you may ski from the stops en route, easily making your outing a day long one, albeit on the slopes.

Aosta—the city—is capital of the *Regione* of Valle d'Aosta—just so you have the confusing terminology clarified. It's but 21 miles southeast of Courmayeur, and though small—population is about 40,000—with half a dozen good reasons for a visit. First is the main square, *Piazza Chanoux*, with the neoclassic *Municipio*, or city hall, its major monument, and snowy Alps as a backdrop. Second are remarkable remnants of once-rich Roman Aosta; *Teatro Romano* (Via Sant' Anselmo) stuns with a still-standing, four-level stone wall as its principal feature. The nearby *Arco di Augusto* remains elegant some 1900 years after its construction, while *Porto Praetoria*—actually a pair of triple-arched gates—is less graceful, albeit built for keeps; and the still-intact Roman-built *city walls* are punctuated by a quartet of towers. The *Duomo* (Piazza Giovanni XXIII) greets you with a severe neoclassic façade, but its two campanili at the rear are Romanesque, and inside, standouts are a gorgeous Gothic carved-wood choir and a Treasury laden with objects of beauty. Best for last: *Sant' Orso complex* (Via Sant' Orso), not unlike the Duomo, boasts a superb choir and important Treasury in its church, but there are, as well, a Romanesque crypt and cloister, with capitals of the latter's columns special. In the onetime priorato, or priory, have a look at the chapel frescoes, moving along, then, to adjacent *Museo Archeologico,* its ceramics and sculpture a celebration of Roman Aosta. *Ristorante Piemonte (Moderate),* conveniently located at Via Porto Pretoria 13 (Phone 40-111) is a sensible lunch choice; *Turin Hotel* (Via Torino 14, *Moderate*), fairly central, is okay for overnight.

A pair of medieval castles: The Valle d'Aosta countryside is liberally sprinkled with medieval castles—some 70 all told, towered, turreted, and crenelated, and invariably topping rocky eminences, backed by snowy peaks. As often as not they have French names—Châtelard and Sarriod de la Tour, St.-Pierre and Sarre, Graines and Cly St.-Denis. Not all are open to visitors. But the top two are. *Castello di Issogne,* in the town whose name it takes, about 15 miles southeast of Aosta, goes back to the fifteenth century, and the frescoes of its three-story courtyard, though faded, remain impressive, as does the pomegranate tree in the central fountain, as well it might: it is made of wrought iron and water still pours forth from its trunk. State rooms were restored and refurnished, in period, toward the end of the last century—and tastefully, so that you want to traipse through chapel and dining room, bedrooms and kitchen, many frescoed. *Castello di Fenis* (nine miles east of Aosta) should by now have served as the set for countless movies with Middle Ages settings. Although I doubt that it has. Its fourteenth-century walls are meticulously crenelated. There are half a dozen towers of as many shapes and sizes. And the treat inside is *Museo dell' Arredamento*—a charmer of a multiroom museum of regional antique furniture.

SETTLING IN

COURMAYEUR VILLAGE

Pavillon Hotel (Strada Regionale 60) has the advantage of a central situation, views of Monte Bianco from many of its 40 terrace-equipped rooms, a restaurant worthy of additional comment in a later paragraph, relaxing bar with deep red-leather seats you can really sink into, copper-hooded fireplace in the cozy lounge, good-sized indoor pool-cum-sauna/solarium, and skilled service. Member, Relais et Châteaux. *First Class.*

Royal e Golf Hotel (Via Roma 83) welcomes with a generously proportioned lobby, high-ceilinged bar-lounge, reputed restaurant, 90-plus nicely designed rooms, swimming pool in the garden-cum-panoramas, and friendly staff. *First Class.*

Les Jumeaux Hotel (Strada Regionale 35) has an ultra-mod look and tastefully large lobby, even larger cocktail lounge, pale-green-accented restaurant, beige-and-brown bedrooms, with the doubles large and the lot equipped with kitchens, and up-to-the-minute baths. *First Class.*

Courmayeur Hotel (Via Roma 158) looks Alpine from without, is smartly contemporary inside, with plaids the basis of its restaurant and bar-lounge décor; and bedrooms (25 all told) are attractive. Good value. *Moderate.*

Cresta et Duc Hotel (Via Circonvallazione) offers just under 40 comfortable rooms, public spaces that include a restaurant, bar-lounge. Very nice indeed. *Moderate.*

Del Viale Hotel (Viale Monte Bianco) sets a stylish standard, with its two dozen rooms, public spaces antique-accented, and fabulous mountain views. Restaurant. *Moderate.*

ENTRÈVES VILLAGE

Des Alpes Hotel has placed its 60 nicely equipped rooms in a six-story pavilion connected to a long, low-slung wing housing the lobby, super bar-lounge with typically Aosta furnishings and accents, picture-window restaurant, and wee-hours disco. *First Class.*

La Brenva Hotel achieves success with its winning country décor—rough-beamed ceilings, flagstone walls, earth-toned textiles of its lobby, restaurant (exceptional enough to warrant later comment), and bar; bedrooms are stunners, too. Friendly. *Moderate.*

La Grange Hotel is a deftly transformed onetime barn, with a long, sloping tiled roof—not unlike those of area farmhouses—flagstone floor in its lobby-bar, and at least one flagstone wall in each of the bedrooms, antique-accented—as are the public spaces. A loquacious myna bird positioned at the front door rarely fails to say *Ciao* to guests arriving or departing. Breakfast only. *Moderate.*

ST. VINCENT

Billia Hotel (Viale Piemonte 18) is closer to Aosta (about 17 miles) than Courmayeur and is among the region's most unabashedly luxurious hotels. It goes back three-quarters of a century, but it has been smartly and thoroughly updated, with, for example, an elaborately equipped health and beauty center, restaurants, and bars and, as a bonus, a glass-roofed casino-cum-nightclub that is among Europe's largest. The 250 rooms and suites are handsome and with excellent baths, and the Alpine neighborhood abounds in skiing but is no less attractive in summer. *Luxury.*

DAILY BREAD

COURMAYEUR VILLAGE

Le Vieux Pommier (Piazzale Monte Bianco 25; Phone 842-281) looks good—the décor is country style Valle d'Aosta, with a reproduction of the full-scale apple tree of the title the centerpiece, its latest appendage a "Big Apple" transported by the boss from New York—and, what's more important, tastes good. The menu abounds in regional specialties, beginning with a help-yourself antipasto buffet laden with, among other things, reputed local salamis. There are a variety of fondute, the local counterpart of Swiss-origin melted-cheese entrées, and meat dishes are special, among them, carne mista al sasso. Order this and you're provided with a Japanese-style hibachi grill to cook your own sausages, beef, veal, pork, and liver. And note: patate fritte (French fries) are on the menu. *First Class.*

Mont Frety (Strada Regionale 21; Phone 841-786) is invitingly contemporary—and tasty. At lunch, start with bresaola della valtellina, the counterpart in these parts of Switzerland's razor-thin air-dried beef, *bundnerfleisch.* Polenta alla valdostana is an interesting starter, too. And pollo alla cacciatore is a super entrée. In the evening half a dozen pizza variations are added to the menu. *First Class.*

Pavillon Hotel Ristorante (Phone 842-420), cheery and capacious, does exceedingly well by the table d'hôte, both at lunch and dinner, with the four-course meal as delicious as it is generous, and, for that matter, authentic, with respect to regional specialties such as hams and sausages, fondute and grilled meats, and a Gallic-origin potato dish invariably among the vegetables. The wheeled-to-table carrello of sweets is irresistible. Fine wines. *First Class.*

Al Vecchio Torchio (Via Roma 122; Phone 842-222) appeals from the moment of entry; you like the vibes, compounded of a loquacious clientele and a smiling staff. Not to mention comestibles. Specialties are grilled—steaks, if you like, lamb, veal, poultry, with hearty regional touches, especially in the matter of antipasti. *First Class.*

La Spiga (Via Roma 89; Phone 842-931) is nothing if not multidiscipline. By that I mean you may have spaghetti al pomodoro or a simple salad, a hamburger, or, yes, even a hot dog. *Moderate.*

Caffè della Posta (Via Roma 51) could be the sitting room of an affluent local squire—antique paintings on stucco walls, heavily beamed ceilings, cylindrical porcelain stoves. But you go for people and patter. This is Courmayeur's No. 1 see-and-be-seen caffè. "Martini Dry" and "Martini Vodka" cocktails head its drinks list, but espresso and ice cream are considerably more popular. *Moderate.*

American Bar (Via Roma 74), given its name, cannot help but lure visiting Yanks and Brits, who enjoy mixing with a Continental *après* (or to use the national language, *dopo*) ski clientele. *Moderate.*

ENTRÈVES VILLAGE

La Maison de Filippo just has to be one of the few restaurants extant with phone-reservation numbers for three countries: 89-968 if you're booking locally, in Italy; 1939-165-89-968 from France; and 0039-165-89-968 from Switzerland. Already you will have gathered that this is a popular spot. Setting is an aged stone-and-frame village house, every rustic, copper-hung room of which hums with apparently voracious diners. Two caveats: you must be very hungry and you must have, minimally, two and a half hours to spend on a prix-fixe meal that you will not soon forget. The antipasti, served to you from mammoth bowls and platters that keep coming, include a mix of salamis and salads, which in themselves constitute two or three superb meals. Then, a range of pastas and soups (in giant tureens). But wait: entrées arrive—you help yourself to as many as you can manage—and include roast or cacciatore chicken, roast veal, and venison, the house's own ragout and fondue. Desserts? Flambé Maison is spectacular and one of ten; with a platter of cheeses to conclude before caffè alla valdostana. Throughout, quality equals quantity. In my view, one of Italy's best restaurants. *First Class.*

La Brenva Hotel Ristorante (Phone 89-285) is the smartest-looking of the public rooms—all of them traditional-style—in this hotel. And with tempting things to eat, either à la carte or by means of the excellent-value prix-fixe, with such hearty possibilities as penne all' arrabbiata and maccheroni al gorgonzola to start, veal piccata or grilled sausages among the entrées. *Moderate/First Class.*

INCIDENTAL INTELLIGENCE

Skiers do well to bear in mind that Courmayeur hotels feature winter White Weeks packages that can be excellent value, and usually include transportation from the nearest transatlantic airport, at Milan. *Further information:* Azienda Autonoma di Soggiorno e Turismo, Piazzale Monte Bianco, Courmayeur; Piazza Chanoux 3, Aosta.

11

Cremona

Lombardian Sleeper Town

BACKGROUND BRIEFING

Any town whose most reputed Renaissance painters are as alliteratively named as Boccaccio Boccaccino and Benedetto Bembo (with Ben's artist brother, Bonifacio, also in the running) can't be all bad. Cremona, a small uncelebrated city in the northerly *Regione* of Lombardy, is anything but. It is, as a matter of fact, an all-Italy sleeper, an aesthetic treasure that, provided with an additional hotel or two of a certain stature, might give giant—and not far distant—Milan (chapter 19) something of a run for its lire.

Always more powerful, Milan played a role in the affairs of much smaller Roman-founded Cremona ever since it demonstrated how, as a medieval *comune*, it was able to make itself wealthy, handsome, and a magnet for artists and architects, teachers and thinkers.

Cremona's Golden Age comprised the eleventh, twelfth, and thirteenth centuries, by which time the ruling Milanese Viscontis stepped in, forcefully absorbing it. Withal, Cremona persisted as a we-try-harder kind of community. The early sixteenth century saw a talented family, Campi by name, establish a Cremona school of painting, with Giulio—trained by Giulio Romano, famed for his work in Mantua (chapter 18)—its guru and brothers Antonio, Bernardino, and Vincenzo his collaborators, along with, of course, Boccaccino and the brothers Bembo.

The Renaissance saw Cremona pioneer in a skilled craft—designing and making violins—with the Amati family, starting with Andrea, the leader, credited with creating the violin as it is known today; and the later Cremonese, Antonio Stradivari, whom we know as Stradivarius—

a pupil of Andrea's grandson, Nicolò. Stradivarius is so famed in the field (he worked well into the eighteenth century—the two hundred fiftieth anniversary of his death was observed in Cremona in 1987) that his name is universally synonymous with the word "violin," and has been given to a violin museum (with some of his own on display) in Cremona.

ON SCENE

Lay of the Land: This is a beautifully walkable city, with its base—indeed its very heart, central *Piazza del Comune*—arguably one of the most scenic in Europe, not only because of the Duomo, its baptistry, and tower, but with manifestations of medieval grandeur like the crenelated and arcaded *Palazzo Comunale,* or City Hall; and a onetime army bastion, *Loggia dei Militi.* Two more recent squares, *Piazza Cavour,* a short block west, and parklike *Piazza Roma,* not far north along Via *Solferino,* are Palazzo Comunale neighbors; *Corso Campi,* a major shopping street, is parallel with *Piazza Roma,* a block west; while *Corso Mazzini* (which eventually becomes *Corso Matteotti*)—the other major shopping street—extends east from Piazza Roma. The railway station is to the north, away from the center.

Duomo (Piazza del Comune): Arrive in a smallish city like Cremona knowing that it had been a substantial art center, and you expect an aesthetically creditable cathedral. But nothing quite so sensational as this. Cremona's Duomo is an all-Italy leader, its multiepoch façade (Romanesque, Gothic, Renaissance) one of those rarely successful melds, with everything working beautifully: graceful pediment, whose four niches frame statues of as many saints; oversized rose window; double row of elegantly narrow loggias, under which is the generously scaled portal; an almost welcoming lion at the base of each column supporting its stone porch. What strikes you first, inside, is the extravagance of the scale; then your eyes light on tapestries—Flemish-woven, albeit with their cartoons the work of the same Giulio Romano who had taught Cremona's own Giulio Campi (above)—wrapped around pillars supporting the central nave. Frescoes surfacing the nave were a collaborative effort by a clutch of painters including Cremonese like Boccaccino, Bembo, and the Campi clan. And there are a pair of exquisitely carved pulpits.

Battistero (Piazza del Comune) next door to the Duomo—the Baptistry—is eye-catchingly octagonal, with a six-column loggia atop each of its eight sides, the façade more interesting than the considerably refurbished interior.

Torrazzo (Piazza del Comune) is what Cremonese call their cathedral bell tower, soaring nearly 400 feet heavenward. It has been a landmark for more than six centuries—with a huge clock that has been telling time for three of those centuries, and an inner stairwell, if you would ascend to the crenelated upper platform, for the view.

Palazzo Comune (Piazza del Comune): Cremona's city hall is a thirteenth- and sixteenth-century remodeling of an older building and welcomes visitors to its grandiose public spaces and a display of aged Cremona violins. Step right in, not only to this palace but to the courtyards of any others whose doors are open, in the course of strolling the city; often, they're veritable alfresco sculpture galleries.

Museo Civico (Via Ugolani Dati) is at once cheap (by that I mean its entrance fee is the lowest of any I have encountered anywhere in Italy, for which a resounding bravo to the city fathers) and charming (by which I mean that it is quartered in a felicitous, high-ceilinged, multi-arched palazzo, Affaitati by name). You'll recognize works by the likes of Magnasco and Salvator Rosa, but the bulk of the paintings are local, by the aforementioned brothers Bembo and Campi, as well as Boccaccino. Charming.

Museo Strudivariano (Via Palestro, an extension of Corso Campi and just around the corner from Museo Civico) is a single-room gallery, displaying violins by renowned Cremona creators, including the Amati family and Stradivarius.

Church of Sant' Agostino (Via Plasio) has a brick Gothic façade, an exuberant Baroque interior. Head for the fresco by Bonifacio Bembo—vaulted ceiling included—in Cappella Cavalcabò, where you'll want to note portraits of a powerful Milanese duke, Francesco Sforza, and his wife Bianca, of the also influential Visconti clan.

Church of Sant' Agata (Corso Garibaldi) is older than you would surmise from its finely detailed neoclassical façade. Look back—way back—at its campanile to detect Gothic origins. Inside, beeline for Bernardino Campi's lovely *Assumption* and the immense Giulio Campi altarpiece, *Martyrdom of Saint Agatha.*

Church of San Michele (at the terminus of Via Cremona) is somber brick Gothic without, older Romanesque within, no two capitals on the columns of its nave alike, and its masterwork a Bernardino Campi altarpiece, *Nativity with Saints.*

Church of Sant' Abbondio (Via Gatti), though small, positively brims with art, frescoes lining the ceiling of its Renaissance nave, sculpture dominating each of eight side chapels, and with a quiet cloister adjacent.

SETTLING IN

Continental Hotel (Piazza della Libertà 26), a ten-minute walk along Corso Mazzini and Corso Matteotti, from the center, is agreeably contemporary, with a pleasant lobby-lounge, well-operated restaurant, not quite 60 full-facility rooms, and a friendly staff. *Moderate/First Class.*

DAILY BREAD

Ceresole (Via Ceresole 4; Phone 23-322)—near the Duomo—pleases with its mix of paneled walls hung with antique prints, Venetian crystal chandeliers illuminating tables set in pale pink linen. Owners are the brothers Botte—Gennaro and Saverio—both out front; their wives (Lucia and Anna) are the skilled chefs. Fare is nouvelle-accented, range of options extraordinarily wide, with exceptional risotto supplementing pastas, and seafood entries (fish is deliciously sauced) supplementing specialties including stracotto di manzo, a beef casserole. This is a spot to break down and have dessert, possibly a slice of torta Cremona, the town's own special cake. In my opinion, one of Italy's best restaurants. *Luxury.*

Aquila Nera (Via Sicardo 3; Phone 25-646)—a near neighbor of the Duomo, heart of town, is known for Cremona specialties. It is *piccolo* and pleasing. *First Class.*

Centrale (Via Pertus 104; Phone 28-701) is indeed *centrale,* with a wide choice of pastas (gnocchi is better than maccheroni pomodoro), veal entries including vitello tonnato, and friendly service. *Moderate.*

Pizzeria Superbar (Via Palestro 56; Phone 24-444) is worth knowing about if you've just come from, or are en route to, Museo Civico, its near neighbor. The Italians' favorite species, Margherita, is reliable. *Moderate.*

Caffè Portici del Comunale (Piazza del Comune) has the best location in town; outdoor tables face the Duomo and adjacent Torrazzo; lovely at sunset. *Moderate.*

Caffè Lanfranchi (Via Solferino 30) beckons with a little clutch of marble-topped tables. Go on in, for a slice of one of their own cakes or a croissant, with coffee. *Moderate.*

SOUND OF MUSIC

Ask your hotel concierge if there's something on—opera, concert, ballet—at sumptuously neoclassic *Teatro Ponchielli* (Corso Vittorio Emanuele) or also handsome *Teatro Filodrammatici* (Piazza Filodrammatici). Both date to the early nineteenth century.

SHOPPER'S CREMONA

Corso Garibaldi abounds in smart stores, and Upim department store is on Corso Mazzini.

INCIDENTAL INTELLIGENCE

Further information: Ente Provinciale per il Turismo, Piazza del Comune 5, Cremona.

12

Ferrara

Grazie, Famiglia Este!

BACKGROUND BRIEFING

Never underestimate, in Italy of all countries, the manifold ways in which a single family can influence the course of a city's destiny. Mantua (chapter 18) owes much to the Gonzagas. Urbino (chapter 36) was put on the map by Dukes of Montefeltro, who did a similarly impressive job with Gubbio (chapter 15). In the case of the north-central cities of Ferrara and Modena (chapter 20) in Emilia-Romagna, the makers and doers went by the name of Este.

There was, to be sure, a pre-Este Ferrara. Its Po River Valley location drew affluent merchants, in the early Christian era, and it was rich enough in the seventh century to have its own cathedral and a citizenry substantial enough to have created an upper class, with inevitable rivalries resulting. In the early thirteenth century, Ferrara witnessed the rise to power of the Estes who, not unlike Mantua's Gonzagas, began their climb, without benefit of titles, only gradually becoming marquesses and ultimately dukes.

The Ferrara Este period—1140–1598—and the Golden Age of Ferrara were one and the same. (Their relatives had much longer staying power in Modena [chapter 20].) The landmark castle—an all-Europe standout of its kind—was built by Nicolà II. The esteemed university was founded by Alberto. The intellectual ferment that came as a consequence of Renaissance philosophers and writers and artists in residence was Lionello's accomplishment. Borso was the first of the Este clan to rate the ducal moniker. Ercole I fostered modern town planning when he commissioned a Renaissance addition to the city, grafted onto Ferrara's medieval core without disturbing it. Alfonso I, recognizing the need for a then-modern defense system, made of Ferrara a force to be reckoned with by means of strong artillery. But, alas, his grandson, Alfonso II, expired without a son to succeed him, the Papal States stepped in to fill the void, and decline set in—not only with the popes but under later Napoleonic and Austrian domination that preceded formation of the peninsula-wide Kingdom of Italy in 1861.

Fortunes of war have taken their toll. Not all the great art of the Este centuries has remained in Ferrara. And the city suffered a hundred World War II air raids. Notwithstanding setbacks, this still little-known city—its population is about 150,000 and it thrives as an industrial center—remains a repository of art and architecture far, far out of proportion to its size.

ON SCENE

Lay of the Land: Unlike other cities like Pisa (chapter 27) and Ravenna (chapter 28), which had been bombed during the Second World War, Ferrara retains its ambience of yore, with certain of its ancient streets—especially *Via Volte,* still framed by Gothic arches, and mansion-lined *Via Savonarola*—crying out for perusal in the course of leisurely walks. Think of the city in rectangular terms, remembering that its principal landmark is *Castello Estense,* the Este dynastic seat, on central *Piazza Castello,* and that the two major thoroughfares are *Corso Martiri della Libertà* (main shopping street running north-south, just west of Piazza Castello) and *Corso della Giovecca* (running perpendicular to Martiri della Libertà, with department stores like Coin and Upim), which becomes *Viale Cavour* in its western reaches, extending to the railway station fronting *Viale IV Novembre.*

Castello Estense (Piazza Castello) is not easily missed. Indeed you half-expect helmeted, breast-plated guards, halberds at the ready, to be patrolling parapets of each of its four corner towers. Work started on the castle toward the end of the fourteenth century and continued into the sixteenth. You enter by means of a moat, pass into a sumptuous courtyard and up a grandly proportioned stone staircase to state rooms on the second floor. Sala dei Giochi's brocaded walls and Rococo furniture are well and good, but look up at the frescoes depicting Renaissance games, and take time to appreciate their minute details; painters were a family called Filippi, also responsible for ceilings in nearby rooms. Shown, too, is a chapel created for the Protestant wife of one of the Estes and—among other features—both a lovely garden and a grim dungeon.

Duomo (Piazza Cattedrale) is not your conventionally façaded Italian cathedral. It is a successful Romanesque-Gothic meld with an entrance wall topped by a trio of pointed porticolike constructions, each with three lower levels of loggias, two of these continuing around the building, one side of which has little shops built into its arcade. The interior—its Baroque décor comes as a surprise—has a choir whose inlaid-wood stalls delineate Este adventures, and paintings by Guercino and the Ferrarese masters, Garofalo and Sebastiano Filippi, best known of the Filippi family of painters, and called Bastianino; you'll see his work all around town.

Museo del Duomo (Piazza Cattedrale) is requisite if only for its paintings—an *Annunciation* and a *St. George* by Ferrara's most celebrated painter, Renaissance master Cosimo Turà. A Della Quercia sculpture, *Madonna and Child,* is memorable, too, as are a dozen reliefs—they had been on a cathedral door—one for each month of the year.

Palazzo di Schifanoia (Via Scandiana) is a fair walk east from Piazza Castello (detour en route to Via Savonarola—a good way to see that venerable street), but you want to take it in. It was built by a pleasure-loving Este as a kind of retreat from rigors of state in the Castello. The façade of red brick is accented by a typically Renaissance front door. What you see inside are a dozen-plus second-floor rooms, with special treats the remaining frescoes by two top Ferrara painters—Francesco del Cossa and Ercole dei Roberti—in Salone dei Mesi (Salon of the Months), with those for March, April, June, August, and September the finest; each an interpretation—full of detail, drama, and color—of the way life was lived in Renaissance Ferrara. A mixed bag *Museo Civico* is in connection—with its range coins and pottery, manuscripts and bronzes, the lot anticlimactic after those fabulous frescoes.

Palazzo dei Diamanti (Corso Ercole d'Este 21): The reference in the title is not to actual diamonds, but rather to the remarkable façade of this fifteenth-century palace that is surfaced with 8500 diamond-faceted squares of marble. As if that were not enough, the principal art museum, *Pinacoteca Nazionale,* is inside. There are appealing paintings, many of Ferrara origin. Zero in on stars of the show: *Death of the Virgin* by the Venetian master Carpaccio; a pair of works by Cosimo Turà that had been part of a church altarpiece; *Madonna with Saints* by Tintoretto; Dosso Dossi's *Rest on the Flight into Egypt.*

Palazzo di Lodovico il Moro (Via XX Settembre 124) is an early-sixteenth-century masterwork, worth visiting if only for its smasher of a delicately arched, two-level courtyard, and original ceilings and frescoes of its Sala del Tesoro, or Treasure Room. But there's another draw:

Ferrara's *Museo Nazionale Archeologico,* its special treasure a cache of pottery from the nearby ruined Etruscan city of Spina, at its height between the sixth and third centuries B.C., and imported by the Etruscans from Greece, with which they had close contact. A dozen rooms brim with vases, footed bowls and kraters, their terra-cotta-and-black decorations still vivid. And there's a bonus of gold jewelry—rings and necklaces, bracelets, and, most memorable, a delicate diadem, the lot from Spina tombs.

Casa Romei (Via Savonarola 28) went up as the town house for an Este relative in the mid-fifteenth century (Lucrezia Borgia, buried across the street—see below—was a frequent visitor, as indeed was Cardinal Ippolito II d'Este, who built Villa d'Este at Tivoli outside of Rome [chapter 2]). Today, alas, there is no furniture, but compensation enough in other respects—beautiful courtyard, range of rooms with original frescoes, many by the prolific local Filippi family; marbles and tablets from Ferrara buildings.

Monastero del Corpus Domini e le Tombe Estense (Via Pergolato 4) is a near-neighbor of Casa Romei (above). It is the fifteenth-century convent of a band of cloistered nuns who, despite vows of seclusion, admit visitors (you must ring the ancient doorbell and wait some minutes for a sister to open up) intent on seeing, in the convent's adjacent church, tombs of a slew of Este luminaries, not the least of which is that of the beautiful Lucrezia Borgia, infamous thanks to both a Donizetti opera and a Victor Hugo play about her life. Daughter of Pope Alexander VI, she had her first marriage to a scion of the powerful Sforza family annulled, and by arrangement with her brother Cesare, her second husband was murdered. It was Spouse No. 3—Duke Alfonso d'Este—who brought her to Ferrara and to his luminary-packed court, where she played an active part until her death in 1519. A nun behind a grille watches as you inspect the tombs, and gives you a brochure about them, as you depart.

Palazzina Marfisa d'Este (Corso della Giovecca 170): Don't let its low-slung façade discourage you. This onetime residence of Principessa Marfisa d'Este—illegitimate daughter of one Este and wife of still another—is the only Este residence you'll visit that's furnished. In addition to its sixteenth-century pieces, there are paintings and frescoes by—you will not be surprised at this point—members of the Filippi clan. Fireplaces are handsome, and there's a fountain-centered garden.

Basilica di Santa Maria in Vado (Via Borgo Vado 3) is the most spectacular of Ferrara churches, with a somber enough Renaissance façade, but an opulent interior, in part designed and executed by the Ferrarese painter Ercole dei Roberti. Look up—the coffered ceiling contains four massive paintings embedded in gilded frames. Then take in the art of the side and high altars, with the four paintings of the latter, especially a *Nativity* by Domenico Mona, surely the most sublime.

SETTLING IN

Ripagrande Hotel (Via Ripagrande 21) is among the better-looking of its category—anywhere in Italy: a clutch of contiguous Renaissance palazzi with smashing public spaces, their original wood beams and natural brick walls complementing antique furnishings. The 40 rooms are something else again—stark modern, with well-equipped baths. There's a bar-lounge and a restaurant worthy of comment in a later paragraph. Central. *First Class.*

Duchessa Isabella Hotel (Via Palestro 70), some blocks north of the Duomo, occupies a romantic fifteenth-century palace, with close to 30 full-facility rooms, restaurant, and bar. Special. *First Class.*

Touring Hotel (Viale Cavour II) has a perky, up-to-date ambience, almost 40 rooms with bath, bar-lounge, breakfast but no restaurant, and a situation a hop and skip from Castello Estense. *Moderate.*

Astra Hotel (Viale Cavour 35) is a traditional-style house, with baths in the majority of its 80 rooms. A bar edges the lobby-lounge; breakfast but no restaurant. Fairly central. *Moderate.*

Europe Hotel (Corso Giovecca 49) is nicely located on the main shopping street, delightfully old-fashioned in the best sense of the term, with a capacious lounge to which a bar is attached, baths in 35 of its 48 rooms, breakfast service and a caffè with outdoor tables, but no proper restaurant. *Moderate.*

DAILY BREAD

Vecchia Chitarra (Via Ravenna 13; Phone 62-204) is an immediately welcoming old-timer, with busily decorated walls—wine bottles, hand-painted plates, copper pots—crowding its walls, tempting tables of antipasti, and an interesting menu, with admirable pastas (try tagliatelle with Bolognese—meat and tomato—sauce) and hearty entrées. Ask if filetti di tacchino—turkey as you will not have had it at home—is on the day's menu. *First Class.*

Ripa (Via Ripagrande 22; Phone 34-942) is a part of the uncommonly attractive Ripagrande Hotel complex (above) and the fare is as appealing as the décor. Open, perhaps, with cappellacci di zucca, a pumpkin-filled species of ravioli, continuing with spiedini di carne alla griglia—Ferrarese mixed grill. This is a restaurant where you may want to have dessert: worth the calories. Fine wines. *First Class.*

Centrale (Via Boccaleone 8; Phone 35-160) is modest in look yet appealing, in large part due to the smiles of its young owning-operating family. Tortellini in brodo—filled pasta in broth—makes a bracing beginning to a meal that might proceed with, say, scaloppa al vino bianco, veal scaloppine in white wine sauce, a simpler grilled paillard of veal, or a beefsteak. *Moderate.*

Piper (Corso Porto Reno 22; Phone 37-423) is indicated when you crave a pizza fix. The Italians' favorite—plain cheese—is good here, but there is a choice of toppings. *Moderate.*

Caffè Cicognani (Corso Martiri di Libertà 68) is heart-of-the-shopping-action; join the foot-weary for an espresso, a drink, and, perhaps, a pastry. *Moderate.*

SOUND OF MUSIC

Teatro Comunale, Ferrara's white-and-gold, eighteenth-century opera house, has annual seasons of opera, ballet, and concerts and prints advance schedules, obtainable from the tourist office.

INCIDENTAL INTELLIGENCE

Further information: Ente Provinciale per il Turismo, Piazza Municipale 19, Ferrara.

13

Florence/Firenze

Heritage of the Medici

BACKGROUND BRIEFING

Florence rates E for Effortless. In no other major Italian city is it as easy to achieve a satisfying holiday. Even Italians from other cities—who do not easily enthuse about towns not their own—become misty-eyed about Florence. The French have not forgotten that Catherine de' Medici took chefs with her from Florence when she went to become Henry II's bride thereby laying the groundwork for the estimable French cuisine. The English remember that Florence was Destination No. 1 on the Grand Tour. (One reason was that its hotels were the cleanest.) Germans, who do more intensive holiday homework than all the rest of us combined, have every Pitti Palace painting committed to memory before they step off the train. Scandinavians, pushovers for all things Italian, are at their most vulnerable in Florence. As for Americans, we have been enthusiasts, if not for as long as the English, with quite as much intensity.

Several factors contribute to the sense of well-being that one feels almost upon arrival. Size, first. Even though it's bigger in area than many of us allow ourselves to discover, it doesn't *seem* big; the scale is intimate. We feel that we can come to grips with this city without strain, rarely finding the need to get about other than on foot—often alongside pairs of nattily uniformed police, astride horses and with long silver swords at their sides. Efficiency is another factor. Florentines are nothing if not well educated and organized, and at ease with foreigners.

A jumble of names evokes the splendor of Florence: Medici dukes and even Medici popes, historic figures like Savonarola and Machiavelli, bankers like the Strozzi and Riccardi families, artists like Giotto, Fra

Angelico, Leonardo, Michelangelo, Raphael, Lippi, Botticelli; sculptors like Donatello and Cellini; writers like Dante and Boccaccio; architects like Brunelleschi and Michelozzo.

But Florence had a quite respectable history even before it gave birth to the Renaissance. We need only travel up to the still beautiful village of Fiesole, high on a minimountain overlooking the city and the Arno, to appreciate how easy it is to visualize what had gone before.

It was in Fiesole that Florence had its beginning. Early-bird Etruscans had established a settlement there, and eventually some of their number descended the hill to the shores of the river and settled in. When Romans headed north it was at the Etruscan settlement that they camped. Ere long the Arno village had a name, *Florentia:* "destined to flourish."

And so it did. Christianity was widespread by the fifth century. (Its earliest missionary was the same Saint Miniato for whom a splendid Florence church is named.) Progress was interspersed with war and with invasion. Florence was to know Goths and Byzantines and Lombards before, in the twelfth century, it became a *comune,* ripe for thirteenth-century emergence into the alliterative, albeit confusing, era of Guelphs and Ghibellines—antagonists who fought for control of the city. Which was which? Guelphs (with the shorter name) were papists and the more democratic of the two groups, while Ghibellines (the longer name) were on the side of the longer-titled Holy Roman Emperor. Matters became more complex when victorious Guelphs split into Black and White factions (with Blacks, among other things, expelling Dante because he was White). All this transpired while merchants, bankers, and manufacturers' guilds enriched the city.

There were losses (more than half the populace died in the fourteenth-century Black Death) and gains (Florence warred with and won control of cities like Pisa and Arezzo). Eventually it took the form of a republic, in which a remarkable family called Medici achieved power. Time was the fifteenth century (the Century of the Medici, as it came to be known) and the first major Medici was Cosimo the Elder. The best of the Medici succeeding him were, like himself, strong-willed, dictatorial, and patrons of the arts. In importance after Cosimo the Elder came his grandson, Lorenzo the Magnificent.

The Renaissance continued for two brilliant Florentine centuries, which did not preclude political turbulence. Lorenzo put down a plot hatched by Pope Sixtus IV and the family was expelled during the rule of his son Piero, to be succeeded for four years by Savonarola, the priest who got himself into such trouble with his anticorruption, anti-worldliness campaign that he was hanged as a heretic.

The Medici made a comeback, first as dukes of Florence, later as grand dukes of all Tuscany, until the last of the line died in the early eighteenth century. The House of Lorraine–Hapsburg took over (the

Napoleonic era excepted) until Florence became not only an intrinsic part of the new United Kingdom of Italy in 1861, but, in 1865, its capital, following Turin (chapter 35). Today's visitors may see the throne room in the State Apartments of the Pitti Palace, seat of the royal family until 1871, when it moved to Quirinale Palace—from which the popes were displaced—in Rome.

ON SCENE

Lay of the Land: No major Italian city is easier to get about, and, more often than not, by foot. Principal landmark is the Arno River. But unlike cities that are nearly bisected by a river, the bulk of Florence is on a single bank—the north (or "right") side of the Arno. Eight bridges span the river; of these, *Ponte Vecchio* is the most picturesque, easiest to distinguish, and most central. The heart of town has three principal squares. *Piazza del Duomo* fronts the cathedral. One may walk south from it, along *Via dei Calzaiuoli* to Via Speziali, and then head west to *Piazza della Repubblica,* the busiest commercial square, leading along *Via Strozzi, to Via Tornabuoni,* principal shopping street. Returning by Piazza della Repubblica to Via dei Calzaiuoli, one may proceed south, a few blocks, to historic *Piazza della Signoria,* whose landmark is spindly-towered Palazzo Vecchio. Cross shop-lined Ponte Vecchio, over the Arno, and in a few moments you've arrived at the *Palazzo Pitti* museum and *Giardini di Boboli,* formal gardens that constitute Florence's finest park. To the east lies elevated *Piazzale Michelangelo,* affording fine views of the city. Back on the right bank, walk north on Via dei Servi, from Piazza del Duomo, to reach *Piazza Annunziata* and the church it takes its name from and nearby Piazza San Marco, with the *Church and Museum of San Marco* and neighboring *Galleria dell' Accademia.* Walk west from Piazza del Duomo, on Via de' Pecori, Via d' Aglio, and Via del Trebbio (one leading into the other) and within a few minutes *Piazza Santa Maria Novella*—and the major church for which it is named—is reached, with *Piazza della Stazione* and the railway station beyond.

THE ESSENTIAL FLORENCE

The Duomo complex (Piazza del Duomo) is not without surprises. It is at once medieval Florence (work began on the Duomo near the end of the thirteenth century) and, if one might use the term in Italy, Victorian; the façade is third-quarter nineteenth century. The painter Giotto was one of the building's early designers. The intricately worked dark and light marble design is joyous and eye-catching, and the adjacent campanile is quite as elegant as befits a Giotto work. But it is the overscaled

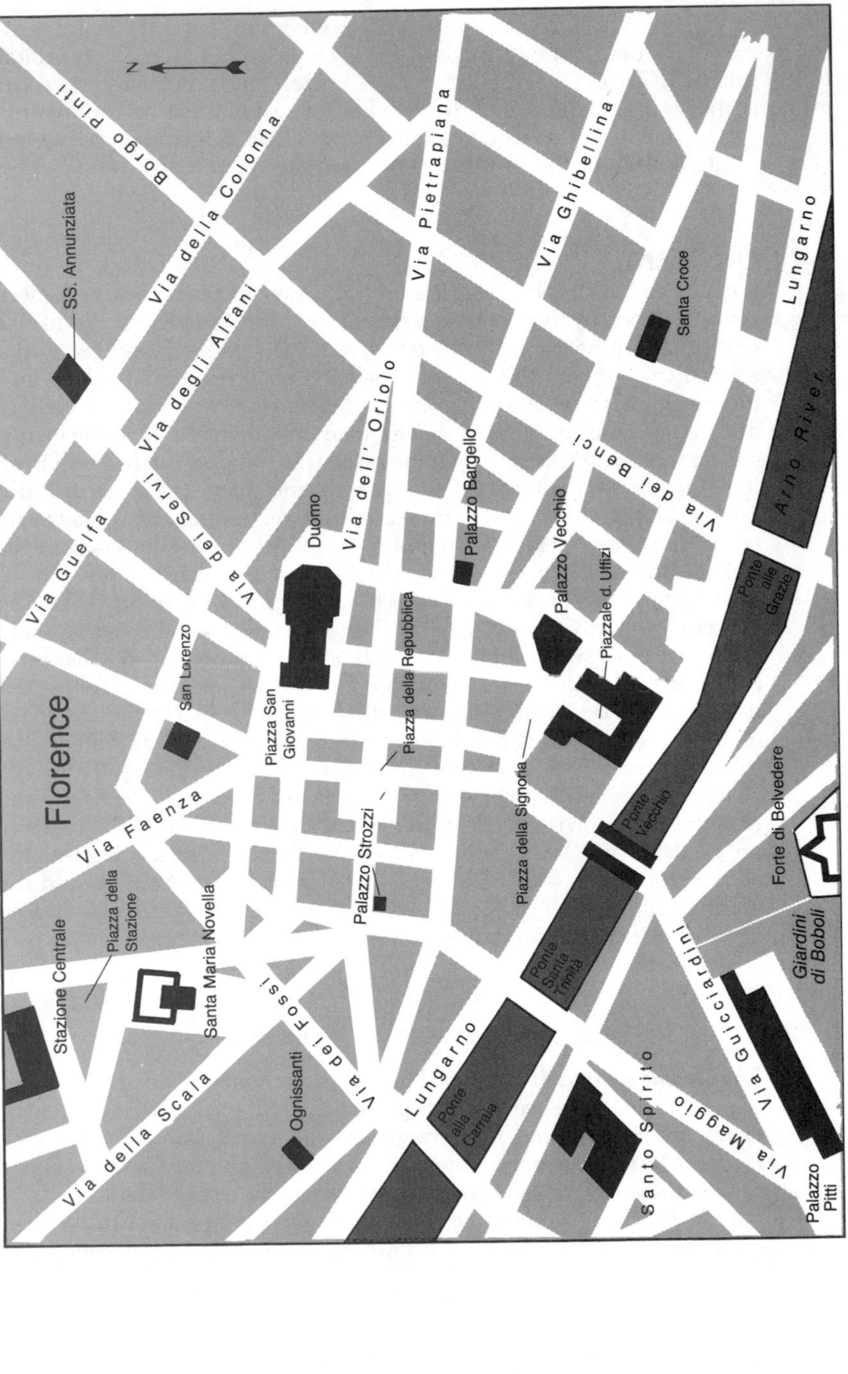
Florence
N
Borgo Pinti
Via della Colonna
SS. Annunziata
Via degli Alfani
Via Pietrapiana
Via Ghibellina
Santa Croce
Lungarno
Via dell' Oriolo
Via dei Servi
Via Guelfa
Duomo
Palazzo Bargello
Palazzo Vecchio
Via dei Benci
Arno River
Ponte alle Grazie
Piazzale d. Uffizi
San Lorenzo
Piazza San Giovanni
Piazza della Repubblica
Via Faenza
Piazza della Stazione
Stazione Centrale
Santa Maria Novella
Palazzo Strozzi
Piazza della Signoria
Ponte Vecchio
Forte di Belvedere
Giardini di Boboli
Ponte Santa Trinità
Via dei Fossi
Ognissanti
Via della Scala
Lungarno
Ponte alla Carraia
Santo Spirito
Via Guicciardini
Via Maggio
Palazzo Pitti

351-foot-high Brunelleschi-designed dome that is the Duomo's glory. Inside, though, the building, despite splendid scale, is gloomily anticlimactic. Move over, then, to the octagonal baptistry—well over a millennium in age, and Florence's cathedral before the current Duomo was erected. It is not always easy when there are groups of observers, but try to tarry at the trio of bronze doors. They are fourteenth- and fifteenth-century, with the choicest the east, or Paradise Door; its ten panels depict Old Testament stories and took their creator—a sculptor named Lorenzo Ghiberti—more than a quarter century to complete. But there's more: a brilliant mosaic Christ embellishing the dome within.

Palazzo Vecchio and Ponte Vecchio: This pair of landmarks represents the secular city much as it was in the Middle Ages. The silhouette of Palazzo Vecchio—a pinnacle-like tower jutting upward from a crenelated stone box (which in recent seasons has happily remained open nonstop 9 A.M.–7 P.M. weekdays, along with the Uffizi Gallery, below)—is itself evocative. Within, this onetime Medici residence embodies the lavishness of the Renaissance, with its Salone del Cinquecento—the biggest room in town (72 feet by 1 74 feet) but, more important, it's the most ravishing. Nearly two-score ceiling frescoes—each framed in gold—depict Florence's history. So do frescoes on the walls. And there is a startling Michelangelo sculpture called *Victory.* Ponte Vecchio is indeed an old bridge, originally eleventh century. Since the seventeenth century, the shops that have always lined its lanes have been mostly those of dealers in gold, silver, and jewels. It is under the Vecchio that we still find a corridor connecting the Uffizi and Pitti palaces, dating back centuries, when it was devised as an escape route for palace occupants wanting to get from one palace to the other in an emergency.

Four great museums: Bargello, Uffizi, Pitti, San Marco: *Il Museo Nazionale Bargello* (Via del Proconsolo) is not the most reputed of Florence museums, it is the most evocative of the medieval city; that is why I lead off with it. Formidable from without, with a single corner tower and Gothic windows, it is somberly grand within and, as would befit a long-time police chief's palace, with prisoners' cells. A vaulted downstairs hall opens into an arcaded courtyard whose stone stairwell leads to upper chambers. Exhibits are eye-popping, most especially the sculptures by Donatello (this is where one sees his bronze *David*), Michelangelo (a *David* of his, too), a bronze *Mercury* by Giambologna, lovely Della Robbias, and among much more a frescoed chapel with its treasure the death mask of Florence-born Dante.

Galleria degli Uffizi (Piazzale degli Uffizi) takes its name from the building it occupies—a U-shaped stunner that went up in the sixteenth century at the behest of Cosimo I, the Medici grand duke of the moment, who sensibly decreed that all government offices, or uffizi, be combined into a single headquarters, and that there be space, as well, for his works of art. And so began what is one of the world's finest art museums, and certainly the most important in Italy, with samplings of the whole range of Italian painting, Middle Ages through Renaissance. There are moving medieval masterworks—innovative Cimabues, Giotto with his pioneering interpretation of perspective, and on along the line—Uccello, Mantegna, Correggio, Filippo Lippi (who was Botticelli's teacher), Botticelli himself (his *Birth of Venus* is probably the most reproduced of Uffizi paintings), Leonardo, Giovanni Bellini, the earlier-mentioned Vasari portrait of Lorenzo the Magnificent, Michelangelo's noted *Holy Family*, a Raphael interpretation of one of the two Medici popes—Leo X, with a pair of cardinals—and Titian's exquisite *Venus of Urbino*. There are standout foreigners, too, including Rembrandt, Van der Weyden, Cranach, Memling, Velázquez, Dürer, Van Cleve, and Holbein. You will stay a solid day and want to return, but for this you will pay more than in other Italian museums. Still, the stiffer tab is undoubtedly what has made possible the Uffizi's pioneering, Italy-wide lead as the first museum to be open nonstop, day-long—Tuesday through Saturday 9 A.M.–7 P.M., with shorter Sunday and holiday hours. But even with these hours, the eminence of the Uffizi is such that, once inside, you must count on the possibility of lines for those rooms with the most celebrated paintings, unless you go at the tail end of the day when—in my experience, at least—you may be virtually alone, admiring masterwork after masterwork, in gallery after solitary gallery of the palace that shelters what is surely Italy's single most satisfying collection of paintings.

Palazzo Pitti is for me the most beautiful in town. It is just across Ponte Vecchio from the Uffizi, straddling the formal Boboli Gardens, and it shelters three museums as well as the former Royal Apartments. I don't know of any museum where art is displayed in a more opulent environment, one knock-'em-dead Renaissance reception room after another displays a collection that dates back to an initial group provided by Grand Duke Cosimo II (grandson of the Uffizi's Cosimo I). There are foreign stars here—a Murillo *Madonna and Child*, a Van Dyck cardinal, Rubens's *Four Philosophers*, a Velázquez (Philip IV on horseback). But the collection is mostly Italian Renaissance—Lippi, Raphael, Fra Bartolommeo, Titian, Perugino, many Del Sartos. You will be able to see the gold-and-ivory state dining room, the crimson throne room, the chapel with its paintings, in the Royal Apartments. And you'll stroll past sculpture (a chubby *Bacchio* is Florence's answer to Brussels's *Mannekin Pis*), and the amphitheater of Boboli Gardens.

Museo di San Marco (Piazza San Marco), last of my quartet, is the most moving experience of the lot, a purely Florentine adventure at once leading into realms of architecture, religion, politics, and art. It is the only one-man show in town—a former monastery commissioned by no less eminent a Medici than Cosimo the Elder. Architect was the prolific Michelozzo, order was the Dominican, and the interior designer was a resident monk originally called Vicchio di Mugello, whose work earned him the name—sanctioned by the church—of Blessed, or Beato, Angelico, which comes through to us as Fra Angelico. Adjacent to a church of the same name (below), San Marco is first seen through Michelozzo's cloister. One ascends, then, to the upper floor, and in cell after convent cell (including those inhabited by the fanatic monk Savonarola and, in the course of prayer retreats, Cosimo the Elder) there are Angelico masterworks—extraordinarily beautiful people, with the oddly gentle quality peculiar to Angelico, against a background of his lovely, luminous colors. The founder of his order, St. Dominic, has surely never been better portrayed. But there are so many more: *Annunciation, Transfiguration, Coronation of the Virgin, Flight into Egypt, The Last Supper,* our favorite Christmas cards, every one.

A trio of churches: Santa Croce, Santa Maria Novella, San Lorenzo complex: If Florence has a single most beloved church it is *Santa Croce* (Piazza Santa Croce), the Franciscans' showplace (and the largest of their churches anywhere) that is at once a place of worship, an art museum both in its sanctuary and in a separate building, and a burial ground of distinguished Italians. Friars have been on the scene since 1212 and are fond of pointing out that their church has known such visitors over the centuries as St. Francis, St. Anthony, and several popes. Santa Croce warrants geographic orientation. There is the church proper, and there is the adjacent monastery area (entered from the right), which embraces both First and Second Cloisters. Pazzi Chapel and the church's art museum are in the former; the latter is a Brunelleschi-designed masterwork, where friars live as they have for centuries. The Gothic church is monument enough. But there are nearly three hundred tombs and cenotaphs. Michelangelo's tomb was designed by Vasari in the late sixteenth century. Donatello's sculpted *Annunciation* is one of his finest works. There is not one but a pair of chapels—Bardi and Peruzzi—decorated with Giotto frescoes. The earlier-mentioned Pazzi Chapel was designed by Brunelleschi, and its interior is a veritable gallery of Della Robbia ceramics. The museum has treasures by Cimabue, Giotto, Donatello, and Bronzino. (And there is a leather-goods shop, with wares made by students of the church's leather school.)

Santa Maria Novella (Piazza Santa Maria Novella) is the Dominican counterpart of the Franciscans' Santa Croce: a Gothic monument—massive and magnificent—that also is a repository of art treasures. Like its Franciscan counterpart, it dates to the thirteenth century. The Strozzi Chapel—named for an important Florentine family—is resplendent with frescoes by Filippino Lippi. Still another chapel has Ghirlandaio frescoes, and there are masterful wooden crucifixes by both Giotto and Brunelleschi. Then comes the cloisters, operated—please note—as a municipal museum with precise open hours and an admission charge. Principal reason for one's visit is the Spanish Chapel—so called because the town's Spanish colony once used it as a place of worship—with a series of murals believed to be the work of Andrea di Buonaiuto, in which the history of the Dominican order—black-and-white-robed friars appear throughout—is celebrated in infinite detail.

San Lorenzo complex is triple-threat. First comes the church, off the piazza bearing its name, with an unfinished façade, apparently still awaiting the execution of Michelangelo's design for it. It's a Renaissance work by Brunelleschi, with a Michelangelo loggia, pulpit and other work by Donatello, a Bronzino fresco, and a Filippo Lippi *Annunciation* in its Martelli Chapel. Brunelleschi's domed sacristy designated as Old to contrast it with a newer one later described—is adjacent. Church and Old Sacristy inspected, one exits to the piazza, walks to its left through a cloister to a stairwell that leads to the second major aspect of the complex: the *Laurentian Library,* designed by Michelangelo, who was also creator of the unique stairway leading to it; I urge you to study the steps before you mount them—no one seems ever to have copied them. The library is a great oblong of a room, fitted with Michelangelo-created furnishings and containing illuminated manuscripts. Next come the *Medici Chapels,* requiring an exit without, and entrance from Piazza Madonna degli Aldobrandini. No single Florence destination more strikingly conveys the power of the Medici. The Princes' Chapel is a marble mausoleum with tombs of half a dozen Medici rulers. From it one moves along to the New Sacristy. In contrast to the multicolored marbles of the Princes' Chapel, it is neoclassic Michelangelo, with an uncompleted tomb and two completed tombs—one of Lorenzo de' Medici, Duke of Urbino (and Lorenzo the Magnificent's grandson), and the other of Giuliano de' Medici, Duke of Nemours, and a son of the Magnificent Lorenzo, each with statues of the deceased and allegorical sculpture surrounding.

A drive to Fiesole: Older than Florence, and superseded by it as long ago as the Roman occupation, Fiesole—atop a little mountain a few miles northeast of town—makes for a diverting excursion. It can be taken in comfortably in a sunny morning or afternoon. What one first wants to do is ascend the hill leading from its main square to a rest stop named for a stone visitors' bench—*Banchina.* The pause is as much for the spectacular view of Florence, way below, as to catch one's breath, before continuing farther upward, beyond the little *Church of Sant' Alessandro* (really ancient, dating to the fifth century) to the *Church of San Francesco,* early Gothic, art-filled, with a honey of a cloister, even a little museum whose theme is the Franciscans' missionary activity in the Orient. Descend, then, all the way to the town's principal square, *Piazza Mino da Fiesole.* What one wants to inspect in this quarter is the remarkable Romanesque Duomo—dating all the way back to the eleventh century; a surprise of an amphitheater that is an intact souvenir of the Roman era and adjacent to a little museum of local Roman artifacts; and *Museo Bardini,* a small but worthy repository of assorted local treasures, none great perhaps, but all with the patina of age. Pause, then, at Piazza Mino da Fiesole, for coffee.

BEYOND THE BASICS: SELECTED MUSEUMS

Galleria dell' Accademia (Via Ricasoli) is where one beelines to see the original of Michelangelo's great *David;* it had remained exposed to the elements in Piazza della Signoria for three and a half centuries when, in 1873, it was finally brought indoors and replaced in the square by a good copy. The original dazzles, but so do other Michelangelo sculptures, including a *Pietà,* this one designated *Palestrina.* There are paintings, too—including work by Botticelli, Lorenzo Monaco, Bernardo Daddi, even Raphael. Location is just across the piazza from Museo San Marco (above), so that it makes sense to take these two museums in on a single visit.

Museo Archeologico (Piazza Annunziata): There are literally scores of galleries devoted to Etruscan art and artifacts, with the setting an atmospheric Renaissance palace. Note, too, the exceptional collection of ancient Egyptian works.

Museo Bardini (Piazza de' Mozzi) is housed in a beautiful early-nineteenth-century mansion, with remarkable ceilings. Its contents are the bequest of a nineteenth-century antique dealer, whose passion was collecting and who knew what he was about. Nothing is labeled, but no matter. There are paintings and portraits, furniture and fragments, a Della Robbia cluster of angels, a polychrome Virgin in red and white garb, *Archangel Michael* in combat with a ferocious dragon, and a gilded medieval crucifix. And very few visitors.

Museo Horne (Via de' Benci 6) is still another private collection in still another stunner of a palace. Mr. Horne was a turn-of-century English collector who restored this elegant thirteenth-century house and filled it with fine things—furniture and furnishings as well as paintings that include a Giotto of San Stefano and works by Masaccio, Daddi, Filippino Lippi—to name some of the choicest. It is seeing the lot in the Horne house that makes the experience memorable.

Museo dell' Opera del Duomo (Piazza del Duomo) houses the cathedral's treasures. Its special lure is a masterful *Pietà* of Michelangelo, for centuries in the Duomo proper, that, at least to this appraiser, is infinitely more moving than his more celebrated *Pietà* in Rome's St. Peter's. A Donatello sculpture of a ravaged *La Maddalena* is easily the second most exciting piece. But there are Byzantine mosaics, medieval paintings, a stone choir carved by Luca Della Robbia, and sculptured saints that once graced the Duomo's campanile.

Museo Stibbert (Via Frederick Stibbert 26) is considerably away from the center, by no means easy to find, and wonderfully, wildly, eccentrically eclectic. Mr. Stibbert was a Victorian Briton who collected compulsively, filling his mock-Moorish palace with a dozen-plus life-size horsemen in Renaissance armor aboard Renaissance steeds; the clothes chosen by Napoleon for his coronation as king of Italy; regalia worn by the military and aristocrats of such lands as India, China, and Japan; rooms full of European and Oriental porcelain; Rococo and Renaissance furniture; and paintings by Titian, Tiepolo, and Longhi. Among much, much more. There are so few visitors that guards welcome those who do come with enthusiasm, if with no foreign-language skills, as they personally tour them about. Mind-boggling.

Museo di Storia della Scienza (Piazza dei Giudici 1) may sound boring—but it isn't. Location is an originally twelfth-century palace. And consider such exhibits as a sixteenth-century brass quadrant, an even older copy of a book by Galileo, globes and glass cones, early telescopes and microscopes, scales and weights. Unlike any other museum of my acquaintance.

BEYOND THE BASICS: PALAZZI

Casa Buonarroti (Via Ghibellina 70): You will have recognized the name as that of Michelangelo's family. I don't know why this structure is termed a *casa*. It is quite as big as many palazzi. More to the point, it is the house that the master bought for his family, which bequeathed it to the municipality in the mid-nineteenth century. A long time before, a descendant of Michelangelo hired a crop of seventeenth-century artists to embellish the house as a memorial. It is today full of Michelangelana and some of his work including marble sculptures and—my favorite—a carved-wood *Crucifixion.*

Palazzo Medici Riccardi (Via Cavour) is a typically sober and somber Florentine Renaissance palace, the model for countless American banks, and designed by Michelozzo for Cosimo the Elder in the fifteenth century. The Riccardi family succeeded the Medici. The prefect of Florence is in contemporary residence. But you are welcome to have a look at the monumental fresco in the chapel—*Il Viaggio dei Magi*—with various Medici luminaries in its cast of beautiful characters, and, as well, sumptuous frescoes of Luca Giordano in the upstairs Galleria.

Palazzo Davanzati (Piazza Davanzati) is also known cumbersomely, though accurately, as Museo della Casa Fiorentina Antica. It's the Middle Ages and early Renaissance in three dimensions, an absolutely enchanting fourteenth-century stone residence—severe in line, vivid with frescoed and stenciled stone walls, ceilings, fireplaces. Three floors of splendidly furnished rooms (including original lavatories) evoke upper-class town life of half a millennium ago. Magical.

Palazzo Strozzi (Piazza Strozzi) is one of the great fifteenth-century houses, named for the powerful merchant family that built it, with a memorable courtyard—look up at the double rows of balconies—and a little basement museum with models of the building's restoration.

BEYOND THE BASICS: SELECTED CHURCHES

Annunziata (Piazza Annunziata) has an unusual arched Renaissance façade. Beneath the elaborately coffered ceiling of the elongated Baroque nave are artworks by a number of masters, most especially Andrea del Sarto. The square is one of the handsomest in town, with another of its occupants, an art-rich hospital, later recommended.

Apostoli (Piazza del Limbo) is intimate in scale, charming of ambience, with a Romanesque stone front. Within, art works include Della Robbia terra cottas.

Carmine (Piazza del Carmine) startles with the utter plainness of its unfinished façade. Walk in, though, and it is richly if not entirely

Baroque. The frescoed ceiling of the nave is a joy. But special treasures are the Masolino and Masaccio frescoes in the Brancacci Chapel—the former, of Adam and Eve, especially beautiful; with exquisite Filippino Lippi works as well, and a don't-miss cloister.

Ognissanti (Piazza Ognissanti) was where Amerigo Vespucci worshiped (it contains his family's tomb) and today, appropriately enough, is the site of English-language masses, traditionally said at ten on Sunday mornings. At any time, this art-rich church warrants inspection. Originally Gothic, it has Ghirlandaio frescoes, handsome sacristy and cloister, and a main altar under a graceful minidome.

Orsanmichele (Via dell' Arte della Lana) looks more like a medieval town house than a house of worship. Statues of saints in wall niches are its only giveaway from without. The interior is compact and ornate, with a number of finely wrought tabernacles the highlights. While you are in the neighborhood, pop into little *San Carlo,* just opposite, and note the fine painting over its altar.

San Firenze (Piazza San Firenze) is striking Baroque, with a coffered ceiling that is among the finest in town and good paintings along either wall of the nave.

San Gaetano (Piazza degli Antinori): Statues filling niches of the gray stone façade of this Baroque beauty catch your attention and draw you inside to the perfectly splendid interior, embracing half a dozen side chapels, with a sculpted Della Robbia *Madonna and Child* in the first chapel on the right. San Gaetano is impressive in scale and dramatic in height.

San Giovanni di Dio (attached to the *spedale,* or hospital, of the same name, on Borgo Ognissanti) is not only handsomely Baroque, but worth knowing about in that masses are traditionally said in English at 10 A.M. on Sundays.

San Marco (Piazza San Marco) is so often overlooked because visitors concentrate on the Fra Angelico frescoes in its monastery-museum (above) that I make mention of it here. Façade is Baroque, and the church embodies refurbishings extending over several centuries. Look for the School of Giotto wooden crucifix and Byzantine mosaics.

San Miniato al Monte (Piazzale Michelangelo) is awesome Romanesque, high on a hill overlooking the city. Its situation alone makes it worth visiting. But then there are the green and white marble façade, a peculiar two-story altar, and—among much art—Paolo Uccello frescoes in the cloister and a mosaic-decorated apse.

Santa Croce (Piazza Santa Croce)—east of the center—is among the city's most beautiful churches. Its big draw is Michelangelo's tomb, but there are, as well, frescoes by Giotto, a sculpted Donatello *Annunciation*, and—among other treasures—a crucifix by Cimabue in the church's museum and a Brunelleschi-designed chapel.

Santa Maria Novella (Piazza Santa Maria Novella) is at once massive, with a dazzler of a main altar, extra-wide nave, and fabulously frescoed walls. Note Ghirlandaio's *St. John the Baptist* and the thirteenth-century Strozzi chapel, with a golden altar.

Santa Trinità (Piazza Santa Trinità) could stand alone, aesthetically, on its Gothic interior. But you want to zero in on the Renaissance art. There is a luminous *Annunciation* (note the extraordinary height of the lily carried by the kneeling angel) by Neri di Bicci; still another by Lorenzo Monaco; and—most significant—frescoes in Cappella Sassetti by Ghirlandaio, including *Adoration of the Magi.*

Santo Spirito (Piazza Santo Spirito) has a stucco façade, Baroque and pleasing. Within, it is somber Renaissance, with Corinthian columns flanking a central nave. There's a precious Lippi *Madonna and Saints* and a similarly titled painting by Lorenzo Credi.

A FLORENTINE MISCELLANY

Forte Belvedere is a near neighbor of earlier-recommended Church of San Miniato al Monte and below-recommended Piazzale Michelangelo; all three can be taken in on a single journey. The Belvedere is a sixteenth-century military complex, dramatically sited and architecturally striking.

Galleria delle Spedale degli Innocenti (Piazza SS. Annunziata) is the No. 1 panorama spot, on a hill across the Arno from the main part of town, with views of river, bridge, and skyline from a broad terrace; earlier recommended Forte Belvedere and the Church of San Miniato al Monte are near neighbors.

Sinagoga (Via Farini): Florence's synagogue is elegant, opulent, and Byzantine-style, with an interior rich in mosaics and frescoes. Topped by a green copper dome, it dates back about a century.

Villas: The Medici and other rich Renaissance families were very big on country homes as a change of pace from their town palaces; indeed, they were European innovators in this respect. A number of these beautiful—and beautifully situated—villas are just outside of town, and visitable, but with limited open hours in recent seasons. (Double-check before you go by phoning the Agriturist organization at 55-287-838.) One—a few miles north of the city—is *Villa della Petraia,* with very grand reception rooms, exceptional Flemish and French tapestries, an immense terraced garden, and fine views of the city. Its near neighbor is *Villa di Castello,* whose first landlord was Lorenzo the Magnificent. See both the rich interiors and the fountain-embellished gardens.

Arezzo, an easy 45-mile journey from Florence, is based on *Piazza Grande,* framed by multiepoch porticos, palaces, and the Romanesque *Church of Santa Maria della Pieve,* brilliant of façade, with a Pietro Lorenzetti high-altarpiece. Nearby is the *Duomo,* in an enchanting piazza bearing its name, its principal treasure a Piero della Francesca fresco, which will prepare you for an entire series of Della Francesca works covering three walls of the *Church of San Francesco* (Piazza San Francesco). Break for lunch at venerable *Ristorante Buca di San Francesco* (Phone 23-271; *First Class*), on the square taking the church's name, proceeding then to *Palazzo Bruni Ciocchi* (Via Garibaldi), in whose Renaissance halls is a cache of paintings by such masters as Signorelli and Vasari, Magnasco and Rosa.

Montecatini, 25 miles from Florence, is the quintessential Italian spa town, a still-grand counterpart of, say, Germany's Baden-Baden, packed with Europeans who come simply to unwind or take a cure. There are seven monumental *stabilimenti termali,* or bathhouses (*Tettuccio,* ancient Roman in style, with an atmospheric caffè and adjacent gardens is the most spectacular) in the *Bagni di Montecatini* quarter, at the terminus of shop-, restaurant-, and caffè-lined *Viale Verdi,* the main street, on which there's a branch of the *Gucci* chain (leather, gifts), *Ceramica Montecatini* (porcelain, alabaster eggs), and *Beppina*—one of a number of shops with locally produced table linens. Branches of *Cartier, Gianfranco Ferre, Fendi,* and *Gianni Versace* are on Corso Matteotti. *Museo della Medaglia* (Viale della Libertà) surprises with exhibits that include composer Giuseppe Verdi's piano; scores of still another composer—Puccini; correspondence of the great tenor Caruso; and no less than half a dozen paintings by the Spanish master Joan Miró—a gift of the artist. *Grand Hotel e la Pace* (Via della Torretta 1; *Luxury*) could easily be the setting for a Henry James novel and is no less than one of the most beautiful hotels in Italy (it's a member of Leading Hotels of the World) with sumptuous main-floor lounges, a delightful bar, excellent restaurant, and 150 no-two-alike rooms, a good portion of which are individually decorated suites. Other worthy hotels that I've inspected—and this is a town full of hotels, worth knowing about when nearby Florence is jam-packed—include the lovely, 100-room *Hotel Locanda Maggiore* (Piazza del Popolo)—the oldest in town, deftly updated with an exceptionally good-looking early-nineteenth-century main lounge *(First Class)*; and the central 85-room *Hotel Ercolini and Savi* (Via San Martino 18, *Moderate*). *San Francesco* (Corso Roma; Phone 79-632) is a reliable *First Class* restaurant, quite central; *Cascina Igea* (Viale Verdi 82) is a pleasant Moderate restaurant-caffè; and there are concerts and other entertainment at Viale Verdi's *Teatro Verdi*. Cure or no cure, it is fun to relax, window-shopping, and caffè-hopping.

SETTLING IN

Adriatico Hotel (Via Maso Finiguerra 9) is a neat-as-a-pin, essentially modern house (eighteenth-century Venetian furniture is scattered about for contrast) with 110 pleasant rooms, all with bath or shower; restaurant and bar. Between the railway station and the Arno. *Moderate.*

Anglo American Hotel (Via Garibaldi 9) is an old-timer beloved of Anglos and Americans. There are 130 lovely rooms with bath, gracious lobby-cum-bar, a honey of a crystal chandelier–illuminated restaurant, and a nice situation. *First Class.*

Astoria Hotel (Via del Giglio 9) occupies a capacious sixteenth-century palazzo (you must insist on seeing the party room with a Luca Giordano ceiling fresco, and the lavishly Baroque Salone dei Seicento) and has 90 bath-equipped rooms (some with super views of the Duomo), restaurant, cocktail lounge, with the Medici Chapel its near neighbor. Atmospheric. *First Class.*

Augustus Hotel (Vicolo dell' Oro 5) is tucked into the heart of town near Ponte Vecchio. There's a winning lobby-lounge-bar—Italian Modern at its best—with 67 pleasant rooms, original framed drawings on their walls. Breakfast only. *First Class.*

Balestri Hotel (Piazza Mentana 1) edges the Arno River and has been operated over the past century by four generations of the same family. There are 50 rooms. Breakfast but no restaurant. *Moderate.*

Baglioni Hotel (Piazza Unità Italiana 6): Old-school and of considerable elegance; 215 smart-looking rooms, restaurant (which moves to the roof in summer), bar-lounge. Near the station. *First Class.*

Berchielli Hotel (Lungarno Acciaiuoli 14) is central, recently refurbished throughout, beloved of Americans over an extended period, and with 74 rooms and suites, the most sought-after of which are those with views of the Arno River, just across the street. Congenial lobby-bar, breakfast. Charming. *First Class.*

Bernini Palace Hotel (Piazza San Firenze 29)—just behind Palazzo Vecchio (above) is good-looking, traditional in style, and conveniently central. There are 86 rooms—including very nice twins, a breakfast room where Italy's Parliament assembled when Florence was the capital, and a cozy bar-lounge where you sink into black leather chairs. *First Class.*

Bonciani Hotel (Via Panzani 17) is a venerable, albeit updated, palazzo, still with some original painted ceilings, and with antique furniture scattered about. More than half of the 70 rooms have baths (the bath of Room 214 is a former chapel with a painted ceiling!) and they vary in degree of comfort. Restaurant, bar. Near the station. *Moderate.*

Brunelleschi Hotel (Piazza Santa Elisabetta), a near neighbor of the Duomo, is a comfortable and convenient Florence headquarters. There are 94 rooms and suites, a welcoming restaurant, and a bar-lounge. The hotel is a restored sixteenth-century watchtower. *First Class.*

Calzaiuoli Hotel (Via Calzaiuoli 6) is strategically sited on a heart-of-town pedestrian shopping street. Its traditional façade belies an up-to-the-minute interior, with a pleasant reception-bar area and breakfast room, along with 44 clean-lined rooms, all with modern baths, some with tubs, some with showers. Friendly. *Moderate.*

Classic Hotel (Viale Machiavelli 25), a neighbor of the Boboli Gardens, is a relatively recently restored mansion—note marble floors and decorated ceilings—with just 19 rooms and suites (all are antique-accented), and a pretty garden. Breakfast only. Lovely. *Moderate.*

Continental Hotel (Lungarno Acciaiuoli 2) is a step from Ponte Vecchio. Don't let the tiny lobby throw you off. There's a bar-lounge-breakfast room a flight up, and 67 bath-equipped rooms, with many of them handsome, most especially a duplex tower suite. No restaurant, but a rooftop terrace where summer breakfasts are served. *First Class.*

Croce di Malta Hotel (Via della Scala 7, just off Piazza Santa Maria Novella) is a seventeenth-century convent turned, relatively recently, into a hotel, with 120 no-two-quite-alike bedrooms and duplex suites, a restaurant (reviewed on a later page), casual bar-lounge, dilly of an outdoor-pool-cum-terrace. The lot is a modish meld of the antique with the mod. The staff is delightful. Ask for one of the attractive, spacious rooms overlooking the garden and the pool. Good value. *First Class.*

De la Ville Hotel (Piazza Antinori 1) is at once central, spacious, traditional-style with nearly 80 attractive rooms and a cocktail lounge. Breakfast only. *First Class.*

Le Due Fontane Hotel (Piazza Annunziata 14) overlooks a substantial square near the Duomo. Though it retains its Renaissance façade, the Due Fontane's interiors—including a main-floor lounge edged by a bar and a breakfast room—are contemporary. Bedrooms, all with bath, are either striped-fabric modern or in the style of the eighteenth century. *Moderate.*

Excelsior Hotel (Piazza Ognissanti 3) is the modern-day descendant of Florence's first proper hotel. It opened in 1865, occupying a contiguous pair of Piazza Ognissanti palazzi with Renaissance roots that were joined and refurbished, according to the standards of the era, to function as lodgings for VIP visitors to the capital of unified Italy when the crown and government moved from Turin. Even after Rome became the new capital in 1871, the hotel—Italie by name—continued to thrive for more than half a century to the point where, in 1925, the Swiss owners at the time closed it for a couple of years for a thorough and extensive rebuilding and a new name—Excelsior Italie. In 1958 Ciga Hotels took possession, and in the decades since dropped "Italie" from the title, the while carefully creating a hostelry that has become one of Italy's most prestigious. Grandly Renaissance in style, the Excelsior is based on a ceremonial stairway edging a lobby whose high, chandelier-hung ceiling is supported by marble columns. Go on, then, to a paneled winter restaurant (evaluated on a later page) accented with venerable stained glass; an atmospheric bar-lounge; the restaurant's summer quarters on the Arno-view roof; and 186 rooms along with a score of antique-accented suites (they lead from corridors hung with fine paintings) with superb baths and—in the case of accommodations facing the river, some terraced—memorable panoramas. *Luxury.*

Grand Hotel (Piazza Ognissanti)—an across-the-square neighbor of its sister hotel, the Excelsior (above)—goes back to the closing years of the last century when, as the Hotel Continental Royal de la Paix, and in competition with the Excelsior, it welcomed guests to a building whose high, glass-roofed, palm-cluttered winter garden was the venue for daily mandolin concerts at teatime. Ciga Hotels bought the Grand in 1957, closed it in 1974, eventually reopening in 1986 following a restoration that was slow but splendid. Those of the 107 rooms and suites I have either inhabited or inspected are generous-sized, high-ceilinged, with décor following the style of the early nineteenth century in pastel tones, and with spectacular marble baths. There's a particularly engaging bar and a breakfast room that has to be the handsomest in Florence. Grand guests are welcome to sign meals to their account, at the restaurant of Ciga's Excelsior Hotel (see above) just opposite. *Luxury.*

Jolly Hotel (Piazza Vittorio Veneto 4), away from the center of town, is ultramodern—not unlike so many of the Jolly hotels in the excellent Italy-wide chain, with a cavernous lobby, very good restaurant, rooftop swimming pool that's most welcome in summer, big cocktail lounge, and 150 thoughtfully equipped rooms. *First Class.*

Kraft Hotel (Via Solferino 2) is uncentral (near Teatro Comunale) but attractive; 70 rooms with excellent baths, a restaurant that goes outdoors in summer, cocktail lounge, rooftop pool, and nice touches such as fresh flowers in the corridors. *First Class.*

Loggito dei Serviti Hotel (Piazza SS. Annunziata 3) pleases with its smart interiors, antique-dotted. There are just under 30 quiet rooms. Breakfast only. Location is the square named for the church edging it, somewhat north of the core. *Moderate.*

Londra Hotel (Via Iacopo da Diacceto 16) is restrained-modern in look, with 100-plus rooms with bath, restaurant, bar-lounge. Near the station. *Moderate.*

Lungarno Hotel (Borgo San Jacopo 14) is left-bank, near Ponte Vecchio and Palazzo Pitti, with its rear rooms directly on the water, affording views of the skyline. There are 71 rooms and suites, some with terrace. Attractive lobby and cocktail lounge. Breakfast only. *First Class.*

Mediterraneo Hotel (Lungarno del Tempio 42) is a biggie—334 rooms with bath. Twins tend to be smallish, but they're comfortable; so are singles. Look throughout is ultramod if not distinguished, with a sprawling lobby and restaurant; away from the center. Groups a specialty. *Moderate.*

Michelangelo Hotel (Viale Fratelli Rosselli 2) is good Italian Modern, embracing some 140 handsome rooms (beds are a little narrow), smart public spaces including restaurant and bar-lounge. Near the station. *First Class.*

Minerva Hotel (Piazza Santa Maria Novella 16) has an inspired setting as next-door neighbor to the Church of Santa Maria Novella (above). It occupies a venerable though smartly updated palazzo. There are 110 comfortable rooms with bath, lobby-lounge that looks out on a patio-garden, good restaurant, and rooftop pool that's a joy in summer. Very comfortable indeed. *First Class.*

Pendini Hotel (Via Strozzi 2) is enviably central, with 17 rooms-cum-bath, comfortable public spaces (green plants at every turn), warm ambience. Restaurant and bar-lounge. *Moderate.*

Pensione Bencista (Fiesole) keeps busy with a loyal cadre of regulars—drawn to its pleasant accommodations, stick-to-the-ribs breakfasts and dinners (included in the room rate) and views of Florence from the dramatic on-high location. City buses (there's a stop a hop and a skip distant) connect you with central Florence. Good value. *Moderate.*

Porta Rossa Hotel (Via Porta Rossa 19) is the genuine old-fashioned article, attractive, heart-of-town, and with baths in about a third of its 60 quite simple rooms; congenial bar. Breakfast only. *Moderate.*

Principe Hotel (Lungarno Amerigo Vespucci 34) is a beauty of an eighteenth-century palazzo, river front, near Teatro Comunale. All 21 rooms have bath; intimate bar-lounge, breakfast room with its original painted ceiling, pretty garden. Charm with a capital C. *First Class.*

Regency Hotel (Piazza D'Azeglio) fronts a square some seven or eight blocks east of the Duomo. This is a relatively small house—there are just over 30 rooms and suites—occupying an impressive villa set in a lovely garden of its own. The same talented Amadeo Ottaviani who created Rome's Lord Byron Hotel (chapter 2) employed his good taste in the Regency's interiors—wallpapered, crystal-chandeliered, stained-glass-windowed lounge; paneled restaurant (cuisine is exemplary) with picture windows giving onto the garden; congenial bar; and individually decorated rooms that are essentially contemporary (the use of color—yellow, blues, and greens—is striking) and with fine baths. *Luxury.*

La Residenza Hotel (Via Tornabuoni 8) is agreeable, with cozy bar-lounge, pleasant rooms (14 of the 23 have bath), small restaurant, roof garden. Many guests stay on a demi- or full-pension plan. Location is Florence's smartest shopping street. *Moderate.*

Ritz Hotel (Lungarno della Zecca Vecchia 24) is up to the minute; all 33 of its neat rooms have bath and front ones are river view. There's a lobby-cum-cocktail-lounge. Breakfast but no restaurant. *Moderate.*

Savoy Hotel (Piazza della Repubblica 7): Florence's vibrant main square, a late-nineteenth-century replacement of a demolished quarter that had been the city's ghetto, is caffè-dotted, near the Duomo, as well as shops of Via Tornabuoni, and is the inspired setting for this long-on-scene, traditional-style house that opened in 1893 and has been a hotel ever since, except during part of World War II, when it quartered British Army officers. Named to honor the then-reigning royal house, the Savoy's lures are capacious, high-ceilinged public spaces (the bar is congenial, the restaurant worthy of comment on a later page), alert and smiling concierges who know just about all that is worth knowing about Florence, and comfortable accommodations, with oversized rooms fronting on the square especially delightful, and the ones to aim for. A link of the Ata Hotels chain that is also a member of the Leading Hotels of the World. *Luxury.*

Della Signoria Hotel (Via delle Terme 1) is near the downtown piazza from which it takes its name. There are 32 cheery rooms, all with bath, and a nice traditional feeling. Bar and breakfast, no restaurant. *Moderate.*

Tornabuoni-Beacci Pensione (Via Tornabuoni 3) is almost too elegant to be true—as a pensione, that is. Antique-accented lounge, restaurant, and terrace, 35 rooms with bath, management by the same family for some 60 years, and a location on the principal shopping street. *Moderate.*

Villa la Massa Hotel (in Candelli, a 20-minute drive from town, on the banks of the Arno) embraces a pair of rambling villas; the larger has a covered atrium that is the main lounge. The bar is adjacent, the restaurant is handsome (it moves to a terrace in summer), and the 50 rooms and suites have been individually decorated with a sense of style. Bonuses include a late-hours disco, pool in the garden, fresh flowers everywhere. Ideal for travelers with cars (for those without, the hotel provides minibus transport to town) or for conference groups. *First Class.*

Villa Medici Hotel (Via il Prato 42): Behind an original seventeenth-century façade is a beauty of a 100-room and -suite hotel, with a swimming pool in its ample garden. Lobby is traditional style with an adjacent cocktail lounge; the restaurant moves poolside in summer. Rooms are oversized (ask for a refurbished one) with tile murals in the baths, and a number have terraces. There are sumptuous suites, overlooking the garden. Ambience is intimate, service quite in keeping. Between the station and Teatro Comunale. Member, Leading Hotels of the World. *Luxury.*

Villa San Michele Hotel (Via di Doccia 4, high on the hill of Fiesole, overlooking Florence, with which it's connected by shuttle bus) is hardly without background. Its Renaissance façade is attributed to Michelangelo, and saw a meticulous late-1980s refurbishing, in cooperation with art historians and other experts concerned with protected monuments. Its occupants, from the time of founding in the fifteenth century until the early eighteenth, were Franciscan monks. A New Yorker, Henry Cannon, bought and restored the premises in 1900. It was bomb-damaged in World War II, but in 1950 a Parisian with taste, Lucien Teissier, purchased it with the idea of living in it. His meticulous refurbishing was so costly that M. Teissier conceived the idea of a hotel. And so this exquisite hostelry came about. A sixteenth-century fresco of *The Last Supper* dominates the main lounge. A Della Robbia *Madonna* frames the main stairway. Wines are stored in a cellar dating to the thirteenth century. In summer, the restaurant (worthy of comment on a later page) moves to a loggia, and drinks are served in the sculpture-dotted garden. The 32 rooms and the pair of suites are no-two-alike (some with original fireplaces and canopied beds, all with jacuzzis in their baths). And there's an outdoor swimming pool. An Orient Express Hotel (along with Venice's Cipriani and Portofino's Splendido, in Italy) that's a member of Leading Hotels of the World and is affiliated with Relais et Châteaux. *Luxury.*

DAILY BREAD

Florence is gastronomic as well as political and cultural capital of Tuscany. And as any traveler in Italy learns, every city has its Tuscan restaurant; the food of this region is perhaps the most popular country-wide. There is an admirable penchant for grilled meats; beef is the best in Italy—steaks are super. Broiled chicken is popular too; when well seasoned with garlic, sage, salt, and pepper, it emerges as pollo alla diavola. Fritto misto—composed of seafood elsewhere in Italy—is a meat and vegetable mix in Florence. Beans are deliciously prepared as a basis for soup—zuppa di fagioli—as a vegetable, or in casseroles. Rice has many fans, when made into a risotto—slowly simmered with chicken giblets. Pasta is a pleasure—pappardelle, noodles with hare sauce; a variation on the ravioli theme called agnellotti; Tuscan-style cannelloni, with chicken livers in the filling; and with beans, as pasta e fagioli. Tuscan game dishes—hare and various birds—are notable too.

Anita (Via Parlascio 2; Phone 218-698): Nothing fancy here; the drill chez Anita is good value. Okay soups and pastas. *Moderate.*

Antico Fattore (Via Lambertesca 1; Phone 2381-215) is indicated for a robust lunch after a morning at the nearby Galleria Uffizi. Tasty standbys like minestrones, tortellini bolognese, roast lamb, and grilled chicken breast. *Moderate.*

Il Bargello (Piazza della Signoria 3; Phone 214-071): If it's warm and sunny, you want to take an outdoor table on this splendid square, perhaps making a meal of tomato salad, lasagne, and veal piccata. Very pleasant. *Moderate.*

Caffè Giacosa (Via Tornabuoni 15 at Via degli Strozzi) is packed with Florentines—shoppers and toilers come for cappuccino accompanied by this house's celebrated pastry. *First Class.*

Caffè Giacosa (Via Tornabuoni 23): A shoppers' caffè on a shop-filled street. *Moderate.*

Caffè Gilli (Piazza della Repubblica 9) is indicated for people-watching, the while partaking of refreshment—coffee or tea, sandwiches, ice cream, drinks. Praise to the proprietors: their exterior clock is one of the few such in all Italy, those of railway stations excepted, that indicates the correct time! *First Class.*

Caffè Rivoire (Piazza della Signoria 3—just opposite the palace for which the square is named) could not be more scenically situated. In fine weather, an outdoor table is indicated, for espresso, a snack, and the view. Or move inside—the setting is smart—and consider the makings of a meal. *Moderate/First Class.*

Caffè Scudieri (Piazza San Giovanni) is just opposite the Duomo. Head for the beige-cloth-topped tables at the rear to take a load off your feet. The pastry is delicious. *Moderate.*

Cammillo (Borgo San Jacopo 57; Phone 212-427) buzzes with a mix of affluent locals and visitors. Aged chandeliers illuminate a pair of stucco-walled chambers, hung with good contemporary art. Food is delicious; try fritto di zucchini as a starter, or tortino di carciofi—an artichoke omelet. Rice dishes and pasta are commendable. So is chicken, in a variety of styles. Super service. *First Class.*

Cantinetta Antinori (Piazza Antinori 3) is worth knowing about for snacks in the course of exploration, or simply a glass of wine when you pass by. Near the Duomo. *Moderate.*

Cantinetta di Palazzo Antinori (Piazza Antinori 3; Phone 292-234): A restaurant in Italy that serves no pasta? Well, here's one. Idea is to sample purely Florentine specialties. You may have no more than a panino casalingo, a smallish sandwich—with a glass of wine. But a proper meal might comprise pappa al pomodoro, a thick tomato soup, basil-scented; fagioli all' uccellotto (grilled sausages and beans); or vitello al forno (roast veal). Setting is a high-ceilinged room of a venerable palace, and service is swift. No credit cards. *First Class.*

Il Cantinone (Via Santo Spirito 6; Phone 218-898): Tuscan-accented fare—soups, pastas, poultry, meats, and sweets—beneath an arched brick ceiling. Open for candle-lit dinners. *First Class/Luxury.*

Cava di Milano (Via della Cave 16, Fiesole; Phone 59-133) is lovely in summer, when you're at a table in the garden. Open with pasta, following with a steak. Not dressy. *First Class.*

Il Cestello (Hotel Excelsior, Piazza Ognissanti; Phone 294-301) is framed by an intricately coffered ceiling, accented by vases of fresh flowers, which bring out hues of antique paintings lining the walls.

Open with carpaccio, smoked salmon, or a well-sauced pasta, following with a grilled veal chop or skewered shrimps and cubed sole—a Cestello specialty—or a roast. And if it's summer, take the elevator to the roof; you'll dine under the stars—and memorably. Super service. *Luxury.*

Il Coccodrillo (in the Croce di Malta Hotel with its own entrance at Via della Scala 5; Phone 28-36-22) makes for a pleasant meal—pause when you're in the neighborhood of Piazza Santa Maria Novella. Prosciutto with melon is a refreshing first course, although the choice of pastas is generous, and the grills—of steak, veal, or for that matter, fish—are delicious. Consider bananas flambé for dessert. Friendly. *First Class.*

Dante (Via Verrazano 5; Phone 24-45-28): You've visited Santa Croce Church and overspent in its leather shop. Okay, then, a simple lunch—pasta-based—is indicated at neighboring Dante. *Moderate.*

Dino (Via Ghibellina 51; Phone 241-452) is undistinguished but reliable, with favored standbys like minestrone or stracciatella as soup choices, mixed grill or grilled chicken as entrées, and grainy hunks of Parmesan cheese with coarse bread for dessert. Setting is a series of clean and antiseptic rooms. *Moderate.*

Doney (Piazza Strozzi; Phone 248-206) is at once a proper restaurant and a caffè. If the weather is mild, take a table on the piazza, for coffee, a drink, or lunch. *Moderate.*

Enoteca Pinchiorri (Via Ghibellina 87; Phone 24-27-77) is what you might label Nouvelle Franco-Italiano, and rather elegant, at that, with the nouvelle aspects inspired by the French wife of the owner, who—himself Italian—is responsible for dishes of his country on the bill of fare. Dressy. *Luxury.*

Le Fonticine (Via Nazionale 7; Phone 28-2106) is noteworthy for its own, made-in-house pasta, broiled steaks, and any dishes containing truffles. Gents: a tie is not necessary. *First Class.*

Giannino (Borgo San Lorenzo 31) embraces a self-service section, with pizza among the specialties, and a sit-down restaurant with a standard menu. As I have tried both, it's the self-service section I'm recommending as quick and *Moderate.*

Il Granduca (Via dei Calzaiuoli 57): I defy you to pass this ice-cream parlor by on a hot day. Chocolate and lemon—*mezzo-mezzo,* half and half—is an inspired cone combination. *Moderate.*

Harry's Bar (Lungarno Vespucci 22; Phone 296-6700) is riverfront. There is a popular cocktail lounge (go only for a drink if you like) and a dining room smartly understated in look, with generally swift service and lovely things to eat, most especially the chef's own scampi, several veal—and a number of poultry—dishes. Conclude with Harry's baked-in-house apple tart with cream. Unusually good wine list. *Luxury.*

I Latini (Via Palchetti 28; Phone 210-916): If you enjoy sitting at long tables with strangers (I don't, particularly), you'll like I Latini—casual, with satisfactory fare, and tabs *Moderate.*

Mamma Gina (Borgo San Jacopo 37, on the left bank of the Arno, and not far from Ponte Vecchio; Phone 296-009) used to be a hole-in-the-wall trattoria, with Mamma hopping about, her slip showing and the food delicious. Mamma's slip no longer shows, the place is vastly expanded in size, and it's considerably more attractive. But the food remains exceptional. Minestrone is unbeatable; so are any of the pastas and grills. Always busy. *First Class.*

La Martinicca (Via del Sole 27; Phone 21-89-28) fills the bill when you seek an unassuming spot in the vicinity of Piazza Santa Maria Novella. It's plain but neat, with an alert staff. Ravioli, deliciously sauced, is a specialty, grilled entrecôte, though hardly as choice as pricier bistecca fiorentina, is tasty, and the house Chianti satisfactory. *Moderate.*

La Nandina (Borgo SS. Apostoli 66, at Piazza Trinità) occupies a pair of agreeably decorated rooms, the first with a bar. Start with a plate of Tuscan salami or spaghetti carbonara and go on to the broiled veal chop, veal piccata, beefsteak, or mixed grill. The house's own cakes are indicated for dessert. *First Class.*

Natale (Lungarno Acciaiuoli 80; Phone 21-39-68) is a worth-knowing-about source of middle-category sustenance, in an attractive enough setting, edging the Arno, not far from Ponte Vecchio. Antipasto toscano is a good bet for an opener, if only for the species of salami. Bistecca fiorentina is well-priced here, and a house specialty is fried chicken, not often come upon. A massive wrought-iron chandelier illuminates Natale, with the service—by waiters in wine-hued jackets—reasonably cordial. *Moderate/First Class.*

Otello (Via Orti Oricellari 19; Phone 215-819) goes on, room after room after room. It is beloved of locals as well as, for some reason or other, of French tourists. Decibel count is high, service may be slow, food is variable. Steaks—a specialty—can be okay, but pastas—including agnellotti and pappardelle—are commendable. Mixed grill is a good bet; you select all you want from a trolley brought to the table. Desserts are wheeled to you, and irresistible. *First Class.*

Ottorino (Via delle Oche 12; Phone 215-151): You're surprised at the contemporary quality of Ottorino, given its situation in venerable quarters. Begin with seafood antipasto or one of the excellent pastas. Entrées are tempters, breast of chicken, especially. *First Class.*

Paoli (Via de' Tavolini 12; Phone 21-62-15) is mock-Renaissance, with intricately embellished ceiling vaults and wall frescoes an agreeable foil to the solid—and delicious—food. Pasta—agnellotti, tagliatelle, cannelloni—is tasty and the carrozza of antipasto is wheeled to table. Osso bucco con riso (veal shank with rice) and pollo alla cacciatore (a classic chicken preparation) are good entries. *First Class.*

Da Pennello (Via Dante Alighieri 4; Phone 294-848) typifies blue-collar Florence at its leisure—plain but animated. Help yourself to antipasto (in my experience one of Italy's most fabulous) from a groaning buffet—baby clams and sardines, mussels and octopus, a variety of bean and vegetable specialties, stuffed mushrooms, eggs and peppers, a pair of pasta salads—that totals 20-plus dishes. If you're able to carry on, pastas-to-order, veal, beef, and poultry are tasty too. Well-tabbed house wine. No credit cards. *Moderate.*

Pizzeria Marchetti (Via Calzaiuoli 109, near the Duomo) is just the spot for a casual meal; it's self-service, with a variety of pizzas and other substantial fare, as well. No credit cards. *Moderate.*

Pizzeria Nuti (Borgo San Lorenzo; Phone 21-04-10): Pizza in Florence is not necessarily to be ranked with pizza in Naples. Still, there are a dozen species of it in this unpretentious, open-all-day-and-evening spot, core-of-town. Watch your order expertly shoveled from the oven; accompany it with draft beer. No credit cards. *Moderate.*

Il Profeta (Via Borgo Ognissanti 93; Phone 21-22-65) makes a specialty of Florentine dishes, does lovely things with mushrooms. The staff is kindly and your bill will be *First Class.*

Sabatini (Via Panzani 41; Phone 211-559) is a beloved old-timer, upper-echelon in style (and, for that matter, price) with unusual openers, mouth-watering pastas interestingly sauced, and no-nonsense meat entrées. Believe me, it's worth having Sabatini's celebrated chocolate dessert. *Luxury.*

La Sagrestia (Via Guicciardini 27; Phone 21-88-83) is a hop and a skip from Palazzo Pitti, and indicated for a festive lunch in connection with Pitti exploration. The three-course prix-fixe is good value and good-tasting, opening with risotto or a pasta, continuing with grilled trout or a veal dish, concluding with fresh fruit. Attractively paneled. *First Class.*

Savoy Hotel Ristorante and Coffee Shop (Piazza della Repubblica 7; Phone 283-313): 1 was reminded on my first visit here of the maxim repeated by Curt Strand, for long president of Hilton International, to his managers round the world: Treat your guests well at breakfast and they're likely to return for lunch or dinner. Breakfast in Italian hotels is habitually made so little of—rarely does one encounter anyone supervising the staff—that when a smiling captain came to take my order in the Savoy Coffee Shop I perked up. The caffè completo proved to be the best I have encountered in Italy: a croissant than which France produces no fresher or flakier, and coffee that was bracing but not overly strong. I did indeed return to the smartly formal restaurant for dinner. Service is skilled, linen crisp, flowers fresh, and fare—despite a largely foreign clientele—admirably Italian, with pasta authentic, insalata verde adroitly mixed at table, veal piccata first rate, and—yes, I succumbed—zuppa inglese, wickedly rich. *First Class/Luxury.*

Silvio (Via Parione 74, with another entrance at Via Vigna Nuova 17; Phone 21-40-05) is conveniently central, near Piazza Goldoni and the Arno. Entrances on two streets notwithstanding, it could not be simpler of ambience. Withal, it packs in Florentines and visitors alike who appreciate corking good food served by Signora Patrizzia's small but alert staff, at reasonable prices. There are half a dozen piatti del giorno, or daily specials—vegetable soup, risotto alla Milanese, and roast lamb, for example. And a fairly extensive à la carte. Antipasto misto di salami toscani is just what the name implies: a platter brimming with assorted Tuscan sausages, and absolutely fabulous. Spaghetti al pomodoro, deliciously sauced, is super, too. Paillard of veal, expertly grilled, is a favored entrée, and you do well to order a green salad to accompany it, as well as the house Chianti. Outstanding. *First Class.*

Sostanza (Via della Porcellana 20; Phone 213-529) is a plain-as-an-old-shoe trattoria with an illegible menu, no-nonsense waiters, and an invariably happy clientele, both local and imported. And why not, with such good food? The steak is the biggest and most succulent I know of in Florence. The vegetable soup is hearty. And wonders are worked with chicken breasts. Fun. *First Class.*

Il Teatro (Via degli Alfani; Phone 247-93-27) is quite central and quite tasty (go with an order of pasta, followed by scaloppine with a carafe of house wine). *Moderate.*

Trattoria Bordino (Via Stracciatella 9; Phone 212-048) occupies a stone-walled, flag-hung cellar, with illumination from wrought-iron chandeliers, and the fare is substantial, with especially good sweets. Worth knowing about after a late night on the town: dinner is served until 1:00 A.M. *First Class.*

Trattoria Drago Verde (Via del Leone 50; Phone 224-002): The charm of the Green Dragon—to translate—is its garden, open the summer long. Cooking is typically Florentine, which means that you may enjoy such treats as grilled sausages and beans washed down with the house Chianti. *First Class.*

13 (pronounced Tray-dee-chee) Gobbi (Via della Porcellana 9; Phone 298-769) is winning. Nice to look upon, with picture-crammed walls, fresh flowers, smiling staff. Then there is the food: the house's own tortellini and pappardelle among the pastas; veal scaloppine and sausage with beans, peasant-style, among the entrées; a special menu of Hungarian specialties as a surprise; splendid cheeses; good wines as expected; but also Löwenbrau beer, from Germany, for a change. *First Class.*

Villa San Michele Hotel Ristorante (Via di Doccia 4, Fiesole; Phone 594-512): It's a fine day and lunch in the country is indicated. Head for Villa San Michele: its indoor winter restaurant is quietly handsome, the niches of its walls studded with antique sculpture, calla lilies on each table, a view of potted orange trees in the garden. In warm weather, setting is a splendid loggia and you are faced with conflicting stimuli—fare (on the table) or Florence (spread out below). Service is white-glove, and by that I mean impeccable. Try tagliolini verdi (you will not taste more delicious green noodles), with grilled scampi as your entrée; and one of the house's own sweets—choose from the wagon that is rolled tableside—to precede coffee in the bar or garden. *Luxury.*

Vittoria (Via Fonderia 52; Phone 22-56-57): You can't be hungry for, say, a steak or veal if you're Vittoria-bound. This is a restaurant for pasta and for seafood. And a standout restaurant, at that. *First Class.*

SOUND OF MUSIC

Teatro Comunale (Corso Italia) is Florence's opera house-concert hall and principal seat of its celebrated spring music festival, *Maggio Musicale.* The Comunale is home to the Orchestra del Maggio Musicale Fiorentino, as well as chorus and opera companies. The main—or winter—opera season is repeated in July—much to the delight of summer visitors—with both early spring and autumn concert seasons, and Maggio Musicale taking place in May. The theater, unlike traditional-style opera houses in other Italian cities, is essentially modern, and, to understate, more functional than beautiful.

SHOPPER'S FLORENCE

All of the Florentine mercantile centuries—the tradition of the Medici, Riccardi, Strozzi, and all the families that traded and aided throughout Europe—come into play when one shops in Florence. No medium-sized European city—Florence's population hovers around half a million—surpasses this one. Via Tornabuoni is the most celebrated of the shopping streets, but by no means alone. Via Calzaiuoli, Via Parione, Via Roma, Borgo San Jacopo—all are areas where one finds clothes, shoes, gloves, leather, luggage, pottery. Via Por Santa Maria and the Ponte Vecchio are for silver and jewelry. One finds antiques on Via dei Fossi and Via degli Strozzi, where gentle bargaining can be the rule. Established merchants are reliable overseas shippers. Herewith a selection of interesting spots to spend your money, alphabetically by category.

ANTIQUES—for which Florence is an all-Europe leader—are concentrated on Via dei Fossi, Via degli Strozzi, the smart street called Borgo Ognissanti, downtown; and across the Arno on such Left Bank streets as Via Maggio and Borgo San Jacopo. Most merchandise is Italian (late medieval polychrome, gesso, Renaissance, and Baroque), but because English antiques are popular in Italy, you'll encounter quite a few of them as well (with subject matter embracing furniture, paintings, ceramics, and doodads) at such shops as *Alberto Bruschi* (Piazza de' Ruccelai), with the specialty seventeenth-century furniture, tapestries, and paintings; *Berti* (Via dei Fossi 29), for eighteenth- and nineteenth-century pieces from the Orient as well as Italy; *Bruzzichelli* (Borgo Ognissanti 33), heavy on the nineteenth century; *Cose del Passato* (Via dei Fossi 27) with a mix of small things—mirrors, pottery, fragments, and some paintings; *Fuiretti* (Borgo Ognissanti 41), where the lure is antique carpets; *Giuliano Freschi* (Via della Vigna Nuova 85), with seventeenth-century paintings, many of them museum caliber; *Palloni* (Borgo Ognissanti 21) for eighteenth-century painted furniture, overdoors, and panels; *U. del Guerra* (Via Parione 53) for antique ceramics; and *Studio Fiorentino,* nineteenth-century paintings and antiques.

BOOKS: *BM Bookshop* (Borgo Ognissanti 4): English-language books are the specialty. *Libreria Seeber* (Via Tornabuoni 66) is big on art books as well as books in English.

CLOTHING: As throughout Italy, stocks for both men and women are the rule in clothing shops, many of which also deal in small leather goods and accessories. You might want to get an idea of the prices Florentines pay at the city's branch of the department-store chain *Upim* (Piazza della Repubblica), where both style and value can be very good indeed. Then consider pricier places, including *Gherardini* (Via della Vigna Nuova 57)—both women's and gents', as well as leather goods; *Emilio Pucci* (Via Ricasoli 20); *Gianfranco Ferre* (Via degli Strozzi 24, with the men's shop up one flight, women's on main); *Giorgio Armani* (Via della Vigna Nuova 51); *Fendi* (Via Tornabuoni 27); *Lord Brummel* (Via della Vigna Nuova 79)—despite its masculine title—is a good source of women's clothes, as well as men's; *Valentino* (Via Vigna Nuova 47); *Mila Schön* (Via della Vigna Nuova 32); *Marina Yachting* (Via Porta Rossa 21); *Neuber* (Via degli Strozzi 32, with British as well as Italian duds); *Principe* (Via Strozzi 21); *Salvatore Ferragamo* (Via Tornabuoni 16—and probably the handsomest of this firm's shops throughout Italy); *Renard* (Via de Martelli 21), with suede and leather clothing its specialty; and *Bottega Veneta* (Piazza Ognissanti).

DEPARTMENT STORE: *Coin* (Via Cenci) is a big branch of an Italy-wide chain.

FABRICS—for draperies and the covering of furniture—are an ancient Florentine specialty. *Antico Setificio Fiorentino* (Via della Vigna Nuova 97) features hand-loomed materials; *Lorenzo Rubbelli & Figlio* (Via Tornabuoni 1) deals in silks, cottons, and brocades; *Zinelli & Petrizzi* (Via Tornabuoni 27) is particularly good for cut velvets; and *Casa dei Tessuti* (Via Pecori 20) specializes in fashion fabrics.

FANCY FOODS: Procacci (Via Tornabuoni 33) is a Florentine counterpart of Milan's Peck and Paris's Fauchon; chocolates, cheeses, cookies, salamis, other tempters.

GLOVES, invariably good value in Italy, and ideal gifts because they're light in weight, are high-styled and relatively pricey at long-on-scene *Ugolini* (Via Tornabuoni 20—with attractive neckties as well) and relatively inexpensive at *Martelli* (Via Por Santa Maria 18) and *Giotto* (Via Guicciardini 58, near Palazzo Pitti), with beautiful wallets as well.

JEWELRY AND SILVER: Mario Buccellati (Via Tornabuoni 71) has been a leading firm for half-a-century-plus.

LEATHER: Gucci (Via Tornabuoni 43 and Via Tornabuoni 57) is the multifloored Mother House of the internationally reputed chain, invariably mobbed by Americans and Japanese who would no more think of missing it than they would the Botticellis at the Uffizi. Range includes luggage, small leather goods, shoes, clothing, and accessories, with neckties (watch for sales of discontinued models) and silk scarves special. Cheaper than in the U.S., but hardly cheap; *Bottega Veneta* (Piazza Ognissanti) has beautiful things, but is very expensive. *Morris* (Via Guicciardini, Left Bank) has big stocks of small objects, wallets, and the like, as indeed does *Cellerini* (Via del Sole 37). *Mario Cintolesi* (Piazza Pitti 25, opposite Palazzo Pitti) specializes in typically Florentine work, gold-tooled desk sets—comprising blotter pads, memo-paper holders, and *carte busti*, or envelope boxes—especially; *Stalls of Loggiato degli Uffizi* (Uffizi Gallery Arcades) operated by long-established merchants (some take credit cards, and they're all open Sundays), including two that I like—*Silvano Fanetti e Figlio*, for leather boxes, and *Antonio Ladisa* for passport cases; *Santa Croce Church Leather School/Scuola del Cuoio* (in the church complex on Piazza Santa Croce) operates an excellent retail shop for well-priced articles made by students, with the range pillboxes to jackets, and with good buys in its "sale" room; and the *Straw Market* (Loggia del Mercato Nuovo), a Renaissance landmark that, despite its name, is a source also of locally produced leatherware—bags, wallets, and the like—not necessarily top quality but moderately priced and suitable for minor gift-giving.

LINENS: Emilia Bellini (Via Tornabuoni 19) features handworked table and other linens, scarves, and blouses (also in Rome); *Pratesi* (Lungarno Vespucci 15) sells its exquisite, own-design bedlinens and towels here, as well as at branches in Rome and New York. *Ghezzi* (Via Calzaiuoli 110) has lovely linens, too.

NECKTIES: *Roxy* (Via Calzaiuoli 110), a branch of a Rome firm with shops in other Italian cities, too, has nothing less—in the opinion of this necktie buff—than the best-value ties in Italy; the silk is good quality, designs are tasteful, workmanship is excellent, and you can't beat the prices. *Stanganini* (Piazza Santa Croce 25)—near Santa Croce Church—is as known for its fine leather gloves as for its tasteful ties.

PAPER GOODS are uniquely Florentine, relatively inexpensive, and ideal gifts. They include hand-printed paper for gift wrapping and shelf lining, stationery, Christmas and note cards, paper-bound memo holders, and the most elegant notebooks you are going to encounter anywhere. Five sources, each distinctive: *Bottega Artigiana del Libro* (Lungarno Corsini 38); *& C.* (Via della Vigna Nuova 91 and Via de' Pucci 22); *Il Papiro* (Via Cavour 55); *Giulio Giannini e Figlio* (Piazza Pitti 37); and *Pineider* (Via Tornabuoni 76, with branches in Rome, Milan, and New York).

PERFUME AND COLOGNE: *Officina Profumo-Farmaceutica di Santa Maria Novella,* adjacent to the noted church (above) for which it is named, has been on scene since 1612, is Gothic-vaulted, and sells its own-made scents.

PHARMACY: *Farmacia Santa Maria Novella* (Piazza Santa Maria Novella) opened in the seventeenth century—and is still going strong.

PORCELAIN AND POTTERY: *A. Menegatti* (Via Tornabuoni 77) is long established for traditional-design majolica, with hand-painted ceramic dinnerware made by noted Deruta and other factories; *Inter-Gallo* (Lungarno Guicciardini) has vast assortments, Deruta among much more.

SHOES, like clothes, are generally sold in shops stocking women's as well as men's models: pricey *Tanino Crisci* (Via Tornabuoni 3); moderately priced *Romano* (Piazza della Repubblica at Via degli Speziali); *Pollini* (Via Calimala 12); *Salvatore Ferragamo* (Via Tornabuoni 16)—a celebrated outlet, with shoes, and clothing as well, for both men and women; *Tanino Crisci* (Via Tornabuoni 34)—a pricey chain with links in Italy and abroad; *Beltrami* (Via Tornabuoni 48)—another ranking firm; *Rive Gauche* (Via Guicciardini 31); with good buys on men's glove-soft loafers; *Cole-Haan* (Via della Vigna Nuova 77), a U.S.-origin chain popular with Italians; and *Raspini* (Via Por Santa Maria 70), with leather coats and jackets as well, are eight of many.

INCIDENTAL INTELLIGENCE

Florence, in the late 1980s, at long last opened an airport of its own. It's called Peretola, it's small but well operated (with a convenient caffè), and it's less than a quarter-hour's drive from the center. Hitch is that terrain precludes wide-body aircraft of the type that fly transatlantic. Still, there are worth-knowing-about flights to Milan's Linate Airport and Rome, with service as well to such foreign points as Paris and Munich, London and Barcelona. The larger airport at not-far-distant Pisa (chapter 27) still is used by travelers to and from Florence, with which it is connected by frequent trains (travel time is about an hour) that serve the airport proper as well as Pisa's central station. Hotel concierges have gratis copies available of *Florence-Concierge Information*, a what's-on publication, but they tend to hide them; ask and you shall receive. Daily newspapers, *Nazione* and *Città*, are valuable for schedules of cultural events. If you would like to make an excursion out of Florence to visit a winery, contact *Consorzio Vino Chianti* (Lungarno Corsini 4, Firenze; Phone 210-168). *Further information:* Azienda Autonoma di Turismo, Via Tornabuoni 15, Florence; Azienda Autonoma di Turismo, Piazza Risorgimento 116, Arezzo; Azienda Autonoma di Turismo, Viale Verde 66, Montecatini.

14

Genoa/Genova and the Riviera

Exploring the Mediterranean

BACKGROUND BRIEFING

The point about the ancient and beautiful Mediterranean port-metropolis of Genoa is that it has attracted visitors of one sort or another for well over two thousand years. But when the transatlantic liners that plied between New York and its harbor were succeeded a few decades back by transatlantic jets to Rome and Milan, treasure-laden Genoa, surely the most underappreciated of the principal Italian cities (only Rome, Milan, Naples, and Turin are larger), became a touristic *terra incognita*. Or almost.

Ignominious may be too strong a term for the consequences of this development. Genoa remains, after all, Italy's premier port, on a regional par with France's Marseilles, capital of the *Regione* of Liguria, and the urban excursion destination of holiday-makers at the Riviera resorts surrounding it. But the time is long since past when Genoese seafarers—Cristoforo Colombo is the most universally celebrated—ranged the oceans, their exploits filling pages of Renaissance geography books.

Antoniotto Usodimare gained the mouth of Western Africa's Gambia River; Lanzarotto Malconcello discovered the mid-Atlantic Canaries where Columbus would later pause en route to the New World; John Cabot—Giovanni Caboto before he sailed under the English flag—discovered Newfoundland.

By that time, Genoa—founded by the prehistoric Ligurians who gave their name to the modern *Regione* of Liguria, later a flourishing Roman colony (its name derives from their Janua)—had become a rich and aggressive maritime power, making and breaking allegiances in the fashion of the epoch. With also-powerful Pisa, it collaborated in routing Arab forces from Corsica and Sardinia, later battling Pisa for control of those adjacent Mediterranean islands. It achieved additional riches through Crusades shipping to the Holy Land. And as a consequence of wealth begetting wealth, it traded profitably in ports extending from the Iberian peninsula all the way east to the Black Sea.

Whereas other Italian city-states had dynastic families that spurred them to pinnacles of influence, Genoa's expansion was fostered in the early fifteenth century by a remarkably influential bank, San Giorgio by name (whose headquarters palazzo remains in use today as seat of the city's Port Authority). Battles with rivals like Milan and Venice, squabbles between antagonistic local clans, and the ascent to absolute power of the dictatorial mariner, Andrea Doria, did not impede development. As the Renaissance era became the Baroque, great Flemish artists like Rubens and Van Dyck came to Genoa, influencing the city's own school of art. The core of the city became dotted with enormous palaces, many of which remain, in a Città Vecchia, or old town, that is rivaled in size among Italian cities only by Venice, and where niches of houses remain to this day studded with marble images of the Virgin Mary, called *Madonnette*.

Later centuries saw foreign control—Austrians, French (to whom Corsica was ceded), Spanish—and Genoa was attached in the early nineteenth century to the Turin-governed Kingdom of Sardinia, well in advance of the unification of Italy later in that century. Its immense natural harbor, at the foot of the idyllic hills it climbs, was badly damaged in World War II, and as if that were not enough, again by mid-1950s storms. But it has been splendidly rebuilt. Genoese jealously protect not only the grand palazzi but the picturesque narrow alleys as well. Genoa's big year touristically was 1992, when its months-long Expo celebrated the five hundredth anniversary of native son Christopher Columbus's landing in the New World, with *Museo Colombo* exhibit-packed. Its people—kind and generous—are proud of what Italians for centuries have affectionately dubbed *Genova superba*. Stay long enough to understand why.

ON SCENE

Lay of the Land: This is a big-in-area city, with upper sectors, those straddling the hills, reached by funicular railways as well as elevators and, of course, surface streets, not to mention a new Metro, or subway, whose first line opened in 1991. But it's the historic core that you want to concern yourself with. It is based on the half-circle *Porto di Genova*, with the bulk of the area you'll want to explore lying largely between the two railway stations: westerly *Stazione Principe*, on the pretty *Piazza Acquaverde* (its landmark is a towering statue of Columbus), and *Stazione*

Brignole, on *Piazza Verdi.* Strolls on history-architecture-art-rich streets and squares linking the stations are enthusiastically counseled. From west to east, these would include *Via Balbi* (with the onetime seat of the royal House of Savoy among its palazzi) and church-flanked *Piazza Nunziata,* which leads to antique-shop-lined *Via Cairoli,* that soon widens and becomes *Via Garibaldi* (among whose palaces are a pair of opposite-each-other and quite brilliant art museums). Via Garibaldi terminates at *Piazza Marose.* From that square, short *Via XXV Aprile* takes one south to very grand *Piazza Ferrari*—Genoa's nerve center—based on a splendid fountain. Important shopping streets like smart *Via Roma,* arcaded *Via XX Settembre* terminating at immense *Piazza della Vittoria,* and *Via San Vincenzo* (ending at *Stazione Brignole*) extend from Piazza Ferrari.

SELECTED PALACES

Palazzo Reale (Via Balbi) had been the Genoa home of the royal House of Savoy, and I don't know of any destination to better orient you to the meld of architecture, art, and furnishings that typify the grandeur of Baroque Genoa. The palace positively dazzles with its audience hall, throne room, ballroom, royal bedrooms, a hall of mirrors smaller but no less beautiful than that of Versailles, frescoed ceilings and gilded stucco work throughout, and a bonus of superb paintings, as for example a Van Dyck *Crucifixion,* a local lady as interpreted by Tintoretto, and Guido Reni's *Saint Mary Magdalene.*

Palazzo Doria (Via Garibaldi), the sixteenth-century home of the sailor-turned-dictator, Andrea Doria, is among the more lavish of Via Garibaldi's palazzi. A range of antique-filled-and-accessorized rooms, with art comprising both framed paintings and a spectacular fresco-surfaced atrium.

Palazzo Tursi (Via Garibaldi) is today Genoa's Municipio, or City Hall. (Credit city fathers for taste in selecting the seat of their government.) Have a look at the strikingly arcaded courtyard, and, among other things, the ashes of Genoa's own Christopher Columbus, as well as letters written by the explorer.

Palazzo Carrega Cataldi (Via Garibaldi) is the contemporary headquarters of Camera di Comercio, or Chamber of Commerce, and not even the former royal palace (above) is more breathtakingly beautiful. The barrel-vaulted room in which the receptionist sits, with frescoes inlaid among the stucco work, is dazzling enough, but it's only for starters; the kicker of the mansion is the accurately labeled Gilded Gallery, a masterwork of eighteenth-century Rococo.

Banco America d'Italia (Via Garibaldi): The Renaissance frescoes of this palace's entrance hall and high-ceilinged banking room (you are welcome, during banking hours) are striking enough to impel you to forgive the bank's California-based namesake for replacing New York's beloved Biltmore Hotel with a Manhattan headquarters skyscraper in the 1980s. Lovely.

Palazzo Ducale (Piazza Matteotti, the square adjacent to Piazza Ferrari) was the longtime seat of the dukes, or doges, of Genoa, considerably more aged than its elegant eighteenth-century façade suggests. It was treated to a major seven-year restoration completed for the 1992 Columbus celebrations. Have a look at its pair of massive, fountain-centered courtyards and the extravagantly frescoed Great Hall, sensibly put to good use for public concerts.

SELECTED MUSEUMS

Galleria di Palazzo Rosso (Via Garibaldi): Forget about the reddish hue of the stone with which this fine Baroque palace was built and for which it is named. Go right in to see a connection of master paintings in an appropriately smashing setting. Bernardo Strozzi, the Genoa school's most reputed artist, painted *La Cucineria,* portraying a cook plucking a soon-to-be-eaten goose. And you will see such treasures as Veronese's *Judith* and a Genoese lady in black ruff and feathers painted by Van Dyck during his Genoa residence; with Pisanello, Caravaggio, and Guercino among other Italians represented, along with such foreigners as Dürer, Teniers, Rigaud, even Spain's Murillo.

Galleria di Palazzo Bianco (Via Garibaldi, opposite Palazzo Rosso, above): It's touch and go which of these museums, Rosso or Bianco, will more interest you. The beautiful Bianco (a century older than its neighbor) welcomes you to a foyer with one of the ranking stairways of the city (on a par with that of Via Balbi's Palazzo dell' Università). Climb up a flight to the galleries for such works as *The Madonna of the Candle* by Genoa's own Luca Cambiaso; Flemish Primitive representation by Van Cleve and Gerard David; later Flemings like Van Dyck (with six paintings) and Rubens (you will immediately recognize his *Venus and Mars*); Dutchmen including Steen, Van Ruisdael, and Maes; Frenchmen like Simon Vouet; Spaniards like Zurbarán; and Genoa's eminent eighteenth-century master, Alessandro Magnasco, whose work anticipated the later Impressionists.

Galleria Nazionale Palazzo Spanola (Piazza Pellicceria): Once you accustom yourself to having to identify the paintings with a plastic-covered card that viewers in each room share—sadly, there are no labels on individual works—you come to enjoy this wealth of art in an enchanting setting: a Renaissance palace with frescoed ceilings, gilded woodwork, seventeenth- and eighteenth-century furniture, and a knockout hall of mirrors. There are four Van Dycks, a Rubens *Holy Family*, a Guido Reni *(Sacred and Profane Love)*, Giordano and Bassano, Strozzi and Ribera; and, for me at least, the highlights: two works by Van Cleve, one a *Madonna* in prayer, the other an immense triptych, *Adoration of the Magi.*

Pinacoteca dell' Accademia Linguistica di Belle Arti (Piazza Ferrari 5) is not nearly as big as its name is long. It occupies the high-ceilinged third floor of a Piazza Ferrari building. Works are predominantly Genoese with paintings by Bernardo Strozzi, a *Pietà* and a *St. John the Baptist*—outstanding.

Museo Chiossone (Via Martin Piaggio at Piazza Corvetto): You have to like to climb steep hills by foot, and Oriental art, if you're to appreciate this distinguished collection of a nineteenth-century Genoese—amassed during thirty years' residence in Tokyo—bequeathed to the city government. There are Ming-era seated Buddhas, paintings of Japanese geisha, ravishingly decorated folding screens, an exceptional cache of ancient Japanese paintings and prints, a substantial section of Thai sculpture. And the parklike setting is verdant.

Museo di Villa Luxuro (Via Aurelia, in Nervi, closest to town of the eastern Riviera resorts, a few miles from the center) is set in a turn-of-century house, and its thrust is the decorative arts, mostly of the eighteenth century: commodes, chairs, silver, ceramics, sculpture, with prints and paintings as well, including a fine Magnasco entitled *Capriccio.*

SELECTED CHURCHES

Duomo (Via San Lorenzo): Genoa is so church-rich that its cathedral (often referred to as San Lorenzo) can get lost in the shuffle. Don't let it. This essentially Gothic structure stuns, first off, with the black and white stripes of its façade and superbly sculpted frames of its three portals. The central nave, gilded capitals atop two levels of columns flanking it, is no less breath-catching, and the high altar and choir occupying the apse are dazzlers. Allow time for the Treasury, in the adjacent Archbishop's Palace, with, among much else, a cup from which Christ is said to have drunk at the Last Supper and a reliquary said to contain St. John the Baptist's ashes.

Church of Santissima Annunziata (Piazza della Nunziata) deceives—to understate—with a somber neoclassical façade that in no way prepares you for the sumptuous Renaissance-Baroque splendor that awaits within: gilded columns support gilded capitals, which in turn support a barrel-vaulted central nave, brilliant with gilt-framed frescoes. And the side chapels brim with paintings by Genoese painters, Bernardo Strozzi, among them.

Church of Gesù (Piazza Matteotti): Jesuits' churches in Italy invariably reflect the brilliant architecture and art of the Counter-Reformation, and Genoa's is no exception, with its finely detailed Baroque façade and a lavish interior—marble pulpit, gilded organ, frescoed main nave, and paintings by such masters as Rubens (there are two by him), Guido Reni, and Simon Vouet, represented by a beautiful *Crucifixion.*

Church of Santa Maria di Castello (Via Santa Maria di Castello) is typically Genoese Gothic without—all black and white horizontal-striped stone. Chapels within are adorned with paintings, and resident Dominicans operate an art museum of consequence in their adjacent monastery. Ask in the church's sacristy if there is a priest available to show you about, if only to see the *Annunciation* by Giusto di Alemagna. Cloister, too.

Church of San Matteo (Piazza San Matteo), black and white striped, not unlike Santa Maria di Castello and the Duomo (above), is interesting because it was built through the largess of the powerful Doria clan (Andrea Doria's tomb is within); mansions on the square were originally inhabited by Doria relatives.

Church of San Donato (Via San Donato) is dwarfed by the immense Romanesque campanile adjacent. Its interior is one of the most profoundly beautiful in Italy, with columns of its central nave striped horizontally, in blue and white stone, no two capitals alike. Look for Joos Van Cleve's sublime altarpiece, *Adoration of the Magi.*

Church of Santo Stefano (Via XX Settembre) is black and white striped out front, somber Romanesque–Gothic within, with the exterior of its apse noteworthy. This is where Columbus is believed to have been christened.

Church of Santa Marta (Largo Lanfranconi) is a case of big things in small packages. By that I mean it is very generous with respect to décor. Every inch of the interior of this Baroque beauty is embellished, gilded arches through frescoed ceilings. Special.

A TRIO OF RIVIERA RESORTS

Camogli, least known to transatlantic visitors of my selected trio of Riviera Levante (meaning East of Genoa) resorts, is a charmer of a little town set in a delightful horseshoe of a harbor, with a range of hotels and restaurants, an enormous piscina comunale, or public swimming pool, to supplement beaches, modern *Museo Marinaro* (model vessels, sailing prints, other nautical exhibits), and *Aquarium* with local marine life swimming about behind glass, and several interesting churches—*Vecchia di Ruta* (its façade and bell tower fashioned of local stone) especially. Genoa is but 14 miles distant.

Portofino, smallest of our Riviera group, albeit the most celebrated, is at once very pretty—it was beloved even of ancient Romans, who dubbed it *Portus Delphini*—and very pricey, with its shops quite the most expensive I have researched anywhere in Italy. (Even postcards cost more in Portofino than elsewhere along the coast.) Withal, this is a class act, with restaurants, boutiques, and caffès enclosing a small beach that fronts a horseshoe of a harbor that is among the most photographed in Italy. A centuries-old castle, high on a hill over the village, is visitable. And there are just five hotels (see Settling In), one of which is among the best to be found at any of the Italian resorts. Genoa is 21 miles away.

Santa Margherita Ligure, surely the most euphoniously named of my trio, is also its largest. It edges a long and lovely crescent of a beach-harbor, brims with hotels of all categories (some beachfront, some across the road from the beach, some inland and elevated), restaurants, people-watching caffès, a busy central square, a seventeenth-century church (Santa Margherita logically its name), and its own sixteenth-century castle. Distance to Genoa is 18 miles.

SETTLING IN

GENOA

President Hotel (Corte dei Lambruschini 6) is a popular modern hostelry, with just over 190 rooms and suites, good restaurant, and often-busy bar-lounge. *First Class.*

Jolly Plaza Hotel's (Via Martin Piaggio 11) capacious lobby, with deep leather chairs, fairly invites you to relax over a drink. There are not quite a hundred rooms and suites, and a restaurant. Just off flower-filled Piazza Corvetto, and an immediate neighbor of another hotel of the same chain, *Jolly Plaza Hotel Dipendenza,* a kind of annex, at Via Martin Piaggio 3, with 68 rooms and its own restaurant and bar. Both Jollys are *First Class.*

Bristol Palace Hotel (Via XX Settembre 35) could not be more central, on a principal shopping street in the heart of the city. It's good-looking, with a crystal-chandeliered lounge, as well as a decidedly contemporary bar with red-leather banquettes. There are 115 rooms and suites, the bigger ones pleasant. *First Class.*

Savoia Majestic Hotel (Via Arsenale di Terra 5) is a refurbished old-timer with 120 adequate rooms and a restaurant, located opposite Stazione Principale. I wish the staff was friendlier; meanwhile, this is not a place I can recommend. *First Class.*

City Hotel (Via San Sebastiano 6) is near central Via Roma and worth knowing about as you can walk everywhere. All 71 neat rooms are bath-equipped; bar and breakfast, but no restaurant. *First Class.*

Aquila & Reale Hotel (Piazza Acquaverde 1) is friendly, functional, and convenient to Stazione Principale, just opposite. There are 85 rooms of varying sizes and degrees of comfort; most have baths. Restaurant and bar. *Moderate.*

Londra & Continental Hotel (Via Arsenale di Terra 1) is adjacent to the Savoia Majestic (above), sharing not only the same management, but a main entrance. You walk through the Savoia to reach the Londra. Forty-eight rooms. *Moderate.*

CAMOGLI

Cenobio dei Dogi Hotel (Via Cuneo 34) is made to order for relaxation, a handsome house set in a meticulously maintained garden, with its terrace sea-view. There are 89 rooms and suites, restaurant that becomes alfresco in warm weather, cocktail lounge, swimming pool, and tennis courts. *Luxury.*

Casmona Hotel (Salita Pineto 13) is nicely situated (ask for accommodations with a view), with 34 rooms, restaurant, bar-lounge. *Moderate.*

SANTA MARGHERITA LIGURE

Miramare Hotel: Picture it: a gleaming white châteaulike structure edging a low hill, just close enough to the western edge of the vast bay of Santa Margherita to afford vistas of sea, town, and mountains. To the side are meticulously manicured gardens, punctuated by a good-sized kidney-shaped swimming pool, with the beach just across the road. Within, the 74 rooms are no two quite alike, though traditional in style and with super baths. Specify a sea-view one, preferably with balcony. The restaurant is worthy of additional comment on a later page; it's supplemented by a poolside midday buffet in summer. Smiling service, razor-sharp management. Member, Leading Hotels of the World. *First Class.*

Metropole Hotel is an elderly, old-fashioned house that has been gracefully updated, with commodious public spaces (the dining room moves to a terrace in summer), mod-look cocktail lounge, just over half a hundred rooms, pretty garden leading to the beach. *First Class.*

Regina Elena Hotel, which appears wholly contemporary as you consider its façade, is a surprising mix inside, with a striking circular restaurant in contrast to an antique-accented crystal-chandeliered lobby-lounge-cum-bar. There are 94 well-equipped rooms and, if you please, a tunnel through the road out front that takes you to the beach. Congenial. *First Class.*

Continental Hotel is enviably well positioned, on an eminence fronting a garden that leads directly to the beach. Public spaces are gracious; the restaurant has a terrace for summer, and there are 76 rooms. I would prefer one in the main building to the few in an across-the-garden annex. *First Class.*

Helios Hotel is agreeably intimate, well located, beachfront, with pleasant lounge-bar and restaurant-cum-summer terrace, and baths in all 20 rooms. *First Class.*

Lombardia & Bristol Hotel is small but choice, at least for the traveler on a budget. It's a short walk inland from the beach, with baths in 7 of its 10 rooms, bar-lounge, worth-knowing-about restaurant later called to your notice. *Moderate.*

Imperial Palace Hotel crowns a hill at the eastern edge of town—an old house that has been modernized in a manner that I find infelicitous, with old and new not coordinating as gracefully as they might. Better rooms (there are nearly a hundred, all told) are very nice indeed, and there is a reliable restaurant (which I have enjoyed), cocktail lounge, and swimming pool. But in my view, the only luxury-category hotel in town is not sufficiently luxurious to justify selecting it over a less-pricey first-class hotel. *Luxury.*

PORTOFINO

Splendido Hotel: If there was ever a hotel that did *not* resort to hyperbole in the selection of its name, it's the splendid Splendido. Situation, for starters, is superb: high on a hill overlooking the picture-book Portofino harbor. And then the hotel itself: a buff-colored pavilion meticulously maintained (it's been operating close to 90 years) with low-key, high-ceilinged public rooms accented by antiques and old prints. There are just 65 handsomely furnished rooms and suites, 80 percent with terraces made to order for sunset cocktails. The restaurant—outstanding enough to warrant later comment—is picture-windowed, with a terrace for service in summer, when there's the option of a barbecue lunch, poolside. Tennis courts are on premises, and the garden paths made for scenic promenades. Member, Relais et Châteaux. *Luxury.*

Nazionale Hotel is small but charming, with welcoming lobby-bar-lounge, pretty vistas from its facing-town rooms (most of which have baths), and a location a pleasant walk away from the center. Breakfast only. *Moderate.*

San Giorgio Hotel is comfortable and quite central, with a score of functional rooms, bar-lounge, and breakfast—but no restaurant. *Moderate.*

DAILY BREAD

GENOA

Zefferino (Via XX Settembre 20; Phone 591-990) is as good a spot as any in Genoa to sample the region's most celebrated pasta, trenette al pesto (the pesto being a delicious sauce, fresh-basil flavored), entrées like grilled veal scaloppine, and desserts including a chocolate zuppa inglese. Lots of the local wines of Liguria are stocked. The walls are busily decorated, with black wrought-iron chandeliers illuminating a sprightly scene enhanced by swift and smiling waiters. Central. *First Class.*

Cinque Lampadi (Piazza Cinque Lampadi; Phone 291-751) calls itself an osteria, but serves not only oysters but other seafood—and seafood-sauced pasta—as well. Its prix-fixe is good value. *First Class.*

Gran Gotto (Via Fiumell; Phone 564-344) is still another top fish restaurant—catch of the day, super shrimp, and shrimp-embellished spaghetti. *First Class.*

Ippogrifo (Via Gestro 9; Phone 592-764) is a neat, though aesthetically standard Genoa restaurant, where the willing staff surpasses the mostly undistinguished fare. Antipasto frutti di mare is a mix of fresh sardines, octopus, shrimp, and crayfish; and bronzino, a local fish, can be good simply grilled. *First Class.*

Tre Stelle (Salita San Giovanni 1; Phone 257-341) is an unpretentious source of such openers as mixed salami and satisfactory pastas. *Moderate.*

Caboto (Salita Pallavicini) exudes the atmosphere of Genoa's old quarter, with arched ceilings, simple appointments, but tasty food. It's known for pastas and grilled fish-of-the-day. *Moderate.*

Moody (Via XII Ottobre 14) is a drop-in self-service for a casual lunch, perhaps following a bout of shopping at La Rinascente department store, just opposite. *Moderate.*

Primo Piano (Via XX Settembre; Phone 540-284), recommended to me by a Genoa Tourist Office guide as well as a hotel concierge, was distinctly disappointing, drawing foreign and some Italian business travelers, with an edible albeit unexciting and nondescript Italo-international menu. I can't recommend this one. *Luxury.*

Caffè Mangini (Via Roma 91), which fronts handsome Piazza Corvetto, has been sustaining customers since 1876 with pastries and coffee—and celebrated candy to go, as well. Crystal-chandeliered. *Moderate.*

Skipper (Calata del Porto 6) is the only restaurant in Italy so named—at least in my experience. And its title, at least to English-speakers, is a clue to its specialty: seafood, of course. Very nice. *First Class.*

Caffè Romanengo (Via Orefici 62) is a core-of-town, wood-paneled, stopping-off point for an espresso accompanied by the house's own cookies. The menu advises that composer Giuseppe Verdi was a patron of yore. *Moderate.*

SANTA MARGHERITA LIGURE

La Paranza (Via Ruffini 46; Phone 283-686) specializes in local seafood. Open with spaghetti alla marinara, continuing with fritto misto (a mix of the day's marine catch), or scampi della casa. Attractive. *First Class.*

Cloe (Piazza Martiri della Libertà 47; Phone 87-444) is centrally located, and with tasty fish, nicely grilled and served with a glass or carafe of house white. *Moderate.*

Da Alfonso (Piazza Martiri della Libertà 57; Phone 87-436) is a full-service restaurant, but it's the pizza—with a choice of toppings—that's the prime lure. *Moderate.*

Da Nino (in the Lombardia e Bristol Hotel; Phone 87-505) features grilled specialties—beef, lamb, pork, veal—that turn out very well indeed. *First Class.*

Cesarina (Via Mameli 2; Phone 286-059) is justifiably noted for its seafood—shrimp or the house's special salmon dish to open, perhaps the deliciously garnished fish of the day as your entrée. *First Class.*

Miramare Hotel Ristorante (Phone 87-014) is Riviera hotel dining at its best. In-house guests favor the prix-fixe lunches and dinners (the second course—a pasta like tortellini alla panna or orecchiette saltate al pomodoro e basilico—is invariably super). But the à la carte menu, with prepared-to-order specialties—beefsteak Florentine style, for example—is exemplary, too. And it is worth noting that the Riviera dress code wisely and sensibly decrees that gents need wear neither jackets nor ties the summer long. Bravo! *First Class.*

PORTOFINO

Splendido Hotel Ristorante (Phone 69-551): I can't imagine a Portofino visit—even if you're headquartering in another hotel—without a meal at the Splendido. You may order what you like à la carte, but prix-fixe lunches and dinners are as tasty as they are copious, with openers at lunch including the house's marvelous antipasto, and as a main course, a generous buffet. Dinner might range from carpaccio—the thinly sliced raw beef delicacy—continuing with a choice of chilled or hot soup or pasta. The menu features a half dozen entrées (including beef), with potatoes among the vegetables. Not surprisingly, the cellar is exemplary. Likewise the service. *Luxury.*

Puny (Phone 69-037) fronts the main piazza, with a look that's a felicitous mix of blond wood chairs, red and white linen, and glass wall sconces. The pasta that I have had here—spaghetti alle vongole (with clam sauce) and pappardelle al pesto—is the best I have had in Liguria. Pesce al sale, fish prepared in a rock-salt encasing removed before service, is the surprisingly delicious specialty. No credit cards. *First Class.*

Delfino (Phone 69-081) charms with a saucy blue and white interior (there are outdoor tables, too) and pleases with such favorites as the Ligurian-origin pasta called panzotti (a kind of walnut-sauced ravioli, triangular-shaped), fish soup, and gamberoni in umido—tomato-sauced shrimp. On the main square. *First Class.*

Stella's (Phone 69-007) specialties include minestrone alla Genovese, a tasty insalata di pesce or seafood salad, and sogliola—that's sole, if you hadn't guessed—simply grilled. On the waterfront. *First Class.*

Caffè Sottocoperta is an on-the-piazza gathering place for coffee, ice cream, drinks, and Portofino's prime pastime: people-watching. *Moderate.*

La Gritta bills itself as an "American bar"; draws an amusing evening crowd to banquettes within and alfresco waterfront tables. *First Class.*

Scafandro competes with La Gritta (above) as a watering hole. The bar and blue and white striped banquettes of the interior are classy, and there are harbor-view tables outside. *First Class.*

SOUND OF MUSIC

Teatro Margherita (Via XX Settembre, Genoa)—for many years the principal venue for opera, ballet, and symphonic concerts—now has company: *Teatro Carlo Fenice* (Piazza dei Ferrari), heavily bombed during World War II, was a long time rebuilding, finally opening in 1991. Ask your concierge for *L'Agenda,* a monthly "What's On" booklet.

SHOPPER'S GENOA

Department stores are big: *Upim* (Piazza Campetto), *Coin* (Via XII Ottobre), and *La Rinascente* (Via XX Settembre). Via Roma has its share of smart shops. Via Garibaldi's gorgeous palazzi contain elegant antique shops, with *D. Villa,* for contrast, a fabulously fancy candy shop. Adjacent Via Cairoli is dotted with antique shops too. Pedestrians-only streets include Via Luccoli and Via San Luca (lined with potted daisy plants).

INCIDENTAL INTELLIGENCE

It is worth my repeating that there are two Genoa railway stations, *Stazione Principe* (Piazza Acquaverde) and—at the other end of town—*Stazione Brignole* (Piazza Verdi). *Aeroporto Cristoforo Colombo* is four miles west of town, with domestic and foreign flights. *Further Information:* Ente Provinciale per il Turismo, Stazione Principale, Genoa; Azienda Autonoma di Soggiorno e Turismo, Via XXV Aprile 2-B, Santa Margherita Ligure; Azienda Autonoma di Soggiorno, Via XX Settembre 33, Camogli; and Via Roma 35, Portofino.

15

Gubbio

Medieval Mountain Stronghold

BACKGROUND BRIEFING

The secret of Gubbio's success—by that I mean remaining virtually medieval, save for such amenities as electricity and plumbing—is the railroad. Or, more accurately, the lack of same. If you want to visit this enchanter (it climbs a mountain in the Umbria countryside), you arrive by car or bus. And, chances are, you depart grateful for the way this little town has resisted the advances of progress.

Earlier visitors made do with earlier modes of transport. One has only to consider Gubbio's previous names to appreciate its substantial background. The ancient Umbrian people—with a culture embracing a written language—called it *Ikuvium.* Later, invading Romans changed the nomenclature to *Eugubium.* (The brilliant theater they built still is to be seen and, indeed, still is in use.) Medieval Gubbio—at first a *comune,* or independent city-state, later under the aegis of the dukes of not-far-distant Urbino—was called *Agobbio.* This period (the fourteenth century) constituted the city's Golden Age. It was then that it took on the look—stone mansions lining narrow streets climbing the slopes of Monte Ingino, monumental palazzi fronting broad squares created for the pageantry of the epoch, churches mellowed over the centuries—that, quite miraculously, it retains today.

The Papal States absorbed Gubbio in the seventeenth century, and with its rule creativity, vitality, and industry ebbed. Then, in the middle of the last century, Gubbio became a part of the modern kingdom of Italy. It remains small—the population hovers at 30,000—though boasting a crafts tradition way out of proportion to its size, and still another tradition, hospitality, that succeeds in evoking the spirit of centuries past, for even the shortest-term of visitors.

ON SCENE

Lay of the Land: Of course, what goes up must go down—including people. Still, it must be pointed out that Gubbio is a very vertical town and, withal, one you want very much to walk about in. Flat, rubber-soled shoes are desirable. Think positively as you ascend, always remembering that the descent is easier. The town revolves around a trio of central squares: northerly *Piazza della Signoria*, the most significant; middling *Piazza San Giovanni;* and southerly *Piazza Quaranta Martiri* (named, incidentally, for an incident in the town's modern history: the mass murder of 40 citizens by World War II Nazis). Principal streets feed traffic into and away from the squares, with *Via dei Consoli, Via Savelli della Porta, Via XX Settembre,* and *Corso Garibaldi* among them. This is a small town. Don't hesitate to walk aimlessly, because virtually every street is loaded with atmosphere and it's difficult to get lost—at least for long.

Palazzo dei Consoli (Piazza della Signoria) is the medieval masterwork that most typifies the glory that was Gubbio—with a slim bell tower in one corner, a crenelated roof framing its four super-high stories, a situation on one of the most beautiful (and beautifully situated) squares in Italy, with its across-the-piazza neighbor Palazzo Pretorio, the city hall. Within the Consoli, on the second floor, is an art museum *(Pinacoteca Comunale)* brimming with treasures (many of which are works of the Gubbio school of painting) from the same period—the fourteenth century—when the palace was built. For me, the most memorable work is Piero Francesco Florentino's utterly beautiful *Madonna*—blond-headed, a black robe covering her red gown—contemplating a reclining Christ child, while a towheaded young St. John the Baptist looks on. The high-ceilinged, exquisitely vaulted rooms in which paintings are displayed are so eye-filling as to almost fight with the art. On your way out, pause in *Museo Civico,* on the main floor, to pay your respects to the *Tavole Eugubine,* so-called Tablets of Gubbio, that go back to the dawn of the Christian era but were discovered as relatively late as the fifteenth century. They relate the accomplishments of the dozen governing priests of ancient Ikuvium, in both the Umbrian and Latin languages.

Palazzo Ducale (Via Ducale) commemorates the rule of the dukes of Urbino, who took over in the fourteenth century. The very same Federico of Montefeltro, who was so highly respected in his hometown of Urbino (chapter 36), built himself this fifteenth-century palace in Gubbio on the remains of an older structure. It is by no means as beautiful as Palazzo Ducale in Urbino, which is hardly to admonish against having a look at it. If the scale and difficult-to-achieve grandeur of the Urbino counterpart are absent, attention to detail—vaulting, capitals, door and window frames, fireplaces—is not. And the exterior is handsome.

Duomo (Via Ducale): Gubbio's Gothic cathedral is smaller than many and has but a single nave. But what a nave! Its ceiling is supported by pointed stone arches—ogival, they're termed—that create a brilliant geometric look. Take in the ravishing frescoes (including some by the Gubbio master Timoteo Viti) that embellish the high altar. The façade—with reliefs of the apostles framing its rose window—is lovely. So are many works of art in the adjacent *Museo del Duomo.*

Church of San Francesco (Piazza Quaranta Martiri): Gubbio is especially fond of this church because St. Francis had Gubbio connections: a local family took him in after his father had made him unwelcome at the family home in Assisi (chapter 3). This church, named for the saint, remains pure Gothic without, but with an interior that has been tampered with over the centuries and that is now essentially Baroque. There are some lovely frescoes, with the local Ottaviano Nelli among artists whose work graces the high altar. And the original cloister charms.

Church of Santa Maria Nuova (Via Ottaviano Nelli): Behind a weathered and severe Gothic façade lie some eminently inspectable treasures in this much-restored church; namely, the side chapels' intricate altars and some paintings, especially *Madonna della Belvedere* by Nelli.

Church of Sant' Agostino (Via Porta Romana) is originally Gothic, albeit with a Baroque façade. You go for the frescoes completely covering walls and ceilings in the apse, by the prolific Nelli. Their theme is St. Augustine's life, but in the telling, Nelli portrays, as well, scenes of domestic life of the Renaissance.

Basilica of Sant' Ubaldo (Monte Ingino): Up you go on a funicular from the in-town station near Church of Sant' Agostino (above) to the church that houses remains of the patron saint of Gubbio. It's attractively Baroque with a Renaissance portal, in a setting affording panoramic views of town and countryside.

Teatro Romano (Viale del Teatro Romano) has achieved the ripe old age of 1900+. The travertine of its walls is rusticated, unlike the smoother-surfaced material of other Roman theaters. And the perspective of the town below is striking.

SETTLING IN

San Marco Hotel's (Via Perugina 5) ace in the hole is an alert staff that's all smiles. Not that it is without other attributes: 60-plus rooms, no two quite alike, with baths in most; a handsomely brick-vaulted restaurant, about which more in a later paragraph; a congenial bar-caffè and inviting lounges. *First Class.*

Bosone Hotel (Via XX Settembre 22) is a history-packed palazzo converted with panache into a modern hotel. There are 28 rooms, some with original Renaissance décor, some contemporary. Bar and breakfast, but no restaurant. *Moderate.*

DAILY BREAD

Federico da Montefeltro (Via della Repubblica 35; Phone 927-3949): A restaurant named for the gifted fifteenth-century duke who built Gubbio's Palazzo Ducale has to have something going for it—and does: delicious cuisine and a friendly staff. Consider such pasta openers as quill-shaped penne with a piquant arrabbiata sauce or the excellent cannelloni—with entrées embracing veal (piccatina all' Eugubina) or chicken (pollo arrosto), crisp green salad accompanying. *First Class.*

Fornace di Mastro Giorgio (Via Mastro Giorgio 2) is, to understate, romantic, given its location in quarters dating to the Middle Ages. Notable pastas and veal entrées. *First Class.*

San Marco Hotel Ristorante (Via Perugina 5; Phone 927-2349) is atmospheric enough, framed by brick vaults, but when the weather is fine it moves to an arbor-covered garden. Select a pasta sauced with local truffles or mushrooms, with a grill—beefsteak or veal chops—to follow. Umbrian wines. *First Class.*

Porta Tessenaca (Via Piccardi 21; Phone 927-2765): You're but steps from Piazza della Signoria at this well-located, well-priced restaurant. Open with antipasto, specifying some of the good Umbrian salami as part of your selection. Simply sauced spaghetti ad aglio e olio—with oil and garlic—is a possibility; so are the day's meat specials. *Moderate.*

Caffè Bargello (Via della Repubblica 45) is indicated for a coffee pause, mid-morning or mid-afternoon. Central and *Moderate.*

AFTER DARK

Gubbio's *Teatro Romano* becomes a summer theater—plays are performed in Italian, though—mid-July through mid-August.

SHOPPER'S GUBBIO

In no Italian city is the ancient handicrafts tradition—pottery, especially—more a vital part of the economy. Earmark a couple of hours to make the rounds of shops (they double often as studios) on streets leading from the central squares. Besides potters, you'll find woodcarvers, stonecarvers, weavers, wrought-iron workers, even cabinetmakers at their work. But it's ceramists whose wares are most popular. Their shops line central streets, especially Via dei Consoli, site—at No. 71—of a permanent exhibition of artisans' work.

INCIDENTAL INTELLIGENCE

If you haven't your own (or rented) wheels, you may travel by train north from Rome, alighting at Fossato di Vico, to complete the remaining 10 miles to Gubbio by bus. There is bus service, as well, from Perugia (35 miles) and lesser points. *Further information:* Azienda Autonoma Comprensoriale di Soggiorno e Turismo, Piazza Oderisi 6, Gubbio.

16

Lecce

and Beyond to Brindisi

BACKGROUND BRIEFING

Lecce? A smallish city in the interior of southerly Apulia (the region that constitutes the heel of the peninsular boot), it is *terra incognita* to most Italians, not to mention visitors from foreign shores. Quiet and unassuming, as modern cities go, it is nothing less, architecturally, than southern Italy's urban sleeper. The city boasts a core—a substantial core, to be sure—that is a veritable symphony in Baroque, finely detailed by Lecce architects during a period spanning the late sixteenth to the eighteenth centuries, when the town enjoyed its Golden Age.

There were earlier history-rich Lecce centuries. Legend decrees its founder, one Malennio, king of the ancient Salentines. (The peninsula on which it is situated to this day is referred to locally as Salento.) Invaders from across the waters to the east followed, and Lecce became part of Magna Grecia. Romans—whose amphitheater in the heart of the city was unearthed as recently as the third decade of the present century—followed, to be succeeded by cultivated Normans, whose courtiers and kings (Frederick of Swabia, especially) made of it a splendid medieval city.

But it was during the late Renaissance and Baroque centuries (when merchant princes reigned and the church became powerful) that Lecce became opulent—with monumental gates and massive palaces, monasteries and churches, fountain-centered squares and serene gardens. Today's visitor wants to pay close attention in the course of exploration, for it is the intricately detailed carving of Lecce Baroque that is distinctive: saints and warriors, flowers and fruits, warriors and hunters, ribbons and garlands—the lot bespeaking a peculiarly Lecce brand of exuberance.

ON SCENE

Lay of the Land: The city revolves around central *Piazza Sant' Oronzo,* with shop-lined *Via Vittorio Emanuele* running westward, the quite marvelous Roman Amphitheater to the south and a positively monolithic sixteenth-century castle—trapezoidal in shape—the landmark to the west. Perfectly beautiful streets lead to perfectly beautiful ceremonial gateways cut into medieval walls—*Porta Napoli* (erected in 1548 for a proposed visit of Holy Roman Emperor Charles V, which never materialized), *Porta Rudiae, Porta San Biagio.* Before zeroing in on specific monuments, make casual forays along such thoroughfares as *Via Rubichi, Via Petronelli, Via Paladini, Via D'Aragona, Via dei Conti di Lecce*—to name but a handful.

Basilica di Santa Croce (Via Umberto) represents Lecce Baroque at its most spectacular. The architect Giuseppe Zimbalo—responsible for more important Lecce works than any other—completed it in 1689. The interior is almost anticlimactic after the dazzler of a façade, subdivided into top and bottom sectors by a gallery above the three entrances. With an intricately bordered rose window its focal point, the upper half of the façade is a meld of saints in niches, cherubs in flight, fantastic animals acting as supports for a gallery, a fanciful pediment topping it all off. Within, a giant painting, *The Assumption,* has been placed in the center of a gilded, coffered ceiling over a long nave flanked by columns whose carved capitals are a minor glory. Next door, a former convent, now *Palazzo del Governo,* still another work by architect Zimbalo, bears scrutiny. Observe its two-story façade before popping in to have a look at the sumptuous onetime cloister—now, alas, a parking lot for civil servants' cars.

Duomo complex (Piazza del Duomo) stuns, with both detached campanile (a quintet of tapered levels, with the top one a little octagon) and cathedral proper (the work of the same Zimbalo who created Santa Croce). Its standouts are a wooden ceiling studded with paintings, lavishly decorated altars, and a crypt whose principal décor consists of carved capitals (no two alike) of the network of columns supporting its ceiling. That leaves the somewhat later and adjacent *Palazzo del Seminario*—with the masterfully embellished well in its courtyard topped by a sculpted *Madonna.*

Church of SS. Nicolò e Cataldo (Via Cimitero) is a ten-minute drive from the center, on a street named for a cemetery just off the highway to Brindisi. It's worth stopping off to inspect, because of the unusual aesthetic success that has been achieved in combining such disparate architectural styles as Romanesque (from the twelfth century) and late Baroque, with a late Renaissance cloister recently restored to its original charm.

Museo Provinciale Sigismondo Castromediano (Viale Gallipoli 29): The kicker here is futuristic interior design—a three-level exhibition space united by spiral ramps, with the substantial collection mounted against stark black and white. Most important are remnants of ancient Greek Lecce, especially a slew of the two-handled vessels called kraters, decorated with scenes of mythology and domestic life, in black and terra-cotta. There is also a sampling of Roman Lecce (fragments of monumental sculpture), of medieval Lecce (a luminous altarpiece by Antonio Vivanni), a cache of the work of later Lecce painters (eighteenth-century Oronzo Tiso is hands-down standout), and of other Italian masters, an *Adoration of the Shepherds* by Bassano among them.

Anfiteatro Romano (Piazza Sant' Oronzo) is so dead-center that you're not likely to miss it. It is open to view only from the outside. But I make mention of it here just in case—and with the notation that it is believed to have had a capacity of some 25,000 when it was built eighteen centuries ago.

Other Baroque churches to savor in the course of Lecce promenades include *Santa Maria delle Grazie* (Piazza Sant' Oronzo), with paintings by the same Oronzo Tiso whose work I admire in the museum (above); *Santa Irene* (Via Vittorio Emanuele), with a classic façade of considerable dignity; *San Matteo* (Via del Perrone), with a façade half-convex, half-concave, and an interior made brilliant with architectural detail; *Gesù* (also known as *Buon Consiglio*, on Via d'Amelio), with a main altar that alone makes a visit memorable; *San Nicolò dei Greci* (Via Umberto 1), Italian with its Baroque design, Greek with the iconostasis-type altar framing a mass of icons—typical of Orthodox churches; *Santa Chiara* (Piazza Vittorio Emanuele), generously art filled; and *Del Rosario* (Via Libertini), another work by Zimbalo, with his touch evident in both vibrant façade and well-detailed interior.

BRINDISI

Brindisi is the little port city, known principally as a take-off point for Greece, some 30 miles north of Lecce. Visitors for centuries long—

Greeks, Romans, Crusaders, Normans—have known this strategically situated town, and it is easy to come to terms with, geographically.

The main shopping street, *Corso Roma,* later becoming *Corso Garibaldi,* cuts though town southwest to northeast ending at the waterfront, with two other important streets leading from it: mercantile *Corso Umberto* (a link of the Upim department-store chain) and historic *Via Duomo,* whose terminus, *Piazza del Duomo,* is a major stopping point. The *Duomo,* with statues of apostles topping its Baroque façade, has an interior notable for its thirteenth-century mosaic floor at the high altar, behind which is a superbly carved sixteenth-century choir. A mellow cloister that belonged to the crusading Knights Templar is next door, and just behind the square is a quite magnificent freestanding Roman column, *Colonna Terminale,* which marked the terminus of the ancient Rome–Brindisi Appian Way and dates to the turn of the second century A.D.

The Crusaders left behind a surprising number of churches. Two that I like are *San Giovanni al Sepolcro* (on the piazza taking its name), still adorned with original frescoes and with eight splendid columns supporting a reconstructed dome; and *San Paolo* (Piazza San Paolo), a mix of epochs, with five Baroque chapels its highlights. Brindisi's *Museo Archeologico Francesco Ribezzo* (Via del Duomo) is a modern structure housing exhibits (three good-sized floors of them) that are testimony to the town's remarkable history, with emphasis on Greek treasures—sculpture, ceramics, coins—and mementos of Roman Brindisi (splendid busts and capitals, especially). There remain manifestations of maritime Brindisi—no less than a trio of harbor areas: *Porto Interno,* closest to downtown and departure point for passenger ships to Greece; *Porto Medio,* for middle-sized freighters; and *Porto Esterno,* the outer harbor, for the biggest ships.

OSTUNI

Ostuni (some 20 miles north of Brindisi, almost twice that distance from Lecce) looks as though it could be across the water in Greece. Pristine, almost entirely whitewashed, it climbs a minimountain, a period piece with nary a discernible contemporary structure within its limited—nearly vertical—confines. Still, it's agreeable to have a walk around, starting at central *Piazza della Libertà,* through a maze of delightful narrow streets, past houses with coats of arms of owning families over entrances, stopping at handsomely Baroque *Church of Monacelle* (Via Pietro Vincenti), concluding at the Gothic *Duomo* (Largo Trinchera) towering above the town, with a stunning rose window a standout feature. If your trek is at midday, pause for lunch at *Ristorante Spessite* (Rione Antico; Phone 972-866), moderately tabbed.

SETTLING IN

LECCE

President Hotel (Via Salandra 6) pleases with its contemporary good looks—a witty foil to the dominant Baroque of Lecce. There are 150 good-sized, full-facility rooms and suites, capacious lobby, congenial bar-lounge, ranking restaurant of which more later, and professional staff whose credo is "service with a smile." Core of town is a 10-minute walk away. *First Class.*

Risorgimento Hotel (Via Augusto Imperatore 19): It's a pity that on my last visit mattresses tended to be thin, light bulbs weak, fare disappointing, staff barely civil, in a hotel occupying such a handsome nineteenth-century budding. Chalk it up to location—the best in Lecce—a step from Piazza Sant' Oronzo and the historic core; management is downright spoiled. There are nearly 60 rooms in traditional style (like the public spaces, they are not unattractive) along with a restaurant and bar-lounge. This could—and should—be a first-class house. But it's *Moderate.*

Grand Hotel (Viale Oronzo Quarta 28) is turn-of-century Art Nouveau with not quite 50 rooms, about half of which have baths. Restaurant, bar, fairly central location. *Moderate.*

BRINDISI

Internazionale Hotel (Lungomare Regina Margherita 26) is an old-timer from a gentler age. There are 87 rooms with bath (ask for one with a view of the port, which the Internazionale fronts), high-ceilinged lobby, convenient restaurant, honey of a bar-lounge, even a pretty garden, Nicest of all: experienced, congenial staff. *First Class.*

Majestic Hotel (Corso Umberto 1) is modern, tasteful, and functional, with not quite 70 smallish rooms, whose principal attraction is smart checkered-tile baths. Restaurant, bar-lounge, central location. *First Class.*

Hotel Regina (Via Cavour 5) is a step from Corso Umberto in the center of town, quite recently refurbished, with 42 functional rooms (the majority with private bath) and a pleasant lobby. Breakfast and bar. *Moderate.*

DAILY BREAD

LECCE

President Hotel Ristorante (Via Salandra 6; Phone 860-076) is the classiest eatery in town—high-ceilinged modern, in hues of pale pink and sea green. Order at will from the à la carte—perhaps risotto (a northern specialty here in the deep south) or Apulia's own pasta, orecchiette; with entries ranging from braised rabbit to grilled steak. *First Class.*

Birreria Dolomiti (Via Achille Costa; Phone 27-881): You may or may not associate this spot with the snowy peaks of the northerly Dolomites. Be that as it may, tuck into a range of pastas. Salads are good; sweets, too. And you may have wine as well as the beer that gives the place its name. *Moderate.*

Guidi & Figli (Via 25 Julio; Phone 58-342) is a short block from Piazza Sant' Oronzo, unpretentious and white-walled, with swift and polite waiters. Open with the orecchiette or antipasti assortiti, continuing with grilled fish of the region. Lots of locals. *Moderate.*

Campari (Piazza Sant' Oronzo) is at once pasticceria, tavola calda, and just plain caffè—with tables out front so that you can watch the world go by. On the principal square. *Moderate.*

BRINDISI

La Botte (Corso Garibaldi 72; Phone 28-400) is core-of-town, on a principal shopping street. It draws citizens as well as visitors with lures that include fresh seafood that serves as the basis of sauces for pasta and as entrées. *First Class.*

La Lanterna (Via Tarantini 14; Phone 224-026) is at its pleasantest in warm weather, when you may lunch or dine outdoors. Good Lecce grub. *First Class.*

Caffè dei Portici (Piazza della Victoria) is a congregating place of consequence. Snacks, drinks, coffee. *Moderate.*

SHOPPER'S LECCE

Via Vittorio Emanuele and satellite streets are an area shopping district of significance, and with branches of national chains.

INCIDENTAL INTELLIGENCE

The Brindisi Airport serves the area with flights to domestic points. And several companies' ships transport passengers (and their cars) between Brindisi and Greek ports including Corfu, Patras, and Athens (Piraeus). *Further information:* Azienda Autonoma di Soggiorno e Turismo, Via Rubieli 25, Lecce; Piazza Dionisi, Brindisi; Piazza della Libertà, Ostuni.

17

Lucca

Tuscan Town That Tries Harder

BACKGROUND BRIEFING

Talk about competition: Lucca, the still walled Tuscan town a dozen miles north of Pisa (chapter 27)—and like it, just inland from the Tyrrhenian Sea—rivaled Pisa in centuries past as a political and economic power, to the point of doing battle with it on more than one occasion.

Today, in the competition for tourist income, the Lucchese city fathers must be excused if, occasionally, they yearn for a tilt in the splendid and perfectly erect campanile of their opulent cathedral. Alas, they cannot compete with the Leaning Tower of their longtime antagonist. Lucca, despite all of its treasures, remains placid, with a much lower visitor count.

Still, the canny traveler does well to take advantage of this lack of visitor congestion. Better to move right along and become acquainted with this town, whose patina of age becomes it.

Lucca dates back to ancient Ligurians who came south from what is now the Italian Riviera, centuries before Christ—to be succeeded by Romans (who bequeathed the contours of a fabulous amphitheater in the heart of town). In the early Christian centuries—beginning about 500 A.D.—the Duchy of Lucca emerged, ruled by Lombardian nobles. Next came a more democratic system, with the town becoming a *comune* and self-governing. By the time Lucca evolved as a proper republic, all the while spatting at regular intervals with nearby Pisa and somewhat more distant Florence, it had become a mercantile center as famed then for the quality of its silk and the shrewdness of its bankers as it is today for the purity of its olive oil.

Wealth impelled construction, and no Italian city has a higher proportion of medieval churches, not to mention a cathedral that remains one of the most underappreciated in Italy. In the early nineteenth century, Napoleon, never averse to nepotism, liked Lucca well enough to have dubbed it a principality and installed his sister Elisa and her husband as its rulers. Then, for a brief period after the Congress of Vienna (before it became part of the united Kingdom of Italy), it changed governments twice more, first becoming a territory under the thumb of still another Napoleonic relative—the emperor's second wife, Maria Luigia, reigning as Duchess of Parma (chapter 25)—then switching allegiance to the Florence-based Grand Duchy of Tuscany.

ON SCENE

Lay of the Land: Unlike nearby Pisa, Lucca was not bombed during World War II. Centuries-old walls surround it, streets are lined with ancient palaces, squares of yore are dominated by ravishing Romanesque churches, and you feel as you walk about (the town within the walls is conveniently compact) that you've stepped back into the Renaissance and the centuries that preceded it. Walled Lucca is rectangular, with *Piazza Napoleone,* just south of the center, its focal point. Shop-filled *Via Vittorio Emanuele* leads west. Smaller *Piazza XX Settembre* and *Piazza del Giglio* (contiguous with Piazza Napoleone) flank it on the east and connect with *Via del Duomo* and, at its terminus, Piazza San Martino, site of the cathedral. *Via Vittorio Veneto,* another major commercial street, takes you north of Piazza Napoleone to *Piazza San Michele,* named for the church that vies aesthetically with the Duomo. Train and bus terminals are outside the southern walls, beyond *Piazza Vittorio Emanuele.*

Duomo (Piazza San Martino): Medieval Lucca set great store on the height of its towers. They were status symbols of the era, and inasmuch as no structure could be taller than the eleventh-century cathedral's campanile, it is not surprising to behold this veritable skyscraper of seven splendid levels. Look down, then, at the Duomo's façade: three tiers of loggias are supported by a triple-arched portico, sculpted in part by Nicolò Pisano of a famed Pisa family of sculptors. But the thrill of Lucca's Duomo is what greets you when you step inside: a staggeringly stupendous space with the painted Renaissance vaults of its nave framing a multitude of art treasures. You want not to miss Lucca sculptor Matteo Civitali's *San Sebastiano,* the same master's pair of angels in Cappella SS. Sacramenti, Fra Bartolommeo's painting, *La Madonna del Santuario,* Tintoretto's *The Last Supper,* Ghirlandaio's *Sacra Conversazione,* and an altarpiece of Filippino Lippi saints.

Church of San Michele (Piazza San Michele) stuns with the joyous Romanesque opulence of its façade—four strata of exquisitely arched loggias on the front, topped by a wonderful statue of St. Michael killing his dragon. Loggias are repeated on the sides. In the impressive interior, gaze on an enameled Della Robbia terra-cotta *Madonna* and still another Lucca work by Filippino Lippi—this, an altar panel of four saints.

Church of San Frediano (Piazza San Frediano) is celebrated, with good reason, for the giant mosaic depicting *The Ascension* that occupies the top of its otherwise plain Romanesque façade. The sculpted baptismal font is superb, and there are works by, among others, Matteo Civitali and Andrea della Robbia.

Church of San Giovanni (Piazza San Giovanni) is so central—next door to the Duomo (above)—that you want to pause and admire the extraordinary sculpture of its portal and, within, fairly recently excavated remnants of its original sixth-century edifice, this being the church that served as the first Lucca cathedral.

Pinacoteca Nazionale and Museo di Palazzo Mansi (Via Galli Tasi): Unless the situation will have changed by the time of your visit, you'll have to work a little harder here than in most art museums. There are no individual labels, but rather a single typed list of objects for each room. Still, rewards can be considerable. What you're experiencing are atmospheric period rooms of a Baroque palace: Camera degli Sposi, or bridal chamber, exuberantly gilded and with an extraordinarily high canopied bed, fabulously frescoed ballroom, drawing rooms rich with seventeenth- and eighteenth-century Italian furniture, and a slew of fine paintings. These, to give you an idea, include Pontormo's riveting study of a young Medici prince and works by such masters as Veronese, Van Dyck, Del Sarto, Giordano, and Tintoretto. A treat.

Museo Nazionale di Villa Guinigi (Via Quarquonia) occupies a capacious Renaissance residence that has been restored—perhaps with too severely contemporary a touch—for museum purposes. Withal, two floors of oversized galleries are treasure-filled. What impresses me most is an entire room full of luminous paintings by Fra Bartolommeo, with one, *Virgin and Child with Saints Sebastian and Rocco,* the standout. But there are works as well by Lippi and Botticelli, Pontormo and Batoni, along with significant caches of sculpture—ancient, medieval, and Renaissance.

Anfiteatro Romano (Piazza del Mercato) is like no other Roman amphitheater you'll encounter. It's a generous-size, elliptically shaped space enclosed by medieval houses that follow the precise contours of the original second-century theater.

Giro delle mura (A walk around the walls): Though newer than much of the town (they date back only to the sixteenth and early seventeenth centuries), the city's walls remain not just intact, but with tops wide enough so that, during the nineteenth-century aegis of Napoleon's widow, Duchess Maria Luigia, they were transformed into a public park. Enter on or near any of the city's lovely classic-style gates—Porta San Pietro, Porta Santa Maria, Porta San Donato, Porta Santa Elisa, Porta Sant' Anna, or Porta San Jacopo—and enjoy a scenic walk, with views to one side (*dentro,* within) of Lucca and to the other (*fuori,* outside) of the walls.

Casa di Puccini (Via di Poggio, near Piazza San Michele): A stone plaque over the front door of this plain brick house indicates that composer Giacomo Puccini (who died in 1924) was born within, in 1858. He studied piano and organ in Lucca before going on to the Milan Conservatory. If you are a devotee of such Puccini operas as *Manon Lescaut, La Bohème, Tosca,* and *Turandot,* you will of course want to pay your respects. Contents: Pucciniana in quantity enough to satisfy the most partisan fan.

Villas in the countryside went up in quantity during the fourteenth and fifteenth centuries, built by Lucchese merchant princes and not unlike those near Florence. A trio of the most spectacular are: *Villa Reale,* "royal" by reason of early-nineteenth-century habitation by Napoleon's sister Elisa (ruling as Lucca's "princess") and only four miles from town; *Villa Torrigiani,* with a statue-studded façade no less elaborate than its sculpture-filled garden, and richly furnished staterooms; and *Villa Garzoni,* immense and fresco-filled, with a somewhat newer annex edging parklike gardens. Before you set out, make sure the villa(s) of your choice will be open. Lucca's tourist office (below) will know and will help with directions.

SETTLING IN

Universo Hotel (Piazza Puccini) is the kind of traditional, really old-school hotel that lots of us cross the Atlantic to inhabit. It could have done with some refurbishing when I last inspected, but it is heart-of-town, friendly, with a good proportion of rooms with bath. Restaurant and bar. *Moderate.*

Ilaria Hotel (Via del Fosso 20) is a nicely refurbished building of some age, well located ten minutes by foot from Piazza San Michele or Piazza Napoleone. There are 17 rooms with bath and a bar-lounge, but no restaurant. *Moderate.*

Rex Hotel (Piazza Ricasoli) is just opposite the train station (you'll save on taxis to and from) and within walking distance of the center. There are 22 rooms with bath, bar-lounge, and breakfast, but no restaurant. *Moderate.*

DAILY BREAD

Buca di Sant' Antonio (Via della Cervia 1; Phone 55-881): Silk-shaped lamps dropping from a gracefully arched ceiling illuminate the principal room of this restaurant, located in an aged core-of-town house, with a jumble of hanging copper pots accenting the décor. Welcome is formal but cordial, smiling green-blazered waiters expert, food exceptional. A meal might embrace risotto al funghetto (with mushrooms) or ravioli di ricotta al pomodoro basilico (with ricotta cheese, tomato, and basil), continue with such entrées as capretto allo spiedo (grilled kid, a house specialty), bracciole di cinghiale al cartoccio (roast wild boar), or a more prosaic bistecche alla fiorentina, and conclude with a sumptuous sweet. Accompany with a Lucca-area wine. In my experience, one of Italy's best restaurants. *Luxury.*

Giglio (Piazza del Giglio; Phone 44-058) is as attractive without (it is situated in a substantial Baroque palazzo) as within, with the ambience appropriately traditional. Antipasto makes a delicious opener; veal (prepared any number of ways), a good main course. If you've ordered a red wine—the choice is wide—consider concluding with cheese. *First Class.*

Trattoria da Leo (Via Tearmi 11; Phone 4-22-36): The friendly brothers Buralli welcome you with a smile and serve up a satisfactory meal. A soup and pasta-cum-salad lunch is a good bet. *Moderate.*

Antico Caffè delle Mura (Piazza Vittorio Emanuele): How about unwinding over an espresso at a caffè atop the city wall? Snacks and drinks as well—and lovely views. *Moderate.*

Antica Locanda dell' Angelo (Via Pescheria 21) is well situated—between the Duomo and the old town—and atmospheric. *First Class.*

Caffè dei Mercanti's (Piazza Scarpellini) tables extend into a pretty little square that, on a fine day, can be the setting for a happy rest pause. Near Anfiteatro Romano. *Moderate.*

SOUND OF MUSIC

Lucca's classic-style *Teatro del Giglio* (Piazza del Giglio) presents operas, concerts, and ballets. The tourist office (address below) has seasonal programs.

INCIDENTAL INTELLIGENCE

If you are contemplating a visit to Lucca from nearby Pisa, or vice versa, note that bus service between the two towns is quick, cheap, and frequent. *Further information:* Entre Provinciale per il Turismo, Via Vittorio Veneto 40, Lucca.

18

Mantua/Mantova

Glory of the Gonzagas

BACKGROUND BRIEFING

It is simplification to be sure, but when you get down to it, Mantua's color-drenched past can be divided into three. There is early, early Mantua—possibly (but not definitely) Etruscan before it became Roman and eventually (in the early Middle Ages) a self-governing *comune*. Then, to skip past a substantial period, there is post-mid-nineteenth-century Mantua, when this city (southeast of Milan, in the *Regione* of Lombardy) joined the united Kingdom of Italy, which preceded the present republic.

Remaining are the exciting Mantua centuries (early fourteenth through early eighteenth), when the city-state was ruled by marquises (later styled dukes) of the Gonzaga dynasty, whose *dramatis personae* are the stuff of which pre-World War II movie melodramas were churned out with style and verve. (Where are you Errol Flynn, George Brent, Bette Davis, Flora Robson, Sir C. Aubrey Smith?)

For, make no mistake, Mantua remains today the ultimate locale for the derring-do costume adventure embracing a succession of historic eras displayed in magnificent environments. It is not absolutely necessary to tour the town with a genealogical chart of Gonzagas in hand. But a little background is not out of order. After all, it is the Gonzagas who wrought—or at least caused to be wrought—monuments of this still smallish but surprisingly monument-filled city.

Trick is to concentrate on the culture-vulture Gonzagas, makers and doers found among a dozen-plus of the family's rulers. It is enough, for example, briefly to note that the first Gonzaga, Luigi, took over Mantua in a bold *coup d'état* from the then ruling Bonacolsi clan. The year was

1328. The third ruler, Gianfrancesco, bought the title of marquis (the tab was 12,000 gold florins) from the Holy Roman Emperor in 1433. He gets credit for hiring the painter Pisanello. But his son, Ludovico II, was the first intellectual Gonzaga—at once a vigorous exponent of the Renaissance's then novel humanist concepts, builder of consequence, and patron of the artist Mantegna. That genius-painter worked at the court some four decades, creating among much else a fresco-lined room, which in and of itself is reason enough for a Mantua visit.

Skip, then, to Francesco II, best remembered for his choice of wife: Isabella d'Este, who in the late fifteenth century lured painters, sculptors, writers, and philosophers to Mantua, making it one of the most talked-of European courts. All the while, Isabella collected art objects—some still to be seen—with consummate taste. Francesco's heir, Federico II, succeeded in having the ruler's title upped from marquis to duke and was responsible for the importation from Rome of artist-architect Giulio Romano, responsible for much of the brilliance of Renaissance Mantua.

Remember, also, Vicenzo I. Handsome and dynamic, he brought painters like Rubens and composers like Monteverdi to Mantua—and was the last of the great Gonzagas. The second Vicenzo sold off a cache of the family's choicest paintings (by the likes of Titian, Correggio, Bellini, and Mantegna) to King Charles I of England, whose Mantua acquisitions were a substantial part of what became recognized (alas, after Charles was beheaded) as one of the great European art collections.

More Mantuan art left the city before the dissolute tenth and last duke died in 1708. But quite enough Gonzaga-inspired brilliance remains to dazzle the visitor. It is no wonder that Verdi's *Rigoletto* opens in the Gonzagas' Mantua palace; Italian opera librettists have never shied away from the visually spectacular.

ON SCENE

Lay of the Land: Three lakes—sensibly named *Maggiore, Mezzo,* and *Inferiore*—surround as many sides of the city. The railway station, fronting *Piazza Leoni* with Lago Maggiore as a backdrop, is detached from the historic core, which centers about two squares: *Piazza Erbe* (flanked by landmark structures and dotted with caffès and restaurants that go outdoors in warm weather) and, connected with it by shops lining arcades of *Via Broletto, Piazza Sordello* (larger than Piazza Erbe but, like it, restaurant-filled and the site not only of the cathedral but of the palace complex of the Gonzagas). Two more squares—*Piazza Mantegna* and contiguous *Piazza Marconi*—lead in the opposite direction from Piazza Erbe (via the boutiques of *Corso Umberto, Via Roma,* and *Via Principe Amadeo*) to still other sections of the city, detached from the core but with destinations of consequence, as I shall try to make clear in succeeding paragraphs.

Palazzo Ducale complex (Piazza Sordello): I employ the word "complex" advisedly. The palace is a collection of structures built mostly between the early fourteenth and late seventeenth centuries, embracing some 500 rooms—sleeping chambers through banquet halls—and 15 courtyards. These last, the courtyards, along with the corridors, are themselves aesthetically noteworthy. But there's a catch, a major catch. Unlike (to cite one example) admittedly smaller Palazzo Ducale in Urbino (chapter 36), Mantua's powers-that-be insist that you go through on frequently departing guided tours—or not at all. The problem with these expeditions (and I appreciate that authorities must cope with the crush of crowds, especially in summer) is that you are taken too quickly through the bulk of the vast, treasure-filled palace—which is bad enough. But the real heartbreaker is the specific time limit guards allow visitors—who must queue up before entering—in the single most fascinating room, the Mantegna-frescoed Camera degli Sposi, where you may remain but a niggardly three minutes. What I seriously propose, therefore, is that you embark on two guided visits; you miss far too much on one alone.

The painters comprise a staggering group: Pisanello (whose frescoes were discovered only in 1969), as well as Rubens, Correggio and Titian, Tintoretto and Mantegna. The diversity, with respect to size, proportions, and décor of staterooms, staggers—the embellished corridors, a gallery of mirrors, intimate living quarters of Isabella d'Este, Giulio Romano's exuberant frescoed Sala di Troia, marble-walled Sala di Mano, Brussels tapestries based on cartoons by Raphael in Appartamento degli Arazzi, Baroque splendor of Salone dei Fiumi, intricate ceiling of Sala del Labirinto (a small-scaled suite of rooms presumably designed for dwarfs who served as court jesters), classic-style Cappella Santa Barbara, not to mention the maze of courtyards (some with formal flowerbeds, some flanked by elegant loggias, some utterly and simply severe).

That leaves best for last: the only remaining Mantegna art in a city where that master worked for 46 years—painting frescoes commissioned by Marquis Ludovico II for the Castello di San Giorgio part of the complex. Mantegna took almost a decade, starting in 1465, to portray (on walls and ceiling of the Camera degli Sposi, or Bridal Chamber, of the Palace) the three generations of Ludovico's family in a pair of wall paintings beneath a *trompe l'oeil* sky that covers the ceiling. This is a masterpiece that bears repeated observation—depicting Ludovico, his wife, children, and a clutch of courtiers in one fresco and Ludovico with family members greeting his son Francesco (just appointed a cardinal) in the other. Clothes, hairstyles, accompanying dogs and horses, furniture and décor, background land- and townscapes, most of all character as delineated in courtiers' facial expressions—Mantegna has captured it all.

Palazzo Te (Viale Te) is a celebration—generous and joyous—of the genius of the painter-designer Giulio Romano: a rural retreat for Duke Federico II, where he and his mistress could get away from court ritual. Palazzo Te, built between 1525 and 1535, is set off by a formal garden. Its principal salons are gained from a central court, itself reached from a statue-studded loggia. The Romano frescoes take your breath away: Cupid and Psyche's wedding feast in the Sala di Psiche; Federico's beloved horses, life-size and painted in profile, in Sala dei Cavalli; a clutch of paintings, one for each sign of the zodiac, in Sala dello Zodiaco; Federico's dazzler of a bedroom; and the smasher of the lot, a graphic depiction of the Fall of the Titans (you feel the crumbling columns are about to engulf you) in Sala dei Giganti.

Palazzo d'Arco (Piazza d'Arco) is a leap from the Renaissance to the Rococo—an impeccable late-eighteenth-century mansion, inspected by means of regularly departing tours that take less than an hour and that are—in contrast to the rushed group inspections of Palazzo Ducale (above)—eminently satisfying. You see quite a lot in each room—family portraits and still lifes, exquisite architectural detailing, fine antique fabrics, frescoes and ceramics, musical instruments and porcelain, a kitchen and a chapel, along with a garden setting off the Palladian-style façade of what is one of the most evocative manifestations of the eighteenth century anywhere in Italy outside of Venice.

Duomo (Piazza Sordello): From the front and—for that matter—inside, the Duomo is classic-style Renaissance (homage to the fine hand of Giulio Romano), with coffered ceiling and Corinthian capitals of columns lining the long, wide nave. But bits and pieces of the original cathedral happily remain—the right outer wall (still Gothic), and Gothic frescoes brightening an entire chapel.

Church of San Lorenzo and Piazza Erbe: San Lorenzo is an eleventh-century gem, a perfect circle of a little church, with a fine cupola that is but one of Piazza Erbe's landmarks.

Piazza della Regione's up-a-flight Sala di Justicia has sixteenth-century frescoes and is still used for public exhibitions. And *Palazzo del Podestà* has been City Hall since it went up in the thirteenth century.

Church of Sant' Andrea (Piazza Mantegna) is essentially the work of a master Mantua designer of the Renaissance, Leon Battista Alberti. It is immense and rather coldly serene, with Giulio Romano and Correggio among those whose paintings are within.

Casa del Mantegna (Via Acerbi) is forbiddingly severe from without. But do go in, if only for the distinctive courtyard (pebbles of its floor are arranged in the shape of an eight-point star). Mantegna is believed to have designed the house in the late fifteenth century.

A pair of theaters: Most Italian cities the size of Mantua are pleased to have one traditional-style theater; Mantua has two. The elder, *Teatro Scientifico* (Via dell' Accademia), is so called because it went up under the aegis of Empress Maria Theresa during the post-Gonzaga Austrian period—as a part of the Empress's Academy of Science. Mozart came from Vienna to conduct the opening concert, and it is the seat of the Mantua Symphony to this day. *Teatro Sociale* (Piazza Cavallotti) went up in 1818 in still another period of Austrian rule: the repressive post-Napoleonic period. Still, there is no denying its neoclassical good looks. Open only for performances.

SETTLING IN

San Lorenzo Hotel (Piazza Concordia 14) occupies a clutch of contiguous houses (of advanced age and considerable patina) on a little square but steps from Piazza delle Erbe. Public spaces are mostly furnished with nineteenth-century antiques, and there are fresh flowers all about. The nearly 50 rooms are no-two-alike, except that almost all have rocking chairs—an unusual touch. A bar edges the lobby, part of which doubles as a breakfast room. And there's a rooftop terrace. On my last visit, the owner-managers were twins—one bearded, the other not. No restaurant, but lots of charm. *First Class.*

Rechigi Hotel (Via Calvi 30) is functional-modern and central, with a lobby-lounge furnished with comfy leather chairs its most attractive aspect. There are 50 rooms. Bar and breakfast but no restaurant. *Moderate.*

Italia Hotel (Piazza Cavallotti 8) is a worth-knowing-about little house on a major square (just opposite Teatro Sociale and a step from Upim department store) that's a short walk from the old town. Pleasant lobby-bar-lounge, agreeable rooms, and convenient restaurant. *Moderate.*

Dante Hotel (Via Corrado 54) welcomes with a chandeliered lobby, off which is a good-sized lounge-bar. There are 40 rooms, and location is fairly central. *Moderate.*

Mantegna Hotel (Via Fabio Filzi 10) does not, alas, evoke the great Renaissance painter's work. It is severely contemporary with a neat little lobby-cum-bar, breakfast but no restaurant, close to 40 rooms, and a location on a nondescript street that's a 10-minute walk from the center. *Moderate.*

DAILY BREAD

Trattoria Romani (Piazza Erbe 13; Phone 323-627) is one of several restaurants on atmospheric Piazza Erbe. Its barrel-vaulted ceiling is hung with copper cooking implements. Tables are set with gold-hued linen; paneled walls packed with contemporary paintings. In warm weather, you sit out on the square. The food is corking good, with tagliatelle con funghi (with a mushroom sauce) or con la selvaggina (with a game sauce) as tasty starters. Entrées include punta del vitello (rolled breast of veal) and lamb prepared in several delicious ways. *First Class.*

Trattoria al Ducale (Piazza Sordello 13; Phone 324-447) is just opposite Palazzo Ducale, with the Duomo also in full view. You're seated in the piazza at the least sign of fair weather. Fare tends to be as easy to take as scenery—competently prepared risotto, delicious veal, tempting cakes from the trolley. *First Class.*

Trattoria da Franco (Via Pescheria 28; Phone 362-784) is a bit away from the core, with neighborhood workers its regulars. Open with maccheroni al torchio, or have the same pasta sauced with basil. Bistecca di manzo (grilled beefsteak) is excellent, bracciole di vitello (rolled veal roast) is a good bet, and green salad mixed at table is tasty. Smiling welcome, smiling service. *Moderate.*

Il Cigno (Piazza d'Arco 1; Phone 327-101) is just opposite eighteenth-century Palazzo d'Arco (above) and itself is an old palace—albeit with a stark, white contemporary interior relieved by massed plants and modern art. Fare is essentially Mantuan, *nouvelle*-accented, with pastas the most successful dishes—at least in my experience. Entrées tend to be oddly sweetish as, for example, poached chicken with oil, vinegar, and raisins. Desserts are conventional; service can be pretentious though polite; prices are among the steepest in provincial Italy. *Luxury.*

Caffè Benincasa (Piazza Broletto) could not be better placed, if one would watch comings and goings of both Mantuans and visitors alike on the square adjacent to Piazza Erbe. *Moderate.*

Caffè Mantegna (Piazza Sordello): Tired feet after a trek through Palazzo Ducale? Take a chair here. Order a gooey sundae, for consumption as you check the passing parade. Result: instant revival. *Moderate.*

SOUND OF MUSIC

Both of Mantua's beautiful old theaters (above) are in operation. Your hotel porter can advise you if there are any opera or ballet performances at *Teatro Sociale* or any concerts at *Teatro Scientifico.*

INCIDENTAL INTELLIGENCE

Further information: Ente Provinciale per il Turismo, Piazza Mantegna 6, Mantua.

19

Milan/Milano

Congenial Colossus of the North

BACKGROUND BRIEFING

It is fair neither to the Milanese nor their countrymen to remark upon the un-Italian qualities of this richest and most contemporary of Italian cities. Still, there is no denying that outwardly both Milan's look and its demeanor are oddly unlike what one encounters elsewhere in urban Italy. Which is not to be critical.

It is simply by way of explaining to the first-timer the underlying reasons for the orderly taxi queues at the railway station, the immediately apparent low decibel count, the unchoked progression of vehicular traffic (without benefit of blaring horns, outstretched fists, or expletives from drivers), all the startling contrasts—especially with cities in the south—in the way ordinary transactions are effortlessly undertaken.

What it comes to is that if Milan is perhaps less exotic, even less adventuresome, and less fun than, say, Rome or Naples (especially to an outlander from northern climes), it has its reasons. It is as culturally hybrid as any single Italian city. Location has seen to that. If a case can be made for being too strategic, let Milan make it. Its Lombard Plain situation became a major intersection in Europe's transport scheme. While it gained tremendously in the areas of commerce and manufacturing, it was to pay a price for easy accessibility for many centuries, down to and including our own.

This respectably long history (it goes back to the Etruscans and later to Celts conquered by Romans who dubbed it *Mediolanum*) is not as easy to perceive in Milan as it is in, say, Florence or Venice, because its industrious citizenry, always impatient with the course of progress, obliterated much of the old in order to make the new possible. The antique features of Milan must, therefore, be searched for with more diligence than often is the case in Europe. Still, a backward glance reveals that it wasn't always locals who were to blame for a succession of new looks. Hostile invaders were frequently culprits.

Early Milan was orderly enough. Romans made it the seat of their Western Empire, and early Christian centuries saw it hold its own with Rome—to the point that a poet dubbed it *Roma Secunda.* It was in Milan that a local bishop, later sainted Ambrose, promulgated use of the Ambrosian Rite wherein—among other features—the congregation joined in the service by singing hymns for the first time.

Warlike Goths came to destroy—and, later, warlike Huns—with the same successful goals. By the sixth century, the Lombards (whose name the region still bears) had conquered Milan, and succeeding centuries saw it evolve commercially and politically to become powerful—all the while fighting battles, external as well as internal.

There was a century of independence (the twelfth), but then two great ruling clans came upon the scene. It was Viscontis first and then Sforzas—best-known of whom was Lodovico the Moor—who followed as dukes of Milan. The Renaissance saw the city a pawn in one battle or political intrigue after another, with such landlords as Spain, Austria, and France. Indeed, Napoleon made the city capital of his Cisalpine Republic and later of his Kingdom of Italy.

Finally, in 1861, Milan became an integral part of a unified Italy, able to concentrate on industry. But it was earlier (in the eighteenth century) that a pattern of development had evolved, whereby the old—meaning historic structures—was to be sacrificed for the new. The post-Industrial Revolution era saw further evolution in that direction, much as was the case in the eastern United States, which today has so few architectural souvenirs of a history that extends back four centuries. Even more of the old Milan was obliterated as a result of devastating World War II air raids. Decades since have seen remarkable restoration.

If today's Milan is hardly an Italian leader when it comes to ancient architecture, it compensates with distinction in other areas. It is gifted in matters musical (who does not covet a seat at La Scala?) and as a conservator of the fine arts, with a cluster of museums and galleries that are among the most underappreciated of any major European city's. Remaining are grace, style, and *éclat.* Milan excels at all three.

ON SCENE

Lay of the Land: Milan's modernity makes for a kind of uniformity of contour. Once one leaves the central core, there is a dearth of the distinctive landmark structures that exist in many other cities. The central sector is ringed by an artery that goes by a number of names—

Via Mulino delle Armi, Via Santa Sofia, Via Francesco Sforza, to cite some. Then, like spokes of a wheel, other wide streets lead from periphery to center; most important of them is *Via Manzoni.* The core to which they lead is *Piazza del Duomo,* the square named for the cathedral that is its landmark. From the *Duomo,* one passes through still another landmark structure—the shop-filled *Galleria*—to *Piazza della Scala,* which takes its name from the opera house at its edge and which leads into earlier-mentioned *Via Manzoni* and other principal streets. One can continue along Via Manzoni to *Piazza Cavour,* crossing to *Via Manin,* passing the park called *Giardini Pubblici* to *Piazza della Repubblica* (site of leading hotels) and, continuing northeast, to still another important point—*Stazione Centrale,* principal railway station (colonnaded and cavernous), with an important group of hotels surrounding it. *Castello Sforzesco,* another historic landmark, is northwest of Piazza del Duomo, with *Arco della Pace* (a Milanese variation on the theme of Paris's Arc de Triomphe) just beyond and not far from an enormous stadium, *Arena Civica.*

THE ESSENTIAL MILAN

Duomo (Piazza del Duomo): One senses the importance of the Duomo to the Milanese simply by considering its location: smack in the center, on a piazza that has intentionally been kept broad—the better to afford perspective. All of the major avenues that encircle Milan lead to the Duomo. Milan life revolves around the Duomo; no major European city regards its cathedral with more affection. Fortunately, this exceptional Gothic building is worth the attention. Work began in 1386 and went on, with interruptions, until as recently as 1965, when five bronze doors—started at the turn of our century—were completed. Consider the most vital of the building's statistics. It's enormous—the second-longest of Europe's major churches, just after St. Peter's in Rome. There are some 3500 pieces of sculpture not counting the 150 marvelous gargoyles. There are 135 pinnacle-like spires, including a central one with an elegant gilded Madonna atop it. Within, the central nave is supported by half a hundred chunky columns, topped with embellished capitals. The stained glass in and of itself is a treat. The Duomo has a Treasury of very old things as well as a museum—in a detached building across the square (below). A piece of advice with regard to outdoor viewing: The front façade is impressive enough, but nothing like the Duomo as seen from either side or from the rear. And a final Duomo suggestion: If the sun is shining on a lovely, clear day, ascend to the roof (there are elevators) for the lacy perspective of the flying buttresses, crowned with sculpted saints. You may walk all around it, and views are unforgettable. You make the journey by elevator with a ticket obtained on the main floor.

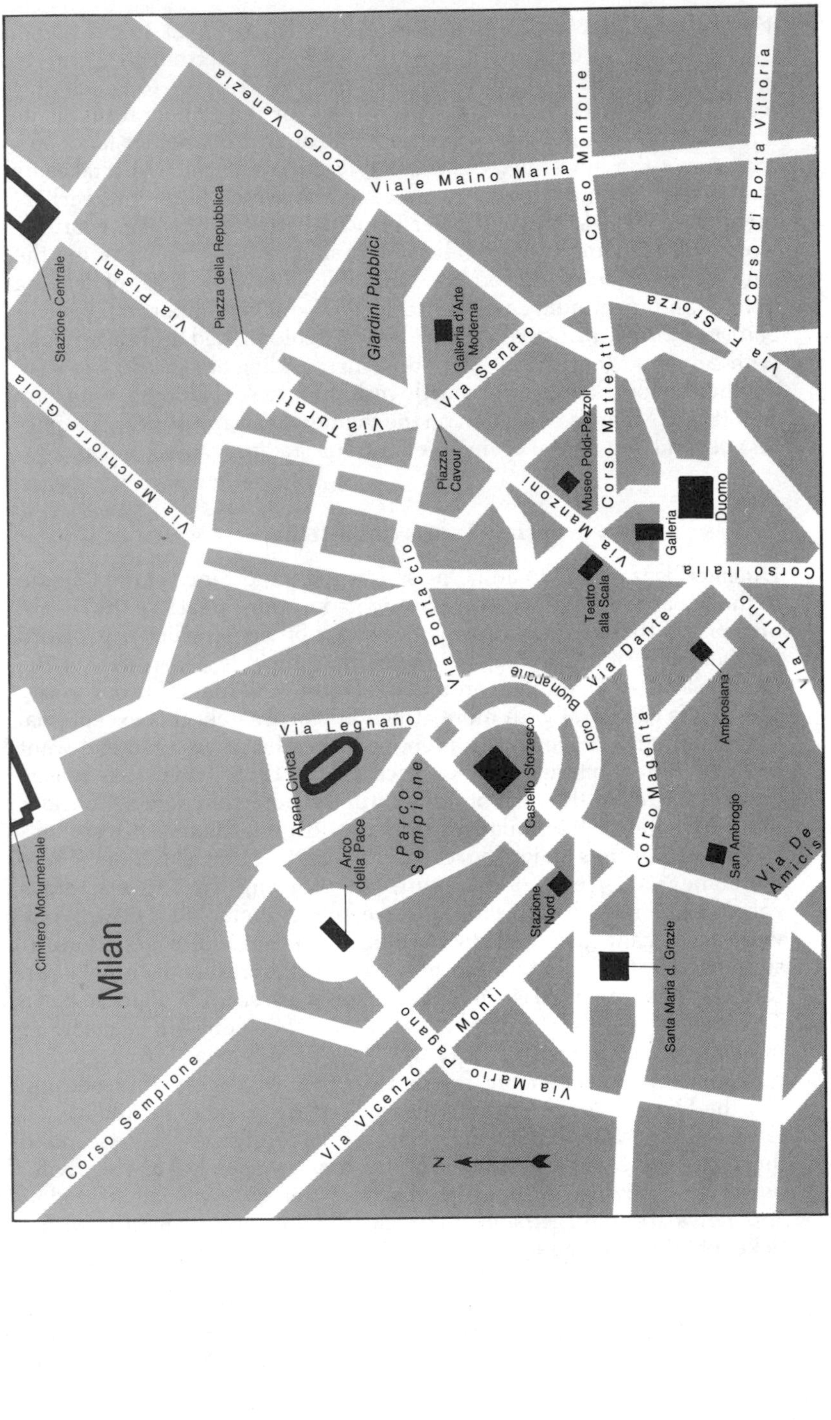
Milan
Corso Venezia
Viale Maino Maria
Corso Monforte
Corso di Porta Vittoria
Via F. Sforza
Via Pisani
Piazza della Repubblica
Stazione Centrale
Giardini Pubblici
Galleria d'Arte Moderna
Via Senato
Via Turati
Via Melchiorre Gioia
Piazza Cavour
Museo Poldi-Pezzoli
Corso Matteotti
Via Manzoni
Duomo
Galleria
Corso Italia
Teatro alla Scala
Via Pontaccio
Via Dante
Via Torino
Foro Buonaparte
Ambrosiana
Via Legnano
Arena Civica
Castello Sforzesco
Parco Sempione
Corso Magenta
San Ambrogio
Via De Amicis
Arco della Pace
Stazione Nord
Cimitero Monumentale
Santa Maria d. Grazie
Corso Sempione
Via Vicenzo Monti
Via Mario Pagano
N

Teatro alla Scala (Piazza della Scala): Americans can easily remember the date of the building—1776. The name is that of a church that had been on the site, Santa Maria alla Scala. Performances have been taking place since 1778. The façade is low-key, a cream-and-putty-colored building in neoclassic style that surprises one, after passing through its portico, with the opulence to be found within. La Scala is open to the public during the day, along with its separately entered museum (below). One must not expect an eighteenth-century gem like Venice's La Fenice or Naples's San Carlo. La Scala was remodeled in 1867, updated in 1921, and restored in 1946 after World War II bombing; Toscanini conducted the reopening concert. A monster of a crystal chandelier dominates a gilt and ivory auditorium embracing half a dozen levels of boxes and balconies superimposed over a single-aisle orchestra. Capacity is 2800. The onetime royal box is embellished with the five-point star of the Italian Republic's insignia, but the coat of arms of the old royal House of Savoy has been left over the proscenium. A daytime visit is better than none. Ideally, though, one attends a performance of either an opera (the season, *Stagione Lirica,* is December to May) or a concert (the season, *Stagione Sinfonica,* is spring through fall). Besides the opera company, there is l'Orchestra della Scala (120 instrumentalists) and Il Coro della Scala (90 voices).

The first opera produced at La Scala, back in 1778, was *Europa Riconsciuta,* by Mozart's rival, Salieri. It was in La Scala that premières of operas by any number of greats were sung—Bellini's *Norma,* Puccini's *Madama Butterfly* and *Turandot,* Verdi's *Falstaff* and *Otello* among them, with still other premières of operas by such composers as Donizetti, Mascagni, and Rossini.

Acoustics are unsurpassed; the ambience is coldly elegant. La Scala ushers, in formal black with silver necklaces (each bearing a likeness of the theater's façade on medallions), are so striking that one almost forgives them their arrogance. *Carabinieri,* in resplendent uniforms of an earlier century, strut about in pairs, not unlike soldier-characters in an opera. The audience is dressy (there is no better observation post to appraise the chattery Milanese), with the intermission bar crush as much a part of the La Scala experience as the architecture and on-stage performances.

The Great Museums: Brera, Sforzesco, Arte Moderna: Pinacoteca di Brera (Via Brera 28)—For someone like myself, who had observed the depths to which the Italian government had allowed the great Brera to sink in the 1970s, its rehabilitation is indeed cause for rejoicing. Originally a medieval convent, later a Jesuit college, in the eighteenth century (while Maria Theresa's Austrians were in control) the Brera turned Institute of Art and Science. Then, when Napoleon suppressed Italian churches, it became an important gallery, with fine paintings sent to it from throughout the peninsula.

Post–World War II decades saw budget cuts, deterioration, and the closing of exhibit spaces. But that sadly shabby Brera has made a comeback. Its splendidly proportioned halls are again repositories for a collection that is a leader in Italy, along with others in Florence, Venice, Naples, and Rome. Take your time as you pass through the courtyard (noting Canova's statue of Napoleon), up the grand staircase, and through the collection. What should you watch for? Let me name a few personal favorites: Vicenzo Poppa's archer taking aim at a martyred St. Sebastian; Bernardino Luini's *Madonna and Child* with flanking saints and donors; Bramantino's exquisitely rendered *Crucifixion*, angels flanking Christ on the cross; portraits of gents in black by Andrea Solario and Filippo Mazzola; Correggio's expressive *Adoration of the Magi;* Titian's revealing *Last Supper;* Carpaccio's architectural *Presentation of the Virgin at the Temple;* the Bellini brothers' monumental *St. Mark Preaching at Alexandria;* Mantegna's *Madonna and Child*, framed by *putti* in a drift of clouds; Veronese's *Jesus in the Garden;* Bramante's closeup *Christ at the Column;* and most memorable, Raphael's *Marriage of the Virgin*—the Brera's trademark. But it's not only the collection. The Brera has what must be the biggest shop of any museum in Italy (not that there are many such), and an even more distinct bonus: the only caffè of any museum that I know of in the entire republic. Bravo, Brera!

Museo d'Arte Antica al Castello Sforzesco (Piazza Castello)—Talk about walled castles: The Sforzesco, bearing the name of the Renaissance family that gave Milan a line of governing dukes, is first of all a grand structure with turreted walls, towering entrance gate, vast inner court—the lot going back to the fifteenth century. A long period of deterioration ensued before turn-of-century and post–World War II restorations took place. Today, the castle shelters a sleeper of a museum of both the fine and applied arts. The paintings alone make it worth a trip—local Lombards and other Italians like Bellini, Lippi, Lotto, Correggio, Tintoretto, and Mantegna. But then there is gallery after gallery of tapestries, ivories, glass, gold, silver, and most especially china and furniture, with pieces from three centuries, concluding with the eighteenth. You will, to be sure, do a lot of walking and, for that matter, of climbing—up and down centuries-old ramps and stairwells. (Women will want to wear flat-heeled shoes.) No matter, the Sforzesco is full of ravishingly beautiful things. And the setting is extraordinary.

Galleria d'Arte Moderna (Via Palestro 16) is about as misleading a museum name as one is likely to encounter. Modern art is but a part of the picture. This collection is housed in a park-enclosed palace away from the center—*Villa Reale*—that went up in the neoclassic style of the late eighteenth century. And it is well that you know before you go to allot enough time to look over the eye-popping suite of state rooms, as well as the paintings. Modern art, in the case of this museum, means most of the nineteenth century, especially Italian. Upstairs, though, is the Grassi Collection, which embraces French artists whom we always enjoy running across: Corot, Manet, Cézanne, Renoir, Gauguin, Vuillard, Bonnard. A next-door pavilion has more recent works by, among others, Italians such as Manzu, Marini, and Modigliani.

***Leonardo's* Last Supper** (Church of Santa Maria delle Grazie, Piazza Santa Maria delle Grazie), known locally as *Il Cenacolo,* occupies an entire wall of what had been the refectory of the convent attached to this church. Leonardo painted it in the late fifteenth century, at the request of the most famous of the Sforza dukes, Lodovico the Moor. And it has been the object of a number of subsequent restorations, the most recent in 1987. The refectory is operated as a museum by the Italian government and is well lighted, so that one is able to study faces and expressions of those attending this most decisive of historic dinners. On the opposite wall is a fine fresco of the Crucifixion by Montorfano. The church itself (fifteenth century) is distinguished by a massive and marvelous dome, and a charmer of a cloister (gained by a walk through the church interior)—both of them by Bramante.

Galleria Vittorio Emanuele II is but one of a number of these earliest of all shopping centers in Milan. To Milanese, it is simply the Galleria. Visitors come to know it straight off as it connects Piazza del Duomo with Piazza della Scala. It goes back a century and is cross-shaped, with an immense glass dome and a mosaic floor. Lures within are shops, restaurants, caffès (some later recommended), and (most fun of all) ambulatory Milanese.

BEYOND THE BASICS: SELECTED MUSEUMS

Museo Poldi Pezzoli (Via Manzoni 12): As if its alliterative name were not enough to draw one, the Poldi Pezzoli adds another ingredient: charm. This is a lovely mock-Gothic mansion a century or so old, with the nucleus of its collection the property of the man whose name it takes. Not unlike New York's Mr. Frick, Boston's Mrs. Gardiner, and Stockholm's Countess von Hallwyl, he left his home-cum-treasures to be operated as a museum. There have been newer acquisitions—the lot embracing one of the choicest of the smaller museum collections in Europe. A smashing *Portrait of a Young Woman* by Pollaiuolo has become this museum's trademark. But the second floor is full of eye-openers—Tiepolo's *The Fortitude and the Wisdom,* Cranach's *Martin Luther* (a subject rarely come upon in Italy), a Guardi of Venice, a Botticelli *Madonna,* a Bellini *Pietà,* to give you an idea. Downstairs is a quintet of sumptuous rooms brimming with bronzes, tapestries, china, furniture, rugs, docks, and glass.

Pinacoteca Ambrosiana (Piazza Pio IX) bears the name of the early Milanese bishop-saint. The gallery goes back to the collection of a seventeenth-century cardinal. It is housed in an early-nineteenth-century structure that is also home to the Ambrosiana Library, a treasure trove of illuminated manuscripts and other works, including Leonardo's *Codice Atlantis.* But it is the gallery that most visitors find important. Its fourteen rooms are evenly divided between two floors. Downstairs one does well to take in works of Lombard painters of the Renaissance. But it is upstairs that most excites—not only with Italian art but a higher proportion of foreign masters than is often the case in Italian museums. Suffice it for me to skim the surface: Botticelli, Ghirlandaio, Lippi, Vivarini, Luini (a slew of exquisite paintings), Leonardo and his school, Bronzino, Reni, Giordano, Bassano, Tiepolo, Titian. Not to mention sculptors out of the Middle Ages and gorgeous Flemish works. My favorites: Ghirlandaio's *Adoration of the Child* and (what has to be the most sublime of still lifes) a leafy basket of fruit by Caravaggio.

Museo Archeologico (Corso Magenta) is tucked into a onetime monastery adjacent to the Church of San Maurizio (below). Setting alone makes a visit enjoyable. There are a number of choice relics of the classical past—capitals, sarcophagi, handsome busts, a striking sculpture of Hercules, and some dazzling mosaics. The lot impresses upon the visitor the very great age of Milan.

Museo Civico di Milano and Museo Civico di Storia Contemporanea (Via Sant' Andrea 6) share quarters in a gracious eighteenth-century house. You come upon the latter first (its period is from World War I to World War II), when you should actually come upon it last, but no matter. It brings to mind (sometimes with ferocious honesty) that not always felicitous period, which included the fascistic Mussolini era. Museo di Milano is mostly seventeenth through eighteenth century in scope. There are furnished rooms from the house's original period and gallery after gallery of objects, including many delightful paintings.

Museo Civico del Risorgimento Nazionale (Via Borgonuovo 23) zeroes in on Milan's role in events (late eighteenth through mid nineteenth centuries) that led to Italy's unification. There are paintings, prints, documents—even including souvenirs of the 1805 Duomo ceremony at which Napoleon was crowned king of Italy. Later exhibits concentrate on the trio of heroes whom we remember from school: Mazzini, Garibaldi, and Cavour.

Museo Teatrale alla Scala (Teatro alla Scala) has its own side entrance and is indicated for opera buffs, with its documentation (paintings, prints, programs) relating to composers, singers, performances, Scala firsts, and Scala history. There are two rooms devoted to Verdi alone and still other exhibits relating to ballet and nonmusical theater, including Italy's commedia dell' arte.

Museo del Duomo (Palazzo Reale) occupies part of a fine old palace just across the way from the Duomo. Here are bits and pieces (and beautiful ones at that) from the six-century-long history of the cathedral—stone gargoyles, sculptured saints, jewel-encrusted crucifixes, rich tapestries, ancient stained glass, even architects' drawings from various eras.

Tecnica Leonardo da Vinci (Via San Vittore 21) is technologically advanced Milan putting its best foot forward. It's in a onetime monastery, with a monk's cell and a monastery pharmacy the only remnants of the building's former function. Technical matters—metallurgy, engineering, oil research, modern vehicles—fill the basement and overflow upstairs. For us nonspecialists, the lure is on the second floor: a socko presentation of the achievements of the genius for whom the museum is named.

Art Galleries: Milan is a major city for commercial art galleries: there are easily 40 rankers. If you're interested in visits, ask your hotel concierge (or the Milan tourist office, below) for the gratis brochure, *Artshow: Guida alle Mostre d'Arte.*

BEYOND THE BASICS: SELECTED CHURCHES

Sant' Ambrogio (Piazza Sant' Ambrogio) is a Romanesque beauty named for the sainted early Christian bishop who gave the Catholic church the Ambrosian Rite. Indeed, St. Ambrose consecrated the original church in A.D. 387. One enters its successor through its cloister. Within there is a Bramante-designed portico and memorable mosaics. After the Duomo, tops in town.

Sant' Eustorgio (Piazza Sant' Eustorgio) is something like a millennium old—a Romanesque souvenir of importance. To be noted within are the chapels—especially the one dedicated to the Three Kings and another, behind the apse, with superb frescoes.

San Lorenzo Maggiore (Corso di Porta Ticinese) has a smashing location, just opposite a cluster of sixteen gorgeous Corinthian columns—all that remains of an early Roman temple. The domed church is the Renaissance successor to an ancient original. Its chapels are embellished with mosaics.

San Maurizio (Corso Magenta 15) was earlier mentioned in connection with the Archaeological Museum, in its monastery. The church is sixteenth-century, and odd in that a wall separates one part of its nave from the other. The walls are the lure, for they are surfaced with frescoes by Bernardino Luini.

San Satiro (Via Torino) is a Renaissance replacement for an earlier church. Designer of the present building was the master Bramante. We may thank him for its splendid proportions and a lovely baptistry. There are fine frescoes.

EXCURSIONS TO PAVIA AND BERGAMO

Certosa di Pavia: A long-time Carthusian monastery that goes back to the fifteenth century, it is oddly and excessively ornamented, but is nonetheless architecturally impressive. The monastery is interesting in that its monks were under a rule so strict that each lived, ate, prayed, and worked in his own little stone house, a series of which surrounded the larger of the two cloisters. Only on feast days did they gather for communal meals and prayers in the chapel. The Carthusians departed in 1947, and a band of white-robed Cistercians are their successors. The drive south from Milan takes about an hour—each way, on ugly, traffic-clogged roads. And while in Pavia, you might want to visit the *University of Pavia,* founded in 1361, although its main building was begun in the seventeenth century and enlarged thereafter, with later buildings complementing it and with history and art-history museums. A closer destination is *Abbazia di Chiaravalle,* four miles southeast of town and architecturally more felicitous. There is a towering campanile, a Renaissance church with a frescoed dome, and a fine cloister.

Bergamo: No provincial city is more made-to-order for a day's excursion, either from Milan—25 miles southwest—or from Lake Como (chapter 7), the same distance northwest. Venetian-controlled for some 350 years, until the late eighteenth century, Bergamo comprises upper and lower towns. It's the former, Città Alta, to which you want to beeline. Around *Piazza Vecchia* are clustered the *Duomo* (with paintings by Tiepolo), an octagonal *Battistero* (baptistry) dating to 1340, with an exterior statue for each of its eight sides, and the chief treasures: next-to-each-other *Church of Santa Maria Maggiore,* with a Baroque, tapestry-filled interior, and *Cappella Colleoni,* with a spectacular Renaissance façade. Have lunch right on the piazza at venerable *Taverna dei Colleoni* (Phone 232-596, *First Class*), proceeding to *Accademia Carrara* (Via San Tommaso) where the lure is paintings—Fra Angelico's *Virgin Enthroned with Angels,* Raphael's *San Sebastian,* Pisanello's *Portrait of Lionello d'Este,* more works by greats like Botticelli, Carpaccio, Giorgione, and Guardi. If you're a fan of composer Gaetano Donizetti (*Lucia di Lammermoor, The Daughter of the Regiment* are but two of his operas), take in *Museo Donizettiano* (Viale delle Mura)—and perhaps one of his operas in *Teatro Donizetti,* named for him, in which case you might overnight at *Excelsior San Marco Hotel* (Piazza della Repubblica), full-facility, central, and *First Class.*

SETTLING IN

Ambasciatori Hotel (Galleria del Corso 3) is a neighbor of Stazione Centrale with 103 so-so rooms (the beds are not for large people), most, but not all, with bath. Nice restaurant, bar, and breakfast terrace. *Moderate.*

Anderson Hotel (Piazza Luigi di Savoia 20) is a chromy-modern house adjacent to Stazione Centrale, with an inviting lobby, restaurant, cocktail lounge, and nice-looking rooms. *First Class.*

Ariosto Hotel (Via Ariosto 22) is a friendly hostelry, with just over half a hundred rooms, west of downtown. Pleasant. *First Class.*

Ascot Hotel (Via Lentasio 305) is recent, with comfortable enough rooms, all bath-equipped. Agreeable lobby, bar. Breakfast only. *Moderate.*

Berna Hotel (Via Napo Torriani 18) has some 75 bath-equipped rooms; they shine. Welcoming lobby-lounge. Breakfast only. Near Stazione Centrale. *First Class.*

Bristol Hotel (Via Scarlatti 32) is functional-modern, with 71 pleasant rooms with bath. Congenial bar-lounge. Breakfast only. *Moderate.*

Carlton Hotel Senato (Via Senato 5) is on a quiet street near Stazione Centrale with some 70 exceptionally pleasant rooms, all of whose beds are equipped with insert-a-coin massage machines. Baths are big. Handsome restaurant, cocktail lounge. *First Class.*

Cavour Hotel (Via Fatebenefratelli 21) is a conveniently located downtown house—modern, with a chandelier-lit lobby, rather grand restaurant, and bar-lounge. About a hundred well-equipped rooms. *First Class.*

Diana Majestic Hotel (Viale Piave 2) occupies an imaginatively updated early-twentieth-century mansion still with original Art Nouveau detailing. Location is a trendy quarter southeast of the Duomo. There are not quite 60 doubles (most of them generous-size) and not quite 40 singles, and all with fine baths. There's no proper restaurant, but the bar-lounge, which extends into a lovely garden in warm weather, is a source of snacks as well as breakfast, which is also served in rooms. A Ciga hotel. *First Class.*

Duca di Milano Hotel (Piazza della Repubblica): Using quite the same degree of imagination that was employed in the case of the reborn Casanova Grill in the same square's Palace Hotel (Daily Bread), Ciga Hotels transformed this completely detached, modern building (which had served as an annex to its next-door Principe di Savoia Hotel), installed a restaurant (reviewed on a later page) to supplement an already popular bar-lounge, and refurbished its 100 one-bedroom suites. There are, as well, a pair of good-sized conference rooms off the lobby and a range of services execs need when they're on the move. *Luxury.*

Excelsior Hotel Gallia (Piazza Duca d'Aosta 9), recently thoroughly refurbished to become one of the smartest hotels in northern Italy, is a veritable Milan institution, beautifully run, with 252 rooms and suites in a variety of décor motifs, each elegant and fully equipped, and with superb baths. There's a spacious lobby, one of the city's buzziest cocktail lounges, good restaurant, and fitness center/sauna. A Trusthouse Forte Exclusive Division hotel that's a member of Leading Hotels of the World. *Luxury.*

Executive Aerhotel (Viale Don Luigi Sturzo 45) is capacious (420 rooms and suites) and contemporary with good-looking rooms, several cocktail lounges, and a restaurant. It's adjacent to the in-town Air Terminal, near Stazione Centrale. *First Class.*

Fieramilano Hotel (Viale Boezio 20) is popular with exhibitors and visitors to the annual Milan International Fair; and just across from its entrance. It's ultramod, with sweeping lobby and full facilities—bar, restaurant, conference rooms—and 238 rooms, all of them convenience-packed. *First Class.*

Grand Hotel Duomo (Via San Raffaele 1) is accurately titled; it's a next-door neighbor of the Duomo. The look is contemporary, and the 160 rooms include smart duplex, or two-story, suites, some with double-sink baths. Attractive—and delicious—restaurant. Nice. *First Class.*

Grand Hôtel et de Milan (Via Manzoni 29) is an old-timer with an enviable downtown location. There are 100 rooms and, among other pluses, a popular cocktail lounge. *First Class.*

Hilton International Milano Hotel (Via Galvani 12) is a modern house with 200-plus fully equipped rooms and suites with U.S.-style baths, main-floor cocktail lounge that sports an English clublike look, rooftop disco, second-floor restaurant. Location is near Stazione Centrale. Popular with Italian as well as international travelers. *Luxury.*

Jolly Hotel Milano 2 (Via Flli. Cervi in the Segrate—or Milano 2—quarter, some distance east of the center) adjoins a Congress Center, not to mention a bucolic lake. It is broad and low-slung with quite the most futuristic interiors of any Jolly Hotel that I know, comprising a honey of a bar-lounge, restaurant, and coffee shop, and attractive rooms. Just the spot for convention and business groups. *First Class.*

Jolly Hotel President (Largo Augusto 10) has a splendid near-Duomo location and the sprightly mod look common to the Jolly chain. The lobby-lounge is capacious. Picture windows of the restaurant (see Daily Bread, below) look out to the Duomo; and there are 200 rooms, fully equipped. *First Class.*

Jolly Hotel Touring (Via Tarchetti 2) edges broad Piazza della Repubblica, a ten-minute walk from the Duomo, past the prime shopping area. The look here is of brown leather easy chairs in a relaxing lounge-bar, restaurant evaluated on a later page, typical Jolly rooms, by which I mean thoughtfully planned and with good baths. *First Class.*

Lloyd Hotel (Corso di Porta Romana 48) is smallish (under 60 rooms and suites) with a situation near the Duomo. The severe façade puts one off, but the interior is handsome. Comfortable lobby-cocktail lounge and fine rooms with massage machines for the beds and, if you please, second phones in the bathrooms. *First Class.*

Manzoni Hotel (Via Santo Spirito 20) edges the center of town, to its north. Half a hundred rooms, breakfast. *First Class.*

Michelangelo Hotel (Via Scarlatti 33) is big, bustling Milan Modern, opposite Stazione Centrale, with 400 compact but well-equipped rooms with bath. Basement restaurant, busy bar-lounge. *First Class.*

Milanofiori Hotel (Strada 1, Milanofiori) is indicated for the traveler whose business is to the west of the city in the Milanofiori quarter, with its score of contemporary office buildings and Milan's World Trade Center. The hotel has 250 sprightly rooms, restaurant, cocktail lounge, and caffè that extends to an alfresco terrace. *First Class.*

New York Hotel (Via Pirelli 5), hardly evocative of Manhattan, is a tranquil 72-room house, modern and agreeable, near Stazione Centrale. All rooms have bath. Bar-lounge and breakfast, but no restaurant. *Moderate.*

Palace Hotel (Piazza della Repubblica) is a long-time Milan leader with 200 rooms and suites, lively cocktail lounge, and the exceptional Casanova Grill (accorded a review on a later page). If you knew the Palace a few years back, be prepared for a change—and for a marked improvement—in room décor. The severely plain contemporary accommodations created in the 50s, presumably to lure young middle-level execs, have happily been redone in period style, with superb taste in matters like textiles (draperies and bedspreads) and accessories. All baths are new, even to marble-sheathed walls and floors, and in many, two sinks. But service—always a Palace standout—remains as it was: super. With especially skilled concierges. A Ciga hotel. *Luxury.*

Pierre Milano Hotel (Via Edmondo de Amici 32) is a respected hotel, in the area of the Genoa train station; 50 rooms. Breakfast but no restaurant. *First Class.*

Plaza Hotel (Piazza Diaz) is heart-of-downtown on a square in the shadow of the Duomo, with 120 agreeable rooms with bath, welcoming atmosphere, amusing bar. Breakfast only. *First Class.*

Principe di Savoia Hotel (Piazza della Repubblica): When the Principe—Milanese shorten its name—opened in 1927, the square it dominates was called Piazzale Fiume, and the main railway station was just opposite. Well, times have changed. The station has long since moved some blocks north, the square has been renamed and is now a tranquil parklike oasis in the midst of the city. And the Principe has kept pace with the times. Ciga Hotels, which had taken it over in 1938, refurbished it entirely after World War II, added a pair of wings in the mid 1950s, even embellished its Salon Galilei (you want to have a look) with frescoes by Tiepolo. Every European city has a *grande dame* hotel. In Milan, the Principe—and to a great extent, the also old-school Excelsior Gallia (above)—fills that role. No lobby in town is busier or buzzier. There's a fabulous bar with a stained-glass dome that is a major Milan congregating spot, Ristorante Galleria (there's no better source in town of *risotto alla milanese*), Caffè Doney (which puts you in mind of its namesake in Rome), and an extraordinary range of accommodations, inside singles through to the presidential suite, with its own swimming pool, eighteenth-century furnishings and a trio of baths. Most rooms—there are 287 all told, including 15 suites—lie somewhere in between, with big twins, smartly Empire in style rather typical. The Principe plays a not insubstantial role in the social, political, and business life of Italy's richest city. A stay is absorbing. A Ciga hotel. *Luxury.*

Regent Hotel (Via Gesù 10) is conveniently close to the shops of Via Monte Napoleone, and a recent addition to the city's group of top-rank hostelries. Good-looking and, to understate, full-facility. *Luxury.*

Rosa Hotel (Via Pattari 5), a traditional-style, 125-room house behind (the most interesting part) the Duomo. All rooms have private baths. There's a restaurant and bar-lounge. Very pleasant. *Moderate.*

Royal Hotel (Via Cardano 1), midway between the Central and Garibaldi railway stations, though good-size, serves breakfast but no other meals. Those of the 215 rooms I've inspected are decorated with paisley-pattern draperies. The 11 suites are fax-equipped, and all accommodations have hair driers in the bathrooms. *First Class.*

Select Hotel (Via Barracchini 12) is a modern, 140-room house not far from the Duomo. Bedrooms are at once cozy and functional. There's a welcoming bar-lounge. *First Class.*

De la Ville Hotel (Via Hoepli 6) recently refurbished, has 102 compact rooms with bath, cocktail lounge, and a super downtown location that could not be more central. *First Class.*

Windsor Hotel (Via Galilei 2) is at once central (it's near the landmark Principe di Savoia, above) and comfortably full-facility, with close to 120 rooms and pleasant public areas that include restaurant and bar. *First Class.*

DAILY BREAD

It should not be surprising that so rich a city—culturally as well as financially—eats as well as Milan does. There are restaurants with foods of the various Italian regions. But Milan's own cooking is hardly to be despised. Supreme specialty is *risotto alla milanese*—northern-grown rice that is slowly simmered in butter, chicken broth, and white wine, flavored with saffron and Parmesan cheese. *Osso bucco* (stewed shin of veal) is another Milanese dish. Veal chops with a white wine sauce are also popular. Locals claim that fish is nowhere fresher than in Milan markets. Typically northern emphasis on rice by no means obliterates pasta's popularity.

Alemagna manufactures its own chocolates and bakes its own cookies, all of which it distributes to retail outlets throughout Italy and abroad. Additionally, it operates a chain of multifunction eateries, offering so many good things one doesn't know where to begin—pastries, cakes, little sandwiches, pizza, soda-fountain ice-cream concoctions, and drinks. Proper bars, too, with retail sections in conjunction. In Milan, important Alemagna locations for the visitor are Piazza del Duomo, Via Monte Napoleone at the corner of Via Manzoni, and Via Croce Rosa at Via Manzoni. *Moderate.*

Alfio (Via Senato 31; Phone 700-633): Well, if you're a Hawaii buff like me, you smile when entering Alfio. The look is Waikiki Beach of about a decade back—all bamboo and transplanted jungle. But Polynesia ends when the menu is presented. If the queue is not overlong, it is worth lining up for salamis and salads in the antipasto buffet. Soups—di verdura (vegetable), di cozze (mussel)—are super; likewise pastas. Bistecca alla fiorentina is no better in Florence; roast lamb is delicious; and, if you attempt a sweet, no other will do save the profiterolles con cioccolata calda—ice-cream-stuffed cream puffs blanketed with hot chocolate syrup. *First Class.*

Amico (Via Orefici, near the Duomo): You're on the run, but hungry. This is a sleek-look self-service run by the Motta confectionery firm, featuring sandwiches, ice cream, hot plates. *Moderate.*

Antica Osteria del Laghetto (Via Festa del Perdono 1; Phone 79-3656) has two special pluses: a central situation behind the Duomo and super seafood: oysters (from which the restaurant takes its name), of course, but fish—sole especially—as well. And seafood-sauced pastas. Friendly. *First Class.*

Antico Boeucc (Piazza Belgioioso 2; Phone 7602-0224): Don't attempt to pronounce it; just enjoy a meal. If you haven't a nobleman's palazzo in which to lunch or dine, Boeucc might well substitute. On a quiet square near Via Monte Napoleone, this aged establishment comprises a trio of salons (whose high-vaulted ceilings are supported by Doric columns) with crystal chandeliers in each and draperies of burnished gold that match table linens. You forgo a trip to the groaning antipasto buffet at your own peril. Afterwards, tackle a pasta (clams are sweet and tiny in the spaghetti alle vongole). Then, as a main course, consider osso bucco, a Milanese veal dish. Salads are special and pastries are wheeled about on a wagon. Wines have been chosen impeccably (ask to see the list). Captains do not smile but waiters are congenial. *Luxury/First Class.*

Bagutta (Via Bagutta 14; Phone 7600-2767) is a beloved old-timer. There seems to be no end to its continuing series of high-ceilinged rooms. And at mealtimes they are all jammed and noisy. There's a help-yourself buffet at lunch (you pay for what you pick up, dish by dish). But for both lunch and dinner, there's a printed menu as well. Antipasti are gorgeous to gaze upon and to taste. Rigatoni alla bagutta is the pasta specialty. Then go on to the vast range of meat and fish dishes, and a salad, if you can manage it. *First Class.*

Bice (Via Borgospesso 13; Phone 702-572) occupies attractive enough but cramped quarters. Rarely in Italy are tables so close together. Red-shaded sconces illuminate what can be a pleasantly frenetic scene. The menu (even extending to the house red—a Chianti—and the coarse country bread) is deliciously Tuscan. You want to start with pasta (fusilli con salsa pomodoro or olive-flecked maccheroni alla coraso are good choices). Florentine grilled sausages served with beans are also indicated, as is—in season—asparagus Bismarck (the vegetable is topped with sunnyside eggs). Location is a street just off Via Monte Napoleone, and Bice has a branch in New York. *First Class.*

Biffi (Galleria; Phone 808-437): Ascend a flight to this favored eatery, where the lure is a remarkable—and remarkably well-priced—buffet that runs an extraordinary gamut. By that I mean you take your choice of a score of tempters from the antipasto table (dishes both hot and cold, pasta through *pesce*), going on then to entrées and desserts, with wine and service included in the one-price tab. Caveat: you had better be hungry. *First Class.*

Biffi Scala (Piazza della Scala; Phone 876-332): A principal charm of Italy (in Milan, overwhelmingly so) is the dearth of disagreeable restaurants. I afford this one precious space only because it may appear a wise selection, given its location, for post-Scala sustenance. For me, that has not been the case. Service has been abrupt, impatient, and patronizing. (It appeared to be pleasanter in the case of Italian customers.) Supper menu was limited. Cooking—at least what my party ordered—was substandard, and prices steep. I can't counsel this one. *First Class.*

Brasera Meneghina (Via Circo 10; Phone 808-108) is no-nonsense comfortable, with stick-to-the-ribs food—zuppa di verdura (vegetable soup) or osso bucco, for example. Kindly service. *First Class.*

La Carbonella (Via Terragio 9; Phone 861-835) specializes in grilled meats—steaks, lamb chops, ribs, mixed grill—ideally preceded by pasta. Have an appetite. *First Class/Luxury.*

Casanova Grill (Palace Hotel, Piazza della Repubblica; Phone 6336): What happened was this: Ciga brass determined that the restaurant of their Palace Hotel needed a new image. So they ripped out what was there, calling in a team of designers who created a salon in the style of the early-nineteenth-century Italian Regency–gilded wall sconces and lyre-back chairs, bar-lounge settees upholstered in pastel stripes, porcelain and table linens in pristine white. Fare is cucina nuova (the emphasis is light) albeit with traditional Italian overtones, built around a superb range of risotti—risotto alla milanese (saffron-scented) and risotto black as the ink of cuttlefish, with mushrooms and truffles in its sauce. Pasta takes on new looks, as in, for example, ravioli with sugo noci (nut sauce). Wines are exceptional, and service the most skilled I know in any restaurant in the Ciga chain. In my view, one of Italy's best restaurants. *Luxury.*

Cavallini (Via Mauro Macchi 2; Phone 669-3174): Once you accept its overbright lighting and monotonous white décor, you enjoy Cavallini for its very good fare—stracciatella or risotto to open, grilled sausage teamed with spinach, or Venetian-style calf's liver among considerable entrées. Swift service. *First Class.*

Cova (Via Monte Napoleone 8): You may not have spent a solitary lira window-shopping Via Monte Napoleone, but that's no reason to forgo a visit to Cova for a casual lunch or pastry and coffee mid-morning or mid-afternoon. Well-heeled and well-dressed Milanese are bound to occupy neighboring tables. *Moderate/First Class.*

Galileo (Via Galileo 12; Phone 720-5928) makes a point of veal—with an exceptional range of veal entrées. But pastas are hardly neglected.

There are 20-plus, with the sauces I've tasted delicious. Central. *First Class.*

Galleria (Hotel Principe di Savoia; Phone 6230) is a prime example of how really good hotel restaurants can be in Italy. Daily specials—carpaccio with mushrooms, grilled swordfish, a selected pasta—are indicated, and there's an à la carte, too. Go for lunch. *First Class.*

Gelateria Passerini (Via Spadari near Museo Ambrosiana): Viewing Old Masters at the Ambrosiana has resulted in a mild case of museum feet. A dish of ice cream (they'll give you a selection of two or three flavors, if you like) served at a Passerini table will perk you up pronto. *Moderate.*

Gianni e Dorina (Via Pepe 38; Phone 606-340) matches white table linen with white walls and pleases with pasta and poultry among entrées and a range of cheeses to accompany your wine. Well-staffed. *First Class.*

Giannino (Via A. Sciesa 8; Phone 545-2765) is all that a luxury restaurant should be: capacious and handsome, warm and smiling, with absolutely delicious food and an all-Italy wine list. The look (one gaily decorated room after another) is of a massive winter garden. There are flowers everywhere, and you peep into the glass-walled kitchen as you move along to your table. Pasta is superlative. Ask for a plate embracing two or three specialties—whatever the captain counsels, unless, of course, you are unable to resist the risotto prepared with seafood. Fritto misto (a mix of deep-fried seafood) is sublime. So are veal piccata and tournedos Rossini. For dessert: omelet confiture flambée. In my view, this is one of Italy's best restaurants. *Luxury.*

Ai Giardini (Via Ludovico Settola 2; Phone 2940-0788) is at once good-size, good-looking, and good-tasting. Start with antipasto from the buffet, following with pasta (penne al tonno, for example) or pizza—with a choice of toppings. Central. *First Class.*

Gran Sasso (Piazzale Principessa Clotilde 10 [Phone 659-7978]—which just has to be the grandest-sounding address in town) is anything but grand. It's a noisy, crowded, imaginatively overdecorated tavern, where waiters—in costumes from the Abruzzi *Regione*—are so overworked that you expect them at any moment to snarl. Instead they carry tray after tray of a traditional fourteen-course meal that has not varied for as long as anyone can remember. Go for dinner when you've plenty of time. Along with an enormous pitcher of house wine and huge hunks of coarse bread, you are served, in this order: skewered mixed grill, eggplant and peppers, frittata (a kind of omelet), beans in oil with parsley, black olives, salami and prosciutto, pastina in brodo (a soup), spaghetti with tomato sauce, a chicken casserole, roast lamb, a cheese platter, the day's cake, a monstrous basket of unshelled nuts, ice cream, coffee, and an assortment of liqueurs. *First Class.*

Al Grattacielo (Via Vitto Pisani; Phone 6704-962) cannot be faulted for its fare—a dozen pastas, exceptional osso bucco, good grilled soles—but for its unfriendly , even faintly hostile management—which can put a damper on a meal. I don't counsel this restaurant. *First Class.*

Idea (Via Scarletti 22; Phone 2951-0656) is a good idea when you're pressed for time: it's self-service—a cafeteria (albeit with a waiter-service dining room as well). The cafeteria is *Moderate.*

Jolly Hotel Touring Ristorante (Via Tarchetti 2; Phone 6335) is agreeable enough with respect to ambience. But a relatively recent meal constituted quite the most unhappy dining experience I have had in any Jolly hotel, and I know the lot of them, Turin to Taormina. The faintly hostile, patronizing air of the maître d'hôtel was more or less emulated by grim-visaged waiters, and the fare—pasta and an entrée—was adequate albeit no more. Disappointing. *First Class.*

Luciano (Via Ugo Foscolo 1), handsome of façade (with a sidewalk caffè especially tempting in summer) and inside as well, is a neighbor of La Scala, remaining open late enough to attract opera-goers for a *dopo*-Scala supper that might well embrace risotto alla milanese and one of the veal specialties. Fine wines, skilled staff. *Luxury.*

Motta (Via Foscolo 1) is the same tasty Motta you may know from elsewhere in Italy; ideal for sustenance on the run, with its fresh-fruit drink, frullati di frutta, a standout. *Moderate.*

Motta (Piazza del Duomo extending into Galleria Vittorio Emanuele II): This branch of Motta is a competitor to neighboring Alemagna (see above) and similar to it in almost every respect. *Moderate.*

La Nôs (Via Amedei 2; Phone 805-8759) occupies a turn-of-century house and is appropriately turn-of-century within—very grand indeed, to a point where the pretentiousness shows through. The menu, in bothersome-to-foreigners dialect, is in the shape of a folding fan and difficult to negotiate. Stick to classic dishes like risotto (which is very tasty), gnocchi (likewise), osso bucco, roasts, and grills. I recall a refreshing lemon sherbet for dessert. *Luxury.*

Peck (Via Victor Hugo 4; Phone 875-774): A century-plus in the retail food business (see Shopper's Milan), Peck decided it was time, in 1983, to open a restaurant. Occupying a couple of subterranean levels (décor is Milanese Modern) beneath their retail wine shop, Ristorante Peck is the prototype of the contemporary Milanese eatery. Staff is skilled, swift, smiling. The à la carte menu is extensive, though not overlong, with a substantial group of daily specials appended. To begin, how about risotto alla monzese—the rice spiked with sausages in a light tomato sauce? Or, perhaps, delicate tortellini in consommé? A day's entrées might include costoletta alla milanese (the filet expertly breaded and served with French fries) or costolettine di agnello alla griglia (a grilled lamb chop, appropriately garnished). As any customer of Peck's retail shop knows, pastries are irresistible. And the wine list warrants study—what with more than 300 entries, including 14 species of spumante alone and 30-plus vintages from the ranking *Regione* of Piedmont. *Luxury.*

Il Piccolo (Duca di Milano Hotel, Piazza della Repubblica; Phone 6284) is a bar-caffè-ristorante with a pleasantly intimate quality, and a tempter of an à la carte, for example, bresaola con scaglie di parmigiano (air-dried beef topped with Parmesan cheese) or velluta di pollo (cream of chicken soup) to start, spaghetti pomodoro e basilico or crespelle Duca (the house's own crêpes), branzinetto alla griglia (grilled sea bass) or filetto di bue (filet of beef). Or go, simply, for an abbreviated snack, coffee and cake, or a drink. *First Class.*

A' Riccione (Via Terramelli 70; Phone 66-86-807) is for seafood—fresh, delicious, and professionally served. One must excuse the eccentric décor. Consider instead the good things to eat, such as fresh shrimp with a homemade mayonnaise dressing, grilled fish of the day, pasta with fresh clam or seafood sauce, or the enormous (and delicious) fried-seafood platter. *Luxury.*

La Rinascente (Piazza del Duomo): Hie yourself to the seventh floor of this department store for an extraordinary view of the Duomo from picture windows of the Bistrot and a delicious lunch—antipasti, salads, pasta; the prix-fixe afternoon tea; or cocktails, for that matter. Attractive and *Moderate.*

Rovello 18 (Via Rovello 18; Phone 864-346) welcomes with intimate scale, white linen, and traditional cuisine, pastas through pastries. *First Class.*

St. Andrew (Via Sant' Andrea 23; Phone 793-132) is the name of the street cleverly translated into English—the better to give this restaurant a slight snob air. And why not? It is among the smarter-looking in Milan, with good food, both at lunch and dinner, but also (worth knowing, this) for late suppers. *Luxury.*

Il Salotto (Galleria) is one of a number of Galleria caffès with outdoor tables, ideal to watch the passing parade over an espresso. *Moderate.*

San Fermo (Via San Fermo 1; Phone 655-1734) is, ideally, taken in tandem with a trek through nearby Pinacoteca di Brera (above). Prix-fixe lunches are the best buy, the made-on-premises pasta and the day's fish—simply grilled—the best bets. Pleasant. *First Class.*

Caffè Sant' Ambroeus (Corso Giacamo Matteotti near Via Monte Napoleone) is for a splurgy afternoon tea. Pastries are nowhere more delicious. The clientele is Milan at its most stylish and good-looking, and there's an overseas branch on New York's Madison Avenue. *First Class.*

Savini (Galleria Vittorio Emanuele II; Phone 805-8343): If you are going to dine in style after a performance at La Scala—*dopo*-Scala ("after Scala") is the expression—it's going to be at Savini. The look is crystal chandeliers and red-silk-lamp-shaded tables. Captains know their old-time customers' every whim, but are equally solicitous of newcomers. Risotto is indicated for starters—saffron or al salto style. Fritto misto (a seafood mix) or scampi savini, or veal cutlet Milan style—all are main-course specials. Cassata is but one of a number of masterful desserts. *Luxury.*

Da Serafino (Via Bramante 34; Phone 318-5363) is for the specialties of the neighboring Piedmont *Regione.* It embraces a pair of oversized, blue-walled chambers, with gregarious waiters and topnotch food. The mixed antipasto—including mortadella sausage, salami, and pheasant pâté—is advised. The Piedmontese variation on the theme of Swiss fondue—fonduta—is a main-course novelty. Pastas are delicious, and so are entrées such as rolled veal with prosciutto. *First Class.*

Al Tavolino (Via Pirello at the corner of Via Fara; Phone 670-3520) packs in area regulars at lunch and is as filled with plants as with people. The buffet is a winner, ditto spaghetti with clam sauce, pizza, and veal entrées. Friendly. *First Class.*

Tina Fontana (Piazza Diaz 5; Phone 860-598) occupies Art Nouveau-style quarters near the Duomo and is a rarity among restaurants in Italy, with nonsmokers' and smokers' sections. Super pastas, ditto the seafood. Go for a special meal. *Luxury.*

Torre de Pisa (Via Fiorchiari 21; Phone 9218-3645) is at its best *dopo*-Scala—after a performance at the nearby Opera—when it teems with hungry music buffs intent on a pleasing meal. *First Class.*

Caffè Verdi (Via Verdi 4) is more than its name implies: a satisfactory source of sustenance, especially pasta, including spaghetti carbonara, lasagna, and the house's own—and special—penne. *Moderate/First Class.*

Il Verziere (Jolly Hotel President, Largo Augusto 10; Phone 7746) is exemplary, soups onward—lobster bisque or onion among them. Crêpes and broad noodles augment standard-style pastas. There are French-style snails, T-bone steaks, and irresistible sweets. *First Class/Luxury.*

SOUND OF MUSIC

La Scala is earlier recommended as a requisite attraction, open daily with its museum. Opera season is early December to early spring. For remaining months, there are concerts performed by the Orchestra Filarmonica della Scala and visiting groups; and ballet as well, by the Ballo della Teatro alla Scala, as well as other troupes. The theater's ticket office, *Ufficio Collettività* (Via Filodrammatici), is usually open daily from 12 noon to 7 P.M. and publishes a seasonal schedule, which details ticket reservation procedures in English as well as Italian. There is always the possibility of customers wanting to sell an unneeded ticket just before the performance. (I was able to buy my first La Scala ticket this way.) Don't hesitate to stand outside an hour or so before curtain, looking for a likely seller. La Scala can be fussy; it sells no more than two tickets per person, insists that you check cameras, hats, and umbrellas, requests that you check coats, recommends that you wear formal dress opening nights and that men appear in jacket and tie at all other performances, and asks that "patrons behave in a suitable fashion whilst in the auditorium . . . and not disturb other patrons in any way during the performance." As if we wouldn't conduct ourselves properly without management's outrageous instructions.

Piccola Scala (Via Filodrammatici) is an alternative to the mother company, or a supplement. It is 1950s modern, with performances of both traditional and contemporary works.

Teatro Lirico (Via Larga) sees performances of La Scala's ballet and of an occasional opera as well.

Piccolo Teatro (Via Rovello) is a municipally operated theater. One might call it a Milanese counterpart of the New York City Center. The idea is culture for the masses at popular prices.

Conservatorio (Via Conservatorio): Symphonic and chamber concerts, recitals.

SHOPPER'S MILAN

Make no mistake, Milan is rich. Milan has style. And Milan has business visitors with money in their pockets. It follows that shops should be among the best in Italy. They are. Via Manzoni is the main street, and streets leading from it are important too. Via Brera is full of art galleries, while Corso Buenos Aires has chain and department stores. Via Monte Napoleone is Milan shopping at its most elegant, along with streets leading from it to Via della Spiga and Corso Vittorio Emanuele II (these include Via Borgospesso, Via Santo Spirito, Via Gesù, and Via Pietro Verri). Herewith, my personally scouted selections in categories of interest to visitors, arranged alphabetically.

ANTIQUES: Florence is Italy's preeminent antiques city, but Milan, with its wealthy industrialist class and a substantial proportion of correspondingly affluent visitors, has many sources, too. No matter how fancy the shop, ask if the price requested is indeed the final price. (Sometimes, it is *not.*) *Bellini* (Via Gesù 17), mostly seventeenth- and eighteenth-century furniture and accessories; *Frecchini* (Via Gesù 11), china, paintings, furnishings—most of it sixteenth- and seventeenth-century; *Old Silver* (Via Gesù 14); *Piva* (Via Sant' Andrea 12) specializes in the nineteenth century; *Zecchini* (Via Sant' Andrea 14) vends an agreeable mix, large and small, over a range of centuries; *Gladform Due* (Via Monte Napoleone 16) has eighteenth-century furnishings; and *Pontremoli* (Via Monte Napoleone 21) specializes in antique paintings, chandeliers, and furniture of the eighteenth century.

BOOKS: *Rizzoli* (Galleria Vittorio Emanuele 79) is an enormous—and attractive—outlet illuminated by crystal chandeliers and featuring foreign-language art books. One of a chain, with U.S. branches.

CLOTHING is a bottomless Milan pit. Sources of smart duds are interminable. For moderately tabbed merchandise—men's, women's, kids', both clothing and accessories—I counsel department stores like *La Rinascente, Coin,* and *Upim* (below). But all of the name designers have boutiques, as for example: *Valentino* (women—Via Santo Spirito 3; men—Via Monte Napoleone 20); *Trussardi* (Via Sant' Andrea 5); *Giorgio Armani,* both Uomo and Donna, at Via Sant' Andrea 10; *Gianni Versace,* (Via Monte Napoleone 11); *Salvatore Ferragamo,* with men's and women's boutiques on opposite sides of Via Monte Napoleone; *Mila Schön,* with separate men's and women's boutiques on Via Monte Napoleone; *Gianfranco Ferre,* with women's wear at Via della Spiga 11 and men's clothing at Via della Spiga 13; *Fendi,* with women's clothes, furs, and luggage at Via Sant' Andrea 22; and *Laura Ashley* (Via Brera 4). Worth noting, too, for men's wear: *La Rusmiani,* a veritable male-clothing department store, at Corso Vittorio Emanuele 12; and branches of such chains as *Beltrami, Valentino, Daniel Hechter,* and *Ungaro*—all on Via Monte Napoleone. *Gucci*'s Milan branch is at Via Monte Napoleone 5. Neckties are, of course, to be found in all the men's shops. But those at the Milan branch of the Rome-based *Roxy* chain (Via Grossi)—where nothing else is sold—are of exceptional style, quality, and value. *Cravatterie Nazionali* (Via Pietro Verri 5) sells ties exclusively too.

DEPARTMENT STORES in Milan are Italy's finest, almost on a par with the great ones of London, Paris, Tokyo, and the United States. *La Rinascente,* with an inspired location adjacent to the landmark Duomo, is a seven-floor giant, offering women's clothes on main, 2nd, and 3rd floors; men's clothes on main, balcony, and 1st (up a flight); children's clothes on 5; such other departments as china, housewares, and while-you-wait shoe repair, as well as a restaurant/bar and fancy grocery (with well-wrapped chunks of Parmesan cheese—easily carried transatlantic—among its wares) operated by Fini of Modena (chapter 20); and a hairdressing salon and bank. *Coin,* like La Rinascente a national chain, has a handsome store on Piazza Loretta at Corso Buenos Aires. Its clothing departments are exemplary. *Upim,* a welcome sight in smaller cities throughout Italy, is on Corso Matteotti.

DUTY-FREE SHOPPING: If you're flying transatlantic from Malpensa Airport, it's not a bad idea to give yourself an hour or so before boarding to scout duty-free shops, where you'll find well-packaged

Parmesan cheese from Fini (the same Modena-based firm that sells it at Rinascente, in town); a good variety of Italian bottled goods (including Campari, Amaretto di Saronno, Galliano, Stock brandy, and various labels of spumante—Italy's variation on the theme of champagne albeit usually if not always sweeter); diverse selections of Perugina chocolates, including their universally admired *baci,* or chocolate kisses, nut-centered; some Gucci leather goods and doodads—among much else. Prices of Italian merchandise are generally lower at Malpensa, but you've less choice and, invariably, less shopping time than in the city.

FABRICS by the meter are a specialty at *Carlo Colombo* (Via Monte Napoleone 7) and *Galtrucco* (Via Monte Napoleone 11 and Piazza del Duomo).

FOOD AND WINES: *Alemagna* (Piazza del Duomo, other locations) is a chain whose outlets are at once caffès and food shops—with the latter good for cookies, candy, crackers, other comestibles; *Motta* (Piazza del Duomo and other locations) is a competitor of and not unlike Alemagna; *Peck* has been a Milan institution for more than a century—a worthy counterpart to Fauchon of Paris and Fortnum & Mason of London, with several locations. Most important, for a range of fancy-food shopping, is its *Gastronomia* at Via Spadari 9, where the range embraces just about everything that is at once Italian and delicious—jams and chocolates, cheeses and crackers, hams and salamis (of which there are, to give you an idea of this firm's dedication, 150-plus species!). Peck's *Casa del Formaggio* (Via Speronari 3) is the definitive Italian cheese shop, with some 350 types, including the coveted Parmesan. There are, as well, a wine shop, *La Bottega del Vino* (at Via Victor Hugo 4, same address as Ristorante Peck above); a butcher shop, *Bottega del Maiale* (Via Victor Hugo 30); and a *Rosticceria* (Via Cantù 3) for take-out spit-roasted poultry and meat. *Salumaio* (Via Monte Napoleone 3) vends a variety of luxury foodstuffs, but accepts no credit cards.

JEWELRY AND WATCHES: *David Colombo* (Via Monte Napoleone 18) has costly costume jewelry in addition to precious jewels. *Mario Buccellati* (Via Monte Napoleone 16) makes a specialty of traditional Florentine jewelry, along with heavy and chunky silver; also in Florence and New York. *Dal Vecchio* (Via Monte Napoleone) sells silver as well as jewelry. *Ebel* (Via Monte Napoleone 4) is noted for its gold necklaces and bracelets, as well as watches. *Scala*'s (Via Spiga 9) diamonds are dazzlers.

LEATHER AND LUGGAGE: *Gucci* occupies a pair of capacious two-floor stores opposite each other on Via Monte Napoleone. One specialzes in the leather goods, luggage, and shoes on which Gucci built its reputation (with jewelry, watches, and silver, as well). The other features men's and women's clothing, accessories (including coveted neckties and silk scarves), and assorted doodads, none of them inexpensive, but less pricey than in United States branches. *Bottega Veneta* (Via della Spiga 8) is for ever-so-elegant women's bags, small luggage, engagement calendars, and desk accessories—all very costly, if less so than at the branch in New York. *Colombo's* (Via della Spiga 12) forte is milady's handbags in original designs. *Zilli* (Via Monte Napoleone 27) is for leather and suede clothing and accessories. *I Santi*'s main shop, for luggage and smaller leather goods, is at Corso Lodi 1, and there are a number of other branches in Milan, Rome, and other Italian, as well as foreign, cities.

LINENS: *Pratesi* (Via Monte Napoleone 16) is an outlet of a firm with branches elsewhere in Italy and in the U.S. It carries own-design bed linens and comforters, with steep tabs attached. *Frette* (Via Monte Napoleone at Via Manzoni) is still another high-quality linen chain, like Pratesi; it's also in New York.

PHARMACY: *Farmacia Carlo Erba* (Piazza Duomo 21; Phone 720-231-20) is worth knowing about in that it never closes.

PORCELAIN AND GLASS: *Richard-Ginori* (Via Monte Napoleone 7) is Italy-wide (and abroad) with its own superb porcelain and other makes as well, in addition to glassware and crystal.

SHOES: Shops generally sell men's as well as women's. *Bruno Magli* (Corso Vittorio Emanuele 38) has shops throughout the country—high-styled, fairly pricey; *Divarese* (Corso Vittorio Emanuele 42) is one link in a nationwide chain that has the advantage of big selection, smart design, and moderate prices. *Flli. Rossetti* (Via Monte Napoleone 3) is high-style, expensive, and with outlets in major Italian cities and New York. *Tanino Crisci* (Via Monte Napoleone) is at least as elegant as Rossetti, and certainly as expensive; also in New York.

INCIDENTAL INTELLIGENCE

There are two airports. *Malpensa Airport* is a long drive—much of it interesting—north of town in the shadow of snowy mountains. It is used for intercontinental flights, including transatlantic ones. Much closer to town (and used for flights within Italy and Europe) is *Linate*

Airport. Most economical means of transport to and from both airports is via bus to or from the in-town *Air Terminal* (Via Galvani 12), not far from Stazione Centrale. Arrival and departure by train generally involves use of *Stazione Centrale* (Piazza Duca d'Aosta)—a formidable specimen of Mussolini Modern equipped with lots of everything except waiting taxis. There are no less than eleven other railway stations for domestic, mostly regional runs; ascertain which you will be using. *Taxis* are metered, with the usual maze of *supplementi* tacked on for a variety of reasons—luggage, dogs, skis, nights, holidays, whatever; and do not be surprised if you queue for a taxi for as long as an hour upon arrival from a rail journey. As in all large cities, taxis are scarce during rush hours. To telephone a cab: dial 117. There are extensive and modern bus routes. Last, there is the *subway*, or Metropolitana. Its stations are designated by the bold "MM" logo. There are two lines. M-1 embraces about a score of stations between Sesti Marelli and San Leonardo. M-2 joins Stazione Centrale with Stazione Lambrate—another rail terminal. Hotel concierges usually have copies of gratis giveaway "What's-On" publications. Check newspapers, too. Most noted (indeed it is the most famous of all Italian newspapers) is *Corriere della Sera. Il Giornale* and *La Repubblica* are two others. *Further information:* Ente Provinciale per il Turismo, Palazzo del Turismo, Via Marconi, Milan; Azienda Autonoma di Turismo, Viale Vittorio Emanuele 4, Bergamo.

20

Modena

Five Centuries a Dukedom

BACKGROUND BRIEFING

If you've been reading this book from the beginning, you will have encountered the extraordinary Este family in their roles as rulers of Ferrara (chapter 12). But the Ferrara Estes, who governed that city from mid thirteenth to late sixteenth centuries, were short-term in contrast to their Modena cousins. Here, in this handsome Emilia-Romagna city (locals tell you it has the highest standard of living in Italy) lying between Bologna (chapter 5) and Parma (chapter 25), the Este clan was in charge, first of all, from 1288 to 1796 and—in a different guise, as the House of Austria-Este—again from 1815 through to the establishment of the Kingdom of Italy in 1861.

Pre-Este Modena was at first Etruscan. Later (under the Romans) it got the name *Mutina* that has stayed with it, albeit Italianized. (Pronunciation, incidentally, is *MOH-day-nah.*) By the time it became a *comune* in the eleventh century—after a long period of post-Roman decline—it had achieved enough commercial, military, and intellectual status to have attracted the eye of the Estes, who became powerful enough for the Holy Roman Emperor to create the title Duke for Borso Este in 1452. Later, when the family lost control in seventeenth-century Ferrara, the clan consolidated itself in Modena. Through the years, it fostered architecture (the Ducal Palace remains in service, appropriately enough, as a military school) and art (the Este picture and book collections are among Italy's more dazzling).

ON SCENE

Lay of the Land: This is a delightfully easy city to walk about. Accurately labeled *Piazza Grande* is its center, with the fabulous campanile of the Duomo (it has its own name, *La Ghirlandina,* as well it might, with an altitude of 285 feet) a landmark, towering over the city. Main Street—here dubbed *Via Emilia*—is crammed with smart shops (a lot of Modena's wealth is generated by the Ferrari auto plant and other industries) and department stores. The street runs east to west through the core. From it, animated *Via Farini* leads north to *Piazza Roma* and still another landmark, *Palazzo Ducale.* Another major square, *Piazza Matteotti,* lies immediately northwest of Piazza Grande. The railway station fringes the northern edge of town, on *Viale Monte Kosica.*

Duomo (Piazza Grande): Modena's cathedral is an all-Italy Romanesque standout surprisingly—and surpassingly—beautiful, with respect both to its façade (reliefs of its central portal are by a twelfth-century sculptor named Wiligelmo) and to its soaring interior. A first glance inside indicates the splendid scale of the vaulting that frames the nave and of the capitals that top columns lining the nave. Stellar works of art dot the interior, not the least of which is Dosso Dossi's *Madonna and Saints.* Take time to descend to the crypt for a look at a cluster of five superb sculptures (the work of Guido Mazzoni), collectively called *Madonna della Pappa.*

Palazzo del Comune (Piazza Grande) is City Hall, and you are welcome to wander inside. Be sure to request that you be directed to *Sala del Fuoco,* very grand in the manner of the Renaissance and superlatively frescoed.

Palazzo dei Musei (Largo Porta Sant' Agostino) is not misnamed. It shelters no less than a half dozen museums, the most important of which, without any doubt, is *Galleria Estense,* housing a collection of paintings fabulous enough by themselves to warrant a Modena visit. This collection of the Este dukes over the centuries is, to understate, an eye-opener. Consider a triptych by El Greco, *The Baptism of Christ;* still another triptych by Veronese, portraying a quartet of saints; a Bassano of *Saints Peter and Paul; The Martyrdom of St. Peter* interpreted by Guercino; Andrea del Sarto's *Madonna and Child with St. Anne;* Lorenzo di Credi's *Martyrdom of St. Sebastian;* and works by such masters as Mabuse and Palma Il Vecchio, Mantegna and Luini, Correggio and Dosso Dossi, Tintoretto and Brueghel, the Venetians Guardi and Rosalba Carreira, the Spaniard Velázquez (a piercing study of an Este duke), even the celebrated Baroque English woodcarver, Grinling Gibbons. Of the remaining museums in the palazzo, I would concentrate on the following: *Museo Estense,* for the family's sculpture (Bernini and Sansovino are among the artists), bronze, and coins, *Biblioteca Estense,* for its gorgeous illuminated manuscripts (Duke Borso's Bible is a standout, lavishly featuring 1200, yes 1200, illuminated pages); and *Museo Civico,* if you enjoy mixed-bag repositories: pottery, guns, needlework, that kind of thing.

Palazzo Ducale (Piazza Roma) wants to be seen, if only from without, for its massiveness. It is among the biggest such in Italy and dates back, primarily, to the seventeenth century. Although now a military academy, you should be able to have a peek at the central courtyard.

Church of San Pietro (Via San Pietro) is a wonder of the Renaissance, with an elegant façade and an enormous five-nave interior that abounds in art—including such memorable works as a sculpted *Pietà* in the apse, an altarpiece (*Madonna with Saints Sebastian and Jerome* by Francesco Ferrari), and still other works attributed to the locally prolific Dosso Dossi.

SETTLING IN

Canalgrande Hotel (Corso Canal Grande 6) is an enchanter of a seventeenth-century palazzo transformed with a sense of style into a hotel that seems far more intimate in scale than its capacity of nearly 80 rooms would indicate. The restaurant is worthy of additional comment, and there is a congenial cocktail lounge. One of Italy's more charming hotels. Central. *First Class.*

Fini Hotel (Via Emilia Este 441), relatively contemporary, and not as central as the Canalgrande (above), makes its point—that of grandeur—with a marble-walled lobby and an attractive bar-lounge. There are just over 90 smartly styled rooms and breakfast service, but no restaurant, although the management owns one, at another address some distance away (below). *First Class.*

Roma Hotel (Via Farini 44) has, as a major plus, a situation on the busy street leading from the Piazza Grande, heart of the city. There's a pleasant lobby bar-lounge and 56 rooms, many with bath. Breakfast but no restaurant. *Moderate.*

Palace Hotel (Via Emilia Este 27) is a reliable modern house near the core, with agreeable public spaces. These include a cocktail lounge and just over 50 functional rooms with bath. Breakfast, but no restaurant. *Moderate.*

DAILY BREAD

La Secchia Rapita (Canalgrande Hotel, Corso Canal Grande 6; Phone 217-160) is evocatively old-style and as good a spot as any to sample Modena specialties, including the pasta called maltagliati (as well as better-known tortellini), bollito misto (a melange of boiled meats), and zampone (sausage-stuffed pig's foot)—Modena's most celebrated delicacy. *First Class.*

Fini (Largo San Francesco; Phone 223-314)—at another address, please note, than the Fini Hotel (above) with the same management—is smart to look upon and can pride itself on delicious food, deftly presented. Pastas are so good that they are packaged and retailed elsewhere in Italy as well as exported to fancy groceries in America. It's fun to order a bollito misto—a mix of meats and vegetables in its own broth—as an entrée, carved and served (with a piquant sauce) by the waiter from a trolley wheeled to your table. Turkey, just-caught trout, and beefsteak are tasty, too. Splurge on dessert here, and take advantage of the excellent wine list. *Luxury.*

Da Enzo (Via Coltellini 17; Phone 225-177) is a good bet for a hearty lunch after a morning in and around the nearby Duomo. Soup followed by grilled sausage and a salad would go down well. *Moderate.*

Caffè Molinari (Via Emilia Este 47) is Modena's No. 1 see-and-be-seen spot. Stop for coffee, ice cream, or a snack; you're on the main shopping street. *Moderate.*

SOUND OF MUSIC

Teatro Comunale (Corso Canal Grande 85): Opera in the hometown of super-tenor Luciano Pavarotti? But of course. Modena's opera house—note the fine bas-relief on its façade—dates to 1841. Try to take in a performance.

INCIDENTAL INTELLIGENCE

Further Information: Ente Provinciale per il Turismo, Via Emilia Centro 174, Modena.

21

Naples/Napoli and the Bay

The Classicist's Italy

BACKGROUND BRIEFING

Let me preface what follows by making clear that Naples is well worth the considerable effort that must be expended to appreciate it. But Naples is special. From the very moment of arrival at the train platform there may be a hassle to find a baggage porter, a hassle claiming baggage, a hassle finding a taxi to get to one's hotel, a hassle with the driver, upon arrival, over the amount of the fare, the added amount for *supplementi,* and—regardless of its generosity—the amount of the tip. And so it goes.

It has always been so. Certainly in the decades I have known Naples. It is a matter of conditioning, a point of view toward strangers often embracing suspicion, that has evolved over the centuries in the case of the less well educated rather than with more sophisticated Neapolitans, than whom no Italians, anywhere in Italy, are more hospitable or more kind.

Glancing backwards, one is astounded at the complexity of the Naples story. To see what I mean, one has only to take a look at the façade of the Royal Palace. There, in niches, one after the other, are larger-than-life statues of kings representing eight different countries that have ruled. And by no means always wisely or well.

Beginnings were uncomplicated enough. Greek colonists drifted westward and established a couple of settlements—*Paleopolis* (Old City) and later *Neapolis* (New City), the name that stuck. (A third ancient name was *Partenope;* it evolved from a Greek legend.) It was only a question of time before others would be as enchanted as the Greeks with the situation of Naples—flanking a natural gulf, on the slopes of a range of hills, the tallest of which is actually a volcanic peak, Vesuvius.

Romans came south in the fourth century before Christ and fought with success for control of the area.

With good reason: they adored the mild climate, the pretty bay, the dramatic silhouette of Vesuvius; and they took to the Greek culture as ducks to water. Indeed, it was in and about Naples that the first vacation villas came into common use; royal Romans—like Emperors Nero and Claudius—lived there; rich Romans built country houses there; Roman poets, like Virgil, worked there. Roman politicians absorbed the nearby and also-beautiful islands of Capri and Ischia into the Naples colonial government.

It did not last much longer than a century. Barbarians came, and later, Byzantines. In the twelfth century, Normans took over—the first of a line of European powers. They were there one after another lasting some six centuries. The range embraced various French, Austrian, German, and Spanish houses, with Napoleon and his family of Bonapartes the last of the lot. There were good guys and bad guys, but the crowd that did the most lasting damage were the Spaniards. They were on hand for two centuries—the sixteenth and seventeenth—ruling what had long since become the Kingdom of Naples, embracing all of Italy south of the Papal States around Rome.

Murat—a brother-in-law of Napoleon who ruled for less than a decade in the early nineteenth century—is remembered for reforms in government and encouragement of the independence movement, which didn't gain strength until some decades later, when Risorgimento leader Giuseppe Garibaldi led forces that conquered what had come to be called the Kingdom of the Two Sicilies, a part of which was the southern mainland area dominated by Naples. Neapolitans welcomed Garibaldi and the consequences of his victory—the united Kingdom of Italy and the post-World War II republic following.

Political domination over the centuries notwithstanding, it is Neapolitans who have been the winners in one major respect; not even the cumulative power of assorted foreigners reigning as kings was able to dissipate or dilute the city's culture. Indeed, it has been quite the reverse. Despite economic privations, no *Regione* of Italy is more sublimely Italian than Campania, of which Naples is capital and sole metropolis. In Naples one finds art forms at which Italians excel—painting (there was a major Neapolitan school), music, dance, architecture, cuisine. All the Austrians or Frenchmen or Spaniards or Germans on the throne do not seem to have made any less brilliant the folk dance called *tarantella,* voices like Naples-born Caruso's, or, for that matter, the savory, Naples-invented pie called *pizza.*

ON SCENE

Lay of the Land: Once one comes to grips with its infuriating traffic jams, Naples emerges as a one-of-a-kind city of astonishing drive, ebullient street life, considerable architectural beauty, and many more artistic treasures than it is generally given credit for. This is principally because most visitors stay an average of a day and a night. What is needed is a stay of several days, enough time to acquire acquaintance with aspects of the city more flattering to it than the taxi drivers and baggage porters who are its own worst enemies.

Remember that the more one walks, the fewer taxi encounters are necessary. The bay is south; inland from it is north. Areas of town fronting the bay are *Santa Lucia,* near which a number of hotels are clustered, and the adjacent *Margellina* area, to the west, with *Posillipo* the most western of the sea-front districts. There are three main downtown squares. Start at No. 1—*Piazza Plebiscito.* Continue in a northerly direction and, poof, you're in square No. 2—alliteratively named *Piazza Trento e Trieste. Galleria Umberto I,* the high-ceilinged late-nineteenth-century shop- and caffè-studded arcade, is at this point, and due northeast is the No. 3 square—*Piazza Municipio,* whose landmark is the principal downtown skyscraper housing the Jolly Hotel. Main shopping street is *Via Roma,* running north-south a block west of Piazza Municipio (and also easily gained from Piazza Trento e Trieste). Via Roma changes its name at *Piazza Dante,* continues north with a succession of names—including *Via Toledo* and *Via Santa Teresa degli Scalzi,* on which one finds the important Museo Nazionale Archeologico; beyond, it becomes *Corso Amedeo di Savoia,* terminating at the park dominated by Palazzo Capodimonte and, within it, a world-class art gallery. Return to Via Roma, the main shopping street, and take it to *Piazza del Gesù;* turn right and you find yourself on *Via San Biagio dei Librai* in *Spaccanapoli*—the heart of Old Naples—a requisite area for walking.

THE ESSENTIAL NAPLES

A pair of museums—Museo Nazionale Archeologico and Museo Nazionale di Capodimonte: Thrust of the first named, *Museo Nazionale Archeologico* (Via Foria 27), is Pompeii, with a dazzling collection of its art treasures removed from the nearby ruined city that thrived some two millenniums ago, only to be buried—and astonishingly well preserved—by an eruption of Vesuvius in the first century. The building itself is a grim palazzo with a respectable four-century history of its own. But before you ascend to Pompeii on the second floor, tarry on the main. Less celebrated than upstairs exhibits are galleries of classical sculpture that will take your breath away. Greeting you is a tough-looking but striking pair of *Tyrant Killers,* copied by Romans some two thousand years ago, from a Greek original half a millennium older. You go on from there to likenesses of Athena, Apollo, Orpheus, Diomedes, a drunken Silenus, and an also inebriated Hercules, a reposing Hermes, a

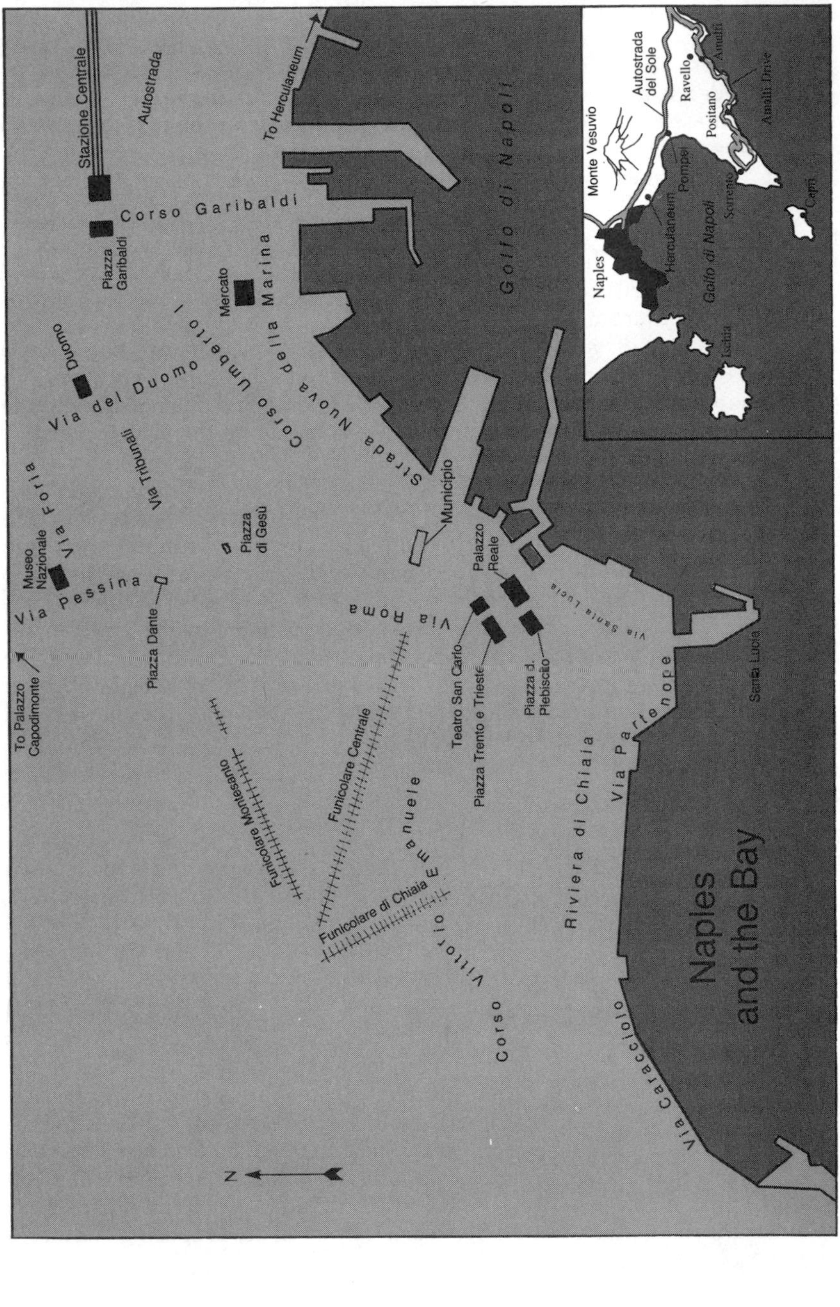
Naples
and the Bay
Stazione Centrale
Autostrada
To Herculaneum
Corso Garibaldi
Piazza
Garibaldi
Mercato
Golfo di Napoli
Corso della Marina
Duomo
Via del Duomo
Corso Umberto I
Strada Nuova
Via Tribunali
Museo
Nazionale
Via Foria
Via Pessina
Piazza Dante
Piazza
di Gesù
Municipio
Palazzo
Reale
Via Roma
Via Santa Lucia
To Palazzo
Capodimonte
Teatro San Carlo
Piazza Trento e Trieste
Piazza d.
Plebiscito
Santa Lucia
Via Partenope
Riviera di Chiaia
Funicolare Montesanto
Funicolare Centrale
Funicolare di Chiaia
Corso Vittorio Emanuele
Via Caracciolo
N
Monte Vesuvio
Autostrada
del Sole
Naples
Herculaneum
Pompei
Golfo di Napoli
Ischia
Sorrento
Capri
Positano
Ravello
Amalfi
Amalfi Drive

pair of wrestlers, a sleeping satyr. Up a high flight, then, to Pompeian mosaics and frescoes of Alexander in battle, a still life of fish and other edibles from the sea that you've seen reproduced on cookbook covers, portraits of beautiful Pompeian ladies, fresco after fresco with scenes of daily life on Pompeian red backgrounds. It is a show manifesting skill, style, and technique that would honor late-twentieth-century artists; when one considers its antiquity, the beauty is all the more extraordinary.

Museo Capodimonte (Parco Capodimonte): There are two royal palaces in town: one heart-of-downtown (below); Capodimonte is the other, on the northern fringe, in its own park. It is unusual in that it was built for the purpose it still serves. Its patron was Charles III, most enlightened of the Spanish Bourbon kings (who, not incidentally, sided with the Yanks in our Revolution and won back Florida for Spain—temporarily at least—as a consequence). The paintings' range is extraordinary, and the quantity is equally so; this is an all-Italy ranker of a museum—on a level with Florence's Uffizi, Venice's Accademia, and Milan's Brera. Ideally, one wants a day to cover the forty-odd galleries, for Capodimonte is a survey of Italian painting and its schools, both regional and chronological, with foreign works, medieval primitives through nineteenth-century Goyas. One finds Lippi *(Annunciation)*, Raphael *(Pope Leo with Two Cardinals)*; Bellini *(Transfiguration)*, Caravaggio *(Flagellation)*; rooms full of Lombardians (Luini, for example); Venetians (a number of the very best Titians, *Pope Paul III with His Nephews*, for example); Neapolitans, century by century, including many Luca Giordanos, whose works are to be seen in a number of the city's churches; and such non-Italians as Van Cleve *(Crucifixion)*, Holbein *(Erasmus)*, Brueghel *(The Blind)*, and Van der Weyden *(Pietà)*. Down a flight—and, sad to report not always open these days—are the State Apartments, full of fine eighteenth-century furnishings, not to mention remarkable collections of china (including the local Capodimonte) and tapestries.

Palazzo Reale (Piazza del Plebiscito): For a country with a rich monarchial past, Italy has surprisingly few royal palaces to show visitors in the cities. The most spectacular of the lot—Palazzo Quirinale in Rome (chapter 2)—is the presidential residence and not open to the public. The Royal Apartments of Florence's Palazzo Pitti Museum (chapter 13) are rarely in my experience (if, indeed ever) open; nor, for that matter, are the Royal Apartments of Naples's Museo Capodimonte (above). That leaves an urban trio that keep regular and reliable open hours: the Royal Palaces of Genoa (chapter 14), Turin (chapter 35), and—the subject at hand—Naples. The in-town palace of the kings of Naples (who lived, as well in the considerably larger palace at nearby Caserta in what had been the countryside, below), Palazzo Reale has seventeenth-century roots but is mostly eighteenth-century, with nineteenth-century and post-World War II restorations. Considerable of its treasures—paintings, furniture, accessories, carpets—have disappeared over the years, and successive municipal administrations have installed various offices in the palace precincts. It serves, as well, as the venue of the separately entered *Biblioteca Nazionale,* or National Library (a repository of precious antique books and manuscripts, with its *Sezione Americana* the United States Information Service-operated J. F. Kennedy Library. And its beautiful *Teatro di Corte*—the Court Theater—is put to frequent use for musical and other presentations. You will, of course, see the theater (meticulously rebuilt after partial World War II bombing) in the course of a self-guided palace tour. But—starting with an extraordinarily broad and high ceremonial grand staircase—there's a lot more, a dozen and a half state rooms all told. The Throne Room, resplendent with Rococo furniture, gilded stucco, massive tapestries, and royal portraits is quite the most dazzling space. But the immense Ballroom—its original parquet floor covered with an also-original eighteenth-century carpet—is impressive, too, as are such other rooms as the Ambassadors' Salon, with intricate barrel vaulting; the small but striking Queen's Chapel; the Royal Audience Chamber, with red and gold brocaded walls framed by a glorious frescoed ceiling; and the Blue Reception Room, with superb early-nineteenth-century furnishings.

Teatro di San Carlo (Via San Carlo): Along with the Fenice in Venice, no Italian opera house has more outrageous charm. San Carlo stands out because it goes back to the eighteenth century—1737, when it was built. There were early-nineteenth-century additions—especially the loggia above the entrance. But unlike Milan's La Scala and Rome's Teatro dell' Opera, San Carlo is the genuine Rococo article, open regularly during the day for non-performance inspection. There are seven levels—a vast orchestra and half a dozen balconies, in a red and gold auditorium, with the onetime royal box framed by a gilded plaster canopy in the shape of a monster crown, adoring royalist angels guarding either side.

A trio of beautiful churches—San Gregorio Armeno, Santa Chiara, Sant' Anna dei Lombardi: If Naples's museums are underappreciated, its churches are virtually unknown to the outer world. The visitor with any feeling for art and architecture misses a sampling at his or her own peril. (The relatively unattractive, multiepoch *Duomo* [Via Duomo] is visitable mainly for Domenichino frescoes.) If I had time for but a single church, it would be *San Gregorio Armeno* (Via San Gregorio Armeno), a Renaissance meld in which there is not an unembellished square inch, with the decoration—slightly crumbly with a mellow patina—as beautiful as it is profuse. Frescoes covering the walls are by the Neapolitan master Luca Giordano. There is a pair of exquisite Baroque organs, a delicate dome over the altar, a finely coffered ceiling over the nave, a rear grille behind which cloistered nuns attend mass. Around the corner is the convent of the Sisters of the Crucifixion of San Gregorio Armeno. Ask for one of the nuns if you would like a peep at the convent's cloister. *Santa Chiara* (Via Trinità Maggiore) is Naples's most elegant church—a masterful post–World War II restoration of a tragically bombed complex. Gothic arches of the now severely simple nave are striking. The choir, with two hundred Baroque stalls, is an achievement in itself. But the real treat is the cloister, whose pillars and benches are of gaily painted majolica tiles, accented by leafy arbors and tubs of plants. *Sant' Anna dei Lombardi* (Via Monteoliveto) has as its most remarkable treasure a *Pietà* taking the form of a group of eight life-size figures sculpted of terra cotta in 1492. But there is so much more—an exuberantly designed Rococo organ; works of art fashioned of inlaid wood; an intricately carved choir; one gorgeous art-filled chapel after another.

Spaccanapoli: A stroll on Via San Biagio dei Librai: What to see? Good heavens, what not? Street vendors, shops selling gold and jewelry, once-great palazzi, elaborate churches, banks and pizza parlors, tall tenement old houses with wash on the lines extending streetward, *cambios* for money changing, and caffès. Most of all, pedestrians—intent, attractive, and in quantity—as authentic a cross section of Neapolitans as one is going to find, with the admission charge absolutely gratis. Take half a day, if you've time, and wander onto side streets, popping into churches and shops, even continuing on to Via del Duomo, a major intersection, at which you may turn left for a walk of several blocks to the Duomo (above) for which the street is named.

Posillipo—the elevated western sector of town—is surprise-filled and warrants an excursion by taxi (or rented car, if you have one) from the center. From its *Parco della Remembranza* there are absolutely smashing views not only of the bay, but of Capri, Ischia, and Sorrento in the distance. Closer to hand is the phenomenon of the park: a rarely depleted mass of parked cars. Not unusual, you say. But note their windows: covered over with taped newspapers, the lot of them, the better to afford privacy to occupants taking time from a busy day for a bit of love-making. Move along, then, to the highest part of the quarter, *Posillipo Alta,* from whose *Via Petrarca* there are still additional bay panoramas, especially striking from the belvedere of the Baroque *Church of San Antonio Posillipo.* Nearby, at the point called *Capo di Posillipo,* is *Villa Rosebery,* an early-nineteenth-century classic-style mansion originally German-owned but contemporarily the official Naples residence of presidents of the republic.

The ruins of Pompeii: I have not known it to fail. Take a look at the treasures from Pompeii in the National Museum (above) and of course you want to make an excursion to the ruined city. There are organized day tours by bus, or you may go by ordinary train from Stazione Centrale (Piazza Garibaldi)—*diretto* trains take about 45 minutes—to the Pompeii town station near the main entrance to the ruins, called Porta Marina. Note also that there are even quicker trains—as little as half an hour; they depart from a station near the main one, on Corso Garibaldi, called Circumvesuviana, and take you to still another station in Pompeii, closer to the entrance and called Porta di Nova. The ruins are operated by the Italian government as a museum, with regular hours and an admission fee. Traditionally, in summer at least, there have been evening as well as daytime hours, with highlights illuminated, and dramatic presentations in the amphitheater. Pompeii is considerably larger than many visitors expect; a full day is just enough to take it in thoroughly. Begin at the on-site museum, the Antiquarium—with its most memorable and rather ghoulish exhibits those of people and their pets whose bodies were petrified as a result of the eruption of Vesuvius that destroyed the town in A.D. 79—seventeen years after an earlier eruption that had been only minimally disastrous. You will already have learned of the advanced state of Pompeian civilization from your National Museum visit in town. What you want to concentrate on, at the site, is the broad city picture. After the Antiquarium, visit the expansive Forum; what remains of a temple dedicated to Apollo; temples to Jove and Jupiter; well-designed baths; marble floors, frescoed walls, and other architectural details of House of the Faun; frescoes—in royal blue and Pompeian red—on the atrium walls of Vetti House; and the eye-popping décor of the Amorini, Dorati, and Orpheus houses. With the amphitheater as a finale. There is a restaurant-caffè (washrooms are upstairs) on the site, where you may have lunch.

BEYOND THE BASICS: SELECTED MUSEUMS

Museo Nazionale di San Martino (Collina di Sant' Elmo al Vomero): This hilltop *certosa,* or monks' charterhouse, is essentially Baroque, with an elegant cloister, and chamber after handsome chamber housing a collection that relates the story of Naples historically, culturally, and artistically, with varied documentation—maps, prints, coins, medals, clothes, locally made applied arts such as china and glass, paintings by Neapolitans from the sixteenth through nineteenth centuries, and, perhaps most charming, eighteenth-century Christmas crèches—with hundreds upon hundreds of exquisitely detailed figures—that were a Neapolitan specialty.

Museo Civico Filangieri (Via del Duomo) occupies a formidable Renaissance palazzo—Cuomo by name—that is intimate and treasure-filled.

Collections, mostly all relating to Naples, are a mixed bag, filling galleries on two floors. There are two Luca Giordano paintings, another by Bernardino Luini, eighteenth-century porcelains, other objects, coins to armor. The galleried upstairs hall and a small paneled library are treats.

Museo Duca di Martina (Via Cimarosa al Vomero) makes its home in an early-nineteenth-century, park-surrounded palace a quarter hour's drive from downtown. Subject matter is the applied arts—furniture, porcelain (French and German especially), crystal, enamels, and silver. Then there is the white colonnaded house with original parquet floors, beautifully painted ceilings, and a formal garden in which you'll want to stroll.

Museo Principe di Aragona Pignatelli Cortes, in the park called Riviera di Chiaia, near the Aquarium (later recommended) is, to be sure, a mouthful. Neapolitans call it simply Pignatelli, and the late-eighteenth-century mansion in which it is situated—unusually triple-porticoed—is beautiful enough to have served as the subject of an Italian postage stamp. The house is quite as treasure-filled—with furnishings in their original position—as when the Pignatelli family was in residence. Have a look at the twin-chandeliered ballroom, its walls of red brocade. Take in furniture and paintings in Conference Room, Music Room, Drawing Room (brimming with china from Berlin, Vienna, and Meissen to complement a cache of local Capodimonte), Library (impressive with walls surfaced in gilded leather, and seventeenth-century furnishings), Dining Room (furnished in early-nineteenth-century Italian Regency, still-life paintings on the walls), and as a bonus, a three-room pavilion in the garden that's a museum of antique carriages.

Banco di Napoli Galleria d' Arte (Via Roma 420): Bravo, Banco di Napoli! It was this civic-minded firm that helped finance the restoration of the church and cloister of Santa Chiara (above), and this same bank has one of its branches in an ancient palazzo with an exemplary chapel (below). This gallery is devoted to choice Neapolitan works, sixteenth through nineteenth centuries.

BEYOND THE BASICS: SELECTED CHURCHES

Cappella, Banco di Napoli (Via San Biagio dei Librai): This branch of a major bank is located in a handsome antique of a palazzo. Walk through to the far side of the courtyard to the chapel, among whose treasures is a

Luca Giordano fresco; even when it's closed, you can look in the windows.

Gesù Nuovo (Piazza del Gesù Nuovo) is distinguished by its massive gray façade and an elaborate Baroque dome. Within it is busy with frescoes and sculptures, the lot under a magnificent coffered ceiling.

Santa Brigida (Via Santa Brigida) could double as a gallery of Neapolitan Baroque paintings. You must go back to the sacristy for a look at the ceiling frescoes by Luca Giordano, but there are works by other seventeenth-century locals, especially Giacomo Ferelli and Massimo Manzione.

San Domenico Maggiore (Piazza San Domenico Maggiore) could be taken for a medieval castle, at least from without. Inside, there is a very long and narrow nave under a gilded ceiling and a Baroque organ behind the altar. Glittering.

San Ferdinando di Palazzo (Piazza Trento e Trieste) is a near neighbor of the Royal Palace and is quite as richly embellished. Every inch of this superior Baroque specimen is decorated.

San Francesco di Paola (Piazza Plebiscito) is masterful neoclassic: strong, severe, and monumental. Behind a long, curved colonnade and central portico is an immense cupola sheltering the interior, around whose walls stand 34 Corinthian columns.

San Lorenzo Maggiore (Piazza San Gaetano) is Baroque without, Gothic within, at once cold and splendid, with Luca Giordano paintings as a bonus.

Cappella di Sansevero (Via Francesco de Sanctis) is what is meant when one says big things come in small packages: an exquisite study in Baroque at its most exuberant, with sculpted angels in an over-altar sunburst, and on walls and ceiling.

A NEAPOLITAN MISCELLANY

Acquario (Via Caracciolo), appropriately enough, faces the sea in the pretty Villa Comunale park. This is an old-time aquarium established more than a century back, and the contents are local. By that I mean every one of the 200-plus species of marine life is from this corner of the Mediterranean.

Castel Nuovo (Piazza Municipio) is the heart-of-town landmark that looks as though it could be an opera set: crenelated medieval towers wrapped around a somber stone façade, originally thirteenth-century. Pass through the Renaissance entry arch and you're in an open court leading to the castle's great hall with an oversized fireplace and a charming Gothic chapel whose claim to fame is that it once held frescoes—long since missing—by Giotto.

Catacombs (Al Tondo di Capodimonte): This two-story underground cemetery bears the name of San Januaris, the very same to whom the Duomo is dedicated. Fine mosaics were discovered relatively recently in a maze of niches carved from rock and decorated with frescoes.

Vesuvius: It is 4200 feet high, buried Pompeii in A.D. 79, and last erupted in 1943. Go by train to Herculaneum, then by bus to the mountain's funicular station for the final lap by foot to the crater at the summit and memorable vistas of the city and the bay.

CULTURAL COUNTRYSIDE: A TRIO OF EXCURSIONS

Herculaneum, considerably smaller than Pompeii, was buried at the same time, as a result of the Vesuvius eruption of A.D. 79. Most of the excavation is within the last half century—much more recent than Pompeii's. The special excitement here is the remarkable art that remains—still-bright frescoes, lovely mosaics, capitals, columns. (Californians will recall that the J. Paul Getty Museum in Malibu is a reconstruction of a Herculaneum villa—one of a number of upper-class houses that are more elaborate than those of Pompeii and a prime reason for a visit to this smaller city.) The area to head for, if one's visit is abbreviated, is the south, where houses—including Tramezzo and Cervi—are the most sumptuously decorated. There are still-lavish public baths, a theater, and a museum exhibiting mosaics and other art and artifacts found on the site. Access is via train (Circumvesuviana Railway), bus, and cab. Distance from town is only five miles.

Paestum, so much less contemporarily celebrated than Pompeii and Herculaneum, deserves more attention. It is a onetime Greek colony, conquered by Romans in the third century before Christ, and still with structures in remarkable stages of preservation, almost all in Doric, the simplest of the three classical styles (the other two are Ionic and Corinthian). The Temple of Neptune is, in its way, quite as majestic as the Parthenon in Athens. The Temple of Ceres, though much more in ruins, remains impressive nonetheless. So do the basilica and forum. There is an on-site museum, too. Paestum is about 50 miles south of Naples, accessible by car, bus, or train.

Caserta is the relatively unheralded site of a magnificent eighteenth-century royal palace bearing its name. Builder was King Charles III, and the idea, at least partially, was to make Louis XV sit up and take notice. Caserta was, then, an attempt to compete with Versailles. Consider that it is built around a quartet of enormous courtyards and is six stories high with a score and a half of staircases, some 1800 windows, and no less than 1200 rooms. The visitor, have no fear, is not shown about in anything like detail. Just enough to get an idea of how the kings of Naples and their families and courtiers squeaked by. Usually shown are the principal royal apartments, with king's and queen's bedrooms and the rooms in which they worked, entertained, and relaxed. As in the Royal Palace in Naples, southern Italian variations of Baroque furniture are less subtle than those of northern Italy, France, or Germany. But quite beautiful. As are paintings and frescoes, most especially those on the ceilings of the Hall of Alexander, the Great Room, and the Throne Room. The fountains of the surrounding park are a major Caserta treat. The late U.S. President—then General—Dwight D. Eisenhower was a post–World War II Caserta resident, and especially enjoyed strolling its gardens. Distance is about 15 miles from Naples via bus or train, with the palace conveniently across the street from the railway station. Overnight, if you like, at *Caserta Hotel Jolly* (Via Veneto 9, *First Class*)—89 rooms, restaurant, bar.

EXPLORING THE BAY OF NAPLES

The Amalfi Drive (Positano, Amalfi, Ravello, Sorrento) is the most celebrated of our planet's single-day motor excursions: a magnificently mountainous promontory whose steep slopes are dotted with venerable smallish towns—some at the top, some climbing from beach to plateau, some a combination. Leaving Naples, head south along the coast to Castellamare, thence turning westward onto the elevated peninsular coastal highway that is actually the Amalfi Drive. You go in the direction of Sorrento, but just short of it, at the little town of Meta, turn inland and take a southerly road over the peninsula to the south coast, driving eastward to *Positano*—an enchanting village that climbs the coastal hills, with as much charm per cubic meter as any resort in the area. If you're not settling in *(below)*, alight and walk about; caffès, boutiques, restaurants, and a Baroque parish church compose the engaging and compact core flanking the beach.

From Positano, move along a few scenic miles east to *Amalfi*, the town that gave its name to the drive. What you want to see is the *Duomo*, at once Romanesque and Gothic, with strong Moorish-Sicilian lines, and an exterior that surpasses what lies within, except for the cloister—aptly called Chiostro del Paradiso. Surrounding Amalfi streets are hilly, narrow, shop-filled, and fun to explore.

From Amalfi, head directly inland just a few miles to an enchanter of a little town, *Ravello*. Its situation is easily the equal—as regards vistas—of the coastal communities. And there is so much of beauty that one easily understands why Richard Wagner settled there for a while in 1880. Little Ravello is no longer the see of a bishop, but had been for centuries after its cathedral first went up nearly a millennium ago. Take a look at the *Duomo* and also visit neighboring *Villa Rufolo*, a curious Moorish-Gothic palace that dates to the thirteenth century, with a splendid cloister and a view of the Amalfi coast from the garden terrace that Wagner exclaimed over (he turned it into the Garden of Klingsor in *Parsifal*), and that is the site, traditionally in summer, of Wagnerian concerts. Other Ravello delights: *Villa Cimbrone*, with its medieval garden-cum-view, and the cloister and *Duomo* of the next-door village of *San Lorenzo*.

From Ravello return to Amalfi on the coast and drive west along the sea; you will be backtracking as far as Positano, but from then on the route will be new territory, taking you almost to the tip of the peninsula for a curve north and east to superbly situated *Sorrento*. Sorrento is a convenient point of departure—one goes by boat and the distance is much shorter than from Naples—to the island of Capri. But tarry to have a walk along the hotel-lined promenade on a dramatic cliff high above the bay; inspect the surprising mix of treasures—paintings through porcelain—in the pretty palace housing *Museo Correale di Terranova*; and pop into the multiepoch *Duomo*.

Capri: It would be hard to beat Capri's staying power. Roman emperors—Augustus first, and later his stepson, Tiberius—were among its first holiday makers, a couple of millenniums back. (Still to be seen are ruins of the estate where they lived.) Capri fortunes, ever since, have more or less followed those of Naples. There are perfectly good reasons Capri should never have made it. It is not, to begin, a beachy island. There are places to swim but they can be a bother to reach. It is more than hilly; it is mountainous, which means that getting about entails huffing and puffing. And by virtue of being surrounded by water, it is, like all islands, more difficult of access than competing mainland resorts. Indeed, arrival or departure in the rain—the case on a recent visit of mine—can be a thoroughly disagreeable experience.

But nobody has ever seemed to mind. In the quarter century that I have known it, Capri has, to its credit, changed less than any other major resort with which I am familiar. It remains small-scale, casual, charming, and in its own hard-to-define way, just zippy and modish enough to be fun. It would never, for example, go to the extremes of, say, St. Tropez. But, by the same token, one should not expect England's Bournemouth or New England's Rockport. There has always been a healthy, forthright, live-and-let-live attitude toward a remarkable clientele—multinational, multilingual, young through elderly, gay through macho-straight, all having themselves a good time.

In order to be successful, it seems ordained that a resort area should have a minimum of the kind of distractions—museums, galleries, churches, theater—that attract visitors to the big cities. Capri conforms in this respect. What it mostly offers are magnificent vistas of the gulf, neighboring Ischia and mainland points, and the oddly shaped rock formations—*Faraglioni*—that extend from its shore. Views, in other words, are sublime.

Geography is relatively simple on this smallish oblong of an island. Boats from Naples and Sorrento disgorge passengers at a north coast settlement called *Marina Grande;* they invariably proceed without delay to a little funicular railway that takes them to another settlement, elevated and mid-island, called, simply enough, Capri. And to hotels, restaurants, caffès, shops, after-dark activity, and, for proper sightseeing, a charterhouse, with a spectacular cloister and handsome chapel. *Grotta Azzurra* (the Blue Grotto), popular because of the phenomenon of the eerie light within, is on the northwest corner of the island and is entered by sightseeing boats—at least on days when water is at the proper level. *San Michele* is the name of a charming house built some decades back by a Swedish physician-writer named Axel Munthe, and imaginatively furnished with antiques emanating from Capri's classical era as well as pieces from more recent centuries; it operates as a museum. *Anacapri* is the top-of-the-island town, with the most sublime views of all, and some hotels. One gets about in Capri by foot, otherwise by little public buses and taxis, not to mention the earlier-noted Capri town–Marina Grande funicular. Still, when all is said and done, the most popular diversion is taking coffee or drinks—the while checking on who is with whom and what the day's new arrivals look like—at caffès on the *Piazzetta,* which no one ever calls by its proper name, Piazza Umberto I.

Ischia: Ischia is bigger in area, bigger in population, in its own way quite as beautiful as Capri, and with the kind of beaches that Capri simply does not have. Withal, it has never had quite the celebrity of the smaller island, and certainly not the international clientele. Contemporarily, the overwhelming majority of visitors are German—many, but by no means all, come for thermal cures. Which is not to say that other nationalities are not welcome, nor that their languages are not spoken.

As on Capri, sightseeing takes second place to relaxing atmosphere. Boats from Naples dock on the north shore of this roughly oblong island, usually at the *Ischia Porto* sector of *Ischia town.* (Although some boats dock at the marina in the nearby community of *Casamicciola*—a few miles west of Ischia Porto and hydrofoils link Naples with the Ischian port of Forio.) A day-long tour can be rewarding. Ideally, one would take in the tiny island connected to the mainland by the bridge at *Ischia Ponte;* its landmark is a storybook castle on the scene since medieval times.

The route would then be roughly clockwise. Stop next at *Barano,* just inland from the south shore, with a view of the long strand of *Maronti Beach* below. *Fontana,* a pretty town even farther inland, is near *Monte Epomeo,* the vineyard region where originates the good white wine that is the mainstay beverage of the Bay of Naples. At *Serrara Fontana,* there is a belvedere with tables, for a drink stop, and the best of the south shore views. I would detour a tiny bit south then, to *Sant' Angelo,* a resort community on a mini-isle connected by causeway to the mainland, and fringing *Maronti Beach.* Access to Sant' Angelo's hotels is by foot, over elevated paths leading to a cluster of inns on a high perch with perfectly sublime views of my favorite corner of the island. Move along to the west coast and *Forio,* a picture-book settlement with four crenelated medieval towers (of which Torrione is the most noted) and the *Church of Soccorso*—glistening white in the sun—tucked onto the edge of a sea-straddling cliff, and surely the most photographed single structure on Ischia. It is at Forio that its German proprietors have created *Poseidon*—an extraordinarily good-looking complex that is primarily a thermal center—with no less than a score of pools dotted about, as well as a massive Roman-style sauna and facilities for *fango,* or mud baths, physiotherapy, and cosmetic treatments. There are, as well, a long and lovely beach and a pair of attractive restaurants with outdoor tables. Onward, then, to the same north shore where we landed and *Lacco Ameno,* with its lure (built on Roman foundations a millennium ago), *Santa Restituta Sanctuary; Casamicciola,* an older resort-thermal community, is next door.

SETTLING IN

NAPLES

Britannique Hotel (Corso Vittorio Emanuele 133) is far enough uphill to afford good views from some of its 80 rooms. Still, it is a fair distance from the core. And press colleagues whose opinions I value report that service, in the course of their stay, was hardly hospitable. Restaurant, bar. *First Class.*

Excelsior Hotel (Via Partenope 48): Thank a firm of canny Swiss hoteliers not only for erecting the Excelsior in the first decade of this century, but for its inspired location: directly on the bay, with fabulous views from rooms on two of its four sides. The city's No. 1 hostelry from the day it opened, the Excelsior in its early years knew visits by King Victor Emmanuel III, his consort, and other members of the Royal Family, who made frequent forays to Naples. Its Swiss owners sold the hotel to Ciga in 1935, and although no hotel in Italy, certainly to my knowledge, has known more thorough refurbishing in recent seasons, Ciga has wisely retained the Belle Époque look and ambience in the capacious lounges, bar, and restaurant (evaluated in a later paragraph) of the main floor. The 114 rooms and suites have been treated to lavish new baths and smart early-nineteenth-century-style furnishings. Those I have inhabited or inspected are generous-sized and delightful; make a point of insisting on a view of the bay and Vesuvius from your window or, better yet, book premium terraced accommodations. No hotel that I know has a more cordial staff. *Luxury.*

Jolly Hotel (Via Medina 70) is the slim skyscraper of a Piazza Municipio landmark that old-timers remember as the Ambassador's Palace. The astute Jolly chain took over some years back, completely refurbishing and redecorating, with the result a handsome hotel with a vast lobby bar-lounge, popular with Neapolitans and guests alike, thirtieth floor restaurant-cum-view (so good that I amplify on it in a later paragraph), 278 well-equipped rooms and suites, and the most central location in town. *First Class.*

Majestic Hotel (Largo Vasto a Chiaia): I had problems here during a stay some years back—surly service, Italian the only language spoken, tiny room and bath whose toilet needed cleaning, so that I wouldn't go back. But things may be better on your visit. *First Class.*

Mediterraneo Hotel (Piazza Municipio) greets one with a contemporary lobby of multihued marbles and an attached bar. There is a restaurant on the roof with a terrace for summer dining, affording panoramas of the bay; and there are 230 spotless, well-equipped rooms. *First Class.*

Oriente Hotel (Via Diaz 44) is an attractive modern house—full facility, with restaurant and bar and an enviably central situation, just off Via Roma. *First Class.*

Royal Hotel (Via Partenope 38), most modern of the Via Partenope group, is a well-run 273-room house with a big, buzzy, mural-decorated lobby, balconies attached to bay-view rooms (the more recently redecorated accommodations feature blond-finish furniture and tasteful textiles), a rooftop saltwater swimming pool, mezzanine picture-window restaurant (evaluated on a subsequent page), and piano bar. Nice. *First Class.*

Santa Lucia Hotel (Via Partenope 46) is one of the Via Partenope quartet, along with the Excelsior, Vesuvio, and Royal—all of which are nicer. The elderly Santa Lucia has 132 spotless rooms, all with bath; bar-lounge and breakfast but no restaurant, and, in my experience, a not especially cordial staff. Only so-so. *Moderate.*

Vesuvio Hotel (Via Partenope 45)—considerably spruced up in recent seasons—is smartly situated facing the bay. Public spaces—big and humming lobby, serene second-floor lounge, bar with leather club chairs surrounding tables, on-high terraced restaurant later reviewed—are inviting. And those of the 170 rooms and suites I have inspected are clean-lined, comfortable, and with good baths; most but not all of those facing the bay are terraced. Friendly. *First Class.*

POSITANO

San Pietro Hotel (Locanda San Pietro) is high on its own eminence with fabulous vistas of the sea, way below, and the village less than a mile distant. There are just 60 suites and rooms, no two alike. Décor theme throughout is essentially traditional with uniquely San Pietro touches—Virginia creeper coming in from the outdoors to cover ceilings, picture-window bathrooms, gilded wood fragments salvaged from Baroque palaces as headboards of beds, Rococo furniture and accessories. The restaurant (about which more later), cocktail bar, and lounges are handsome. And this is the only Positano hotel with its own beach; you take an elevator, and may have lunch while below. A San Pietro stay is a unique experience and there are not a few repeaters, many of them Americans. *Luxury.*

Le Sirenuse (Via Colombo) is a sumptuously updated eighteenth-century townhouse that charms with an ambience of special style. There are just 60 individually designed suites and rooms, many with terraces; a super restaurant that moves outdoors in summer; delightful management and staff. Swimming pool-cum-bar, with snacks. Member, Leading Hotels of the World. *Luxury.*

Miramare Hotel (Via Trara Genoino) has an enviably elevated in-town position that affords views of the beach just below. Each of the antique-accented rooms has its own terrace—ideal for breakfast and cocktails. And the excellent restaurant is picture-windowed. *First Class.*

Poseidon Hotel is phototypically Positano. By that I mean situated on a hilltop affording fabulous views, with inviting public spaces that include strategically sited restaurant and bar as well as half a hundred charming rooms, all terraced and with fine baths. Friendly. *First Class.*

Palazzo Murat Hotel (Via Drimalini) has as its ace in the hole an in-town location, adjacent to the beach. The look is essentially traditional, with some rooms in a newer wing; lovely antiques throughout. Bar and breakfast but no restaurant. Friendly. *Moderate.*

Marincanto Hotel (Via Colombo): You can walk down to the beach from this elevated hotel. There are precisely 26 traditionally furnished rooms (all with baths), lounge-cum-bar, terrace for breakfast (there is no restaurant), and sun baths. *Moderate.*

Casa Albertina Hotel (Via Tavolozza) is intimate (there are 27 pleasant rooms with bath) with an on-high setting affording smashing vistas, breakfast terrace, restaurant, and bar. *Moderate.*

Villa Franca Hotel (Viale Pasitea) is high enough up for management to offer complimentary bus service to and from the beach. There are 42 rooms and those I have inspected tend to be small, but I like their baths; ditto the restaurant and bar-lounge. *Moderate.*

Tritone Hotel (Triano, two miles from Positano) lies high over the beach (there are elevators), with a pool as well, restaurant-bar, 62 rooms with extraordinary views. *First Class.*

SORRENTO

Excelsior Victoria Hotel (Piazza Tasso 34) has the patina that comes only with graceful advanced age: the kind of old-fashioned house—superbly situated on a steep cliff overlooking the bay—that we cross the Atlantic to experience. There are 114 rooms, restaurant and bar. *Luxury.*

Sorrento Palace Hotel (Via Sant' Antonio) first welcomes the visitor from without: setting is a honey of a garden with no less than half a dozen interconnected swimming pools. Go on in, then. Public spaces are handsome and include a quartet of restaurants (one of them a convenient coffee shop) and quite as many bars, as well as an indoor pool and tennis. There are close to 400 thoughtfully equipped, terraced rooms and, as frosting on the cake, a state-of-the-art conference center with facilities (including three auditoriums) for 1700 delegates. *Luxury.*

Parco dei Principi Hotel (Via Rota 1) is centered in a lovely, swimming-pool-equipped, bay-view garden from which there's an elevator to the beach way below. This is a modern full-facility house (nice places to dine and to drink) with close to a hundred pleasant rooms. *First Class.*

Bristol Hotel (Via del Capo 22) is a cliffhanger—quite literally. It hugs the bayfront promontory, affording scrumptious views from front rooms (there are 132 all told) and a swimming-pool terrace. Restaurant, bar. *First Class.*

Carlton International Hotel (Via Correale 15) is functional-modern, with 70 rooms, restaurant, bar, swimming pool, and central situation. *Moderate.*

Gran Paradiso Hotel (Via Privata Rubinacci) is a worth-knowing-about house with 86 comfortable rooms and a swimming-pool-centered terrace from which there are memorable views of the bay. Restaurant, bar. *Moderate.*

RAVELLO

Palumbo Hotel (Via San Giovanni del Toro 28) was originally a twelfth-century palace. It is at once elevated and sea-view with just 20 terraced rooms (baths are special), smart indoor–outdoor restaurant-bar, and pretty garden. A super spot. *Luxury.*

CAPRI

Quisisana Hotel (Via Camerelle) is heart-of-town, neoclassic—even to urn-filled niches on its pedimented façade, with sweeping public spaces; 150 rooms and suites, no two quite alike, but all that I have either lived in or inspected quietly smart. The restaurant (worthy of later comment) moves in summer to a terrace in the garden. There's entertainment in the paneled cocktail lounge, and a big oval of a swimming pool. Very nice, indeed. Member, Leading Hotels of the World. *Luxury.*

Punta Tragara Hotel (Via Tragara 57) is a onetime private villa with 33 terraced suites (there are only a few regular twins), excellent antique-furnished restaurant, bar-lounge, pool, and dining terrace-caffè affording exciting panoramas of the shore. The clublike ambience and imaginative decorative schemes appeal. *Luxury.*

Scalinatella Hotel (Via Tragara 8) is small (there are just under 30 terraced and tile-floored rooms and suites, some of the latter with two baths, the lot delightful and accented by antique furnishings) but choice, affording splendid views of the sea way below from its elevated setting in a pretty garden, which has a honey of a swimming pool. The staff is skilled and smiling. A special place. Breakfast only. *Luxury.*

La Pazziella Hotel (Via Giuliani 4) is a near neighbor of the Piazzetta—Capri's main square—and is agreeably intimate with but a score of smartly traditional rooms, handsome public spaces, with a capacious veranda the most popular. Breakfast only. *First Class.*

Europa Palace Hotel (Anacapri): Given a yen to headquarter topside on this beautiful island—there's no question about the spectacular vistas from Anacapri—the indicated hotel is the Europa Palace, long on scene albeit spiffily updated in contemporary style with just over 90 smart rooms with fine baths (including a score of spiffy two-bath junior suites). There is a big swimming pool in the garden, trio of nearby tennis courts, ranker of a restaurant, nice spots to enjoy a relaxing drink. Lovely. *Luxury.*

Luna Hotel (Viale Matteotti 3) is splendidly sited, with striking views of a striking coastline—it faces the jutting rocks called Faraglioni—with the key word with respect to facilities "big": lobby, 44 balconied bedrooms, restaurant (on a terrace in summer), cocktail lounge, swimming pool, garden. *First Class.*

La Palma Hotel (Via Vittorio Emanuele 32) pleases with its central situation, 80 tile-floored, terraced rooms, an especially elegant restaurant-cum-terrace, bar-lounge, and pool. *First Class.*

Gatto Bianco Hotel (Via Vittorio Emanuele 38): The White Cat, to translate, is a winner, with cozy lobby, cocktail lounge, and attractive if compact rooms, 44 all told and all with bath; and a pretty terrace restaurant. Super-central location. *Moderate.*

Flora Hotel (Via Serena 26) is small-scaled. There are 22 terraced rooms in a close-to-the-Piazzetta location, with a pleasant bar, sea-views, and breakfast service, but no restaurant. *Moderate.*

Pineta Hotel (Via Tragara 6) is a departure from the usual traditional-style Capri hotel, spiffily mod-look, with 50-plus neat rooms, pool surrounded by a big sun-terrace-cum-vistas, restaurant, and bar. *Moderate.*

ISCHIA

Jolly Hotel delle Terme (Via de Luca 42, Porto Ischia) is a honey of a 208-room modern house in a verdant setting, with a distinguished restaurant, bar-lounge where guests get to know each other, big swimming pool in the garden, and a well-equipped thermal spa—isn't it time you had a mud bath?—adjacent. *First Class.*

Punta Molino Hotel (Lungomare Telese, Porto Ischia) affords smashing views of the medieval castle at Ischia Ponte (above); rooms are nice (close to 90 all told); restaurant, bar, and beach. *First Class.*

Terme di Augusto Hotel (Lacco Ameno) is a contemporary heart-of-Lacco-Ameno house, garden-surrounded, with the beach steps away. There are 120 smartly styled rooms, enjoyable restaurant, along with swimming pool, tennis courts, and thermal treatment center. *First Class.*

San Michele Hotel (Sant' Angelo) has half a hundred modern rooms with bath, inviting public spaces including restaurant, bar, terrace caffè, swimming pool, and top-of-the-world setting overlooking nearby Maronti Beach. *Moderate.*

Regina Isabella e Royal Sporting Hotel (Lacco Ameno)—hugs the shore (with its own beach) and has wisely placed one of two restaurants and both its swimming pools at dramatic points overlooking the sea. The main lounge—in the style of the eighteenth century—is arguably the most elegant on the island, and there are just over 130 no-two-quite-alike rooms and suites; those I have inspected are very nice indeed. The Regina Isabella's special feature is its own superbly equipped multi-facility spa, with mineral and mud baths, inhalation treatments, massage, gym-fitness center, cosmetic treatments, and thermal pools. *Luxury.*

Excelsior Hotel (Via Gianturco 19, Porto Ischia) is a thoroughly delightful 72-room house, seafront, with handsome public spaces—rambling main lounge; crystal-chandelier-hung, picture-windowed restaurant, cozy bar, a swimming pool in the garden, and the beach adjacent. Those of the rooms I have inhabited or inspected—including some duplex suites—are charmers. And the staff is super. A lovely experience. *Luxury.*

Il Moresco Hotel (Via Gianturco 21, Porto Ischia—just opposite the Excelsior, above) flanks its own garden and the sea. The lobby-lounge combines club chairs with Murano chandeliers. Those of the 73 bedrooms I've inspected are smartly traditional. The restaurant is exemplary, and there's a big outdoor pool and a thermal spa–fitness–beauty center. *First Class.*

Aragona Palace Hotel (Via Porto, Porto Ischia) is directly on the harbor, heart of the Porto Ischia action. There are just over 60 modern rooms with counter-sink baths, competent restaurant, terraced bar-lounge, outdoor pool strategically situated so as to afford fine views, and thermal facilities, the range mud baths through massages. *First Class.*

La Reginella Hotel (Lacco Ameno) embraces half a hundred bath- or shower-equipped rooms, attractive restaurant and bar, both indoor and outdoor thermal swimming pools, a well-equipped spa–beauty center, tennis courts, and beach. *First Class.*

Solemar Hotel (Via Battistessa 45, Porto Ischia) has the advantage of a beachfront location. Swim from and sun on the sands—or in the hotel's own big pool. Those of the 72 rooms I've inspected are okay and have shower-equipped baths and balconies; you want to book one facing the sea. Restaurant, bar, and thermal spa. *Moderate.*

Bristol Terme Hotel (Via Venanzio Marone 10, Porto Ischia) is conveniently heart-of-town, with 40 neat rooms, restaurant, bar, pool, and thermal spa. *Moderate.*

AMALFI

Santa Caterina Hotel (Amalfitana 9) straddles a verdant seaside eminence; with a pair of elevators to and from the beach, 72 terraced rooms and suites, pair of restaurants and of bars. Views are extraordinary. Special. *Luxury.*

DAILY BREAD

It is possible to approach the cuisine of Naples and the *Regione* of Campania of which it is capital somewhat patronizingly. We have, in the back of our minds, too many Italian-American restaurants where touch is anything but light, tomato sauce heavy, scaloppine thickly breaded, minestrone more pasta than soup. Naples food, at its best, is something else again. Tomato sauce—the famous *pommarola* of the region—tends to be light and delicate and fresh. Pasta is encountered in limitless variety—spaghetti, to be sure, but variations on the theme like *bucatini, vermicelli, ziti,* and *cannelloni.* Pizza is Naples-born and -bred. And seafood is significant. It might be *spigola* (sea bass), *orate* (sea bream), *triglie* (red mullet), or *tonno* (tuna). Order pasta with any number of superb seafood sauces—made with clams *(vongole),* mussels *(cozze),* shrimp *(gamberi),* lobster *(aragosta),* squid *(calamari),* eels *(anguille),* or oysters *(ostriche).* Look for *zuppa di pesce* (fish soup), *casseruola di pesce* (fish casserole), *frittura di pesce mista*—an assortment of seafood (usually featuring squid or octopus), deep fried and delicious.

NAPLES

La Brace (Via Silvio Spaventa 16; Phone 417-034) is handy to the central train station and a super source of pizza and fresh-as-this-morning seafood—the basis for pasta sauces and simply but deliciously prepared entrées. *First Class.*

La Caffetiera (Piazza dei Martiri) is relatively recent: at once a smart and popular caffè; gossipy Neapolitans crowd it late afternoon, to see and be seen. *Moderate.*

La Cantinella (Via Cuma 42—a few blocks east along the bay from the Via Partenope hotels): The look is what might be termed gentrified rustic—white lace cloths over red linen on the tables, stuccoed walls. You take your time reading the extensive à la carte. Antipasti take up a page—shrimp cocktail and seafood salad through sautéed clams and prosciutto with mozzarella. Pasta options are among the most extensive of any restaurant I know in Italy—simple (but expertly sauced) spaghetti al pomodoro through three-times-as-pricey risotto al salmone (the salmon, of course, being smoked). Florentine-style steak and veal dishes are good bets. But I counsel seafood—grilled swordfish, lobster thermidor, a casserole of mussels (delicious, this), a frittura embracing samples of the day's diverse catch. Extensive wine list. Smiling red-jacketed staff. *First Class.*

Caffè Caflish (Via Toledo 253) is a good-sized sit-down caffè, with principal lures delicious cakes to accompany coffee, and a candy counter. *Moderate.*

Caffè Gambrinus (Piazza Trieste e Trento) is the perfect downtown observation point for Neapolitans on the go, with mellowed frescoes framed by wood panels, Palazzo Reale as a backdrop. Drinks, coffee, snacks. *Moderate.*

Caffè Marino (Via dei Mille 18) is the prototypical Neapolitan stand-up coffee bar—for an espresso or a cappuccino. Celebrated. *Moderate.*

Casanova Grill (Excelsior Hotel, Via Partenope 48; Phone 417-111): Framed antique prints line the beige walls of this understatedly handsome room, whose tables are surrounded by Thonet-type chairs. Cold antipasti and salads top a central counter. Best buy is at midday when there's a three-course prix-fixe lunch. Or select from the à la carte, opening with sliced tomato and mozzarella doused with fresh basil and olive oil, or the house's delicious carpaccio. Sorrento-style gnocchi and linguine Posillipo (with clams) are pasta treats. Of course you may order pizza; specify Margherita style (plain cheese—the favorite of Neapolitans). Veal dishes—including, in summer, vitello tonnato—are no less delicious than mixed grill or spit-roasted chicken. And desserts are wheeled to table on a trolley. *Luxury.*

Don Salvatore (Strada Mergellina 4; Phone 681-817) is framed by stucco arches, with red-shaded lamps at tables, an alert staff, and mighty good things to eat. There's a prix-fixe menu but the à la carte is favored by many regulars, who choose from an interesting menu largely printed in Neapolitan dialect; your waiter will give you whatever help you need. Open with a seafood-accented pasta—tuna-sauced bucatini, for example. Follow with lobster, simply grilled fish, or a frittata of seafood. Satisfying. *First Class.*

Ciro Santa Brigida (Via Santa Brigida 71; Phone 324-072) occupies two good-looking floors of a heart-of-downtown building, with the look a meld of palest of blue walls and draperies. Service is swift and cordial.

Clientele is business and professional Neapolitan—chatty, animated, attractive. Menus are computer printouts, with all of the typical Naples dishes included, and a lot from other regions. Few restaurants that I know have a more enticing selection of pastas. A good bet is linguine alla puttanesca, with a sauce of oil, anchovies, and olives, accented with sweet basil and a hint of garlic. A tasty entrée is granantine alla Ciro, a mini meatloaf blanketed by melted cheese and a delicate tomato sauce served with escarole, steamed, as a vegetable. Focaccia—which might be described as piping hot pizza whose sauce is replaced by a drizzle of olive oil—supplements the crusty bread served. Sound regional wines. In my view, one of Italy's best restaurants. *First Class.*

Da Luigi (Via Domenico Morelli 14) is a good spot to remember if you're quartered in one of the Santa Lucia hotels; it's on a street to their rear, modest-looking but with fresh and tasty pastas and seafood and happy customers. *Moderate.*

Grapalù (Via Roma 16) is, to be sure, Neapolitan, but with a pleasing—and not jarring—contemporary accent: pastas, entrées, made-on-premises sweets. *Luxury.*

Jolly Hotel Ristorante (Via Medina 70): Up you go to the thirtieth floor—ideally for lunch on a clear, sunny day, the better for picture-window vistas of the Royal Palace and other city landmarks, with the bay and Vesuvius beyond. Concentrate on seafood, opening perhaps with risotto posillipo (with a seafood sauce), continuing with grilled fish of the day, a crisp Ischian white wine accompanying, a typically Neapolitan pastry to conclude. *First Class.*

Motta (Via Toledo 152) is a branch of the Italy-wide chain selling its own pastries, cookies, candies, ice cream—even potato chips. And, in addition, sandwiches and a variety of other snacks, invariably delicious. Proper bar, too. *Moderate.*

Peppino (Via Palepoli 8) lines its walls with tile plaques, fills its tables with a lively clientele, specializes in seafood. Near Santa Lucia hotels. *Moderate.*

Pizzeria Trianon (Via Pietro Colletta 46, near Stazione Centrale): Since Naples is pizza's place of origin, Neapolitans take their pizza seriously. The Trianon is as plain as an old shoe. There are a variety of pies but the favorite of locals is the species labeled Margherita, which means with mozzarella, tomatoes, and just a sprinkle of olive oil. Beer and cola are the usual accompaniments. *Moderate.* (Other leading pizzerie include *Port' Alba*—reputedly the oldest in town—and centrally situated at Via Port' Alba 19, phone 459-713; *Bellini,* Via Santa Maria di Costantinopoli 80, phone 459-774—near Museo Archeologico Nazionale; and *Lombardi di Santa Chiara,* Via Benedetto Croce 59, Phone 206-46, near Church of Santa Chiara. All are *Moderate.*)

Rosolino (Via N. Sauro 5; Phone 415-873) is herein given space only because of its proximity to Via Partenope hotels; you might be tempted to go, as you pass by. If the stodgy dinner I experienced—served in a ballroom-size space to the accompaniment of a band whose decibel-count precluded table conversation—is typical (the setting might have been Nebraska rather than Naples), you might well prefer to move along to something more typical. To understate: disappointing. *First Class.*

Royal Hotel Ristorante (Via Partenope 38; Phone 400-244) occupies light and bright quarters, picture-windowed and overlooking the bay. Red-leather chairs enclose tables set in starched white linen, and the best bet is the prix-fixe menu, varying each day at lunch and dinner, and possibly consisting of the day's special pasta or a salad (one, for example of beans, tuna, and onions) to start, veal scaloppine with mushrooms or the day's fish among entrées, fresh fruit or pastry to conclude. *First Class.*

Rugantino (Via dei Fiorentini 45; Phone 325-491) is heart-of-downtown, modern with gracious service, and a first-rate kitchen. Contorni—cooked vegetables of the season—make a good first course here; paglia e fieno—straw and hay—is a tasty pasta of two hues for starters; roast chicken is good, and so is grilled fresh fish. *First Class.*

La Sacrestia (Via Orazio 116; Phone 761-1051): Smart, stylish restaurants are not in oversupply in Naples; La Sacrestia is one such, high on a hill overlooking the city, with good portraits of priests and cardinals lining its walls, the better to do justice to its name. Service is professional, food exceptional. Why not begin with a platter of three species of pasta—rigatoni, scarpiello, and spinach-stuffed ravioli in a cheese sauce? Then order the jumbo shrimp—spiedini di gamberoni—grilled and delicious. Or involtini alla papalina—sautéed veal rolled in prosciutto and cheese. *Luxury.*

Santa Lucia complex: A clutch of restaurants straddle the pier, and adjacent floats, at Santa Lucia, on the bay, with about that many Via

Partenope hotels to feed them foreign customers. One should not be surprised, then, that service can be patronizing if not downright nasty. Cooking, with such a largely non-Italian clientele, can be mediocre, despite fresh ingredients. Of the group I would not return to *Ciro*, so hostile have I found the service and so inadequate the fare. The others include *Starita, Transatlantico,* and *La Bersagliera* (Phone 415-692), with the last-named my preference of the group. *First Class.*

Umberto (Via Alabardieri 30; Phone 418-555) is good-looking and comfortable, with a wide-ranging menu. Pizza—light, puffy, with a sauce of fresh basil, tomato sauce, and garlic—is superb. Spaghetti alla provencale—with capers and olives—is tasty. So is frittura di pesce—mixed fried fish—and saltimbocca alla romano—the veal and cheese classic. Crispy green salads, too. The wine list is unusually extensive; the staff kind. *First Class.*

Vesuvio Hotel Ristorante (Via Partenope 45; Phone 417-044) occupies the hotel's roof, so that views of the bay can be striking, especially if you snag a table on the terrace. There are daily specials and a tempting à la carte, from which a satisfying meal might run to penne ai quattro formaggi (pasta with a sauce of four cheeses), frittura di calamari e gamberi (a shrimp and squid combo), or costoletta Valdostana—a thick grilled veal chop; with prepared-at-table crêpes Suzette a properly festive dessert. *Luxury.*

Dante e Beatrice (Piazza Dante 44; Phone 349-905) fronts a broad downtown square, is unpretentious, family-run, friendly, and with corking good food. The platter of five little grilled fish of the day is recommended; so are the pasta dishes with seafood sauces—any of them. Meals are served on the piazza in warm weather. Remember now, very simple. *Moderate.*

POSITANO

San Pietro Hotel Ristorante (Locanda San Pietro; Phone 875-455): I can't imagine a visit to Positano—regardless of one's headquarters—without a dinner at this hotel (above), miraculously perched atop its own cliff, with the fare as memorable as the panorama. Specialties include pennette San Pietro and the chef's specially sauced spaghetti, among pastas; involtini di vitello, fegato alla veneziana, and a range of beef dishes (to please invariably present Yanks) among entrées; with super salads, sumptuous sweets, and a distinguished wine list. *Luxury.*

Chez Black (Positano beachfront; Phone 875-036) is a Positano institution, and with good reason. Location is central and scenic, service is swift and smiling, and food is delicious, be it the mixed antipasto, zuppa di verdure (its vegetables are fresh), any of the pastas—cannelloni through linguini al pesto, with spaghetti alle cozze (with fresh mussels) especially good—or such entrées as grilled steak and paillard of veal. In the evening pizza is on the menu. *(Le Tre Sorelle,* next door, with similar fare and prices, is Black-owned.) Both are *First Class.*

Capurale (Via Marino 12, Positano; Phone 875-334) tries a little harder, with respect to décor; its walls are hung with striking Picasso-like murals. Try a seafood-sauced pasta and the featured fish, grilled. *Moderate.*

Caffè la Zagara (Via dei Mulini 12) is indicated for coffee, pastry, and crowd-watching. *Moderate.*

SORRENTO

Al Cavallino Bianco (Via Correale 11; Phone 878-5809) is central and not far from the Carlton Hotel (above) and a reliable source of hearty soups, deftly tossed salads, well-prepared entrées, either fish or meat. Ask for zabaglione, as a sweet. *First Class.*

Parrucchiano (Corso Italia 71; Phone 878-1321)—big, bold, and with cuisine that epitomizes that of the south. Open with the antipasto specialties, follow with pasta and a seafood entrée, if you can handle both. *First Class.*

Minervetta (Via del Capo 25; Phone 878-1098) is a bit away from the center, but with compensations: striking vistas of the bay, and tasty marine-accented fare. *Moderate.*

CAPRI

La Capannina (Via delle Botteghe 14; Phone 837-0732) hangs plants from rafters, sets tables with crisp linen, places pots of fresh flowers all about, and delights with good service and good food that might include ham in cream sauce, pappardelle, or a Caprese variation of grilled red snapper served with fried zucchini. Veal dishes—piccatine al limone, scaloppine al marsala or alla pizzaiola—are tasty, too. Top rank. *First Class.*

Sceriffa (Via Acquaviva 29; Phone 837-7953) makes a point of seafood-accented pasta and admirable antipasto—displayed spectacularly as you enter. Reliable fish entrées, but chicken, rather surprisingly, is a specialty, too. Take enough cash along; no credit cards, but otherwise pleasant. *First Class.*

Paolino (Via Palazzo a Mare 7; Phone 837-6102) makes for an agreeable alfresco meal. You want to open with the antipasto here—the assortment is extraordinary and everything is delicious. Ditto the pastas and the fish. Have an Ischian white to accompany. *First Class.*

Faraglioni (Via Camerelle 75; Phone 837-0320): Go when the weather is fine so you may lunch or dine al fresco. Delicious first courses, both antipasto and pasta; choose red meat or the catch of the day as an entrée. Smart. *First Class.*

Certosella (Via Tragara 115; Phone 837-0713) is indicated for lunch on a sunny day and at an outdoor table; take your swimsuit along, so that you may have a dip in the pool. Salads, pastas, seafood. Fun. *Luxury.*

Tip Top (Via Vittorio Emanuele 41; Phone 837-1432) is hardly a run-of-the-mill name for a restaurant in Italy; this one is cozy; little lamps—one on each table—illuminate it at dinner, when you want to start with the clam-flecked spaghetti, proceeding to one of the day's special entrées. *Moderate.*

Caffè Tiberio, Caffè Caseo, Gran Caffè, and Caffè al Piccolo have business on the Piazzetta sewn up among them, and you get to check out the island's new arrivals over coffee, ice cream, or a drink from any of them. *Moderate.*

ISCHIA

Giardini Eden (Via Nuova Cartaromanna; Phone 99-3909) is delightful midday—and at a terrace table. The emphasis is on food from the sea: pasta or bivalves to open, catch of the day to follow. *First Class/Luxury.*

Dal Pescatore (Sant' Angelo; Phone 999-206) virtually balances on the edge of the Sant' Angelo peninsula. Not surprisingly, the menu is maritime; you want to base your meal on the seafood platter—lobster, shrimp, clams—and conclude with chocolate cake. *First Class.*

Alberto (Bagno Lido, Porto Ischia; Phone 98-12-59) occupies stilted quarters giving onto the sea. The look is tentlike, the fare absolutely delicious. Steamed mussels and clams or spaghetti alle vongole (with clam sauce) are indicated first courses, not that seafood risotto is to be despised. The catch of the day—fish simply broiled—is the desired entrée, with fresh fruit—strawberries, perhaps, to conclude, and a good Ischian white to accompany. Congenial. *First Class.*

Gennaro (Via Porto 68; Phone 99-29-17) is among the poshest of the maze of restaurants facing the port. This is an attractive spot based on a green and white color scheme that does well by seafood-sauced pasta, with seafood—steamed, sauced mussels, for example—as entrées; refreshing sweets. Fun. *First Class.*

'O Padrone d'ò Mare (Lacco Ameno; Phone 98-61-59): Up a flight you go, to a glass-walled pavilion, the better for sea views. Antipasto assortito is a marvelous maritime sampler, but seafood-sauced spaghetti alla Padrone is as well, along with the unusual pizza alla Padrone d'ò Mare. Go for frittura di calamari e gamberi (fried squid and shrimp), broiled sole, or fabulous lobster stew as entrée choices. And choose from among nine or ten Ischian whites to accompany. *First Class.*

SOUND OF MUSIC

Teatro di San Carlo (Piazza Trento e Trieste): Earlier-recommended as a sightseer's requisite, this eighteenth-century beauty is Performing Arts Center No. 1 (it celebrated its 250th birthday a few seasons back), with its own exemplary opera (the range Bellini's *Norma* through Prokofiev's *Romeo e Giulietta*), ballet, chorus, and symphony. The opera season is February through June. Autumn into January sees symphonic concerts, with chorus and/or guest soloists. It pays to book a San Carlo seat immediately upon arrival in Naples, either through hotel concierges or by yourself, at the box office, which has traditionally kept weekday hours from 10 A.M. to 1 P.M. and 4:30 to 6:30 P.M., and which prints seasonal schedules. (Watch, also, for concerts performed in the *Auditorium della RAI*—the Italian TV-radio networks—on Via Marconi.)

SHOPPER'S NAPLES

Naples has the advantage of a compact, easily walkable central shopping district, with Via Roma the not-long main thoroughfare, and Via Chiaia a relatively brief extension of it. Via Costantinopoli and Via Domenico

Morelli have antique shops; Via Santa Brigida, off Via Roma, is lined with smart boutiques. What follows is my own personal selection, alphabetized by category, and within each category.

ANTIQUES: *Bowinkel* (Via Santa Lucia 25) is a mine of old prints and etchings. *Brandi* (Via Domenico Morelli 49) specializes in eighteenth-century Italian furniture and bibelots. *Lombardi* (Via Costantinopoli 4) deals in antique books and maps.

CANDY AND FOODSTUFFS: *Gay-Odin* is a venerable Naples candy company, at two points on Via Roma and on Via Chiaia, as well; fancy boxes for gifts. *Motta* (Via Roma at Via Ponte de Trappia) is a link of a national chain that's convenient for snacks, with train-ride nourishment to go as well. *Perugina* (Via Roma at Piazza Carità) is indicated when you crave *baci,* this Perugia-based candy firm's habit-forming chocolate almond kisses.

CLOTHING: *Mario Valentino* (Via Roma 18) is pricey, modish, and for women. *Monetti* (Via Roma 26) is a long-on-scene source of stylish men's clothing and accessories. *Old England* (Via Roma 39) deals in English imports, both men's and women's; stocks Italian things too. *Fendi* (Piazza dei Martiri) is a branch of the Rome-based firm, very smart and very costly. *Giorgio Armani* (Via dei Mille) features advanced designs, for both men and women, in Naples, as in his other shops. *Portolano* (Via Chiaia 11) is for ladies' casuals, including raincoats. *Roxy* (Via Roma 14) is also on Via del Corso in Rome; the kicker is pure silk neckties; with the quality and style excellent and the prices low.

DEPARTMENT STORES are smaller than in other major cities, but with the advantage of being near one another. Check out *La Rinascente* (Via Roma near Via Diaz); *Standa* (with a worth-knowing-about supermercato that's handy for snack foods and wines), on Via Roma at Via Diaz; and *Upim* (Via Diaz).

LEATHER: *Giannotti* (Via Roma 36) runs a wide gamut, wallets through two-suiters. *Gucci* (Viale dei Mille) purveys clothes and accessories, too.

INCIDENTAL INTELLIGENCE

Naples's principal railroad station, *Stazione Centrale,* is on Piazza Garibaldi, a fairly long taxi ride from downtown. Note also—this can be confusing—that another station, called *Stazione Piazza Garibaldi,* is underground—directly below Stazione Centrale—and is at once a subway stop and where many long-distance trains (often the faster Rapidos) arrive and depart. To complicate matters, there is still a third important station, *Mergellina* by name. Besides the subway system there are buses, trolley-buses, and trolleys; conductors can be surprisingly helpful. Taxi drivers may quote fares that include *supplementi* that one never dreamed existed. There are nearly a dozen legal *supplementi*—enough so that one simply accepts the drivers' quotations or risks a high-pitched argument. Do as the Italians do: allow *supplementi* to take the place of tips. Keep in mind, too, that there are ordinary steamers linking Naples with Sorrento, Capri, and Ischia, year-round, but also much faster—and pricier—hydrofoil vessels that are, in my opinion, well worth the premium fare; there is a similar choice between Sorrento and Capri, in summer, when there are also Positano-Amalfi-Capri hydrofoils. You may, as well, travel between Naples Airport and Capri by helicopter; flying time is ten minutes. There are flights linking Naples with Rome and other Italian points, and there is air service to certain European cities, too. Ente Provinciale per il Turismo publishes a monthly multilingual "What's-On" booklet called *Qui Napoli,* with current information, including transport schedules and open hours of museums; ask your hotel concierge for a copy. Don't overlook local dailies including *Il Mattino* and *Corriere di Napoli. Further information:* Ente Provinciale per il Turismo di Napoli, Via Partenope 10, Naples; Azienda Autonoma di Soggiorno e Turismo, Piazza Umberto 1, Capri; Via Iasolino, Ischia; Via del Saracino 2, Positano; Via Luigi de Maio 35, Sorrento; Corso delle Repubbliche Marinare 25, Amalfi; Piazza Duomo 10, Ravello.

22

Orvieto

Fairytale Wine Town

BACKGROUND BRIEFING

It has never been easy for a wine town to be loved for itself rather than its wine.

Take Bordeaux. It is easily, at least in my view, one of the most elegant cities in France. But I suspect the Bordelais have long since resigned themselves to its being recognized as little more than a name on a label.

So it is with Orvieto. If it is much smaller than its French counterpart, it is at least as impressive, in its way. Still, think Orvieto and what comes to mind is a crisp white with an agreeable bouquet that is surely the most celebrated, globally, of any such produced in the Italian peninsula.

Then you pay a visit to the town of origin—a veritable medieval fairytale high on its own protective cliff in southwest Umbria, just over the border of the *Regione* of Lazio (where Rome is situated)—and unless you are a dedicated oenophile, urban entity will take precedence over outlying vineyards. Orvieto charms.

As how could not a compact city erected on the table-like surface of a 600-foot-high stand of the Italian stone called tufa? Especially when you consider that it has a pedigree with Etruscan origins. It was Etruscans (remains of temples and tombs dot the area, and local Etruscan artifacts are on view in one of the city's museums) who are believed to have built the city of *Volsinii,* a part of the pan-Italian Etruscan League, which disintegrated only when Romans came north in the third century. Post-Roman Orvieto became a sovereign city-state. The Renaissance saw it change hands from time to time, while thriving economically—and building.

By the time it passed to the Papal States in the fifteenth century it had become one of the most monument-rich towns of central Italy. And so, to its great credit, it has remained these succeeding five centuries, ancient walls and quartet of gateways still separating it from the late-twentieth-century Italy that surrounds it.

ON SCENE

Lay of the Land: Arrive by car and you drive up into the elevated town through any number of points of entry. Arrive by train and you alight below the old town. If you have heavy baggage, I suggest a taxi directly to your hotel, although it is more fun to make your entrance by means of the nineteenth-century funicular, adjacent to the station, which will take you up the cliff to *Piazza Cahen,* at the eastern edge of the city. Orvieto's main street, *Corso Cavour,* cuts through it, west to east, with the most interesting parts of town in its western quarter, centered about *Piazza del Popolo,* which is connected by means of *Via del Duomo* with *Piazza Duomo* and the cathedral that is Orvieto's reigning beauty. Streets that exude the flavor of the Renaissance and earlier medieval centuries—Gothic arches still frame many of them—lead south and west from the Duomo—*Via degli Alberici, Via del Paradiso, Via della Cava,* to name but three—past gardens tucked into courtyards behind stone gateways, across squares punctuated by detached towers of weathered churches.

Duomo (Piazza del Duomo): Some Italian cathedrals are so severely somber without that you can't wait to go inside. Not so Orvieto's. This essentially Gothic masterwork—the cornerstone was laid in 1290 by Nicholas IV, one of the many popes who knew the city in the Middle Ages—catches you up as you approach. As well it might, given the brilliance of its mix of art forms: mosaic panels created as early as the fourteenth century, as late as the nineteenth; intricately sculpted fourteenth-century rose window framed by two dozen finely chiseled saints; quartet of marble pillars whose sculpted reliefs are among Italy's finest. A good measure of sculpture surmounts the three portals, including a *Madonna and Child* under a canopy framed by angels. The bronze doors' biblical scenes were sculpted as recently as the 1960s. But you haven't gone inside yet. Within, a motif of horizontal black-and-white stone walls and pillars dazzle. You focus on art. Painted walls of the apse, six levels all told, recount the Virgin Mary's life. Cappella del Corporale's walls are luminously frescoed. Cross the nave to Cappella di San Brizio. Fra Angelico started its frescoes in 1447 (two of his works still are to be seen), to be succeeded by Luca Signorelli, whose graphic- and detail-filled panels—*End of the World, Stories of the Antichrist* (with a self-portrait of the artist, alongside Fra Angelico on the left side), *The Resurrection, The Damned*—are said to have inspired Michelangelo's Sistine Chapel masterworks. Have a look—Signorelli celebrated the human anatomy with masses of nude figures—and you'll see why.

Museo dell' Opera del Duomo (Piazza del Duomo) occupies Palazzo dei Papi, so called because popes inhabited it after it was built in the thirteenth century; you reach the high-ceilinged hall of the museum by means of a steep exterior stairway. It is possible to quarrel with the crowded arrangement of the works—not only from the Duomo but other local churches—but not with their beauty: Simone Martini's *Madonna and Child Surrounded by Four Saints;* a Signorelli *Maddalena,* rich in scarlet and gold; a two-panel *Annunciation;* a massive *St. Sebastian;* mosaic fragments and crucifixes; vestments and wood sculptures, the most memorable a seated *Redeemer* carved 600 years ago.

Museo Etrusco (Piazza del Duomo) is a relatively recent exhibit space, with its own separate street-level entrance in aforementioned Palazzo dei Papi. The kicker is a group of Etruscan frescoes—they go back to the fourth century before Christ—taken from neighborhood tombs, with the most looked-at a graphic representation of two men kissing one another on the lips—possibly accepted practice in the Etruscan culture—while women watch.

Museo Archeologico Claudio Faina (Piazza del Duomo) brims with scenes of daily life painted in black and terra-cotta, bronzes, and coins; a lovely lady sculpted of marble—the *Venus of Canicella*—is the most spectacular exhibit.

Church of San Giovenale (Piazza di San Giovenale) is probably the most interesting in town after the Duomo. It is pure Romanesque, with a thousand-year-old altar, fine lectern, and—biggest treat—spectacular frescoes on each wall.

Church of Sant' Andrea (Piazza della Repubblica) is as good a reason as any for a stroll to a historic square. St Andrew's is almost dwarfed by its unusual, twelve-sided Romanesque campanile. Do go in, for this is a very old church, dating back nine centuries.

Church of San Francesco (Piazza di San Francesco) had papal origins in 1266, and a Gothic façade that is more interesting than its Baroque interior. French history buffs will want to know that the pope who canonized Louis IX of France is buried within.

Pozzo di San Patrizio (Piazza Cahen, adjacent to the funicular station) is Orvieto's oddball attraction: a 200-foot-deep well dug in the sixteenth century by order of a resident—and thirsty—pope. What makes the well unusual is not only a network of 70 windows that illuminate it, but a pair of concentric staircases, so designed that if you're going down and I'm on my way up, somehow or other, we don't meet. Try it, if you like, bearing in mind, though, that there are 248 steps.

SETTLING IN

Aquila Bianca Hotel (Via Garibaldi 13) is perfectly located, core of town, in a smartly—and relatively recently—restored and refurbished Renaissance palazzo, with coffered and painted ceilings in public spaces, not quite 40 good-looking rooms with snazzy baths, relaxing bar-lounge; breakfast, but no restaurant. Beautifully appointed. *First Class.*

Maitani Hotel (Via Maitani 5) is within view of the cathedral (the breakfast terrace overlooks its façade), with 44 distinctively decorated rooms, none quite like its neighbors, inviting lobby—contemporary art lines the walls—and bar-lounge. There is no dining room, although Ristorante Morino (below) some blocks distant is under the same management. *First Class.*

Virgilio Hotel (Piazza del Duomo) could not be more strategically situated; you can almost touch the cathedral. This is an ancient building, still with its original façade, but totally modernized within, in sleek Italian Modern style. Sixteen rooms, bar and breakfast, but no restaurant. *Moderate.*

La Badia Hotel (outside the town of La Badia) is a deftly converted medieval abbey, now sporting a couple of dozen spiffy rooms with restaurant, bar-lounge, outdoor pool, and tennis. *Luxury.*

DAILY BREAD

San Giovenale (Piazza San Giovenale; Phone 40642) leads my group, not so much because of its food—which is delicious—but because (a) its situation at the western edge of town impels you to walk through atmospheric old streets to reach it; and (b) the restaurant itself is an architectural marvel: a desanctified Gothic church that has been transformed—motif is modern—with style, wit, and a sense of drama. Then comes fare: If agnello all' arrabbiata—roast mountain lamb—is on the menu, order it, preceded by one of the excellent soups or pastas. Friendly staff. *First Class.*

Morino (Via Garibaldi 37; Phone 35152) represents Orvieto's attempt at gastronomic grandeur. And with success. Overstuffed leather chairs beckon in the cocktail lounge. The two-level restaurant's tables sparkle. Staff is professional. Consider local prosciutto and salami as antipasto requisites, ravioli in a truffle sauce among the pastas, roast kid among entrées; washed down with a regional red bearing the house's own label. Huge cellar. *Luxury.*

Maurizio (Via del Duomo 78; Phone 32212) attracts with its aged good looks—stucco walls enclose an intimate interior—and does not disappoint with its fare. Why not an entrée of, say, roast chicken, in company with a ration of Orvieto white? *First Class.*

Trattoria Rocchio (Via Maitani 12; Phone 43317) is invariably populated by locals who appreciate good value: Pastas or the hearty zuppa di verdura, reliable veal, and a reputation for well-priced wines, including many from Umbria. *Moderate.*

Del Cocco (Via Garibaldi 4; Phone 42319), just opposite Hotel Aquila Bianca (above), is neat as a pin with starched white linen, competent spaghetti al pomodoro, nicely prepared scaloppine of veal. *Moderate.*

Caffè Montanucci (Corso Umberto 74) is Orvieto's favorite caffè; join the gossipy locals. *Moderate.*

INCIDENTAL INTELLIGENCE

Orvieto's celebrated white wine is sold at outlets all over town. One such, *Cantina Barberani* (Via Maitani 1), has big selections, including three-packs, and offers free sips. *Further information:* Azienda Autonoma di Cura, Soggiorno e Turismo dell' Orvietano, Piazza del Duomo 24, Orvieto.

23

Padua/Padova

Once All-Powerful, Still Art-Rich

BACKGROUND BRIEFING

Look at a map. There is Padua, with Venice (chapter 37) a few miles to the east, and Verona (chapter 38) about equidistant to the west. Between the two of them, this once great military-mercantile-cultural center contents itself with backwater status on the northeast Italy tourism trail. Which is hardly to say that the alert explorer does well to bypass it. World War II bomb devastation notwithstanding, enough pockets of extraordinary beauty remain to tempt the traveler who would come to grips with the city where Mantegna was born, Giotto painted, Dante studied, and St. Anthony is enshrined.

Under the Romans, some two thousand years ago, the colony of *Pativium* thrived to the point where it came close to rivaling the capital to the south with respect to economic prowess. But good news traveled fast, even as long ago as the seventh century, and warlike Lombards from the northwest virtually leveled Padua in the course of conquest.

It grew strong, though, gradually evolving as a *comune,* no less aggressive than its earlier aggressors. For two centuries, twelfth through fourteenth, it did battle with neighboring cities, ultimately controlling a fair-sized chunk of what is now the *Regione* of Veneto. For nearly nine decades of that period, starting in the early fourteenth century, a Padua family—Carrara by name—held the political reins, the while fostering art and culture not unlike ruling clans I bring to your attention in other chapters of this book.

By the time of the Carraras, Portuguese-born St. Anthony of Padua (identified thus so as not to be confused with the early Christian era's St. Anthony Abbot) had preached, died, been canonized, and buried in

Padua; Florence-born Giotto had begun his masterwork fresco cycle in Padua, and the University of Padua—second-oldest in Italy after Bologna's—had been established by renegade Bologna teachers and students, ultimately to attract such scholars as Petrarch and such professors as Galileo.

With the Renaissance, the Venice of the Doges had become so fabulously rich and strong that it engulfed more vulnerable Padua, to rule it through to the arrival of Napoleonic troops in the late eighteenth century, from which point on its fortunes were those of Venice, right into affiliation with the last century's pan-Italian kingdom. There is no gainsaying Padua's largely infelicitous reconstruction after World War II bombings. Still, today's Padua is a lively industrial city of a quarter million without, to be sure, anything like the hotels and restaurants of visitor-packed Venice or even Verona. (It does much better with shops.) Withal, a day or two of Paduan exploration, perhaps in connection with its neighbor cities and the also-nearby Palladian villas of the countryside (chapter 39) can be time spent profitably.

ON SCENE

Lay of the Land: No Italian city that I know has a cluster of so many contiguous central squares. They are, going clockwise, *Piazza Garibaldi* (from which shop-lined *Corso Garibaldi* leads north to Giotto's frescoes in Cappella degli Scrovegni and the railway station); *Piazza Cavour* (off which are smart shopping streets like *Riviera dei Conti Romani* and *Via VIII Febbraio*, site of the University of Padua); *Piazza delle Erbe* (with a traditional alfresco market that spills over into adjacent, appropriately named *Piazza della Frutta*); and *Piazza dei Signori*, ringed by Renaissance palaces, graced by loggias, with gold stars on the blue face of a towering clock. *Piazza del Santo*, named for the church complex dedicated to St. Anthony, is an easy walk south, via *Via del Santo*.

Cappella degli Scrovegni (Corso Garibaldi): In Assisi (chapter 3) it is the basilica dedicated to St. Francis where Giotto painted. Here, the Florentine master who was the first artist of consequence to depart from Byzantine technique—thus pioneering the course of Western painting—devoted several years, beginning either in 1304 or 1305 (his Assisi work had been done earlier) to create a series of 38 frescoes that easily constitute one of the great Italian art experiences. Reason enough for a Padua visit, they are a testament to Giotto's genius at perspective, design, and color, and as a superb storyteller. Look first at the inner surface of the front wall of the chapel, where the theme is *The Last Judgment*. Then go on to Giotto's interpretations of immortal incidents in the lives of Jesus and the Virgin Mary. You'll find familiar themes like

The Annunciation, The Nativity, The Flight into Egypt (most beautiful such of any that I have seen), *The Last Supper, The Crucifixion, The Deposition,* among much more to study and ponder, including a set of panels symbolizing Virtues and Vices.

Palazzo della Regione (a.k.a. Il Salone) is the massive medieval monument lying between Piazza delle Erbe and Piazza della Frutta—elongated, green-roofed, with frescoes lining its sometimes visitable Great Hall.

Museo Civico (Piazza del Santo) deceives with its modest-appearing façade, that of a long-ago monastery positively dwarfed by the square's Basilica of Sant' Antonio (below). But you want to allow time for what is one of Italy's more important art museums. There are, to give you an idea, a Veronese *Last Supper* (interesting to compare with that of Giotto, at Cappella Scrovegni, who himself is represented by a *Crucifix* that came from the Scrovegni); a male portrait by Giovanni Bellini, noted for his Madonnas; a clutch of the paintings of domestic life in eighteenth-century Venice by Longhi, with such other masters as Tintoretto, Vivarini, Giorgione, and Tiepolo represented. I wager you will buy postcard reproductions of the lot, from the enterprising guards who sell them at the exit.

Church of the Eremitani (Corso Garibaldi) wins honors, at least from me, as the single most all-around beautiful church in town (with the understanding that Giotto's frescoes in the Scrovegni [above] are in a class by themselves). This Romanesque-Gothic structure catches you up, once you step inside, its walls horizontally striped in terra-cotta and gold, enclosing an extraordinarily long nave, with a splendid *Crucifixion* gracing the frescoed high altar, and still more frescoes in side chapels. Of these, most requisite are on the high altar—all that remain of two by Padua-born Andrea Mantegna; nothing to compare with his output in Mantua (chapter 18), but withal, masterful Mantegna.

Duomo (Piazza del Duomo), while hardly in the same aesthetic category as Scrovegni and Eremitani (above), is visitworthy if only for the surprise of a Baroque interior contrasting with an incomplete Gothic façade. Scale is superb, likewise the pattern of the marble floors and Corinthian capitals of the columns lining the nave. You want also to go inside the adjacent *Battistero,* boxlike Romanesque baptistry of the cathedral, to take in its extravagant frescoes—especially the ceiling, centered by Christ giving his blessing—the masterpiece of the Giotto school's Giusto de Manabuoi.

Basilica of Sant' Antonio (Piazza del Santo) dominates the Padua skyline with a mix of eastern-inspired domes (half a dozen all told) and spires, at its best when viewed from Via del Santo. This is a Romanesque-Gothic church-cum-cloister on which work started only a year after the death of the saint—a Franciscan credited with accomplishing many miracles—in 1231, continuing well into the succeeding century. Make your way through crowds of pilgrims to the estimable art within—including bronze sculptures on the high altar by Donatello (who also created the equestrian statue on the square outside) interpreting incidents in the saint's life, and still more sculpture (by Sansovino, among others) in the transept. There is a museum that relates St. Anthony's story. But my favorite part of the complex is the lovely—and refreshingly serene—cloister.

Scuola di Sant' Antonio and Oratory of San Giorgio (Piazza del Santo) are appendages of the basilica (above); the so-called scuola, or school, is the more aesthetically exciting of the pair, with an upstairs series of Renaissance frescoes—the theme is St. Anthony's life—by a mix of masters, Titian among them. Still more frescoes line the walls of the oratory.

Università degli Studi (Via VIII Febbraio): Padua's university, Italy's second-oldest after Bologna, dates to 1222, although its main building is a Renaissance palazzo through whose elegant courtyard you pass, en route to an extraordinary six-level wooden spiral of an anatomy theater—Europe's oldest such (1544) and surely its most unusual—and the Great Hall, its walls hung with faculty and student coats-of-arms.

Abano Terme, eight miles south of Padua and pronounced AH-bano, is among the bigger of the Italian spas, with a clientele principally German (although there are French and, of course, Italian visitors, as well). With the dearth of English-speaking clients, a relative paucity of English-speaking hosts should not be surprising. (Exceptions include reception and concierge staffs in bigger hotels and captains in their dining rooms). What lures crowds to Abano—and packed it is, indeed—are *fango,* or mud baths. It is the preeminent mud therapy spa (popular with arthritis, neuritis, neuralgia, and gout patients) and unusual in that treatment centers are in hotels rather than a central bathhouse. Shopping can be good—the town is cut through by Viale delle Terme, the main street lined with emporia, caffès, and restaurants. But Abano, to this visitor at least, lacks the charm of Salsomaggiore (chapter 25), the beauty of Montecatini (chapter 13), or the relaxed diversity of Ischia (chapter 21), which is, of course, at least as much a resort-island as spa. I bring it to your attention only because Padua—but a hop and skip distant—has a dearth of hotels, while Abano has scores of them in all categories, and if you've a car, you might want to consider headquartering at an Abano hotel. There is but one in the Luxury category—*Hotel Orologio* (Viale delle Terme 66); while it is full-facility (there are 165 modern rooms, thermal-water swimming pools in the garden, restaurant, bar) I find its ambience chilly, and service patronizing. Hotels I can recommend include *Bristol Buja* (Via Montirone 2, *First Class*)—family-owned and operated, with a perfectly delightful staff, close to 150 rooms (those I've inspected are very nice indeed), indoor and outdoor thermal swimming pools, good restaurant-bar, and tennis courts; *Trieste & Victoria* (Via Pietro d'Abano 1; *First Class*)—an attractively updated 100-room old-timer, with crackerjack management, smiling staff, and fine restaurant; and two full-facility, central *Moderate*-category hotels: 113-room *Aurora Terme* (Via Pietro d'Abano 13) and 101-room *Terme Milano* (Viale delle Terme 169). *Rifugio Monte Rua* (in Torreglia, outside of town; Phone 511-049; *First Class*) is indicated for a hearty, anything-but-dietetic meal, with fare delicious—pasta through dessert.

SETTLING IN

Plaza Hotel (Corso Milano 40) is the city's largest, with 142 plain and smallish rooms; a restaurant that keeps limited open days and hours; bar-lounge; and a not-too-central situation. A plus is the kindly and efficient reception/concierge crew. *First Class.*

Donatello Hotel (Piazza del Santo) has the virtue of a location in a part of town you'll be concentrating on, with pleasant public spaces, just over 40 functional rooms (request one with a basilica view), and a restaurant I detail in a later paragraph. *Moderate.*

Majestic Hotel (Piazzetta dell' Arco 2) is well situated about midway between Piazza del Santo and the Scrovegni chapel neighborhood and Corso Garibaldi's shops. About 40 rooms, restaurant, bar-lounge. *Moderate.*

DAILY BREAD

Antico Brolo (Vicolo Cigolo 14; Phone 664-555) pleases with its high-ceilinged, rather formal look. Ask about the pasta dishes and meat entrées that sound unfamiliar; they can be very good. *First Class.*

Dotto (Via Squarcione 23; Phone 25-055): Paduan business types mix with visitors at this centrally positioned source of regional fare. If you haven't tried pasta e fagioli, a long-esteemed macaroni-and-beans combination, this is the place to order it. The Veneto region's liver and salt-cod favorites are on hand, too. But worry not; so are a range of other pastas and more prosaic veal and chicken entrées. *First Class.*

Sant' Antonio (Piazza del Santo in the Donatello Hotel; Phone 24-123): If the weather is fair, you want to take a table on the big terrace, facing the basilica. Fellow-lunchers or diners will speak a babble of languages; you're in the heart of tourist territory, but pastas are authentic, withal; solid entrées and wines, too. *First Class.*

Costantino (Via San Pietro 95; Phone 32-975) is Padua at its smartest, stylish early-nineteenth-century in look, with creditable cuisine, the range a seafood-accented risotto or a mix of salami and prosciutto as starters, a French-style entrecôte or a choice of veal entrées, Sardinian wines, and that same island's crackerlike bread—carta da musica. Friendly. *First Class.*

Al Santo (Via del Santo 56; Phone 35-445) is one of a number of restaurants on this street leading to the basilica; it's attractive, with green linen on the tables and a canopy sheltering additional sidewalk space. A green salad and pasta lunch would be satisfactory. *Moderate.*

Cavalca (Via Manin 8; Phone 39-244) is long-on-scene, conveniently central, friendly, and animated, with the fare nourishing if undistinguished. *Moderate.*

La Bussola (Via degli Zabrella 48; Phone 34-231) is among the better-looking of the city's eateries, with such starters as carpaccio—not to mention a range of pastas, a variety of beef entrées, and an interesting wine list. Near Coin department store. *First Class.*

Caffè Pedrocchi (Piazza Cavour) is a Padua landmark, somberly neoclassical from the early decades of the last century, with outdoor tables under a portico supported by Ionic columns. The ice cream is celebrated. *Moderate.*

Caffè delle Erbe (Piazza delle Erbe): How can you miss, seated at an outdoor table with the location a landmark Padua square? *Moderate.*

Caffè Museo (Piazza del Santo) is named for adjacent Museo Civico, but views are of St. Anthony's Basilica and the never-ceasing crowds. *Moderate.*

SOUND OF MUSIC

Teatro Comunale Verdi (Via Livelio 32) features annual seasons of opera, concerts, and ballet.

SHOPPER'S PADUA

This good-sized city does well by shops, with more than its share of smart ones. Piazza Garibaldi is the core of the department-store area, while there are good shops on Corso Garibaldi, Via Zabarella, Via Emanuele Filberto, and Riviera dei Ponti Romani.

INCIDENTAL INTELLIGENCE

Brenta Canal tours—along the fabulous villa-lined waterway connecting Padua with Venice—are one-day boat trips going in either direction that include a lunch stop and visits to selected country mansions, of the caliber designed by Palladio (chapter 39) for wealthy Venetians, fifteenth through eighteenth centuries; they operate summer only. *Further information:* Ente Provinciale per il Turismo, Riviera Mugnai 8, Padua; Azienda Autonoma di Soggiorno e Turismo, Via Pietro d'Abano 18, Abano Terme.

24

Palermo

and Sicily's Great Greek Ruins

BACKGROUND BRIEFING

It seems inconceivable that so many of us persist in stereotypical concepts of Sicily. We have little difficulty conceptualizing a scenic resort town like Taormina (chapter 32). Still, relatively few of us can easily appreciate that Syracuse (chapter 31) was a center of ancient Greek culture and a rich medieval city. Nor, more to the point of the present chapter, that the capital of 180-mile-long, 120-mile-wide Sicily—almost twice the size of Connecticut and largest of the Mediterranean islands—is a thriving metropolis-seaport of three-quarters of a million that had been seat of a kingdom whose most influential rulers were a French count (its brilliant founder) and a resident Holy Roman Emperor of Teutonic origin.

But Palermo considerably predates its regal status. Phoenicians settled in as long ago as the eighth century before Christ, for a couple of hundred years, productive enough to have attracted Carthaginians from across the Mediterranean, who in turn were ousted by Romans come south, in the third century B.C. As was the case in so many Roman-colonized European places, it was its Latin name—*Panormus*—that stuck, with subsequent Italianization.

Byzantines, who controlled so much of post-Roman Italy, stormed Palermo in the early sixth century, remaining through the early ninth. That was when Arabs came, staying on for two brilliant centuries, a fitting prelude to Palermo's evolution as capital of the Kingdom of Sicily, a consequence of victory by Frenchmen serving under a Norman count who came to be known as Roger I, and whose son, Roger II, was crowned first king by an antipope and rival of the pontiff Nicholas II.

Pope Nicholas eventually had to cede mainland territory to Roger, who attracted a circle of courtiers, artists, philosophers, and writers to an increasingly wealthy Palermo. The city evolved the following century when Holy Roman Emperor Frederick II—skilled as a scientist and artist as well as a statesman—reigned, the while adding monuments that, with those of earlier and later periods, combine to create the historic core of a still woefully underappreciated destination.

ON SCENE

Lay of the Land: Backed by the formidable gray mass of Monte Pellegrino, fronted by one of the most splendid Italian harbors, Palermo has long since rebuilt—tastefully and extensively—following World War II bombings. Key to understanding it geographically is a central artery that bisects its core, running north-south, and named *Via Maqueda* until it reaches verdant *Piazza Verdi*—whose landmark is massive Teatro Massimo—when it becomes *Via Ruggero Settimo,* again changing names as it passes through a pair of contiguous squares, *Piazza Castelnuovo* and *Piazza Ruggero Settimo,* continuing as *Via della Libertà,* even as it divides a pretty park—partly called *Giardino Inglese,* partly called *Villa Gonzaga*—terminating at *Piazza Vittorio Veneto.* Select a downtown hotel and you can walk just about everywhere, including to shops that border the main street, spilling over into adjacent ones, especially *Via Roma. Mondello,* edging a crescent-shaped strand, is the city's beach resort, six miles northwest of town. Which leaves suburban *Monreale,* whose major monument is of such significance that I lead off with it, straight away.

Duomo of Monreale (scenically elevated on a mountain called Caputo, five miles west of Palermo): There is, to be sure, a considerably greater quantity of mosaics in Ravenna (chapter 28). But no mosaics—anywhere—are more beautiful than those of this cathedral, the supreme Palermo testament to the long-ago presence of brilliant Byzantine craftsmen. The marvelously high Gothic nave leading to an equally elevated apse, draws your eye to the most striking of the mosaics: a giant Christ giving His blessing, with the Virgin Mary, flanked by apostles, saints, and angels, on two lower panels. But that's not all. Additional mosaics—their themes the Old and New Testaments—line the nave's walls. Take your time making the rounds—not missing the exquisitely painted beams of the ceiling, and ending in the cloister, most all of whose columns retain original no-two-alike decorations.

Palazzo dei Normanni (Corso Vittorio Emanuele): Back in Palermo, this onetime royal palace was Norman-built eight hundred years ago and remains in service, currently housing the legislature of the Sicilian regional government. Visitors are welcome, first to inspect—without the need for guides—separately entered *Cappella Palatina*—much smaller than the Monreale cathedral, but hardly to be dismissed, given its sumptuous Arabic-style carved wood and gilded ceiling (which will put you in mind of Seville's Alhambra and palaces and mosques of Morocco) and its mosaics, a variation of Monreale's mosaics, in the apse, lining walls of the nave as well. Subjects are biblical, including a *Baptism of Christ* quite unlike any you have ever seen before, and a charming *Flight into Egypt*, the Virgin's horse oddly elongated. Elsewhere in the palace, you'll wait your turn for a guard to show you about (his narrative is in Italian, but no matter) the relatively compact but elegant *Aula di Re Ruggero.* King Roger's Hall is properly regal, its ceilings a mix of mosaic birds and animals, with the lions not in the least bit threatening. You end in a range of relatively newer palace rooms, an Audience Hall the most elaborate.

Galleria Nazionale della Sicilia (Via Allora) makes its home in a honey of a Renaissance palazzo, architecturally a fine foil, not only for introductory sculpture—a bust of *Eleonora d'Aragona* is sublime—but, more important, the second floor's paintings. You will have seen reproductions of the gallery's trademark, the blue-veiled Virgin of Antonella da Messina's *Annunciation.* Mabuse, a Flemish Primitive master, is represented by a lovely altar painting. And there are works by Sicilians with which you may be unfamiliar, including a *Nativity* (among several) by Renaissance-era Antonello Gagini.

Museo Nazionale Archeologico (Piazza Olivella): Sicily abounds in so much ancient art and artifacts that there is a temptation on occasion to take it for granted. In the case of this repository of not only Greek and Roman work but Etruscan as well, my counsel is, in a single word: Don't. Note particularly work from temples of the Greek colony of Selinunte (below)—still clearly defined sculptures, sarcophagi, inscribed tablets. Other souvenirs of Magna Grecia colonies in Sicily are to be seen, a bronze ram from Syracuse, most memorably. Etruscan ceramics are extraordinary; and so is a Roman sculpture—Hercules attacking a deer on the run—come south all the way from Pompeii.

Duomo (Piazza della Cattedrale): Palermo's cathedral makes no attempt to compete with Monreale's (above). There is no question but that it is at its best from without, with the perspective of its elongated, mostly Gothic sides—you take in a trio of towers, crenelated walls that could be those of a castle, and a late Baroque dome—quite unlike that of any other Italian cathedral. Inside, the surprise is a quite plain, classical-style motif, unexceptional save for a pair of medieval chapels containing tombs of long-ago Sicilian kings.

Church of San Giovanni degli Eremiti (Via dei Benedettini) transports you to the twelfth-century reign of beloved King Roger II, its red-orange domes Arab-influenced, a severe interior, and a cloister—fragrant with jasmine and mimosa—relatively little altered from the time of its twelfth-century construction.

Church of Martorana (Piazza Bellini) looks—and most certainly is—Baroque. But that's an overlay. You go for the lavish Byzantine mosaics inside, one of which depicts the coronation of Roger II, the others essentially—and spectacularly—biblical.

Church of San Cataldo (a Piazza Bellini neighbor of Martorana above) is not without its share of mosaics, but I mention it primarily for its squat, boxy shape and a trio of domes like none you will have seen surmounting any other church.

Oratorio and Church of San Domenico (Piazza San Domenico) is a triple treat. A Baroque monument to the saint—topped with a likeness of him—in the square; the ornate Baroque façade of the church; and, most memorable, the adjacent oratory, for two reasons: splendid stucco work and a Van Dyck painting representing the Virgin surrounded by a cluster of saints, Dominic, not surprisingly, among them.

Church of Gesù (Via Ponticallo): If the Jesuits were rarely subtle in the décor of their Baroque-era churches—art was put to service in the cause of the counter-Reformation—they rarely lacked taste, invariably commissioning the best available artists and architects. Palermo's Gesù Church is typical in the best sense, lavish with respect to frescoes, paintings, stucco work, the lot embellishing virtually the entire surface of a generously scaled interior.

Segesta (42 miles southwest of Palermo): Little remains of this once thriving Greek colony—a foe of stronger Selinunte (below) to the south. But it is worth going out of one's way to see first a gloriously situated theater built into the top of a mountain, Barbaro by name, still with some twenty stone rows of semicircular seating intact and affording wide-angle views; second, a still-pedimented temple graced by three dozen Doric columns, quite elegant in its solitary splendor.

Selinunte (64 miles southwest of Palermo)—a once-powerful enemy of Segesta (above) and westernmost of the colonies of Magna Grecia when it was founded some 2700 years ago—was largely destroyed by later Carthaginians, with near-finishing touches attributed to a medieval earthquake. Palermo's Museo Nazionale Archeologico exhibits a wealth of Selinunte treasures, as I point out in an earlier paragraph. On site, there is more to see than at Segesta: a clutch of eight temples—some in better shape than others—on a pair of hills, the lot reduced by contemporary archeologists to ignominious identification by letters of the alphabet. Most important, Temple E, with nearly 40 columns still with original Doric capitals, and even more intact Temple C.

Agrigento (71 miles directly south of Palermo; farther, of course, if the route is via Segesta and Selinunte, above) is at once an ancient Greek colony and a small city with a relatively undistinguished Città Vecchia, or old quarter, and—not unimportant—good hotels, which makes it a logical layover point in the course of exploring western Sicily.

Established five centuries before Christ by the Greeks, ancient Agrigento became a city to be reckoned with—militarily, culturally, financially. It vaunted its wealth with status symbols of the era, splendid temples. Succeeding Romans dubbed it *Agrigentum,* and although it is not without its share of medieval-Renaissance-Baroque monuments (the *Duomo* on Via Duomo melds all three periods), it is ancient Agrigento—in a detached area (Zona Archeologica, a.k.a. *Valle dei Templi*) south of the old quarter—that beckons the visitor for its hotels (below) as well as its monuments.

Temple of Concordia, best preserved of a handful in the area, surmounts a dramatic hill—a visit at sunset is unforgettable—and though roofless, remains pedimented and ringed with not quite three dozen Doric columns. Sadly, much less remains of the other temples: *Juno,* still with 25 pillars, and *Hercules,* with 8, are in the best condition. There are, as well, fairly substantial remains of a *Roman theater,* with a dozen-odd rows of the original stone seats. *Church of San Nicola,* originally a Greek temple is essentially Gothic but with visible consequences of later remodelings. Next door is the excellent *Museo Nazionale Archeologico,* a 24-foot-high reconstructed statue dominating its high-ceilinged central hall. Wander through a score of rooms to see vases, mosaics, coins, with a clutch of paintings, Middle Ages onward.

Piazza Armerina is the name of a town—not a square—mid-island, 50 miles northeast of Agrigento, where the lure is *Villa del Casale,* a fabulous vacation villa built by a moneybags Roman in the fourth century A.D., with colonnaded courtyard, pool-centered, and—principal point of a visit—a range of rooms, Roman baths included, with original mosaic floors brilliantly intact, the themes both of the Roman life of the period, colorful hunts most especially, and of mythology. If you've time, look at the Baroque Duomo, heart of town. *Pepito* (Via Roma 138; Phone 82-737, *Moderate*) is an okay lunch stop.

SETTLING IN

PALERMO

Grand Hôtel et des Palmes (Via Roma 398) persists in maintaining a French-styled name from the late-nineteenth-century period when French names signified grandeur, which indeed must have been the case a century back. The original architecture remains, with a spectacular lobby and succession of even more opulent lounges, as well as a restaurant, cocktail lounge, and a suite in which management claims Wagner wrote *Parsifal,* a claim made also by city fathers of the Bay of Naples village of Ravello (chapter 21). (Perhaps the composer created the opera in both places?) There is a good deal of variety in the 184 rooms—have a look at accommodations suggested before you agree to them. Considering its ancestry and good looks, this hotel should be luxury-category. Instead, it's a notch below. *First Class.*

President Hotel (Via Crispi 230) is at once central and brightly traditional in look, with nearly 130 well-equipped rooms, rooftop restaurant, and cocktail lounge. *First Class.*

Politeama Palace (Piazza Ruggero Settimo 15) has the virtue of a situation on a principal square and is agreeably contemporary in style and full-facility, with just over a hundred rooms. *First Class.*

Mediterraneo Hotel (Via Rosolino Pilo 44) is central, with more than a hundred neat rooms, bar-lounge, breakfast and restaurant for registered hotel guests only. *Moderate.*

Touring Hotel (Via Mariano Stabile 136) is an adequately equipped small house (not quite two dozen rooms), with bar and breakfast but no restaurant. Central. *Moderate.*

Villa Igea Hotel's (Via Belmonte 43) problem is that it's a quarter-hour's drive away from the center of the city, completely isolated. But it is, at the same time, beautiful: a turn-of-century mansion transformed into an exquisitely appointed 120-suite-and-room hostelry, overlooking Palermo harbor, which it flanks. There's a swimming pool in the pretty garden, with a ruined Greek temple adjacent; a pair of exemplary restaurants supplemented by a summer dining terrace; and a cocktail lounge. *Luxury.*

Jolly Hotel (Foro Italico) is, like Villa Igea, detached from the core of the city, a ten-minute drive away, ocean-front. This is a sprawling, modern house, with a capacious lobby, restaurant, cocktail lounge, swimming pool, and 290 rooms, a capacity that endears it to groups. *First Class.*

AGRIGENTO

Jolly Hotel (Parco Angeli) is sprightly ultra-modern, with 150 handsome rooms (doubles are really generous in size), sweeping lobby that combines with a friendly cocktail lounge, restaurant. A fabulous buffet breakfast is a feature, but authentic Italian fare at lunch and dinner (with Sicilian specialties) is excellent, too; topnotch staff. *First Class.*

Tre Torri Hotel (Parco Angeli) is modern: a trio of towers tucked into mock-medieval façade. There are just under 120 well-equipped rooms with bath, capacious restaurant, bar-lounge, outdoor/indoor pool. Smiling staff. *Moderate.*

DAILY BREAD

Gourmand's (Via della Libertà 37; Phone 323-431) attracts with modern paintings, tables of starched yellow linen, attentive waiters, and a display of just-caught fish and seafood that impels you to concentrate on a maritime meal, opening perhaps with trenette Genovese (one of many pastas), possibly substituting a costoletta di vitello (a grilled veal chop) for the fish. *First Class/Luxury.*

Cuggagna (Via Principe Granatelli 21; Phone 587-267) makes a point of pasta, seafood-sauced, with sound veal and fish entrées. Locals are generally in attendance (the ambience is buzzy). Central. *First Class.*

Trattoria al Buco (Via Principe Granatelli 33; Phone 323-661) is unpretentious, to be sure, but neat as a pin, central, popular with locals, and a purveyor—via swift and skilled waiters—of perfectly delicious food, starting with the help-yourself antipasto buffet or a pastalike fusilli quattro formaggi, the sauce a mix of four cheeses; entries as simple as frittata (an omelet), or more substantial veal. Super sweets. *Moderate.*

Charleston (Piazzale Ungheria 30; Phone 321-366): The name, at least to Americans who will associate it with South Carolina, is a put-on. This is an attractive house that pleases northerners homesick for risotto, makes a specialty as well of calf's liver prepared the house's own way, and is hardly lacking in tempting pastas and delicious veal and fish entries. *First Class/Luxury.*

Lo Scudiero (Via Turati 7; Phone 581-628) is an easy-to-locate near neighbor of the opera house and is indicated for a reliable repast, starting with, say, a seafood-accented antipasto, and continuing with the fish of the day, simply grilled. *Moderate.*

Caffè Roney (Via della Libertà 49): Take one look at the green-upholstered wicker chairs and you want to sink into one of them for an espresso; adjacent tables are bound to be occupied by Palermo business types. *Moderate.*

Caffè Extra (Via Ruggero Settimo 11) makes a specialty of pastries; stop in for a sampling, or purchase some to go. *Moderate.*

SOUND OF MUSIC

Teatro Massimo (Piazza Verdi): Work was started on Palermo's opera house in 1866 and wasn't completed until 1897, not surprising considering its enormity. A Corinthian colonnade supports the elegant portico of its entrance wing, backed by both an exuberant dome and contours of the proscenium; go for opera, ballet, or whatever is on. A treat.

SHOPPER'S PALERMO

Via Ruggero Settimo is lined with big stores and posh boutiques. Via Maqueda, Via della Libertà, Via Roma, and Via Belmonte are other mercantile thoroughfares. You'll find branches of top-rank mainland chains and fine local firms as well.

INCIDENTAL INTELLIGENCE

Aeroporto di Punta Raisi is 18 miles north of town, with service to and from domestic and foreign points. *Further Information:* Ente Provinciale per il Turismo, Piazza Castelnuovo 34, Palermo; Azienda Autonoma di

Soggiorno e Turismo, Viale della Vittoria 255, Agrigento; and Piazza Garibaldi in the town of Piazza Armerina. (Note that two additional chapters of this book deal with Sicily: chapter 31 [Syracuse/Siracusa: and North to Catania] and chapter 32 [Taormina: In the Shadow of Mt. Etna]).

25

Parma

City of the Charterhouse

BACKGROUND BRIEFING

If ever the relationship between literary associations and travel needs to be illustrated, cite Parma. My first visit was predicated on the opportunity to inspect the ancient charterhouse, or monastery, which is the title of the classic Stendhal novel about passions and power drives of the upper classes in early-nineteenth-century Parma.

Alas, the Charterhouse of Parma is, today, a semiruin in the suburbs. But it was fictional curiosity that converted me into a fan of this too-little-inspected medium-small northern city, with attributes way out of proportion to its size. The charm of Parma evolves from sophistication that can come only from so cosmopolitan a background.

Early on a Roman colony, it evolved in the twelfth century as a *comune* thriving enough to attract attention of larger powers as distant as Milan, and even France, a country that would dominate Parma through Napoleon (not to mention his second wife) in later centuries.

Still, there was the intervening Golden Age of the Renaissance, when sixteenth-century Pope Paul III designated the then provincial city seat of the Duchy of Parma, tapping his son, a scion of the influential Farnese family—first of a line of dukes whose court lured artists and intellectuals well into Parma's elegant eighteenth century. In 1748, Bourbon rulers—quite as culture-conscious as the Farnese dukes—took over, continuing to enrich an already monument-laden town, quite to the taste of Napoleon, whose troops annexed it to France at the turn of the nineteenth century.

Fate stepped into Parma's history when the Congress of Vienna in 1815, decreed that the new ruler of the duchy would be none other than

Austrian-born Marie Louise, at once daughter of a Holy Roman Emperor and second consort of Napoleon. Slightly modifying the spelling of her name, Maria Luigia ruled—not always prudently, according to some historians, in collaboration first with a lover who became a morganatic husband, and upon his death, with a count who was Husband No. 3—as Duchess of Parma for three decades.

Not long after, this long-royal capital city—where Correggio and Parmigianino painted, Bodoni invented what may well be the most famous of typefaces, Verdi composed, and Toscanini was born—dispensed with privileged status in favor of sublimation to the pan-Italian Kingdom of Italy. Visit it today, though, and enough past associations surface to evoke the Parma of Maria Luigia and of the Stendhal novel—surely reason enough for a visit.

ON SCENE

Lay of the Land: This is a Right- and Left-Bank city; the river dividing it—Parma by name and a tributary of the Po—cuts through, north to south, with the Left—or East—Bank the more important. Orient yourself around significant *Piazza del Duomo,* from which *Via XX Marzo* leads south to the major east-west thoroughfare, called *Via Mazzini* in its department-store-and-shop-clustered area, *Strada della Repubblica* after it passes through *Piazza Garibaldi* (site of the arcaded Municipio, or City Hall), and *Via Massimo d'Azeglio* after it crosses *Ponte di Mezzo* to the Right, or West, Bank. Back on the Left Bank busy north-south *Via Cavour* is enjoyable for shopping strolls, with major monuments in its vicinity; *Strada Garibaldi,* another important shopping thoroughfare, takes one north to *Piazzale Marconi* and the requisite *Palazzo della Pilotta* complex. The railway station edges the northern part of town, on *Viale Bottego.* If you've time for a leisurely walk, cross the river on *Ponte Verdi* (near Palazzo della Pilotta) to the well-manicured garden of *Parco Ducale,* just opposite, and bordered by *Palazzo Ducale,* longtime residence of the duchy's rulers, an eighteenth-century rebuilding of an originally Renaissance structure, closed to visitors.

Duomo (Piazza del Duomo): Work began on this spectacular church—among the loveliest of Italy's cathedrals—nine hundred years ago. The Romanesque façade—relatively simple but striking—is graced with three levels of loggias with an exquisitely sculpted porch framing the central portal, and a landmark campanile adjacent. The extravagantly art-laden interior, to be appreciated, needs to be savored slowly. I counsel looking first—so you don't risk missing it—at the cupola; its fresco, *Assumption of the Virgin,* is a Correggio masterwork. Look up, also, at Renaissance frescoes surfacing vaults of the nave. Take time for paintings of the side chapels, noting especially Cappella Verli; and for the atmospheric crypt.

Battistero (Piazza del Duomo): The cathedral's baptistry is not the only octagonal-shaped one in Italy, but it is surely the most brilliant. This Romanesque-Gothic work is especially splendid from without—a roof ringed with eight delicate minispires; four levels of galleries, with the reliefs by a Parmesan sculptor named Antelami. Note, too, frescoes and sculpture, also by Antelami, in the architecturally distinctive interior.

Palazzo della Pilotta complex (Piazzale Marconi): I append the word "complex" because this rambling Renaissance palace shelters three museums (one of major importance), a theater unlike any you will have seen unless you've visited Vicenza (chapter 39), and a library. *Galleria Nazionale*—Parma's principal art museum (there's another—*Pinacoteca Stuard,* Via Calvastro 14)—brims with master paintings. Important ones. There are, to start, works by the two great local painters, Correggio *(Madonna and St. Gerolamo, Madonna and Child)* and Parmigianino *(Self-Portrait, Portrait of a Young Woman).* There are works by other Italians—Fra Angelico's *Madonna and Child,* Dossi's *Saint Michael,* Canaletto's and Belotto's cityscapes, Tintoretto's *Deposition.* And foreigners are on hand, too, including Van Dyck *(Isabella of Spain),* Holbein *(Erasmus),* El Greco *(Christ Heating the Blind),* a Brueghel landscape, a Pourbus of a local Farnese duke. With a bonus of original frescoed ceilings and early nineteenth-century chairs dotted about, for rest pauses. *Teatro Farnese*—a spectacular symphony in paneled wood originally built in 1618 by an architect named Argenta that was inspired by Palladio's sixteenth-century Teatro Olimpico in Vicenza—suffered badly from World War II bombs and has been meticulously rebuilt over a sustained period, reemerging as one of the supreme Italian interiors. It is cathedral-sized (with respect to height as well as width and depth), its seats not unlike those of a crescent-shaped amphitheater, with two levels of loggias backing them, and a stage that was the first such extant to be designed for changeable—as distinct from permanent—sets. Special. *Museo Nazionale d'Antichità* emphasizes finds from a neighboring Roman settlement, including imposing imperial statues, but there is more: Etruscan and Greek pottery most especially. *Biblioteca Palatina* is hardly your run-of-the-mill public library; this one abounds in illuminated manuscripts, old leather-bound books, with—at any given time—an exhibit of selected treasures from among its 600,000 objects. *Museo Bodoni:* I first became taken with the now-classic typefaces designed in the eighteenth century by Giambattista Bodoni while learning how to set type as a journalism student at Syracuse University. Parma is where Bodoni made his reputation, while in the service of the dukes, producing elegant folios and quartos of ancient Greek poets, for courtiers' leisurely perusal. If you're at all taken with graphic design, have a look.

Museo Glauco Lombardi (Via Garibaldi 15): You wouldn't suspect it from the title, but this smallish museum is a celebration of the reign in Parma for some three nineteenth-century decades—just following Napoleonic rule—of Duchess Maria Luigia, by coincidence Napoleon's second empress. If you are a sucker for this kind of memorabilia—as I confess to being—you'll have fun with this mix of clothes and correspondence, jewels and paintings, including a portrait of Maria Luigia's first husband—the Emperor—who was succeeded, in Parma, by two others.

Church of San Giovanni (Piazzale San Giovanni) went up in the sixteenth century, and despite a newer façade from the succeeding century, remains original within, as well it had better, given the pedigree of its frescoes. Parmigianino painted those in a quartet of side chapels, while Correggio was responsible for those in the dome.

Church of Madonna della Staccata (Via Garibaldi), unusually square-shaped in the manner of Greek Orthodox churches—even though it is the work of an Italian Renaissance architect—warrants inspection if only for the group of frescoes by Parmigianino on biblical themes, that of *Adam and Eve* the most memorable.

Camera di San Paolo (Via Malloni) is my final Parma destination for Correggio aficionados. Originally a room in the apartment of the superior of a convent, its ceiling was frescoed—themes are charmingly allegorical—by the master in 1518, so that this is among his earliest works.

Salsomaggiore Terme, a charming spa town set among rolling hills 20 miles west of Parma, achieved a certain celebrity during the early-nineteenth-century period when Maria Luigia (Napoleon's second wife) was Grand Duchess of Parma, thanks to thermal springs that were the nucleus of its treatment centers. Contemporarily, visitors tend to be Italians, Germans, and other continental Europeans, and a principal problem for English speakers is a dearth of locals with whom to converse, apart from the reception and concierge desks of major hotels. Bathing in iodine-salt water is the principal therapy, mainly for rheumatic and gynecological ailments. But there are other types of therapy, including mud baths, and such typical spa diversions as concerts and fashion shows. And there are no less than 170 hotels (a number with their own treatment centers) and pensiones, which makes Salsomaggiore worth noting for motorists in the region anxious for a comfortable bed. *Grand Hotel et de Milan* (Via Dante) is so delightful—it's an old-timer with a swimming pool in its lovely garden that has been modernized, but not overly so, with some of its 112 rooms nicer than others and with some baths that could have done with a bit of refurbishing on my last visit—that I recommend it and its restaurant, as delicious as it is handsome. *First Class.* It's a few minutes' walk from the center, where *Hotel Regina* (Largo Roma 3)—a handsome, 100-room turn-of-century house, also *First Class*—is counseled. *Hotel Porro* (Viale Porro), elderly albeit updated, has 85 rooms (those I've inspected are very pleasant), is set in its own park, and serves excellent cuisine in a chandelier-hung restaurant. *First Class.* I'm impressed, too, with *Hotel Valentini,* away from the center in a park, with 100 rooms, most with showers rather than tubs in their baths and a reliable restaurant. *Moderate.* And I have dined very well—a meal might run to house-cured prosciutto con melone, tortelloni alla Parmigiana, and a super grilled beefsteak—at *Ristorante Tartufo* (Viale Marconi 30; Phone 573-696; *First Class*).

SETTLING IN

Park Hotel Stendhal (Piazzetta Bodoni): A hotel named for the author of *The Charterhouse of Parma* on a square named for the great typographic designer has got to have something going for it. The Stendhal does. It is an easy walk north from the Duomo and has 60 attractive rooms and equally felicitous public spaces that include the locally esteemed restaurant named for the city's museum-filled palace, Pilotta. Cocktail lounge, too. *First Class.*

Palace Hotel Maria Luigia (Viale Mentana 140), more distant from the cathedral area than the Stendhal (above), is an agreeably modern house, with a cozy lobby-lounge, popular Maxim's restaurant, and 105 pleasant rooms. *First Class.*

Torino Hotel (Via Mazza 7) is strategically situated near the Duomo, and not far, either, from the Palazzo Pilotta museums. There are just over 30 bath-equipped rooms, bar-lounge, and breakfast but no restaurant. *Moderate.*

Button Hotel (Strada San Vitale 7) is a few blocks south of the Duomo, near Strada della Repubblica. It contains some 40 functional rooms, bar-lounge; breakfast but no restaurant. *Moderate.*

DAILY BREAD

La Filoma (Via 20 Marzo 15; Phone 234-269). You are in the city of Parmesan cheese, of Parmesan hams, of Italy's first pasta factories (it was all handmade until the 1870s), and of pastry chefs who consider themselves heirs of French and Austrian predecessors imported by the ducal court in earlier centuries. What I am saying is that the food is good in Parma, and La Filoma is an ideal spot—attractive, intimate, and cordial—to sample a meal that might include Parma ham-sauced tagliatelle or anolini (Parma's answer to ravioli) in broth; a local entrée like picaia (stuffed breast of veal); concluding with an extravagant sweet. Extensive wine list. Near the Duomo. *First Class.*

Parizzi (Strada della Repubblica 71; Phone 285-952) does well with pasta, of course, but try its specialties of duck and of mushrooms, too. Popular. *First Class/Luxury.*

Angiol d'Or (Via Scutellari; Phone 22-632) is an esteemed cathedral-area restaurant, attractive and delicious, with specialties Parmesan cheese-accented, pasta as well as poultry. *First Class.*

Canòn d'Or (Via Nazario Sauro 3; Phone 285-234) is an apt choice for a hearty meal; make sure that you start with antipasto assortito. *Moderate.*

Caffè Provinciale (Via Cavour 53) is a centrally located source of pastry, taken in tandem with coffee, tea, or a drink, in the company of loquacious locals. *Moderate.*

SOUND OF MUSIC

Teatro Regio (Via Garibaldi) is among Italy's most reputed opera houses (it went up in 1829) and among its most beautiful, as well; a blue ceiling fresco, scarlet bordered, crystal-chandelier-centered, highlights a six-level auditorium where you want to try to take in opera, ballet, or a concert. There are daytime tours but only if your hotel concierge or the tourist office (below) has made advance arrangements. *Teatro Ducale* (Via Bixio) is the No. 2 house.

INCIDENTAL INTELLIGENCE

Further information: Ente Provinciale per il Turismo, Piazza del Duomo 5, Parma; Azienda Autonoma di Soggiorno e Turismo, Viale Romagnosi 7, Salsomaggiore Terme.

26

Perugia

The Essence of Umbria

BACKGROUND BRIEFING

If it is true that Umbria—stretching south of Tuscany, its aged stone-built towns climbing the slopes of emerald hills—is quite the prettiest non-Alpine Italian *Regione*, it follows, too, that Perugia is the quintessential Umbrian city. Surely no other beats it, with respect to relevant criteria: advanced age, world-class art and architecture in a setting of splendor, and an intuitive sense of style that has been magnetlike in drawing settlers of consequence over a span exceeding the twenty centuries of our own era.

Perugia began as a settlement of the ancient, primitive people—about which relatively little still is known—who gave their name to the region, the Umbrians. They were hardly a match for gifted Etruscans who made of their city of Perusia—today's Perugia—an important center of a civilization adept at working with materials like iron, bronze, and gold, developing a written language, becoming expert as merchants, seamen, and administrators of governments that extended even to colonies as far distant as Spain.

Romans came north in the fourth century B.C., to govern a prosperous Perugia. The early Christian epoch was not a proud one. But Perugia made a comeback—as a self-governing *comune*—in the twelfth century, to the point where it became ruler of much of Umbria, the while developing as a city of substance. Churches and palaces filled its core. The Perugia school of painting—Perugino and Pinturicchio, many of whose works remain on view in the city, were its leaders—became known throughout Europe. And the University of Perugia—supplemented in modern times by a second university that teaches the Italian language and Italian culture to students from all over the world—was established as long ago as 1308.

ON SCENE

Lay of the Land: Umbrian hill towns, because of partially vertical terrain, can seem more geographically complex than is the case. Perugia—biggest of the lot (with a population of about 140,000) and he regional capital—occupies a substantial hill that affords vistas of the Tiber River valley, way below. The historic center—riddled with landmarks—is based on a sumptuous square, *Piazza IV Novembre,* centered by a fountain significant enough for later comment, and flanked by the Duomo and a medieval palace. The principal shopping street—smart *Corso Vannucci*—extends west from this complex to *Piazza Italia* and an ancient city gate, *Porta Mandorla.* The railway station is on *Viale Roma* in the southwest part of town. If you are going to zero in on a single medieval street with character, make it *Via dei Priori,* which runs north from *Piazza IV Novembre* to *Piazza San Francesco* and a pair of noteworthy churches—of which this city has many. Or head south from the center, along *Via Derini, Via Cartolari,* and *Via delle Conce* with your destination the complex embracing the *Church of San Domenico* and *Museo Archeologico.* A pleasant eastbound stroll would take you from the core, following *Via Rocchi,* right through *Arco Etrusco*—Perugia's principal Etruscan souvenir, going back to the third century before Christ, albeit with a Renaissance loggia and fountain appended to it—to *Palazzo Gallenga,* its intricately detailed eighteenth-century façade enclosing *Università Italiana per Stranieri,* Perugia's university for foreigners.

Fontana Maggiore (Piazza IV Novembre) translates as Major Fountain, and is accurately enough named for me to accord it prominence that I do not customarily devote to fountains. This one, completed near the end of the thirteenth century, is a marvel of medieval sculpture unlike any other that I know, except possibly Nuremberg's fourteenth-century Schöner Brunner (See *Germany at Its Best*). The Maggiore, topped by an elegant clutch of bronze nymphs, is double-basined. The upper basin is embellished with precisely two dozen statues, mostly of saints and civic figures, while the lower basin's décor consists of 48 bas-reliefs on an extraordinary mix of subjects, the range months of the year—always popular in medieval art—through zodiacal signs. The fountain's creators were a father-son team, Nicola and Giovanni Pisano, the latter known also for later work in the Duomo of Siena (chapter 29).

Duomo (Piazza IV Novembre): Perugia's cathedral, unheralded in contrast to many in Italy—perhaps because its Gothic façade is unfinished (to me it is quite beautiful, with horizontal brick stripes at uneven intervals punctuated by a Baroque portal)—resembles that of Lucca (chapter 17), with similarly painted vaults framing a long, high nave. Features to note: beautiful bishop's throne, exquisitely carved choir, Cappella del Sant' Anello (with what legend decrees is the Virgin Mary's wedding ring), and Cappella di San Bernardino, with the Renaissance painter Barocci's stunning *Deposition,* and a blue-robed *Madonna delle Grazie* by a pupil of Perugino's, Giannicola di Paola.

Galleria Nazionale dell' Umbria (Piazza IV Novembre) occupies the high-ceilinged third floor of Palazzo dei Priori, a crenelated Gothic structure that could be out of a fairy tale. It attracts, first off, with the pair of not very ferocious lions guarding an elaborate front door; lures, as well, with its second-floor Sala dei Notari, or Notaries' Hall, whose ceiling is supported by eight frescoed arches; and climaxes on the third floor where some 30 rooms contain works of the National Gallery of Umbria, among Italy's more important. Route yourself leisurely through this treasure trove, mostly, but not entirely, of Umbrian art. Look out for the painted thirteenth-century crucifix of Maestro di San Francesco, interpretations of the *Madonna and Child* by such masters as Fra Angelico, Pinturicchio, Pietro da Cortona, and Duccio di Buoninsegna. Don't miss the multilevel altarpiece by Piero della Francesca, topped by a geometric *Annunciation,* unlike any other you will have come across. And there are memorable Perugino works—*Christ in the Tomb,* a *Nativity,* and a *Madonna,* among much more.

Museo Archeologico Nazionale dell' Umbria and Basilica of San Domenico (Piazza Giordano Bruno) constitute an odd—but compatible—coupling, with the museum occupying space in what had been the monastery attached to the church. It works like a charm, with exhibits in halls overlooking a handsome cloister, with Etruscan exhibits—most from this onetime Etruscan capital and its environs—the standouts: bronze statues, sculpted stone urns, ceramics, sarcophagi, and—not to be overlooked—the Perugian Memorial Stone, a slab of travertine inscribed in the Etruscan language, not unlike the similarly significant Gubbio Tablets (chapter 15). Which leaves the church proper, massively Baroque to the designs of Carlo Maderno, whose name you will recall from his Rome works. The stained-glass window in the apse is fifteenth-century—as lovely as it is large—and side chapels are art-filled.

Collegio del Cambio (Corso Vannucci): Talk about big things coming in small packages. This Renaissance money-changers' guild—a section of

Palazzo dei Priori but separately entered—is a celebration of the genius of Pietro Perugino. Move through the entry room into Sala dell' Udienza, or Audience Hall, for the wall and ceiling frescoes—*Adoration of the Shepherds, Transfiguration, Nativity*—as well as a self-portrait of the artist, red-capped and double-chinned.

Church of San Pietro (Via Borgo XX) ranks with the Duomo as Perugia's most important church. Indeed, because of its paintings alone, it outranks the cathedral. Romanesque in origin, it is essentially Renaissance—and sumptuous. The wide nave is covered by a coffered and gilded ceiling, flanked by decorated arches beneath rows of oversized paintings—nearly a dozen all told—by an artist called Aliense who studied under Veronese. But there is so much more: a moving *Pietà* and four portraits of saints by Perugino; a Caravaggio of *Santa Francesca Romana;* a baby Jesus with an equally young *St. John the Baptist* that the church attributes to Raphael; Parmigianino's *The Holy Family;* an *Annunciation* by Sassoferrato; and works, as well, by Guido Reni and Vasari. Also note the frescoed sacristy and no less than a trio of cloisters.

Church of Santa Maria Nuova (Via del Roscetto) stands out, first off, for its gem of a campanile, gracefully Renaissance-arched on each of several levels. The capacious interior is no less appealing, given a plethora of art—frescoes on the columns and arches of the nave, paintings by a range of Renaissance Perugians in side chapels, carved-wood choir, vaulted cloister.

Oratorio of San Bernardino (Piazza San Francesco) is visitable for the bas-relief of its Renaissance façade, more than for its plain interior. The saint himself is centered in the lunette—flanked by angels—over the pair of stone-framed portals. Still more angels—musicians, these—are at the other side of the doors, with a mix of saints and angels in niches completing this symphony in marble. The sculptor, out of Florence, was Agostino di Antonio di Duccio. Bravo!

Church of Sant' Angelo (Via del Tempio, adjacent to Porta Sant' Angelo, a fourteenth-century city gate, and a fair walk from the center) goes back to the fifth century, is rotunda-shaped with a simple circle of a dome, and an interior ringed by sixteen columns, their Corinthian capitals the principal decoration. Worth the walk.

SETTLING IN

Brufani Hotel (Piazza Italia): Time was—and for a long time—when you came to Perugia seeking a luxury hotel, you stayed at the old

Brufani Palace. Well, what has happened is that this distinguished hostelry is now two hotels, each separately owned, and occupying one of the two joined buildings of the old hotel. The Brufani, smaller of the pair, occupies the senior of the structures, with 25 traditional-style rooms—each refurbished—smartly pastel-hued and with smashing Tiber Valley views from most. Service is skilled, smiling, and personal; bar and restaurant. *Luxury.*

Palace Hotel Bellavista (Piazza Italia): You have surmised, if you have read the paragraph above, that this is the remaining section of the former Brufani Palace Hotel, with new name and management, and 85 completely renovated rooms with bath or shower, capacious public spaces including a bar-lounge-cum-terrace, restaurant, and fine vistas from those of its rooms that are valley-view. *First Class.*

Rosetta Hotel (Piazza Italia) occupies venerable quarters that have been nicely updated; the lobby, to give you an idea, is in dramatic browns, with a welcoming bar attached to it. There are nearly 100 rooms with bath or shower, and a restaurant worthy of later comment. *First Class.*

Posta Hotel (Corso Vannucci 97) is positioned on the city's attractive—and central—main street. And it is hardly without staying power, having been in business since the late eighteenth century, with a clientele—according to its literature—that included Goethe and Hans Christian Andersen. Public rooms remain traditional in style, but I am glad to report evidence of the current century: an elevator to the upper stories where all 40 rooms are bath-equipped. Bar and breakfast, but no restaurant. *Moderate.*

Signa Hotel (Via del Grillo 9) is neat, functional, and fairly central. A majority of its 23 rooms have baths. Bar and breakfast, but no restaurant. *Moderate.*

DAILY BREAD

La Bocca Mia (Via Rocchi 36, Phone 23-873) is a brick-walled and atmospherically vaulted space, respectably advanced in years, that has been brought up to date by the two friendly women who operate it, with the accent on yellow—menus, table linen, even upholstery of the chrome chairs. Everything that I have sampled is delicious. Ask if typically Umbrian spaghetti ai tartufi neri—black local truffles, these—is available, or, among the entrées, also regional agnello all' arrabbiata—

a lamb specialty. Bocca Mia's wines are well priced, and its desserts—especially the pastries—tempting. *First Class.*

Rosetta Hotel Ristorante (Piazza Italia; Phone 20-841) is at its best in summer when tables are set out front, on the piazza, and you watch the passing parade as you dine. Pastas are first-rate, with the range wide; there is always a good choice of veal entrées, and you do well to accompany yours with a green salad. Professional service. *First Class.*

La Taverna (Via delle Streghe 8; Phone 610028) is indicated for an antipasto to start, with good Umbrian salamis among its tempters. And a beefsteak or petti di pollo—chicken breasts, done the chef's own way—are sensible entrée choices. *First Class.*

Caffè Ferrari (Corso Vannucci 43) is where Perugians bump into fellow Perugians and are brought up to date on contemporary affairs. Delicious ice cream, coffee, drinks. *Moderate.*

Caffè Sandri (Corso Vannucci 64) is justifiably noted for its pastries and little sandwiches; perfect pick-me-ups. *Moderate.*

SOUND OF MUSIC

Teatro Comunale Morlacchi (Piazza Morlacchi) is opulent Rococo, a lovely late-eighteenth-century monument, still going strong, with opera, ballet, and concerts, bookable through hotel concierges; the tourist office (below) will have printed schedules.

SHOPPER'S PERUGIA

Department and other stores are on Corso Vannucci, Via Alessi, Via Calderini, and Via Rocchi.

INCIDENTAL INTELLIGENCE

Further information: Azienda Autonoma di Cura, Soggiorno e Turismo, Via IV Novembre 3, Perugia.

27

Pisa

What the Leaning Tower Hath Wrought

BACKGROUND BRIEFING

The pity of Pisa is that it has allowed itself to come so close to being a tourist trap. It is not that, of course; no city with such a glorious history and with so much glorious art and architecture to show for it could possibly be.

Pisa's problem, or so it would seem to one observer, is twofold. The first is heavy World War II bombing followed by a rebuilding that could have been vastly more felicitous; one must search out pockets of beauty, for there is precious little to be found in the ambience in the course of a casual stroll. The second, it should be apparent to anyone who has gotten through fifth-grade geography, is the tilt of the Romanesque campanile adjacent to the cathedral—180 feet high and 15 feet out of the perpendicular.

It is the Leaning Tower that has made of Pisa a mass-tourism destination like no other in provincial Italy, with countless busloads flocking in just long enough to have a look, or possibly a climb, buy a dreadful souvenir from an appalling ribbon of stands edging the cathedral square that constitute Italy's most egregious example of visual pollution, and move along.

The consequence of this pattern of tourism is, without any doubt, full coffers for bus operators and vendors of miniature towers. But because precious few of us have enough curiosity to stay at least overnight, Pisa beyond the tower rarely gets a fair shake, and there is so relatively little demand for hotel space, that there's nary a solitary luxury category hostelry in this globally famous Tuscan city that was, during its Golden Age, a substantial international power.

When Romans came north to this Arno River city, it probably still edged the shores of the Tyrrhenian Sea (from whose beach resorts it is now six miles distant). That was in the second century B.C., by which time Etruscans—and possibly even Greeks—had settled it. The early Middle Ages saw the city emerge as a sovereign maritime republic battling Arabs from the south shore of the Mediterranean, allying itself with France's Normans, cannily competing with also-rich Italian city-states like Venice, Florence, Genoa, not to mention neighboring Lucca, the while creating a culture that drew on influences as diverse as the ancient Romans, Middle Eastern Turks, and Islamic Moors.

In the fifteenth century nearby Florence conquered a Pisa that had already built a great cathedral in the style that has come to be known as Pisan Romanesque, fostered its own school of art, founded a university (Pisa-born Galileo was a professor), and even for a period ruled Sardinia as a colony.

ON SCENE

Lay of the Land: Easy. The Arno River neatly slices the core of town in half. Centrally situated Stazione Centrale, the main train station, fronts *Piazza Vittorio Emanuele,* leading to *Corso Italia,* the main shopping street, which takes one to its terminus at *Ponte di Mezzo* (Middle Bridge) and over the Arno—have a look in both directions as you cross, at palazzi lining the water, for this is one of the few scenic vistas of post-World War II Pisa—to *Piazza Garibaldi.* From this point it's an easy walk along *Borgo Stretto* through *Piazza dei Cavalieri*—the handsomest nonecclesiastical ensemble in the city, from the Renaissance, when Florentine Medici ruled Pisa—to *Via Santa Maria, Campo dei Miracoli,* and the *Duomo,* with its campanile and other satellite structures.

Campo dei Miracoli (a.k.a. Piazza del Duomo): Resign yourself to the reality of the traffic here and you'll enjoy it more; you will not have seen proportionately heavier crowds at St. Peter's in Rome, St. Mark's in Venice, or the Duomo in Florence. The miracle of the Field of Miracles—to translate the complex's title—is that it remains exquisitely beautiful nine centuries after it was begun. If you will forgive me for not allowing the tail to wag the dog, I will start with the *Duomo* proper, rather than its detached bell tower. Pisa's cathedral demands exterior inspection before going inside. Its façade—one of the great ones in a land of many such—stands out if only for the four levels of delicately carved loggias above a trio of portals, the arches of which are repeated on both sides of the building. Even the front doors' bronze panels—depicting scenes from the life of Jesus and the Virgin Mary—warrant study. The interior, for me at least, is at its best when taken in from the entrance, the better to appreciate the design of its black-and-white striped stone walls, Corinthian capitals of the nave's columns, and gilded, coffered ceiling. Take time, then, to amble about what at first appears to be an overdecorated crossing, altar, and apse area, but with superb art. Take notice of Giovanni Pisano's sublimely sculpted pulpit, the attributed-to-Cimabue mosaic of *Christ Pantocrator,* above the apse; and, among a number of fine paintings, Andrea del Sarto's *Saint Agnes.* Then, start all over again, for a second tour; you'll have missed a lot, in the dizzying course of the first.

Battistero, or Baptistry, is, in contrast, severely simple—a giant domed circle that is partially the work of the same Pisano (Giovanni) who created the Duomo's pulpit, with still another Pisano (Nicola), responsible for the Battistero's pulpit, and, with Giovanni, a clutch of striking statues. The giant baptismal font is splendid.

That leaves, of the Duomo trio, the *Leaning Tower,* or *Campanile,* which started to tilt shortly after construction began some 800 years back and hasn't stopped since. Even forgetting its posture, the tower is exceptional if only for its good looks. In part the work of still another Pisano—Bonanno by name—it embraces eight levels, six of them ringed by handsome loggias, with seven bells in the belfry, gained by a circular flight of nearly 300 steps. And, yes, if you have the strength or the youth, or both, you may ascend.

Camposanto, most unusual component of the cathedral complex, is a great rectangle of a walled cemetery, originally thirteenth-century. Do go in; you wouldn't know it from the name, but this is a corking good museum. In four immense galleries enclosing a grassy courtyard are displayed a rich mix of works—Greek and Roman sarcophagi, monumentally immense frescoes, medieval Madonnas, mosaics, and bronzes.

Museo delle Sinopie, newest addition to the Campo dei Miracoli, is indeed a surprise package: a display of *sinopie,* technical term for a red-hued pigment used to delineate sketches or cartoons for paintings—a technique that was not discovered until after the Camposanto (above) was struck by World War II bombs, after which authorities came upon frescoes that had been damaged, and the red-pigment underlay beneath them was exposed. A clutch of remarkable drawings-in-pigment-going back to the fourteenth century—is the subject matter of this not-to-be-missed museum. Fascinating.

Museo Nazionale di San Matteo (Lungarno Mediceo) flanks the Arno, is a brief and pleasant hike from Piazza Garibaldi, and takes the name of the originally Romanesque convent it occupies. The building—especially its cloister—is mellow enough to warrant inspection. But the exhibits—of Pisan Romanesque paintings and sculpture—are what give the museum its importance: painted crucifixes, polychrome saints, illuminated manuscripts, a room full of sculpture by the Duomo complex's Giovanni Pisano, Simone Martini altarpieces, painted saints by Masaccio, tapestries and jewel boxes, ancient coins, and fragments of antique capitals. Special.

Church of San Michele in Borgo (Borgo Stretto) goes back, in part, to the tenth century and is rich with works of art in its evocative Romanesque-Gothic interior, an altar triptych of the Madonna surrounded by saints and angels most especially.

Church of Santo Stefano (Piazza dei Cavalieri) is the best reason for a visit to this fine Renaissance square. It is essentially the work of Giorgio Vasari, who designed the Uffizi Gallery (as offices) in Florence—among much more. Beneath a sumptuous gilded wood ceiling, there are a number of Vasari objects, and works by others, including a bust by the same Donatello you will also associate with Renaissance Florence.

Church of Santa Caterina (Via Cardinal Maffi): Prime draw here is the enormous—and enormously beautiful—altarpiece, *Apotheosis of St. Thomas,* by a fourteenth-century master named Francesco Traini and works by members of the medieval Pisano family.

Church of San Paolo a Ripa d'Arno (Via San Paolo): Ripa d'Arno translates as "Banks of the Arno," and this church is indeed alongside the river. It has, for me, the handsomest ecclesiastical interior in town—long, gray-stoned, and somber—with the Corinthian capitals of its nave and the apse's stained glass almost its only decorative elements. If it's open, pop into little *Cappella di Sant' Agata,* out back.

Church of Santa Maria della Spina (Piazza Saffi) is a small, busily detailed species of Gothic—too detailed, in my view—that borders the Arno, is much commented upon, and is rarely open; you may, however, look, through the windows.

SETTLING IN

Cavalieri Hotel (Piazza della Stazione 2) is Pisa's No. 1—a well-operated, compact 100-room red-brick structure just opposite the railway station, near air and bus terminals, and steps from Corso Italia, the main shopping thoroughfare that leads directly to the Arno and the Duomo complex. Restaurant-bar, friendly concierge. *First Class.*

D'Azeglio Hotel (Piazza Vittorio Emanuele) occupies a slender eight-story high rise near the bus and railway stations. The look is contemporary, with a bar off the lobby-lounge and terraces attached to the 29 rooms. Breakfast only. *First Class.*

Mediterraneo Hotel (Via Turati 35) is just a block off Corso Italia, with 100 relatively recently refurbished rooms; bar and breakfast. *Moderate.*

Roma Hotel (Via Bonanno Pisano) is agreeably modern and close to the Duomo complex, with 27 rooms, bar, and breakfast. *Moderate.*

Touring Hotel (Via Puccini 24) welcomes with a comfortable lobby-lounge and 34 nicely equipped rooms. Location is near the railway station. *Moderate.*

DAILY BREAD

Trattoria da Bruno (Via Bianchi 12; Phone 560-818) is indicated after a morning at the Duomo ensemble, which it's near. This is an old-fashioned (it's past the half-century mark) trattoria that draws a mix of Pisans and visitors. The minestrone is hearty; pasta—the house's penne alla cacciatore, especially—is delicious; and entrées, including osso bucco and agnello arrosto (roast lamb), are good, too. And the whole staff is friendly. *First Class.*

La Buca (Via Queirolo 25; Phone 24-130) is on a quiet street behind Piazza Vittorio Emanuele, near the railroad station. The look is prosaic but the food is tastily Tuscan. Open with insalata di mare, the seafood salad, continue with grilled sausages or perhaps an entrée-sized order of asparagus, if it's in season, concluding with macedonia di frutta, fresh fruit cup. A carafe of the house Chianti is a well-priced accompaniment. *First Class.*

Ivaldo (Via Toselli 11; Phone 27-372) is nicely situated between Corso Italia and the Arno, close to both shops and monuments. *Moderate.*

Buzzino (Via Cammeo 44; Phone 27-013) is counseled only if you book in advance; or, if lunch is the meal in question, arrive early enough to precede the crowd from the nearby Duomo. Then relax over a repast of, say, mushroom-sauced risotto and Florentine-style beefsteak, with a salad. *First Class.*

Sergio (Lungarno Pacinotti 1; Phone 48-225) tries very hard—unsmiling waiters, pretentious décor, patronizing attitude—to be very grand. But does not, in my experience, succeed. And although prices are steep (assorted cheeses, served from a trolley, are a notable exception), fare—again in my experience—disappoints, the friandises—little French-style pastries served with coffee—an exception. The menu includes non-Italian selections—shrimp cocktail, smoked salmon, fried and au gratin potatoes, French-style crêpes—as well as national soups, pastas, and entrées. Withal, though, disappointing. *Luxury.*

Caffè La Borsa (Piazza della Stazione 7) lures locals and visitors alike, for coffee, pastry, and crowd-watching. *Moderate.*

Caffè Salza (Borgo Stretto 67) has been on scene since 1898; 1 don't know what the ice cream was like then, but it's irresistible now. *Moderate.*

SOUND OF MUSIC

Teatro Verdi (Via Palestro) has annual seasons of opera, ballet, concerts, and plays. Your hotel concierge can book.

SHOPPER'S PISA

Pedestrians-only *Corso Italia* has department stores and good shops.

INCIDENTAL INTELLIGENCE

Marina Pisa, the city's satellite beach resort on the Tyrrhenian, is a scant five miles west and with wide white sands, should you crave a dip or some sun in the course of a summer visit. Pisa's *Aeroporto Galileo-Galilei* is all of a mile from downtown; you're there in five minutes with a taxi from your hotel, or from the air terminal near the railway station. *Further information:* Ente Provinciale per il Turismo, Piazza del Duomo, Pisa.

28

Ravenna

The World's Greatest Mosaics

BACKGROUND BRIEFING

Of course there are others. Beauties, to be sure, in Turkey's Istanbul, Greece's Salonica, Sicily's Monreale, Venice and nearby Torcello, Rome and Pompeii. And at so many other points where the ancient Greeks and succeeding Romans were partial to telling stories in compositions created with bits of rock and glass.

But no city has such an easily accessible concentration of mosaics—the mosaics of the early Christian churches, extravagantly surfacing basilicas' walls and domes and apses—as Ravenna. This now quiet town of Emilia Romagna—just inland from the Adriatic and 85 miles south of Venice on the coastal Via Roma route—was, during its heyday, so strategically situated that it became a center—governmental, military, cultural, maritime—of the world as it existed before the Middle Ages.

Romans, for example, tapped Ravenna as capital of their Western Empire in the fourth century, with Ravenna's then port, Classe (now an inland suburb with a magnificent church its major monument) the seat of their Adriatic fleet. In the fifth century barbarians came—Germanic Ostrogoths whose kings Odoacer and Theodoric were adherents of the then quite prevalent Arian sect. They made Ravenna a royal seat, and churches that Theodoric built for Arian worship—considered heretical by Christians because Jesus' divine status was lessened—remain major Ravenna monuments. These same churches became Christian with the demise of Arianism by the time Ravenna was a Byzantine capital, at the start of the seventh century. Ceded to northern Italians out of Lombardy to whom the Byzantines lost a decisive battle in the middle of the eighth century, Ravenna's fortunes were not all that different from many others in the Italian peninsula. Its period of glory had ebbed.

Venice, followed by a Venice-origin family, and the Papal States governed it until the mid nineteenth century when the united Italian Kingdom was created. World War II saw it bombed—blessedly, major monuments were either spared or rebuilt—so that the city, contemporarily, is hardly more felicitous in ambience than, say, also-bombed Pisa (chapter 27). Still, like Pisa, pockets of extraordinary beauty remain. For transatlantic visitors whose orientation in Italy is more westward, eastern aspects of this city—artistic, historic, geographic—open eyes to a dimension of Italy that is oddly and appealingly exotic.

ON SCENE

Lay of the Land: Despite substantial size—population is 140,000—Ravenna is walkable. Places you'll want to inspect are dotted about town, but you can take them in, mostly, on foot. The square-shaped core is linked directly with beaches, in and around *Marina di Ravenna,* on the Adriatic to the east, by *Canale Candiano,* whose terminus is on *Via Darsena,* running north-south. Going west from *Piazza Farini,* near the canal's city terminus, *Viale Farini* soon becomes Ravenna's Main Street, *Via Armando Díaz* (lined by specialty shops and department stores), with its termination in the city's handsomest square, *Piazza del Popolo.* Dominated by a pair of freestanding statue-topped Renaissance columns, this is where visitors gather in caffès that spill onto the pavement, against a background of rather grand Venetian-design palazzi, one of them the *Municipio,* or City Hall.

Basilica of San Vitale (Via San Vitale) is quite the most ravishing of the mosaic-surfaced Ravenna spectaculars—and has been, since it went up in the first quarter of the sixth century. If your experience of mosaics has been Roman floors faded from footsteps of many centuries, you will no doubt vociferously exclaim at the brilliance—should one say vitality?—of San Vitale's colors, quite as fresh as they must have been some 1460 years ago. Note mosaics surfacing the dome (saints surrounding the symbolic mystical lamb), covering the walls of the colonnaded space before the high altar (medallions of saints, groups of saints, animals, birds, and flowers), inset in vaults and arches at every turn (depicting angels in flight and biblical Bethlehem), and in the apse (of Emperor Justinian flanked by clergy and courtiers, and of his Empress, Theodora—decreed a onetime prostitute by legend—and her ladies).

Basilica of Sant' Apollinare Nuovo (Via Roma) went up in the sixth century as an Arian place of worship—the Ostrogoth king, Theodoric, was its builder—eventually becoming Catholic. Your eye will be drawn to long walls of the nave, to beautiful capitals of columns supporting graceful arches, then to the spaces above, each with three magnificent levels of mosaics; on the left, depictions of Christ's parables and miracles, and an extraordinary formation of white-robed saints; and on the right the mosaicists' interpretation of Christ's Passion and Resurrection and a procession of twenty-plus Byzantine Virgins. Now then, observe the word *nuovo* (new) in this church's name; it is there to distinguish it from still another stellar structure a ten-minute drive south of the center on *Via Cesarea: Sant' Apollinare-in-Classe.* Classe is the ancient name of the port of Ravenna. This church—similar in general design to its in-town namesake, albeit with a detached circular campanile—has sarcophagi lining its walls and mosaics like none in town, most especially the ceiling of its apse in grounds of green, centered by a great gold cross embedded in a star-studded blue circle.

Tomba di Galla Placidia (Via Galla Placidia) is a neighbor of Basilica di San Vitale (above) and of the National Museum (below). It's lower down in my grouping than San Vitale because it's difficult to see. It's a smallish mausoleum, believed to be the burial place of a fifth-century empress whose name it takes. Its dome—royal blue dotted with gold stars and centered with a gold cross—is superb, as is the red-white-and-blue circular pattern of its barrel vault. But only licensed guides who show groups about know where to turn on the lights, and if you enter on your own—managing to squeeze into this always-packed destination—you may or may not have illumination.

The pair of baptistries can confuse. Elder of the two, *Battistero degli Ortodossi* (a.k.a. Battistero Neone) on Via Rasponi (adjacent to the essentially eighteenth-century, devoid-of-mosaics Duomo), predates its counterpart by some 50 years of the fifth century. It is the more impressive, a quite marvelous octagon with its décor a mix of marble reliefs and mosaics, chief of which are in the dome, which depicts a naked, albeit bearded, Christ, half submerged in water, being anointed by St. John the Baptist. In the smaller, charming *Battistero degli Ariani* (Via degli Ariani), erected by King Theodoric and, as the name implies, Arian before it was Catholic, the mosaic of the dome has the same theme: Baptism of Christ, with the Christ figure half in water and naked as in the bigger baptistry, but—unusual this feature—without a beard.

Pinacoteca Civica (Via Rome) is a triple treat. First, part of it is Basilica of Santa Maria in Porto—exuberantly Baroque, with a splendid façade, a carved-wood Renaissance choir, and—in its transept—a lovely 900-year-old marble likeness of the Virgin, called the Greek Madonna.

Second is the also lovely—and adjacent—monastery of the church, with an elegant marble loggia and a serene cloister its standout architectural features. Third is the city's art museum, in the ex-monastery, with a cache of eminently inspectable medieval and Renaissance paintings. The most requisite are two paintings of the *Crucifixion*, one by Lorenzo Monaco, the other by Antonio Vivarini. Have a look.

Museo Nazionale (Via San Vitale and a neighbor to Basilica of San Vitale and Tomba di Galla Placidia, above) is notable, first, for contemporary good looks, two capacious floors of smartly presented exhibits, with special treasures upstairs: Roman busts, capitals from columns of long-vanished churches, finely worked little bronzes, generous samplings of early Ravenna pottery from a mix of epochs, bas reliefs and sarcophagi, and—biggest surprise—a room brimming with icons, gold-backed Orthodox religious paintings, the most memorable a boyish, scarlet-robed St. George, his elongated sword in the fiery mouth of the dragon.

SETTLING IN

Bisanzio Hotel (Via Salera 30) is somewhat north of the center, not far from San Vitale Basilica. There are not quite 40 rooms (not all have baths), bar-lounge, and breakfast service, but no restaurant. *First Class.*

Centrale-Byron Hotel (Via Quattro Novembre 14) is indeed *centrale*, on an agreeably busy street just off Piazza del Popolo, with nearly 60 rooms, most with baths. Bar-lounge and breakfast. *Moderate.*

Argentario Hotel (Via Roma 45) is just down the street from Sant' Apollinare Basilica; has baths in most of its 14 neat rooms, a bar-lounge, and breakfast. *Moderate.*

DAILY BREAD

Tre Spade (Via Rasponi 37; Phone 32-382) is smart, smallish, and satisfying, with a tempting antipasto among starters, tasty pastas (ask if garganelli—Ravenna-invented macaroni—is available), and a range of entrées, possibly including locally hooked tuna. *First Class.*

La Gardèla (Via Ponte Marino 3; Phone 27-147) is just north of the core, and good value. *Moderate.*

Caffè Roma (Piazza del Popolo) is one of a trio of such establishments on this scenic and central square, where crowds gather at almost any given hour for sustenance—coffee, drinks, pastry—and people watching. If there are no tables, cross over to the competition—*Caffè Italia* or *Caffè Marino.* If all there are packed—which can be the case—move along to *Caffè Giovanni* on not-far-distant Piazza Farini. *Moderate.*

Al Porto (Via della Nazione 20, Marina di Ravenna; Phone 43-0105) is just the ticket for lunch, should you have taken off for sun and Adriatic surf at the adjacent-to-town beach. Order a seafood-sauced pasta and grilled catch-of-the day. *Moderate.*

SOUND OF MUSIC

Teatro all' Aperto della Rocca Brancaleone—Ravenna's summer theater—embraces both opera and jazz and takes place under the stars in the Renaissance-era Brancaleone fortress (Via Rocca Brancaleone).

INCIDENTAL INTELLIGENCE

Further information: Azienda Autonoma di Soggiorno e Turismo, Via Salera 8, Ravenna.

29

Siena

Medieval Movie Set

BACKGROUND BRIEFING

Credit Siena with persistence. Its citizens have quite obviously been of the same mind over long centuries, in wanting to preserve its Middle Ages ambience. Lesser Italian towns have done likewise; Gubbio (chapter 15) is perhaps a prime example. But none as celebrated has so resisted motels of plastic and high rise towers of glass and steel.

The name, as you may remember from long-ago schoolbooks, came from the legendary son, Senus, of the legendary Remus, who with Romulus founded Rome. Post-Roman centuries were good to the *comune* of Siena, which evolved into a proper republic—and a thriving one, notwithstanding intraclan quibbling and intercity battles with rivals like nearby Florence.

By the time of the powerful Florentine Medici in the late sixteenth century, Siena had been fought over by the French and the Spaniards and the Holy Roman Empire, the while its school of art—this is the town of Simone Martini, Guido da Siena, both Pietro and Ambrogio Lorenzetti, Duccio di Buoninsegna, the father-and-son sculptors named Pisano—became one of Italy's greatest, and its twice-each-summer Palio horse race (the dates are always July 2 and August 16) became celebrated.

Prices are paid for Siena's brilliant historic core and several of these affect the visitor. First is that Siena gets packed—but packed—early spring well into the autumn, but especially in summer; it appears at times simply not big enough to contain the crowds. Second is that there has been, for the most part, no space in the core for the better hotels to locate (of the majors, cheers for the Jolly, which is central), and they're mostly a fair distance from the action. And third is that Siena, despite its international ambience, has never become a major restaurant city, or, for that matter, a shopping city of consequence. You must not expect anything like, say, larger, cosmopolitan Florence. But these are minor matters, quibbles almost, when one considers the consequences of *not* taking a giant step backward into this medieval movie set, and, to similarly ancient, albeit much smaller, San Gimignano, nearby and for that reason included in this chapter.

ON SCENE

Lay of the Land: No Italian city—save possibly Milan, in the case of its Piazza del Duomo, and Venice, with Piazza San Marco—is more closely identified with its central square. Siena's shell-shaped *Piazza del Campo* (a.k.a. Il Campo) is world-class; *Palazzo Pubblico,* the Town Hall, and its landmark campanile *Torre del Mangia* are surrounded by lower but equally aged structures mostly out of the fourteenth century, with a beautifully sculpted fountain, *Fonte Gaia,* in the center, and enough space for both mounted horsemen and spectators, at the twice-each-summer Palio. *Via di Città,* central Siena's principal shopping street, is one of the several that lead from Il Campo and is important because from it one gains *Via San Pietro,* on which Pinacoteca Nazionale is situated; another is *Via Pellegrini,* which takes one to *Piazza del Duomo* and the cathedral complex; while *Via Fontebranda* is the way to both the Dominican church and the shrine of Saint Catherine. The railway station is away from the center, on *Viale Sardegna;* but the bus station is closer in, on *Piazza San Domenico,* and—because taxis are not always easily come by in this city with a number of important noncentral hotels—let me note that there's a taxi-rank on *Piazza Matteotti,* where you line up for them.

Duomo complex (Piazza del Duomo): There are many reasons to visit Siena, but you don't need more than one: its cathedral—easily one of a handful of the most significant in Italy, which in a country abundant with beautiful churches is saying a lot. Siena's Romanesque-Gothic Duomo excites in every respect—immensity of scale (it is enormous and its horizontally striped campanile towers over the city); Giovanni Pisano-designed trio of portals punctuating the exuberant marble façade; and an interior—framed by a sumptuous blue and gold ceiling—so art-filled that you want to schedule at least one return visit to take it all in: Nicola Pisano's intricate altar; Pinturicchio frescoes; Donatello sculpture; inlaid marble floors, pillars, and walls with the same striking striped-marble designs of the campanile; sculpted bronze of the high altar. Move, then, to the *Battistero,* where the fifteenth-century baptismal font sculpted by Jacopo della Quercia is reason enough for an inspection, but where, as well, there are sculptures by Donatello. Conclude in the cathedral's *Museo dell' Opera Metropolitana,* a multistory building whose exhibits had all been in the Duomo or Battistero at one time or another and run an extraordinary gamut—a number of luminous, gold-backed paintings by Duccio di Buoninsegna most spectacularly, but with Pisano sculptures and significant works by the likes of Simone Martini, Ambrogio Lorenzetti, and Giovanni di Paolo.

Palazzo Pubblico (Piazza del Campo), advanced age of some 700 years notwithstanding, remains in service, doing double duty as Siena's *Municipio,* or City Hall, and as an art museum *(Museo Civico),* its treasures in a setting that is an architectural work of art. A horseman, Guido Riccio da Fogliano—whom Simone Martini painted in the same black-diamond-patterned cloth-of-gold with which his horse is adorned, riding along in profile with a pair of castles in the background—is the museum's mascot. Frescoes by Ambrogio Lorenzetti, marvelously named *Effects of Good Government* and *Effects of Bad Government,* are outstanding, too, along with Della Quercia sculptures, Renaissance tapestries, and a number of other treats. You'll have a good time.

Pinacoteca Nazionale (Via San Pietro 29) makes its home in a Gothic palazzo, Buonsignori by name and—I want to advise at the outset—is much bigger than it looks, with the bulk of the collection a survey of Sienese painting—medieval through Baroque—that takes your breath away. Surely the most unexpected painting of the lot is Federico Zuccari's smashing study of *La Regina d'Inghilterra*—England's Elizabeth I—very regal in black and white, wearing a bosom-length strand of giant pearls, and with four courtiers in the colonnaded background. But what you want to concentrate on are the great Sienese—Guido da Siena's *Life of St. Peter,* a clutch of multipanel altarpieces by Duccio di Buoninsegna, a Simone Martini *Madonna,* Ambrogio Lorenzetti's *Annunciation,* Giovanni di Paolo's *Presentation of Jesus in the Temple.* These painters and their works are less familiar to most of us than what we see in places like Rome, Florence, and Venice—although hardly less appealing.

Archivio di Stato (Via Banchi di Sotto): Archives are rarely open to visitors in Italy, but Siena's are. Or at least a selection of the most spectacular, in a second-floor museum of Palazzo Piccolomini, a severely façaded Renaissance structure that puts you in mind of many you see in Florence. Stars of the archives show are tavoletti, elegantly painted covers of medieval Sienese government record books. To be admired, as well, are illuminated manuscripts, papal bulls, and imperial proclamations. Fascinating.

Basilica of Santa Maria dei Servi (Piazza Manzoni) impresses with a somber Romanesque façade. Inside, it is essentially Renaissance; principal reasons for a visit are a clutch of paintings by Sienese masters, including Pietro Lorenzetti's *Massacre of the Innocents,* Taddeo di Bartolo's *Adoration of the Shepherds,* Lippo Memmi's *Madonna del Popolo,* and Giovanni di Paolo's *Madonna della Misericordia.*

Basilica of San Domenico (Piazza San Domenico) is massive Gothic, and plain, but with such works of art as frescoes by Il Sodoma illustrating the life of Catherine of Siena, the fourteenth-century saint designated Patroness of Italy by Pope Pius XII, in the chapel taking her name; a Pietro Lorenzetti painting, *Madonna with St. George;* still another *Madonna* by Sano di Pietro; and a frescoed cloister. (A hop and a skip distant, on Via del Tiratoio, *Santuario e Casa di Santa Caterina* embraces the house in which the saint lived and several later oratories, decorated with paintings about her life, all nineteenth-century.)

Church of Sant' Agostino (Via San Pietro): Work was begun on this big church in the thirteenth century and concluded in the eighteenth. You go principally for the exquisite altarpiece depicting the life of St. Augustine, by Simone Martini; and for such other works of art as a highly respected *Epiphany* by Il Sodoma; a moving *Crucifixion* by Perugino; and an enthroned Madonna surrounded by saints, by Ambrogio Lorenzetti.

San Gimignano—a kind of mini-Siena celebrated for its cluster of medieval towers—is 22 miles to the northwest, and an ideal excursion point from Siena or from Florence (chapter 13). Still walled, straddling an impressive hill, it was, like Siena, a *comune* in the Middle Ages, and again like Siena it was later governed by Florence. It abounds in atmospheric streets, palazzo-lined; squares that are quite as they were centuries back; and churches sheltering art by painters you will have become acquainted with in Siena and in Florence as well.

San Gimignano (pronounced *gee-meen-yahn-oh*) is centered with a pair of contiguous squares, *Piazza del Duomo* and unusually triangular *Piazza della Cisterna,* the later named, as you will have guessed, for a well in its midst; the former for the cathedral, here called *La Collegiata.* Romanesque in origin and with the work of such artists as Taddeo di Bartolo (a superb *Last Judgment*), Pollaiuolo, and Domenico Ghirlandaio (an *Annunciation*). In *Palazzo del Popolo's* Sala di Dante, see the huge and marvelous *Virgin Enthroned with Saints,* by Lippo Memmi, moving then to the building's *Museo Civico,* where such painters as Filippino Lippi, Pinturicchio, Guido da Siena, and Taddeo di Bartolo are represented. Conclude your visit in *Church of Sant' Agostino,* early Gothic with a series of frescoes by Benozzo Gozzoli on the life of St. Augustine. You might enjoy walks on the main streets—*Via San Matteo* leading south from *Piazza del Duomo,* and *Via San Giovanni,* leading north from *Piazza della Cisterna,* not to mention narrower side streets leading from them. If lunch is indicated, have it at *Ristorante le Terrazze (First Class),* in the attractive, period-style, *Moderate*-category *Cisterna Hotel,* (Piazza della Cisterna), where you might also want to stay the night.

SETTLING IN

Certosa di Maggiano Hotel (Strada di Certosa 82): It is surely safe to assume that when a band of Carthusian monks built themselves a monastery in what was then countryside—construction ended in 1314—they did not contemplate that the result of their efforts would be a luxurious hotel six and a half centuries later. The Certosa, as it is called locally, is not the only onetime religious house serving as a hostelry; Taormina's (chapter 32) San Domenico Palace comes immediately to mind as another such. But what distinguishes this hotel is the charm of the public spaces. A firm of Milanese interior designers has employed an enviably light touch, deftly combining superb antiques—the odd piece of furniture, paintings, etchings, accessories—with contemporary textiles like flowered chintz and cotton plaid in a connected series of large rooms, one a bar, another a restaurant. There are just 14 delightful, no-two-alike suites and rooms, a graceful cloister (to which the restaurant moves in summer), a chapel that remains consecrated, operating as a parish church; and a swimming pool in the garden. Lovely. Member, Relais et Châteaux. *Luxury.*

Jolly Hotel (Piazza la Lizza): Jolliest aspect of the Siena Jolly (a.k.a. Jolly Excelsior) is location; it's the only centrally situated of the city's top-category hotels, a few minutes' walk from Il Campo. Not that it is without other pluses. Hardly. There are 126 snappy, well-equipped rooms, a typically Jolly restaurant—which means authentic Italian fare *and* a fabulous breakfast buffet; and a popular bar-lounge. *First Class.*

Park Hotel (Via Marciano 16): The name offers a clue, with the setting a verdant hilltop park, and the hotel itself a picture-postcard villa, dating to the fifteenth century, its interior stylishly refurbished, and comprising close to 70 pleasant rooms (ask for one with a view of the city, beyond), rambling lounge space, indoor/outdoor restaurant, cozy bar, typically Tuscan garden with a swimming pool, even a pair of tennis courts. *Luxury.*

Athena Hotel (Via Paolo Mascagni 55) is fairly central, with a contemporary-look lobby and bar-lounge, and 110 rooms in a mix of styles, all bath-equipped. Breakfast but no restaurant. *Moderate.*

Villa Scacciapensieri Hotel (Via di Scacciapensieri), after you learn to spell and pronounce it, emerges as an attractive country villa turned hotel, with vistas of the city from better rooms (there are 27 all told), smart restaurant that moves to a terrace in summer, mod-look cocktail lounge, formal garden, swimming pool, and tennis. Very nice. *First Class.*

Villa Patrizia Hotel (Via Fiortina 58) is still another country house seeing service as an agreeable, full-facility hotel; big rooms (a total of 33) are a feature; garden, pool, tennis. *First Class.*

Palazzo Ravizza Hotel (Piano dei Mantellini 34) is indeed a palazzo—with Baroque origins, and nearly 30 rooms, most with bath; well-priced restaurant, bar, and fairly central situation, not far beyond the Duomo. *Moderate.*

Chiusarelli Hotel (Via Curatone 9) is still another of the modest houses that are central—it's near San Domenico Church. This one has baths in many of its half a hundred rooms. Restaurant and bar. *Moderate.*

DAILY BREAD

Al Marsili (Via del Castoro 3; Phone 47-154) makes its home in a venerable core-of-city palazzo, wonderfully brick-vaulted, with delicious pastas and the beefsteaks that Americans so enjoy in Tuscany. An enoteca, or wine-shop-cum-tastings bar, is connected, ensuring a wide choice to order with your meal. *First Class.*

Botteganova (Strada Chianigiana; Phone 284-230) presents classic dishes—a marvelous mix of antipasti, pastas in profusion, substantial entrées, house-made sweets that tempt. *First Class/Luxury.*

Nello-La Taverna (Via del Porrione 28; Phone 289-043) occupies brick-walled quarters in a respectably venerable house, just far enough distant from Il Campo to be relatively serene. Pleasant waiters serve up the likes of pasta dishes like paglia e fieno—translated as straw and hay—and a creditable risotto alla Milanese, with a range of entrées, tasty salads, and well-priced house wines. *Moderate.*

Benzo (Piazza Indipendenza 46; Phone 323-953), with sprightly modern décor, welcomes with a choice of table d'hôte menus; good value. *Moderate.*

Severino (Via del Capitano 36; Phone 574-442) is nicely situated on an ancient street leading from Piazza del Duomo. The look is snappy black and white, the three-course menu, opening with spaghetti al pomodoro and continuing with well-prepared veal, is indicated. *Moderate.*

Al Mangia (Piazza del Campo 42; Phone 281-121) is one of several restaurants on the Campo, where smashing views are as much lures as cuisine; this one has photo-embellished walls, tables out front for warm weather, and a fairly standard menu, with pasta and salad good bets. *Moderate/First Class.*

Caffè Fonte Gaia (Piazza del Campo 30) is a case of having the Campo view while seated, but without having to order a meal. The ice cream here is creditable; or settle for coffee. *Moderate.*

Caffè Mannini (Piazza Matteotti 45): If you're staying in an outlying hotel, and are without a car, chances are you'll find your way to this square's taxi rank. In advance of queuing up for a cab, coffee at Mannini will sustain you. *Moderate.*

INCIDENTAL INTELLIGENCE

I repeat the dates of the annual Palio horse-race spectacle that takes place on Il Campo: July 2 and August 16; if your visit coincides with either, make certain you've confirmed hotel space, which must be booked well in advance. *Further information:* Azienda Autonoma di Turismo, Piazza del Campo 55, Siena.

30

Spoleto

Festival City in the Hills

BACKGROUND BRIEFING

There's nothing like an annual international performing arts festival to position a long-obscure town in the hills of Umbria on the tourist map. For long overshadowed as a visitor destination by such neighboring points as Perugia (chapter 26) and Assisi (chapter 3), ancient Spoleto made a comeback in 1958. It was in that year that Italian-born, U.S.-trained composer Giancarlo Menotti (celebrated for such operas as *The Medium, The Consul, The Saint of Bleecker Street,* and *Juana la Loca*) collaborated with the late American composer Thomas Schippers in presenting a mix of music, dance, and drama in historic Spoleto settings, with such success that Spoleto became the first European festival to branch out with a transatlantic counterpart—each June in Charleston, South Carolina.

If twentieth-century travelers had been bypassing Spoleto pre-Menotti, it had not been overlooked in earlier eras. Hardly. Early Spoletani were the highly developed ancient Umbrians with likewise gifted Etruscans following, before Romans—encountering a thriving city—took over in the third century B.C. Early Christian Spoleto was the seat of a Lombard-governed duchy whose territory encompassed a fair-sized chunk of central Italy.

The Papal States gained control of this rich territory, holding the reins through to 1861, when the unified Kingdom of Italy was born. Not surprisingly, given such a long stretch of clerical authority, Spoleto—idyllically situated beneath a fairy-tale castle high above a valley spanned by a multiarched bridge—amassed a disproportionate quantity of beautiful churches so filled with works of art that one overlooks the relative weakness of its museums.

ON SCENE

Lay of the Land: Look up, and what you see on the table-like plateau over the town is a six-tower castle, *La Rocca,* built by a fourteenth-century pope, for a period home to the daughter of still another pope, the infamous Lucrezia Borgia, and, alas, since the early nineteenth century, a prison. The brilliantly engineered *Ponte delle Torri* (Tower Bridge) beneath it went up in the thirteenth century as an aqueduct and is one of the finest such in Italy. Lower down, the town bases itself on a clutch of major squares: easterly *Piazza del Duomo* and adjacent *Piazza della Signoria,* center of the action at festival time, from which *Via del Duomo* leads westerly to a pair of piazze—*Pianciani* and *Mentana,* off which shop-lined *Corso Giuseppe Mazzini* makes a connection with southerly *Piazza della Libertà.* Among Spoleto's charms are atmospheric palace-lined streets—*Via dell' Arringo,* a kind of long-distance stairway; *Vicolo della Basilica,* in an ancient quarter; *Via dei Duchi,* with traditional craft shops and leading to *Piazza del Mercato,* with an eighteenth-century fountain; and *Via di Fontesecca* for its wealth of Middle Ages houses.

Duomo (Piazza del Duomo): The cathedral is set off by a square that serves as site of the final program of each summer's festival and contains a plaque honoring the memory of festival cofounder Thomas Schippers. Its chief attribute is a superb Romanesque façade, with a mosaic fresco above the rose window, gracious portico, and well-proportioned campanile. The undistinguished Renaissance interior is redeemed by art, most especially Filippo Lippi's apse frescoes: *Annunciation, Nativity, Death of the Virgin,* and Pinturicchio's *Madonna and Child with Saints.* To be seen, too, is Lippi's tomb (he died in Spoleto) in the transept, the work of his artist son, Filippino.

Church of Sant' Eufemia (Via Saffi) is quite possibly the most atmospheric of the churches—twelfth-century Romanesque, small and severe, with its only decoration a fresco atop the apse; occasional festival performances take place here.

Church of SS. Giovanni e Paolo (Via SS. Giovanni e Paolo) is about the same age—and of the same sobriety—as Sant' Eufemia (above) but with still smashing frescoes, including one of the martyrdom in England's Canterbury Cathedral of St. Thomas à Becket, not a usual subject in Italian churches.

Church of San Domenico (Piazza San Domenico) attracts with a horizontally striped reddish tan and white brick façade. Its Gothic interior brims with sixteenth-century paintings, *Madonna and Child with Four*

Saints, most importantly. And its Cappella Montevecchio has a Baroque silver reliquary containing what is believed to be a nail of the Holy Cross.

Church of San Nicolò (Via Cecili), though desanctified, remains much visited—as a major venue for festival events. It is a massive Gothic work, still with original frescoes and a pair of cloisters, the elder of which is also taken advantage of for festival exhibitions.

Church of San Ponziano (Via delle Lettere) stuns with its Romanesque façade. It is named for Spoleto's martyred patron saint. Head for the crypt's frescoes, their colors still brilliant, with the most impressive depicting a gold-winged angel against an emerald-green background.

Basilica of San Salvatore (Via delle Lettere) is the oldest church in town: originally fourth-century, albeit with updates. Still, Roman columns from a long-disappeared temple—with original Corinthian capitals—are in themselves reason for a visit.

Pinacoteca Comunale (Palazzo Comunale, Piazza del Municipio): Spoleto's art museum is situated in an elaborate second-floor reception room of the originally thirteenth-century town hall, and if my visit is typical, you get a chance to see the unlabeled paintings only if a guard with a key to the locked room happens to be present, and lets you in. None are by celebrated artists, which is hardly to say they are not worthy, most especially those by Renaissance master Giovanni Spagna; his *Madonna con Santi* is a standout.

Museo Civico (Teatro Caio Melisso basement, Piazza del Duomo): Down you go, into subterranean depths for a mix of Roman and Middle Ages sculpture, with Roman works—fragments of columns, inscribed tablets, finely chiseled sarcophagi—the handsomest.

SETTLING IN

Dei Duchi Hotel (Viale Giacomo Matteotti 2) is an agreeably contemporary house, within walking distance of the center, containing half a hundred functional rooms, convenient restaurant, bar-lounge, and a pretty garden. *First Class.*

Gattapone Hotel (Via del Ponte) has a nice sense of style, is agreeably intimate (there are but 15 rooms with bath), with a bar-lounge, views of the valley surrounding Spoleto, and, important this, a location but five minutes' walk from the center of town. Breakfast only. *First Class.*

Albornoz Palace Hotel (Viale Matteotti) is somewhat south of the core, but full-facility, with close to a hundred okay rooms, restaurant and bar. *First Class.*

Europa Hotel (Viale Trento e Trieste 201) is modern, functional, and friendly. There are just two dozen full-facility rooms and a lobby bar-lounge. I wish, though, that location were more central; the Europa is almost adjacent to the railway station some distance north of the core of town. *Moderate.*

Manni Hotel (Piazza Collicola) is well-equipped—there are 18 rooms, bar-lounge, breakfast but no restaurant. Location is a central square not far from the landmark Teatro Romano. *Moderate.*

DAILY BREAD

Tartufo (Piazza Garibaldi 24; Phone 40-236)—neat, modern, capacious—is as good a spot as any to tuck into such Spoleto specialties as the pasta called stringozzi; lamb, chicken, or game birds lard-roasted on a spit; and any of many dishes prepared with the local truffles for which the restaurant is named. *First Class.*

Del Quarto (Via Carlo Catteo; Phone 31-108) is typically Spoletano with respect to cuisine—pastas and entrées especially, with roast kid an interesting suggestion—and serves dinner in the garden during warm weather months. *First Class.*

La Barcaccia (Piazza Fratelli Bandiera 3; Phone 21-171): The decibel count is just audible enough for you to appreciate that the crowd is enjoying itself. Antipasto is a good starter, with a roast following. *Moderate.*

Pentagramma (Via Martani; Phone 37-241): The name of the game here is pizza, as good as you'll find in town, accompanied by a glass of beer. *Moderate.*

Caffè del Teatro (Teatro Caio Melisso, Piazza del Duomo) is in the foyer of this nineteenth-century theater when it's cool, moves out onto the piazza during the festival and throughout the summer. A see-and-be-seen source of coffee, drinks, pastry, snacks. *Moderate.*

Caffè Canasta (Piazza della Libertà): If you crave ice cream while in Spoleto, this is the place for your fix. Lots of locals. *Moderate.*

Caffè Vincenzo (Corso Mazzini 89): Strategically situated for shoppers. *Moderate.*

INCIDENTAL INTELLIGENCE

If, when you arrive at the railway station, your eye catches a massive abstract metal sculpture that looks for all the world like an Alexander Calder, it is. He titled it "Teodelapio" and it went up in 1962. *Festival dei Due Mondi* (Festival of Two Worlds) is a late-June through mid-July event that takes place in two mid-nineteenth-century theaters (*Nuovo* and *Caio Melisso*) and a number of atmospheric locales around town, even including *Teatro Romano,* dating to the first century A.D. The festival issues a free printed schedule well in advance of each season; it has offices in Spoleto (c/o Teatro Caio Melisso, Piazza del Duomo) and in Rome (Via Margutta 17), through which mail bookings may be made. *Further information:* Azienda Comprensoriale di Soggiorno e Turismo, Piazza della Libertà 7, Spoleto.

31

Syracuse/Siracusa

and North to Catania

BACKGROUND BRIEFING

Even with the heroically proportioned theater that remains—and the lovely pieces in its Museo Archeologico—it is difficult to conceive of this placid provincial Sicilian port as having been one of the great colonial outposts—culturally as well as militarily—of the ancient Hellenes. But it was, indeed. Speak of the glory that was Greece, and you speak, substantially, of Syracuse.

Its situation—with a covelike natural harbor fronting the Ionian Sea on Sicily's east coast—is what first drew settlers from Corinth as long ago as the eighth century before Christ. Ere long, democratically governed Syracuse became strong enough to establish satellite colonies. But its wealth made it attractive, eventually, to autocrats bent on taming it and all of Greek Sicily. In the fifth century B.C. a chap called Gelon had achieved the dubious distinction of the title of Tyrant, but saved his reputation by repudiating invading Carthaginians come from across the Mediterranean in what is now Tunisia.

The defeat was a major Greek victory against Punic forces. Syracuse had become a city of substance, and of power struggles, with history-book immortals like Hiero I and Hiero II, Dionysius the Elder and Dionysius the Younger battling protagonists—and the Punic enemy—the while fostering cultural development. The playwright Aeschylus, the poet Pindar, the philosopher Plato, the mathematician Archimedes all lived and worked in Syracuse, whose Golden Age—from about 406 B.C., with the rise to power of Dionysius the Elder, to 212 B.C., when it fell to the Romans—constituted a chapter of achievement in the annals of ancient Greece.

Contemporary Syracuse, with a population of about 100,000, keeps busy operating its port, at minor manufactures, and—not unimportant this last—as a magnet for visitors from abroad who come to experience its links not only with the ancients, but—and this is a Syracuse surprise—with the centuries of the last half-millennium wherein were created monumental art and architecture of the medieval, Renaissance, and Baroque eras.

ON SCENE

Lay of the Land: There are in effect, two Syracuses, old and new. *Città Vecchia* the former, occupies *Ortigia Island,* with a principal thoroughfare, *Corso Matteotti,* linking northerly *Piazza Pancali* and adjacent *Largo XXV Luglio* with central *Piazza Archimede,* centered with a Baroque fountain named Diana. *Via Roma* leads south from it, concluding at *Piazza Duomo* with cathedral and archaeological and art museums nearby. *Città Vecchia* is linked to mainland Syracuse by *Ponte Nuovo,* a bridge that leads to wide *Corso Umberto* and still another principal street, *Via Catania,* at right angles with it, and later becoming *Corso Gelone*—worth keeping in mind because it is the major shopping street and because it leads to ancient Syracuse, in the northwest corner of town, edging the extension of Corso Gelone, and called *Viale Teracati.*

MAINLAND SYRACUSE

Teatro Greco (Viale Rizzo) is the single most spectacular monument in town and, for that matter, one of the great ancient masterworks, either in the mother country or Sicily. The wonder of this vast semicircular shaped theater—its original seating capacity when it was built in the fifth century B.C. was 30,000—is that it remains so intact (it still is used for summer performances), with excellent acoustics.

Grotta dei Cordari (Viale Rizzo) is an immense lichen-surfaced grotto—large enough for a football game—that has traditionally been headquarters to the ropemakers of Syracuse; chances are you'll see some of them at work when you pass through.

Orecchio di Dionisio (Viale Rizzo) is so named because its natural entrance is in the shape of a giant ear, in this case that of the ancient tyrant of Syracuse, Dionysius. The interior is, to understate, capacious—some 200 feet long, some 60 feet high, with a capacity for the production of echoes that just about every visitor tests out.

Anfiteatro Romano (Largo Anfiteatro) is considerably younger, considerably smaller, and in considerably less good shape than Teatro Greco (above). It was built between the second and fourth centuries A.D. Still, you get an idea of its originally elliptical design, and you perceive, as well, that public entertainments in the Sicilian provinces of the Roman Empire were a good deal smaller in scale than at the Roman Colosseum.

San Giovanni complex (Via San Giovanni) embraces the Church of San Giovanni Evangelista, a beautiful near-ruin of a Byzantine church, through whose multiarched cloister you proceed to what remains of a maze of catacombs—watch for frescoes on the walls here and there, and the crypt of San Marziano, named for the martyred first bishop of Syracuse.

Church of Santa Lucia (Piazza Santa Lucia, not to be confused with the Church of Santa Lucia alla Badia, in Città Vecchia, and below recommended): The church was originally early—very early—Christian, built on the presumed site of the fourth-century martyrdom of St. Lucy. It is a mixed bag, architecturally, with its prime lures the Caravaggio painting (in the apse) depicting the saint's burial and the masterful eight-sided chapel with a niche originally containing Lucy's remains.

CITTÀ VECCHIA

Museo Regionale di Palazzo Bellomo (Via Capodieci): Syracuse's art museum is so often missed by visitors (locals, including hotel concierges who should know better, are not always cognizant of it) that I open this section with it. Setting is a stone-walled two-story Gothic palace out of the fifteenth century that is one of the most beautiful such in Sicily. You pass through an elegantly arched portal into a dazzler of a courtyard, ascending to the series of galleries on the second floor by means of a stone stairway, a Bellomo fan before you've seen a single exhibit. Antonello da Messina's celebrated *Annunciation,* painted for a Syracuse church in 1474 and allowed to deteriorate over the centuries, is the best-known painting at the Bellomo. But there are memorable objects at every turn, with the range extraordinary: Renaissance pottery and priests' vestments in cloth-of-gold, Baroque busts and altar triptychs, models of eighteenth-century ships and marble sarcophagi, Flemish missals and plaques of inlaid precious stones, sculpted Madonnas and paintings from Syracuse churches. Special.

Museo Archeologico Nazionale (Piazza Duomo): Behind a traditional neoclassic façade is a smartly updated series of galleries containing superb souvenirs of Greek Sicily, with some post-Greek exhibits as a bonus. Single most memorable object is a headless, one-armed, and ravishingly beautiful Venus. Pottery—painted vases and kraters with scenes of mythology as well as of domestic life—is first rank. So are sculptures, be they of lions or ladies.

Duomo (Piazza Duomo): Of the Italian Baroque cathedrals that I know, the façades only of those in Lecce (chapter 16) and Urbino (chapter 36) are in a league with Syracuse's, with its two levels of colonnades, each exuberantly flanked by sculpted saints. And the interior is hardly anticlimactic: a presumed Antonello da Messina painting of San Zosimo, an altarpiece with more than a dozen luminous panels of Christ and selected saints, and—among much more—an abundance of frescoes and carved marble.

Church of Santa Lucia alla Badia (Via Santa Lucia, fronting Piazza Duomo) is at its best from without. The façade is at least as joyously Baroque as that of the Duomo. It is narrow and vertically elongated, with a wrought-iron balcony above the portal.

Church of the Collegio (Via Collegio) is handsomely massive and Baroque, if much less elaborate in its decorations than either the Duomo or Santa Lucia della Badia. Within, quiet pastel walls are a foil for a brilliant high altar.

Basilica of San Martino (Via Capodieci) is small but exquisite with sixth-century origins, a somber Gothic façade, and a wood-ceilinged interior that abounds in art, with a gilt-framed altarpiece of the Virgin surrounded by Saints Martin and Lucy, the choicest.

A day in Catania, Sicily's No. 2 city and 35 miles up the coast from Syracuse, can be a day well spent. Start in the core, at fountain-centered Piazza del Duomo, edged by palazzi, with the elaborately Baroque *Duomo*—its interior highlighted by the art-filled Cappella di Sant' Agata, with the tomb of opera composer Vincenzo Bellini its centerpiece. Allow time in *Museo Civico* (Via Auteri) whose quarters, in a venerable castle, exhibit a mix of paintings (none by artists whose names are household words, but many lovely), antique Italian furniture, and an impressive collection of Greek and Roman sculpture. Then relax over lunch at either *Ristorante Pagano* (Via Roberto 37; Phone 53-045, *Moderate*) or in the dining room of the *Jolly Hotel;* neither is far from *Via Etnea,* Catania's main street, lined with shops and caffès. (And if you're an opera buff, ascertain in advance if there will be a performance at sumptuous *Teatro Bellini*—an all-Italy ranker—in which case plan to overnight at the full-facility, 160-room *Jolly Hotel* (Piazza Trento, *First Class*).

SETTLING IN

Jolly Hotel (Corso Gelone 45) is among the smaller Jollys; there are just 100 rooms, all relatively recently refurbished, along with public spaces of the hotel. Location is central—heart of the shopping district, as convenient to Città Vecchia as the classical ruins. There is a nice warm feeling here, partly because it's relatively small, partly because of a congenial staff. The restaurant is worthy of comment in a later paragraph. *First Class.*

Motelagip (Viale Teracati 30) is fully equipped, with 76 rooms, restaurant, bar-lounge, and a location adjacent to the archaeological zone, albeit a fair distance away from the center of town or Città Vecchia. *First Class.*

Panorama Hotel (Via Necropoli Grotticelle 33) is still another modern house, with just over 50 rooms; breakfast service but no restaurant—and a location near the ruins, but not close to the core or the old town. *Moderate.*

DAILY BREAD

Darsena da Ianuzzo (Riva Garibaldi 6; Phone 66-104): The area of Città Vecchia, through which passes the canal that divides the old city from the new, is atmospheric, and the ideal setting for a meal. Darsena da Ianuzzo is good at fish and seafood as entrées. *First Class.*

Jolly Hotel Ristorante (Corso Gelone 43; phone 64-744) has the virtues of central location (perfect lunch stop if you're shopping), low table count (it's intimate), and exceptional fare. Open with tortellini in brodo, at once a soup and a pasta (the Jolly's pastas are among the best I've had in Sicily), continue with grilled fresh fish of the day or a veal specialty, ending with one of the excellent pastries or the very good ice cream. Well-selected wines. *First Class.*

Minerva (Piazza Duomo; Phone 66-532): You've spent a morning in the cathedral and Museo Archeologico and you're hungry. The Minerva, next door to the museum and opposite the Duomo, is indicated for a competent lunch embracing, say, antipasto or a pasta, the day's special entrée, with house wine. *First Class.*

Caffè Archimede (Piazza Archimede): I can't come up with a prettier spot in Syracuse for coffee than fountain-centered Piazza Archimede, flanked by palazzi. *Moderate.*

Caffè Trinacria (Corso Gelone 67): Just the place to pause after, say, a bout of shopping in nearby stores or boutiques of neighboring Via Ciane. *Moderate.*

INCIDENTAL INTELLIGENCE

The nearest airport is at Catania (see above) with flights to a number of domestic points. *Further information:* Azienda Autonoma di Turismo, Via San Sebastiano 43, Syracuse; Ente Provinciale per il Turismo, Largo Paisiello 5, Catania. (Note that two other chapters of this book deal with Sicily: chapter 24 [Palermo: And Sicily's Great Greek Ruins, including Agrigento, Segesta, and Selinunte, as well as Piazza Armerina] and chapter 32 [Taormina: Mt. Etna, Messina, and Regio Calabria].)

32

Taormina

Mt. Etna, Messina, and Reggio Calabria

BACKGROUND BRIEFING

Talk about pedigree: How many resort towns do you know with a population of, say, 10,000, that have been luring visitors of consequence for two dozen centuries? And are, to understate, still going strong?

There is believed to have been a Taormina eight centuries before the Christian era. But even if you discount the original settlement, Carthaginian colonists, come from across the southern shore of the Mediterranean in the fourth century B.C., are known to have reestablished this ravishingly situated community on Monte Tauro—Etna, Europe's highest volcanic peak, backs it; Sicilian east coast beaches are way below—in the fourth century B.C.

Greeks, in the course of developing their Magna Grecia empire, followed, leaving what must be the most sublimely located of amphitheaters and ruins of their temples. Succeeding Romans, no mean builders themselves, have left bits and pieces of their handiwork. Arabs took over in the tenth century, Normans in the eleventh, and Taormina knew wealth through the Middle Ages into the Renaissance, after which decline set in, to be reversed centuries later with the onset of modern tourism. Today's Taormina—the name derives from the Greek *Tauromenion* and the later Latin *Tauromenium*—bases its economy exclusively on visitors from harsh climes—northern Europeans (with Germans leading) most particularly. Americans have been going in numbers since after World War II. But sprinklings of many European groups are present, with not a few Italians down from what Sicilians call the Continente, or mainland, to see if reports of ethereal beauty have been exaggerated. They have not.

ON SCENE

Lay of the Land: Key word is precipitous. What has to be the granddaddy of hairpin-curve roads, *Via Pirandello* winds its way up the slopes of *Monte Tauro,* to the plateau whereon lies a delightfully walkable town that is a kind of east–west oblong, cut through by shop-caffè-and-restaurant-lined *Corso Umberto,* a trio of virtually contiguous squares—*Piazza San Antonio, Piazza del Carmine,* and *Piazza del Duomo* at its western end, with *Piazza Vittorio Emanuele Badia*—leading to *Teatro Greco*—at its eastern extremity. *Giardino Pubblico,* a jewel of a park, is gained by *Via Bagnoli Croce,* going south from Corso Umberto. *Lido Mazzaro,* edged by a clutch of hotels and the principal beach, is connected with the town by a funicular (the station is on Via Pirandello); and still other beaches-cum-hotels—*Lido Spisone* and *Lido Mazzeo*—are due north of Lido Mazzaro. Hotels and pensiones? There are nearly a hundred, and they literally dot the town and shore, with some sort of smashing view, I wager, from even the simplest of the lot.

Teatro Greco (Via Teatro Greco): If you've declared a sightseeing moratorium for the course of your Taormina respite, lift it, please, for the Greek Theater. Second-largest in Sicily (after Syracuse), it went up in the third century B.C. and was expanded a century later. Location is nothing short of sublime. By that I mean seats are positioned so that spectators look for miles along the Ionian coast with one eye, and at snowy Etna with the other.

Antiquarium (Via Teatro Greco) is nicely combined with Teatro Greco, and a repository of reminders of Classical Taormina—Roman as well as Greek—in the form of fragments, busts, and other sculpted pieces—a torso of Apollo is memorable—and still-readable stone tablets.

Duomo (Piazza del Duomo): You expect a small cathedral in a small town. The surprise of Taormina's is the charm of its compressed thirteenth-century proportions, with a crenelated roof, later Renaissance portal, choice paintings and sculpture within.

Palazzo Corvaia (Piazza Vittorio Emanuele Badia) is, not unlike the Duomo, distinguished by a crenelated façade. Its moment of glory was in 1410, when the Sicilian parliament sat within its walls. Have a look at the legislators' hall, not missing the handsome courtyard. Then pop into next-door *Church of Santa Caterina,* fronting Largo Santa Caterina, and an attractive remembrance of the Renaissance.

Mount Etna (15 miles southwest of Taormina) is, at 10,958 feet, Europe's highest active volcano. It makes an adventuresome day's excurion. Even its vegetation zones are interesting: oranges, olives, and wine grapes grow in the lower reaches; the next zone is woodsier; and after about 9000 feet you're in a lunar landscape, with massive drifts of lava all about. A cable car takes the curious to an observatory near the immense crater, which is gained by foot. Go all the way, though; a look into the bowels of Etna is not soon forgotten.

Messina and Reggio Calabria: If your arrival in or departure from Sicily is via surface, you go through Messina—the island's northernmost city, on the strait that takes its name—a ferryboat ride away from Reggio Calabria on the mainland, just opposite.

Though ancient, *Messina* was leveled by a 1908 earthquake, and intelligently rebuilt so as to be as earthquake-proof as possible, with houses no higher than 36 feet. Concentrate on three destinations. First and foremost is *Museo Nazionale* (Piazza Unità d'Italia), whose pinacoteca excites with some splendid paintings, including Antonello da Messina's altarpiece, *San Gregorio,* a pair of Caravaggios, with the *Resurrection of Lazarus* the most celebrated. Its other sections brim with treasures, too, the works from destroyed Messina churches, Roman sarcophagi, Sicilian jewelry, ceramics and furniture, prints and coins. Move along, then, to the *Duomo* (Piazza del Duomo), pausing on the square to admire an exuberantly sculpted late Renaissance fountain and the cathedral's campanile, of this century but in the style of the Middle Ages, with what is said to be the biggest mechanical clock in the world; it's fun to watch its figures chime the time. The interior can be anticlimactic, despite great size, but have a look at the Treasury. Stop No. 3: *Church of Annunziata dei Catalani* (Piazza dei Catalani), Romanesque, with an unusual dome setting off the blind arches of its exceptionally wide apse. Extraordinary vaulting graces the interior. Consider lunching at *Ristorante Pippo Nunnari* (Via Ugo Bassi 157; Phone 293-8584; *First Class*). Should an overnight stay be indicated, be assured that you'll be comfortable at the full-facility, 100-room *Jolly Hotel* (Corso Garibaldi 126; *First Class*).

Reggio Calabria, capital and metropolis of the mainland *Regione* of Calabria (there's another Reggio in Emilia-Romagna), just across the Strait of Messina from Messina, was destroyed by the same 1908 earthquake, and again like Messina, was rebuilt, grid-style, with obligatory low-slung buildings, so as to withstand any future earthquake damage. It is agreeable to stroll its seafront promenade, *Lungomare Matteotti,* but if time is of the essence, beeline for *Museo Nazionale* (Piazza de Nava) where the hottest items have been on display only since their discovery in the waters of the Ionian Sea near Riace, as recently as 1980. They're a pair of larger-than-life figures already celebrated as The Bronzes of Riace, which were Greek-created in the fifth century B.C. In mint condition and brilliantly sculpted, these bearded nudes are believed to represent gods, as yet specifically undetermined. There is, of course, plenty more in the museum, including an enormous cache of Greek sculpture, pottery, mosaics, and glass; and a pinacoteca of substance, with Luca Giordano and Antonello da Messina among painters represented. If you're staying the night, consider the *Miramare Hotel* (Via Fata Morgana 1), full-facility, overlooking Lungomare Matteotti, and *First Class*. *Ristorante Conti* (Via Giulia 2; Phone 29-043, and near the Miramare) is a good bet for a *First Class*–category seafood lunch.

SETTLING IN

San Domenico Palace Hotel (Piazza San Domenico) has nothing if not advanced age; it went up in 1430 as a monastery of the order founded by the saint whose name it took—and still takes, five and a half centuries later, as one of all Italy's legendary hotels. The 101 rooms—surprisingly capacious when one learns that most were originally monks' cells—are no longer identified by the names of saints, as was the case during my first visit a couple of decades back. Alas, they are prosaically numbered, but no less handsome, with superb baths and antique accents. Indeed, antiques dot the hotel—in wide corridors, inviting lobbies, cocktail lounge, and restaurant that moves to a scenic terrace in warm weather. An oversize swimming pool edges a luxuriant garden. And there are a pair of cloisters, which perhaps more than any other aspect of the San Domenico evoke its long history. Special. *Luxury.*

Jolly Diodoro Hotel (Via Bagnoli Croce 75) stuns, first off, with its magnificent setting, atop its own cliff, with a superbly situated swimming pool and a flowering terrace just below. Views from the charming traditional-style rooms—100 all told—are either of the Ionian coast, of Etna, or—if you're really lucky on the accommodations you draw—of both. The cocktail lounge is at one and the same time big and cozy. The restaurant is picture-windowed; I detail its virtues in a later paragraph. And location is ideal; you're a short walk from the core of town. Bravo, Jolly! *First Class.*

Bristol Park Hotel (Via Bagnoli Croce 92) has the advantages of a central location, half a hundred fully equipped rooms, reliable restaurant, bar-lounge, pool—and super views. *First Class.*

Excelsior Palace Hotel (Via Toselli 8): You are convinced you're entering a Moorish, rather than an Italian, palazzo, upon approaching the Excelsior. But interiors are relatively recently restyled in trendy, small-patterned traditional motifs. There are not quite 90 agreeable rooms, and snappy public spaces including restaurant, bar-lounge, and pool, with striking vista. *First Class.*

Timeo Hotel (Via Teatro Greco 69), a near neighbor of the Greek Theater (above), is gracious and aged—the owning family has run it for a century—albeit updated. The half a hundred rooms all have terraces, the broad corridors are quite as elegant as the restaurant and cocktail bar, and there's a verdant and panoramic terrace-cum-tables. *First Class.*

Monte Tauro Hotel (Via Madonna delle Grazie) typifies the contemporary in Taormina: an ultra-mod, poured-concrete structure climbing a mountain, with eight floors of just under 70 small terraced rooms (their baths have showers but no tubs) beneath the lobby. Strategically situated pool-sundeck, restaurant, bar. *Moderate.*

Villa Paradiso Hotel (Via Roma 2) is a looker—33 traditional-style rooms with bath, in excellent taste—and equally pleasant public rooms, including a restaurant affording fine vistas and a bar. *Moderate.*

Mazzaro Sea Palace Hotel (Mazzaro) is just the ticket for the warm-weather visitor (season is April–October) who's a beach buff. It's directly on the sands, in Mazzaro, a swift cable-car ride from town. You swim in a calm crescent of a bay or in the adjacent pool. The hotel is smart Italian Modern with spiffy terraced rooms and suites, a likewise well-situated restaurant (which moves poolside on warm evenings), grill for casual lunchtime buffets, kicky bar-lounge-disco. Member, Leading Hotels of the World. *Luxury.*

Ipanema Hotel (Mazzaro) is a short stroll inland from the beach but nicely elevated so that front rooms afford sea views. Restaurant, bar. Good value, this. *Moderate.*

Capotaormina Hotel (Capotaormina) is, to capsulize in a word: dramatic. Clean-lined and half-moon-shaped, it straddles—in lonely grandeur—the rocky summit of Cape Taormina, a few miles south of town. You have to want to utterly relax in a completely self-contained resort to enjoy this hotel. Public spaces are picture-windowed, restaurant and bar-lounge among them. There are 200-plus rooms with terraces and smashing views. Two elevators lead to the beach, which is joined to the saltwater pool and adjacent grill-caffè by an ingenious carved-through-rock tunnel. *First Class.*

DAILY BREAD

Giova Rosy Senior (Corso Umberto 38; Phone 24-411): The unusual name is a come-on, but Giova Rosy—white-walled, nicely appointed, and with a patio—does not disappoint. Pastas—seafood-accented but with traditional sauces as well—are super, ditto fresh fish, or, if you're in the mood, expertly prepared omelets. Congenial. *First Class.*

La Griglia (Corso Umberto 54; Phone 23-980): Book a table in the pretty garden out back. Commence with seafood-accented antipasto with grilled fish of the day as your entrée. Nice desserts. Friendly staff. *First Class.*

Jolly Diodoro Hotel Ristorante (Via Bagnoli Croce 75; Phone 23-312) is high, wide, handsome, and seaview, with a cosmopolitan decibel count, the accents representing just about all major western languages. Special treat is an antipasto buffet that seems a mile long and is as tasty as it looks. Pasta is exceptional—the fettuccine al limone, for example. And so are meat and fish entrées. Interesting wines. *First Class.*

Luraleo (Via Bagnoli Croce 32; Phone 24-279) is just the ticket for a cozy lunch or dinner; it's smallish and smiling, with fish of the day a good bet, preceded by a nicely sauced pasta. *Moderate.*

Chez Angelo (Corso Umberto 38; Phone 240-411): Open with a pasta, the typically Sicilian maccheroni con gamberi (shrimps) or con le sarde (sardines) perhaps, continuing with a roast or fish, ending with cannoli, Sicily's most typical sweet. *Moderate.*

Caffè Wunderbar (Corso Umberto 65) offers *wunderbar* views, coffee, drinks, and pastries, not to mention a chance to size up the day's new arrivals in town. *Moderate.*

Il Pescatore (Mazzaro; Phone 23-460) is, not surprisingly, given its beach location, for seafood—risotto alla pescatora to start, the day's fish with a marinara sauce—washed down with a local Etna white wine. *First Class.*

SHOPPER'S TAORMINA

It's fun to stroll pedestrians-only Corso Umberto, with a wealth of shops for *women's and men's clothing, jewelry,* and *Sicilian handicrafts.*

INCIDENTAL INTELLIGENCE

The regional airport is at Catania (chapter 31), which it links to Italian mainland and other European cities. *Further information:* Azienda Autonoma di Soggiorno e Turismo, Piazza Santa Caterina, Taormina; Via Calabria 301, Messina; Via Demetrio Tripepi, Reggio Calabria. (Note that two other chapters of this book deal with Sicily: chapter 24 [Palermo: And Sicily's Great Greek Ruins, including Agrigento, Segesta, and Selinunte, as well as Piazza Armerina] and chapter 31 [Syracuse/Siracusa: And North to Catania].)

33

Taranto

Ancient Ionian Seaport

BACKGROUND BRIEFING

No, it's not an Italian counterpart of Canada's premier city—with "a's" substituted for the "o's." Whereas the name of Toronto, Ontario, derives from an Indian word meaning "meeting place," Apulia's Ionian Sea port of Taranto was originally named *Taras* by settlers who came from Greece, changed later to *Tarantum* by the Romans, evolving eventually into the Italian Taranto, and pronounced, incidentally, *TAH-ran-tow.*

The Italian Republic's principal harbor city on the Ionian, Taranto is at once very old, very handsome—its waterfront promenade is one of the most strikingly situated in a country where seaside boulevards are not uncommon—and a substantial role-player in the Italian economy, given its status as an industrial center (steel, shipyards) and port of consequence with one of the top two Italian naval bases.

It was Spartans from Greece who first appreciated the town's situation in the eighth pre-Christian century. Within a couple of years, the colony of *Taras* was one of Magna Grecia's richest. It passed, eventually, to Roman aegis, later knowing rule by Byzantines, Saracens, Normans, Swabians, Frenchmen, and eventually becoming a part of the far-flung Kingdom of Naples, with Napoleonic intervention, in advance of the unified Italy of the mid nineteenth century.

Just about everybody, it appears, has gotten into the Taranto act except the contemporary visitor, Italian as well as imported. The fact of the matter is that this agreeably animated city of a quarter-million is not only southern but southeastern—just enough away from the well-beaten path to be too often overlooked. Regrettable, this. Because Taranto likes company.

ON SCENE

Lay of the Land: The key word is "elongated." Taranto occupies a pair of bridge-linked areas on the gulf that takes its name, with the inner harbor, *Mare Piccolo*, to the north, and *Mare Grande*, actually the Gulf of Taranto, to the south. The smaller area is actually an island, *Città Vecchia*, and represents historic Taranto, with major monuments in and about *Piazza Fontana* and *Via del Duomo*. A landmark castle, *Castel Sant' Angelo*, built five centuries ago and a perfect setting for a swashbuckling movie, borders the canal that separates Città Vecchia from the newer city. The crossing is made on *Ponte Girevole*, a late-nineteenth-century revolving bridge (updated relatively recently) that opens twice a day to allow tall ships to pass.

Modern Taranto—*Città Moderna*—is edged on its southern flank by *Lungomare Vittorio Emanuele*, above a high stone embankment, with the sea below, and graced, on its northern flank, by the immaculately manicured gardens of *Giardini Pubblici*, one of Italy's prettier urban parks. *Via d' Aquino*—which changes its name to *Via di Palma*—is the principal shopping street (and site of both Coin and Standa department stores), with a clutch of smart boutiques on *Via Anfiteatro*. Leading hotels are on *Viale Virgilio*, a kind of extension of the Lungomare.

Museo Nazionale della Magna Grecia (Corso Umberto): Just as Museo Nazionale in Naples brings to life the extraordinarily advanced culture of Pompeii, so does Taranto's Museo Nazionale depict the glory that was Magna Grecia—the pre-Christian Greek settlements of southern Italy, with particular reference to the Taranto era. The Taranto museum is second only to that of Naples in the south, in and of itself reason for a Taranto visit. The bulk of what is on display was unearthed from a necropolis that lay beneath the land on which modern Taranto now stands; to date, several thousand tombs have been emptied, and as excavations for new buildings are undertaken, so new finds are made on a continuing basis.

What most visitors, myself certainly included, find most exciting is the gold jewelry. My notes are punctuated with exclamation marks over ravishingly beautiful diadems—one with exquisitely fashioned flowers and vines in enamel as well as gold, others of oak leaves and rose petals. There are rings embedded with jewels, exquisite necklaces, ceremonial earrings, bracelets that would be fashionable this very day. Sculpture is magnificent. The sixth-century B.C. Poseidon di Ugento, a life-size bronze, is understandably the museum's trademark. A winged goddess, known as Nike de Taranto, is another major work. The museum is rich, as well, in busts and ruined torsos. And the pottery: Apulian museums abound in it, but Taranto's is unsurpassed, with some of it from the later Roman era; the lot—cups, bowls, vases, and kraters—fascinatingly decorated with the women demurely draped, the gents invariably nude.

Many of the coins are in amazingly good condition. The terra-cotta figures—5000 all told—are of gods and goddesses, but also of ordinary people in ordinary domestic situations. Legends are in Italian only, but they are clearly printed and you'll find yourself understanding a good bit. (*A final note:* Should you base your Taranto visit around an inspection of the museum, keep in mind that this is an Italian government-operated museum, which means—unless conditions improve, hardly likely—that it closes at 2 P.M. [you had better arrive no later than 1:25], and on Mondays.)

Duomo (Via del Duomo): Unheralded, the city's cathedral comes as an agreeable surprise. Behind a symmetrical Baroque façade—statues of four Apostles occupy as many niches—is a stunning Romanesque interior, with much of the floor still surfaced with original mosaic tiles and a marble-columned nave, the lot framed by a knockout of a late Baroque painted-wood ceiling, embedded with paintings of the Virgin and saints; and with a pair of striking chapels, their walls of inlaid marble, their ceilings frescoed.

Church of San Domenico Maggiore (a.k.a. San Pietro Imperiale, Piazza San Domenico) is originally Romanesque—dating to the eleventh century—but had a Gothic rebuild a couple of hundred years thereafter, only to be restyled once again, in the Baroque era, with a domed transept and four side altars. Given this mix, one might expect little more than an aesthetic hodgepodge. But each of San Domenico's styles is tasteful, and so is the meld.

Concattedrale (at the eastern terminus of Via Dante Alighieri): Contemporary ecclesiastical architecture, with very few exceptions, ranks behind contemporary civil architecture, certainly in my view. The Italian architect Gio Ponti, esteemed for much of his work, designed the Concattedrale, or cocathedral, in the early 1970s. It is, to be sure, a bold statement, stark white, angular, and massive, with a broad horizontal tower, as wide as the building, its principal distinguishing characteristic. Still, my preference is for the Duomo, downtown.

Massafra and Mottola: *Massafra* is an oddball hill town ten miles north of Taranto. I say oddball because in addition to an attractive though conventional cathedral, and an even more impressive medieval castle on high, it is the site of a long-ago troglodyte community, whose remnants are a score-plus early Christian cave-churches, the best preserved of which remain sumptuously frescoed, with that of San Marco the freshest appearing; Candelora and San Leonardo are also worthy of inspection. *Mottola* (a dozen miles northwest of Taranto) lures with its Duomo, built in the thirteenth century, with a chunky campanile added a hundred years later, and still other additions from the Renaissance, including an art-filled, single-nave interior.

SETTLING IN

Delfino Hotel (Viale Virgilio 66) welcomes by means of a low-key lobby—very contemporary in beige and black—with a similar décor scheme continued in nearly 200 nicely equipped rooms, each with a balcony. (You want, of course, to aim for those that are seaview.) Public spaces are high ceilinged and generous, with bar-lounge and open-to-the-sea restaurant (about which more later), both attractive. *First Class.*

Palace Hotel (Viale Virgilio 10) is tastefully modern, the lobby-lounge in green, rust, and dark woods, the half a hundred bedrooms in paler tones, each with an enclosed, windowed balcony. Baths have showers rather than tubs (more hygienic, says the management, and I agree). Restaurant, bar-lounge, caffè. Very pleasant, indeed. *First Class.*

Mar Grande Park Hotel (Viale Virgilio 90) has 90-plus well-equipped rooms (seaview ones are the most sought after), restaurant and bar, and an outdoor pool (with tables for drinks) which is mighty appealing in summer. *First Class.*

Plaza Hotel (Via d'Aquino 46) is heart of the shopping district, modern and sprightly, with 90 of its 110 rooms bath-equipped. Bar-lounge, breakfast only. *Moderate.*

Miramare Hotel (Via Roma 4) is simple, to be sure, but well located, facing the sea, a hop and a skip from Ponte Girevole, linking new and old towns, with Museo Nazionale della Magna Grecia a near neighbor. Most of the 57 rooms are bath- or shower-equipped. Breakfast only. *Moderate.*

DAILY BREAD

Al Gambero (Vico del Ponte 4; Phone 411-190) could not be more scenically positioned, given its specialty: seafood. By that I mean it overlooks both the sea and the city's colorful (albeit ramshackle) fisherman's community. Its owners need only hop over to the returning boats, end of each day, to make their choices. You want, of course, to have a maritime-accented meal here—spaghetti or risotto al gambero (with shrimp sauce) or spaghetti frutti di mare (with mixed seafood sauce) to commence, with the day's fish simply grilled, or perhaps shrimps allo spiedo—roasted on a spit. There's a big meat selection, too, in this, Taranto's premier restaurant. *First Class.*

Delfino Hotel Ristorante (Viale Virgilio 66; Phone 3205): The seafood has to come a greater distance here than to Al Gambero (above), but it's mighty tasty withal. The chef shows a deft hand with a variety of deliciously sauced pastas. And his veal piccata is recommended. Good sweets. Big selection of wines. *First Class.*

Hiding (Piazza Ebalia 7) isn't hiding at all; location is conveniently midway between Viale Virgilio hotels and the business quarter. Ambience is pleasant; likewise staff and fare, seafood-accented. *Moderate.*

INCIDENTAL INTELLIGENCE

Further information: Ente Provinciale per il Turismo, Corso Umberto 113, Taranto.

34

Trieste

with a Foray North to Udine

BACKGROUND BRIEFING

The beauty part of Trieste's checkered past is that it has carried through to Trieste's checkered present. This most northerly of Italy's port cities—with its setting the most uncommonly felicitous of any on Italy's coasts, save, of course, that of Naples—remains a cosmopolitan mix, ethnic as well as linguistic, which surely could not be otherwise, given its meeting-point situation where three nations and the Adriatic converge.

Today's visitor reaps the benefits, with respect to languages—the Triestini are Italy's most skilled linguists, as adept at English and German as Serbo-Croat and, of course, the Italian that is their national tongue. As to cuisines, Austria's Wiener schnitzel and Hungarian goulash are quite as commonplace as risotto alla Milanese or fegato alla Veneziana. Places of worship are far more disparate than is customary in a medium-sized Italian city (the population is a quarter million)—Roman Catholic in abundance, to be sure, but Serbian as well as Greek Orthodox, Jewish as well as Protestant. And still visitable monuments reflect Trieste's connections, over the centuries, with ancient Rome through the Hapsburgs, beyond to the contemporary Italian Republic.

If the visitor traffic is relatively minimal today—Trieste has nothing like the pulling power of, say, Venice, less than a hundred miles down the coast—it was not always thus. It was, indeed, Romans who gave the city its name—Tergesta—when they created a colony two centuries before Christ. The early Middle Ages saw it change hands not infrequently, with forces of Charlemagne its rulers in the eighth century, its own people in charge—governing a *comune*—in the twelfth, and Venice a subsequent—and serious—rival until the late fourteenth century.

That was when Austria took over, allowing Trieste varying degrees of autonomy, over an extraordinarily sustained period, all the way through to World War I, in the present century. By that time Trieste had grown prosperous as the Austro-Hungarian Empire's solitary port, and a crossroads of Italian, Germanic, and Slav peoples, with substantial Greek, Armenian, Hungarian, and Jewish communities as well.

And all this while the city stubbornly retained allegiance to Italy's language and culture, to the point where in the mid nineteenth century it became a center of popular support for Irredentism, the nationalist movement whose goal was annexation to Italy of border areas Austrian-governed, but with Italian ethnic majorities.

Came 1919 and the Irredentists won out: Trieste became a part of Italy. At the conclusion of World War II, though, Yugoslavia wanted it, but the Western powers were opposed. And so Trieste and adjacent coastal zones, in 1947, became an oddball Free Territory, under United Nations Security Council auspices, until, in 1954, the city officially joined Italy, while the out-of-town provincial area went to what was then Yugoslavia.

No longer the rich port or shipbuilding center it had once been, and with tourism a relatively minimal income producer, today's Trieste is placing its economic bets on science and technology, as the co-site (along with India's New Delhi) of an important new center for genetic engineering sponsored by the United Nations with the support of the Italian Government, which itself is planning other projects designed to effect a Triestine Renaissance.

ON SCENE

Lay of the Land: Arrive by plane and by means of the airport bus ride along the Adriatic into town—the most exciting scene of any such that I know in Italy, and free at that—and you perceive the splendid setting of Trieste, climbing hills that enclose the beach-fringed *Gulf of Trieste,* which culminates, in town, as a vast port, flanked center to east by *Piazzale Duca degli Abruzzi* and a waterfront boulevard with half a dozen successive names, each of them starting with the key word, "Riva," and collectively *Le Rive,* punctuated by two principal landmarks. First is a body of water heading inland, known simply as *Il Canale,* lined by substantial neoclassic buildings with the much-photographed domed and colonnaded *Church of Sant' Antonio Taumaturgo*—which could have been designed by Palladio—at its terminus, and—a touch of the territory to the East—the *Serbian Orthodox Church of San Spiridone* to its right. Farther along, fronting Le Rive, is the city's largest and most spectacular square, *Piazza Unità d'Italia*—just plain *Piazza Unità* to locals—an essentially nineteenth-century complex whose principal landmark is a mock Renaissance *Municipio,* or Town Hall, with a tower whose clock's hours are sounded by a pair of mechanical statues, Mikeze and Jakeze. Piazza Unità leads north and west into smaller *Piazza della Borsa*—named for the old stock exchange, or *Borsa Vecchia*, an elegant neoclassic palazzo—and beyond to smart *Corso Italia*—Upim and Coin department stores are among its many shops—which terminates at busy *Piazza Goldoni*, just after passing the worth-strolling pedestrians-only *Via San Lazzaro*. A wide commercial thoroughfare, *Via Carducci*, leads southwest from Piazza Goldoni to the railway station near the harbor. Oldest parts of the city—Roman and medieval/Renaissance—lie north of the center, with *Città Vecchia*, or Old City, embracing a colorful clutch of alleylike streets—*Dei Colombi, Della Bora, Donota*, in and about *Piazza dei Trionfi*, and the cathedral complex flanking *Via Capitolina*.

Castello-Duomo complex (Via Capitolina): *Il Castello* was a contribution of both medieval Venetians and Hapsburgs—and looks that way to this day, every brick and stone of it—with formidably high walls and small windows (better for protective purposes than large ones), capacious courtyards, leftover cannons and cannonballs, and an ever-so-evocative museum in a suite of furnished-in-period state rooms: *Sala dei Capitani* (ceiling frescoed, with a fabulous fireplace); *Sala di Caprin*, with busts of doges among other Venetian mementoes; *Cappella di San Giorgio*, with a School of Carpaccio altarpiece; and passageways put to good use with displays of swords and silver, guns and halberds.

The *Duomo* (a.k.a. San Giusto) has the square, boxy look of Gothic churches in this *Regione* of Italy (awkwardly named Friuli-Venezia Giulia), and it's smaller than you might anticipate, though with a substantial chunky campanile and an enormous—and enormously beautiful—rose window; a portal flanked by sculpted heads of a Roman tombstone, vertically divided into halves for the purpose; and an interior brimming with treasures: dramatically arched nave, mosaic-surfaced apse, and San Giusto (St. Justus)—the city's patron—delineated on silk, in the Treasury.

Museo di Storia ed Arte (Via Cattedrale) is more *storia* (history) than *arte*, or at least than paintings, of which there are a few choice works, including a triptych of St. Claire by Paolo Veneziano and some Tiepolo drawings. There is good Italian porcelain, and a fair amount of Roman artifacts—many of them handsome—both indoors and dotted about the garden.

Teatro Romano (Via del Teatro Romano): It is difficult to believe that this big and beautiful semicircle of a theater—built nineteen centuries ago by the Romans—remained buried until as recently as 1938. There has been a good deal of reconstruction (the theater is put to contemporary use) but enough remains of the original to evoke Roman Trieste.

Museo Revotella (Piazza Venezia) is, truth to tell, more visitworthy because of its setting—an excessively elaborate mid-nineteenth-century palazzo that's a mix of stained glass ceilings, intricately carved, dark-wood stairways, fussily plastered ceilings, and designed-for-the-premises chandeliers—than for the paintings, a mostly nineteenth-century Italian collection willed to the municipality by the rich baron who collected them. Very few were visible in the course of my inspection; more may be, when you go. In all events, the musty house is a nostalgia trip of consequence.

Acquario (Riva Nazario Sauro): You are bound to pass by the enormous sign above this waterfront institution, which shares quarters with the immense fish market, and if you are an aquarium nut, as I confess to being, of course you want to have a look around: the fish are imported as well as domestic. And you are bound to enjoy the reactions of fellow visitors, mostly youngsters in classroom groups.

Castello di Miramare (Viale Miramare, four miles north of town) is an absolute requisite for anyone who has visited Mexico City's Chapultepec Palace and become fascinated with the tragedy of the Hapsburg archduke who was Emperor of Mexico (living in Chapultepec) for three brief mid-nineteenth-century years—before being executed. (The only other association with this couple that I know of in Italy—remote though it is—is Ristorante Ranieri in Rome [chapter 2], which was founded by the chef who worked for Maximilian and his widow, Carlotta, after Carlotta became mentally ill, upon her return to Europe.) It was in Miramare where Emperor Franz Josef's younger brother was offered the Mexican crown. You are shown the bedroom where this occurred and other rooms of a house that has all of the lugubrious heavy-handedness of the period, but virtually none of its charm. But there's a surprise of much older paintings (Veronese, Van Dyck, Rembrandt, Cranach) in the throne room. The crenelated mock-Gothic façade is romantic, and so is the setting—a pretty seaside park. Withal, it is not difficult to understand why Carlotta was said to have been unhappy at Miramare; it's gloomy. *Son et Lumière* (Sound and Light) spectacles tell the Imperial Couple's tragic story on summer evenings.

Muggia (seven miles south of Trieste) is not very euphonious a name, but no matter: this small town—for centuries Venetian-governed—boasts a honey of a Venetian Gothic *Duomo* (Piazza Marconi), with its façade much smaller than that of Trieste's but not all that different, even to the rose window, albeit with a disproportionately large campanile out back. Wander the neighborhood, not missing adjacent *Palazzo dei Terroti* (note its Venetian Lion of San Marco) and the picture-book harbor, with a medieval castle its backdrop. Then head for nearby *Muggia Vecchia,* a hilltop hamlet with the enchanting Romanesque *Basilica of Santi Ermacore e Fortunato,* the walls of its tiny interior frescoed. Have lunch in the *Moderate*-category ristorante of the *Lido Hotel* (Phone 273-338) on Via Cesare Battisti, in Muggia proper.

Udine (pronounced *OOH-dee-nay,* 40 miles north of Trieste) might well be called the *Regione* of Friuli–Venezia Giulia's Second City (population is about 100,000), and if you see only its principal square, strongly Venetian-influenced Piazza della Libertà (Venetians were present from the fifteenth century into the eighteenth), you will have gotten an idea of what a beautiful place it must have been before World War II bombings destroyed a good bit of the core. The square's component parts are a sumptuously façaded palace-cum-loggia, *Del Comune* by name, that represents Venetian Gothic; impressive *Arco Bollani,* a sixteenth-century work by the Veneto *Regione's* great architect, Palladio (chapter 39); an exuberant central fountain; and a masterful clock tower. Towering over the square is *Il Castello,* out of the Renaissance but with its interior badly damaged during the *Regione's* disastrous 1976 earthquake. Its museums are worthwhile. They are *Arte Antica e Moderna* (with a cracking good group of Old Masters by the likes of Bronzino, Carpaccio, Caravaggio, and Giordano) and *Civico* (Roman sculpture, mosaics, and sarcophagi from the neighborhood). The *Duomo* (Piazza Duomo) is a Gothic–Baroque mix, with a smashing façade and Tiepolos of the side altars its big draws. Still more Tiepolos grace the always-locked little *Oratorio della Purità* (just opposite the Duomo, from whose sacristy you must borrow the Oratorio door key) and *Arcivescovado* (the Archbishop's Palace on Piazza Patriarcato, where you'll have to request permission to have a look). Take in, as well, *Church of San Giacomo,* a felicitous Renaissance–Baroque meld on nicely mellow, fountain-centered *Piazza Matteotti.* This is a good shopping city, as you'll perceive from a stroll along *Via Merceria* and adjacent streets. Overnight at the excellent *Astoria Hotel* (Piazza XX Settembre, in the core, *First Class* and with a corking good restaurant), keeping in mind, if you've the occasion for another meal, *Ristorante alla Buona Vita* (Via Treppo 10; Phone 21053; *First Class*), and, if you want to pause over coffee, taking in aforementioned Piazza della Libertà, *Caffè Contarena* is situated on that square.

Cividale del Friuli (10 miles north of Udine) is an ancient university town where you want to see the *Duomo* (Piazza del Duomo), its façade at once Gothic (lower portion) and Renaissance (above). It has fine paintings and a Treasury, but the special lure is adjacent *Museo Cristiano,* with two celebrated eighth-century masterworks: *Battistero di Callisto,* an exquisitely carved marble octagon, and the Ratchis Altar, with stone-sculpted interpretations of the *Adoration of the Magi, Ascension,* and *Visitation. Museo Archeologico,* also on Piazza del Duomo, occupies an eighteenth-century mansion and exhibits illuminated manuscripts and other medieval treasures, with its ace-in-the-hole a seventeenth-century altarpiece by Jacopo Palma the Younger. Don't leave town without seeing the Renaissance frescoes—or at least what remains of them—covering the otherwise plain façade, dwarfed by a giant campanile, of *Church of SS. Pietro e Biagio* (Borgo Brossana). *Ristorante alla Frasca* (Via de Rubeis 10; Phone 731-270) is a good *Moderate*-category lunch stop.

SETTLING IN

Duchi d'Aosta Hotel (Via dell' Orologio 2) has been carefully, skillfully—yes, tenderly—maintained as what might well be the most authentic of the smaller period-piece hotels in urban Italy. The mock-Renaissance façade is not unlike those of other buildings on the city's showplace waterfront square. Lobby and lounges are intimately scaled, authentically furnished. And nearly 50 rooms and suites—ask for accommodation on the Piazza side—are charming, with up-to-the-minute baths; Harry's Grill, the restaurant, warrants additional comment in a later paragraph. *Luxury.*

Jolly Hotel (Corso Cavour 7), well located on a principal thoroughfare between the railroad station and the waterfront, is a clean-lined high rise that welcomes with a high-ceilinged lobby, 177 well-equipped rooms and suites, bar-lounge with deep seats that you sink right into, and a smilingly staffed restaurant that's as agreeable at breakfast (there's a generous buffet) as at lunch and dinner. *First Class.*

Savoia Excelsior Palace Hotel (Riva del Mandracchio 4) is an oldie—public spaces are enormous—that has, in recent seasons, been stylishly refurbished with original ceiling stuccowork retained, in attractive juxtaposition with contemporary furnishings. There are 135 rooms and suites, some with seaview balconies; restaurant, bar-lounge. *First Class.*

Continental Hotel (Via San Nicolò 25) is conveniently central with little more than half a hundred functional rooms, bar-lounge, and breakfast, but no restaurant. *Moderate.*

Abbazia Hotel (Via della Geppa 20) is fairly close to the railway station and offers just over 20 neat rooms, bar-lounge, and breakfast, but no restaurant. *Moderate.*

DAILY BREAD

Suban (Via Comici 2; Phone 54-368): Up you go—in a cab or your rented car—to the hills of San Giovanni, high above the city. The drive will take twenty minutes, but it's eye-filling, and when you arrive at Suban the view of the city and the sea is fabulous. This is a big brick-and-stone-walled place, rustic in ambience, hearty of fare. The kitchen—glass-walled so that you can watch everyone's meals being prepared—specializes in meats, grilled or spit-roasted. And delicious, whether your choice is veal, liver, lamb, or beef kidneys (if you're homesick for Châteaubriand-for-two, this is the place). First courses tend to typify Trieste—sauerkraut and bean soup, called Jota Carsolina, for example, Hungarian goulash and Wiener schnitzel—both usually available. And you may have a baked potato—patate in tecia—with your entrée. That said, let me reassure you that the pasta is delicious—not necessarily always the case in this part of the world—that there's a good choice of regional wines, and that service is swift and cordial. *First Class.*

Harry's Grill (Duchi d'Aosta Hotel, Piazza Unità d'Italia; Phone 7351) is especially buzzy at lunch, when clientele is a mix of Triestini and the likes of you and me, from distant shores. Service is as old-school as the look of the place, and you order from the menu del giorno, or an à la carte that makes a point of regional dishes: pappardelle ai funghi, noodles with mushrooms to start; perhaps an order of luganica, the local sausages nicely grilled, to follow; with also locally popular polenta, cheese-topped. There's no finer wine list in town—nor more tempting sweets. *Luxury.*

Nastro Azzurro (Riva Nazario Sauro 12; Phone 775-985): The name of Nastro's game is frutta di mare: seafood. Open with antipasto di pesce misto dal carrello—with your picking all you like from the wagon wheeled to table. Continue with risotto alla marinara, concluding perhaps with fritto misto dell' Adriatico—a mixed small-fish fry—or a just-caught fish simply grilled to order. Nice waiters. *First Class.*

La Marinella (Viale Miramare 323; Phone 410-986) is indicated if you're en route to—or from—Castello Miramare (above). This place is enormous, but professionally operated so that service can be relatively prompt; antipasto misto—shrimps, mussels, sardines, octopus—is delicious, although I would skip the prepared-in-advance pasta casseroles, moving along to a platter combining grilled fresh sole and crayfish. Strudel, a popular pastry, is more Austro-Hungarian in name than execution. *First Class.*

Elefante Bianco (Riva III Novembre 3; Phone 365-784)—the first restaurant called White Elephant that I've come across in Italy—is somewhat north of the center, with heavy business traffic midday during the week. Fine fare and service. *First Class.*

Caffè degli Specchi (Piazza Unità d'Italia) typifies Old Trieste and is as much a congregating point for locals as outlanders, with tables spilling out into the huge waterfront square. Have coffee, pastry, ice cream, or the little sandwiches. *Moderate.*

Caffè Rex (Corso d'Italia 55) is indicated for a watch-the-world-go-by pause in the course of a shopping stroll along the Corso; in warm weather, take an outdoor table. *Moderate.*

SOUND OF MUSIC

Teatro Comunale Giuseppe Verdi (Piazza Verdi) is Trieste's handsome opera house, with an on-premises theater museum; concerts, too, with additional musical events at also opulent *Teatro Rossetti.*

INCIDENTAL INTELLIGENCE

If you're arriving in Trieste by air, keep in mind that taxis to town are pricey, and that the airport buses are free. *Further information:* Azienda Autonoma di Soggiorno e Turismo, Castello di San Giusto, Trieste; Palazzo Municipale, Cividale del Friuli; Corso Puccini 6, Muggia; Ente Provinciale per il Turismo, Piazza Maggio 6, Udine.

35

Turin/Torino

United Italy's First Capital

BACKGROUND BRIEFING

When you're a city that had been the seat of two prestigious kingdoms, later becoming a mercantile capital of no mean consequence (Turin is where both Fiat and Lancia cars are made), it should follow that this combination—residues of royalty coupled with economic wherewithal—would prove enticing enough to absorb the visitor.

In the case of this northwest metropolis—in the shadow of the Alps to the north, of France to the west, and at the confluence of the Po and Dora Riparia rivers—the formula is not as successful as expected. Exceeded in population only by southerly Rome and Naples and not-far-distant Milan (80 miles east), Turin—despite an extraordinary cultural pedigree, a plethora of good restaurants, and linguistic skills (many Torinese are bilingual in French)—trails behind the Big Three cities in attracting nonbusiness travelers.

It was the Romans who named Turin *Julia Augusta Taurinorum* and who created the grid plan of its core that remains to this day. Early medieval Turin had a variety of landlords, evolving—as did so many Italian city-states—into a *comune* before it was taken over in the late thirteenth century as a consequence of the tangle of Europe's fortunes of war. A Savoyard duke—Vittorio Amadeo II (the family's heads were partial to two names as well as a number)—was ceded the Kingdom of Sardinia under terms of an international treaty, to compensate his duchy for having lost the island of Sicily as a consequence of battle.

The new kingdom embraced not only the island of Sardinia (whose name it confusingly retained, albeit with its seat for the most part in Turin), but the Italian *Regione* of Piedmont (of which Turin is now capital), as well as Nice and the Savoy area of France; and, later for a time, Genoa and surrounding Liguria.

Seven kings later—the mellifluously named Carlo Emanuele III, Vittorio Amedeo III, Carlo Emanuele IV, Vittorio Emanuele I, Carlo Felice, Carlo Alberto, and finally, in 1861, under Vittorio Emanuele II—the Kingdom of Sardinia, having earlier transferred Nice and Savoy back to France, became the Kingdom of Italy, still with a scion of the House of Savoy on the throne.

Alas, even though Turin had been the peninsula's principal focal point in the pan-Italian movement (the chamber in which the first parliament sat is a part of the city's Risorgimento Museum), the royal capital was moved to Florence's Pitti Palace in 1865, until it was transferred to Rome's Quirinale Palace six years later.

ON SCENE

Lay of the Land: Turin is attractive, much of it rebuilt since World War II bombing, with plane-tree-lined streets punctuated by the kind of formal square often come upon in neighboring France, and with streets of its central area—10-plus miles in length—arcaded. Vertically, it is low slung, church spires of course excepted, along with its trademark structure: a mid-nineteenth-century building that had been both synagogue and museum—called *Mole Antonelliana*—with its pinnacle towering above an abnormally bulbous dome. *Via Roma*—small and insignificant on city maps—is the principal shopping street, arcaded and lined by the heavy and graceless façades of Mussolini Modern structures typical of the pre-World War II period. A pair of contiguous squares, *Piazza Castello* and *Piazza Reale,* are at Via Roma's northern flank, with also-significant *Piazza San Carlo*—vast, imposing, and arcaded on two shop- and caffè-lined sides. *Stazione Porta Nuova*—the main train station—is to the south. Surrounding streets—*Via La Grange, Via XX Settembre,* and *Via Cavour* are shop-lined. The Po, more important of the city's two rivers, lies east of the core, with the other, *Dora Riparia,* to the north. Count on the need for motor transport to the two major monuments (below) that are out of town.

Palazzo Reale (Piazza Reale) was home to the Savoy kings from the time it went up in the mid seventeenth century through to the start of the mid-nineteenth-century reign of the first king of Italy, Vittorio Emanuele II. You may have a look, but by means only of guided tours in the Italian language, for which there can be very long outside queues. Italian-speaker or not, long wait or short, this is a palace you want to see; its state rooms are vastly more impressive than those of Palazzo Pitti (most of which is now an art museum) in Florence, while Rome's

Palazzo Quirinale, the ex-papal and later royal palace that is now the presidential palace, is not open to the public. Turin's Reale is Baroque at its most spectacular, starting with a splendid ceremonial staircase, and including a throne room with a royal chair canopied in red damask to match that of the walls; tapestry-lined dining room; and what are, for me, the most exquisite rooms of the palace: Gabinetto Cinese, an Italo-Chinese collaboration in scarlet, black, and gold; Gabinetto di Toletta della Regina—a veritable gilded birdcage where the queen primped and preened; and Sala del Caffè, subtly sublime with its variations on a theme of gold.

Museo Civico d'Arte Antica (Palazzo Madama, Piazza Castello) is something of a double whammy: a former royal residence (*Madama* is the singular of *Madame,* females of the House of Savoy who were in residence) that is essentially Renaissance within, albeit with the brilliant Baroque façade a masterwork by the greatest of northern eighteenth-century architects, Filippo Juvara, designer of several below-recommended Turinese destinations; and with a superlative collection of art and artifacts. Antonello da Messina's suspicious-looking *Ignoto,* or unknown gent, his plain-shaven countenance between a plain black cap and a pleated red tunic, is undisputed star of the painting collections, but there are works as well by the likes of Vivarini and Tiepolo; a wood-sculpted *Pietà* consisting of seven detached figures; a carved choir out of the Renaissance, taken in toto from a church; room after sumptuous period room, with the eighteenth-century Sala di Madama Reale hung with a painting by Rubens, the smasher of the lot.

Duomo (Via XX Settembre) has the dubious distinction of being quite the least aesthetically appealing—plain without, gloomy within—of any of the not inconsiderable number of cathedrals with which I am familiar in Italy. But it is celebrated for the contents of one of its chapels, the domed Baroque-era *Cappella della Sacra Sindone*—with the Holy Shroud, so called because one can see on it an outline of what is believed to be the body of Jesus. The cathedral is of course open daily, but the chapel with the shroud is not necessarily; inquire before you go.

Church of the Carmine (Via del Carmine) is an agreeable antidote to the almost unrelieved dullness of the cathedral (above): a joyous work of Juvara with wide nave and high ceilings embellished with superb plasterwork, half a dozen side chapels art-filled, and high altar enclosed by a glass-topped dome, allowing the sunlight to play upon its portrait of *The Ascension.*

Church of San Filippo Neri (Via Maria Vittoria): Behind a colonnaded neoclassical façade one finds an enormous—and enormously beautiful—Baroque interior that, because its dome collapsed after construction in the seventeenth century, was redesigned and rebuilt by the redoubtable Juvara in the eighteenth.

Church of San Lorenzo (Piazza Castello) is small but elaborately detailed—once you get in. To do so, pass through an even smaller structure that had been an oratory and is now this Baroque church's vestibule: the designer was the same Guarino Guarini of the Duomo's Sindone Chapel.

Churches of San Carlo and Santa Caterina (Piazza San Carlo) immediately put one in mind of Santa Maria dei Miracoli and Santa Maria in Montesanto, the opposite-each-other Baroque near-twins on Rome's Piazza del Popolo (chapter 2). Of this Turin pair, also Baroque and also compact Santa Caterina is by far the more charming. See if you agree.

Museo Egizio and Galleria Sabauda (Via Accademia delle Scienze 6): Because it has the best Egyptian collection in Italy, and because it keeps the limited hours of most Italian government-operated museums, the Egyptian Museum is often so jam-packed that it can be difficult to take in its indisputably superior exhibits. Among treasures are frescoed walls of a reconstructed tomb, jewelry and painted busts, pottery and weapons, mummies and statues (yes, there's one of King Tut), sarcophagi and sphinxes. Still, for those of us familiar with great Egyptian collections—New York's Metropolitan, London's British Museum, Cairo's Egyptian Museum are but three—Turin's Egizio may disappoint. *Galleria Sabauda,* Turin's Old Masters museum, is located in the same seventeenth-century *palazzo* as the Egizio. (You climb a long, steep stairway; there's no public elevator.) Memling and Van Dyck, Veronese and Mantegna, Fra Angelico and Brueghel, Bronzino and Lippi, Bellini and Clouet, Rembrandt and van Ruisdael are among painters represented.

Carlo Biscaretti di Ruffia Motorcar Museum (Corso Unità d'Italia 40) is indicated for car buffs, not unlike the Daimler-Benz Museum in Germany's Stuttgart. This one, in Italy's No. 1 auto-manufacturing city, is modern and capacious, an appropriate setting for a fantastic range of antique autos, Fiats and Lancias in abundance, not surprisingly, but other makes as well. Gosh, but those oldies could be beautiful!

Palazzina di Caccia di Stupinigi (in Stupinigi, seven miles south of the center): in English, *Mauriziano Hunting Lodge/Museum of Art, Furniture, and*

Furnishings is not one but several mouthfuls. Call it what you will, but if you have any interest in architecture, interior design, and furnishings of the eighteenth century, you will trot out and have a look. From what I can perceive, there is a staff of two, a ticket seller and a guide, and while the guide is showing a group through (doubling as sole vendor of postcards at the end of each tour) you wait outside for him. This so-called hunting lodge of the Savoy royals was no more rustic than were the so-called "cottages" of turn-of-century millionaire Americans in Newport, Rhode Island. Stupinigi was—or certainly could have been—a palace for all seasons, the residential masterwork of the prolific Juvara, with a fabulously felicitous plan based on a tall and immense central pavilion, from which radiate four lower wings. The guide, droning on in Italian, takes you on a really extensive tour: some 40 rooms. Juvara's ingeniously proportioned Salone Centrale, frescoed and chandelier-hung, is No. 1, but you recall as well the red-canopied bed of the queen's bedroom; the deceptively octagonal look of what is actually a rectangular Stanza da Gioco, or games room; the Salotto degli Specchi, spectacularly mirrored and frescoed; the hunting theme of the king's bedroom, and—at every turn—inlaid tables, lacquered consoles, carved-walnut chests, porcelains and bronzes, damasks and brocades, chairs and settees, many with original brocade upholstery. You want no more to miss Stupinigi than you would Versailles.

Basilica di Superga (seven miles east of the center): Having presumably inspected at this point two town palaces and a country estate of the long-ruling Savoys, and seen a number of works by the architect-designer Juvara, you may—or may not—want to see this Juvara-designed church, with its subterranean royal House of Savoy tombs. But if it's a fine day, you're guaranteed a fine view from this church atop a mountain, superbly domed and colonnaded, with a pair of side bell towers for good measure.

Centro di Arte Contemporaneo di Castello Reale (Castello di Rivoli, on the outskirts of Turin) went up in the eighteenth century as a royal country house; Filippo Juvara, about whose other Turin work I write in this chapter, was the architect. Only in the early 1980s, after long neglect, was the palace restored to shelter Italian modern art in some 40 rooms turned galleries. Unless you're a buff of contemporary art in Italy, you may not know the painters' names, which should not deter you from a tour of inspection.

Museo Nazionale del Risorgimento (Piazza Carignano): Italy abounds in museums documenting the ever-so-important years leading to unification in the middle of the last century. They are of greater interest to Italians, who are familiar with the period, than to foreigners, and I rarely recommend them in this book. Torino's is an exception because it is situated in handsomely Baroque Palazzo Carignano, wherein visitors may see the chamber that served, in 1848, as the first parliament of the Kingdom of Italy. Among other exhibits is a reconstruction of the study of Camillo Cavour, prime minister of the Kingdom of Sardinia during the reign of Vittorio Emanuele II, who—with (as we learn in U.S. high schools, or at least did in my time) Giuseppe Garibaldi and Giuseppe Mazzini—played vital roles in the Risorgimento.

SETTLING IN

Jolly Principe di Piemonte Hotel (Via Gobetti 15) quite belies the sobriety of an imposing, clean-lined façade. Lobby, cocktail lounge, restaurant and, for that matter, 107 generous-sized, high-ceilinged rooms and suites are stylish reproductions of the Rococo of the eighteenth century. Service, at the combination reception–concierge desk that is a chain-wide Jolly feature, is as cordial as it is professional. And location could not be more central. This is a warm, welcoming hotel. *First Class.*

Turin Palace Hotel (Via Sacchi 8): Its opposite-the-train-station location was convenient when it opened more than a century back, and the Turin Palace remains well located today. It also remains tastefully traditional, with 125 pleasing rooms and suites, gracious public spaces including restaurant and bar-lounge, and alert service. *First Class.*

Jolly Hotel Ambasciatori (Corso Vittorio Emanuele 104) is a good-looking contemporary house. Public spaces feature deep leather chairs, bedrooms feature rust and beige color schemes and super baths. There is a stool-equipped bar in the cocktail lounge and a reliable restaurant. *First Class.*

Jolly Ligure Hotel (Piazza Carlo Felice 85), one of three Turin links of the invariably reliable Jolly chain, offers 156 neat rooms, restaurant, and bar. Central. *First Class.*

Concord Hotel (Via La Grange 47), well positioned between the main train depot and the air terminal, is flanked by smart shops of a boutique-dotted street and has 130 nicely equipped rooms, restaurant, and friendly lobby bar. *First Class.*

Nazionale Hotel (Via Roma 254) is central, with its décor engagingly modern, its 63 bath-equipped rooms comfortable, and with bar-lounge, breakfast, and a restaurant reserved for the groups it serves. *First Class.*

Gran Mogol Hotel (Via Guarini 2) is a handsomely maintained house with pleasant public spaces and 45 well-equipped rooms. Breakfast only. *Moderate.*

Venezia Hotel (Via XX Settembre 70): Down-home old-fashioned is how you might categorize the Venezia, with antimacassars on its lobby chairs and a mix of period furniture in its bedrooms (not all of which have baths). Bar and breakfast, but no restaurant. *Moderate.*

Victoria Hotel (Via Nino Costa 4) offers 75 functional rooms, bar-lounge, breakfast, and a central situation. *Moderate.*

Bramante Hotel (Via Genova 2) is smallish, with just over 40 neat rooms; bar-lounge, breakfast, and heart-of-the-core location. *Moderate.*

DAILY BREAD

Cambio (Piazza Carignano 2; Phone 543-760): There is something to be said for the staying power of a restaurant operating since 1757. In the case of Cambio—occupying quarters in a venerable palace that it redecorated in the eighteenth century—there is a *lot* to be said. White-marble tables of its intimate bar-lounge are agreeable enough. But the restaurant proper—illuminated by a trio of crystal chandeliers, the stucco of its ivory walls picked out in gold, windows dressed with damask Austrian shades, fresh flowers on tables complementing its frescoes—is, in my view, among the most beautiful in Italy. Traditionally uniformed waiters—white tie, black jackets, and long white aprons—offer a menu dotted with specialties as well as traditional standby dishes. Antipasto embraces vitello tonnato, breasts of chicken, shrimp and other seafood, and a range of salads. Or opt for a platter of assorted salamis and carved-at-table hams to start, unless you prefer truffle-sauced risotto, or pasta. There are always nine or ten entrée specials—veal steak and fresh salmon, for instance. Sweets come to table on a trolley and are superb, cakes especially. The wine list, by my count, has three dozen Piedmont reds alone, with the other regions well represented. And service is as friendly as it is faultless. In my view one of Italy's best restaurants. *Luxury.*

Gelati Pepino (Piazza Carignano 6) is a near-neighbor of Cambio (above). Go for the excellent ice cream. *Moderate.*

Due Lampioni (Via Carlo Alberto 45; Phone 83-97-409) is understated in ambience—the look is plain but proper—with reliable enough fare: fettuccine Corsaro a good pasta bet, roast rabbit with polenta and French-style tournedos among entrées, okay mixed salad. Service is correct but can be chilly. Not, in my experience, either friendly or fun. *Luxury.*

La Smarrita (Corso Unione Sovietica 244; Phone 390-657) is a taxi ride from the center. (The Torinese are fair-minded: there's a USA Boulevard, too.) At any rate, this intimate spot, located in a rather grand apartment house, is low key and trendy, with a clientele largely composed of execs from the nearby Fiat works, their families, and foreign guests. There is no menu—rather waiters announce the day's specials and standard dishes, as well. Everything that I have tried is delicious: shrimp variously prepared or such pastas as tagliolini with asparagus or artichokes; a tasty mushroom soup; basil-flavored pork chops from the grill; Châteaubriand as tasty as it might be across the frontier in France. And how about house-made whiskey ice cream to conclude? *First Class.*

Vecchia Lanterna (Corso Re Umberto 21; Phone 537-047): It is not only a lantern that is old here. Vecchia Lanterna is *vecchia* throughout—Gothic chairs, antique paintings on the gold-brocaded walls illuminated by sconces from earlier centuries. Even place plates on the tables—removed when your meal arrives—are of advanced age. Tuxedoed waiters are almost too polite and proper, smiling gingerly rather than heartily. And the sommelier tastes the wine before serving it, a practice more French than Italian. The food—a meal might run to risotto quattro formaggi (with a four-cheese sauce), broiled lamb chops with also-broiled tomato, chocolate mousse—is competent but expensive, to the point where you feel you are paying an awful lot for the pretentious ambience. *Luxury.*

Vittoria (Via Carlo Alberto 34; Phone 54-19-23) is at once animated, engaging, and delicious. Vitello tonnato—Italy's famed tuna-veal dish—is nowhere better. Pasta—tagliatelle, pesto-sauced, for example—is excellent. Ditto veal entrées. And the price is right: exceptional value. *Moderate.*

Carignano (Piazza Carignano 7; Phone 539-793) is situated on the same handsome square as Cambio (above), makes a specialty of pizza, and sets tables out front in warm weather. *Moderate.*

Buca di San Francesco (Via San Francesco da Paola 27; phone 839-84-64) is just the ticket for a tasty but informal lunch—risotto is special—in the core of town; have the house wine. *Moderate.*

Perbacco (Via Mazzini 31; Phone 88-21-10) comes up with tasty fare—antipasto, pasta, reliable entrées—but it tends to be pricey. *First Class.*

Caffè Torino (Piazza San Carlo 204) is the city's oldest, most atmospheric, and most antique-accented caffè: Luigi XV chairs covered in brown leather, lace-bordered tablecloths, brocaded walls, gilded mirrors, marble fireplace, with a typically Vecchia Torino clientele. You do very well to emulate the three impeccably dressed, busily gossiping ladies at the next table and have hot chocolate with little sandwiches. Or do as the elderly gents in the corner do, order tea and pastries. An institution. *First Class.*

Caffè San Carlo (Piazza San Carlo) presents one of the most spectacular interiors in town: a great crystal chandelier, gilded stuccowork. Meals include a good-value prix-fixe menu and there are drinks, even live concerts in winter. *First Class.*

SOUND OF MUSIC

Teatro Regio (Piazza Castello) retains its eighteenth-century façade but is spankingly—and strikingly—contemporary within, and you are urged to take in an opera or ballet performance. The city's *Conservatorio* (Piazza Bodoni) is where major symphonic, chamber, and other concerts take place. Turin is a theater town—dramas as well as musicals. Theaters include *Stabile, Carignano,* and *Alfieri.* The plays can be imported (O'Neill, for example), but the language employed is, of course, Italian.

SHOPPER'S TORINO

La Grange (Via La Grange) is the ranking department store and is combined with *La Rinascente;* the former has the first two floors and basement, the latter occupies floors 2, 3, and 4. There are *Upim* and *Standa* department stores on Via Roma, whose other stores include *Luisa Spagnoli* (women's clothes), *Pulloveria* (sweaters), *Divarese* (moderately priced men's and women's shoes), *Maglio* (expensive men's and women's shoes and bags), *Longhi* (leather and suede), *Durando* (furs), *Santagostino* (moderately priced clothing for all the family), and such high-fashion houses as *Ferragamo* and *Gianni Versace.* Via La Grange's pricey boutiques—*Ceramiche d'Arte* (pottery and porcelain), *Varzino* (copper and brass), *Fiorucci* (way-out clothes and accessories), *Lucarelli* (old books and prints)—are browsable. And there's a branch of *Gucci* (leather, men's and women's clothes, accessories) on Via Pietro Micca.

INCIDENTAL INTELLIGENCE

Aeroporto Città di Torino is nine miles north of town; domestic and international flights. *Further information:* Ente Provinciale per il Turismo, Via Roma 226, Turin.

36

Urbino

Roots of Raphael

BACKGROUND BRIEFING

Of course the early birds flocked to Urbino. Check its location—on a minimountain, just enough inland from the Adriatic coast to be protected, but still a halfway point between northerly Venice and southerly Rome—and you can appreciate how it appealed to ancient peoples who preceded the Romans, Urbino's first substantial builders.

But it is not for pre-Roman or even Roman remnants that Urbino—in the east-central Italian *Regione* called Marche *(MAR-kay)*—is visited. This small, simple, unpretentious town, without so much as a single first-class hotel, is a celebration of the grandeur that exemplified the Renaissance.

What happened was that as the Early Christian centuries evolved into the Middle Ages, the Holy Roman Emperor tapped scions of a clever family named Montefeltro to be overlords of Urbino. Time was the twelfth century. Between then and the early fifteenth, the same family—under emperors and popes—tenaciously retained control, and Urbino might have remained a relatively obscure settlement into our own time, had it not been for a remarkable Montefeltro descendant whose turn came to take over.

This was the famed Federico. His father had wisely sent him to the brilliant court of the Gonzagas in Mantua (chapter 18) to be educated, and he grew up with more brawn and brains than good looks, and with dual interests, both of which he developed to the hilt: culture of the Renaissance on the one hand, and the profitable profession of soldiering—in the employ of whatever power paid the most—on the other. Federico was the prototypical soldier of fortune, with emphasis on the final word of that term. Students of his career have estimated that various rulers for whom he fought paid him the medieval equivalent—per annum—of several million dollars, in terms of today's spending power.

But he was not a hoarder. In 1455, a decade after assuming control of Urbino, he imported an architect—Luciano Laurana—as principal designer of a palace that would become one of the great Renaissance achievements of Europe. With his wife, Battista Sforza, of the Milanese Sforza clan, he made his court a melting pot for the continent's leading painters, sculptors, artisans (for detailing of the palace's décor—plasterwork, inlaid woodwork), and other thinkers and doers of the age.

Urbino's decline was sad. The last duke of the dynasty died in the early decades of the seventeenth century, and the town's administration passed to an envoy of the pope, by which time riches amassed by Federico began to disappear, and Palazzo Ducale became a shell of what it had been; when Urbino became a part of the United Kingdom of Italy in the mid-nineteenth century, the palace was in such pitiful condition that it was put to use as a prison. Only in this century did government agencies attempt to right past wrongs, with a meticulous restoration that culminated in use of a fair-sized portion of the palace (by no means all of it) as site of the National Gallery of the Marche *Regione.*

ON SCENE

Lay of the Land: What it lacks in amenities—hotels tend to be away from the historic center—Urbino compensates for with atmosphere. Original walls still encircle it. *Palazzo Ducale,* towered and turreted and broad at the beam—is its principal landmark. And once within the walls, one may walk about everywhere, most enjoyably, perhaps, in hilly steplike alleys little wider than ordinary sidewalks, with centuries-old houses at their extremities: *Piolo Santa Margherita* and *Piolo San Bartolo* are two such. But these minor thoroughfares are best reserved for leisure strolls after hitting the highlights. Central Urbino is based on two squares fronting Palazzo Ducale—*Piazza Duca Federico* and *Piazza Rinascimento.* This last works its way north into shop-lined *Via Pacinotti,* which passes the façade of the *Duomo* and leads to *Via Vittorio Veneto* and always-animated *Piazza della Repubblica,* whose landmark is the *Church of San Francesco,* and which one crosses to continue north on *Via Raffaello,* which terminates at *Piazzale Roma,* on which has been erected a modern monument to the painter Raphael, Urbino's most globally celebrated native. The newer part of the city, beyond the walls, lies farther north in and about *Viale Comandino;* while the railway station is at the extreme southern end of town, beyond the walls, on *Via delle Stazione.*

Palazzo Ducale and Galleria Nazionale delle Marche (Piazza Rinascimento) are, as I point out in an earlier paragraph, one and the same, with the former serving as setting for the latter. The combination, to understate, is inspired. And unlike the Palazzo Ducale in Mantua (chapter 18), which can be inspected only on rushed guided tours, you are blessedly on your own here in Urbino, taking as much time as you like, so long as you follow arrows that (not always too clearly) define the prescribed visitors' route. By no means compact—but still much smaller than the gargantuan Mantua palace—the Urbino palace is a tripartite treat: paintings, architecture, interior design—the lot ingeniously melded. The building itself is one magnificent space following another: Cortile d'Onore, the arcaded courtyard than which there is no surely handsomer of the period; Scalone Grande—the broad principal staircase, with a statue of Federico in an oblong niche at its base; Salone del Trono, the onetime throne room, its walls now surfaced with Gobelin tapestries, with Federico's arms on the fireplace, and with scenes in its doors brilliantly depicted in inlaid woods; Sala delle Udienze Private, where dukes received state guests; Camino degli Angeli—celebrated for its frieze of angels set against their original blue background; the stuccoed fireplace in Camera da Letto del Duca, the duke's now bedless bedroom; and the room that elicits more oohs and ahs than any other: Studiolo del Duca Federico, the study completely walled with three-dimensional scenes created in inlaid wood.

Of the paintings, there is but a sole Raphael, his indelibly beautiful portrait of a bare-shouldered young woman, *La Muta.* Be on the lookout for Piero della Francesca's *La Flagellazione,* after *La Muta* most popular of the palace's works, thanks to character apparent in faces of its three foreground figures, still-sharp color, extraordinary architectural angularity of the background. An elegantly handsome cityscape, *La Città Ideale,* by an unknown genius of the fifteenth century, draws crowds, too, as do Paolo Uccello's set of six red-and-black sequences, *La Profanazione dell' Ostia,* and Pedro Berruguate's riveting study of Federico and a young blond son at prayer.

Duomo (Via Puccinotti) is unexpected in Renaissance Urbino because it is not of the period. Which is hardly to say this superbly detailed Baroque reworking of another church in classic style is to be passed over lightly. Indeed, the façade, with a quintet of sculpted saints atop its portico, ranks with those of also-Baroque cathedrals in Lecce (chapter 16) and Syracuse (chapter 31). Have a look at the impressive interior, taking in works of art—paintings, illuminated manuscripts, reliquaries, other objects—in adjacent *Museo Diocesano* (a.k.a. Museo Albani).

Oratorio di San Giovanni Battista (Via Barocci) is requisite because of frescoes filling its walls, their color still vivid—with *The Crucifixion* perhaps the most brilliant—by a pair of gifted fifteenth-century brothers, Salimbeni by name.

Oratorio di San Giuseppe (Via Barocci, diagonally opposite San Giovanni, above) delights with its life-size crèche, in stucco, and an unusual *Nativity.*

Church of San Domenico (Piazza Gherardi) welcomes with a blue-and-white Della Robbia lunette over its Renaissance portal, which is at least as noteworthy as the interior.

Casa di Raffaello (Via Raffaello): Of course you want to pay your respects at the nicely maintained and furnished fifteenth-century house in which Raphael was born. Walls are lined with paintings by a number of his contemporaries, but don't expect a slew of the master's work—there is but one piece: a frescoed *Madonna* (in profile) and (sleeping) *Child,* among his first efforts, and fascinating.

SETTLING IN

Montefeltro Hotel/Ristorante (Via Piansevero 2; Phone 38-324), modern though it is, will not win a beauty contest. There are 65 plain rooms with bath, a lobby-lounge-bar, and an unprepossessing-looking restaurant that turns out corking good soups, pastas, meat, and seafood entrées, even sweets, with sound wines and swift service. A quarter-hour's drive from the center. *Moderate.*

Bonconte Hotel (Via della Mura 28) is north of the Ducal Palace. There are 20 modern rooms with breakfast, but no restaurant. *Moderate.*

Piero della Francesca Hotel (Viale Comandino 53) cannot be faulted for the artist's name it takes, any more than can the across-the-street Montefeltro (above), for the source of its title. 84 rooms, bar, and breakfast but no restaurant. *Moderate.*

DAILY BREAD

Nuovo Coppiere (Via Beato Vescovo Mainardo 5; Phone 320-092) has a cozy look and a fairly standard menu; you do well enough with, say, a pasta and a veal or fish entrée. *First Class.*

Trattoria del Leone (Via Battisti 5; Phone 4033) is a heart-of-town source of temptingly tabbed sustenance, the roast of the day, for example. *Moderate.*

Vecchio Urbino (Via dei Vasari 3; Phone 4447) is locally popular and humming midday; lamb and veal specialties, super pastas. *First Class.*

Nuovo Carlo (Viale Zara 59, Pesaro; Phone 68-984): You just might have to pass through the Adriatic Sea resort of Pesaro en route to or from Urbino by train/bus; or you might want to spend a day at the beach; in any event, the seafood-sauced pastas and grilled fish here are good. *First Class.*

INCIDENTAL INTELLIGENCE

As I mention directly above, you may reach Urbino by way of Pesaro; the two towns are linked by fast bus, but certain trains serve Urbino as well. *Further information:* Azienda Autonoma di Soggiorno e Turismo, Via Puccinotti 35, Urbino.

37

Venice/Venezia

Canaletto's Paintings Come to Life

BACKGROUND BRIEFING

It is sinking. It is not sinking. The international argument goes on, while concerned citizens the world over—many of whom have never seen Venice—kick in funds to societies dedicated to its preservation. No other living city may make that statement.

The consequences of a makeshift settlement built on Adriatic coastal swamps by refugees fleeing barbarian invaders, Venice went on to become a substantial power, in politics and war, as well as trade and commerce, the funnel through which East and West bartered wealth. That eminence is past, but the meld of architecture and art that its canny citizens created on a canal-patterned maze of muddy islands still draws the curious as flies to sticky paper. Pore over locally written history and one finds that changes have been made here, destruction has taken place there; progress has reared its ungainly head at the cost of precious preservation. Of course these complaints make sense. Still, no other major city on the planet is as similar to look upon today as it was two or even three centuries ago.

There will be changes from the Carpaccio painting one might study at the National Gallery in Washington; the city is no longer quite what it was when that native son portrayed it in bold, precise strokes in the fifteenth century. But if one pops into, say, the Boston Museum of Fine Arts to look at the way Guardi interpreted his city in the eighteenth century, or if the choice is a Canaletto at, say, New York's Metropolitan, Venice is about as recognizable as the snapshots we capture it with today. Piazza San Marco, Palladio's island Church of San Giorgio Maggiore, the joyous Baroque conceit called Santa Maria della Salute, the same Rialto Bridge for which a design proposed by Michelangelo was rejected, the gondola-dotted Grand Canal—even the garb of the gondoliers—are virtually unchanged. Venice is the easiest history lesson on the planet because it is there for us to use and touch and walk through in that rarity of situations, an urban environment without automobiles.

I think that's why we love it so. We seem to want to contemplate what happened in advance of our arrival. Mainland Venice had been part of a province of the Roman Empire. But when aggressive northerners took the offensive, Venetians began retreating to the marshy islands of a lagoon that had long been known principally to fishermen. They came to build houses on log piles, and then they began to dig canals where streams had been. Between the middle of the fifth century and the end of the seventh they organized as a proper ministate, naming their ruler *doge,* after the Latin, *dux,* for leader.

It may well be that they had not realized how much they had going for them with a location that straddled Occident and Orient. They soon learned. Ere long they had organized maritime commerce, and they became strong politically and militarily. They became aggressors, controlling the Adriatic coast and expanding across its waters, to become lords of an eastern empire that brought riches at once commercial and cultural.

All this while, expansion continued. Involvement in the Crusades won more territory. Envoys to foreign courts were forerunners of the diplomatic corps that was to become a requisite of every sovereign state's foreign policy. Thirteenth-century accounts of the eastern travels of native son Marco Polo were to serve as the West's primary frame of reference on the Orient.

The originally representative Venetian Republic turned repressive. Its much-feared Council of Ten was ruthless in wiping out enemies and gradually usurped many of the doge's powers. Withal, Venice, as the Middle Ages turned into the Renaissance, prospered as the maritime power that linked East and West, as a colonial power dominating the Veneto mainland. And as a fountainhead of culture.

The Renaissance was later in coming to Venice than to the rest of Italy, but it was worth waiting for. The Venetian school of painting began with the Bellini family, most especially Giovanni, but Gentile and Jacopo as well. It continued with Giorgione, Carpaccio, Veronese, Titian, and Tintoretto, not to mention architects like Palladio and Sansovino, later artists like the Tiepolos with vibrant Baroque frescoes, Canaletto and Guardi, with their evocative cityscapes, Longhi, with his charming insights into upper-class domestic life. The lot portrayed in paint what the same era's playwright Carlo Goldoni interpreted in his dramas.

Venetian strength began to subside with the discovery of the New World and the somewhat earlier Turkish conquest of Constantinople;

both tended to lessen the power of Venice while strengthening that of nations directly involved in trade with and settlement in the Americas. By the time Canaletto and Guardi were painting in the eighteenth century, Venice had lost its Adriatic territories and, along with them, much of its riches. The Serenissima—as the officially styled Serene Republic had been called—was subsiding in strength. The early nineteenth century saw it acquiesce as a territory of Napoleon, with a later switch to unwelcome control by Austria.

Early stirrings of the Risorgimento—the national independence movement—came at the right time for Venice. The years before the middle of the last century were a period of struggle. The revolutionary Daniele Manin organized fellow Venetians to resist Austrian domination, eventually resulting in the occupiers' expulsion. Venice joined the new Kingdom of Italy not long thereafter, in 1866.

Through all of these centuries of triumph and defeat, the city has resisted physical change. There is some industry, a modern port (Porto Marghera), and a modern city (Mestre) on the nearby mainland. And a tourist industry wherein the centuries-old skill of the Venetians at dealing with strangers has stood them in good stead, to the point where they have been able to achieve a price level so steep that Venice has become Italy's most expensive city. High cost of living notwithstanding, Venice works very well indeed, and despite the unusual qualities of the Venetian terrain, the newcomer feels immediately welcome. And why should he or she not, in what is, after all, a fantasy city come to life?

ON SCENE

Lay of the Land: There are prefatory points to be made about Venetian exploration. Most important is that *Piazza San Marco* and its environs are only a small piece of the pie. An important piece, of course. But, I repeat, because I know how many well-intentioned visitors never leave the area: only a piece. Second point is that canals and frequent boat rides on them notwithstanding, Venetian sightseeing is synonymous with walking. It is easy walking because it is flat, and because there are no motor vehicles or traffic lights. But the conscientious explorer must not be surprised if he or she walks eight or nine miles a day, even allowing for a lunch break. And not realizing it. (Venetians are the world's all-time champion urban walkers.)

Third point is geography. As soon as one realizes that this is a city of some 120 islands, spanned by some 400 bridges and intersected by some 150 canals, it is easy to become fainthearted. The map on the following page gives you a good idea of Venice's geography, but you want to lay hands on a more detailed map, invariably gratis from your hotel concierge, as well as the city tourist office (address below). Note peculiar Venetian terminology not encountered elsewhere in Italy. Except for

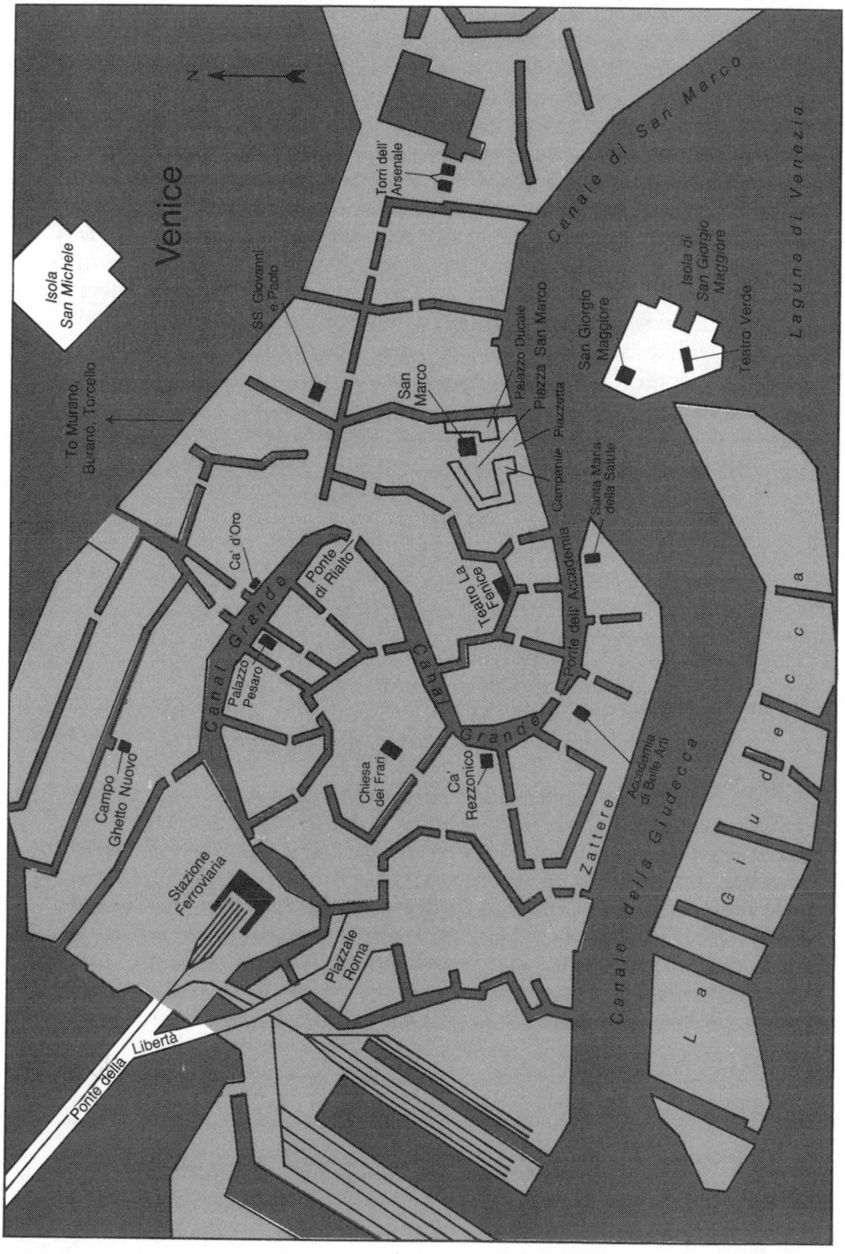
Venice
Isola San Michele
To Murano, Burano, Torcello
N
Torri dell' Arsenale
SS. Giovanni e Paolo
Canale di San Marco
Isola di San Giorgio Maggiore
San Giorgio Maggiore
Teatro Verde
Laguna di Venezia
Palazzo Ducale
Piazza San Marco
San Marco
Piazzetta
Campanile
Santa Maria della Salute
Ponte dell' Accademia
Teatro La Fenice
Ponte di Rialto
Ca' d'Oro
Canal Grande
Palazzo Pesaro
Chiesa dei Frari
Ca' Rezzonico
Accademia di Belle Arti
Zattere
Canale della Giudecca
La Giudecca
Campo Ghetto Nuovo
Stazione Ferroviaria
Piazzale Roma
Ponte della Libertà

Canal Grande and Canale della Giudecca, the word for canal is *rio.* Except for Piazza San Marco, its satellite Piazzetta San Marco, and Piazzale Roma, a square is a *campo.* There are other names for thoroughfares—*larga, fondamenta, riva, ruga,* but most of the time a street is a *calle,* as in Spanish.

Arrive by plane and you land at Venice's aptly named *Aeroporto Marco Polo* near the mainland town of *Mestre.* You may take a relatively reasonably priced public boat *(vaporetto)* direct from Marco Polo to Piazza San Marco. Or go by bus some five miles across *Ponte della Libertà* to *Stazione Santa Lucia,* Venice's railway station on the west side of town at *Piazzale Roma*—precisely where you'll arrive if coming by train. There a porter will take your bags to one of the public canal ferries that operate much like city buses in more prosaic communities, to the stop nearest your hotel. Or, if you're willing to spend a large sum, hire a private motor launch (*motoscafo—motoscafi* is the plural) to take you directly to your hotel's pier. (Most hotels are on a *rio* as well as on a *calle.*) If you are really rich and romantic, you may hire an even costlier gondola, settling the fare with the gondolier before departing.

The body of water on which you first travel is the Grand Canal *(Canal Grande).* It is in the shape of a backward "S" and winds through the core of town, with gorgeous palazzi lining its banks, to the body of water called *Bacino di San Marco,* which is actually a channel to the sea, and changes its name going west to *Canale della Giudecca.* At this point it divides Venice proper from *La Giudecca Island,* whose major landmark is *Redentore Church.* Continuing eastward, with a turn to the south, Canale di San Marco leads to the *Lido,* an oblong strip that is the city's beach resort. Major visitor islands of the lagoon—*Burano, Murano,* and *Torcello*—lie a short distance beyond.

Back then to Venice proper. Bacino di San Marco is at the south end of Canal Grande, and Piazza San Marco is at its southern extreme. The area between the piazza and the water is *Piazzetta San Marco.* Follow it to the harbor, turn left, and the thoroughfare is *Riva degli Schiavoni,* named for the merchant Slavs *(Schiavoni)* from across the Adriatic, who traded there in earlier centuries.

Of bridges spanning the Grand Canal, there are two important ones. *Ponte dell' Accademia,* closer to San Marco, is a relatively modern wooden affair worth knowing about because it feeds directly to the *Galleria dell' Accademia,* most requisite of the museums. Farther north is the much-painted bridge, *Ponte di Rialto,* core of Venice's market area. Now another geographical hint: most direct route between San Marco and Rialto Bridge is via the principal shopping street; it's called *Mercerie.* Another point: No area of the city is without historic, architectural, cultural, or simply social interest, if only because of the vibrant street life. Venetians live in close-together, fairly sunless houses and enjoy being out of doors. The old ghetto, for example, is in the north, around *Campo Ghetto*

Nuovo. There are splendid churches, like *Scalzi,* near the railway station. *Fondamenta delle Zattere,* bordering the Giudecca Canal, is the site of such landmarks as the *Gesuati* and *Spirito Santo* churches. Little *Isola di San Giorgio Maggiore* is the site of a church designed by Palladio, the local architect who gave his name to a style of neoclassic architecture, and whose houses for the gentry in neighboring mainland communities (chapter 39) inspired great English designers like Inigo Jones, William Kent, and Robert Adam. The east end of town is the site of what has to be the world's most beautiful arsenal. *Frari Church* and *Scuola di San Rocco* are near neighbors, west of the Grand Canal. I make mention of this handful of landmarks only to underscore the importance I attach to getting all about the city. And rest assured: every *calle* and *rio* and *campo* is well signposted.

THE ESSENTIAL VENICE

Basilica di San Marco (Piazza San Marco): It is a debatable premise, but not difficult to accept: I submit that there are four rarely confused landmark churches in Europe: Notre Dame in Paris, St. Peter's in the Vatican, Westminster Abbey in London, and St. Mark's in Venice. Of the four, St. Mark's is the oldest, most distinctive, smallest, and surely the most exotic. St. Mark's is Byzantium in western Europe. It is the fortunes of Venice for nearly a millennium. It is the epitome destination of the eighteenth-century Grand Tour—and of today's packages. Devout Venetians stole the remains of their patron saint, Mark, from infidels of Islamic Egypt in the early ninth century, when the doge of the moment began plans for a church in the saint's honor. The first and second St. Mark's were razed; the one we see today is the third. Even so, it dates back nine hundred years, its Eastern architecture embellished over the centuries by gifts of treasures representing a multitude of epochs.

The interior—provided one goes, especially on a first visit, in the sunlight, most especially not at dusk or in the evening—is as ravishing as the façade. St. Mark's is at once history book, art gallery, and, as a cathedral, seat of the patriarch—ancient local name for bishop—of Venice. (A relatively recent occupant of that post was the late Pope John XXIII, beloved of Venetians as of admirers around the world, which is easy to perceive from the photographs of him in churches throughout the city that he visited, either as patriarch or pontiff.)

Cross-shaped, and with five elegant domes, it is recognizable as the same St. Mark's that Gentile Bellini and Carpaccio painted in the fifteenth century, with its five mosaic-embellished entrances, beneath as many similarly decorated arches. These last lie between the still-visitable *terrazza* for views of the square, and the quartet of prancing horses of gilded copper that Napoleon briefly spirited away to Paris.

The domes are lined with mosaics and frescoes. The rood screen, of the kind popular in Eastern churches, separates altar from nave and is outlined with statues of saints. The jewel-embellished golden altarpiece *(Pala d'Oro)* is studded with enamels of episodes from St. Mark's life. The separately entered Museum and Treasury are repositories of art not the least of which—to whet your appetite—is a Veneziano painting of St. Mark afloat, with the patterned sails of his ship surely the loveliest such ever painted.

Doges' Palace (Piazzetta San Marco)—it should be understood from the outset—doubles as one of Europe's most remarkable art galleries. The visitor is, understandably, caught up with the excitement of a trek through the Gothic castle in which a long succession of doges lived from the ninth century onward. The palace is a 3-D fairy tale, and would be even if its walls and ceilings were without priceless frescoes. The courtyard is of a breathtaking grandeur, with its busy mix of styles and an elegant stairway leading to a maze of treasure-laden chambers.

One requires a strong neck for gilt-framed frescoes embedded in ceilings. Consider Bassano and Tintoretto in the Hall of Avogaria, Tintoretto and Veronese in the Square Hall, Tintoretto and Titian in the Four Doors' Hall, Veronese's celebrated *Rape of Europa* in the chamber known as Antecollege; more Veronese, joined by Tintoretto, in the adjacent College Hall. In the magnificently scaled Senate, Tintoretto is on the ceiling *(The Triumph of Venice)* and on walls as well; and in the Council Hall, behind the magistrates' bench, is still another Tintoretto, this masterwork called simply, and accurately, *Paradise.*

I have not mentioned works by lesser-known painters, nor the golden staircase. I will, though, at this point recommend traversing the *Bridge of Sighs,* which links the palace to the also visitable, very grim jail. The idea behind the bridge's name was that prisoners looked out of the marble-framed windows of the bridge, en route to their cells, sighing at the loss of their freedom.

Galleria dell' Accademia (Campo della Carità) is a *vaporetto* (public water bus) ride away from most visitors' hotels. It is justly honored by the boat station bearing its name, and the Grand Canal bridge in its vicinity is also named for it. As well they might be. This is a major gallery, named after a society of eighteenth-century Venetian painters and occupying a onetime church-monastery-school complex that had originally been designed by Palladio but was substantially rebuilt. One begins with sadly lovely Venezianos of the Virgin and of saints. A sublime group of works by Giovanni Bellini—*Pala di San Giobbe, Madonna degli Alberetti, Allegoria dell' Incostanta,* among others—in themselves make a Venice visit worthwhile. So, for that matter, does the Gentile Bellini of a religious procession before St. Mark's. There are brilliant Carpaccios—*Miracolo Della Croce a Rialto*—and other works depicting Renaissance Venice, Giorgione's *Tempest*, Lotto's *Gentleman*, a Titian *Pietà*, Veronese's *Cena in Casa di Levi*, and Tiepolo, Canaletto, and Guardi, from the later eighteenth century.

A Pair of Art-Filled Churches—Frari and SS. Giovanni e Paolo: *Santa Maria Gloriosa dei Frari* (Campo dei Frari), along with SS. Giovanni e Paolo (below), would each, in a city without a St. Mark's Basilica, have achieved the celebrity of St. Mark's. But such are the disadvantages of competition to churches such as this, that they go unseen by many Venice visitors. The Frari, as Santa Maria Gloriosa dei Frari is known to locals, is masterful as much for architecture as art. It is called after Franciscan friars *(i Frari)* who founded it. The present structure, with its somber elongated Gothic façade, is the third Frari church—early-fifteenth-century—with a massive vaulted nave. Newcomers' eyes seem first to focus on the elaborately carved choir, then Titian's *Assumption* at the high altar. But one must take some time and walk about; there are more Titians (not to mention the painter's tomb), one of Bellini's exquisite Madonnas, and works by Vivarini, Sansovino, Donatello, Paolo Veneziano, and Canova. *SS. Giovanni e Paolo* (Campo San Zanipolo) has a façade oddly similar to that of the Frari, which is not surprising in that they are about the same age. The Frari dates to 1420, Sts. John and Paul to 1430. While the former is the principal Venice seat of the Franciscans, the latter is the Dominicans' counterpart. (Both St. Francis and St. Dominic are believed to have visited Venice.) Both churches are the burial places of a substantial number of doges. Sts. John and Paul's great Gothic interior, architecturally masterful like that of the Frari, is also studded with treasures. A Giovanni Bellini polyptych of St. Vincent Ferrer is one such. Also on the scene are Vivarini, Bassano, Lotto, and most especially, Veronese.

Scuola Grande di San Rocco (Campo San Rocco) is the most spectacular of the peculiar group of so-called schools in Venice. These were charitable organizations, religious-sponsored but lay-endowed, to the point where they were able to build sumptuous headquarters, the while carrying on their good works. San Rocco, in a Renaissance building adjacent to a church of the same name, is a treasure trove of Tintoretto. His many and diverse works in the earlier-recommended Doges' Palace are incredible enough. But on San Rocco's second-floor Great Hall there are more than half a hundred wall and ceiling frescoes by that master, who spent nearly two mid-sixteenth-century decades on the project. There is a ceiling fresco of the church's name saint, Rocco, a moving *Crucifixion*, and a *Last Supper*, not to mention a number of Old Testament subjects. Happily, there are benches on which you may sit to study the ceilings.

Ca' Rezzonico (Canal Grande at San Barnaba) is an effortless step into the lilting Rococo grandeur of eighteenth-century Venice—an entire palazzo turned into a museum of that era. Single most splendid aspect is a ballroom to which you would like—without delay—to cable your friends to come at least for cocktails if not for dancing into the wee hours; it has opulent chandeliers and a frescoed ceiling. Two other rooms have ceilings covered with Giovanni Battista Tiepolo frescoes. Chamber after chamber is decorated in period, with the painted furniture peculiar to Venice. Another room is chockablock with paintings by Longhi that show how the Venetian rich lived in the eighteenth century. China, books, clothes, other objects, too. And views of the Grand Canal, which the palace fronts.

Isola di Torcello is to me the most interesting of the major island trio in Venice's lagoon. It was Torcello that the early Venetians first built up in their flight from invading barbarians some fifteen hundred years ago. The gem of the now-quiet island is the *Duomo,* a Byzantine cathedral that dates to the seventh century, with mosaics quite as exciting as those of St. Mark's Basilica in town. As if the Duomo were not enough, there is a fine Romanesque church—*Santa Fosca*—next door, with a brick-walled circular interior, carved capitals of its pillars the principal decorations. Nearby *Museo dell' Estuario* exhibits a mixed-bag clutch of historic lore in galleries on two floors of an aged structure.

BEYOND THE BASICS: SELECTED MUSEUMS

Galleria Internazionale d'Arte Moderna (Canal Grande at San Stae): Ca' Pesaro, the palace in which the museum occupies two floors, is among the more splendid in town. Decorations are in themselves significant; so is the very grand scale. There is a good deal of nineteenth-century and some contemporary Italian work with a sampling of French—Bonnard, Corot, Rouault, Chagall, and other luminaries like Ernst, Nolde, Kandinsky, and Klee.

Galleria Giorgio Franchetti (Calle Ca' d'Oro) is the collection of a turn-of-century baron who had money and taste. He bought fifteenth-century Ca' d'Oro and restored it. Then he filled it with his own art and, not long after, killed himself. His estate gave both house and collection to the Italian government, which added treasures from the Accademia (above). Many Italian masters are represented—Vivarini, Mantegna, Paris Bordone, native Venetians including Carpaccio and Guardi. But there are distinguished foreigners whom you'll recognize, too.

Museo Correr (Procuratie Nuove, Piazza San Marco, directly opposite the St. Mark's Basilica) is the most conveniently located of Venice's museums, and No. 2 after the Accademia. Central situation on a landmark square notwithstanding, the Correr remains virtually incognito. I was pretty nearly alone on my most recent revisit—all the sadder when I came to see that the museum has been expensively and expansively refurbished to the point where it is now one of the most beautiful repositories of art and artifacts in Italy. The Correr is actually a trio of museums, one having to do with documentation relating to the Risorgimento—the nineteenth-century independence movement—another devoted to derring-do Venetian history, with revelations about matters local, doges to gondolas. Most important, though, is the Quadreria, or paintings gallery, a score of rooms brimful of beautiful things: a number of works by Venice's own Giovanni Bellini, including a *Madonna and Child,* a *Pietà,* and a *Crucifixion;* bewigged Longhi gents; a blue-robed Lotto *Madonna and Child* framed by scarlet-robed angels; a prim-lipped, red-capped Baldassarre Estense youth-cum-page-boy-haircut; an extraordinary *Pietà* by Antonello da Messina; unexpected Flemish primitives by the likes of Dirck Bouts and Hugo van der Goes; and several splendid works by Carpaccio, including a study of a pair of most unhappy-looking Venetian ladies.

Museo di Icone dell' Istituto Ellenico (Scuoletta di San Nicolò, Ponte dei Greci): There have been Greeks in Venice for half a millennium. They built a church in the sixteenth century, which developed into a cultural complex embracing a collection of icons; you will find none of better quality in the mother country. They are brilliant of hue, with a scarlet-robed St. George killing a nasty black dragon from his white steed, the most dramatic of the lot; along with an equally fierce St. Minas, golden shield at the ready.

Collezione Peggy Guggenheim (Calle San Gregorio, on the Grand Canal almost opposite the Gritti Palace Hotel) is the cache of modern art amassed by a wealthy long-resident American—between 1938 and 1979, when she died—displayed in what had been her home, an eighteenth-century palace that has been operated since her death—infinitely more professionally than when she ran it—by New York City's Guggenheim Museum, which was endowed by her family. Though largely staffed by young Americans who appear to be junior-year-abroad students in Venice, showing off Italian-language skills in the course of noisy coffee-klatches in the corridors, there is no doubt but that the works on view constitute a collection of caliber. Sculptures by Arp, Moore, Max Ernst, and Alberto Giacometti embellish the garden. You depart remembering Picasso's powerful *On the Beach*, Chagall's *Rain*, Francis Bacon's *Study for Chimpanzee*, Clyfford Still's *Jamais '44*, Jean Dubuffet's *Fleshy Face*, Georges Braque's *The Clarinet*, Mondrian's *The Sea*, Léger's *Men in the City*, and paintings by Gorky and Appel, Duchamps and Robert Delaunay, Gris and Malevich, Sutherland and Kandinsky, Joseph Cornell and Kurt Schwitters. Unusual hours (of course, subject to change) are worth noting: daily except Tuesday from noon until 6 P.M.; on Saturday, closing time is 9 P.M.

Museo Storico Navale (Campo Angelo Emo) occupies an ancient building that was for long Official Granary of the Serene Venetian Republic. It's a five-story stone box, with its most engaging exhibits those having to do with Venice on the High Seas, most especially an elaborate model of the ceremonial galley, an original of which is still used at regattas.

Palazzo Grassi (Canal Grande): If you are of the conviction that it is impossible to see interiors of too many Venetian palazzi, keep the Grassi in mind; it is operated by a private foundation that stages temporary art exhibitions within its originally eighteenth-century precincts, now with contemporary accents. Whatever the subject matter—and Grassi shows are invariably top rank—make it a point to go.

Pinacoteca della Fondazione Querini Stampalia (Campo Santa Maria Formosa): We may thank a nineteenth-century count—Querini Stampalia by name—for leaving to the public his eighteenth-century palace with its scholars' library, beautiful furniture, and painting collection. To have a look at the paintings and furniture, one passes through the ground-floor library to the upper story. There, an attendant—usually glad to have visitors, of which there appear to be precious few—acts as tour escort. There are a score of rooms, a number with the Rococo painted furniture of Venice, all with paintings by such masters as Bellini, Tiepolo, Longhi, and Giordano; most charming of a charming lot is a chubby lady named Laura Priuli painted by Palma Il Vecchio.

Scuola di San Giorgio degli Schiavoni (Calle dei Furlani) is another of the so-called schools of Venice, church-founded, privately funded, of which San Rocco (above) is the best known. This is a Slav-founded fifteenth-century institution that to its everlasting credit commissioned Vittore Carpaccio to decorate it. The artist created a series of vivid, color-splashed paintings that ring the walls of the ground floor. No St. George has ever killed a dragon with more panache. The adventures of Sts. Jerome and Triphon are a bonus.

BEYOND THE BASICS: SELECTED CHURCHES

Carmini (Campo Santa Margherita) is a felicitous hodgepodge: Renaissance façade, a couple of dozen Romanesque columns dividing the naves within, paintings by Lotto, among others; pretty cloister.

Degli Scalzi (Fondego Scalzi) is quite the most dazzling Baroque church in Venice, well worth a trip to Piazzale Roma, even if you're not yet ready to leave town. (An idea: combine a visit with your departure.) The façade is elaborate, on the order of San Moisè and Santa Maria del Giglio. There are half a dozen exquisite chapels; the one dedicated to St. Teresa of Ávila was restored by the Italian government relatively recently and has a fine Tiepolo on its ceiling.

Gesuati (Zattere ai Gesuati facing Canale della Giudecca—not to be confused with *Gesuiti,* on Fondamenta Nuove, Baroque and on the northern fringe of town) is neoclassic-handsome with its lures ceiling frescoes in both main church and presbytery by Tiepolo, as well as a Tintoretto.

Redentore (Isola La Giudecca) is the principal reason for a visit to La Giudecca Island. This is one of Palladio's two complete Venice churches (the other is San Giorgio Maggiore, below). It is beautiful neoclassic, as would be expected of Palladio. The severe interior's sumptuous Corinthian columns are the chief decorations. Ask one of the Franciscan priests on duty to show you the church's pride-and-joy paintings, one each by Vivarini, Bassano, and Tintoretto.

San Barnaba (Campo San Barnaba): You are attracted by the classic-style pediment framing the eighteenth-century façade. Within, architecture takes you back to the Renaissance, although the painted cupola over the high altar is of the same period as the façade. Biggest treat: Veronese's *Holy Family.*

San Francesco della Vigna (Campo Confraternità) is the result of an unusual collaboration: classic-style Palladio without, but by Sansovino within, where attractions include superlative art: works by Veronese, Vivarini, Giovanni Bellini—among others.

San Giorgio Maggiore (Isola di San Giorgio Maggiore) is a scenic little vaporetto ride from Piazzetta San Marco. It's the church that along with Santa Maria della Salute is such an intrinsic part of the Venice skyline; Palladio designed it. Façade has a pediment supported by a quartet of the Corinthian columns he so liked. (See Redentore, his other Venice church, above.) The pale gray interior is sublime in its simplicity; carved-wood choir stalls are as masterful as the choir's geometric-pattern black, tan, and white marble floor. Paintings? Carpaccio, Bassano, Tintoretto, if you please.

Santa Maria Formosa (Campo Santa Maria Formosa) was rebuilt the year Columbus sailed west. Go for the lovely Vivarini triptych.

Santa Maria del Giglio (Campo del Giglio) is a Baroque confection that has never looked better, thanks to relatively recent restoration. The façade is one of the most brilliant in a town where such are commonplace. Within, there is a Rubens *Madonna and Child* in the tiny chapel to the right as you enter and a Tintoretto in the choir.

Santa Maria della Salute (Campo Salute) is the domed Baroque work that is the landmark at the extreme southern terminus of the Grand Canal. Erected as an act of thanksgiving for the termination of a seventeenth-century plague, it is engagingly octagonal—the dome covers all of the interior except the high altar, at one side—and is art-filled with major Titians, a Tintoretto, and a trio of Giordanos.

San Maurizio (Campo San Maurizio) is smallish, early-eighteenth-century neoclassic, with striking marble floors and fine paintings, by the workshop of the Veronese school and that of Tiepolo.

San Moisè (Campo San Moisè) has an everything-but-the-kitchen-sink façade, by which I mean busy—with scrolls and busts, and full-length statues of saints and garlands and columns and a neoclassic pediment. It works. So does the cozy interior, whose considerable art includes a Tintoretto.

San Pantalon (Campo San Pantalon) is among the more successful Baroque churches, because of a smashing eighteenth-century ceiling fresco by a relatively unheralded painter named Fumiani, for whose achievement three cheers.

San Sebastiano (Campo San Sebastiano) might better be called Veronese's Church. It has half a dozen of that sixteenth-century master's works, even including decoration of doors of the organ, under which the painter is buried. But look around also for a Titian, a Tintoretto, a Paris Bordone.

San Stefano (Campo San Stefano) is a Gothic beauty with paintings by Tintoretto and, unusual for Venice, a decorated ceiling that is one of the loveliest in Italy.

San Zaccaria (Campo San Zaccaria) has a broad, expansive, six-level Renaissance façade—strong and handsome. Within, it does not disappoint, what with paintings by Giovanni Bellini, Tintoretto, and Vivarini, to name a few of the artists.

A Venetian Miscellany

Arsenal: The most visitor-neglected of the great Venice buildings. Understandable, because one can't enter. Have a walk around, though. This could be an old Errol Flynn movie set—moated, with a trio of ferocious, though handsome, lions guarding its elegant Renaissance arch and a formidable crenelated wall.

Columns: The two freestanding columns on Piazzetta San Marco are worth a stop and an upward glance. They came from the East some eight centuries ago. The one on the right as you face the water is topped by a statue of St. Theodore, St. Mark's predecessor as Venice's patron saint. Its mate is a lovable bronze lion that, along with copper horses over the entrance to St. Mark's Basilica, was taken to Paris by Napoleon's forces, but later, like the lions, returned.

Ghetto remains a remarkable entity, more so perhaps than that of any other important European city. It's centered in Campo Ghetto Nuovo. What one wants most to see is the sixteenth-century synagogue, *Scuola Grande Tedesca*—elaborately furnished and with a graceful oval of a women's gallery. Italy gave the word *ghetto* to the other languages of the world. The centuries-old houses of its ghetto are the tallest in Venice.

Gondolas: Watch them being made, just as they have been for centuries, at a little piazza called *Squero San Trovaso,* surrounded by low-slung tile-roofed houses of great age.

Islands: *Torcello,* most important of the trio of major lagoon islands, is honored by inclusion in The Essential Venice, above. One might also want to explore quiet little *Burano,* with fishermen's houses painted in primary colors, and lady lace makers busy at their work, alfresco in the good weather, selling what they create, including linen handkerchiefs. Go in the morning and you can take in the action at the fish market, staying on for a seafood lunch, perhaps, at *Da Ramano*—inelegant but delicious. Murano, whose name has for so long been synonymous with glassmaking, attracts masses of visitors. It is possible to see glass hand-blown as it has been for some seven centuries in the factories. Visit *Museo dell' Arte Vetraria*—a onetime palazzo full of glass, with the old stuff the handsomest. Inspect the eight-century-old *Church of San Donato*—one of the most important structures in the lagoon; it has a severe façade and a magnificent apse, with the interior arched Romanesque.

The Lido is Venice's summer resort, an eye-filling fifteen-minute vaporetto ride from San Marco, with a wide white sand beach extending for several uninterrupted miles. A section of the beach is municipally operated, for day-trippers, with lockers for changing. And there are good hotels. After-dark action centers in and about a severe and graceless summer-only Casino. In winter, the Lido shutters and the Casino moves to a Grand Canal palazzo of especial beauty (below).

Palazzi, assorted: As if palaces turned museums, hotels, and what-not-else are not enough, there are others serving more prosaic purposes. *Palazzo Corner* is by the prolific Sansovino—a mid-sixteenth-century work of such substantial proportions that it is now seat of the Prefettura, or municipal government. *Palazzo Contarini* is a Gothic-Renaissance mix with its ace-in-the-hole an exterior spiral staircase. *Fondaco dei Tedeschi,* where German traders stored their wares during the Renaissance, is still seeing service. Function: Main Post Office. *Fondaco dei Turchi* was where the Turks did business, and there are touches of the East in its multiarched façade. The town's Natural History Museum—mostly frequented by students—is within.

Panoramas: Skyscraperless Venice surprises with the possibilities it offers for bird's-eye views. Uppermost, as regards elevation, is the *Campanile of St. Mark's,* early-twentieth-century copy-cum-elevator of an ancient bell tower that collapsed. *Torre dell' Orologio* is another Piazza San Marco landmark, fifteenth-century, with the bell on its visitable terrace surrounded by a pair of darkened copper gents who have been ringing in the hours these many centuries. Below, against a blue and gold background, a gilded lion of St. Mark protects an ancient clock that tells seasons and movements of the sun, rather than the time. Then there is the *terrazza of St. Mark's Basilica.* Ask inside how you may reach it. Once arrived, you're right up there with the copper horses, enjoying a view of the piazza. Last, there is the perspective of the Grand Canal and surrounding territory, to be seen from sixteenth-century *Ponte Rialto,* the Rialto Bridge.

Teatro La Fenice: The only way you're going to see the interior of this opera house is to buy a ticket for an opera, ballet, or concert, unless management decides to open up for daytime sightseeing. La Fenice went up in 1792 but less than half a century later it was pretty much destroyed by fire. To their credit, a pair of brother-architects—pupils of the original architect, Giannantonio Selva—rebuilt, taking great care to reproduce the original. To look at the theater from its own little piazza, one would have no idea of what a large auditorium lies within. The façade is restrained neoclassic, with a little four-column portico leading to the lobby. Under a sky-blue ceiling centered with a crystal chandelier there are six levels of seats. Décor is pink, green, and gold. Electrified antique sconces with pleated silk shades—hundreds of them affixed to the balconies—complement the ceiling chandelier. Opera tradition is strong at La Fenice. Consider the world premieres of Verdi operas alone: they included *Rigoletto, La Traviata,* and *Simon Boccanegra.* And firsts continued into this century, with maiden performances of Britten's *The Turn of the Screw,* Prokofiev's *The Flaming Angel,* Stravinsky's *The Rake's Progress.* Besides the Fenice there are opera and ballet performances upon occasion at *Teatro Malibran,* handsomely designed in turn-of-century Art Nouveau (called Liberty—the English word—in Italy) and concerts at the eighteenth-century *Palazzo Labia* in a onetime ballroom with frescoes by Tiepolo.

Casino Municipale: Warm-weather months see operation in an ugly modern structure at the Lido, with a winter locale that changes to the Grand Canal and Ca' Vendramin Calergi, a fifteenth-century palazzo that is one decorative extravagance after another—grand stairway, beautifully arched doorways, first-rate paintings and salons—Fireplace Room, Gilt Leather Room, Royal Drawing Room, Yellow Room, Red Room—that even the staunchest of nongamblers will want to inspect. Games include craps, vingt-et-un, trente-et-quarante, and roulette.

SETTLING IN

Ala Hotel (Campo Santa Maria del Giglio) is modish—65 rooms, each with bath, corridors lined with black and white antique etchings, beamed lobby, adjacent bar-lounge. Breakfast but no restaurant. *Moderate.*

American Hotel (Fondamenta Bragadin at Campo San Vio) has baths in half its 29 rooms, and is in a quiet quarter near Santa Maria della Salute. Restaurant, bar. *Moderate.*

Bauer Grünwald Hotel (Campo San Moisè): It is odd about the Bauer. Unless you're a Venetian or a Venice regular, chances are you may not know it. Ask first-timers to reel off grand hotels and you're not surprised to hear Gritti Palace, Danieli, and Cipriani. But the Bauer can boast an authentic Gothic *palazzo* on the Grand Canal as its main building and a core-of-town location as convenient as any in Venice. Nor is it by any means Giovanni-come-lately. Named for its German founders—Herr Grünwald was Herr Bauer's son-in-law—its roots go back a century and a quarter. Today, it embraces both an updated medieval palace and a modern building fronting Campo San Moisè, opposite the landmark church (see On Scene, above) for which the square is named. The lobby and the high-ceilinged lounge it edges are impressive. Those of the 214 rooms I have inspected are among the best-looking in town. The Royal Suite is furnished in antique painted furniture that typified Venice's eighteenth century, but all rooms facing the Grand Canal are antique-accented. And even singles, at least those I've seen, are comfortable and with fine baths. There's an engaging bar just off the lobby, and the restaurant is outstanding enough for me to accord it space on a subsequent page. Member, Leading Hotels of the World. *Luxury.*

Bel Sito e Berlino Hotel's (Campo Santa Maria del Giglio) chief attribute is a location at once scenic and central. About 20 of 32 rooms have baths; bar and breakfast. *Moderate.*

Bisanzio Hotel (Calle della Pietà) is near the Arsenal and away from the center, but all 40 rooms have baths. Breakfast and bar, but no restaurant. *Moderate.*

Bonvecchiati Hotel (Calle Goldoni) is a good-looking, good-sized (90 rooms, 81 with bath) house with a restaurant (outdoors in summer) and a location near San Marco. I like. *Moderate.*

Boston Hotel (Ponte dei Dai, just off San Marco) is an agreeable 50 room-cum-bath house, centrally situated. Breakfast, bar. *Moderate.*

Cavaletto e Doge Orseolo Hotel (Calle Cavaletto, off San Marco) is at once attractive and central; 80 rooms (some with brass beds, others with eighteenth-century style painted furniture) with bath or shower, as well as a pleasant lobby, creditable restaurant, and bar-lounge, and delightful staff. Charming. *First Class.*

Cipriani Hotel (Giudecca Island): By the time Natale Rusconi took over at the Cipriani, he had managed two of the great Italian hotels: Rome's Grand (where I first met him) and the Gritti Palace (when I stayed with him, again), just across the lagoon in Venice. But the Cipriani is different: a veritable resort hotel in the city, a four-minute gratis shuttle-boat ride from Piazzetta San Marco to its own landing on Giudecca Island. The Cipriani is a modern building built for the purpose it serves (indeed, it is the only such in Venice, if you except those on the more distant Lido). Public spaces—traditional albeit with welcome rattan touches—are directed to the out of doors, with an awning-covered caffè overlooking a lush garden and an alfresco lunchtime restaurant (later reviewed) edging a whopper of an outdoor pool, surrounded by sundecks interspersed with chaises longues and umbrella-topped tables to which waiters bring drinks. Still another terrace abuts the main restaurant (also evaluated in a subsequent paragraph), and there is tennis. There are just under a hundred rooms. Those I have either inhabited or inspected are lovely: a suite furnished in pale-green-upholstered eighteenth-century furniture, oversized junior suites giving on to the pool, terraced doubles in brown and beige, sprightly singles. There is a penchant for detail: antique accents, holders covered in traditional Florentine paper containing stationery on writing tables in rooms, TV sets that pop up from tables at the push of a bedside button, clear plastic containers of multicolored Emilio Pucci hand soaps on counters of exquisitely fitted bathrooms. There's a beauty and fitness center (sauna, steam baths, massage). And I don't know of a hotel in Italy with a more fabulous breakfast. It's included in the rate (not a bad idea as tabs are indeed steep) and includes fresh-squeezed orange juice, cereals, house-baked croissants, breads and rolls, eggs to order any style, coffee, tea, or hot chocolate, plus whatever you can put away from a buffet laden with Parma ham and salamis, cheeses, baked goods, yogurt, and fresh fruit. Later in the day, a Bellini cocktail at the bar is a Cipriani requisite. Member, Leading Hotels of the World. *Luxury.*

Concordia Hotel (Calle Larga San Marco) is central, nicely updated, with private baths in all 60 period-décor rooms, restaurant, bar-lounge. *First Class.*

Danieli Hotel (Riva degli Schiavoni) was where I stayed on my first Venice visit, and of course I've returned. The setting—a Gothic palace wherein had lived a doge of the long-powerful Dandolo family, and next door to *the* Doge's Palace (see On Scene, above), it is at once historic, opulent, and central. Interiors of the original fourteenth-century *palazzo* are part medieval, part Renaissance, with appreciated contemporary touches. But there are 235 rooms all told, in the original and two newer adjacent buildings. On a relatively recent revisit, management—understandably proud of extensive refurbishing, as part of an ongoing program whereby interiors of rooms and suites are becoming Venetian eighteenth-century in style—pointed out that fabrics are by Rubelli, a long-on-scene Venice-founded firm, and that baths are marble-countered and marble-walled. The high-ceilinged lobby-lounge is arguably the most amusing locale in Venice for a drink (it's always busy and bubbly), and the terraced restaurant on the roof is accorded an evaluation on a subsequent page. But to me, the Danieli is at its most spectacular on the second floor of the original building, now an Italian government-protected national monument. You ascend a masterful staircase to a corridor that's a veritable ballroom, and, leading from it is the Royal Suite, which—with its vast stone fireplace, painted ceiling, Murano chandeliers, Rococo furniture, and gilded mirrors—is the quintessential Venetian interior. A hotel since 1822, the Danieli has been in Ciga Hotels' hands since the turn of the present century. Together with still another landmark palazzo turned hostelry, the Gritti Palace (below), Venice-origin Ciga operates it (not to mention three other Venice hotels) with affectionate expertise. Bravo, Ciga! *Luxury.*

Des Bains Hotel (Lungomare Marconi, Lido) is long, low-slung, glistening white, beachfront. There are 255 rooms, one of the best-looking dining rooms in the area, swimming-pool-cum-snack-bar and disco, underground passage to the hotel's beach, 18-hole golf course in connection. A Ciga hotel. *Luxury.*

Europa & Regina Hotel (Calle XXII Marzo at Canal Grande) comprises a quintet of contiguous eighteenth-century palazzi, the principal one of which was for long seat of the Tiepolo family, the very same that produced the pair of celebrated Rococo-era artists. Arrive by foot and you enter from the rear, but if it's a boat that brings you, go in via the front door, directly on the Grand Canal, adjacent to the terrace-caffè that's attached to the smart restaurant, appropriately named Tiepolo. Public spaces are an antique-contemporary meld, and there are 200 rooms. Those I have inspected—especially including a canal-view suite with rose-hued textiles covering antique-style painted furniture, as well as similarly decorated doubles—are handsome. Because Teatro Fenice, Venice's opera house, is nearby, this is the hotel where singers (not to mention composers) often headquarter. (Verdi was among the hotel's guests.) But even without divas or tenors, the E&R's vibes are good. A Ciga hotel. *Luxury.*

Excelsior Hotel (Lungomare Marconi, Lido) is a Moorish fortress from without, a contemporary playpen within. There are also places to eat, snack, and drink on the hotel's beach, dancing under the stars, and private motorboat service between the Excelsior and Ciga's sister in-town hotels. On-site tennis and 18-hole golf course in connection. The Excelsior is fun. *Luxury.*

La Fenice Hotel (San Marco 1936) lies between the famous theater–opera house (above) and San Marco; pleasant public areas; ditto the rooms I've seen. Breakfast only. *Moderate.*

Gabrielli-Sandwirth Hotel (Riva degli Schiavoni) is a dilly of a waterfront house, with a substantial history (the fourth generation of the owning family is now running the place), 120 rooms with bath (mind you don't get one of the smaller ones), marble lobby, bar-lounge, and restaurant—all framed by a Gothic exterior. Bonuses: a roof for drinks, sun, and vistas, and a patio-garden for dining in summer. *First Class.*

Gritti Palace Hotel (Campo Santa Maria del Giglio): To term the Gritti Venice's most romantic hotel is to understate. Named after a Renaissance doge (his portrait hangs in one of the lounges) who built it half a millennium ago, its name has become synonymous with that of Venice. Ciga Hotels took over this smallish, 99-room house in 1947, wisely keeping the ambience—low-key and blessedly devoid of glitz—quite what it had obviously been when Somerset Maugham first knew it at the turn of the present century. There are two annual events—a winter series of lectures by mostly imported experts, on Venice's history, art, and architecture, and a summer (July–August) series of cooking classes. Suites and rooms have been meticulously refurbished with hand-decorated woodwork, sumptuous Fortuny textiles, Murano chandeliers, antique accents, and lavish marble baths. There are three legendary Grand Canal–view suites—Royal, with furniture Venice-made in the eighteenth and seventeenth centuries; Presidential, facing the sculpted dome of the Church of Santa Maria della Salute and where Maugham stayed; and Hemingway—where the American author wrote part of *Across the River and under the Trees.* But the point of the Gritti is that even singles can charm the pants off you; I had to be torn away from my most recent—a canal-view single from which I looked out the window about as much as I slept. I review the terraced restaurant on a later page; even if you don't stay at the Gritti, you owe it to yourself to have a meal there, or at least a drink. A Ciga hotel. *Luxury.*

Kette Hotel (Piscina San Moisè 2053) is centrally situated on a street leading to Teatro Fenice. There are 44 rooms with bath or shower; sizes vary but they're traditional Venetian in looks; pleasant. Breakfast only. *Moderate.*

Locanda Cipriani Hotel (Island of Torcello) is for a get-away-from-it-all vacation in rustic elegance, on the most interesting of the lagoon islands (above). This is a rambling country house set in a garden. Meals (decidedly among the better in the Venice area) are served on a vast terrace. Each of the half-dozen rooms is a rambling, two-room suite. Visitors have included Queen Elizabeth II and Prince Philip. *Luxury.*

Londra Palace Hotel (Riva degli Schiavoni) is a long-respected old-timer—enviably well situated on the waterfront—that has spruced itself up in recent seasons, employing a sure sense of style. Public spaces—including a restaurant and cocktail lounge—are paneled and inviting, as are those of the 70 rooms I have inspected, some with canopied beds. *First Class.*

Luna Hotel Baglioni (Calle dell' Ascensione)—long popular and center-of-the-Venice action—contends that it is Venice's oldest hotel, operating as a hostelry since 1474. Its facilities are, of course, nothing like as antique as the opening date, but lobby, restaurant, and bar-lounge are agreeably mellow, and those of the 127 rooms I've inspected are pleasant and with good baths. *First Class.*

Metropole Hotel (Riva degli Schiavoni 4149) is smallish (64 rooms and suites), well located, and winning; and by that I mean lobby, cozy cocktail lounge, and bedrooms—the lot in period style. Breakfast only. *First Class.*

Monaco e Grand Canal Hotel (Calle Vallaresso): It was my old friends Betty Adams and Martha Morano—whose New York firm, E & M Associates, makes a specialty of representing unusually good Italian hotels—who brought the Monaco e Grand Canal to my attention. It has a lot going for it. By that I mean a situation that places its entrance on a core-of-Venice street, but another of its façades (and the terrace of its restaurant, reviewed on a later page) fronts the Grand Canal. Key word for the Monaco is intimate. Little lounges off the foyer include a bar with walls of gold brocade complementing blue-upholstered furniture. Those of the 80 rooms I've inspected reflect the ambience of Venice—painted bedsteads in the manner of the city's eighteenth century,

Murano chandeliers, antique prints, but baths are of this very moment. *Luxury.*

Montecarlo Hotel (Calle Specchieri, just off San Marco) embraces 64 small but spotless rooms with bath, in a heart-of-town setting, with an exceptional restaurant in connection. Good value. *Moderate.*

Palazzo Vendramin Hotel (Giudecca Island) is both a next-door neighbor of, and under the same management as, Hotel Cipriani (above). Originally fifteenth-century, it opened only a few seasons back. There are just 9 handsome suites, with kitchenettes of varying sizes. The same fabulous—and enormous—Cipriani-style breakfast is included, and all Cipriani facilities and services are available to Vendramin guests. Lovely. *Luxury.*

Panada Hotel (Calle Larga San Marco) insists, in its brochure, that it is precisely 50 steps from St. Mark's. I haven't counted, but the hotel is scrubby-up spotless, with 45 bath-attached rooms, and breakfast but no restaurant. *Moderate.*

Petit Palais Hotel (Lungomare Marconi, Lido) is a smallish beachfront hotel; all 26 rooms have baths; bar-lounge. *Moderate.*

Do Pozzi Hotel (Corte dei do Pozzi) is a find: a lovely, updated old house on a quiet and central minisquare. Every one of the 35 spacious rooms has bath and contemporary art on the walls. And the Raffaele Restaurant (below) is in connection. *Moderate.*

Quattro Fontane Hotel (Via Quattro Fontane, Lido) is central to both Casino and beach. There are 72 rooms, restaurant, and bar. *First Class.*

Saturnia e International Hotel (Via XXII Marzo)—nicely situated between a pair of landmark hotels (Gritti Palace and Bauer Grünwald, above) occupies a fourteenth-century palazzo that has been updated with a sure sense of style. Public spaces include an inviting restaurant and bar, and those of the rooms I've inspected—there are just under 100—are delightfully period-style, with good baths. Friendly. *First Class.*

Savoia e Jolanda Hotel (Riva degli Schiavoni) is a lovely old waterfront house with not quite 80 spruced-up rooms with bath and a reliable restaurant-caffè. Very nice indeed. *Moderate.*

Star-Splendid Suisse Hotel (Mercerie 760 at Ponte dei Bartteri) has an unusual—but convenient—location on Venice's main shopping street. Its quarters are a venerable palazzo but interiors—lobby, restaurant (which moves to an inner patio in summer), bar, and nearly 160 rooms are clean-lined contemporary. Pleasant. *First Class.*

Torino Hotel (Calle delle Ostreghe 2356) is, like the Saturnia e Internazional (above), midway between the Gritti Palace and Bauer Grünwald hotels. This is a small but worth-knowing-about house in a fifteenth-century palace, with just a score of rooms-cum-shower (those I've inspected are pleasant). Breakfast only. *Moderate.*

Villa Corner della Regina Hotel (near Cavasagra di Vedelago, 20 miles west of Venice and a bit more distant from Padua [chapter 23] and Vicenza [chapter 39]) is an almost-too-good-to-be-true Palladian-style villa—pedimented, porticoed, and with statues topping its façade in the manner of Palladio—that has become a 22-room-and-suite hotel (part main building, part less-pricey annex) that is just the ticket for travelers with cars who are exploring the Veneto and its countryside. To say that no two rooms or suites are alike is to understate. Range is an ivory-hued room with an early-nineteenth-century bed of the Empire period, through to a twin with metal beds sporting blue headboards, and beyond to canopied beds in some of the seven suites. Restaurant, cocktail lounge, swimming pool in the garden, tennis, and a sauna. *Luxury.*

Wildner Hotel (Castello 416) is long-established, with a reputation for good value. Twenty bath-attached rooms, bar, restaurant. *Moderate.*

DAILY BREAD

Venetians claim, with foundation, that it was their ancestors who invented the fork before the rest of the world had given table utensils any thought. With so long a history as middlemen between East and West, they are indeed culinarily sophisticated. Rice is a staple, and *risotti* of Venice are quite as delicious as those of Milan. Look for *risotto con i caparozzoli*—a seafood variation; *risi e bisi* (rice and peas) is everywhere to be seen. *Polenta,* a cornmeal staple beloved also of as diverse peoples as Romanians and American Southerners, is often served as one might potatoes—toasted, grilled, roasted, even boiled. There's a variety of fish—bream, sole, red mullet, sea bass, eels, sardines—as well as shrimp, lobster, and squid. Veal and lamb are popular and everywhere available. So is liver—*fegato alla veneziana*—a prime specialty. And lucky is the diner who comes upon torresani—tiny roast pigeons.

Al Covo (Campiello della Pescaria 3968; Phone 522-3812) is a fair walk from San Marco, but once you tuck into a meal, you're not sorry you went. Mixed antipasto and the house's mussel appetizer are good openers. Clam-sauced spaghetti is counseled, too, as is the seafood mixed grill. *First Class.*

All' Angelo (Calle Langa San Marco 403; Phone 520-9299) is intimate—framed pictures pack paneled walls, flowers center tables—and good-looking. In ordering, bear in mind that both pasta and ice cream are homemade. *First Class.*

Antica Carbonera (Calle Bembo; Phone 522-5479) is as elderly as its name implies, with an interesting near-Rialto location; good for risotto and seafood. *First Class.*

Antico Martini (Campo San Fantin; Phone 522-4121) has been around even longer than neighboring La Fenice opera house—which means early eighteenth century. It is posh and popular, thanks to delicious cooking, smiling service, and touches like crystal chandeliers, Austrian shades framing windows, and amusing frescoes of 1930s flappers. Risotto primavera is sublime; so is cannelloni. Ditto fresh grilled fish and scampi. *Luxury.*

Antico Pignelo (Calle Specchieri 451; Phone 522-8123)—good-sized and convenient to Piazza San Marco—offers seafood as well as roasts and, of course, pasta. *First Class.*

Bauer Grünwald Hotel Ristorante (Campo San Moisè; Phone 523-1520): Dominated by a dramatic mural—the subject is a herd of horses—that takes up much of one wall, the Bauer's dining room employs pink as its dominant color—carpeting, draperies, table linen, flowers—with singular success. There are prix-fixe lunches and dinners, very good, to be sure. But when I say that a meal ordered from the à la carte—printed in English, French, and German, as well as Italian—is extraordinary, I do not exaggerate. Antipasto alla Veneziana is one of the best assortments of appetizers I have experienced in Italy. Spaghetti in tomato and basil sauce is memorable, no less so other pastas I have sampled. Grilled scampi is an entrée that in and of itself makes a Bauer meal worthwhile. Saltimbocca alla Romana is equally worthy. Desserts are made much of here—zabaglione, cassata, crespelle Georgette (the hotel's answer to crêpes Suzette), the pâtissier's exceptional cakes. Wines have been carefully selected; no less so post-meal digestivos, grappa most particularly. And service is nowhere more skilled or smiling in Venice. *Luxury.*

Caffès of Piazza San Marco, including *Florian* and *Quadri* (the best-known and doubling as proper restaurants) as well as *Lavena,* along with *Chioggia*—on adjacent Piazzetta San Marco, have never been inexpensive. Any experienced traveler expects to pay somewhat more for his espresso when it's ordered in as legendary a location as St. Mark's Square. But recent seasons have seen San Marco tabs become positively exorbitant, and they are even higher if you sit down when a clutch of roaming musicians is playing something schmaltzy at the caffè you have innocently selected. In as tourist-trappy a milieu as this, it's conceivable that you will be thanked by the waiter for your patronage. But I wouldn't count on it. *Caveat emptor. First Class/Luxury.*

Caffè Paolin (Campo San Stefano) is included at this point only to serve as a sample of the engaging caffès similar to it in *campos* and *calles* all over town. The point I make is that it's a nice change to eschew caffès of visitor-populated San Marco (below) for the Venice of the Venetians. Unlike Piazza San Marco caffès—where service can be nasty and tabs severely inflated—these places are friendly and prices are easier to take. They're all *Moderate.*

Caffè Segafredo (Campo San Zulian) is noted for cannoli and other Sicilian treats. *Moderate.*

La Caravella (Calle Larga XXII Marzo 2397; Phone 520-8901): Ham-and-salami platter is a choice opener, as is fish soup. This is an excellent restaurant for risotto—in many variations. And why not grilled jumbo shrimp or steak au poivre as entrées? A super spot. *Luxury.*

Cipriani Hotel Ristorante (Giudecca Island; Phone 520-7744) is arguably the single most elegant dining space in town. Beige and ivory vaults of its ceilings are variations on those of Venetian palazzi, with Murano chandeliers hanging from them. Oversized windows give onto the lagoon and a terrace illuminated by freestanding wrought-iron lanterns—where you want to book your table for starlit summer evenings. The à la carte is among the most imaginatively created of any that I know in Italy, and everything I have tasted is delicious. Open with local crab served in its own shell and expertly dressed, carpaccio Cipriani—the house's own—or still another specialty, insalata Shirley—a wedding of arugula, radicchio, foie gras, and truffles. Pasta and risotti—risotto asparagi, especially, if asparagus is in season—are masterful. Gigot d'agneau, a Cipriani interpretation of a French lamb classic, is A-OK; ditto fegato alla Veneziana con polenta—Venice's calf's liver masterwork. The cheese platter—Italo-French—is unsurpassed in

Italy. Desserts—chocolate soufflé combined with housemade bitter-chocolate ice cream, as a prime example—rate a separate card. So, for that matter, do aperitifs and digestifs, including whiskeys (ten Scotches, Yank bourbon, and Canadian Club), cognacs (no less than a dozen French labels), a score plus of eaux-de-vie, grappas, and marcs; and a wide choice of American and English gins, Soviet vodkas, and Caribbean rums. And there's a still another "separate card": a wine list that's a veritable primer (there are both Italian and flawless-English versions) of Italian vintages. In booklet form, it breaks them down as Noble Reds, Medium-Range Reds, Red and Pink Lights, Full and Fruity Whites, Light and Crisp Whites, After-Dinner, and Sparkling Wines; if you're at all an oenophile, you want to beg, borrow, or steal a copy. The Cipriani is very pricey but in my opinion is one of Italy's best restaurants. *Luxury.*

Cipriani Hotel Buffet Lunch (Giudecca Island; Phone 520-7744): Hop aboard the Cipriani's own gratis boat at the Piazzetta pier, ideally selecting a day when the sun shines and clouds are billowy. On arrival—three minutes after departure—head for the outdoor pool restaurant, and tuck into the daily luncheon buffet. The 30 choices of antipasti—hot as well as cold—are superb, and generally include a pasta and a risotto (hope that tagliolini verdi is one of them). Salads are sumptuous, and you've a choice of a pair of the day's entrées, with a vast and delectable selection of desserts. *Luxury.*

Città di Milano (Campiello San Zulian; Phone 5227-002) is the restaurant—with a strategically situated, and very broad, terrace on a charming square near San Marco—of a small hotel. Service can be of the take-it-or-leave-it variety that is, unfortunately, not any longer uncommon near San Marco. But it's not hostile, and fare—mussels in a marinara sauce, pasta such as pappardelle (wide noodles) ai frutti di mare, and reliable veal and fish entrées—is tasty. *Moderate.*

Colomba (Piscina di Frezzeria; Phone 522-1175) is a series of plain rooms, tables close together, good contemporary art on walls, and snooty waiters obviously aware that first-rate food can compensate for bad manners. Seafood is the thing—clam or mussel chowder, shrimp in a variety of styles to start, grilled fresh sardines or lobster thermidor for entrées. Mind, though, steaks are good too. *First Class.*

Excelsior Hotel Ristorante (Lungomare Marconi, Lido; Phone 526-0201): I don't think I would undertake the sea journey from Venice for dinner, but a day's outing, in summer, for a swim and some sunshine on the beach might well include the buffet lunch of this hotel's casual lower-level restaurant. It's the antipasti—you've easily a score-plus of selections, hot and cold—that make this meal a standout, but creditable entrées and dessert (including a choice of ice creams) are included in the prix-fixe tab. For the buffet lunch: *First Class.*

Graspo de Ua (Rialto, near Banco d'Italia; Phone 522-3647) is packed with *ambiente*—busily decorated walls, dazzling displays of edibles, scurrying waiters. And super food. Start with tartufi di mare—big clams or small oysters as you decide, but delicious on the half shell with a squeeze of lemon. Or the ravishing antipasto to which you help yourself from a groaning table. Little fried soles—bambinolli—a grilled shrimp platter, or baccalà—the local cod—are good entrée bets. So is cannelloni. *First Class.*

Gritti Palace Hotel Ristorante Club del Doge (Campo Santa Maria del Giglio; Phone 796-611): Forget the long title; it's the dining room of the Gritti—Venice's most legendary hotel—that's the subject at hand. Ideally, you time your visit to coincide with a lovely day or evening, booking a table on the terrace—you front the Grand Canal with the landmark Church of Santa Maria della Salute just opposite. It is no wonder that the Gritti is the site of annual cooking schools, in which guest experts collaborate with the hotel's chefs. The kitchen turns out beautiful food. Sfogi in saor is Venetian dialect for marinated baby sole in a piquant sauce, sopressa alla Maugham is local salami teamed with pears and cheese and named for a celebrated Gritti guest. Pasta—including the Venetian-origin pasta e fagioli—is special. Risotto di scampi is an inspired combination. But fish and seafood entrées are excellent too—frittura dell' Adriatico, a mix of local fried fish, especially. No restaurant in town prepares veal more masterfully. Gritti sweets—its own ice creams and sherbets, and Soufflé Grand Marnier—are tempting. And the wine list is one of the best in Venice. In my view, one of Italy's best restaurants. *Luxury.*

Harry's Bar (Calle Vallaresso; Phone 528-5777): Downstairs, waiters dart in and out of the narrow spaces between close-together tables with dispatch and good humor. Upstairs is less frenetic but also less fun. If you are going to have a dry martini in Venice, Harry's (which has a branch in New York) is the place. Fish soup is super. So is risotto alla primavera. Choose from a limited group of fish and meat dishes: piccatina di vitello alla pizzaiola is a fine veal choice. Steaks are as good. And bittersweet chocolate cake with whipped cream is perfection. Remember, though, Harry's tabs are mighty high. *Luxury.*

Hosteria ai Coristi (San Marco 1995; Phone 522-6677) is indicated for Venetian tempters—mixed appetizer platter, pasta with local-style sauces, fried fish, and calf's liver in the Venetian way. *First Class.*

Locanda Cipriani (Torcello Island; Phone 730-150) is a smart inn (above) with a good restaurant, nicely combined with a day's excursion to this lagoon island. Count on just about everything being good, most especially homemade pasta and fresh-caught Torcello fish and seafood, with zuppa di pesce outstanding. Setting is a garden-framed terrace. Summer only. *Luxury.*

Marco Polo (Castello San Lio 5571; Phone 523-5018) is unassuming but given its name—in Venice of all places—it does not go unnoticed. It is central and has outdoor tables. There's a tasty, well-tabbed three-course prix-fixe that might open with lasagne or spaghetti, continue with a veal, fish, or chicken entrée, and conclude with macedonia di frutta. *Moderate.*

Monaco & Grand Canal Hotel Ristorante (Calle Vallaresso; Phone 520-0211) is just opposite ever-so-costly Harry's Bar and a worthy (and less costly) alternative. The setting is intimate and lovely—blue and beige brocade surfaces on walls, nineteenth-century chairs flanking tables illuminated by flickering blue candles (with a honey of a Grand Canal terrace indicated for balmy days and evenings). Tuxedoed waiters scurry about, understandably proud of the chef's offerings. Open with the house's own tuna pâté, fish soup, or seafood-sauced spaghetti ai frutti di mare. Grigliate di pesce—an Adriatic mixed grill—makes for a delicious entrée; so does piccata di vitello—veal in a cream of Gorgonzola sauce. And how about strawberry-stuffed crepes to conclude? *Luxury.*

Mondo Novo (Salizzada San Lio 5409; Phone 700-698) boasts on its menu that it offers "tutte le specialità di pesce dell' Adriatico," proceeding, then, to name thirty-plus seafood dishes. My counsel is to open with oysters on the half shell or a shrimp specialty, with one of the day's fish—simply grilled—to follow. Pleasant. *First Class.*

Montin (Fondamenta Eremite; Phone 536-481) is an away-from-the-center choice with a slightly saucy, slightly raffish air, big trellis-covered garden for warm-weather service, and fine fare. Venetians like liver—fegato—and it's popular here. Or how about duck with polenta? More conventional are broiled fish, fried scampi, and spaghetti with clam sauce. For dessert: zuppa inglese. *First Class.*

Osteria da Fiore (Polo; Phone 721-308) is a good bet for an unpretentious meal, with spaghetti alle vongole—with fresh clams—counseled, along with a carafe of the house white. *Moderate.*

Poste Vecie (Pescherie, near Rialto Bridge on the side opposite San Marco; Phone 370-4140) is a neighbor of the fish market, which means that products of the sea are indicated. The antipasto table seems almost to dwarf this friendly, small-scaled Old Venice-style place. Choose from it for starters, or have a pasta, with a piece of broiled fish, and cheese to follow. *Moderate.*

Da Raffaele (Ponte del Ostreghe; Phone 523-2317) is busily, yet amusingly, overdecorated, with tables on the quiet canal it fronts, for summer meals. Menu is standard, which is not to say unappealing—soups, pastas, rice dishes, entrées that include roast chicken. *First Class.*

Rio de la Borsa (Calle del Sartor da Veste; Phone 700-541) is an apt choice for a meal prior to or following a performance at neighboring Teatro la Fenice. It's small but attractive and humming, with the principal reason a four-course prix-fixe—centered, in the course of my sampling, on filet of veal—that's at once good value and good-tasting. *Moderate.*

Da Romano (Murano Island; Phone 730-531) is an unpretentious country seafood house with a well-deserved reputation for quality. Go for lunch on a sunny day and seek out a Lagoon specialty like rospo—a fish species good simply grilled with a squirt of lemon; or canocchi, a Lagoon variation on the lobster theme. Friendly. *First Class.*

Rosa Salva (Calle Fiubera) is at first glance a caffè where you may want to stop for midmorning coffee and a piece of the scrumptious pastry (there is none better in town). It is also, should you be in the market, the town's most distinguished caterer of private parties. For coffee and cake: *Moderate.*

Taverna La Fenice (Calle Fenice, adjacent to Teatro La Fenice; Phone 522-3856) is a lovely sampling of eighteenth-century Venice, appropriately adjacent to the opera house of the same era, bearing the same name. The look is brocaded walls, Rococo chairs, silk-shaded sconces, mullioned windows. A delightful staff serves good things to eat, such as seafood antipasto, the traditional pasta e fagioli (Venice is as good a place as any to try this beans and pasta combination), lombatina, or paillard of veal; or a chicken specialty—petto di pollo principessa. *Luxury.*

Terrazza Danieli (Hotel Danieli, Riva degli Schiavoni; Phone 522-6480) is a top-floor space with an inspired covered terrace that, given its elevation, affords spectacular vistas of the Grand Canal and the lagoon. Book in advance—visibility is best at lunch, which does not have the fairly steep minimum charge imposed at dinner—for a table at the terrace's edge. But I don't want to give the impression that cuisine is incidental to the view. On the contrary. Danieli chefs are Venice rankers. Start with capo sante gratinate—an inspired scallop specialty, *au gratin.* Or opt for pasta as an opener. I wager you'll be the first on your block to have had spaghetti alla Danieli spadellati al tavalo—with its ham-and-egg topping flambéed at table; cannelloni and ravioli are excellent, too. Baked sea bass is the indicated seafood entrée; breast of chicken Marsala-and-mushroom-sauced is special as well. And ask to have the *carrello,* or trolley, of sweets, rolled up, so that you may choose your dessert. Fine wines, alert service. *Luxury.*

Terrazza Tiepolo (Hotel Europa e Regina, Via XXII Marzo; Phone 520-0477): Mealtime vistas of the Grand Canal are not to be despised, certainly at Terrazza Tiepolo, a restaurant among the least pricey of the Ciga hotels in Venice. Which means good value, especially in the case of hurricane-lamp-illuminated tables at dinner, which might embrace a seafood-accented risotto, followed by the day's invariably tasty *plat du jour. First Class.*

Al Theatro (Campo San Fantin adjacent to Teatro la Fenice; Phone 5237-214) is as good a spot as any in town for a pizza. But it's also a proper restaurant—fresh-caught rospo is a fine choice and pasta is first-rate. Attractive. *First Class.*

Todano (Piazza San Marco) is locally favored for its ice cream with justification. A bar as well as a gelateria at the square's edge, lagoon-side. *Moderate.*

Trattoria alla Canonica (Calle Larga San Marco 339; Phone 412-5365) is welcoming, neat as a pin, with candlelight on red-linen-covered tables at dinner, and competent fare; a meal perhaps opening with risotto alla scampi, one of the day's fish simply prepared as an entrée, and Canonica's own pineapply dessert to conclude. Accompany with the house white. *First Class.*

***Trattoria alla Scala*'s** (Calle Lucatello 571; Phone 522-0767) skillfully prepared fare is excellent value—meat entrées as well as pasta. Near St. Mark's. *Moderate.*

Trattoria da Ignazio (Calle Saoneri, just off Campo San Paolo; Phone 34-854): The afternoon is earmarked for the Frari Church and Scuola Grande di San Rocco. Depart early enough for lunch at not-far-distant Ignazio. Within, watercolors of Venice line the walls; without is a garden, pristine with white tables and chairs. To open: zuppa di verdura, with sogliola fritta—fried sole—following. *Moderate.*

Trattoria do Forni (Calle Specchieri 468; Phone 523-7729) is worth knowing about, given its location—steps from Mercerie, the main shopping street. Locals enjoy local dishes, risotto, sole and other Adriatic fish, and fegato (liver) alla Veneziana among them. And there's a garden. *First Class.*

Trattoria El Chef (Campo San Barnaba; Phone 22-815): You've just exited the Church of San Barnaba, and within view of its elegant campanile is El Chef. Find a table in the garden and order up a lunch centered about grilled fresh tuna or frittura mista. *Moderate.*

Vino Vino (Ponte delle Veste 2007; Phone 523-7027) serves corking good pastas, meat, and fish to accompany its wide choices of vino by the glass or bottle, at bar or table. Traditionally open midmorning through 1 A.M. *Moderate/First Class.*

SHOPPER'S VENICE

Venice's main shopping street—Mercerie—is, for some reason or other (probably the magnetism of Piazza San Marco, from which it is only a matter of yards, to the northeast) the least known to foreigners of any such in principal Italian cities. Become acquainted with it by means of a promenade, from one terminus, near San Marco, to the other at Rialto Bridge. Herewith, some personally scouted sources at various locales, alphabetically by category.

ANTIQUES, though without the quality of Florence, or the quantity or quality of Rome, can upon occasion be of museum caliber, are mostly Venetian in origin, and are very often extraordinarily expensive. Dealers tend to be correct if cool, not as welcoming of questions as colleagues in other cities. They include: *Arredi d' Arte* (Ponte delle Ostreghe), with eighteenth-century furniture and accessories; *Pippo Casellati* (Via XXII Marzo), with paintings as well as furnishings; *V. Trois* (Via XXII Marzo), with antique fabrics (as well as contemporarily made Fortuny printed cottons); *Giocondo Cassini* (Via XXII Marzo), a treasure trove of Piranesi prints as well as eighteenth-century books and maps; and *Pietro Scarpa* (Via XXII Marzo), with often superb paintings.

CLOTHING: *Buosi* (Siestere di San Marco) is a men's shop with style. *Elite* (Calle Larga San Marco 274, near Mercerie) is the classiest shop in town for men's clothes and accessories. *Emporio Armani* (Calle dei Febbri 989, near San Marco) is a source of Giorgio Armani-created duds, male and female. *Missoni* (Calle Vallaresso 1312, near San Marco) is an outlet for Missoni-designed clothing and accessories, both women's and men's (including neckties). *La Bauta* (Mercerie) has leather and suede clothing, men's and women's; shoes, too. *Ciro's* (Mercerie) specializes in women's embroidered blouses. *Il Marchese Coccapani* (Sestiere di San Marco): Go for sportswear, men's and women's. *Max Mara* (Mercerie) is a link of a women's clothing chain. *Gianfranco Ferre's* Venice outlet (men and women) is on Calle Larga San Marco. And gents who wear hats will find Borselinos at *R. Bignotti* (Mercerie). *Fendi* (Salizzada San Moisè 1474, near San Marco) attracts with all manner of Fendi-label wares, emphasizing women's clothes, but with men's accessories, as well as luggage. *La Coupole* (Frezzeria 1674) features name-make clothing and shoes, male and female. *Louisa Spagneli* (San Marco 741) is a link of a women's clothing chain. *Mila Schön* (Calle Goldoni 4485) is part of a top designer's chain: pricey. *Milliaccio* (San Marco 4844): trendy men's and women's. *Trussardi* (San Marco 695)—another top chain. *Vinei* (Mercerie) runs a broad clothing gamut, women's and kids', French as well as Italian designers.

DEPARTMENT STORE: *Coin* (Sestieri de Narregio) is a national chain. The outlet is a good-size five-floor emporium.

FABRICS: *Rubelli* (Campo San Gallo) is for damasks and brocades, rich and costly. This is a famous, long-on-scene firm.

FOOD AND WINE: *Mercato Canna Regio* (Ponte delle Guglie) is near the railway station and Ghetto; open-air fish and other food stalls. *The Rialto* quarter—its landmark is its much-painted Grand Canal bridge—has been a marketplace for centuries, one of Italy's most color-drenched. Go as early in the morning as you can, not missing *pescherie* (fish markets) and *erberie* (vegetable markets), among much more, a lot of it excellent-value clothing and leather.

GLASS: Murano Island is the site of a hundred and fifty glass factories, with retail sales made from each. If a word to the wise is sufficient, let it be noted that the tourist office receives the majority of its complaints from visitors who have ordered—but not received—glass from Murano sources that was to be shipped to them. A number of dealers, please note, have a series of little shops in and about Piazza San Marco, which they use to attract customers to their main showrooms, escorting them on foot. Go along if you like, but don't feel obligated to buy. There are no bargains; the good stuff is expensive. Sources include *Venini,* Fondamente Vetrai, Murano, as well Piazzetta Leoncini, Venice; *Salviati,* Fondamente Radi, Murano, with various Piazza San Marco and other Venice locations; and *Cenedese,* Fondamente Venier, Murano, with its main Venice shop at Canal Grande 175 near Salute Church, and a number of others around San Marco. There are, as well, many Venice shops not connected with Murano factories, with typically Murano glass paperweights (super easy-to-carry gifts) among specialties; *Tiozzo Piera* (Calle Fiubera 891, near San Marco) and *L'Isola* (San Marco Mercerie 723) are among the better ones.

GLOVES: *Rialto Market's* open-air stalls have the best buys in town.

LACE AND LINENS: *Brocchi* (Calle Vallaresso, off San Marco) is a source of traditional Venetian lace (it was once a major craft) and of hand-worked linens. *Jesurum* (Ponte del Canonica and San Marco 60) is worth a visit if only for a look at tablecloths, napkins, and lace.

LEATHER: *Gucci* (Piazza San Marco 258), with clothes and accessories, as well; their loafers are famous, their neckties nifty. *Bottega Veneta,* easily as pricey as Gucci, and like it with branches abroad, is on Calle dell' Ascensione. *La Bauta* (San Marco 729) has lovely leather—and it's expensive. *Vogini* (San Marco 1257A) is worth exploring; big selections, varied objects.

PAPER: In no country is paper dealt with as imaginatively as in Italy. To see what I mean, have a look at *Il Papiro* (San Marco 2764).

SHOES: *Santini e Dominici* (Via XXII Marzo 2007, near San Marco) is reputed for its own-design, high-style shoes, men's as well as women's. Both *Fratelli Rossetti* (costly) and *Divarese* (mid-category) are on Campo San Salvador near the Rialto. And *La Paragina* (Mercerie) has well-priced men's loafers.

SILVER AND GOLD JEWELRY: *Rialto Market* has jewelry shops worth inspecting, under the arcade on the far side of the bridge. *Sforso* (Campo San Toma) deals in large silver pieces like trays and bowls, but has small stuff, too, and other work in gold. *A. Cocagna* (Bocca di Piazza San Marco) has for long dealt in lovely antique jewelry. And *Les Must de Cartier* is on Calle Vallaresso. *Chimento* (Campo San Moisè) features bold gold jewelry; watches, too.

INCIDENTAL INTELLIGENCE

Arrival in Venice is unusual enough for me to detail it earlier on; see Lay of the Land. Let me note at this point, though, that there are no direct Venice–North America flights. But there are flights to and from domestic and other international points. Venice's Aeroporto Marco Polo is on the adjacent mainland. *Getting About:* Two ways—on foot and by water. Public water buses—*vaporetti*—operate on a series of half a dozen-odd routes, with the Grand Canal their main artery. Major lines are No. 1 *(accelerato)* and No. 2 *(diretto).* Tickets (priced according to length of journey) are purchased at stations, which have signs indicating route numbers and stops; ticket agents are invariably helpful. Always travel with a good map of the city. Before setting out, go over your itinerary—whether it be sightseeing, shopping, dining, or a combination thereof—with the hotel concierge; in most cases these men know their city intimately—and intricately. *Gondolas*—of which there are only some 400 in operation contemporarily (in contrast to an estimated 10,000 in the seventeenth century)—are expensive. Their high cost can be obviated by group charters, either for sightseeing or evening serenades, complete with schmaltzy music. For an ordinary journey—on which as many as five persons can be accommodated on standard-size gondolas (fewer on the smaller craft called sandoli)—one is advised to determine with the gondolier a fee *in advance of boarding—not hesitating to bargain.* There are clusters of gondolas at Piazzetta San Marco and Piazzale Roma. Gondoliers are licensed, as would be a taxi driver—worth bearing in mind in case of any misunderstanding or difficulty. Ask your hotel concierge for a gratis copy of *Un Ospite di Venezia,* a "What's-On" monthly. *Brenta Canal tours*—along the villa-lined waterway connecting Venice with Padua (chapter 23)—are one-day trips going in either direction that include a lunch stop and visits to selected country mansions, of the caliber designed by Palladio (chapter 39) for rich Venetians, fifteenth through eighteenth centuries. If this will be a first visit to Padua, plan on staying overnight so that you may explore that city. Venice in late autumn—starting in November—can be rainy (*very* rainy), and with flooded streets and squares, sometimes severely so. Some hotels provide rubber boots for guests at such times, and principal visitor areas—such as Piazza San Marco—are equipped with narrow, elevated boardwalks for pedestrians, who walk slowly, in single file. *Further information:* Azienda di Promozione Turistica, Castello 4421, Venice.

38

Verona

Evocations of Guglielmo Shakespeare

"In fair Verona, where we lay our scene."

Romeo and Juliet

"Act One, Scene One: Verona. An open place."

The Two Gentlemen of Verona

BACKGROUND BRIEFING

The bard selected this ancient northeastern city as the setting not only for *Romeo and Juliet*, in which, as all the world knows, "a pair of star-cross'd lovers take their life," but of the comedy chronicling the amours of a pair of dandies—*The Two Gentlemen of Verona*—Valentine and Proteus, by name. Still, even with half a millennium of free Shakespeare publicity, the overwhelming majority of transatlantic visitors en route to nearby Venice—75 miles to the east—pass Verona by.

A pity, this. For what they miss is a city whose core cannot be all that much changed from the era of the Shakespeare classic, and—to step even farther back into history—which possesses the largest and finest concentration of Roman antiquities in all Italy, after Rome itself.

Indeed, it was Romans who came upon a community on a dramatic curve of the Adige River, as long ago as the first century B.C. Sensing, even then, the strategic significance of the location—on a trade route linking central Europe and central Italy—Romans dubbed the place *Augusta Verona* and set about building a model northern town, a fair amount of which still is to be seen.

Early Christian and Middle Ages conflicts were not dissimilar from others throughout Italy, but two points about these centuries are worth making. First is that antagonism between the alliteratively titled—and invariably confusing—Guelph and Ghibelline factions that spread throughout the center and north manifested themselves in thirteenth-century Verona to the point where they were well enough chronicled to have impelled Shakespeare to base the plot of *Romeo and Juliet* on the enmity of the Guelphs (to whom Romeo's family professed allegiance) and the Ghibellines (to whom Juliet's family was loyal).

Second, it was during the rule of a Ghibelline clan, the Scaligeri, or Scalas—from the early fourteenth through the early fifteenth century—that Verona experienced its Golden Age economically (it became rich), militarily (it extended its domination over much of the surrounding Veneto region and beyond), and culturally (luring not only writers—Dante was one such—but artists whose work remains to be admired). A number of the Scaligeri family's leaders are buried in a remarkable Gothic tomb in front of the church at which they prayed.

Later centuries saw envious city-states—Padua and Venice, Florence and Milan—oppose Verona, often with success; indeed, it was under Venetian aegis for almost four centuries, early fifteenth through late eighteenth, when the Venetian Republic fell and Verona was, successively, French- and Austrian-governed until it became part of the mid-nineteenth-century-founded Kingdom of Italy. It fared badly—as a consequence of Allied bombing—during World War II, with insult added to injury by retreating German forces at the end of the war. But Verona rebuilt with extraordinary finesse and skill, painstakingly restoring long-adored monuments to the greatness of the past, the better to be appreciated by today's inspectors.

ON SCENE

Lay of the Land: This city of a quarter million is not as compact as the newcomer might suspect, and to be done justice requires a few well-planned days. Core of town—and many, but not all, of its major monuments—lies within the hump-shaped central area delineated by the flow of the Adige River. Orient yourself from sprawling *Piazza Brà,* easily identifiable because it abuts the city's principal Roman remnant, the amphitheater known simply as the *Arena.* From Piazza Brà, shop-lined *Via Mazzini,* No. 1 mercantile street, leads north to a clutch of contiguous squares: *Piazza Erbe,* for centuries the seat of produce vendors, and still massed with umbrella-covered stalls; opulent *Piazza dei Signori,* edged with arcades, sculpture, and palazzi, with fifteenth-century *Loggia del Consiglio,* mullion-windowed and magnificent; *Palazzo della Regione* (a twelfth-century Romanesque masterwork whose inner court, *Cortile del Mercato Vecchio,* with horizontal-striped brick walls and a stunner of a Gothic stairway you want to see); *Arche Scaligere* (busily detailed Gothic burial enclosure of Scala rulers, with upright and horizontal statues of each, which Queen Victoria might well have had in mind when she erected Prince Albert's memorial in London, five centuries later); and more contemporary *Piazza Indipendenza,* off which leads another important shopping street, *Via Capello.* Two requisite churches, the cathedral and *Sant' Anastasia,* are in the neighborhood of these squares, gained by *Corso Sant' Anastasia,* whose shops specialize in antiques, often of high caliber. The railway station is a fair distance from the center. Museums and other landmarks are in still other areas of the city. Why don't I lead off with two of these, to make sure they don't get lost in the shuffle, and you don't miss them?

Castelvecchio (Corso Castelvecchio): Old Castle, indeed; Verona tends to understatement. A visit to this fourteenth-century complex—principal legacy of the Scala ruler named Cangrande II and meticulously rebuilt and restored after tragic World War II damage—is a "two-fer" of no mean significance. Which is to say that a single visit produces double rewards. First, you're given an idea of what medieval grandeur was all about in Verona: half a dozen massive towers punctuating crenelated walls, with elevated ramparts and massive inner spaces, the lot put to service with panache and wit—which leads us to the second aspect of the visit, Verona's *Museo Civico.* Even if one ignored the exciting architecture, paintings alone make this an all-Italy standout gallery: a number of brilliant works by Andrea Mantegna, including a searing *Christ Carrying the Cross* and an exquisitely wrought *Holy Family;* Tintoretto *(Concert of the Muses);* Verona's own Veronese (a portrait of an armor-clad soldier); Pisanello (*Madonna and the Quail,* so called because of the bird at the bottom right corner); more foreign painters than are often seen in Italian museums (Rubens and Lely, Jordaens and Mor, to name four); and what—among much more—have come to be Castelvecchio's mascots: a black-hooded young Benedictine monk by Giovanni Francesco Caroto and the same Caroto's *Child with Sketch,* a smiling, redheaded youngster, funny-face drawing of her own in hand.

Basilica of San Zeno (Piazza San Zeno) is a Romanesque-Gothic complex—church, cloister, pencil-slim campanile—that was several centuries in the making. The symmetrical façade stops you short at the front doors; few portals in Italy are so splendidly embellished; each is the setting for a panel of twenty-four bronze panels, illustrating—originally for the illiterate devout, en route to worship within—the life of the saint whose name the church takes, and stories from the Bible, as well; they are mostly twelfth-century. And they are but a prelude to the grandeur lying within—a soaring nave leads to the high altar, with a ravishing Mantegna *Madonna and Child* surrounded by angels and the garlands of fruit that became a trademark of that master; a *Crucifixion* by Lorenzo Veneziano; architecturally superb crypt; quiet cloister.

Arena di Verona (Piazza Brà): Verona's nineteen-century-old amphitheater (capacity 22,000) is northern Italy's answer to Rome's Colosseum, except that unlike the latter, it's still in use—the summer long, as warm-weather quarters of the highly regarded municipal opera troupe, Ente Lirico Arena di Verona. Seeing a performance—*Aïda* with its massive cast, ideally—is the preferred method of taking in the Arena; but it keeps daytime inspection hours, so that you can inspect this extraordinary construction, elliptical in shape and enormous: 365 feet wide by 455 feet long, with its walls comprising two levels of arches, 72 all told.

Duomo (Piazza del Duomo): There is a compact quality to the cathedral's perfectly symmetrical Romanesque-Gothic façade—note carvings of the portal, by the same medieval sculptor, Nicolò, who created the panels at San Zeno (above). But once past them, you find yourself in a grandly proportioned church, alive with embellishment, with its No. 1 lure an *Assumption* by Titian (his only Verona painting, and by no means a copy of the similarly titled work of his in Venice's Frari church). Look at the font in the Battistero, and end in the Cloister.

Church of Sant' Anastasia (Piazza Sant' Anastasia)—despite sculpted borders and faded frescoes of its portals—appears deceptively simple as one approaches (its façade was never completed). But go on in. A dozen tall columns—the capitals are different on each—support a central nave whose Gothic vaults are painted in floral motifs. The pair of baptismal fonts are conversation pieces. There are works by the likes of Lorenzo Veneziano and Stefano da Verona, but the masterpiece of Sant' Anastasia is Pisanello's much-reproduced *St. George and the Princess*, in my view the city's single most beautiful painting.

Church of San Fermo Maggiore (Strada San Fermo): If, like me, you are a Pisanello fan, you will head straight for the Renaissance tomb of Nicolò Brenzoni, in this brimming-with-art, two-level, Romanesque-Gothic church. There it is: Pisanello's *Annunciation*, its blond kneeling angel in profile, profoundly beautiful and reason enough for your pilgrimage.

San Giorgio in Bradia (Lungadige San Giorgio) is as good a reason as any to cross the Adige River. Near Ponte Garibaldi, this domed Renaissance structure, overlooking the water, contains a memorable Veronese, *The Martyrdom of St. George*, on the high altar, and Tintoretto's *Baptism of Christ* on the front wall. Wander through the art-crammed side chapels, too.

Juliet and Romeo's (presumed) houses and Juliet's (legendary) tomb: The first of the trio, which virtually no outlander dares leave Verona without having visited, is centrally situated on Via Capello, and there is said to be strong evidence that it was the Capulet family seat. At any rate, it's an enchanting brick dwelling with a stone balcony on the second floor, and there is a wall plaque that quotes the immortal Romeo speech—"*But, soft! what light through yonder window breaks? It is the east, and Juliet is the sun!*"—in both English and Italian. This proves quite enough, in the case of many visitors, to impel treks to the nearby, also-ancient house on the Via delle Arche Scaligere, called Romeo's (with less documentation than in the case of Juliet), and to the more distant chapel of a partially ruined onetime Capuchin monastery (Via Pallone) in whose crypt is what tradition decrees to be the Tomba di Giulietta.

Teatro Romano/Museo Archeologico (Via Santa Chiara): Not content to build their massive Arena (above), Verona's Romans also erected a theater, near the also-Roman-built (and still in use) Ponte Pietro, the stone bridge you cross from downtown to each. Positioned in the hills, with the river below it, and two ancient Christian complexes adjacent (the little *Church of SS. Siro e Libera* and a onetime monastery), the restored semicircular theater still is used for plays. In the ex-Monasterio di San Girolamo is the town's Museo Archeologico, where exhibits run to bits and pieces of Roman Verona—mosaics and busts, glass and pottery, beautiful sculptures—with the monastery's pair of cloisters and monks' cells cleverly put to service as display space.

Lago di Garda: If Scotland's Loch Lomond is Glasgow's front yard, so is Lake Garda its Verona counterpart. Largest in area of the Italian lakes, but geographically detached from and considerably east of the remaining Big Two (Como and Maggiore, chapter 7), Garda can be visited easily in tandem with Verona. *Sirmione*—a good headquarters point—is a venerable little town on the lake's southern shore, some 20 miles from Verona, that is dotted with hotels (foreign visitors to Garda are mostly German), and is, moreover, dominated by the Gothic profiles of a derring-do fortress, *Rocca Scaligere* by name, with a trio of crenelated towers, a waterfront situation, and a pedigree that dates to the Middle Ages when the same Scala family that ruled Verona built it. There are a few interesting churches—*San Pietro, Santa Maria Maggiore,* and *San Salvadore.* But mainly, Sirmione is for relaxation in the sunshine; ambles along shop-lined *Via Vittorio Emanuele,* with pauses in its caffès; a visit, perhaps, to what still is to be seen of a rather fabulous Roman villa, the so-called *Catullus Grottoes;* and excursions to other lakeside towns such as *Desenzano* and *Salò,* nearby, but also possibly including *Garda,* a kind of north shore counterpart of Sirmione, with quite as many old-school hotels, and even a castle to match southerly Rocca Scaligera. In Sirmione, lunch well—try the lake fish and of course the Soave and

Valpolicella wines from nearby vineyards—at *Ristorante Grifone-da-Luciano* (Via delle Bisse 5; Phone 916-097; *First Class*); you'll enjoy the setting. Overnighting? *Villa Cortine Hotel* (Via Grotte 12), set in a lakefront garden, is full-facility and *First Class,* while *Golf et Suisse Hotel* (Via 25 Aprile 60) is smallish, with pool, bar, and breakfast but no restaurant, and *Moderate.*

SETTLING IN

Due Torri Baglioni Hotel (Piazza Sant' Anastasia 4), named for the two towers of its original Renaissance building, was a Verona home-away-from-home, over earlier centuries, of composers like Mozart and Wagner and poets like Goethe and Heine. The Due Torri's ace-in-the-hole is its décor. There are 100 unusually decorated rooms, not two alike and each furnished with Veronese antiques in one of fifteen distinct styles of the eighteenth and nineteenth centuries—Louis (oops, Luigi) XVI and Directoire, Empire and Biedermeier, and beyond—the lot making for one of Europe's more beautiful hotels, with a vast lobby-lounge and piano bar, not to mention L'Aquila (one of the best restaurants in town). Member, Leading Hotels of the World. *Luxury.*

Colomba d'Ora Hotel's (Via Cattaneo 10) ace-in-the-hole is a super-central location, between the river and Piazza Brà. There are half a hundred rooms, bar-lounge, and breakfast, albeit no restaurant. *First Class.*

Grand Hotel (Corsa Porta Nuova 105): I wish this gracious old-timer—relatively recently updated) were more central, but it's attractive, (there are close to 50 rooms, cocktail lounge and breakfast but no restaurant), and it's close to the railway station. *First Class.*

Accademia Hotel (Via Scala 12) is good-sized—with well over a hundred rooms—and conveniently central, a major plus in its favor; bar lounge and breakfast, with the same management's Ristorante Accademia adjacent at No. 10 (Phone 8006-072). Both hotel and restaurant are *First Class.*

San Luca Hotel (Galleria Volto San Luca 8) is heart-of-town, near the river, and is nicely equipped, with 40 functional rooms with bath, pleasant public spaces, including a bar-lounge and breakfast, but no restaurant. *Moderate.*

Giulietta & Romeo Hotel (Vicolo Tre Marchetti 3): It says something for Italian gallantry, or at least this hotel owner's gallantry, that Shakepeare's title is reversed, with the lady's name coming first. Bravo! This is a small 30-room house with a major advantage its central situation, in the shadow of the Arena. Bar and breakfast. *Moderate.*

DAILY BREAD

Dodici (pronounced *dough-dee-chee* and meaning 12) ***Apostoli*** (Corticella San Marco 3; Phone 596-999) occupies a pair of arched and frescoed rooms in a fourteenth-century, heart-of-Verona building that has been operating since the eighteenth century. Conventional openers—spaghetti al basilico, for example—are delicious, but regional specialties—toasted polenta, the house terrine, or the Veneto area's beloved paste e fagioli—are more interesting. Entrée specialties—a mixed grill brought to you on its own individual grill—is super; so is carbonata Veronese, a beef-in-beer masterwork. There are some 250 wines in the cellar, many from blue-chip Verona-area vineyards. If you've ordered a red, have cheese with it—they're excellent here—in lieu of a sweet. *Luxury.*

Il Desco (Via Dietro San Sebastiano 7; Phone 595-358) lures a clientele at once attractive—like its intimate quarters in what was built as a convent four centuries back—and savvy. Go with a house pasta and rack of lamb. *Luxury.*

Nuova Marconi (Via Fogge 4; Phone 591-910) is indicated for a gala meal that ideally embraces risotto (seafood- or poultry-accented) and simply broiled fish. Fun. *Luxury.*

Veron' Antica (Via Sottorvia 10; Phone 34-124) is intimate, attractive, and with perfectly delicious comestibles, from, say, an authentic risotto alla Milanese through to deftly prepared veal, lamb, and fish from nearby Lake Garda, with correspondingly agreeable wines. *First Class.*

Re Teodorico (Piazzale Castel San Pietro; Phone 834-9990) is a delightful miniexcursion from the center. You cross the Adige River via Roman-built Ponte Pietro and ascend green hills, just opposite, for a festive meal-cum-views, which might center on roast lamb, which follow assorted antipasto, and conclude with a super sweet. *First Class.*

Il Cenacolo (Via Teatro Filarmonico 10; Phone 33-932) is so well located, near Piazza Brà, that it's indicated for a post-Arena or post-Teatro supper, with sound risotti and pastas, or perhaps an omelet. *First Class.*

Greppia (Vicolo Samaritana 3; Phone 800-4577) is unpretentious but satisfactory for a competent meal at a fair price. Central and *Moderate.*

Caffè Dante (Piazza dei Signori): You want to pop into this historic spot—nineteenth-century décor is original—at least once, for coffee and people-watching; if it's summer, take a table in the square. *Moderate.*

Caffè Europa (Piazza Brà): Position yourself at a table under the canopy so that you can observe sidewalk traffic, the while sipping espresso or a drink. *Moderate.*

SOUND OF MUSIC

I allude above to summer opera in the Arena. But if you're in town fall through early spring, the same company—Ente Lirico Arena di Verona—has a winter season (with concerts and ballet, as well) in dazzlingly beautiful *Teatro Filarmonico* (Piazza Brà), the city's eighteenth-century opera house that was bombed during World War II and restored thereafter to its gilt-and-ivory Rococo splendor.

INCIDENTAL INTELLIGENCE

Further information: Ente Provinciale per il Turismo, Piazza delle Erbe 42, Verona.

39

Vicenza and the Villas

Legacy of Palladio

BACKGROUND BRIEFING

Nearby Venice (chapter 37) is, to understate, more beautiful. Nearby Verona (chapter 38) is at least as beautiful—and more cosmopolitan. You go to this city, No. 3 of the northeast Veneto Region's "V" cities, primarily to pay homage to Renaissance architect Andrea Palladio. This is the core of the area where he lived and worked, designing a marvelous mix of urban structures and country houses for wealthy Venetian merchants.

Palladio was the fifteenth-century innovator who changed much of the look of the West, with his special brand of neoclassic mansions, palaces, and churches. Englishmen like Inigo Jones and, later, Robert Adam saw his work in the course of Italian Grand Tours, adapting it to their own designs back home. Eventually Palladian symmetry, with its central domes, dramatic colonnades, pedimented doors, and broad porticoes spread across the Atlantic, to be emulated not only at celebrated rural seats like George Washington's Mount Vernon and Thomas Jefferson's Monticello, but in countless public buildings—National Gallery of Art in Washington, Broad Street Station in Philadelphia, Morgan Library in New York are a random trio—not to mention banks, post offices, and schools the country over.

Palladio's city antecedents are not all that different from nearby (30 miles) Verona. Roman-founded, it evolved, during the Middle Ages, into a *comune,* later warring with northern city-states like Verona and Milan, before Venetians took it over in the fourteenth century, holding power until the eighteenth, by which time commercial eminence had fostered substantial building activity, not to mention a thriving

Renaissance-era school of art, led by Bartolommeo Montagna, not, incidentally, to be confused (it's not difficult) with the same region's Andrea Mantegna.

ON SCENE

Lay of the Land: In effect, an oblong, easily traversed by foot. Key street, aptly named for the town's most famous citizen, is shop-, palace-, and church-lined *Corso Andrea Palladio,* and it cuts through the core, from western *Piazzale Roma* through to eastern *Piazza Matteotti.* The pencil-slim campanile, belonging to the Palladio-designed Basilica of central Piazza dei Signori is, by tradition, the tallest construction in town; you'll see it from everywhere. Most in-town monuments lie on or just off the Corso (locals usually drop "Andrea Palladio" when referring to it). The railway station is southwest of the center, on *Campo Marzio,* and the so-called *Palladian villas*—country houses designed by the master—lie beyond the town in every direction.

Basilica Palladiana (Palazzo dei Signori—its name notwithstanding, a civic structure) dominates the square, with its massive green metal roof, two levels of sumptuously detailed loggias (note that the capitals of the lower one are Doric; of the upper, Ionic), and a series of statues ringing the building. Vicenza's trademark, Palladio designed the Basilica around the shell of an older government building; it was his final work. The upstairs Great Hall, used for special exhibitions, is anticlimactic after the façade. Go on up if only for a perspective of the pavilion opposite.

Loggia del Capitano (Piazza dei Signori) is a two-level Palladian work of stunning beauty—although actually it was never completed—with respect to reliefs on its two-story façade and bold frescoes in its upstairs Great Hall.

Teatro Olimpico (Piazza Matteotti) is, for me, the city's outstanding building, with its interior an all-Italy top ranker; if I had one interior to see in Vicenza, this would be it. Palladio designed it on commission for the town's Olympian Academy (thus the name). There is nothing else quite like it that I know of, save Parma's Teatro Farnese (chapter 25), half a century younger, and indeed based upon the Olimpico. It is not unlike a Greek amphitheater, albeit enclosed and roofed. Indeed, the ceiling is painted to emulate the sky; the elliptical auditorium is topped by a pair of loggias; the proscenium is a kind of built-in stage set, representing a triumphal arch, each of its two levels embedded with sculpture-filled niches. Go for daytime inspection or for an evening production of a classical play. Better yet, both.

Palazzo Chiericati (Corso Andrea Palladio) is almost too much of a good thing: a Palladian-designed two-level palace, its roof exuberantly ringed with sculpture and enclosing treasure-filled *Museo Civico.* By treasures I mean a precious cache of Palladio drawings and ravishing paintings: a *Madonna and Child with Saints* by the city's own Renaissance master, Montagna; still another painting of the same subject, albeit with different saints, by Veronese; a Tintoretto of St. Augustine; and works by such foreigners as Memling and Van Dyck.

Church of Santa Corona (Contra Santa Corona): There is certainly no trace of Palladio in this Gothic church's red-brick façade-cum-campanile. But its Cappella Valmarana is pure Palladian; and there are other treats, including paintings by Giovanni Bellini, Veronese, and Montagna, and an impressive wooden choir.

Duomo (Piazza del Duomo) started out Gothic, gained a striking pink-and-white marble façade during the Renaissance. But do go in, if only to see the gorgeous gold-backed fourteenth-century altarpiece by Lorenzo Veneziano; an eight-century-old font in the Baptistry, frescoes by Montagna; and—across the square as part of the Arcivescovado, or archbishop's palace—a charming inner loggia.

La Rotonda (Via dei Nani, just south of town) is the prototypical Palladian villa. It surely inspired William Kent when he designed Chiswick House in London, Jefferson when he created the University of Virginia, and countless succeeding architects. Only its dome is round; otherwise the building is square with a portico supported by six Ionic columns on each of its four identical sides. I don't guarantee that you'll be allowed to see the interior in the course of your visit, but it's the façades that are what made La Rotonda important.

Villa Valmarana (Via San Bastiano, just south of town and so near La Rotonda, above, that you'll want to visit the two on a single excursion) has nothing to do with Palladio, I must make immediately clear. The lure here is an extraordinarily large group of delightful frescoes by the Tiepolos, father (Giambattista) and son (Giandomenico), that prolific team of eighteenth-century Venetians who here decorated a seventeenth-century mansion and its satellite guest-house.

Palladian villas beyond Vicenza are no more consistent in their open hours (if any) than Britain's country houses—and invariably quite as worth visiting. Villas that have traditionally maintained limited open hours (sometimes only late spring through early autumn) include *Villa Cordellina-Lombardi* (at Montecchio Maggiore, ten miles south of Vicenza), with Tiepolo frescoes as a bonus; *Villa Malinverni* (at Lonedo di Lugo, 15 miles north of Vicenza)—Palladio's first country house, beautifully frescoed and with an art gallery; and *Villa Zen* (at Lisiera di Bolzano, 5 miles north of Vicenza). One that has *not* traditionally kept regular hours that I would ask the Tourist Office (address below) to obtain advance permission to enter is *Villa Volpi* at Maser, 25 miles north of Vicenza, a Palladio masterwork of considerable size (a central pavilion and two arcaded wings) with brilliant frescoes by Veronese, most especially the Great Hall's *Olympus.* Other villas designed by the master, without regular hours, include *Villa Sarego, Villa Foscari* (a.k.a. Malcontenta for the town in which it is situated), *Villa Pisani La Rocca, Villa Caldogna,* and—just a few miles from town—*Villa Gazoto-Marcello.* If visits to any of these are possible while you're in Vicenza, the azienda can so advise you.

SETTLING IN

Campo Marzio Hotel (Viale Roma 21) is at once central (near the Duomo) and full-facility, with 39 bath-equipped rooms, restaurant that closes weekends, more's the pity, and bar. *First Class.*

Castello Hotel (Contra Piazza del Castello 24) is fairly central—a block from Corso Andrea Palladio, with baths in most of its rooms, bar, and breakfast, but no restaurant. *Moderate.*

Cristina Hotel (Corso SS. Felice e Fortunato) is, to be sure, on a beautifully named street, and is well equipped with baths in most rooms, comfortable bar-lounge, and breakfast, though no restaurant. But it's not central. *Moderate.*

Villa Cipriani Hotel (Asolo, 30 miles north of Vicenza) might be just the ticket if you've wheels and would enjoy a relaxing respite at an originally seventeenth-century villa high above a pretty hill town, with 32 period-style rooms (some in a satellite house across the garden), reputed restaurant, and congenial bar-lounge. You're well positioned here for drives to the Palladian villas and Vicenza, not to mention Padua (chapter 23), Venice (chapter 37), and Verona (chapter 38). A Ciga hotel that's affiliated with Relais et Châteaux. Special. *Luxury.*

DAILY BREAD

Tre Visi (Contra Porti 6; Phone 23-964) is indicated for local dishes like polenta e baccalà—an unlikely sounding mix of the starch staple with baked cod that tastes better than would appear to be the case. Less courageous diners will start with a competent pasta, and go on to a veal entrée. Choice local wines. Central. *First Class.*

Cinzia e Valerio (Piazzetta Porto Padova 65; Phone 509-213) is not alas central. You go if you're a seafood buff, opening with a platter of seafood as the antipasto, continuing with maritime-accented fare, fresh fish through to pasta sauces. *Luxury.*

Scudo di Francia (Contra Piancoli 4; Phone 28-665): Start with the locally esteemed risi e bisi—soup based on rice, peas, and ham—continuing with a roast, perhaps, or an order of fegato—calf's liver, Venetian style. *First Class.*

Al Pozzo (Via Sant' Antonio 1; Phone 21-411) is a near-neighbor of the Duomo, with reliably sauced pastas, a range of entrées, and reasonable house wine. *Moderate.*

Gran Caffè Garibaldi (Piazza dei Signori 5; Phone 44-147) is wonderfully atmospheric, with outdoor tables on the splendid square in warm weather. Establishment Vicenza gathers here regularly. Go for an espresso or a drink; or, for that matter, a proper meal; the latter *First Class;* the former *Moderate.*

Offeleria del Meneghina (Via Cavour 18) has at least as venerable a past (it goes back to the eighteenth century) as the Gran Caffè above, with perfectly delicious pastries and little sandwiches to accompany your coffee. *Moderate.*

AFTER DARK

Do try to take in a performance to get an idea of what *Teatro Olimpico* is like when put to proper use; the tourist office (below) will have schedules.

INCIDENTAL INTELLIGENCE

Further information: Entre Provinciale per il Turismo, Piazza Matteotti, Vicenza.

40

Viterbo

and Tarquinia's Etruscan Tombs

BACKGROUND BRIEFING

If every city has a secret touristic weapon, then that of Viterbo—a smallish, contemporarily unheralded city not far north of Rome (chapter 2) and even closer to Orvieto (chapter 22)—is, or at least was, popes. A clutch of Middle Ages pontiffs made of it a kind of home away from home. And much of the architecture their residence inspired—fountain-centered squares, stone-paved streets with their original houses, treasure-laden churches, grandiose palaces—remains very much part of the Viterbo scene.

Etruscan in pre-Roman centuries, Viterbo eventually became the Roman colony of *Vicus Elibii* (only the first two letters of that ancient name remain). Not unlike so many Italian communities, early medieval families—in the case of Viterbo a pair of such, named di Vico and Gatti—vied for control, to the point where, in the eleventh century, stronger papal forces took over. For a sustained period—well into the thirteenth century—Viterbo served as a papal seat, with the pontiffs' palace, heart of town, still visitable.

ON SCENE

Lay of the Land: You want to walk the compact historic center of this beautiful city. (Only its train stations—Piazzetta Fiorentina on *Viale Trento,* along with Roma Nord on *Viale Trieste* [both north of the core] and *Piazza Romana* [at the southern edge]—are peripheral.) Heart of town is *Piazza del Plebiscito,* framed by a marvelous mix of medieval masterworks, with the city hall—*Palazzo dei Priori* (whose public spaces and verdant courtyard you want to inspect) the most impressive. From this square, *Via San Lorenzo* (mercantile as well as atmospheric) leads south to *Piazza San Lorenzo,* edged both by the cathedral and one-time Papal Palace. From the cathedral the street that cuts through the *really* picture-postcard part of town—*Via San Pellegrino*—leads west, enclosed by an extraordinary concentration of stone houses (many with typically Viterbese outer stairways leading to upper precincts), and bisecting a charming minisquare, *Piazzetta San Pellegrino,* site of the landmark church for which it is named.

Duomo (Piazza San Lorenzo) is a case of good things in small packages. What it lacks in scale, this little cathedral (with a late Renaissance façade and older campanile) compensates for with its austerely handsome Romanesque interior, the capitals of columns flanking the nave its principal embellishment. Special.

Palazzo Papale (Piazza San Lorenzo) is where medieval popes made their Viterbo headquarters. Its most felicitous aspect is an unmistakably Gothic loggia, gained by a stone stairwell, and opening into a courtyard centered with a typically Viterbese fountain.

Museo Civico (Viale Raniero Capocci): Whenever they can, Italians place museums in antique settings, the better to create an ambience of times past. Viterbo's is no exception. It occupies the onetime monastery that had been attached to a church (below), with the original cloister still intact. The Pinacoteca section's paintings include a luminous *Madonna and Child* by one of the leading local Renaissance painters, Vitale da Viterbo, and Sebastiano del Piombo's *Christ Descended from the Cross,* not to mention some fine sculpture. Etruscan artifacts—not of the caliber of those in Tarquinia (below)—include some interesting sarcophagi; there are striking Roman pieces as well.

Fontana Grande (Piazza Fontana Grande): You don't miss a pilgrimage to this, the city's oldest fountain, any more than you would to Rome's Fontana di Trevi. Not that they are at all similar. Viterbo's Grande is much older (thirteenth century) and infinitely smaller. It typifies fountains—*del Gesù, delle Birbe, San Faustino, Pianoscarano, Della Morta*—that are to be found at virtually every turn as you stroll this veritable City of Fountains.

Church of Santa Maria della Verità (Viale Raniero Capocci)—next-door neighbor of Museo Civico (above)—is multiepoch (Romanesque,

Gothic, Renaissance) and much restored. But if you are partial to Raphael's *Marriage of the Virgin* (at Milan's Brera Museum, chapter 19), you will want to observe this variation on the same theme by a local Renaissance painter, Lorenzo da Viterbo.

Tarquinia (26 miles west of Viterbo, and a veritable stone's throw from Tyrrhenian Sea beaches) is an atmospherically attractive little town that would not figure on many itineraries, were it not for two remarkable destinations. First, *Museo Nazionale Tarquiniense* (Piazza Cavour, just off Corso Vittorio Emanuele, in the center of town) occupies a fabulous Renaissance palazzo, Vitelleschi by name, with what is one of the ranking collections of Etruscan artifacts in Italy. And second is a cluster of visitable Etruscan tombs, just beyond town. But why in Tarquinia? There's a good reason. It is the modern successor to nearby and ancient Tarquinii (notice that final "i"), which had been the seat of the Etruscan League, central military-political apparatus of the Etruscan people, who were defeated by Rome in the fourth century B.C.

As more is known about this creative pre-Roman people (not all of whom were vanquished by the Romans, but simply absorbed into their population) the aura of mystery that has long surrounded them begins to dissipate. Professor Massimo Pallottino, noted Italian archaeologist whose specialty is the Etruscans, told *Ulisse 2000* magazine in an interview with Graziano Sarchielli, that "over the last forty years, knowledge of the Etruscans has made gigantic steps. . . . We can read all the ten thousand inscriptions which have come down to us. . . . We don't know their political history, but we know a great deal about their culture: the tombs, with their painted scenes, with the banquets illustrated to the last detail; scenes of dancing, hunting, and music at Tarquinia, for example, give us a wealth of information."

But first things first, which means the museum before the tombs. (You can't enter the latter without first visiting the former.) There are, to be sure, non-Etruscan exhibits, most especially a collection of precious painted Greek ceramics. But it is Etruscan objects that take precedence, with the trademark exhibit a pair of remarkable terra-cotta horses, sublimely graceful and in mint condition. In addition, there is a wealth of objects from the nearby tombs where Etruscans, not unlike ancient Egyptians, were buried with amazing assortments of objects for use after life, pottery most especially, with some revealing frescoes of domestic Etruscan life, as well. (Tarquinia's multiepoch *Duomo* is virtually next door to the museum, but if you've time to inspect but one town church, rather make it *Church of Santa Maria di Castello* [Piazza Castello], a Romanesque beauty, with its baptismal font originally a Roman sarcophagus.)

To visit the *Etruscan tombs* (two miles east of town and viewable only on hourly guided tours that traditionally conclude at midday), you must *first* book at the museum in town, proceeding by car, if you are driving, or taxi. There are some three-score tombs all told, in the necropolis, but worry not; you're going to be shown only the half-dozen or so whose revealing wall paintings—some 2600 years old—are the best preserved.

SETTLING IN

Tarconte Hotel (Via Tuscia 19, Tarquinia) is a nicely operated contemporary house, with just over a hundred agreeable, bath-equipped rooms, spacious lobby and cocktail lounge, and on-premises *Ristorante Solengo* (Phone 856-141) where a satisfactory lunch might begin with the generous buffet antipasto, continue with deliciously sauced spaghetti al funghi, concluding with macedonia di frutta, the fresh fruit cup that no restaurant in Italy, at least to my knowledge, is ever without. Hotel is *Moderate;* restaurant, *First Class.*

Mini Palace Hotel (Via Santa Maria della Grotticella 2, Viterbo): There are lots of "Palace" hotels in Italy, but the modern Mini Palace—the only so named that I have encountered—is not all that "mini," with close to 40 well-equipped rooms, lobby-lounge and bar; breakfast but no restaurant. Friendly. *Moderate.*

DAILY BREAD

La Scaletta (Via Marconi 41, Viterbo; Phone 30-003) is a long-on-scene source of Viterbo specialties, including such pastas as agnellotti and pappardelle, and delicious poultry entrées, the house's own chicken casserole most especially. Good local wines, too. And a skilled staff. *First Class.*

Spacca (Via della Pace 9, Viterbo; Phone 340-650), quite as traditionally popular as La Scaletta (above), does well by seafood salad, among its openers; what it calls Etruscan-style cannelloni among its pastas; and a super mixed grill among its entrées. Smiling waiters. *First Class.*

Caffè Centrale (Piazza del Plebiscito, Viterbo) is indeed *centrale;* perfect for people watching and mid-morning or mid-afternoon sustenance. *Moderate.*

Caffè Impero (Corso Vittorio Emanuele, Tarquinia) is well located on Tarquinia's main street, close to the museum. *Moderate.*

SOUND OF MUSIC

Viterbo's *Festival Barocco,* a mid-June into mid-July classical festival taking place mostly in the Church of Santa Maria della Verità and its cloister (above), is worth looking into, if the period of performances coincides with your visit.

INCIDENTAL INTELLIGENCE

Further information: Ente Provinciale per il Turismo, Piazzale dei Caduti 14, Viterbo; Azienda Autonoma di Soggiorno e Turismo, Piazza Cavour 1, Tarquinia.

Acknowledgments

For this third edition of *Italy at Its Best*—with subject matter a land that extends from the Alps to Apulia, from Trieste to Taormina—I am in the debt of many good friends and colleagues in Italy, and on this side of the Atlantic, as well.

Silverio Nardone, the astute press and public relations director of the Italian Government Travel Office in New York, has been kind and cooperative in many ways, and I express appreciation to him, as well as to Umberto Lombardi, the Italian travel commissioner in New York, and to Josephine Inzerillo, a key executive on Mr. Lombardi's staff, whom I was sorry to see retire after a quarter-century's service to Italian tourism, almost at the time of this edition's publication. I'm grateful, too, to Anita Diamant, my agent; and to Max Drechsler, my research editor. To them all: grazie mille!

Let me acknowledge, alphabetically, deeply valued cooperation, in the course of researching and writing this Second Revised Edition, extended by Dr. Carlo Arcolao, Piero Bandini, Paolo Barroncelli, Gianfranco Bassan, Massimo Bassan, Lily Bates, Angelo Bettoja.

Also Gianfranco Biji, Joan E. Bloom, Matilda Salvo Bocca, Roberto Catani, Giampaolo Burattin, Marco Camiciottoli, Enza Cirrincione, Franco Cocquio, Dr. Maria Grazia Contri, Giuliano Corsi, Umberto Costa, Paolo P. Danieli.

Also Edward O. Douglas, Caradio Esposito, Alphonse Falcone, Walter Ferrari, Vincenzo Finizzola, Alessandra Foppiano, Carla Gaita, Eugenio Galli, Maddelena Roman Gallo, Linda C. Gwinn, Mary Homi, Pier Luigi Magrini.

Also Joyce M. Martin, Umberto Martuscelli, Sandro Mattassini, Martha A. Morano, William F. Peper, Giorgio Petracco, Carmelo Pitruzzella, Carol D. Poister, Alessandra Rossi.

Also Dr. Natale Rusconi, Gianni Segalerba, Dr. Gianna Specia, Dr. Patrizia Tartarotti, Marinella di Tomasso, Emilio Varini, and Nadia Villa.

R.S.K.

Index

D

E

I, J, K

L

M

Q, R

T

About the Author

Robert S. Kane's initial writing stint was as editor of the [Boy Scout] *Troop Two Bugle* in his native Albany, New York. After graduation from Syracuse University's noted journalism school, he did graduate work at England's Southampton University, first making notes as he explored in the course of class field trips through the Hampshire countryside. Back in the U.S., he worked, successively, for the *Great Bend* (Kansas) *Daily Tribune, Staten Island Advance, New York Herald Tribune,* and *New York World-Telegram & Sun* before becoming travel editor of, first, *Playbill,* and later *Cue* and *50 Plus.* His byline has appeared in such leading magazines as *Travel & Leisure, Vogue, House & Garden, Atlantic, Harper's Bazaar, Family Circle, New York, Saturday Review,* and *Modern Bride;* and such newspapers as the *Newark Star-Ledger, New York Post, New York Daily News, New York Times, Los Angeles Times, Chicago Sun-Times, Boston Globe, San Diego Union, Dallas Morning News, San Francisco Examiner,* and *Toronto Globe & Mail.* And he guests frequently, with the subject travel, on TV and radio talk shows.

Africa A to Z, the first U.S.-published guide to largely independent, post–World War II Africa, was the progenitor of his acclaimed 14-book *A to Z* series, other pioneering volumes of which were *Eastern Europe A to Z,* the first guide to what was the USSR and the then Soviet Bloc countries as seen through the eyes of a candid American author, and *Canada A to Z,* the first modern-day, province-by-province guide to the world's second-largest country. His current 13-title *World at Its Best* series includes two volumes *(Britain at Its Best* and *France at Its Best),* tapped by a pair of major book clubs, and a third *(Germany at Its Best)* that's a prize-winner.

Kane, the only American authoring an entire multivolume travel series, has the distinction of having served as president of both the Society of American Travel Writers and the New York Travel Writers' Association, and is a member, as well, of the National Press Club (Washington), P.E.N., Authors Guild, Society of Professional Journalists/Sigma Delta Chi, and American Society of Journalists and Authors. He makes his home on the Upper East Side of Manhattan.